# BUSINESS STUDIES

Michael Fardon, with Frank Adcock, Ian Birth, David Cox,
Stuart Oddy, Hugh Padley, John Prokopiw, Richard Wootton

## Osborne Books

Published by Osborne Books Limited,
Gwernant, The Common,
Lower Broadheath, Worcester, WR2 6RP
Tel 0905 333691

Printed by the Bath Press, Avon.

British Library Cataloguing in Publication Data
A catalogue record for this book is available from the British Library

ISBN 1-872962-50-5

# the writers

## WRITER AND GENERAL EDITOR

**Michael Fardon BA MPhil ACIB Cert Ed**
has followed a career in domestic and international banking, in teaching, writing and publishing. His publications include *Finance, Accounting, Business Record Keeping* and *Financial Transactions* from Osborne Books, and banking textbooks from Northwick Publishers. He currently lectures part-time at Worcester College of Technology.

## THE WRITING TEAM

**Frank Adcock BA (Econ) DipM**
has held marketing management posts with the Mars Group, Tube Investments and others. He is currently Marketing Director of New Education Press Limited and a Marketing Consultant. He has had twenty years' teaching experience in FE and has been a BTEC Course Coordinator.

**Ian Birth BA (Econ) MEd**
is Head of Economics and Business Studies at Worcester Sixth Form College.

**David Cox FCCA FCIB Cert Ed**
is a Senior Lecturer in the Management and Professional Studies Department at Worcester College of Technology. He is a fellow of the Chartered Association of Certified Accountants and has twenty years' full-time teaching experience, during which he has taught accounting students at all levels. He is the author or joint author of a number of textbooks in the areas of accounting, finance and banking.

**Stuart Oddy MBA DMS DipM Cert Ed**
is a Management Consultant who has spent over twenty years' in the pharmaceutical industry in sales and marketing positions in multinationals. He has taught business and management studies in FE and HE and has been particularly involved in short practical management courses.

**Hugh Padley MA (Cantab) MSc (Econ) FCMA**
has has had sixteen years experience as Managing Director of various manufacturing businesses. In the last seven years he has built up his own pottery company 'from scratch' in the Stoke-on-Trent area and now employs sixty people.

**John Prokopiw BA (Econ) MA (Industrial Relations) Cert Ed**
has taught business and management studies in FE for over 16 years. He has also worked in a large multinational packaging company. He is a member of the Institute of Personnel Management and has written textbooks and workbooks on personnel management for correspondence and open learning courses.

**Richard Wootton BEd**
is Senior Tutor at Worcester Sixth Form College. He has written educational materials for schools commissioned by Shell UK Ltd, Lloyds Bank, Lever Bros and the Post Office. He is joint author of books published by the Schools Curriculum Development Committee.

# acknowledgements

The authors wish to thank the following individuals for their help with production of this book: Chris Baker, Bryan Coates, Jean Cox, Anne Fardon, Peter Fardon, Chris Hall, George Johnston, Susie Lee, Roger Petheram, Diane Skerm, and Jim Taylor.

The authors are particularly grateful for advice on the interpretation of the GNVQ specifications to Kay Kelly at NCVQ and to Linda Thomas at the Institute of Education, London University. Thanks are also due to BTEC, City and Guilds, and RSA and to the many teachers and lecturers who have discussed the contents and requirements of the GNVQ "Advanced" (ie Level 3) course with the authors.

Practical observation of the workplace has played an important part in the production of this book, and the Editor would like to thank Hugh Padley of Berkshire China and Charles Morgan of the Morgan Motor Company for the time given in factory visits. Thanks are also due to Charles Morgan for allowing the factory to be photographed and illustrated in this book, to the Rover Group for providing photographs of their Longbridge plant and to Terry Symonds for allowing his studio to be photographed.

Osborne Books is grateful to the following for permission to reproduce published material:

The Controller of Her Majesty's Stationery Office for reproduction of a variety of statistical tables from *Economic Trends, Monthly Digest of Statistics and Social Trends*

The Independent for an article "British women gain ground on men"

Lloyds Bank Plc for material from the *Lloyds Bank Economic Profile of Great Britain*, compiled by Trevor Williams

Methuen for maps from the *Atlas of Industrialising Britain 1780-1914* by Langton and Morris

Olympus Sport for their *Customer Care* questionnaire

Phillip Allan Publishing for material from *Economic Review*

W H Smith Ltd and David Young and Associates for their *Customer First* questionnaire

Weidenfeld & Nicolson for statistical figures from *The UK Economy* by Prest and Coppock

# contents

# introduction – for the student

The subject, Business Studies, is a fascinating area to investigate because it is so wide-ranging and because it impinges on every aspect of everyday life. The term "business" for example is not strictly limited to the corner shop and "High Street" names, it includes public bodies such as the local authority and British Rail.

Your study of Business Studies will be equally wide-ranging. You will be expected to read texts such as this, investigate statistics in libraries, collect documents, visit businesses, possibly work in businesses, and maybe set up your own profit-making business within your school or college. All this work will contribute towards your GNVQ Portfolio of Evidence, your "course file".

Your school or college will no doubt provide you with details of the specifications of the eight Units which make up the GNVQ course. These Units are divided into Elements which are are set out as follows:

| | |
|---|---|
| *Element Title* | for example "Element 3.2: Use consumer trends to forecast sales" |
| *performance criteria* | these are essentially what you have to be able to do to gain accreditation in the Unit, eg "characteristics of consumers are investigated" |
| *range statement* | this defines the areas of knowledge covered by the Element, eg "Consumer characteristics: demographic, age, gender, taste, lifestyle . . ." |
| *evidence indicators* | these indicate the student activities – including the external test – that have to be carried out successfully before you can gain your GNVQ, eg "A short term prediction (one to five years) of consumer demand based on identified consumer trends . . . and a sales forecast (one to five years) . . ." |

This book, *Business Studies*, has been specifically written to help you to cover all these Elements. The chapters take you through all the GNVQ Units and provide all the facts covered in the "range statements" which you will need for your external tests. At the end of the book are some Unit tests which will help with revision. The book also has a number of Evidence Collection Exercises which cover the "evidence indicators" and also develop your Core Skills on which you will be assessed.

Enjoy your course and this book, and may you have every success in your future career.

Michael Fardon
Summer 1993

# introduction – for the tutor

*Business Studies* has been specifically written for what was conceived as the GNVQ Level 3 in Business, and what is now known as the GNVQ "Advanced" Level in Business.

## coverage of the syllabus

The writers of *Business Studies* have taken great care to ensure that the right syllabus has been covered, at the right depth, and at the right level. Their aim in writing *Business Studies* has therefore been twofold:

- to produce a book which will provide the *knowledge requirement* of the GNVQ course which will be tested by externally set tests
- to provide a range of *practical activities* – Evidence Collection Exercises – which will satisfy the internal assessment requirements and contribute to the Portfolio of Evidence – the cumulative record of a student's achievement

*Business Studies* therefore:

- covers every Element in the course specification
- covers all the topics covered in the range statement of every Element
- provides student activities in the Evidence Collection Exercises which comply with the requirements of the evidence indicators
- includes at the back of the book a series of Unit Tests which will help prepare for the external testing

In this process Osborne Books has liaised with NCVQ and teachers and lecturers generally to ensure that the course specifications have been correctly interpreted.

## structure of the book

Readers will see from the contents page that *Business Studies* is divided into eight Sections which largely follow the eight Unit structure of the GNVQ course (see page iv). The writers, in consultation with teachers and lecturers who have been drawing up schemes of work, considered that the best starting point was a study of business organisations and systems. The book therefore starts with "Business Systems" rather than "Business in the Economy" and includes in this first section the coverage of types of business organisation specified in Element 4.2 in the "Human Resources" Unit.

Core Skill coverage and assessment have also been important considerations, and pages v and vi set out how they can be achieved by using this book.

The writers hope that you will enjoy using this book, and the Editor will welcome any comments and criticisms you may wish to make.

Michael Fardon
Summer 1993

# evidence collection exercises

# GNVQ Unit coverage

# core skills coverage

GNVQs have been designed to provide a foundation for training for employment, and also to prepare students for further and higher education. At Advanced Level (Level 3) the GNVQ in Business requires three of the core skills to be accredited: *Communication, Application of Number* and *Information Technology*. The Student Activities and Evidence Collection Exercises in this book are designed to develop these skills. Set out below is a summary of the three main skills and the way in which their development is implemented in this book. We suggest that teachers and lecturers may wish to use this summary as a basis for skills assessment of the course.

## communication

Four themes have been identified for development:

> *taking part in discussions*
> *preparing written materials*
> *using images to illustrate points made in writing and discussions*
> *reading and responding to written material and images*

These skills are developed specifically in three chapters:

- Chapter 4 "Communication systems – written communication" deals with the format of written communication: letters, memoranda, faxes, reports
- Chapter 5 "Oral and visual communication" deals with oral skills (telephones, messages, meetings) and visual communication (graphs, bar charts and formal presentations)
- Chapter 22 "Recruitment, job application and interviews" explains how to draw up an advertisement, complete an application for a job (letter, CV, application form); it concludes with interviewing techniques (for interviewer and interviewee).

Study of these chapters and completion of the appropriate student tasks will form useful material for assessment. In addition most other student tasks throughout the book develop these skills. Evidence Collection Exercises 1 and 12, for example will provide a broad basis for assessment.

## application of number

The numeracy skills at this level are equated with National Curriculum Level 7, and tutors are advised to refer to the relevant sections in the DES booklet "National Curriculum Mathematics for ages 5 to 16". Three themes have been identified for development:

> *gathering and processing data*
> *representing and tackling problems*
> *interpreting and presenting data*

Numeracy skills are developed throughout this book, and tutors might like to refer to the following pages:

- numerical calculations on invoices (314 and 316)
- percentages in the form of discounts (316), tax (341), VAT (336, 344, 358)
- averages (160), moving averages (161)

- time series analysis (161)
- linear regression (162)
- index numbers (164, 166 - 167)
- calculations and graphing (182, 256)
- critical path analysis (508 - 509)
- Gannt charts (511)
- formulas (506 – including square root) and throughout Chapter 39 (409)

Evidence Collection Exercises which *particularly* involve numerical techniques include:

- No 8 "Using consumer trends to forecast sales" (166) – averages, indices and tables of data
- No 19 "Monitoring business performance – Toscano Wines" – percentages, formulas, analysis of findings
- No 21 "Calculating the cost of goods and services"

## information technology

Five main themes have been identified:

> *storing and inputting information*
> *editing and organising information*
> *presenting information*
> *evaluating procedures and features of application*
> *dealing with errors and faults*

In this book Chapter 6 "Electronic systems" and Chapter 7 "Information technology and its users" specifically explain this Core Skill.   Evidence Collection Exercises  2 (page 61) and 3 (page 75) develop the use of Information Technology.   Tutors should note the additional use of IT on the following pages:

- spreadsheets: analysis of accounts (421), presentation of final accounts (391), cash flow forecasts (426 onwards and Evidence Collection Exercise 20, p.439)
- word processing  – throughout the book students are recommended to use a word processor for written presentations and, if available, a Desk Top Publishing package (61, 231)
- database: analysis of questionnaires (30, 157)
- use of computer charting facility (53)

# SECTION

# 1

# business systems

## contents

In this Section we look at what a business is, the many different types of business, and how a business is run. We examine in detail the skills that are necessary when working in a business: communication and the use of information technology. These are two of the Core Skills which form an important part of your studies You will be able to appreciate from reading this section that business studies involves both knowledge and skills.

The section is divided into seven chapters:

Chapter 1   We define what a business is, and look at different forms of business in the public sector and the private sector. We obtain an overview of business.

Chapter 2   This chapter looks at the way an individual business can be structured. It examines the different administrative systems functions within an organisation, eg sales and and finance.

Chapter 3   This chapter analyses and explains the various external influences which dictate how a business operates. These influences include legal constraints, the demands of the customer, and the practice of Total Quality Management.

Chapter 4   Communication systems are essential to the efficient running of business. In this chapter we describe the various forms of written communication used within business, including letters and reports.

Chapter 5   This chapter turns to the use of oral and visual communication in business, eg interviewing and presenting data in the form of graphs and charts.

Chapter 6   This chapter explains the setting up and use of electronic systems – computers and telephones – within a business.

Chapter 7   Information technology involves the use of computer equipment and programs. In this chapter we look at the main applications of computers in business and give practical advice on their use.

You should note that the last four chapters deal with the Core Skills of Communication and Information Technology. Your studies in this area will therefore contribute to evidence collected for GNVQ Unit 2 "Business Systems" and also to the Core Skills assessment.

## GNVQ Unit coverage

The writers have decided that for a logical progression in the book that the first seven chapters should cover Unit 2 "Business Systems". They have also included in this section the part of Element 4.2 from Unit 4 "Human Resources" which deals with types of business organisation and organisational structure, an obvious starting point for any study of business.

*For detailed reference of Unit coverage, please see the table on page iv.*

# 1 Business organisations

## introduction

In this chapter we will look at the forms of organisation which businesses take. We will specifically:
- define and analyse what we mean by a 'business'
- distinguish between the 'private' sector and the 'public' sector
- examine businesses in the private sector:
  - sole trader
  - partnership
  - limited companies (private and public)
  - co-operatives and franchises
- examine public sector organisations:
  - public corporations
  - Central Government enterprises
  - Local Government enterprises

Lastly we will look at non profit-making organisations, such as charities, which use business methods.

## what is a business?

### common factors in business

If you ask the person in the street what a business is, you are a likely to be given an example: W H Smith, Tescos, the local garage, British Airways, the window-cleaner, and so on. All these examples of 'businesses' have factors in common:
- they *use* resources which are limited in supply – money, manpower, materials
- they *provide* something in the form of goods or services – books, food, petrol, travel, clean windows
- they are normally in competition with others

- their activity involves specific *functions:*

  - *purchasing* – the order of materials and stock for use in the short-term (books, food, petrol) and the acquisition of items for use in the long-term (premises, vehicles)
  - *marketing the product or service* – this involves researching the need for a product and then promoting it; the promotion can range from TV and magazine advertising to placing an entry in the yellow pages and pushing leaflets through doors
  - *selling and distributing the product or service* – distributing the goods to the consumer, providing the client with the service
  - *book-keeping and accounting* – keeping a record of financial transactions so that performance and financial 'health' can be monitored
  - *management of staff* – this can be organised in the form of a Personnel Department, or in the case of the window-cleaner, making sure that his mate turns up on time

- *decision making* – all businesses are faced with choices which involve decisions:

  "Should we sell this magazine? – it may be pornographic"

  "Should we sell organically grown vegetables? – they go off more quickly"

  "Shall we instal a fast food counter in the garage?"

  "Should we increase the number of flights to Peru?"

  "Should I team up with another window cleaner ? – we may get more business working as a pair "

When one considers all these factors it is possible to come to a definition of a business:

*A business is an activity which involves the making of decisions to use resources for the purpose of selling goods or services*

This definition is useful in that it concentrates the mind on the need for *resources* and the importance of the *decision-making* process, themes which will be taken up later in this book.

## aims of business

If you again approach 'the person in the street' and ask what the aim of business is, the answer will invariably be "to make money, of course." The *profit* motive is understandably high on the list of objectives of any person in business, but there are other aims:

- *growth* – to sell as much as possible (this does not necessarily equate with profit!)
- *fame and reputation* – to become the most prestigious business in the field
- *personal interest* – of the owner of the business
- *to care for the environment* – to use recycled products, to ban CFCs (gases which damage the ozone layer) – again possibly at the expense of profit
- *to care for society* – to donate money to charity, to sport, or to the arts
- *political interest* – to donate money, for example, to the Conservative Party

## the private sector and the public sector

Businesses have traditionally been divided into what is termed the *private sector* and the *public sector*. A definition of these sectors is best achieved by looking first at the public sector:

**The public sector** comprises government owned or government controlled bodies including:

- public corporations such as the Post Office, British Rail and the Bank of England
- Government Departments (the Civil Service)
- local organisations such as County, Metropolitan or District Councils

You will no doubt have heard of discussions about the levels of *public sector pay* which affect teachers, nurses, and also cabinet ministers.

**The private sector** on the other hand, comprises enterprise which is directly or indirectly in private ownership. This sector accounts for most businesses operating within the UK. Private sector businesses include

- sole traders (one person businesses)
- partnerships (groups of people in business)
- limited companies (a limited company is a body owned by shareholders, set up to do business)
- cooperatives (groups of people 'clubbing' together for a specific purpose - eg a farmers cooperative set up for producing and selling grain)
- franchise operations (where a trader can 'buy' a name and set up a business which is already established and used by other independent operators, eg Thorntons and Dynarod)

**Privatisation** is a process whereby *public sector* operations have been 'sold off' by the Government, in order to raise money, to *private sector* shareholders. British Telecom is a well-known example.

### a further definition of business

A business may now be further defined as:

*any organisation which exists for commercial or public service reasons*

So far we have given only a brief introduction to the concept of the private and public sectors. The remainder of this chapter will examine in detail the business organisations which operate in these two sectors.

---

### student activity 1.1 – defining business

(a) Write down a definition of a business *in your own words*.

(b) Form into groups of three or four and decide who has drafted the best definition.

(c) Write down all the business organisations with which you had contact yesterday (eg by buying a magazine, going by bus, going to school, to the hospital, dentist etc). Categorise them by *private* and *public* sector

(d) Write down in each case in (c) above the most important aim of each of the business organisations (eg profit, public service etc)

---

## private sector business

In this section we will examine the following common forms of private sector business:
- sole trader
- partnership
- private limited company
- public limited company

In the next section we will explain how co-operatives and franchises operate.

## sole trader

*A sole trader is an individual trading in his or her name, or under a suitable trading name.*

If you set up in business, you may do so for a number of reasons: redundancy, dissatisfaction with your present job, or developing a hobby or interest into a business. The majority of people setting up in this way do so on their own. If you decide to do so, you become a *sole trader*.

In law a sole trader is an individual who is *solely liable for all the debts* of the business. If the business fails the sole trader will have to repay all its debts, and may have to sell his or her personal assets (house, car, personal belongings) to pay off those debts. The sole trader may be taken to Court and be made bankrupt if the debts are not repaid. If you are a sole trader you can use your own name, or adopt a trading name. You do not have to register a trading name, but you may find yourself in court if you use someone else's name or a name connected with royalty. You cannot, for instance, open a shop and call it 'Marks and Spencer' or 'Royal Designs'.

There are a number of *advantages* of being a sole trader:
* freedom – you are your own boss
* simplicity – there are no legal formalities required before you can start trading – there is less form-filling than there is, for instance, for limited companies, and the book-keeping should be less complex
* savings on fees – there are none of the legal costs of drawing up partnership agreements or limited company documentation

There are also *disadvantages:*
* risk – you are on your own, with no-one to share the responsibilities of running the business
* time – you may need to work long hours to meet tight deadlines
* expertise – you may have limited skills in areas such as finance and marketing
* vulnerability – if you are ill, you may have no cover to enable the business to carry on

It is clear that setting up in business as a sole trader involves total commitment in terms of capital, time, and the risk involved. If you are starting your business with other people or need to raise substantial capital, you may consider establishing a partnership or a limited company.

## partnership

*A partnership is a group of individuals working together in business with a view to making a profit.*

A *partnership* is simple to establish and involves two or more people running a business together. In legal terms, the partners *are* the business. Examples of partnerships include groups of doctors, dentists, accountants, and solicitors.

A partnership – often known as a 'firm' – can either trade in the name of the partners, or under a suitable trading name. For example if M Smith & G Jones set up a glazing business, they could call themselves 'Smith and Jones & Co.' or adopt a more catchy name such as 'Classy Glass Merchants'. You should note that the '& Co.' does *not* mean that the partnership is a limited company.

The essential legal point about a partnership is that each partner is liable for the *whole* debt of the partnership (in legal terms 'jointly and severally liable'). This means that if one partner runs up a big debt, each of the other partners will be liable for it. It therefore pays to take care whom you admit as a co-partner in your business.

Partnerships are regulated by the *Partnership Act 1890*. Most partnerships will operate according to the terms of a Partnership Agreement, a document usually drawn up by a solicitor, and known as the

Articles of Partnership or Deed of Partnership (a more formal document). This document will set out matters such as

- the amount of capital contributed by each partner
- partners' voting rights
- the sharing out of profit (and losses) by the partners
- the procedure in the case of partnership disputes (these are unfortunately common)
- the procedures for new partners coming in and old partners retiring (or being asked to retire)

It must be stressed that a partnership does not *have* to draw up a partnership agreement; it is just that a written document sets out clearly each partner's rights and obligations, a useful factor in th case of a dispute. In the absence of a written agreement, the Partnership Act 1890 sets out certain terms and conditions relating to partners' rights and obligations. If there were a dispute, these terms would be recognised in a court of law.

The *advantages* of a partnership are:

- there is the potential to raise more capital than a sole trader is able to – there are more individuals to contribute funds
- there is more potential for expertise and specialisation – one partner may be a technical expert, another a good salesperson, another a financial expert, and so on
- there is cover for holidays and sickness
- unlike a limited company (see below), a partnership does not have to make its accounts available for the public

The *disadvantages* are:

- each partner is liable for the whole debt of the partnership, to the extent that he or she may be made personally bankrupt if the business fails
- each partner is also liable for the business deals of the other partners (this could be a problem if a deal went badly wrong)
- disgreements can and do occur amongst partners – occasionally this can lead to the break-up of the partnership and the business

Another option if a group of people want to set up a business is the formation of a limited company, to which we will now turn.

## limited company

*A limited company is a separate legal body, owned by shareholders, run by directors.*

A *limited company* is quite different from a sole trader and a partnership in that it has a legal identity separate from its owners. The owners – the shareholders – are not personally liable for the business debts (the company's debts), but have *limited liability*: the most they can lose is the money they have invested in the company.

A company is managed by directors appointed by the shareholders (also known as members). In the case of many small companies the shareholders *are* the directors. A company must be registered at a central office known as Companies House. An annual return and financial statements must be sent each year to Companies House by the company. As you will see there is much paperwork and 'red tape' involved in establishing and running a limited company. The documentation you are likely to encounter is:

- *the Memorandum and Articles of Association*
    - the *Memorandum* is the 'constitution' of the company and sets out the company's name, location, its share capital, and defines in an 'Objects Clause' what the company can and cannot do, often in general terms such as "a general trading company", which means it can do anything legal

– the *Articles* are effectively the 'rulebook' of the company, governing the conduct of directors, calling of meetings, and other administrative matters

• *the Certificate of Incorporation* – the 'birth certificate' of a company – is a single sheet of paper issued by Companies House stating when the company was formed, what its name is, and giving it a number

If you are running a Young Enterprise company in your school or college you will appreciate at first hand the complexity of setting up and running a limited company. If you are forming a limited company outside school or college, a solicitor or accountant will advise you and help you draw up all the necessary documentation. You can either form a new company, or buy an existing company 'off the shelf' and change its name to whatever you want to call it, by registering the change at Companies House.

The *advantages* of forming a limited company are:

• members (shareholders) have limited liability for the company's debts
• capital can be raised more easily, and in some cases, from the public on the Stock Exchange
• expansion is made easier, because of the availability of finance
• status – for the employees and the directors

The *disadvantages* are:

• the expense of setting up a limited company (solicitors' and accountants' fees)
• paperwork – the legal necessity to send an annual return and financial statements to Companies House
• the accounts have by law to be audited, incurring more accountants' fees

## private companies and public companies

It should be noted that a limited company can be referred to as either

• a *private limited company* (abbreviated to *Ltd*), or
• a *public limited company* (abbreviated to *plc*)

Most small or medium-sized businesses which decide to incorporate (form a company) become private limited companies; they are often family businesses with the shares held by the members of the family. Private companies cannot offer their shares for sale to the public at large, and it therefore follows that their ability to raise finance for expansion is limited.

A private company may, however, become and trade as a *public limited company* if it has

• a minimum of two directors (a private limited company needs only one)
• a share capital of at least £50,000
• a Trading Certificate issued by Companies House
• the words 'public limited company' or 'plc' in its name

A plc *can* offer its shares for sale on the Stock Market in order to raise finance, but not all take this step.

**student activity 1.2 – types of private sector businesses**
What legal form of business would you recommend in the following circumstances, and why?

(a) Bob has been made redundant and wants to set up a plumbing business with his redundancy money.

(b) Stan and Oliver want to set up a general 'odd job' business to carry out general building/repair/decorating jobs.

(c) Helen, Olivia and Chloe want to set up an 'up-market' fashion clothing business, and need to raise a substantial amount of capital.

(d) The Government wants to sell off the Prison Services.

## co-operatives and franchises

### co-operatives

A co-operative is a general term applied to two types of trading body:

1. *a retail Co-operative Society – a specific form of trading body set up under the terms  of the Industrial and Provident Societies Acts*

2. *co-operative – a group of people 'clubbing' together to produce goods or to provide a service*

We will deal with each of these in turn.

### retail Co-operative Societies

Co-operative Societies date back to 1844 when a group of twenty eight Rochdale weavers, suffering from the effects of high food prices and low pay,  set up a society to buy food wholesale, ie at the same price as it was sold *to* the shops.  This food was then sold to the members at prices lower than the shop prices,  and the profits distributed to the members in what what known as a *dividend,* the level of which depended on the amount of food they had bought.  These self-help co-operatives grew in number until in 1990 there were around eighty in number.  The best-known example of a retail co-operative is what is known as 'the Co-op', which now operates the Leo's supermarket chain.  The Co-op was founded as the Co-operative Wholesale Society in 1863.

A Co-operative Society is a separate legal body set up under the Industrial and Provident Societies Acts (unlike a company, which is set up under the Companies Acts).   A person becomes  a Co-operative Society member by buying a share;  this confers certain rights:

• one vote (and no more than one vote) at the Co-operative Society's annual meeting at which the governing committe is elected
• discounts at the Society's retail outlets (traditionally in the form of stamps) and use of other facilities (funeral services, for example)

At the time of writing, the retail Co-operatives, which have traditionally been regional, are declining in number, partly because of merger and rationalisation and partly because of the intense competition in the retail sector from public companies such as Tescos, J Sainsbury, Asda and Gateway.

### co-operative ventures

The term co-operative also applies more loosely to co-operative ventures which are not registered as Co-operative Societies under the Industrial and Provident Societies Acts.  At the time of writing there are around two thousand co-operatives which fulfil a  number of different functions:

*the trading co-operative*     Groups of individuals, such as farmers,  who do not have the resources in terms of capital and time to carry out their own promotion, selling and distribution, may 'club' together to store and distribute their produce.  They may also set up co-operative ventures to purchase machinery and equipment.

*the workers co-operative*     A worker's co-operative may often be found where the management of a business is not succeeding and a shut-down is proposed.  The 'workers' step in, with the consent of the management, and take over the ownership and running of the business with the aim of 'making a go of it' and at the same time safeguarding their jobs.  Commonly the workers will contribute capital in the form of a share and thus assume voting rights and control of the business.  It is not uncommon for the workers' share to be funded out of redundancy money.  In 1992, for example, 130 miners invested £10,000 each to re-open Monktonhall Colliery near Edinburgh.

**franchises**

The franchise system was first established in the USA and is now a growing business sector in the UK. A franchise is an operation which involves two separate parties:

- *the franchisor*, a person who has developed a certain line of business, such as clothes retailing, hamburgers, drain clearing, and has made the trading name well-known
- *the franchisee*, a person who buys the right to trade under the well-known trading name in a particular locality, and in return for his investment receives training and equipment

The franchise system is not just confined to *well-known* trading names. It is becoming increasingly common for smaller businesses to franchise parts of their operations. For example, your local department store may *franchise* some of its departments; your local milkman may operate as a *franchisee* of the dairy, his 'round' being his franchise.

The *advantages* of taking on a franchise are

- you are entering into a business which has been tried and tested in the market
- your business may well have a household name such as Benetton, or Dynarod
- you are more likely to be able to raise finance from a bank for a well-known franchise
- you should receive training, and in some cases, be provided with tried and tested equipment
- in short, the *risk* element is low

The *disadvantages* are:

- the initial cost of going into the franchise– the payment to the franchisor – can be high
- a proportion of your profits also go to the franchisor
- you are less independent in that you cannot develop the business as you wish – you cannot change the name or change the method of doing business

In short, you are less independent and could be less profitable than if the enterprise were your own.

---

**student activity 1.3 – co-operatives and franchises**

Find as many examples as you can of co-operatives and franchises in your local area. Analyse them according to

(a) the type of business

(b) the size of business

What conclusions can you draw from your investigations?

---

# public sector 'business'

We turn now to *public sector organisations* – organisations which are directly or indirectly controlled by the government. The Government owns and controls certain areas of activity for a number of different reasons:

- the area provides goods and services for the good of the community, for example, health, education, transport
- the area has to be controlled by the Government because it is supervisory in nature, for example Customs & Excise, the Inland Revenue, the Armed Forces, the Police, the Bank of England

In this section we will examine:

- Public Corporations
- Central Government enterprises
- Local Government enterprises

## public corporations

Public corporations are bodies established by Act of Parliament, and owned and financed by the State.  Examples include the Post Office, British Rail, the Bank of England and the BBC.  Some public corporations are known as *nationalised industries* because at one time they were in the private sector, and were then nationalised (taken into public control) by Act of Parliament.  British Rail, for example, used to be a group of independent private sector regional railway companies before it was nationalised in 1948 by a Labour government.  The tendency now, as we will see in Chapter 11, is for *privatisation*, the return of public corporations to the private sector.

Public corporations are run by a Board of Management headed by a chairperson appointed by the Government.  The public corporation is directly answerable to a Government Minister – the chairperson of British Rail to the Minister of Transport, for example – and also to a select committee of MPs.  Whereas a public limited company will give an annual report to its shareholders, a public corporation will submit its annual report to the appropriate minister, who will then report to Parliament.  The proceedings are, of course, made public and are usually reported in the media.

## central government enterprises

These fall into two categories
- an enterprise run as part of a government department – a Government Minister has ultimate responsibility, and the day-to-day operations are run by Civil Servants;  the Inland Revenue (the 'taxman') is a well-known example
- a public limited company in the private sector in which the Government has a shareholding

## local authority enterprise

*Local Authority* is a term applied to local governing councils which operate both in the county areas and also in urban areas.  In the county areas the Local Authority is normally structured in three tiers:
- the County Council
- the Borough or District Councils
- the Parish Councils

In the urban areas, on the other hand, only *one* level of council exists:  in London there are separate Borough Councils (such as Brent or Westminster) and in other urban areas there are Metropolitan Borough Councils (such as Birmingham or Liverpool).  Proposals for the reform of the structure of local government into single 'unitary' authorities are currently being considered.

Local Authorities taken as a whole have a wide range of services to administer. These include education, environmental health, planning, refuse collection, social services, transport, fire services, libraries and recreational facilities.  They finance these from three main sources:
- Central Government Grants
- local taxation (currently the Council Tax)
- income from local authority enterprise

These enterprises include a wide variety of commercial activities, including, for example:
- leisure – swimming pools, golf courses
- transport – local bus services
- car parks
- lotteries

Not all of these are actually carried out by the Local Authorities: in recent years Local Authorities have engaged in Compulsory Competitive Tendering (CCT), the system whereby services such as waste collection and catering have been offered for tender to private businesses.  It has been proposed that this form of local authority *privatisation* be extended to other areas such as legal services and payroll.

**student activity 1.4 – public sector businesses**

Investigate the services (including transport) supplied to:

(a)   the house in which you live

(b)   your school or college

Discover whether they are provided by the public sector or by the private sector. If they are provided by the private sector, try to discover when the business concerned started that service. What conclusions can you draw from these investigations?

# non-profit making organisations

There are a number of types of organisations which employ business methods but which do not aim to make a profit for the organisers' benefit. These include

- *charities* – both national and local which raise money for humanitarian and social needs; these include well-established international charities (Red Cross), national charities (Mencap, Cancer Research), local charities (the local hospital scanner appeal) or 'one-off' events (Comic Relief)
- *Arts Associations* – national foundations, local dramatics, operatics and choral societies
- *Sports Associations* – national associations and local clubs
- *pressure groups* – examples include Friends of the Earth and Greenpeace

**student activity 1.5 – charities?**

Identify as wide a range as possible of non-profit making organisations active in your area. In each case

(a)   identify the business methods they use

(b)   state whether you think that the funds they raise or the facilities they provide should be provided by the Government – why do you think the funds have to be raised by independent means?

# chapter summary

❑   A business may be defined as *any organisation which exists for commercial or public service reasons*.

❑   The private sector comprises enterprises which are directly or indirectly in private ownership:  sole trader businesses, partnerships, limited companies, co-operatives and franchises.

❑   The public sector comprises government owned or government controlled organisations: public corporations, Central Government enterprises and Local Government enterprises.

❑   Some organisations, eg charities, employ business methods but are essentially non-profit making.

# 2 Business structures and administration systems

## introduction

In the last chapter we looked at the different *types* of business organisation. In this chapter we look more closely at the organisation itself, at the way it is *structured* and *administered*.

All organisations require a system – a structure – for imposing control and making communication possible. We will therefore examine in this chapter:

- the principles of organisational structure
- the different types of organisational structure
- the administration systems within an organisation
- the various functions of the administration system

## basic principles of the organisation

An organisation may be defined as:

*a group of individuals working together for a specific purpose*

Although your course of studies is based around business organisations, where the "specific purpose" is normally the pursuit of profit, it is important to appreciate that any group of individuals may constitute an organisation, for example a club, a local authority. In the study of organisational theory it is common practice to illustrate the organisation by means of a structure chart. Look at the structure of a family – the most basic of organisations – set out on the next page. In this family there are two parents and five children. Note in particular:

- the routes of communication between different parts of the organisation
- the levels of control and authority within the organisation

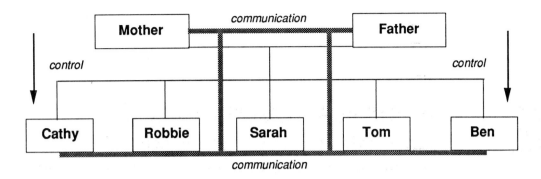

Note the following points:
- the parents are at the top of the diagram as they are responsible for and control the family
- communication flows both horizontally and vertically: the children communicate with each other and with the parents; the parents communicate with each other and with the children

It is not difficult to see that this is the ideal family, where everything works so well. Bearing in mind the way families operate in reality, what problems can you foresee with this structure?

- the parents may not be speaking to each other
- one parent may dominate and control the other
- some of the children may not be speaking to each other
- the parents may not be able to control the children

This example of a family has been discussed because it illustrates the basic principles of how an organisation should function, and can malfunction. Any failure in communication routes or in control will result in serious problems for the organisation.

## organisational structures

You should appreciate that the *shape* of the organisational structure of a business will affect the way in which it operates. Set out on the following pages are some commonly found types of organisational structure.

### hierarchical structure

This is a traditional structure, typified by a limited company business (illustrated on the next page) or by traditional organisations such as the Civil Service. The main features of a hierarchical structure (also known as a 'pyramid' or 'tall' structure) are
- a *hierarchical* structure – a series of levels, each responsible to and controlled by the level above
- as you move up the levels, the number of people or units decreases – hence the 'pyramid' effect
- at the top of the pyramid is the managing director (or equivalent) who is responsible for the success or failure of the organisation

The problems associated with a pyramid or 'tall' structure are
- long lines of communication between the lower levels of employees and top management in their 'ivory tower' – a problem which successful management can overcome
- lack of motivation in the lower levels who see no immediate prospect of climbing up the levels of the pyramid

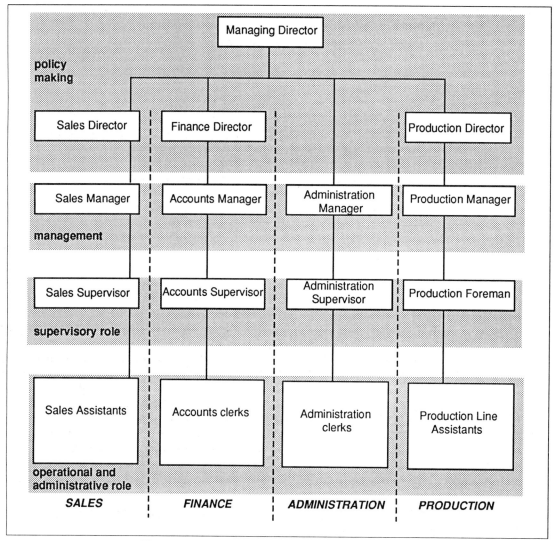

Fig. 2.1  A hierarchical organisational structure

### points to note from the structure chart

You should note that the chart set out above represents a small company – for example a manufacturer – which produces goods.  The levels of hierarchy and functions (sales etc) are only illustrated as an *example* of a pyramidal structure.   The essential point to remember is that the basic pyramidal or tall *shape* of the hierarchical structure will remain the same, no matter how the departmental functions or levels of authority change.

Now note the following points from the chart:

**functions**       Each vertical column represents a separate function or department:

- *sales* – responsible for the marketing and selling of the products
- *finance* – responsible for everyday financial transactions such as invoicing customers, getting the money in, paying for purchases and running expenses
- *administration* – the day-to-day running of the company – employing staff, payroll, running the building, purchasing
- *production* – developing products, controlling the production process

**management levels**   Each horizontal level represents a step in the level of importance and responsibility of the staff:

- the *managing director* is responsible for directing company policy, the other directors are responsible for policy in their defined areas (eg sales, finance)
- *managers* are in charge of the departments, they implement policy and liaise with the directors
- *supervisors* are in charge of the day-to-day running of the departments and normally work alongside the production and administrative staff
- *production and administrative staff* enable the company to function and to communicate effectively both internally and externally

**levels of authority**   Each horizontal level represents a level of authority which must be respected and used in cases of

- *instructions* – passed down the line of authority
- *problems* – referred to a higher level
- *disciplinary matters and complaints–* referred in the first instance to the next level up

## horizontal or 'flat' structure

The horizontal or 'flat' structure (see fig 2.2 below) is becoming an increasingly popular form of organisational structure. Here individual parts of the organisation operate independently of the other parts, but are all under the 'umbrella' control of the higher management. Many large companies have reorganised themselves into groups of smaller operating companies in this way. The main features of a 'flat' organisation are

- degrees of specialisation in the separate parts of the organisation, eg different products, different geographical areas, different functions (eg sales, purchasing, accounts, personnel)
- more motivation for the management of the individual units, who are rid of the bureaucracy of a pyramid structure, and are able to take more decisions without reference to a higher level

The problems experienced with this form of organisation include

- poor communications *across* the organisation – the 'left hand' not knowing what the 'right hand' is doing, either because of geographical separation, or because of rivalries
- weakened control from the top management which has a greater span of control to sustain and a wider spread of resources to manage

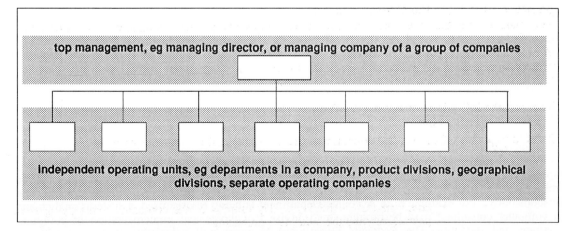

*Fig. 2.2  A horizontal or 'flat' organisational structure*

## further aspects of organisational structure

It is clear that the *hierarchical* structure illustrated in fig. 2.1 is suitable for large organisations, and as such is largely *static:* it will be slow to adapt to change because decisions affecting the whole of the organisation will take a long time to be made, and even longer to implement. The flat structure shown in fig. 2.2, however, allows more independence to the individual operating units which can make decisions and change more rapidly. In this sense the flat organisation can be more *dynamic* – its constituent units can make rapid and effective decisions.

A similar contrast may be drawn between a hierarchical and a flat organisation in that all the functions in a hierarchical structure – eg purchasing and marketing – will be *centralised*, whereas in a flat organisation they will probably be *devolved*, ie the responsibility for administrative functions will pass to the individual operating units.

---

### student activity 2.1 – organisational structures

Draw up a structure chart of your Young Enterprise company or mini-business, having first established:

* the different levels of authority
* the different functional areas, eg sales, production

Include on your chart arrows indicating the lines of control and authority.

State:

(a)  briefly the functions of any individual in each different level of authority

(b)  whether you consider the organisation to be tall or flat

(c)  whether you see any particular problems with this type of structure in terms of communication or control

(d)  whether you consider you could improve on the organisation

*Note: if you are not taking part in a business start-up scheme, you could use a business in which you have a work placement, part-time job, or a business with which your school or college has close links. You should liaise closely with your tutor in this activity. If you are running a small business, activities (c) and (d) could be discussed in small groups within the class, and the results then compared in an open class session.*

---

## relationships within the organisational structure

The organisational structures illustrated on the last two pages show that authority and control are exercised from above, and pass down through the levels of the hierarchy. This is known as a *line* relationship:

### line relationships

In any organisation a clear line of authority and responsibility can be traced from the top to the bottom of the hierarchy:

* policy and instructions pass downwards
* responsibility for actions, errors and complaints passes upwards
* responsibility for decisions can be delegated downwards

Although the line relationship is the most obvious relationship, there are also *other* relationships not shown on the charts. These include:

### function relationships

A function relationship is established when a person is appointed as a specialist to carry out a specific function in an organisation, and takes responsibility for that function. A specialist will be responsible to the higher management (eg directors) and will relieve a line manager of that responsibility. For example if an Accounts Department is being re-organised, a systems analyst and a computer consultant may be brought in to advise the choice and implementation of computer systems and staffing. The Accounts Department Manager will liaise with them, but will not ultimately be responsible for the decisions made.

*staff relationships*

A staff relationship exists when a manager is given *advice* by someone else, possibly a staff member working in another department who does not have a *line* relationship with the manager. The manager accepts responsibility for all decisions taken as a result of that advice; the adviser is free of responsibility.

---

**student activity 2.2 – relationships within the organisation**

Identify the *types* of relationship (ie whether line, function or staff) in the following situations within a business:

(a) The Sales Director tells the Finance Director in confidence that he suspects one of the Accounts Clerks of stealing money from the till.

(b) The Managing Director appoints a computer consultant to oversee the installation of a new computer accounting system.

(c) The Finance Director confirms to the Managing Director that one of the Accounts Clerks has been found stealing from the till; he asks for his immediate dismissal for gross misconduct.

(d) The Managing Director fires the Accounts Clerk.

---

# administration systems

We have already seen in the structure chart of the hierarchical organisation that the business illustrated is organised according to *function* – sales, finance, administration, production. This is by far the most *common* method of organisation and will be explained in more detail in the rest of this chapter. It should be appreciated, however, that there are other methods of organising a business, eg

- by *product* – eg vehicle production where individual factories produce individual types of vehicle
- by *area* – eg transport businesses such as British Rail's Network South East
- by type of customer – eg some banks which have specific branches for business customers

In this chapter, however, we will look at the following functions within a business:

- accounts
- purchasing/production
- marketing and sales
- distribution
- personnel
- administration and support services

## the accounting function

The Accounting Department of a business is responsible for financial record keeping. This involves keeping records – either in manual form, or on computer file – of money received and paid out. The financial records maintained will be used to produce the financial statements of the business (see Chapters 35 to 38), which in the case of limited companies are required by law. The Accounting Department normally also oversees the payment of wages and the handling of cash by the cashier. Full and accurate wages records are also a legal requirement.

The Accounting Department is also responsible for the *management accounts* of the business. These are figures produced for the management of a business showing how well the company is performing in terms of income and expenditure in comparison with *budgets* prepared in advance.

### the production/ purchasing function

If a business is manufacturing a *product*, the manufacturing process will have to strictly controlled in order to maintain quality and keep to production targets.  The business must also monitor the efficiency of production methods and research and develop new techniques in line with modern technology.  A closely controlled purchasing policy is also an important aspect of efficient production and will have a direct effect on profitability.  The purchasing function must ensure that it obtains raw materials from the right supplier, at the right price, at the right time, and of the appropriate quality.

If the business is providing a *service*, the role of the production department will be taken by an *operations department*.

### the marketing and sales function

*Marketing* is involved with satisfying customers' needs at the right price.  It means researching what the customer wants, and investigating how the business can satisfy that need.  Selling, on the other hand, involves persuading the customer to buy the products the business has already produced. Often in an organisation the marketing and selling functions are closely linked, and the danger lies in the business becoming *product* orientated rather than believing that "the customer is king."  The sales function will co-ordinate the selling programme, using a variety of techniques – travelling sales representatives, telephone sales, mailshots and a follow-up schedule.

### the distribution function

Efficient distribtion means that the customer gets the product on time and in perfect condition. Distribution involves warehousing and storage, packing, despatch and transport.  Businesses will vary in their distribution methods, but the most successful businesses will always monitor the *quality* of their distribution.

### the personnel function

The personnel function fulfils a number of needs.  It is responsible for the hiring and firing of employees, for staff training and development, and for dealing with matters relating to industrial relations.  In service industries in particular the personnel function is responsible with senior management for the "customer care" programme which will be  critical in winning new business and satisfying existing customers.

### administration and support services

The administration and support services are essential in keeping the wheels of the business turning. They include maintenance of the business premises and equipment, reprographics, in-house printing (forms, stationery, newsletters), catering and computer services, mail handling and  data storage.

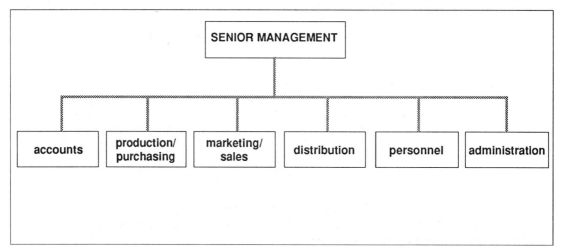

*Fig. 2.3 Administration systems within an organisation*

## the purpose of administration systems

So far in this chapter we have described the various *functions* of administrative systems. We need also to examine their *purpose* in the organisation.

### efficiency
Administrative systems are established so that the organisation can operate *efficiently*. Each function will be clearly defined and job descriptions will normally be drawn up for members of staff who will operate within prescribed routines.

There will also be flexibility so that *non-routine functions* can be dealt with. Some organisations operate under a *matrix* system, which effectively means that any member of staff will be answerable to more than one supervisor or manager.

### support
Administrative systems also provide *support* for:

*human resources*　　ie the employees who receive:
- training and welfare backup from personnel department
- day-to-day services such as car-parking, the canteen, photocopying, security
- payments of wages and salaries

*financial resources*　　the administrative systems provide:
- computer systems for recording and analysing financial transactions
- suitable trained staff for operating financial systems
- security for cash kept on the premises and being collected from the bank

*physical resources*　　the administrative systems provide:
- premises maintenance and security
- machinery and equipment maintenance and security
- supply and safe storage of stock and raw materials
- vehicles and transport
- systems for recording assets (items owned by the business), including stock levels
- insurance cover for all assets – on and off the premises

### recording and monitoring of business performance
Administrative systems record data about the performance of the business which is used by management and outside bodies to judge its level of success. A business will normally make projections about its performance, and it will be the responsibility of the senior management to take action if the actual performance falls short of (or exceeds) the target. Typical examples of data include:
- sales performance both by volume (items sold) and by value (sales revenue)
- profit level
- stock level (too high a stock level means money tied up unnecessarily)
- v arious costs in relation to profit (eg wages, advertising, interest paid on borrowing)
- the level of wastage in the production process
- the nature of customer response to questionnaires about the quality of customer service

---

**student activity 2.3 – administration systems at work**

You go into a local department store. What administration departments or functions will be involved in the following transactions?

(a)   You buy a pair of shorts.

(b)   You return some recently purchased underwear and receive a cash refund.

(c)   You go and have a cup of coffee in the restaurant.

(d)   You want a particular pair of sandals, but your size is out of stock. They will order a pair from the supplier.

(e)   You are asked to fill in a questionnaire on quality of service in the store.

(f)   On the way out you see a notice advertising for part-time weekend sales assistants. You make a note of the telephone number and decide to make enquiries.

(g)   As you go through the door you accidentally set off the alarm and are stopped by a store detective.

Draw up a diagram showing the *administrative* structure of the organisation, adding the function of senior management and any other areas which you think appropriate.

---

# chapter summary

❑   An organisation is a group of individuals working together for a specific purpose.

❑   An organisation may have a hierarchical (tall) structure or a flat structure.

❑   Relationships within an organisation may be line, function or staff relationships.

❑   Administration systems may be organised according to function, product, area or by type of customer. The most common system is organised by function.

❑   Administration functions include:
- accounts
- purchasing/production/operations
- marketing and sales
- distribution
- personnel
- administration and support services

❑   The purposes of administration systems are:
- to ensure the efficient running of the organisation
- to provide support for human, financial and physical resources
- to provide data so that business performance can be monitored

# 3 Administration systems – external influences

## introduction

In the last chapter we examined the purpose and function of administration systems within businesses in terms of the efficiency of *internal* organisation. The operation of administration systems within businesses is also determined by *external* influences. These fall under two main headings:

- the requirements of the law
- the requirements of the customer

In this chapter we will see how these demands affect the way business operations are organised.

Legal requirements of a business include:

- Employment Law
- Health and Safety at Work regulations
- Company Law (for limited companies)
- Value Added Tax (VAT) obligations
- Pay as You Earn (PAYE) – deductions from employees wages

Administration systems are also directly and indirectly dictated by the needs of the *customer;* some of these needs are dictated by *consumer protection law*, and some are responded to by *customer care schemes* and *Quality systems* (Quality Assurance and Total Quality Management).

When a business realises that it is there to help the *customer,* it is then able – through customer feedback – to *evaluate* the efficiency and effectiveness of its operations.

## employment law

There are a number of legal requirements which dictate how the employer treats the employee. These comprise:

- Employment Law
- the regulations generally known as Health and Safety at Work (HASAW)

We will deal with these in turn.

Most employees are protected in law by Acts of Parliament which give them rights in areas such as terms of employment, discrimination on grounds of race and sex, and equal pay.

### Employment Protection (Consolidation) Act 1978

A contract is a legally binding agreement between two people. Most full-time employees will have a written *contract of employment.*   The main terms of a  contract of employment will set down what the job is, what the pay is and the notice period required.  If the contract of employment is *not* in writing – which it need not be – the employer must give a *written statement* to a full-time employee who works more than sixteen hours a week of the terms of employment, within 13 weeks of beginning employment, containing details of:

- names of parties (ie employer and employee)
- date of commencement of employment (and termination if appropriate)
- title of job
- remuneration and when payable
- working hours
- holidays and holiday pay
- sickness provisions (sick pay)
- pensions
- details of grievance procedure (if the number of employees is more than 20)
- length of notice required

### Anti-Discrimination Law

- *Sex Discrimination Act 1975 (and amendments)* makes it illegal for an employer to discriminate against an employee on grounds of sex
- *Race Relations Act 1976* makes it illegal for an employer to discriminate against an employee on grounds of race
- *Equal Pay Act 1976 (and amendments)* makes it illegal for an employer to discriminate against an employee in terms of pay and conditions of work when the employee carries out similar work to another person

Cases in courts of law relating to these statutes (Acts of Parliament) are frequently reported in the media.  You should note that the cases are often taken beyond the English Courts to the European Community (EC) courts which can make rulings affecting practice in England and Wales.

## health and safety at work

### Health and Safety at Work etc Act 1974

The Health and Safety at Work etc Act 1974 is aimed at *people* at work.  Its general aims are to

- maintain or improve the standards of health, safety and welfare of people at work
- protect other people against risks to health and safety arising out of work activities
- control the use and storage of dangerous substances.
- control certain emissions into the air from certain premises

To achieve these aims the Act puts people into categories and gives each category specific obligations.  The categories are:  employers,  employees, the self-employed, manufacturers etc, and those that control premises.

The principle obligation of *employers* is to safeguard, as far as is reasonably practicable, the health, safety and welfare of the people who work for them.

To achieve this aim, employers should provide and maintain:
* safe and healthy plant and systems of work – and maintenance of the equipment
* safe and healthy working environment and adequate welfare facilities and arrangements
* safe and healthy premises with adequate amenities, access and exits
* safe methods for handling, storing and transporting materials
* adequate instruction and training for employees, and adequate supervision
* information to employees concerning health and safety

In addition, the employer must issue a written *safety policy* stating his intention to secure the health and safety of persons employed, and setting out the arrangements made for this purpose. The Act also makes provision for the appointment of safety representatives and states the employer's obligation to form a safety committee.

The area of health and safety at work is subject to constant review, particularly in terms of Directives issued by the EC, which are binding in the UK. The regulations relating to VDUs (computer screens) are a case in point.

### Offices, Shops and Railway Premises Act 1963

This Act covers the maintenance of business premises and requires the employer to provide:
* clean, uncrowded, heated, well ventilated premises
* toilets (for him and for her)
* washing facilities and a rest area
* first aid facilities and fire escapes

---

**student activity 3.1 – treatment of employees by employers**

Using either a work placement, a part-time job placement, or your school/college, carry out the following investigations:

(a) Obtain a written contract of employment and compare the details on the contract with the requirements of the Employment Protection (Consolidation) Act 1978

(b) Gather information about the Health and Safety at Work regulations, and if possible obtain a copy of the organisation's 'safety policy'. Compare the information gathered with the legal requirements.

In order to appreciate the laws relating to discrimination, obtain a copy of your local paper and examine the job advertisements.

(c) Can you find any examples of sexual or racial discrimination?

(d) If you can, are there any circumstances about the job which might justify discrimination?

---

# company law

Limited companies are regulated in law by the Companies Acts 1985 and 1989. These statutes set out how a company and its directors must conduct their dealings. All companies are registered at Companies House, a Government owned organisation in Cardiff which keeps full records of all companies registered in England and Wales. These records are available to the public.

As we saw when looking at companies in Chapter 1, there is a considerable amount of 'red tape' which limited companies (but not sole traders or partnerships) must observe *by law*. These procedures involve:
* the drawing up of doumentation when the company is incorporated (formed) – the *Memorandum of Association* (the constitution of the company) and the *Articles of Association* (the 'rulebook')
* the holding of meetings, including an Annual General Meeting (although companies can now dispense with AGMs if they choose to do so)
* the keeping of formal records – details of directors, shareholdings, minutes of meetings

- the annual filing (sending) of financial statements to Companies House, or abbreviated statements in the case of small companies
- the filing of an annual return (Form 363) stating details of directors, share capital issued, shareholdings, company property charged (mortgaged) for borrowing

A business which is a limited company must have a Company Secretary appointed to administer all these requirements.  The Company Secretary is not a 'secretary' in the traditional 'office secretary' sense, but is often a Director of the Company, and may be the Managing Director.

---

**student activity 3.2 – company administration**
If you are taking part in a Young Enterprise Scheme or are setting up a company as part of your coursework, investigate the role of the company secretary, and make a short written summary of his or her main duties and the annual returns that have to be made.

If this is not possible, interview or arrange a talk with a company secretary from an organisation with which your school or college has contact (in the case of some colleges, it could be the college itself).

---

# financial administration

The accounting function within an organisation has a number of legal requirements to fulfil.  These include:

- the keeping of full records of financial transactions
- dealing with VAT, and VAT registration where appropriate
- maintaining payroll records and deducting tax and National Insurance from employees (PAYE)
- paying sick pay and maternity pay to employees
- arranging pension payments, and in some cases administering pensions

We will deal with these in turn.

### the need for accounting records
All businesses are required to keep accurate accounts of their financial transactions (see Chapter 28) so that they can provide information to:

- the *Inland Revenue*, so that their tax liability can be established
- *H M Customs & Excise* – the body which deals with the collection of Value Added Tax (see below)

The object here is to prevent businesses from evading tax. You should note that limited companies are liable to *corporation tax*, which is worked out as a percentage of their profit.  Sole traders and partners in partnerships are liable to *income tax*, a tax on their personal income, ie the amount of money they receive from the business is pay and in benefits. In all cases, the financial records of the business – all invoices, receipts, the 'books', computer records – must be kept accurately so that the taxable profit (income less expenses) can be verified.

### Value Added Tax (VAT)

*VAT (Value Added Tax) is a government tax on the selling price charged to buyers at every level of sales, from the first supplier to the final consumer.*

VAT is a government tax on spending – it is added to the purchase price of items sold.  In Britain most businesses with a sales turnover (ie the total amount of sales in a given period) of more than

£37,600 must be registered for VAT. This turnover figure is increased from time-to-time as a part of the Chancellor of the Exchequer's budget proposals. The figure quoted here was set in March 1993. Once registered, a business is issued with a VAT registration number which must be quoted on all invoices and on other business documents. It charges VAT at the standard rate (currently 17.5 per cent) on all taxable supplies, ie whenever it sells goods, or supplies a service. From the supplier's viewpoint the tax so charged is known as *output tax*. A number of items are *zero-rated* and no tax is charged when they are supplied: for example, food and children's clothing are zero-rated.

Businesses registered for VAT must pay to the VAT authorities (H M Customs and Excise Department):
* the amount of VAT collected (output tax)
* *less* the amount of VAT charged to them (input tax) on all taxable supplies bought in

If the amount of input tax is larger than the output tax, the business claims a refund of the difference from H M Customs and Excise.

Every three months a form known as a VAT return (Form VAT 100) has to be completed, although some smaller businesses submit a VAT return on an annual basis. Payment of VAT due (if the business is not claiming a refund) is made with the VAT return.


## PAYE – payroll and benefits

Pay as You Earn (PAYE) is a system required by law whereby employers deduct from employees' pay and send to the Inland Revenue on a monthly basis:
* *income tax* – a tax based on the level of income (less allowances) of the employee, and used by the Government as a source of funds for public spending, eg education, health, defence
* *National Insurance Contributions* – a tax levied by the Department of Social Security, and used to pay for benefits and State pensions

The PAYE system is also used by employers to pay certain State benefits *to* employees:
* *Statutory Sick Pay* – a standard rate full-time employees receive when off sick for between four days and twenty eight weeks
* *Statutory Maternity Pay* – a standard rate full-time pregnant employees receive when off work to have a baby, payable for a maximum of eighteen weeks

The majority of the money paid out by the employer to the employees for these benefits is reclaimable from the Inland Revenue, and is normally *deducted* from the monthly payment of income tax and National Insurance Contributions sent to the Inland Revenue.

As you will appreciate from the complexity of these arrangements, the employer will need to keep detailed payroll records and to give each employee a detailed payslip (see page 341), a system required by law. Payroll may either be maintained manually or on computer. After the end of each tax year (April 5) the employer must send to the Inland Revenue a full summary (Form P35) of all pay and deductions made during the tax year.


## pensions

Employers will also be involved in dealing with deductions from employees' pay for pensions. A pension is a 'savings scheme' operated either by the employer, or more often by an independent company, which provides a lump sum or regular pay (or both) to the employee after retirement. There is sometimes confusion about pensions because there are a number of diffrent types:
* *State Pension* – a flat rate State benefit payable to retired people (men aged 65 and over, women aged 60 and over) *and not administered by the employer* – the funds come from National Insurance Contributions (see above)
* *Contributory Pension* – a pension scheme whereby the employer *and* the employee contribute a percentage of pay to a pension fund
* *Non-contributory Pension* – a pension scheme whereby only the employer contributes a

Self-employed people (sole traders and most partners) normally contribute a percentage of their income to an independent pension scheme, and have the added benefit that they will save tax if they do so.

---

**student activity 3.3 – financial administration**

(a)   Obtain a shop or other receipt which shows that VAT is included.

    i    What is the VAT registration number?

    ii   What is the VAT rate and VAT amount (these *may* not be shown)?

    iii  Who actually pays the VAT, and who finally receives it?

    iv  What is it used for?

(b)   Obtain a payslip, or use the example on page 341 and identify:

    i    the amount received by the employee before deductions

    ii   the various deductions to the State

    iii  any pension payments

    iv  the amount received by the employee after deductions

---

# the influence of the customer

Businesses can only survive if they keep their customers.  Loss of custom means loss of business.   It is therefore essential, as we will see in the Marketing section of this book, that the business is *customer orientated* rather than *product orientated*:  in other words the business should operate according to *customer* needs rather than what the *business* wants to produce.

In the remainder of this chapter we will look at how the customer influences the administration systems of business.  We will deal with in turn:

• *consumer law* – ie the protection that the legal system considers that customers need

• *customer care schemes* and methods of obtaining customer feedback for evaluating the success of the business – *user opinions*

• quality systems – Quality Assurance and Certification (BS5750) and Total Quality Management

# consumer protection law

Consumers are given a great deal of protection in law, and a business must be aware of the legal restrictions when it:

• manufactures goods or provides a service

• advertises its product

• sells its product

• provides after-sales service

### the Sale of Goods Act 1979

This Act is  the cornerstone of consumer legislation.  Its main provisions state that:

• the seller has the right to sell the goods – this is assumed in the running of most businesses!

• the goods are sold "as described" – the goods must correspond with the details in any advertisement, or spoken statement

- the goods are of "merchantable quality" – the goods must work properly for their normal purpose, and be in a satisfactory condition, eg a pair of shoes must not let in water
- the goods are "fit for the purpose" – if the seller recommends the goods for a particular purpose, they must perform accordingly, eg "this camera telephoto lens will focus on objects 200 metres away"
- the goods should correspond with any sample provided – eg a small sampler tin of paint should reproduce accurately the colour of a 5 litre tin

If the consumer buys a product which does not fulfil these conditions, the consumer is entitled to return the goods and receive a refund.

### other consumer legislation

- *The Supply of Goods and Services Act 1982* extends the Sale of Goods Act to services or to the hire of goods, eg hiring a car, employing a plumber, having your hair cut.
- *The Unfair Contracts Terms Act 1977* prevents businesses from avoiding responsibility in law in the sale of goods or services, eg by showing notices stating "No Refunds"
- *The Consumer Protection Act 1987* legislates against faulty and unsafe products

You will no doubt encounter other Acts of Parliament relating to consumer protection; these will be studied – along with those mentioned here – if you are studying a Business Law option as part of your course.

### the effect of legislation on administration systems
The statutes listed above clearly affect a number of the administration functions within a business:

- *production* – quality control of the product
- *advertising* – ensuring that descriptions and claims for products are accurate
- *personnel* – providing thorough staff training in product knowledge
- *sales* – providing after sales service for faulty goods

---

### student activity 3.4 – the effect of consumer law
You run a shop which sells electrical goods. What is the legal position of the shop and the customer in the following situations?

(a) A customer buys a radio on Monday and returns it on Wednesday, stating that the tuning control does not work. He asks for a refund, but your sales assistant refuses to give one.

(b) A customer returns a washing machine saying that it makes a lot of noise and wakes the baby; she adds that "it did not make any noise on the TV advert".

(c) A customer buys a small calculator battery and returns the same day very worried, saying that the baby has swallowed it.

What implications do these problems have for the *manufacturer* of the products?

---

## customer care

Customer Care schemes operated by many of the major service industries, eg British Airways and British Rail, have been well publicised and have met with mixed success. What is a Customer Care scheme? It is essentially a focussing of the whole business on the needs of the *customer* rather than the operational needs of the *business*. It is an attitude which should permeate the whole organisation from the Chief Executive to the Sales Assistant. Successful schemes have achieved this "attitude", often involving the senior management spending time on the shopfloor: Sir John Sainsbury, for example, visits 100 stores a year.

## customer care and the organisation

A successful customer care scheme could be developed along the following lines:

- *customer needs* as they relate to the business are researched
- the *structure* of the business is modified to reflect customer orientation – this may mean a 'flattening' of the hierarchy so that customer problems can be sorted out at a lower level
- standards for levels of customer care
- systems are set up to motivate staff to take an active part in the new scheme – quality circles, for example (small voluntary groups of employees who thrash out problems and issues relating to customer care, and report to management with specific proposals for improvements)
- widespread training of staff to "think customer" – this should avoid introducing the irritating veneer of politeness which sometimes passes as customer care, eg the parrot-like "Good Morning. This is Tracey speaking. How may I help you?"
- set up systems for monitoring customer feedback, eg customer questionnaires such as Fig 3.1 below, and the W H Smith questionnaire illustrated on pages 149 to 151.

### OLYMPUS SPORT

Dear Customer,

At Olympus we really care about the service that we give to you, our customer. That's why your feedback is vital in maintaining and improving our standards of Customer Care.

Please spend two minutes of your time to tell us how you feel about the service you have received today and give us your suggestions as to how we can improve.

This information will only be used by Olympus as part of its customer care programme, and will not be passed on to third parties for other uses.

Your reply will be entered into our monthly prize draw where you can win £50 of Olympus gift vouchers.

Thank you for shopping at Olympus.

Yours sincerely

John Fallon
Managing Director

*Please give us your comments.*

Thinking about the service you have received today:

1. Were you made to feel
   - [ ] Special    [ ] Attended to
   - [ ] Welcome    [ ] Ignored

2. Was the speed of service
   - [ ] Prompt & Efficient    [ ] Rushed
   - [ ] Adequate    [ ] Slow

3. Was the product knowledge of our staff
   - [ ] Excellent    [ ] Sufficient
   - [ ] Good    [ ] Poor

4. Were the required products
   - [ ] Stocked & in the right size/colour    [ ] Not stocked
   - [ ] Stocked but size/colour not available

5. Comments
   (How can we improve our service to you?)
   ........................................................
   ........................................................
   ........................................................
   ........................................................
   ........................................................

6. Name & Address
   ........................................................
   ........................................................
   ........................................................
   ........................................................

Signature ......................................

*Fig. 3.1  Olympus Sport customer care questionnaire*

# quality assurance and total quality management (TQM)

Many businesses are currently placing the customer as the focus of their operations by adopting formal schemes which promote *quality*. What is quality in relation to business? It may be defined as:

*providing a product which is fit for its purpose, safe in use, designed and constructed to satisfy the cutsomer's needs*

There are currently two main approaches to the introduction of a quality system:

* Quality Assurance Certification
* Total Quality Management

It must be stressed that these are not *different* methods of approaching the quality problem – they are complimentary, and a business may in fact adopt Quality Assurance Certification *as part of* Total Quality Management.

## Quality Assurance Certification

A business may apply for formal certification by bringing its administration systems in line with published standards:

*British National Standard BS5750*

BS5750 was first published by the Department of Trade and Industry in 1979. In 1987 it was brought in line with the International Standard – *ISO9000*. BS5750 sets down rigorous standards for internal procedures such as

* quality control
* vetting of suppliers
* systems of internal documentation
* after-sales service

These all ensure that the product will be of the standard that will meet customer requirements. The certification process is lengthy and time consuming, but the end-result for the business will be:

* inclusion in the Department of Trade and Industry's Register of 'quality' businesses
* the ability to use the well-known quality *'kitemark'* symbol on products and documentation

The *benefits* tof BS5750 to the business include:

* saving in costs – because internal procedures will be soundly based and efficient
* satisfied customers – the right product at the right time
* reduction of waste in internal processes
* less frequent reviews and re-workings of designs and procedures
* the increased likelihood that the business will be chosen by other BS5750 certified organisations which are looking for quality *suppliers* – in fact some businesses will accept supplies *only* from BS5750 certified organisations!

## Total Quality Management (TQM)

Total Quality Management (TQM) is *not* a certification process, but a proven systematic approach by the management of a business to satisfy customer requirements as efficiently and as profitably as possible. Some businesses may not apply for BS5750 certification, but will adopt TQM, which may be defined as:

*a style of management which*

  *– produces a commitment to quality work by people at all levels*

  *– in order to meet customer requirements*

  *– first time and every time*

On the next page is a typical 'Quality Statement' and the guiding principles of TQM formulated by a business.

**QUALITY STATEMENT**
We have a long-term commitment to continual improvement of the quality of all our systems processes and activities.  By building quality into every stage of the business we are striving to satisfy our customers through precise performance.

**QUALITY POLICY**
1.   Leadership – managers and supervisors will support staff actions and ideas
2.   Quality is needed in every area of the business
3.   The whole workforce is responsible for the business performance
4.   Zero defects – stop mistakes before they happen
5.   Improvement is a continuous process contributed to by everyone

### student activity 3.5 – customer care and quality systems

(a)   Collect examples of customer care questionnaires from shops and businesses and make a list of areas of customer care which concern those organisations.  Comment on those areas and analyse the administration functions within the organisations that are responsible for them.

(b)   In consultation with your tutor design a questionnaire on one side of A4 paper which enquires about 'customer' care at *either* a shop *or* your own Young Enterprise scheme or mini-busines.  Use a word processor or DTP program if possible.  Circulate the questionnaire among a defined group and analyse the findings (using a computer database if possible), discussing them with your tutor.

(c)   Collect examples of 'quality statements' from businesses, eg 'Customer Charters' from public services.  Analyse the main points they have in common.  *Optional activity:* use these points as a basis for a quality statement for your own Young Enterprise or mini-business scheme.

# chapter summary

❑   Administration systems within a business are influenced by external factors.  These include the requirements of the law, and the needs of the customer.

❑   Legal requirements cover the areas of:
  • employment law  the setting out of contractual terms
  • Health and Safety at Work – safeguarding employees and visitors
  • Company law  for limited companies
  • financial administration – accounting records, VAT, PAYE, pensions
  • consumer protection against faulty products and suppliers avoiding responsibility

❑   Customer care schemes show the influence of the needs of the customer affecting the internal systems of a business.

❑   The need to satisfy the customer also accounts for the introduction of quality systems within a business:  BS5750 certification and Total Quality Management (TQM).

# EVIDENCE COLLECTION EXERCISE 1

# *Investigating an administration system*

| Element 2.1 | Investigate administration systems |
|---|---|

Suggested Sources:
- Your school or college administration
- professional administrators
- your fellow students
- local Health and Safety Executive
- textbooks in libraries and resource centres

## INTRODUCTION

You are to form into groups of three or four students. You are to investigate the administration system of your own school or college by undertaking a number of tasks. You should appreciate that the day-to-day running of your school or college places immense pressure on the administration staff, and therefore you should liaise closely with your tutor and ask permission before requesting information.

## TASK 1

Establish what type of organisation your school or college is. It may be part of the local authority education provision, it may be a limited company, it may even be a charity. Give a written description of the *type* of organisation, and state why your school or college has taken this form.

## TASK 2

(a)  Draw up an organisational structure chart of your organisation, showing the levels of *hierarchy*.

(b)  State whether you consider the structure to be tall or flat, giving reasons for your decision.

(c)  Identify and discuss any problems you see in this structure (talking to tutors will give you ideas here).

(d)  Give examples of any line, function and staff relationships you have seen in the organisation.

## TASK 3

(a)  Draw up another organisation chart, this time showing only the administration *functions*.

(b)  Give a *brief* description of each of these functions.

(c)  Identify and discuss any problems you see in the way the functions support each other (talking to tutors will give you ideas here). Suggest solutions to the problems

## TASK 4

Examine the ways in which the Health and Safety at Work Regulations affect your organisation. If possible obtain a copy of the Safety Policy.

## TASK 5

In close consultation with your tutor draw up a 'customer care' questionnaire seeking users' (ie students') opinions about the school or college as a service provider (eg expertise of staff, facilities, efficiency of marking!). Circulate among a defined group. Analyse the findings and discuss them with your tutor.

# 4 Communication systems – written communications

## introduction

Effective communication systems are essential to the efficient running of any organisation. In business, communication systems involve a number of different forms of communication:

- *written* communications – letters, memoranda, reports
- *oral* communications – verbal messages, telephone calls
- *electronic* communication – messages transmitted by electronic means, including by fax, electronic mail and by teleconferencing

In this chapter we will, deal with the written word, one of the more traditional methods of communication, and also one of the most effective. We will explain the format and use of

- letters
- memoranda
- faxes (which also involve electronic communication systems)
- reports

We will deal with oral and electronic communication systems in the next two chapters.

Communicating is also a Core Skill in your Business Studies course, and you will find that the formats outlined in this chapter will be required in Activities and Exercises throughout your course of studies.

We must start, however, by defining what we mean by *communicating*.

## the communication process

If you ask what *communicating* is, you will probably get a variety of responses :

> *"Passing on a message."*
> *"Telephoning someone or writing a letter."*
> *"Getting the message across"*
> *"Making sure that they understand me."*

The first two responses show only part of the process: a message is sent. The second two show an understanding of the full process: the message is understood.

The process of communicating may be broken down into several distinct stages:

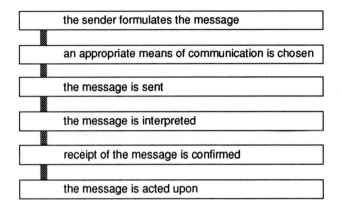

the sender formulates the message

an appropriate means of communication is chosen

the message is sent

the message is interpreted

receipt of the message is confirmed

the message is acted upon

Here the communication process involves

- *formulating the message,* ie deciding what you want to say – this is a critical stage, and too often one where communication problems start – "I am sorry I didn't mean that" . . . "Is <u>that</u> what I said?" . . . "You can read into it what you like. I meant . . ."
- *choosing the appropriate means* – would a telephone call be better than a letter? would it be easier and quicker to send a fax showing the route map?
- *the message is sent and interpreted* – another area where misunderstandings can arise – a message should be read or listened to carefully
- *the message is confirmed and acted upon* – it is essential in business that a communication is confirmed – letters should be acknowledged, faxes will automatically produce a correct transmission report
- *the message is acted upon* – this final stage confirms the success of the communication

You should note that these principles apply equally to oral (word of mouth) communication as to written communications. Oral communication will be dealt with in the next chapter.

## communication systems

### internal and external communication
Communication systems involve both *internal* and *external* communications; for example:

| *internal communications* | *external communications* |
|---|---|
| • staff newsletter | • letter to customer |
| • memorandum from a manager | • sales brochure to customer |
| • report on Health and Safety | • sales invoice |
| • notice of a staff meeting | • job advert in the local newspaper |

---

**student activity 4.1 – internal and external communication**
Analyse the different forms of communication that might be involved if you saw an advertisement for a job in a local newspaper, and then applied for the job. Distinguish between
(a)   the forms of communication with which *you* would be directly involved
(b)   the forms of communication which may take place *internally* in the organisation advertising the vacancy

## information handling and decision making

Businesses require efficient communication systems because they need rapid access to up-to-date and relevant information.  From this information situations can be assessed and informed decisions can be taken.  The type of information which may be needed can be classified in a number of ways:

## internal and external information

Information may be data about the business itself, or it may be information available from external sources such as statistical publications or TV information services (Prestel, Viewdata).  For example, if a business is making a forecast of future sales, it will look at:

* its own past sales record from internal records
* external predictions about factors such as the state of the economy and the industry

When you study Marketing as part of your course you may undertake a similar exercise yourself (see Evidence Collection Exercise 8, pages 166 to 167).  Examples of information sources are set out below:

| *internal information sources* | *external information sources* |
|---|---|
| • sales figures | • trade directories |
| • stock levels | • statistics of the economy/industry |
| • various types of cost | • CD ROM (compact disc) directories |
| • product specifications | • TV information sources |

## past , present and future information

Past, present and future (forecast) information about the business is required for informed decision making:

* *past information* includes data about sales (both by volume and by money received), costs, wages levels, borrowings, profitability, productivity, efficiency
* *present information* about all these subjects – ie the up-to-date figures – enables the business to *monitor* the current position
* *future information* is simply the forecast a business will make about future performance in say, sales, profitability, cost levels, the need for finance

As you will appreciate, the *accuracy* of the information available to the business is of paramount importance.  The maintenance of accurate records, in manual and computerised form, is only possible where the communication channels within a business are open and operating efficiently.

We will now look at the various forms of written communication in detail.

# the letter

## house style

If you work in an organisation or receive letters from an organisation, you will note that the appearance and format of each letter is (or should be!) in a uniform 'house' style, a style which readily identifies that organisation, and is common to all letters which it sends. The letter will normally be sent on standard printed stationery showing the name, address and details of the organisation, and set out with headings, paragraphs, signatures – the 'elements' of the letter – in a uniform way.

The most common way of setting out a letter is the fully-blocked style, explained on the next two pages. The example letter has been prepared by a firm of electrical contractors, Wyvern Electrical Services.  A potential customer, Mr J Sutton, has enquired about the possibility of having his house rewired.

<table>
<tr><td>

**Elements of the letter**
*(see page 36 for a full explanation)*

reference

date

name and address of recipient of letter

salutation

heading

body of the letter

complimentary close

signature

name and job title of sender

enclosure indicator

</td><td>

**Wyvern Electrical Services**
**107 High Street**
**Mereford MR1 9SZ**

**Tel 0605 675365 Fax 0605 675576**

---

Ref DH/SB/69

14 December 19-9

J D Sutton Esq
23 Windermere Close
Crofters Green
Mereford MR6 7ER

Dear Mr Sutton

<u>Rewiring:  23 Windermere Close</u>

Thank you for your letter of enquiry dated 10 December.

We are pleased to enclose a brochure detailing our services and will be pleased to give you a quotation for rewiring your new extension. In order to do this we will need to send our estimator to see your property, and shall be grateful if you will telephone us to arrange a visit at a time which is convenient to you.

We look forward to hearing from you.

Yours sincerely

Derek Hunt
Sales Manager

enc

</td></tr>
</table>

## characteristics of a fully-blocked letter

- the most commonly used style of letter
- all the lines start at the left margin
- use of *open punctuation*, ie there is *no* punctuation, except in the main body of the letter, which uses normal punctuation
- a fully-blocked letter looks neat and clean (no untidy punctuation)
- a fully-blocked letter is easy to type as all the lines are set uniformly to the left margin

# elements of the letter

The references next to the left of the letter on the preceding page describe the *elements of a letter*. These are explained more fully below.

**printed letterhead**
This is always pre-printed, and must be up-to-date.

**reference**
The reference on the letter illustrated -*DH/SB/69* - is a standard format
- DH (Derek Hunt), the writer
- SB (Sally Burgess), the typist
- 69, the number of the file where Mr Sutton's correspondence is kept

If you need to quote the reference of a letter to which you are replying, the references will be quoted as follows:*Your ref. TR/FG/45 Our ref. DH/SB/69'*

**date**
The date is typed in date (number), month (word), year (number) order.

**recipient**
The name and address of the person to whom the letter is sent. This section of the letter may be displayed in the window of a window envelope, so it is essential that it is accurate. Note the difference between the open and full punctuation in the recipient section of the letters; the open punctuation in the blocked and semi-blocked styles appears much 'cleaner.'

**salutation**
*'Dear Sir. . . Dear Madam'* if you know the person's name and title (eg Mr, Mrs, Ms), use it, but check that it is spelt or applied correctly - a misspelt name or an incorrect title will ruin an otherwise competent letter.

**heading**
The heading sets out the subject matter of the letter - it will concentrate the reader's mind.

**body**
The body of the letter is an area where communications skills can be developed. The text must be
- laid out in short precise paragraphs and short clear sentences
- start with a point of reference (e.g. thanking for a letter)
- set out the message in a logical sequence
- avoid jargon, eg "please send your O.P.P. to the I.M."
- avoid slang expressions
- finish with a clear indication of the next step to be taken (e.g. please telephone, please arrange appointment, please buy our products, please pay our invoice).

**complimentary close**
The complimentary close (signing off phrase) must be consistent with the salutation:
*'Dear Sir/Dear Madam'* followed by *'Yours faithfully'*
*'Dear Mr Sutton/Dear Ms Jones'* followed by *'Yours sincerely'*.

**name and job title**
It is essential for the reader to know the name of the person who sent the letter, and that person's job title, because a reply will need to be addressed to a specific person.

**enclosures**
If there are enclosures with the letter, the abbreviation 'enc' or 'encl' is used.

**continuation sheets**
(not shown in the illustrations)
If the text of the letter is longer than than one sheet of paper will allow for, the letter will conclude on a continuation sheet, a matching plain sheet of paper headed with the recipient's name, the page number and the date.

## letter tone and style

You will know from personal experience that if you are writing to your boyfriend/girlfriend/husband/wife you will use a different tone and style than you would if you were writing to the bank manager or writing an application letter for a job. In writing business letters you should use a tone and style appropriate to the situation. You should always

- have a mental picture of the person to whom you are writing
- be aware of his or her status in the organisation
- adopt the appropriate tone for the situation: are you writing an enquiry, an apology, a complaint?

Here are some suggested approaches to different types of letter together with some example texts

| *type of letter* | *tone and style* |
|---|---|
| **enquiry** | • a polite letter |
| | • precise details of the information required |
| | • an indication of where the information is to be sent |
| | • a deadline if the enquiry is urgent |

---

Dear Sir

Photocopiers

I shall be grateful if you will send me an up-to-date catalogue and price list for your range of office photocopiers.

Our company intends to purchase a machine by 30 June, our financial year-end, and we therefore need the information by 31 May.

I look forward to hearing from you.

Yours faithfully

---

| | |
|---|---|
| **complaint** | • a firm, informative and polite letter |
| | • do not be abusive, even if you feel angry |
| | • state what action you want taken: refund, replacement, compensation? |

---

19 November 19-9

Dear Sir

Order 12837

We ordered 100 reams of photocopying paper from you on 5 November for urgent delivery to our office by 14 November. Regretably the paper did not arrive. We telephoned you on 14 November and were promised delivery for 15 November. Again the paper did not arrive, and so we obtained it from another source, and cancelled your order by telephone.

We have today (19 November) received this order in a damaged state. We shall be grateful if you will arrange with your carrier for collection of the paper from our premises as soon as possible, and at your expense.

Yours faithfully

**apology**
- a helpful and polite letter stating the reason for the problem
- accept responsibility - do not blame other people
- apologise but do not overdo it - an over-apologetic letter sounds insincere
- state what remedy you are making available

---

Dear Mrs Simms

Damage to patio doors

Thank your for your letter of 12 February.

I was sorry to hear that the patio doors we installed were shattered last Friday when your children were playing in the garden.

Our doors are made to the highest specifications, including the use of safety glass. They will, however, shatter if they receive a very sharp impact.

We are therefore sending our fitters to your premises to inspect the damage and to make safe the opening; they will be contacting you to arrange a suitable time for a visit. We have also ordered a replacement door, which we hope to be able to fit within ten days.

With apologies for the inconvenience caused

Yours sincerely

---

**selling**
- a persuasive and interesting letter
- state the facts relating to the product or service
- set out the benefits of the product or service
- conclude with an invitation to buy

---

Dear Mr Osborne

Pegasus Telephones

I am writing to introduce to you our exciting new Pegasus range of telephones.

We have just launched a smart modern range of telephone systems which include
- office exchange systems
- cordless handsets
- car telephones
- a new improved combined handset/answerphone/fax unit
We feel these are ideal for the demands of your organisation; they will help increase your efficiency and productivity.

The Hermes range is available for the first three months at special low introductory prices, details of which are set out in the enclosed catalogue.

I will be contacting you within the next week to explain how the Hermes range can help your business.

Yours sincerely

## student activity 4.2 – writing the right letters

You are Lesley Francis, Sales Manager of Francis Furnishings Limited, 34 Galliford Road, Stourminster ST1 2RF, Tel 0685 423142, Fax 0685 421341. You are to draft letters to deal with the following situations:

(a) You receive a letter from Mr I M Cross,"Heatherlea", Milton Green ST4 5RD. The text is as follows:

*"I recently received a sofa from your warehouse, but the colour was wrong. I ordered Mexican Orange draylon, but the sofa received was brown. I am very unhappy about this and would like the correct sofa by the end of the week, beacuse my mother-in-law is coming to stay."*

You check your records and find that you have in fact supplied a sofa in Buffalo Brown. A replacement sofa will take three weeks to arrive.

(b) Your Managing Director asks you to make enquiries of Antico Furniture about their new range of reproduction furniture. He is particularly interested to know their prices as he is seeing a client in a week's time whom he thinks will be interested in the range. The address is Antico Furniture, Unit 14, Great Western Estate, London W15 8HN.

(c) You have received back in your showroom a kitchen table from Mr C Lumsy of 45 Salisbury Crescent, Stourminster ST3 8NB. He purchased the table (in perfect condition) a week ago, but it now has deep cuts on the wooden surface. He said to the sales assistant who saw him that he had been cutting up carrots on it, and thought that it should stand up to such treatment. He then left in a huff saying that he expected to get his money back in the post.

(d) You have received a 50 metres consignment of carpet from Wessex Carpets, Unit 7, Carpenters Estate, Millfield MF5 9JH, purchase order No 7237236. The carpet is Glowing Blossom (foamback, colour pink), and you ordered Apple Blossom (twist, colour green), which you need urgently (within 7 days).

You should produce the letters fully-blocked in typed or (preferably) word processed form, and sign them. Use today's date.

## the memorandum

### format

The *memorandum* (plural *memoranda*) is a formal written note used for internal communication within an organisation. It may be typed or handwritten, and will often be produced in a number of copies which can be circulated as necessary. It can be used for situations such as:

• giving instructions
• requesting information
• making suggestions
• recording of opinions
• confirming telephone conversations

A memorandum is normally pre-printed by the organisation with all the headings in place, and can be half page or full page in size. A completed memorandum is illustrated on the next page.

---

# MEMORANDUM

**To**  Tim Blake, Sales Manager

**From** K Roach, Finance Director       **Ref.** KR/AC/1098

**Copies to** Departmental Managers       **Date** 7 July 19-9

**Subject** COMPUTERISATION OF ACCOUNTING RECORDS

---

Please attend a meeting on 14 July in the Conference Room.  Attendance is
vital as the new system comes on line on 1 September.  Summary details of
the new system are attached.

enc

---

## elements of the memorandum

Most of the headings on the pre-printed memorandum form are self-explanatory, as they are also to be found on business letters.  You should, however, note the following:

| | |
|---|---|
| **heading** | the name of the organisation may be printed above the word 'Memorandum', although this is not strictly necessary, as the memorandum is an internal document |
| **'to' and 'from'** | the name and job title of the sender and the recipient are entered in full, and as a consequence the salutation 'Dear......' and complimentary close 'Yours ...........' are not necessary |
| **copies to** | memoranda are frequently sent (as in the example above) to a large number of people;  the recipients will be indicated in this section of the document |
| **reference** | as in a business letter the reference indicates the writer, the typist, and the file number |
| **date** | as in a business letter the order is day (number), month (word), year (number) |
| **subject** | the subject matter of the memorandum must be concisely stated |
| **text** | the message of the memorandum should be clear and concise |
| **signature** | a memorandum can be signed, initialled, or even – as is often the case – left blank |
| **enclosures** | if material is circulated with the memorandum, the abbreviation 'enc' or 'encl' should be used |

# the facsimile message (fax)

## the technology

*Fax* is an abbreviation of *facsimile transmission*.  A fax machine scans a document and sends an exact (facsimile) image of the document through the telephone system.  A receiving fax machine will decode the message and print out an exact copy of the document.  A fax machine will therefore enable a copy of a drawing, an invoice, a handwritten message, or a letter to be sent instantaneously to the recipient, avoiding postal delays and losses.

## fax header sheets

It is customary for an organisation sending fax messages to precede the actual document (or documents) being scanned with a pre-printed *header sheet*, so that the recipient will know what is being transmitted.  An example is illustrated below.

---

### FACSIMILE TRANSMISSION HEADER

From
THE NATIONAL BANK PLC
6-8 High Street
Mereford
MR3 5RJ
Telephone  0915 921524   Facsimile  0915 926644

---

TO...................................................................................................................

....................................................................................................................

....................................................................................................................

TELEPHONE NUMBER............................................FACSIMILE NUMBER............................

NUMBER OF PAGES INCLUDING THIS HEADER............................DATE..............................

| **message** |
| --- |
|  |

If you have any enquiries regarding this message please telephone the above number and

ask for extension......................

## elements of a fax header

**sender**                 the sender's name, telephone number and facsimile number are present so that the recipient can get in touch if he wants to send a reply, or telephone if there are transmission problems (an extension number is also given in case of need)

**page numbers**           the header will indicate the number of pages being transmitted, this is so that the recipient can check that the whole document has printed out - the document is normally printed out in one continuous roll

**recipient**              the recipient's name, address, telephone number and facsimile number are present so that the recipient can be contacted in case of problems, and also so that the message can be filed correctly after transmission

**message box**            a box is provided for brief messages or notes relating to the pages which follow; it is interesting to note that the fax has become an *informal* written communication – the header sheet and message are often handwritten rather than typed

# written reports

## types of report

There are a number of different types of written report which are used by organisations, for example sales reports, feasibility studies, product performance reports, project reports. The format of the report will depend on the a numbers of factors: is the report an internal report? is it a formal report? is it a long report? The most common types of report are:

- *the full-length formal report* – eg a feasibility study for new premises, submitted to higher management
- *the short formal report* – usually an internal report to higher management on an important matter such as observance of health and safety regulations in the office
- *the informal report* – usually an internal report at a lower level of authority in the organistion, eg a supervisor reporting to a manger on punctuality of staff
- *memorandum report* – an internal report set out in the form of a long memorandum, often used when one department communicates with another

## structure of a report

There are no specific regulations dictating precisely how a report should be written. The report is a flexible form of communication, as can be seen from the many different types described above. *Generally* speaking a report will be structured as follows:

*title*                    the subject matter of the report – what it is about

*terms of reference*       the circumstances and the scope of the report:
- the person(s) who commissioned it
- the ground it has to cover
- the date by which it has to be submitted
- whether it has to make any recommendations

| | |
|---|---|
| *procedures* | this section sets out how the report was compiled |
| | • the use of source documents – the sources should be identified |
| | • interviews – details should be given |
| | • observation |
| *findings* | the information is set out in a structured way and analysed |
| *conclusions* | a summary of the analysis of the findings |
| *recommendations* | if required, specific recommendations can be made on the basis of the conclusions drawn from the findings |
| *appendices* | the inclusion of any relevant material from the findings, eg numerical data, copies of important source material |

The structure set out above is the normal format for the short formal report, and should be adopted for reports which you will from time-to-time compile as part of your studies.

## report layout

The formal report, as well as being structured in a formal way, is often laid out in a formal manner. It should normally be typed or word processed. The increasing use of laser printers and sophisticated word processing or DTP (Desk Top Publishing) systems has resulted in the more 'professional' appearance of many internal documents such as reports.

It has become common practice for reports to be divided into sections by the use of the *decimal point referencing system*. This divides the structure of a report (as set out above) into numbered sections, and identifies subdivisions of those sections by setting out the number of the section followed by a decimal point and a number identifying the subsection. The subsection can *also* be subdivided by placing a decimal point after the subsection number and incorporating a third number.

This is best understood by looking at the plan set out below of the Conclusions and Recommendations sections of a short formal report – note how the sections and subsections are indented from the left margin (ie the text starts further away from the left margin) as the sections become more subsidiary. Note also that the *structure* is illustrated here, *not* the text itself:

```
4.0   CONCLUSIONS
      4.1   first conclusion (main heading)
      4.2   second conclusion (main heading)
      4.3   third conclusion (main heading)
            4.3.1 – first point of third conclusion
            4.3.2 – second point of third conclusion


5.0   RECOMMENDATIONS
      5.1   first recommendation
      5.2   second recommendation
```

Now read on the next page an extract from a short formal report submitted by an Administration Manager to the Managing Director of a small company. The matter under investigation is the introduction of a drinks vending machine in the staff rest room. Note carefully the format of the report, the use of sections and headings in capital letters. Note also the use of *impersonal* language, eg "staff were interviewed" rather than "I interviewed staff". The avoidance of the words "I" or "we" helps make the report more *objective*, and not just a narrative of what the Manager did and thought.

---

**CONFIDENTIAL**

**to**     Howard Neskin, Managing Director        **ref** DS/FT/GH6

**from**    David Salcombe, Administration Manager     **date** 15 February 19-9

**REPORT ON PROPOSED PURCHASE OF DRINKS VENDING MACHINE FOR STAFF REST ROOM**

1.0   TERMS OF REFERENCE

On 6 January 19-9 the Managing Director requested David Salcombe, Administration Manager, to investigate the feasibility of the introduction of a drinks vending machine in the first floor staff rest room. He was asked to assess demand for the machine and types of drink, to compare the cost of buying a machine with the cost of rental, and to investigate the servicing costs. He was requested to forward his written report, with recommendations, to the Managing Director by 20 February 19-9.

2.0   PROCEDURE

The following investigations were made:

2.1  A questionnaire to staff (for copy see Appendix 1) was circulated on 15 January and completed by 20 January 19-9.

2.2  Details of vending machines were requested and received from five companies. These details were:

    2.2.1   The comparative costs of purchase and rental

    2.2.2   The servicing and maintenance costs

3.0   FINDINGS

3.1  <u>Questionnaire to staff</u>

58 Staff members completed the questionnaire. The questionnaire established that the majority of staff wanted the installation of a drinks vending machine. The results showed that

    3.1.1   89% of staff wanted a machine installed

    3.1.2   67% wanted *all* of the following available drinks: soup, hot chocolate, coffee, tea

*extract from a short formal report*

---

**student activity 4.3**

(a)    Lesley Francis (see Activity 4.2) is reviewing the discounts given to trade customers. Draft a Memorandum from Lesley to Julie Moore, Accounts Supervisor, asking for details of any bad payers whose discount should be reduced or stopped, and any good customers whose discount could be increased. A list of the current discounts given should be enclosed with the memorandum. (Note: you are not required to draft this list)

(b)    Design on A4 paper a fax header for an organisation of your choice. If you are taking part in a Young Enterprise or similar scheme, use your own business. You may find it useful to obtain specimen fax headers from businesses with which you have contact.

(c)    Draw up on A4 paper a *structure chart* of a short formal report, setting out the headings and the accompanying decimal point referencing system.

(d)    There is a proposal by your school/college to instal a new drinks machine in your common room/canteen. Draw up one questionnaire for the class (see Chapter 14 "Marketing Research") to establish demand for the machine and also to establish which drinks are required. Complete the questionnaire, analyse the results in smaller groups, and each write a short formal report addressed to your teacher/lecturer setting out the findings. Note: *ignore all cost aspects.*

# chapter summary

❑ The communication process involves the stages of formulating a message, choosing a means of communcation, sending the message, and ensuring that the message is understood.

❑ The communication system of a business involves *internal* and *external* communication.

❑ The communication system should assist management in the decision-making process by making available:
  • internal and external information
  • past, present and future information

❑ The letter is presented in a 'house' style and is normally fully-blocked.

❑ Appropriate letter tone and style should be adopted for the circumstances.

❑ The memorandum is a formal written note used for internal communication.

❑ The fax, transmitted over the telephone network, is an increasingly popular form of written communication.

❑ The written report can take a number of forms, all of which have the same basic structure.

# 5   Oral and visual communication

## introduction

Oral and visual communication are essential skills in business, and an important element of the Core Skills which form part of your course of studies.

*Oral communication* means communication 'by word of mouth', and in this chapter we will examine the processes involved in
* interviewing customers and clients face-to-face
* speaking on the telephone
* organising meetings

*Visual communication* is also crucial in getting a message across. Visual communication is involved in
* body language – giving people messages by gestures and facial expressions
* effective presentation of text and pictures, eg in advertising, promotional literature
* effective presentation of information in the form of tables, graphs, and charts

Oral and visual communication come together in the exercise known as the *presentation* – for example the launching of a product, the briefing of colleagues. Your course of studies may involve you in making a group presentation to your fellow students or teacher/lecturer. This chapter therefore concludes with a section explaining how to make an effective presentation.

## oral communication

Good oral communication is essential to the efficient running of a business. Oral communication can be:
* *internal* – passing on messages promptly, giving your colleagues relevant information, being prepared to listen to others, contributing at meetings, pointing out difficulties and being prepared to sort out other people's problems
* *external* – dealing with customers and clients face-to-face and over the telephone

Good *internal* communications will mean that a business will operate efficiently, staff motivation will be enhanced, and no unpleasant 'atmospheres' or tensions will develop.  Good *external* communications will give the business an enhanced image.  As we have seen in Chapter 3, a business is judged by the way it deals with its customers;  good external communications can actually increase sales.

It is not possible in a book of this nature and level to explain in full how to operate a telephone or how to talk to people.  You should be able to gain experience in your school or college in simulated situations involving oral communications –  interviews, telephone conversations – and you may possibly have part-time jobs which give you this experience.  The following hints are therefore offered to help you develop communication technique.

## passing on information

If you have to pass information to someone, you must do so clearly and accurately.  If you have played the game of 'Chinese Whispers' you will know how a message can get corrupted as it passes from person to person.  The information may be a short message or it may be an account of a customer interview or an appraisal of a new product from a competitor.  The information may be passed on face-to-face, or it may be relayed over the telephone.  Whatever the circumstances you should:

• think of what you have to say before you say it
• have to hand any relevant written material such as letters, files and figures
• speak clearly and precisely – do not rush
• be pleasant and polite!
• ensure that the message has got through by asking relevant questions:

  *"Are you happy with that?"*

  *"Do you want me to repeat any of that?"*

Always ensure that you are clear if any follow-up action is expected of you.

---

### student activity 5.1 – passing on information

(a)  Divide into groups of four or five.  One of the group is to make up and write down a complex message (maximum 50 words) involving a foreign name, a telephone number, and a set of instructions.  This written message should be kept from the other members of the group.  The person who has made up the message should then relay it *verbally* to another member of the group, who in turn passes it on *verbally* to someone else, and so on. The last person to get the message should write it down.  The two written messages can then be compared and any differences noted and analysed.  What *conclusions* about verbal communication can be drawn from this exercise?

(b)  As an exercise on oral report giving you are to investigate:

  i  the structure of the course you are taking, involving the duration and the subjects studied (both compulsory and optional)

  ii  the way the course is assessed

  You are to give a verbal explanation of the course and its asessment, assuming that the person to whom you are speaking has no prior knowledge of it.

---

# meetings

Your course will inevitably involve meetings.  They may be part of your course organisation (eg you may be a student representative on a course team), they may form part of your coursework or they may be held if you take part in a school/college business 'start-up' scheme.

Many people do not like meetings because many meetings are not well organised.  Taking part in meetings is an essential part of the development of your Core Skills – involving both communication and also problem-solving.

There is no standard format for a business meeting.  Some are *informal* (a discussion at the pub!) and some are very *formal*, for example the Annual General Meeting of a limited company, and the formal meetings of a Local Authority.

Meetings can be held for a variety of purposes:

* planning
* informing/briefing
* liaision between management and staff
* quality circles
* compulsory,  eg Annual General Meeting

We set out below the generally accepted procedures for a formal meeting.

## written documents prepared and circulated in advance

* *written notice* – giving time, date and place to those invited
* *minutes* – a written record of the previous meeting
* *agenda* – a list of the items for discussion (see below)
* *documents for discussion*, eg feasibility study, financial accounts, menus for Christmas meal!

## duties of participants in the meeting

*chairperson*
* approves the agenda in advance
* starts the meeting
* controls the meeting – calls order, introduces items on the agenda
* closes the meeting and checks the minutes

*secretary*
* prepares documentation (notice, minutes, agenda)
* takes minutes (unless this is delegated to a 'minutes secretary')

*members*
* discuss, make proposals, vote

There may also be a *treasurer* who records and reports financial transactions and draws up (or helps draw up) the financial statements, if these are required.

A typical agenda illustrating the 'running order' of a meeting is shown below.

```
          OSBORNE ELECTRONICS PLANNING COMMITTEE


     Agenda for meeting on 23 July 19-9 at 14.00 in Room 45


     1.  Apologies for absence

     2.  Minutes of previous meeting

     3.  Matters arising

     4.  New customer car park

     5.  Quality Assurance

     6.  Any other business

     7.  Date of next meeting
```

## visual communication

Visual communication is used in business in a number of ways:
- body language
- presentation of text and pictures
- presentation of numeric information in the form of tables, graphs and charts

### body language

Body language – the use of gestures, posture and facial expressions to express your inner thoughts and feelings – is a form of communication that people on the whole engage in without thinking. If you are sitting down to read this book, how are you sitting? Are your legs crossed or uncrossed, are you stretched out watching the TV News at the same time, or are you hunched up over a desk in deep concentration? The chances are that you will not *know* how you are sitting until a subject like body language is brought to your attention.

Body language is useful in business situations in that it can:
- enable you to assess how other people are thinking and feeling: are they going to buy your product? are they bored? do they know what you are talking about? are they telling the truth?
- allow you to put other people at ease when they look at your body posture

### assessing body language

We set out below some common examples and interpretations of body language. Try them out yourself and see if you agree with the suggested interpretations.

| *gestures* | *interpretation* |
|---|---|
| nodding the head | agreement |
| shaking the head | disagreement |
| head held in hands | concentration or despair |
| stroking hair slowly | contemplation |
| scratching hair vigorously | unable to find solution |
| hands clenched | frustration and anger |
| finger pointed | emphatic explanation of point |
| foot tapping | irritation, impatience, unease |
| placing hand to mouth or nose or earlobe | lying |

| *facial expresions* | |
|---|---|
| wrinkling of nose | doubt or disgreement |
| raised eyebrows | surprise, disbelief |
| knitted eyebrows | anger, doubt |

| *posture* | |
|---|---|
| arms crossed | defensive |
| legs crossed | defensive |
| legs uncrossed | relaxed |
| whole body spread out | relaxed and confident |
| whole body hunched up | nervous |
| body leaning forward | aggressive |

**student activity 5.2 – interviewing and body language**

Divide into groups of two.  One person should play the part of a sales manager, and the other the part of a customer.  The customer has come to the shop and wishes to make a complaint about a faulty washing machine purchased.  The first time it was used the waste water flooded the kitchen floor, ruining a carpet in the next room.

The interview should be staged in a room (the sales manager's room) with a table and two chairs, the chairs either side of the table.  The interview should be video recorded, and no other students should be present.

The recordings shold be played back to the whole class:

(a)     *with sound*
        The group should be asked to comment about how successful the customer was in communicating the complaint, and how well the manager dealt with the problem

(b)     *without sound*
        The group should be asked to comment about the body language used by the customer and the manager

Note:  if no video facilities are available, the exercise could be carried out with a lecturer present to assess the oral communication skills, and to point out the type of body language used.

## presentation of numerical data in visual form

There are a number of situations when you will find it necessary to produce visual representations of numbers.  For example you may want to produce a report on sales or profit trends for management, or for the shareholders of a limited company, or you may want slides for a presentation.  It is generally accepted that a picture can often  provide a better idea of a trend or a proportional breakdown than any number of words.

The traditional forms of presentation are:
• the line graph
• the bar chart
• the pie chart
We will deal with each of these in turn.

## graph, bar chart and pie chart

The starting point for any visual presentation of numbers is the ' raw' information, which will often be found in the form of a table.  The table below sets out the sales in money terms of two cars – the Corsair and the Tornado over a period of four years.  These figures are presented in the form of a graph and a bar chart on the next page.

|                  | Year 1 £000's | Year 2 £000's | Year 3 £000's | Year 4 £000's |
|------------------|---------------|---------------|---------------|---------------|
| Sales of Corsair | 1,000         | 1,250         | 1,500         | 1,250         |
| Sales of Tornado | 1,500         | 1,000         | 500           | 250           |

## line graph

Note that

- the graph is given a title
- the time scale is set out on the horizontal axis and a label added
- the sales figure in £000's are set out on the vertical axis and a label added
- a key is produced to distinguish between the two lines

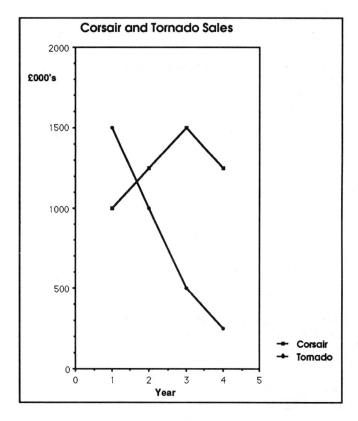

## bar chart

Note that

- the chart is given a title
- the time scale is set out on the horizontal axis and labelled
- the sales figures in £000's are set out on the vertical axis and labelled
- there is a distinctively shaded bar for each type of car
- the bars are of equal width
- a key is produced to distinguish between the two types of bar
- the chart is known as a 'compound' bar chart, as there is more than one bar per year
- each bar *could* be subdivided into different shaded sections to show, for example, the sales of each car by region – this type of chart is known as a 'component' bar chart

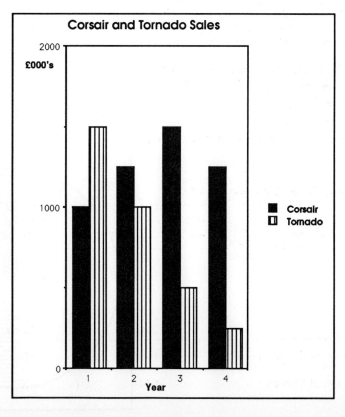

## pie chart

A pie chart (illustrated below) is a circle divided into a number of parts, just as an edible 'pie' is divided into slices. Whereas the line graph and bar chart are useful in showing a *trend* over a period of time, a pie chart is used to illustrate how a single figure is made up from its constituent parts. For example total sales for an organisation for one year may be divided into sales by region, and illustrated by means of a pie chart.

A pie chart might be used, for example, to show the worldwide sales by region of Tornado Cars:

**Sales of Tornado Cars by area  In Year 1**

| Area | £000's |
|------|--------|
| UK | 250 |
| Europe | 500 |
| USA | 625 |
| Japan | 125 |
| Total Sales | 1 500 |

The total sales of £1.5M will become the whole circle of the pie divided into segments, each of which will proportionally represent a geographical sales figure. As the angle at the centre of a circle is 360° it is necessary to work out the angle for *each* segment individually before drawing in the 'slices' of the pie. The formula is as follows:

$$\frac{\text{Figure for the part of the whole}}{\text{Figure for the whole}} \times 360° = \text{the angle at the centre for the segment (°)}$$

The angle for the UK sales 'slice', for example, is therefore $\dfrac{250}{1,500} \times 360 = 60°$

The pie chart therefore appears as follows:

## pie chart

Note that

- the chart is given a title
- the angles are not written in
- each segment is shaded distinctively
- a key is shown which indicates the different geographical regions

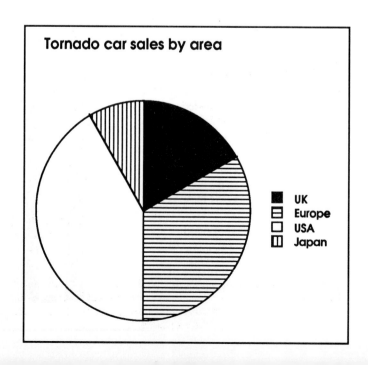

Tornado car sales by area

■ UK
⊟ Europe
☐ USA
Ⅲ Japan

**student activity 5.3 – giving visual meaning to numbers**

You are processing Osborne Electronics Limited's sales figures for the last six months.  The figures are as follows: January £45,000;  February  £40,000;  March £35,000;  April £35,000;  May £40,000; June £45,000.

The figures for the previous year were:

January  £35,000;  February  £35,000;  March £30,000;  April £25,000;  May £35,000; June £40,000.

You also note that the total sales for the last six  months were split as follows:

| Type of customer | £000s |
|---|---|
| Commercial | 120 |
| Professional | 60 |
| Educational | 30 |
| Other | 30 |
| Total | 240 |

**You are to:**

(a)  Present the sales figures for the first six months of the year so that they can be compared with the figures for last year.

(b)  Show the different types of customer sales for the last six months in a visually meaningful way.

Note:  you may use a computer graphics package if it is available.

# the presentation

Oral and visual communication are combined in the exercise known as the 'presentation'.  In business presentations are used in a number of contexts:

• internal briefings, eg telling sales staff about a new product range
• public product launches
• exhibition presentations

As part of your school or college business studies course it is likely that you will be asked to make presentations, usually working in groups.  It must be admitted that they are hard work to put together, and even harder to 'bring off' on the day.  The guidelines set out below are intended to make the process run as smoothly as possible.

*define the topic*  It is essential first to define exactly what you are going to talk about: for example you may be working in a business and preparing an internal briefing about a new product;  you may be in a school or a college and preparing a talk on employment law.  Defining the topic may sound an obvious requirement, but is surprising how often presentations can stray from the point or not 'hang together' because the topic has not been adequately defined.

*define the audience*  Establish to whom is the presentation being made – colleagues, trade buyers, the general public?  Each type of audience will have a different level of knowledge, different motives for listening to you, and will therefore require different treatment.

*assess the material*   You will need to collect a wide range of material, which will vary with the situation involved. A product brief will require examples of the product, details of its market and expected sales; a talk on employment law will require accurate and up-to-date factual information and case studies.

*group roles*   If you are in a school or college undertaking a group project you will need to establish who in the group is doing what, both in terms of research and in terms of taking part in the presentation. Once roles are established, the group members should *liaise* constantly so that the final presentation is a coordinated group effort. All too often group projects and presentations degenerate into "Bob, you look at this and talk about it, Jim you look at this and talk about it . . ." and so on. The result is a disjointed presentation involving a series of individual talks which are boring for the participants and for the audience.

*plan the sequence*   An individual or a group presentation needs careful planning. Most presentations should include

- an introduction setting out what the presentation is about
- the main points in a logical sequence
- a summary and conclusion

A group presentation gives the opportunity for group members to share out the talking. Effective techniques include

- using one individual to act as introducer or 'compere'
- alternating between individuals when a list of points/ideas has to be given (much as the newsreaders do on the TV)

This sequencing should be carefully planned and controlled.

*plan visual aids*   The visual aids used will depend on the resources available. Even the simplest and cheapest aids are highly effective when used properly. Facilities may include:

- image sequences, together with sound, which are produced on a large screen from a computer disc – this is known as multi-media presentation, and is becoming popular in business contexts
- slide projectors with a predetermined order of slides
- overhead projectors – slides can be prepared with coloured pens, or on a computer and laser printer, or images can be photocopied (take care with the film if using a photocopier or laser printer – some types melt!)
- paper flip-charts
- hand-outs on paper

In addition videos and audio tapes can be used for a limited timespan.

*assess the venue*   It is essential to assess the venue for

- facilities such as power points, curtains (if slides are being shown)
- the need for a public address system (if it is a large hall)
- seating and visibility

Nothing detracts more from the proceeedings if the speaker has to disappear under a table to plug in a projector, or if a microphone is not working or screeching because of acoustic feedback.

*giving a performance*   A successful presentation calls for a performance from all the participants, who are essentially acting a part. Many people hate speaking to a group of people; some positively relish it. Here are some hints for would-be actors:

- rehearse the presentation – run it through with all the visual aids, and most importantly, time it (there may be a time limit)
- when giving the presentation, speak to the audience and do not read from a sheet of paper (it induces sleep in the audience)
- use cue cards (small cards with key points written on them) or a piece of paper with list of key points – it is very easy to miss something out in the heat of the moment
- vary the tone of voice and introduce jokes (of an acceptable type) to keep the interest of the audience
- observe the audience reaction – it has been said that you should worry if someone looks repeatedly at his watch, and you should stop if he starts to shake it!
- be prepared for questions from the audience and accept them when appropriate – make sure that everyone else has heard the question
- watch the time carefully – particularly after lunch when the tendency for the audience to sleep is at its strongest

*dealing with props*   Ensure that you know how to use the equipment. An overhead projector can cause major problems:

- ensure that it is in focus
- if you want to point to something use a pencil on the slide (do not point to the screen)
- do not stand in front of the projector – the writer remembers well a lecturer who used unintentionally to project slides onto his shirt front for long periods of time

---

**student activity 5.4 – the presentation**
If you are engaged in a Young Enterprise or mini-enterprise scheme, prepare and deliver a presentation of your product or service. Your audience (your fellow students) are members of the general public at an exhibition centre. You should use all the resources which your school or college can provide.

---

# chapter summary

❑   Good oral communication is essential to the efficient running of a business.

❑   Oral communication can be internal (with colleagues) or external (with customers).

❑   Oral communication can be face-to-face or over the telephone.

❑   The conduct of meetings also involves oral communication.

❑   Visual communication is used in a number of ways
- body language (also known as non-verbal communication)
- the presentation of numerical information in the form of tables, graphs, bar charts and pie charts

❑   Oral and visual communication are both involved in the formal presentation, an exercise which involves careful planning, the use of visual aids and oral skills on the part of the presenter(s).

# 6 Electronic systems

## introduction

The increasing business use of electronic systems – ie computer networks and telephone communication links – for internal and external communication has become an accepted fact of life.  The reasons for this increase include:
- the need to communicate with other businesses which already operate similar systems
- ease of use and increased efficiency of operations
- the fall in the cost of installing and maintaining systems

In this chapter we examine the different forms of electronic systems:
- computer networks
- electronic mail
- enhanced telephone systems
- electronic information storage

We discuss the ways in which they are used and their benefits: accuracy, cost-effectiveness and security.

## computer networks

### the need for a network
If you mention a "computer" to someone, they will undoubtedly immediately think of the desktop workstation or PC (personal computer) – a screen, keyboard and processor 'box' – which is commonly seen in schools, colleges, public libraries and shops.  This machine may carry out a variety of functions:
- word processing – producing letters and other written documents
- database – storing and manipulating records in an electronic filing system
- spreadsheet – performing specified calculations
- communicating – linking with other computers

These functions will be examined in detail in Chapter 7.

If you consider the needs of an organisation with more than one PC you will see that the workstations will benefit greatly from linking up in a *network system*, served by a central storage device – a *file serve*r – which will store the programs and data needed.   This will enable the users of the individual workstations in the system to:

- share programs – wordprocessing, database, spreasdsheet
- ensure that the data stored on computer – eg stock levels, prices, customer details – is up-to-date and immediately available to all users
- share other computer equipment which can be linked in, eg laser printers and document scanners
- communicate with other workstation users

The *file server* itself may be a separate unit, or it may be a workstation which has been upgraded with extra memory and loaded with all the necessary programs and storage capacity.  It can:

- *multi-serve*, ie it will deal with  a large number of workstations at the same time
- *multi-task*, ie it will download programs and accept files and messages at the same time

## types of computer network
Computer networks are classified in a number of ways:

*LAN (Local Area Network)*   The Local Area Network is a simple term used to describe a computer network in a single location such as an office.

*WAN (Wide Area Network)*   The Wide Area Network extends the principle of the LAN over a wider geographical area, linking computers in different locations (and countries) by telephone link, radio and satellite.  It would be used, for example by a travel company operating worldwide.

The networks (LAN and WAN) can be organised in different configurations to suit the demands of the individual business.  In the diagram below the star network is the only system with a *separate* file server; the linear and the ring systems use one of the workstations as a fileserver.

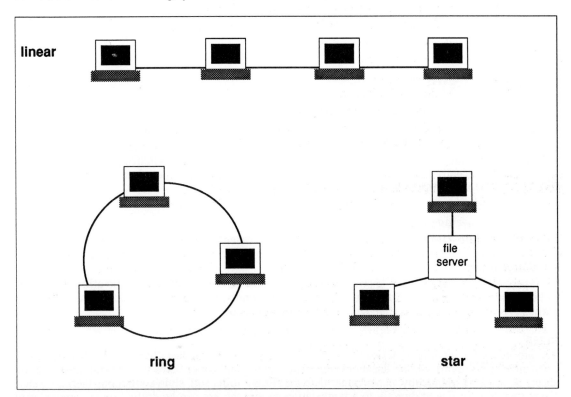

*Fig. 6.1 Computer network connection systems*

## electronic mail

*Electronic mail* (E-mail) enables you to send a text document such as a letter or a memorandum from one computer work station to another, without the need for any paper.

• *internal E-mail*

Electronic mail can be used within the office in a local area network (LAN), ie a group of computer terminals linked by cable, as seen on the previous page. A document can be input by one employee and sent to another.

• *external E-mail*

Electronic mail is especially useful when used between organisations. British Telecom's *Telecom Gold* system, for example, gives an electronic 'mail box' with a special number to each subscriber. If you want to send an E-mail message to a subscriber, the details and the number are sent down the telephone line and will appear on the recipient's terminal, and will be stored if the recipient is not there. This can be very useful if you want to send an E-mail letter to Australia or any destination in a different time zone when the recipient's office is likely to be empty in the middle of their night and your day.

---

**student activity 6.1 – computer networks**

Under the supervision of your tutor, investigate the computer system in your school or college resource centre or administration office. Describe:

(a)  the type of computer used

(b)  the type of programs used

(c)  the type of network used (if any) – draw a diagram to illustrate it

(d)  the security procedures for using the system – why do you think these procedures exist?

---

# telephone systems

## CABX – the switchboard

Most businesses link with the telephone network through what has been traditionally known as a PABX (Private Automatic Branch Exchange) – commonly called a "switchboard". The modern switchboard is usually computerised and is known as a CABX (Computerised Automatic Branch Exchange). It will perform a number of useful functions:

• transfer and hold calls

• play music to waiting callers!

• record the usage – ie enable management to see which extensions use the phone the most

## answerphones

Most people dislike speaking to answerphones, but it must be conceded that they do allow a business to keep open the communication channels while there is nobody to answer the telephone. They are particularly useful for small businesses where the owner is out.

## faxes

The procedure for sending a facsimile message was described in the last chapter. The technology is constantly being improved, the latest developments being plain paper faxes which print onto separate sheets of standard 'photocopy' paper rather than the flimsy 'toilet roll' style continuous thermal paper. Faxes may also be linked directly to a workstation so that the fax can be drafted *on screen* and sent directly down the telephone line via a modem to the recipient.

## portable telephones and pagers

Business communications have also been made easier by the portable 'mobile' telephone, which operates on a radio transmission 'cellular' basis. The 'cell' is the geographical area covered by a particular transmitter; as the telephone moves from one part of the country to another, it moves from 'cell' to 'cell'. The two main operators are Telecom-Securicor and Racal-Vodaphone. The phones may either be car-based (a cheaper alternative) or completely free ranging 'pocket' models.

Pagers are 'bleep' devices carried by employees, hospital doctors, for example. They can be activated by a radio signal and indicate that the carrier must telephone 'base' as soon as possible. The writer recalls a lecturer who carried a pager around his college when his wife was expecting a baby!

## enhanced telephone systems – ISDN 2

The traditional telephone lines allow the passage of electrical signals carrying voice and fax messages. New methods of transferring signals, largely made possible by the use of fibre optic cables, enable the messages to be encoded digitally, ie converted into streams of digits (numbers). The volume of information which a single cable can take has therefore been dramatically increased. BT's *ISDN 2* system, which sets up two separate 'channels' in a single telephone line linked at both ends to the users' computer, provides the subscriber with many enhanced facilities and cost savings, as the following examples show:

*data transfer* Computer files can be transmitted via ISDN2. This is of particular use to publishers and printers. A large text and graphics computer file – an entire sales brochure, for example – can be transmitted from London to Manchester in 17 minutes via ISDN 2 at a cost of just over £1 (cheap rate). A four hour courier service would cost over £200.

*desktop conferencing* ISDN 2 enables users in different locations to share data on computer screens, and to discuss the information displayed. In the example given above, the sales brochure could be discussed and amended on screen in London and in Manchester.

*videoconferencing* ISDN2 enables businesses to communicate internally and with clients at remote sites in video. The parties involved talk over the telephone and simultaneously appear on the computer screen. This technique is commonly used for TV news interviews. Videoconferencing clearly saves enormous costs in terms of travel and accommodation.

# electronic information storage

## document image processing (DIP)

Another area in which electronic systems are transforming the operation of businesses is in the electronic storage of documents. A traditional filing system physically stores documents in drawers and cabinets according to a specific alphabetic or numeric system. The system takes up much space and is labour intensive. It is also vulnerable to mishaps like lost files and misplaced files. Another method of storing documents is to photograph them onto microfilm. This is relatively cheap (approximately 0.1p per A4 page), but access to the documents requires a special reader machine, and is relatively cumbersome.

*Document Image Processing (DIP)* is an electronic system which offers many advantages. Each original paper page is scanned using Optical Character Recognition (OCR) software which turns the written page into computer data. The data is normally stored on optical disks. Although the business has to stand the capital cost of the equipment (a minimum of £20,000), the cost of storing each page is relatively low, at 1.2p per A4 page. Many large institutions which hold large numbers of files are now turning to DIP: Abbey National Property Insurance and Royal Life Insurance being examples.

**student activity 6.2 – advantages of electronic communication systems**

What forms of electronic communication systems would you recommend for:

(a)   a travel agent shop with five counter positions

(b)   a company selling and servicing business machines (ie computers, fax  machines, photocopies)

(c)   a graphic designer

(d)   an insurance broker

(e)   a time share agent dealing with properties worldwide

# chapter summary

❏   Computers are often linked in networks and served by a file server.  The networks can be
   • Local Area Networks (LAN)
   • Wide Area Networks (WAN)

❏   Electronic mail (E-mail) enables a business to send a message from one computer to another, either internally, or through an electronic 'mail box'.

❏   Telephone systems in business normally operate through a CABX (Computerised Automatic Branch Exchange).  Other telephone facilities include:
   • answerphones
   • fax machines
   • portable telephones and pagers

❏   Enhanced telephone systems, operated through ISDN 2, provide the following facilities:
   • transfer of data files between computers
   • desktop conferencing
   • videoconferencing

❏   Document Image Processing (DIP) is a system used by a business to scan its written documents for storage on computer file, normally on optical discs.

# "Babycare" – setting up communication systems

| Element 2.2 | Investigate communication systems |
|---|---|

Suggested Sources: • suppliers of computer equipment
• suppliers of communication equipment
• local newspapers
• textbooks in libraries and resource centres

## INTRODUCTION

Ann Spain and Julie Saunders have formed a partnership which will trade under the name of "Babycare". The business will recruit foreign nationals with work permits – particularly Americans and Australians – who have trained as nannies, and will act as sgents, selling their skills to families in London and the Home Counties. Ann and Julie have rented an office in North London (3A Muswell Parade, London, N29 OAP) where they have installed a telephone (081 625 5216). They have also invested in a small photocopier and a PC with an integrated program offering word processing, database, spreadsheet and communications functions. They also have a basic DTP program. There are a number of tasks they have to complete in connection with their communication systems. You are to carry out the following tasks in pairs.

## TASK 1

Using a word processor or preferably a DTP (Desk Top Publishing) package, draft a suitable letterhead and fax header sheet for the partnership (which is not VAT registered). Then design *two* local newspaper advertisements for Babycare, one *asking* for nannies and one *offering* Babycare's services.

## TASK 2

Draft two letters and sign them (the date is 5 July 19-9)

(a) Mrs. L Hopcraft of 54 Rosebury Road, London N10 9JH has written as follows (letter dated 3 July 19-9):

"Dear Babycare,
I feel I must write to complain about Maria whom you sent to me last week. I know that she comes from Sydney, and she is very pleasant, but she smokes in the house. The children are bound to suffer, and I am very worried about what may happen to their health in the long run.
Yours sincerely, L Hopcraft."

(b) To Elgin Machines, 65 High Road, London N27 OHP, complaining about a faulty F500X photcopier: it keeps chewing up the paper it is copying, and the mechanic failed to turn up on 2 July 19-9.

## TASK 3

Investigate the electronic communication systems and machines which are commercially available to the partnership, obtain costings of the equipment required, and present the findings in a short formal report to the partners, making suitable recommendations. Use your own name and the date 9 July 19-9.

## TASK 4

The partners are concerned about the security of their proposed equipment and data. Investigate the precautions they could take to protect both the equipment and the data held in the office.

# 7 Information technology and its users

## introduction

Information technology is a term given to describe the way in which information is *used* within an organisation. Traditionally information has been stored and distributed manually, ie in filing cabinets and on pieces of paper. Increasingly, however, information is being stored on computer discs of varying sophistication and transmitted from one electronic machine (eg fax, computer) to another.

In your studies you will need in the first place to appreciate the importance of the storage and use of information as part of the efficient functioning of a business organisation.

In the second place, 'Information Technology' is an essential Core Skill on which you will be assessed in your course of studies. The various computer applications described in this chapter will be used by you in your work: word-processing for presenting projects, databases for collecting evidence from market research activities, spreadsheets for presenting financial statements and forecasts.

In this chapter we will give an overview of information technology applications in business and then look in more detail at databases and spreadsheets. We will also look at the effect of information technology on its users:
- in legal terms – the Data Protection Act
- in Health and Safety terms

## purposes of information technology

### storage of information – manual systems
Information may be stored within an organisation *manually*, ie the data is stored on paper (or filmed copy) and organised – *filed* – in a number of ways depending on the nature of the document

involved:

* alphabetically
* numerically
* by geographical region
* chronologically (in date order)

---

**student activity 7.1 – manual storage methods**

State which filing method you would chose to file the information in the following circumstances (choose from alphabetical, numerical, geographical, chronological):

(a)　an insurance company's customer files

(b)　an insurance company's records of its insurance policies

(c)　a company's sales statistics

(d)　a builders merchant's sales invoices (copies of the documents issued)

(e)　the correspondence in an individual's customer file

Note:　there is not always a definitive answer!

---

### storage of information – electronic systems

Information is increasingly being stored, as we saw in the last chapter, by electronic means:

* on floppy disc
* on hard disk
* on optical disk

The information stored may either be a computer file, eg a list of customer names and addresses maintained on a database (see page 67), or it may be paper records which have been electronically scanned and stored on disc.

### distribution and communication of information

Information is only of use if it can be distributed and communicated effectively, both within and outside the organisation.　Examples of the distribution of information by a business include:

*internal*
* updated customer information – names, addresses, sales data
* product information – specifications, prices
* regulations and restrictions, eg new consumer legislation

*external*
* routine correspondence
* product information – brochures and prices, special promotions
* public relations – advertising, events, media articles

All these functions can be carried out using manual information processing methods, but, as we will see in this chapter, the computer information technology available enables a business to function far more efficiently.

### the use of information – decision making by managers

Management information systems enable businesses to make decisions rapidly and on the basis of accurate information.　Computer systems are particularly useful as all the information required can usually be displayed on a screen at the decision maker's desk, or processed by the computer. Examples of the types of information available include:

* reports on sales – by region, by comparing one time period with another, by comparing products
* reports on staffing – comparing productivity, costs, location of staff

# use of information technology in the workplace

In this section we will will look at the whole range of available systems to give you an overview of modern technology in the workplace. Some of the applications have been covered in the last chapter, but are included here to give a full picture. The use of the *database* and the *spreadsheet* are covered in more detail later in the chapter. The word processor is not covered in detail later as it is assumed that you are able to use one, or at least soon will be able to!

**word processing**  We have already looked at written communications in Chapter 4, and you will be aware of the format of a letter, memorandum or report. The ability to process text on a computer, to file it and to amend it are the major advantages of word processing. If you have a standard letter or text format on file you can also *mailmerge,* ie automatically retrieve names and addresses from a database file (see below) and insert them in the text file to produce a batch of documents on the printer, for instance:
- a letter to your customers promoting a new product
- a demand letter to customers who have not paid their bill
- labels for addressing Christmas cards to selected customers

You will see from this that word processing is both an efficient and also a time-saving process. If you have access to a word processing program at home, school or college, you should use it to process evidence for your Portfolio of Evidence.

**DTP**  DTP is short for Desk Top Publishing, a widely accepted name for a sophisticated word processing program which can present and format text in combination with lines, boxes, shadings and imported pictures (graphics), all on the computer screen. The program can be used for producing in-house documents, forms, newsletters, and also for external publicity material – advertisements asnd brochures. The finished design is then printed out on a laser or bubble jet printer which gives a high quality finish. DTP is used by some publishers  – this book was produced entirely on a computer DTP program.

**database**  A computer database is essentially a computerised 'card index' filing system for organising information  and can be used for purposes such as maintaining:
- customer names and addresses, and accounts
- stock records
- staff files

As noted above, the database can usefully be integrated with a word processing program in a *mailmerge* exercise.  A database is described in more detail in the next section of this chapter.

**spreadsheet**  A spreadsheet is a useful and widely used computer program which enables the operator to set up simple or complex calculations on a grid on the computer screen. Once the basis of the calculation has been set up (the 'mask'), figures can be entered and the calculations will be performed automatically. It is commonly used for:
- financial forecasting – comparing future income with expenditure
- presenting financial statements

The advantage of a spreadsheet is that once the calculation structure – the 'mask' – is set up on the screen, you can enter and change figures, and the computer will carry out the calculations for you automatically.

**integrated programs**
Many software manufacturers combine the word processing, database and spreadsheet programs into one 'integrated' program. This type of program has the advantages of savings in cost, and the ease with which data can be transferred from one program to another.

**accounting programs**
Many organisations record their financial transactions (sales, purchases, bank payments, payroll) on specialised accounting programs. Many of the business documents described in Chapter 29 can be generated by an accounting program and printed out on a computer printer.

**fax**
Fax (facsimile transmission) machines are able to transmit to another fax machine over the telephone system an exact copy (facsimile) of a document fed into the transmitting machine. They have a number of advantages:

• they are easy to operate
• transmission takes a short period of time
• they can be backed up with a telephone conversation to explain what is being sent
• they can transmit text, drawings and documents
• they can also double as photocopiers, ie you can use them to copy documents in the office (some machines are now sold as fax/photocopiers)

**electronic mail**
*Electronic mail* (E-mail) enables you to send a text document such as a letter or a memorandum from one electronic machine to another, without the need for any paper.

• *internal E-mail*
Electronic mail can be used within the office in what is known as a local area network (LAN), ie a group of computer terminals linked by cable. A document can be input by one employee and sent to another.

• *external E-mail*
Electronic mail is especially useful when used between organisations. British Telecom's *Telecom Gold* system, for example, gives an electronic 'mail box' with a special number to each subscriber. If you want to send an E-mail message to a subscriber, the details and the number are sent down the telephone line and will appear on the recipient's terminal, and will be stored if the recipient is not there. This can be very useful if you want to send an E-mail letter to Australia or any destination in a different time zone when the recipient's office is likely to be empty in the middle of their night and your day!

**viewdata**
Viewdata is a means of obtaining information on a VDU from a central information source. It also enables the user in some cases to send information back. You will probably have seen viewdata in operation if you have been to a travel agent, and seen the agent calling up holiday details on the screen, and possibly making a booking.

Viewdata may be made available as a *public* service – in the UK a common example is Prestel, a British Telecom service giving information about a wide range of topics. It is also possible to access other databases through Prestel via computer 'gateways.' Viewdata is also available on a *private* basis, as in the travel agent example, when an organisation has a number of computer terminals linked to a central database. Each terminal will have access to the central information – for example, holidays available – which will be updated as individual holidays are sold.

---

**student activity 7.2 – using information technology**
Investigate your school, college, part-time job or work placement and reaearch into the forms of information technology used.  Write a short report setting out:

(a)   a description of the computer hardware and software used

(b)   the *types* of information stored

(c)   *how* it is stored (in terms of both hardware and software)

(d)   who in the organisation makes use of it, and for what purpose

Note:

•   the information processing systems investigated may be highly confidential – always make sure you have the permission and co-operation of the organisation when making your investigations

•   the report should be short and not go into too much detail about the individual systems – the object is to obtain an overall view of the application of  information technology

---

# the database program

## what is a database?

Organisations *record* and *store* information - details of customers, employees, stock held, and so on. They also need to have *access* to that information.  Traditionally a good filing system fulfilled that need, but in recent years the development of computers has  made the task of storing, sorting and retrieving information much simpler and faster.  A computer database is therefore nothing more than *a collection of related pieces of information,*  for example the names, addresses and telephone numbers  of your customers.

You might ask why a computer is used.  Why not keep all the names, addresses and telephone numbers of your customers on index cards?  You could do this, but imagine the time it would take if:

• you wanted the names of all the customers who lived in London
• you wanted to sort the cards in alphabetical order of the towns/cities in which the customers lived
• you dropped all the cards on the floor and had to resort them in alphabetical order!

The computer can take all the hard work out of these types of tasks and can perform them almost instantaneously.

## database programs

Database programs can be

• 'stand alone' programs which operate independently of other programs and may be specially written for the business
• part of an integrated software program which may also include a wordprocessing program and a calculation program known as a 'spreadsheet'
• 'flat' databases which contain independent records of information, or 'relational' databases which link up individual records so that if you amend information in one record, the data will change in related records

Whichever form the database program takes, it can usefully link up with other programs.  Suppose, for instance, that you wanted to send out a standard letter to your customers.  You would link up the addresses in your database with a standard letter format – with a gap for the address – in your word processing program, and the computer would print out all the letters, and possibly also address labels to match, if they were required.  Database programs can also perform calculations on numerical data entered.   Some businesses consequently use databases to produce invoices and other financial documents which require calculations (eg number of items sold multiplied by the price).

## database terminology

Set out below is an explanation of terminology which is common to all database programs, and you will need to familiarise yourself with the various definitions.

**data**　　　　　　　　information, either 'text' or 'numeric'

**database**　　　　　a collection of data organised so that the data can be added to, amended, sorted and accessed

**file**　　　　　　　　a collection of records in a specified format – eg all the records of customer names and details

**record**　　　　　　an individual record containing data – eg a customer's name and details – comparable to an index card in a manual system

**field**　　　　　　　a separate item of data contained in a record – eg a customer's name, a customer's initials, the first line of a customer's address are all *fields* and will have
- a specified maximum number of characters (letters/numbers)
- a specified format (all numbers, or all letters)

**form**　　　　　　　A form is the record (or part of the record) *as it appears on the computer screen* (see the illustration below).  It is like a card index record, showing all the fields available, their names, and the spaces in which you can type the required information.

The *organisation* of a computer database is set out in diagramatic form below.

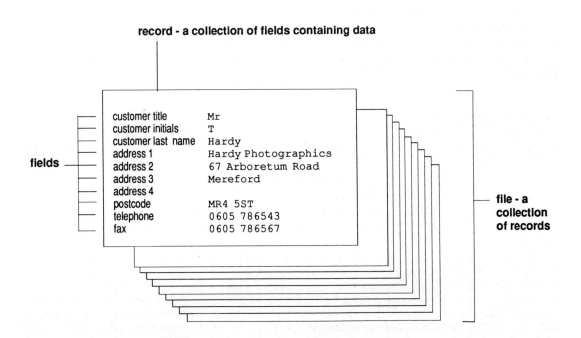

**record - a collection of fields containing data**

| | |
|---|---|
| customer title | Mr |
| customer initials | T |
| customer last name | Hardy |
| address 1 | Hardy Photographics |
| address 2 | 67 Arboretum Road |
| address 3 | Mereford |
| address 4 | |
| postcode | MR4 5ST |
| telephone | 0605 786543 |
| fax | 0605 786567 |

**fields**

**file - a collection of records**

The completed record on the computer screen will look like this:

```
customer title       Mr
customer initials    T
customer last  name    Hardy
address 1        Hardy Photographics
address 2        67 Arboretum Road
address 3        Mereford
address 4
postcode         MR4 5ST
telephone        0605 786543
fax              0605 786567
```

## database functions and uses

Databases are fast, flexible and efficient in the way in which they manipulate data.  They can:

• *sort* data in a field alphabetically, numerically and in date order

• *select* records from  a file, eg all customers living in London, all customers with a fax number

• *calculate* numerical data in a record, eg total sales to a customer, an invoice function

• *export* data, eg into a word processor file for letters and labels, a process known as 'mailmerge'

Databases are therefore widely used in business for:

• maintaining customer records

• personnel records

• stock records (you often see stock records on screen in DIY stores)

• analysis of market research questionnaires

As part of your studies and your 'Information Technology' Core Skill assessment you should become familiar with computer databases and use them when apppropriate.

## computer spreadsheets

### what spreadsheets do

If you wanted to carry out a budget calculation – for example working out how much money you have available to spend in a week after you have met all your expenses – you could set it out in column form on a sheet of paper – a *worksheet* –  and use a calculator or your brain for the calculations.  The budget would look something like this:

| | | |
|---|---|---|
| Wages | | £150 |
| *less expenses:* | | |
| food and housekeeping | £45 | |
| rent | £50 | |
| petrol | £15 | |
| clothes | £15 | |
| entertainment | £10 | |
| total of expenses | | £135 |
| | | |
| *Money left for spending* | | £15 |

All you have done is to perform a simple budget: you have added up the expenses (total £135) and have deducted them from your wages (£150) to give the spending money total of £15. Suppose that you then discover that your rent is to be increased. You will have to cross out some of the original figures and do all the calculations again. Suppose you wanted to do the same calculation the following week, but decide that you are not going to spend any money on entertainment – you will have to draw up the figures again and recalculate the totals. In short the process involving paper and calculator takes time and involves much crossing out and recalculation.

A computer spreadsheet is specifically designed to speed up tasks of this type, and can be used by the individual for personal finance, or by organisations. *A spreadsheet is a calculation worksheet displayed on the computer screen.* Once you have input the figures and given the instructions for the calculations, the spreadsheet carries them out on the screen. You can change the figures and the totals will be re-calculated automatically. You have created what is known as a 'mask'. Spreadsheets are used for a wide variety of tasks by organisations: projecting budgets (estimating income and expenditure), maintaining financial records, and keeping track of the bank account.

Before we examine how to enter the figures in a spreadsheet to carry out calculations we will first look at how a spreadsheet is set out on the computer screen.

### the spreadsheet on the screen

If you want to access a spreadsheet on your computer screen you will either load a specific program (from hard or floppy disk) or load a spreadsheet option from an integrated package. You will then access a spreadsheet file; this may either be a new file (the equivalent of a blank piece of paper ready for calculations) or it may be an existing file set up to perform a specific calculation. Whatever the case, the format of the screen will always be the same. Look at the example below.

| | A | B | C | D | E | F |
|---|---|---|---|---|---|---|
| 1 | | | | | | |
| 2 | | | | | | |
| 3 | | | | | | |
| 4 | | | | | | |
| 5 | | | | | | |
| 6 | | | | | | |
| 7 | | | | | | |
| 8 | | | | | | |
| 9 | | | | | | |
| 10 | | | | | | |
| 11 | | | | | | |
| 12 | | | | | | |

*a new spreadsheet file as it appears on the screen*

A new spreadsheet file is set out as a series of blank boxes in rows and columns into which data can be entered. The terms used in this 'grid' layout are as follows:

**rows**          each horizontal *row* is given a *number* (shown in the left margin)

**columns**       each vertical *column* is given a *letter* (shown at the top of the screen)

**cells**         each box is known as a *cell* and is used for entering data; the location or 'reference' of each cell is determined by its column (letter) and row (number), for example A1, B2, C3 and so on . . .

The screen shows only a limited number of cells, often 20 rows and 8 columns. In fact a typical spreadsheet file can provide over 4,000 rows and over 250 columns. As there are only 26 letters in the alphabet, columns after the letter Z are given a two letter reference: AA, AB, AC, AD, AE, and so on. You can move around the spreadsheet file by using the 'cursor' keys or by inputting a specific command indicating the reference (eg F6) of the cell to which you wish to move the cursor.

The illustration below shows a spreadsheet file into which data has been entered. The calculation is the expected sales income and expenses (budget) for Electra Limited, a business. The principle behind the calculation is exactly the same as that of the personal budget on page 68.

| | A | B | C | D | E |
|---|---|---|---|---|---|
| 1 | ELECTRA LTD | | | | |
| 2 | Budget for Jan-March | | | | |
| 3 | | January | February | March | Totals |
| 4 | Sales | 10000 | 10000 | 10000 | 30000 |
| 5 | | | | | |
| 6 | Expenses: | | | | |
| 7 | Purchases | 5000 | 7500 | 2500 | 15000 |
| 8 | Wages | 1000 | 1000 | 1000 | 3000 |
| 9 | Overheads | 750 | 500 | 750 | 2000 |
| 10 | Total expenses | 6750 | 9000 | 4250 | 20000 |
| 11 | Profit | 3250 | 1000 | 5750 | 10000 |
| 12 | | | | | |

*a completed spreadsheet file as it appears on the screen*

## entering data into the cells - labels, values and formulas

The cells of the completed spreadsheet contain different types of data – *labels, values* and *formulas*. We will deal with each of these in turn by looking at columns A and B.

For the technicalities of input, ie which keys and commands to use, you should refer to your instruction manual. In the descriptions below we concentrate on what labels, values and formulas actually *are* and *do*.

**labels**   A *label* is a piece of *text* input into a spreadsheet cell, ie a word or a phrase. A label does not *normally* contain any numerical information, except where it is used for the purposes of illustration, eg a year '1992' or '1993'. A label is used to explain what appears in the row or column to which it applies. Your computer program may enable you to print a label in **bold type** or <u>underlined type</u> for emphasis. Column A is made up entirely of labels:

cell A1            the title **ELECTRA LTD**

cell A2            the subtitle **Budget for Jan-March**

cell A3            the descriptions of the figures in each row, eg Sales

Column B has one label – the name of the month in question: January (B3)

**values**

A *value* is a *number* which is input into a spreadsheet cell. Column B contains the following values which will have been input (note the column/row reference used for each cell):

| | |
|---|---|
| cell B4 | 10000 (money received from Sales for the month) |
| cell B7 | 5000 (money spent on Purchases for the month) |
| cell B8 | 1000 (wages for the month) |
| cell B9 | 750 (other standard expenses for the month) |

Note that B10 and B11 are *not* values, but are totals calculated from the values by means of formulas, which we will examine next.

**formulas**

A *formula* is an equation input on the computer keyboard into a spreadsheet cell. It automatically performs a calculation on the value cells which you specify in the equation, and displays the result in the formula cell.

The cell B10 on the previous page is the total of B7+B8+B9. The equation input on the computer keyboard at cell B10 is

*=B7+B8+B9.*

The cell B11 is B4 *less* B10. The equation input at cell B11 is

*=B4-B10*

Note that:
- the formula starts with the 'equals' sign: = (see the note below)
- the formula specifies the cells which are to be used in the calculation
- most programs include other useful arithmetic functions which can be entered into a formula, eg multiplication, division, percentages and averages of value cells
- if the figures in the value cells are changed, the result shown in the formula cell will automatically change

### uses of computer spreadsheets

Computer spreadsheets are widely used in business because they are an accurate, fast and efficient way of handling numeric data. The critical factor in the use of spreadsheets is to start with the 'right' calculation grid – *mask* – and time should be spent on planning it.

Examples of the use of spreadsheets include:
- payroll calculations
- VAT calculations
- invoice production
- presentation of financial statements – the trading and profit and loss account and balance sheet
- budgets – including the cash flow forecast

In this book we suggest ways in which a spreadsheet can be used:
- Chapter 35 "Final accounts – extended trial balance format"
- Chapter 40 "Budgeting – the cash flow forecast"

If you have access to a spreadsheet program in your school or college you should spend time familiarising yourself with the way it works, with your tutor, or with a tutorial manual. It forms an important part of your Core Skill 'Information Technology'.

# information technology and its users

Information technology
- provides *benefits* to its users – speed of use, cost savings, accuracy, improved access to information
- imposes extra requirements: security of data, training obligations
- imposes *legal obligations* – the Data Protection Act and Health and Safety Regulations

We will deal with each of these in turn.

## benefits of information technology

*speed*

This chapter has already shown that information technology can greatly speed up business operations:
- a database of customer records, for example, can sort automatically, print reports, print labels for mailshots in a fraction of the time it would take manually
- a spreadsheet can dramatically reduce calculation time – look, for example, at the way a cash flow forecast can be amended (Chapter 40)

*cost*

Speed means less time used and therefore a cost saving to the business. Against this cost saving must be set the capital cost of buying the computer and program, and training the staff. In the long run there is little doubt that information technology saves money.

*accuracy*

The "garbage in, garbage out" principle states that a computer system will provide accurate information when the input is correct! As long as a business has a system for checking the accuracy of its input, the output, eg for spreadsheet calculations, will always be accurate.

*access*

Records maintained on paper can get lost or sit unnoticed on someone's desk – they will be unobtainable. Information maintained on computer, particularly if a network is installed, will be readily accessible on screen, as long as access is authorised.

All these factors contribute to the level of *efficiency* within an organisation. It must be remembered that efficiency is only possible if the *staff* are also efficient and follow internal procedures correctly. There is nothing more irritating that being told that a mistake is "due to the computer"!

## requirements of information technology

*security*

The ready accessibility of data also has its dangers, and businesses often need to restrict access to information, eg to personnel records. This may be achieved by a password system whereby a computer program or file can only be accessed if a restricted codeword is input. Another development is the use of an encoded plastic card which is needed to gain access to equipment.

The data itself must be preserved securely. Computer data storage systems (eg hard disks) can "crash" and lose the data that has been input. Businesses therefore should set up elaborate backup systems, using floppy disks (stored away from the computer) and additional storage devices linked to the computer. It is common practice for backup disks to be stored in a fireproof safe on the business premises

*skills training*

The use of information technology is an acquired skill (it forms part of your Core Skills assessment). In business, time and money has to be set aside to train staff in the use of equipment and software. The most effective method is "on the job" training. Often the firm supplying the equipment and software will provide training and an advice "hotline" as part of the overall package.

## Data Protection Act 1984

The Data Protection Act was passed in order to protect the rights of individuals who have data relating to them stored on *computer* file (not on paper-based files) by an organisation, the *owners* of the data.  Concern had been growing at the time about the dangers to privacy when organisations passed on or sold personal information – eg records of non-payment of debt – to other organisations. All organisations who maintain customer data on computer file *must* register with the Data Protection Registrar.  The Registrar's job is to maintain a public register of data users and computer bureaux.

Exceptions to the registration rules include data used:
* in payroll programs
* in accounting programs, or other records of purchases and sales
* in mailing lists
* in word processing documents

This exception list, as you will appreciate, covers many of the business uses of computer data.

The main provisions of the Act are:
* to give individuals the right to *know* what details relating to them are stored on computer file
* to enable the individual, on payment of a fee, to obtain a *copy* of any computer data file
* to enable the individual, if the entry is *incorrect*, to apply to the Registrar for correction or deletion of the record
* to enable the individual to seek compensation if the records are either *inaccurate*, or *disclosed without authority*

The implication of the Act for businesses is that they should make enquiries of the Registrar if any use of personal data on computer file *may* require registration (which merely involves the completion of a form and the payment of a small fee).   As noted above, many routine business uses do not require registration.

## health and safety aspects of information technology  – EEC Directive 87/391

It has been recognised for some time that *ergonomics* – the study of the way the workplace conditions affect the human body – are important both for the employer and employee.  The growth in health disorders related to the use of computer workstations has received wide coverage in the media.   Public attention has been drawn to the dangers of radiation to pregnant women from computer screens and to RSI (repetititive strain injury) from keyboard operation.

From 1 Janaury 1993 an EC Directive required that any new installations of computers must conform to certain standards:
* employers are obliged to analyse workstations to evaluate safety and health conditions relating to risks to eyesight, physical problems and mental stress
* provision of training in the use of the workstation
* employees' activities must be planned to give them periodic breaks from computer input
* employees should be given periodic eyesight tests, and be provided with glasses if necessary
* computer screens must tilt and swivel and not flicker
* keyboards must be tiltable and separate
* the work surface must be the right height, adjustable and non-reflective
* the chair should be adjustable and have arms and a backrest
* the room lighting must be sufficient and non-flourescent
* equipment noise must be regulated and radiation reduced

It is the responsibility of the employer to ensure that these stringent regulations are implemented.  It is also up to the employee to see that the various precautions are observed, even if it means wearing glasses!

### student activity 7.3 – uses of a computer database

Consider how the following businesses might make use of a computer database to maintain customer records. State in each case what forms of information will need to be maintained – ie what 'fields' will be required, what 'sorting' processes might be used and what security (if any) will be needed to protect the data.

(a)  a bank

(b)  a double-glazing firm

(c)  a school or a college

### student activity 7.4 – uses of a computer spreadsheet

Construct a worksheet *on paper* setting out the monthly *income* and *expenditure* of a typical family of four, along the lines of the illustration on page 68. You can obtain the figures from your own family, from discussion with your fellow students, or by reference to statistics in the Household Expenditure Tables in "Social Trends" published by HMSO. Discuss your calculations with your tutor and then set out the table on a computer spreadsheet. When you have successfully completed the spreadsheet, vary the figures by:

(a)  increasing income by 25%

(b)  decreasing income by 25%

What effect will this have on your monthly budget? In both cases change any expense figure which you *can* change and which you *want* to change.

### student activity 7.5 – legal requirements of information technology

An insurance broking business is introducing computer workstations so that all members of staff can have access to a new customer database which the firm is setting up. What advice would you give to the partners about:

(a)  legal requirements relating to the maintenance of customer records on computer file

(b)  regulations governing the working conditions of the staff

# chapter summary

❑  Information technology involves the manual and (increasingly) computer-based storage, manipulation and communication of data.

❑  Computer technology covers a wide area of operations, including word processing, DTP, database, spreadsheet, accounting, fax, electronic mail and viewdata.

❑  The computer database is used for the storage and sorting of data; more sophisticated programs also allow calculations to be carried out.

❑  Computer spreadsheets are calculation worksheets which have a number of useful applications: payroll, invoicing, presentation of financial statements and budgets.

❑  Information technology provides the benefits of speed, cost-saving, accuracy and easy access to data. It also requires security systems and skills training.

❑  Legal requirements imposed on computer users include the Data Protection Act 1984 which protects the privacy of personal records, and the EEC Health and Safety regulations which require a high degree of comfort and safety for computer users.

# *Villas International Ltd – the application of information technology*

| Element 2.3 | *Investigate information processing systems* |
|---|---|
| Suggested Sources: | • computer and office machine companies |
| | • British Telecom shops and catalogues |
| | • talks from computer consultants |
| | • school or college information technology centres/practice offices |
| | • textbooks in libraries and resource centres |

## INTRODUCTION

You work as a clerical assistant for Villas International Ltd., an independent travel agent which specialises in the rental of foreign villas and apartments to UK holidaymakers. The company, which is situated at 34 The Hop Market, Stourminster MR8 6TF, comprises the owner, a secretary and yourself.

Villas International Limited is a old-fashioned business started by Miles Ludlow twenty years ago. It has relied very much on traditional methods of selling its holidays – small advertisements in the local paper and word-of-mouth recommendations. Recently, however, competition from other firms who advertise in the Sunday newspapers and promote a much more 'glossy' image has resulted in a substantial decline in business. Last month Miles Ludlow, who is 65, decided to retire and to sell the business to someone who was much more go-ahead and up-to-date in approach. The buyer was Paul Robinson, a young and energetic executive in the travel business. You heard him say on his first morning when he toured the office that a lot of changes would have to be made.

The main areas of operation of the business are

• keeping in touch with owners of apartments and villas abroad in locations which stretch from Europe to Honolulu
• booking flights through the main airlines
• marketing the holidays to UK holidaymakers

The office itself is very old-fashioned, although it functions very efficiently. The records of apartment and villa owners are kept in filing cabinet drawers in alphabetical order, while the client (holidaymaker) details are kept in a card index file in a drawer.

The business relies very much on the telephone for keeping in touch with its villa and apartment owners and also for booking flights.

Marketing and advertising are very low key and are based on regular adverts in the local Stourminster Echo and an annual newsletter to regular clients, typed in the office and sent out by post. It is your job to type out the envelopes each year for the newsletter.

The only electrical equipment in the office is an elderly electric typewriter, a small desk-top photocopier, and a coffee percolator (Mr Ludlow was very particular about his coffee).

## TASK 1

Paul Robinson asks you to write a *formal report* covering the following areas (use your own name and the current date):

1.       The opportunities there are there in the office for the introduction of new technology, and the advantages to be gained, particularly in the areas of

(a) word processing
(b) DTP
(c) a database program
(d) a spreadsheet program
(e) a fax machine
(f)  electronic mail
(g) viewdata

2.       Miss Preece, the secretary, has no experience of computers and states quite firmly to Mr Robinson:

*'If those machines come in here,  I'm off somewhere else, even if it's feet first!  They are terrible things to  work with  – you get headaches, backaches and there is a cancer risk from radiation!"*

What *can* you and *should* you do to keep Miss Preece happy?

3.       Paul Robinson mentions to you that he has heard at the local Business Club about the Data Protection Act.  He wants to know what it is, and if it applies to him.

## TASK 2

It has been  assumed in this Exercise that not *all* students will have access to *all* forms of new technology, and therefore Task1 is theoretical, ie it does not involve 'hands on' experience of computers and related technology.  If you *do* have access to computers you should attempt some of the following exercises:

(a)     Using a database program, set up  a file of thirty clients;  each record should contain the client's name, address and telephone number, together with a series of fields for the dates when they booked holidays with you, and the destinations in each case.  Sort the records so that you can print out reports to show which destinations are the most popular from year to year.
Note:  invent the client details.

(b)     Using a word processor write a letter to your clients telling them of the change of management and giving them an assurance of continued good service.  If your computer system and resources permit, carry out a mailmerge exercise and print out a letter to each client on the word processor, headed with the client's name and address from the database.  You can either design your letter so that window envelopes can be used, or alternatively you can use the database and word processor to print a series of address labels to stick on plain envelopes.
*Note: if resources are limited, set the system up and print out a single specimen letter.*

(c)     Using a DTP program design an advertisement for Villas International to place in the local newspaper. Look at other travel advertisements to give you an idea of the format required.  Your advertisement should include a notice of the change of management.

# SECTION

# 2

# business in the economy

## contents

In this section we turn from looking at individual businesses and the way in which they operate to the subject of the *economic background* of business. In the next five chapters we examine in turn:

## information sources

You are recommended to research and read as widely as possible when studying this area. The list below sets out a number of useful sources.

STATISTICAL INFORMATION (HMSO)
United Kingdom National Accounts (CSO Blue Book), Bank of England Quarterly Bulletin, Economic Trends, Economic Trends Annual Supplement, Employment Gazette, Department of Employment, Social Trends

EC SOURCES
EC Commission General Reports, Europe in Figures, Eurostat

MEDIA
Newspapers: The Economist, Financial Times, The Times, The Daily Telegraph, The Guardian, The Independent
TV and Radio: Radio 4 is a particularly good source of very up-to-date information

TEXTS

| | | |
|---|---|---|
| *Investigating Economics* | Hocking & Powell | Longman |
| *Economics: a new approach* | Alain Anderton | Hyman and Bell |
| *Economics* | Alain Anderton | Causeway Press |
| *Economics Explained* | Peter Maunder et al | Collins Educational |
| *The UK Economy* | M J Artis (Ed) | Weidenfeld & Nicolson |

BUSINESS SOURCES
Company Reports and Accounts
Chambers of Commerce
The Confederation of British Industry

# 8 The products and purpose of business

## introduction

In this chapter we shall consider:
- why there was a movement away from a system where everyone produced all the goods and services they needed for themselves to one where individuals *specialised* in the activities to which they were best suited
- the advantages and disadvantages of specialisation and the wider applications of this principle
- how the combination of unlimited wants and limited resources gives rise to the need to make choices, and how economists classify the activities of firms and the goods and services they produce

We shall conclude by looking at the range of factors which motivates firms to produce goods and services.

## the development of specialisation

In the earliest days of human development people were *self-sufficient*. They provided all their basic *needs* – food, shelter, clothing – themselves. In order to survive people would be forced to spend a very large proportion of their time finding enough food to eat and ensuring that their other needs were satisfied. People probably lived in this way for thousands of years, but eventually it became apparent that this was not the most *efficient* way to live. Individuals found that they were better able to perform some tasks than others. Some may have discovered that they were particularly well suited to hunting while others became skilled at making tools. This then was the beginning of *specialisation*. People discovered that through specialisation they were able to use their time more efficiently and thus increase the production of food and the other items that they wanted.

# specialisation and the division of labour

## specialisation

At the present time the evidence of the existence of specialisation is all around us. Few people attempt to provide all their needs themselves.  Some people may attempt to produce all the food that they need but the range and variety of human wants is so enormous – personal stereos, computers, electricity, education – that it is virtually impossible to achieve self-sufficiency. Instead people concentrate on producing just some of society's needs and become bricklayers, lawyers, doctors and airline pilots.

Even within these occupations further specialisation often occurs.  Lawyers may concentrate on criminal or business law and doctors may become specialists in dealing with certain aspects of the human body.  Mainly as a result of specialisation individual efficiency has increased and people can now produce more of the *goods* and *services* that are needed than could ever have been the case through self-sufficiency.

## the division of labour

The principle of specialisation is closely associated with the *division of labour* where large tasks are broken down into a number of smaller and easier operations.  The best example of the division of labour is probably the modern car assembly line where the production of each vehicle has been divided into literally hundreds of smaller and separate jobs.  One of the major advantages of this system of production is that it makes it easier to introduce machinery into the process.

# specialisation within and between countries

The principle of specialisation extends beyond the individual to
- regions within a country
- whole countries

In the UK some regions are associated with particular activities.   In the same way that individuals discovered they were better at doing some things than others, so regions and countries have discovered that they too are better at some types of activity than others.  This may be related to climate, or natural resources.  Thus the availability of clay in the area around Stoke-on-Trent led to the development of the pottery industry.  Similarly the combination of climate and soil has led to the growth of the wine industry in France.

## student activity 8.1 – regional specialisation
Make a list of six regions of the UK, including the area in which you live, and the main activity with which each is associated.  In each case state the key economic reasons which explain why regions have specialised in the products or services you give.

## the gains from specialisation

The main benefit of specialisation is undoubtedly the increase in the quantity of goods and services that can be achieved.

To demonstrate this factor, consider the tables on the next page which set out the *hypothetical* quantities of cars and wine produced in the UK and France before and after specialisation has taken place.

| BEFORE SPECIALISATION | | | AFTER SPECIALISATION | | |
|---|---|---|---|---|---|
| | wine (000s litres) | cars units | | wine (000s litres) | cars units |
| UK | 100 | 500 | UK | 0 | 1,000 |
| France | 500 | 100 | France | 1,000 | 0 |
| Total | 600 | 600 | Total | 1,000 | 1,000 |

Notice that before specialisation and with both countries allocating their resources equally between the two commodities, total production of wine and cars is 600 units. If each country then specialises in the good (product) at which it is best, ie the UK in cars and France in wine, then total production increases to 1,000 units of each – an increase of 400 units of both cars and wine.

### student activity 8.2 – specialisation and the division of labour

Make a list of FIVE possible advantages and FOUR disadvantages associated with specialisation and the division of labour.
Try to suggest how some of the disadvantages might be overcome.

# the problem of unlimited wants

Most people who live in the UK would probably accept that they are able to satisfy their essential needs. Relatively few people go hungry or are unable to find accommodation on a regular basis. Equally there are probably very few people who would claim that all their wants have been satisfied. It seems to be a fact of life that no matter how much people have they always want more. Unfortunately there are limited resources available to satisfy people's wants. Given these two conflicting realities – *limited resources and unlimited wants* – individuals and countries cannot obtain all the goods and services they want, and they are forced to make economic choices.

For example, a country may be considering building a new airport. If it chooses to do so, it must be understood that it will have to forego spending money on another project, perhaps building three new hospitals. The real or *opportunity cost* of the airport is the next best alternative that has to be sacrificed — the three new hospitals in this example.

### student activity 8.3 – opportunity cost

State the likely opportunity costs in each of the following situations:

(a)   you decide to buy your mother some flowers

(b)   you get up very late on Sunday morning

(c)   a student stays on at college beyond the age of 16

(d)   the government decides to build a second channel tunnel between the UK and France

## production possibility curves

The range of choices open to a country and the related opportunity costs are often represented on a *production possibility curve*. In the diagram below a country must choose between two types of goods: guns and butter. The curve shows the maximum amount of guns and butter that could be produced given existing resources and the current state of technology. Notice that if the country wants to produce *more* guns, then the opportunity cost of this decision is the butter that it will need to go without, as resources are moved from butter to the production of guns.

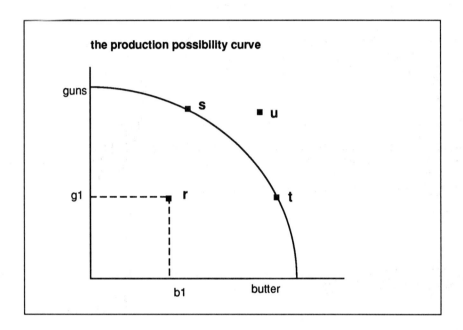

Points **r** to **u**  represent the following possibilities:

**r** a combination of guns and butter (g1,b1) below the maximum it could achieve – the country is thus making *inefficient* use of its resources

**s** a combination of guns and butter where the *most efficient* use is being made of its resources.

**t** a different combination of guns and butter where it is also making the most *efficient* use of its resources

**u** a combination of guns and butter that *cannot be achieved* given existing technology

## the need for markets

One of the main benefits of specialisation has been the increase in the quantity of goods and services produced. Individuals, regions and countries produce more goods and services than they themselves need. These additional amounts are known as *surpluses* but the benefits of these surpluses can only be achieved if they can be *exchanged* for the surpluses produced by others. The importance of exchange to the existence of specialisation has led to the development of *markets*. Without markets sellers of goods and services would need to spend a lot of their time seeking out those who might wish to buy and vice versa.

Markets may be defined as:

*situations that make it possible for buyers and sellers to meet*

Markets may range in sophistication from car boot sales to the international currency markets, where buyers and sellers of foreign currencies are linked through a highly complex network of electronic communications systems. Despite such differences the aim of all markets is the same: to keep the costs involved in exchanging goods and services to a minimum.

### the importance of money and transport
The need to exchange goods and services and the development of markets has also resulted in the development of *money* and *transport networks*. Money is simply:

*anything that can be used to settle a debt*

The direct exchange of goods – *barter* – has enormous drawbacks and, with the occasional exception, is unworkable in a modern economy. Without money those who wish to sell goods would need to find not only someone willing to buy but also a buyer who is willing to offer the 'right' goods in exchange. A person willing to exchange his surplus of watches for shoes has to find not only someone with a surplus of shoes but, who is also willing to exchange shoes for watches (the *double coincidence of wants*). Just think of the time it would take for shoppers to discuss what they might offer Tesco or Sainsbury's at the check-out having completed their weekly shopping.

It must also be appreciated that an efficient transport network is needed to bring goods from wherever they have been made in the world to the markets where they are to be sold.

### EC transport policy
In the light of the creation of the single (European) market with common standards and the free movement of goods and services, a common transport policy is a priority within the EC. For many years the European Parliament and the European Commission have been active in pursuing an open market in transport by seeking the elimination of national restrictions and barriers in the operation of various means of transport – shipping, inland waterways, road, rail and airlines.

---

**student activity 8.4 – problems with barter**
Apart from the double coincidence of wants mentioned above, give FOUR other problems that would be encountered in a barter economy.

---

# classification of goods and businesses

### classification of goods
In the example given above guns and butter have been used to represent the range of products that a country might wish to produce. In reality the goods and services that a country produces depends on the *demand* (needs and wants) of individuals (see Chapter 10). Note that the demand for goods such as cars also gives rise to a demand for other goods and *factors of production* (ie land, labour and capital) used to make cars. This is known as *derived demand*. The idea of derived demand applies most obviously to machinery or *capital goods* and to two additional factors of production *labour* and *land*. It should also be recognised that in most countries governments demand goods and services such as education on behalf of its citizens.

In summary, the production of goods can be classified under the following headings:

| | |
|---|---|
| *consumer goods* | These are goods and services wanted by consumers for their own sake and include computer games, clothes and holidays. |
| *producer goods* | Producer goods (capital goods) are goods and services wanted not for their own sake but for the contribution that they make to the production of other goods and services. They include items such as trucks, lathes and accountants. |
| *public goods* | These are goods and services such as jet fighters and street lighting which are not normally demanded by individuals. Such goods are provided by local and central government and are normally paid for through the raising of taxes. |

## the classification of businesses by sector

As well as classifying goods and services in terms of who demand them, it is also usual to divide the activities of the businesses into three broad sectors:

| | |
|---|---|
| *primary* | This is the first stage of the production process and refers to the extraction of raw materials that are needed in the production process. It includes activities such as mining, fishing and agriculture. |
| *secondary* | As the name suggests, this is the second stage of the production process where the raw materials are processed and made into products for sale. This stage is also known as *manufacturing*. |
| *tertiary* | This is also known as the service stage and includes intangible activities such as banking and tourism. |

# the motives of firms

## the profit motive

The existence of demand for a good or service does not automatically mean that a firm will produce or *supply* a good or service. Firms need to be offered some kind of incentive or reward for their activities. In most cases the reward for production is *profit*. Profit is essentially the difference between the amount of money a firm receives from selling its output *(revenue)* and the expenses it incurs *(costs)* such as labour and raw materials. This simple definition of profit is employed in the *accounting* statements of a business (see Chapter 28). An *economic* definition of profit also takes into account the less obvious costs incurred, such as the risk, initiative, time and effort undertaken by the firm's owner(s). Once all these costs have been deducted then what remains is referred to by economists as *normal profit*.

## profit and customer satisfaction

Profit should not only be seen as a reward for production. The existence of profit may also help to indicate what goods and how much of them are wanted. As will be seen in the next chapter, goods for which the demand is very high often give rise to high profit levels which can stimulate further production. Low profit levels may indicate that firms are producing inefficiently and that the best possible use is not being made of resources. Similarly low profit levels may indicate that the good is not sufficiently valued by consumers to make its production worthwhile. The primary function of all businesses, regardless of their motivation, is to satisfy their customers. Any businesses that consistently do not produce what its customers want will eventually fail.

## public services and charities

Profit is not, however, the only reward for production and risk taking. In the UK the government provides a number of *public services* for the benefit of the community as a whole. Education and the

National Health Service (NHS) are examples of services organised by the state, but which do not aim to make any profit. Those activities that are organised by either central or local government are part of what is termed the *public sector*. Other organisations such as the Terence Higgins Trust which offers help to AIDS sufferers, depend on volunteers to form the largest part of their labour force. Most organisations like these are registered *charities* and they are motivated by the wish to help others. Some businesses have several aims in that they try to make profits but then give a portion of their profits to help the local community. The Northampton-based chemical firm Scott Bader is one such example.

## the motivation continuum

The range of motives can be represented on a continuum (straight line), as in the diagram below. On the extreme left of the line, business motivation can be characterised by high profits and purely private benefits. An example might be a drug pusher who charges the highest prices he or she can, and who has no regard for the welfare of those who buy the drugs. On the extreme right of the line, business motivation can be characterised as philanthropic (charitable) or humanitarian and profits are zero. The National Society for the Prevention of Cruelty to Children (NSPCC) is a good example. In reality most firms lie somewhere between the two extremes.

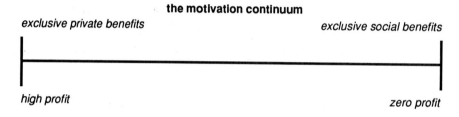

the motivation continuum

exclusive private benefits          exclusive social benefits

high profit          zero profit

## student activity 8.5 – business motives

Look at the business organisations in your neighbourhood. List FIVE examples where a business is not motivated wholly by the profit motive. What benefits do you think the business achieves in each case?

## student activity 8.6 – analysis of UK economic output

The questions set out on the next page are based on the table below which shows the output of the UK economy by the main sectors of economic activity.

| Main sectors of economic activity | Employees* '000 March 1992 | Value added £ billion 1991 | % share of gdp 1990 | Volume change in output % pa 1982-1991 |
|---|---|---|---|---|
| Agriculture, forestry and fishing | 265 | 8.8 | 1.8 | 2.5 |
| Energy and water supply | 408 | 28.3 | 5.7 | 0.7 |
| Manufacturing | 4,522 | 104.3 | 21.0 | 2.1 |
| Construction | 843 | 33.7 | 6.8 | 4.0 |
| Distribution, hotels and catering | 4,454 | 73.0 | 14.7 | 3.2 |
| Transport and communications | 1,322 | 34.8 | 7.0 | 3.3 |
| Financial services | 2,615 | 88.2 | 17.7 | 6.1 |
| Ownership of dwellings | 128 | 34.8 | 7.0 | 0.8 |
| Education and health | 3,260 | 49.6 | 10.0 | 1.2 |
| Public administration | 1,570 | 34.8 | 7.0 | -0.1 |
| Other services | 1,884 | 33.9 | 6.8 | 3.1 |
| Adjustment and residual | | -27.2 | -5.5 | |
| Gdp | 21,271 | 497.0 | 100.0 | 2.5 |

*Figures for Great Britain only. The other columns in the table are for the UK as a whole.

SOURCE: LLOYDS BANK PLC

The column headings on the table may be explained as follows:

"value added"     Output is expressed in terms of value added, or the values of outputs minus inputs, so as to avoid double counting when the sales of different units are added together

"gdp"     gdp (often written as GDP) stands for Gross Domestic Product – this is the total value of the output of goods and services produced in the UK in a year

## questions

(a)     What percentage of total output is accounted for by the primary, secondary and tertiary sectors respectively?

(b)     Which were
    (i)     the fastest growing sectors in the period 1982-1991?
    (ii)     the slowest growing sectors in the period 1982-1991?

(c)     How might you account for your answers to question (b)?

(d)     In 1992, distribution, hotels and catering employed 4,454,000 workers while manufacturing employed 4,522,000 workers, yet their percentage shares of GDP(1990) were 17.7 and 21.0 respectively. How might this difference in the number of workers employed in relation to their share of total output be explained?

(e)     Although it is not evident from the data, energy was the fastest growing sector in the early 1980s. How might you account for its apparent growth and subsequent decline?

# chapter summary

❑ Originally people were self-sufficient but they soon learnt that production could be increased through specialising in activities to which they were best suited.

❑ The principle of specialisation can also be applied to countries. It is more efficient if each nation concentrates on producing the goods and services for which their climate and natural resources makes them most suited, as opposed to producing all their needs themselves.

❑ The problem of unlimited wants and limited supply creates the need to make choices about what can be obtained and what must be sacrificed.

❑ The development of specialisation has led to the creation of markets, money and sophisticated transport systems to facilitate the efficient exchange of goods and services.

❑ Goods and services are normally classified under the headings of consumer, producer and public goods.

❑ Business activities are normally classified into primary, secondary or tertiary sectors.

❑ Firms are motivated by a variety of rewards the most common of which is profit.

# 9 The price of goods and services

## introduction

In this chapter we shall investigate how the prices of goods and services are determined in a free market economy. We shall look at in turn:

- the theories of *demand* and *supply*
- the factors that cause *changes* in the levels of demand and supply
- the way in which the theories of demand and supply are combined to show how the concept of *equilibrium price* can be derived.
- the concepts of *elasticity of demand and supply* which help to explain how changes in prices influence quantities bought and produced

## demand

In simple terms *demand* refers to the desire of consumers to obtain the goods and services produced by firms. In economics, however, the term has a more precise meaning and is usually referred to as *effective demand* and is defined as:

*the amount of a good that consumers desire to purchase over a certain period of time.*

The basic *law of demand* states that:

*the quantity demanded is inversely related to the price of the good*

All this means is that, all other things being equal, at higher prices the quantity demanded will be low and at lower prices the quantity demanded will be high. Alternatively it could be said that there is an *indirect relationship* between price and quantity demanded.

The phrase "other things being equal" means that all the other factors that can affect demand are held constant. Unless this condition is met it would be impossible to know whether a change in quantity demanded was due to a change in the price of the good or due to another factor such as a change in consumers' incomes.

## the demand schedule

In order to achieve a better understanding of the law of demand it is helpful to consider a hypothetical example: the quantity of compact discs demanded over a period of one month in relation to their price. The relationship between price and quantity demanded is shown in the table below.

| the demand schedule for compact discs (CDs) | |
| --- | --- |
| *price of CDs*<br>*£* | *quantity demanded*<br>*(000s) per month* |
| 30 | 10 |
| 25 | 20 |
| 20 | 30 |
| 15 | 40 |
| 10 | 50 |
| 5 | 60 |

Notice that when the price is £30 the quantity demanded is relatively low at 10,000. Similarly, when the price is only £5 the quantity demanded is relatively high at 60,000. If these combinations are plotted on a graph, with price along the vertical axis and quantity demanded along the horizontal axis, then the shape and position of the demand curve can be ascertained, as in the diagram below. Note that it is called a demand curve even though it is actually a straight line.

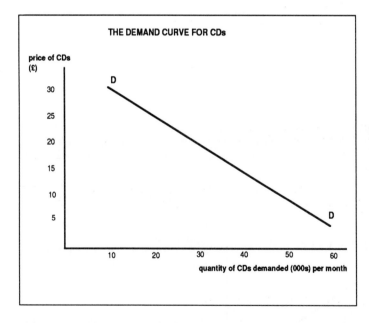

The demand curve in this example slopes downwards from left to right. This is known as a *normal demand curve*. The demand curves for the vast majority of goods and services would look rather like this although they may not actually be straight lines.

## why does the demand curve slope downwards?

The law of demand is one of the most fundamental laws in economics and is the basis of an enormous amount of economic theory developed over the last one hundred years or so. Not surprisingly, economists have been anxious to demonstrate that the law is sound and have come up with a number of explanations to support the view that people will buy more of a good as its price falls. One such explanation is that consumers derive diminishing amounts of satisfaction (utility) as their consumption of a good increases. In other words, a person who eats successive chocolate bars will gain a lot of satisfaction from the first but may be sick after the twenty first. Thus, in order to tempt people to buy more of a good the price must be reduced. This reflects the fact that consumers put less value on each extra unit purchased.

## the determinants of demand

It was mentioned above that a demand curve is drawn on the assumption that "other things remain equal." These other things are the *determinants of demand*. The determinants of demand are:

### 1. income
The demand curve for compact discs derived above was drawn on the assumption that consumers enjoyed a given level of income. If there were to be a rise or fall in consumers' incomes this would result in a change in the level of demand for compact discs. The table below shows the effects of a rise and fall in consumers' incomes on the quantities demanded.

**the demand schedule for compact discs following a change in consumers' incomes**

| price of CDs £ | quantity demanded after a rise in incomes (000s) per month | quantity demanded after a fall in incomes (000s) per month |
|---|---|---|
| 30 | 20 | 0 |
| 25 | 30 | 10 |
| 20 | 40 | 20 |
| 15 | 50 | 30 |
| 10 | 60 | 40 |
| 5 | 70 | 50 |

Both sets of figures have been plotted on the graph below, alongside the original demand curve (DD). Its easy to see that where there has been an increase in consumers' incomes the demand curve

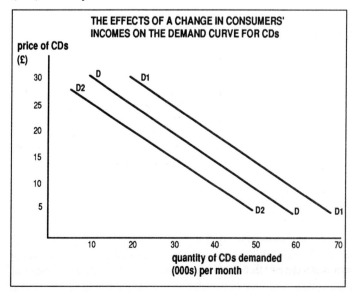

THE EFFECTS OF A CHANGE IN CONSUMERS' INCOMES ON THE DEMAND CURVE FOR CDs

quantity of CDs demanded (000s) per month

has *shifted to the right* ($D_1D_1$) and where there has been a fall in consumers' incomes it has *shifted to the left* ($D_2D_2$). The changes in the level of income have produced a movement of the whole curve. This is called a *change in demand* and means that a new quantity of a good will be demanded at *each and every price*.

A change in demand is quite different from a change in quantity demanded. A change in demand results in a shift of the whole curve whereas a change in quantity demanded results in a *movement along the curve* as the result of a change in price.

## 2. credit availability

Many consumers prefer to be able to buy the goods they want today and pay for them over a given period of time in the future. Goods obtained in this way are purchased *on credit*. The ease with which consumers can obtain credit has a considerable influence on demand. If credit became easier to obtain then the demand curve for compact discs may well shift to the right. If credit became more difficult to obtain the demand for CDs would be expected to shift to the left. Factors affecting the ease with which credit can be obtained include the length of the repayment period, the size of the initial deposit required and the level of interest payable.

## 3. expected price changes

If the price of goods is expected to rise in the near future consumers who are considering buying the good might well bring the date of their purchase forward to avoid paying the higher price. If the Chancellor of the Exchequer was expected to increase the rate of VAT in a forthcoming budget, consumers may be tempted to buy CDs in advance of the expected announcement and thus avoid paying the higher tax rate. In this case the demand for CDs would increase and the demand curve would shift to the right.

## 4. tastes and fashion

If people became more interested in listening to music in their own homes then one would expect the demand for compact discs to increase and thus the demand curve for CDs would shift to the right. Likewise changes in fashion have led changes in the demand for particular products. The trend in ladies fashions in favour of tights resulted in a large fall in demand for stockings and thus a shift to the left in the  demand curve for stockings.

## 5. advertising

Advertising has a significant affect on the demand for a wide range of goods and services.  An increase in advertising for compact discs which highlighted their improved sound quality over vinyl recordings and cassettes would be expected to result in an increase in demand for compact discs. Note that the demand  for CDs refers to the demand for CDs in general and not the demand for CDs by a particular artist.

## 6. changes in the prices of related goods: complements and substitutes

If there were to be a significant rise in the price of compact disc players, a *complement* to CDs (as CDs cannot be played without them), one would expect to see a shift to the left in the demand curve for CDs. A fall in the price of compact disc players would probably shift the curve to the right as consumers buy more CD players. The effects on the demand curve for CDs, of a change in the price of a complement, are shown in the diagram below.

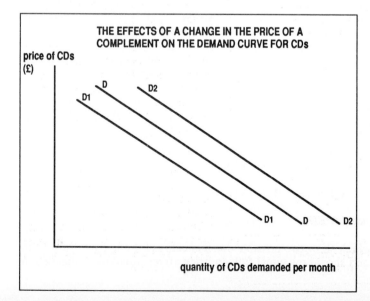

THE EFFECTS OF A CHANGE IN THE PRICE OF A COMPLEMENT ON THE DEMAND CURVE FOR CDs

The original demand curve is DD. $D_1D_1$ represents the demand curve following a rise in the price of a complement. $D_2D_2$ represents the demand curve after a fall in the price of a complement.

A significant fall in the price of pre-recorded cassettes, a substitute for CDs, would probably lead to a shift of the demand curve for CDs to the left as people switched to buying the cheaper alternative. A significant rise in cassette prices would probably shift the curve to the right as people change their purchases in favour of CDs. The effects on the demand curve for CDs, of a rise and fall in the price of a substitute good, are shown in the diagram below.

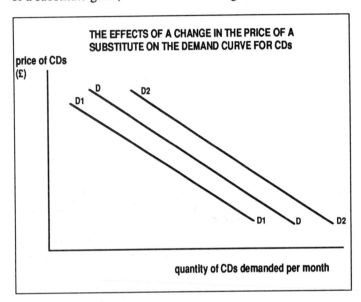

The original demand curve is DD. D₁D₁ represents the demand curve after a fall in the price of a substitute. D₂D₂ represents the demand curve after a rise in the price of a substitute.

---

### student activity 9.1 – the determinants of demand

Show, on separate diagrams, the effects of the following changes on the demand curve for CDs:

(a) an increase in the rate of income tax

(b) a substantial fall in the price of DAT (digital audio tape) equipment

(c) a rise in the price of CDs

(d) a fall in interest rates

---

## elasticity of demand

It has been established that for the vast majority of goods and services a change in price, other things being equal, will lead to a corresponding change in quantity demanded. While it is obviously helpful for a business to understand the basic law of demand, the law says nothing about how large the change in quantity demanded might be. Without this information a business will not be able to determine whether a change in the price of its products will be beneficial.

*The amount by which quantity demanded changes in response to a change in the price of a good*

is known as the *price elasticity of demand (PED)*.

Look at the graphs on the next page which show two possible demand curves for compact discs. Both curves are drawn on the same scale and show how equal falls in price affects quantity demanded in each case.

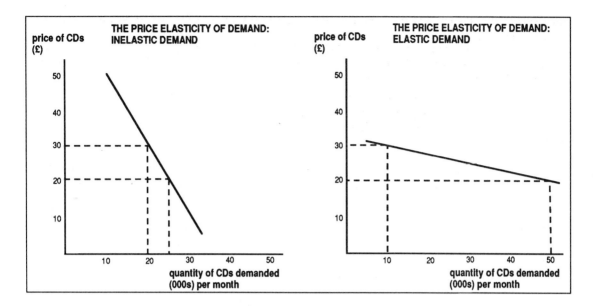

In the graph on the left a fall in price from £30 to £20 leads to a 5,000 increase in quantity demanded from 20,000 to 25,000 whereas the same fall in price leads to a 40,000 change in quantity demanded, from 10,000 to 50,000, in the graph on the right. Clearly quantity demanded is much more responsive to changes in price in the right-hand graph than is the case with the left-hand graph. In the left-hand graph demand is said to be *inelastic* and in the right-hand graph demand is said to be *elastic*.

The important points to note when considering PED are not merely the absolute changes in price and quantity that are being compared, but the *percentage changes*. In the examples above the percentage change in price is 33.3% (10/30 x 100). This leads to a 25% (5,000/20,000 x 100) and a 400% (40,000/10,000 x 100) increase in quantity demanded in the left-hand and right-hand graph respectively.

To obtain a more precise numerical value of PED the percentage change in quantity demanded is divided by the percentage change in price.

$$PED = \frac{percentage\ change\ in\ quantity\ demanded}{percentage\ change\ in\ price}$$

Therefore, in the first graph PED is 25%/33.3% = 0.75 while in the second PED is 400%/33.3% = 12. Wherever the value obtained is greater than one (PED > 1) demand is said to be elastic, where it is smaller then one (PED < 1) demand is said to be inelastic.

### student activity 9.2 – elasticities of demand

For each of the following goods state which you would expect to have high or low price elasticities of demand. Justify your answers.

(a)     luxury sports cars

(b)     all brands of petrol

(c)     Esso petrol

(d)     salt

# supply

Supply refers to the total amount of goods produced by firms. More accurately quantity supplied is:

*the amount of a good that firms are willing to produce over a given period of time*

The law of supply states that *at higher prices a larger quantity will be supplied than at lower prices.*

This means that, all other things being equal, quantity supplied will increase as price increases. Alternatively it could be said that there is a *direct relationship* between price and quantity supplied.

## the supply schedule

The possible relationship between the price and quantity supplied of CDs is shown in the table below.

| the supply schedule for compact discs | |
| --- | --- |
| *price*<br>*£* | *quantity supplied*<br>*(000s) per month* |
| 30 | 60 |
| 25 | 50 |
| 20 | 40 |
| 15 | 30 |
| 10 | 20 |
| 5 | 10 |

Notice that at a relatively high price of £30 the quantity supplied is 60,000, whereas at the relatively low price of £5 the quantity supplied is much lower at 10,000. If these figures are plotted on a graph, with price along the vertical axis and quantity supplied along the horizontal axis the supply curve will be produced, as shown below.

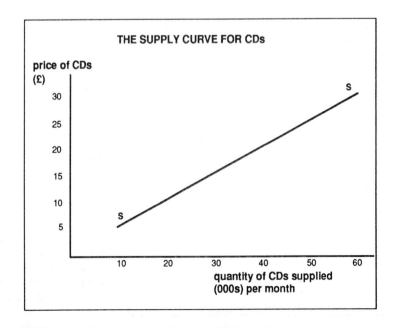

THE SUPPLY CURVE FOR CDs

### why does the supply curve slope upwards?

Generally speaking, as price rises the potential for firms to make higher profits also increases. Higher profit levels give producers a greater incentive to work harder, and employ more resources (factors of production) in the production of the product, thus increasing production. Higher prices also allow other less efficient firms to enter the market.

## the determinants of supply

As in the case of the demand curve, the supply schedule is drawn on the assumption that all other things remain equal. These other things are the *determinants of supply* and will be considered in detail below.

### 1. the costs of factors of production

It is impossible to produce anything without using some of the three factors of production - land, labour and capital. If the price of these factors were to change, the cost of production would change. This would affect the supply schedule in the way shown in the table below.

| the supply schedule for compact discs following a change in the costs of production | | |
| --- | --- | --- |
| *price of CDs* | *quantity supplied after a rise in costs* | *quantity supplied after a fall in costs* |
| *£* | *(000s) per month* | *(000s) per month* |
| 30 | 50 | 70 |
| 25 | 40 | 60 |
| 20 | 30 | 50 |
| 15 | 20 | 40 |
| 10 | 10 | 30 |
| 5 | 0 | 20 |

Both sets of figures have been plotted on the graph below along side the original supply curve (SS).

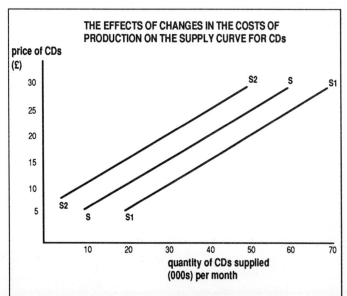

THE EFFECTS OF CHANGES IN THE COSTS OF PRODUCTION ON THE SUPPLY CURVE FOR CDs

It can be seen that a rise in the costs of production has resulted in a shift of the supply curve to the left ($S_2S_2$) and a fall in the costs of production has shifted the curve to the right ($S_1S_1$). A rise in the costs of production has produced a *decrease in supply* while a fall has produced *an increase in supply*. This means that more or less will be supplied *at every single price*.

A change in supply is quite different from a change in quantity supplied. A change in supply results in a shift of the whole curve, whereas a change in quantity supplied results in a *movement along the curve* as the result of a change in price.

## 2. taxes and subsidies
The imposition of a tax on CDs will move the supply curve for CDs to the left as at any given level of output price will now be higher. A reduction in tax on CDs will shift the curve to the right.

Governments sometimes give subsidies to producers if they wish to reduce the price of a product. A subsidy on CDs would thus shift the supply curve to the right. The removal or reduction of a subsidy would shift the curve to the left.

## 3. technology
Improvements in technology normally mean that it becomes easier, or cheaper to produce goods and thus the supply curve for CDs will shift to the right.

## 4. the aims of firms
It is generally assumed that firms aim to maximise profit. However, as was shown in the previous chapter, this is not always true of all producers. It is difficult to be precise about the effect of changes in the aims of firms on the supply curve, although a firm that wanted more people to enjoy listening to music in their own homes and which was less concerned about high profits, might well supply more CDs than a firm which simply aimed to maximise profit.

Similarly a firm trying to break into a new market might sacrifice profits in the short term to ensure that more of its products were available in the shops. In both these examples the supply curve is likely to shift to the right.

## 5. a change in the price of other goods
A change in the price of, for example, miniature TVs will ultimately affect the supply of CDs. This is because an increase in miniature TV prices suggests that profits in the industry have increased and suppliers of CDs will be tempted to stop producing CDs and move into miniature TV production. The supply curve for CDs will, therefore, shift to the left. A fall in miniature TV prices and thus a fall in profit levels, will ultimately result in producers stopping or reducing the output of miniature TVs and moving into CD production where profits are higher. The supply curve for CDs will, therefore, shift to the right.

In terms of the supply of goods and services all products can be thought of as substitutes. Over time producers will move out of industries where profits are low and into industries where profits are high. Without this flexibility a country would not be able to produce the goods and services that consumers want and its economy would stagnate. Such changes will not happen overnight. The speed with which a country can move resources from one area of production to another is dependent on the mobility of factors of production. As will be seen in Chapter 12 one of the aims of government economic policy is to implement policies that improve factor mobility.

### student activity 9.3 – the determinants of supply

Show, on separate diagrams, the effects of the following changes on the supply curve for CDs:

(a)  an increase in the rate of VAT

(b)  a fall in the price of DAT (digital audio tape) equipment

(c)  a rise in labour costs for CD producers

(d)  the discovery of a new and cheaper method of producing CDs

# elasticity of supply

As well as knowing that an increase in price, all other things being equal, will lead to an increase in quantity supplied it is also important to know how large the change in quantity supplied will be. The actual size of the change in quantity supplied will depend upon the *elasticity of supply (ES)*.

The graphs below show two possible supply curves for compact discs. Both curves are drawn on the same scale and show how equal increases in price affect quantity supplied.

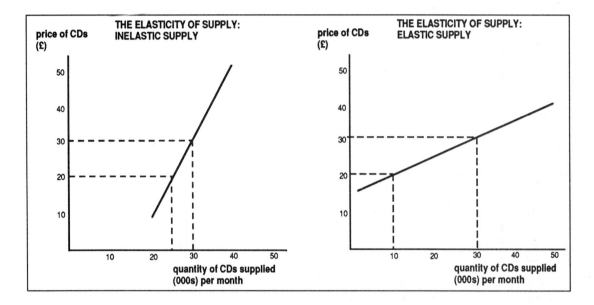

In the graph on the left a rise in price from £20 to £30 leads to a 5,000 increase in quantity supplied, from 25,000 to 30,000, whereas the same rise in price leads to a 20,000 change in quantity supplied, from 10,000 to 30,000, in the graph on the right. Clearly quantity supplied is much more responsive to changes in price in the right-hand graph than is the case with the left-hand graph. In the first example supply is said to be *inelastic* and in the second supply is said to be *elastic*.

As before, the critical point to note when considering elasticity of supply (ES) is the proportional or percentage changes in price and quantity supplied. In the examples above the percentage change in price is 50% (10/20 x 100), however this leads to a 20% (5,000/25,000 x 100) and a 200% (20,000/10,000 x 100) increase in quantity supplied in the first and second graph respectively.

As with the price elasticity of demand (PED – see page 91), to achieve a numerical value of ES the percentage change in quantity supplied is divided by the percentage change in price.

$$ES \quad = \quad \frac{\text{percentage change in quantity supplied}}{\text{percentage change in price}}$$

Hence in the first graph ES is 20%/50% = 0.4 while in the second graph ES is 200%/50% = 4. Wherever the value obtained is greater than one (ES > 1), supply is said to be elastic; where it is smaller then one (ES < 1) supply is said to be inelastic.

# the determination of prices

To understand how the prices of goods are determined the demand and supply curves need to be put together. In the table below figures are given for the demand and supply curves for CDs. This information has then been plotted on the graph below.

### the supply and demand schedule for CDs

| price £ | quantity supplied (000s) per month | quantity demanded (000s) per month |
|---|---|---|
| 30 | 40 | 10 |
| 25 | 35 | 20 |
| 20 | 30 | 30 |
| 15 | 25 | 40 |
| 10 | 20 | 50 |
| 5 | 15 | 60 |

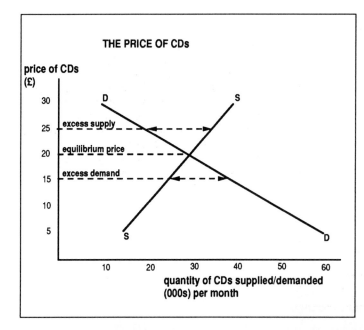

THE PRICE OF CDs

quantity of CDs supplied/demanded (000s) per month

Notice that when the price is £25 the quantity supplied (35,000) is greater than the quantity demanded (20,000). In other words there is an excess supply of 15,000. At this price suppliers of CDs will be unable to sell all their output – there is a surplus on the market. Eventually market forces will result in a fall in price until the market clears.

When the price is £15, quantity supplied (25,000) is smaller than quantity demanded (40,000). There is an excess demand of 15,000. At this price suppliers are not producing enough CDs to satisfy demand – there is a shortage on the market. Eventually market forces will result in a rise in the price until the market clears.

## equilibrium price

The equilibrium price in this example is £20. This is the point where quantity demanded is equal to quantity supplied and at this price the market will clear. There will be neither a surplus nor a shortage. It is also the price where *there is no tendency for change*. If an attempt is made to raise the price above this level, market forces will operate to return to the equilibrium price. If an attempt is made to lower price below this level, market forces will operate to restore the equilibrium price.

## changes in demand and supply

The concept of equilibrium price implies stability - a price where there is no tendency for change. It is, however, possible for the equilibrium price to change if there is a change in the determinants of demand or supply. The aim of this final section is to show how changes in demand and supply affect equilibrium price. The four diagrams below refer to changes in the supply and demand for CDs.

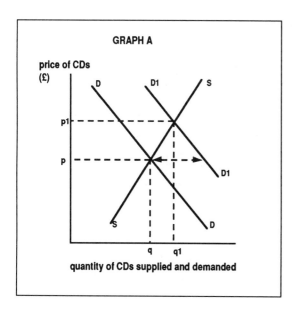

## diagram A – an increase in demand

The original demand curve is (DD) and the original supply curve (SS). Quantity supplied and demanded is q. Initially equilibrium price is at p but an increase in the demand for CDs ($D_1D_1$) leads to a temporary shortage (excess demand) in the market, as indicated by the arrows. This shortage will cause price to rise to p1. At this new higher price quantity demanded is again equal to quantity supplied and equilibrium is restored.

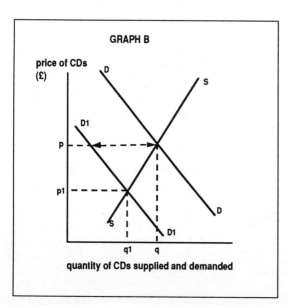

## diagram B – a fall in demand

The original demand curve is (DD) and the original supply curve (SS). Quantity supplied and demanded is q. Initially equilibrium price is at p but a decrease in the demand for CDs ($D_1D_1$) leads to a temporary glut (excess supply) in the market, as indicated by the arrows. This glut will cause price to fall to p1. At this new lower price quantity demanded is again equal to quantity supplied and equilibrium is restored.

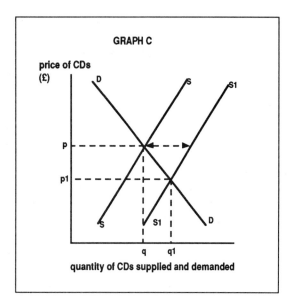

### diagram C – an increase in supply

The original demand curve is (DD) and the original supply curve (SS). Quantity supplied and demanded is q. Initially equilibrium price is at p but an increase in the supply of CDs ($S_1S_1$) leads to a temporary glut (excess supply) in the market, as indicated by the arrows. This glut will cause price to fall to p1. At this new lower price quantity demanded is again equal to quantity supplied and equilibrium is restored.

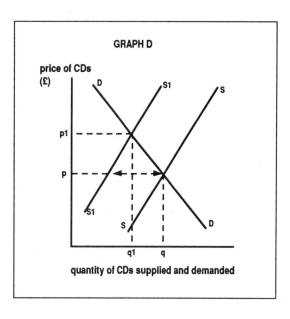

### diagram D – a fall in supply

The original demand curve is (DD) and the original supply curve (SS). Quantity supplied and demanded is q. Initially equilibrium price is at p but a decrease in the supply of CDs ($S_1S_1$) leads to a temporary shortage (excess demand) in the market, as indicated by the arrows. This shortage will cause price to rise to p1. At this new higher price quantity demanded is again equal to quantity supplied and equilibrium is restored.

### conclusion

Four predictions about the effects of changes in supply and demand on price can be derived from these diagrams. All other things being equal:

- an increase in demand leads to an increase in price
- a fall in demand leads to a fall in price
- an increase in supply leads to a fall in price
- a fall in supply leads to an increase in price

## student activity 9.5 – equilibrium price

On four separate diagrams show the effects of the following changes on the equilibrium price of CDs:

(a)     a fall in personal income taxes

(b)     a subsidy given to CD manufacturers

(c)     a successful advertising campaign by CD manufacturers

(d)     a rise in the factory rents of CD manufacturers

## student activity 9.6 – investigating house prices

Using advertisements in local newspapers and property details provided by estate agents, collect information about house prices in your area. Categorise the information you obtain to try and discover what are the typical prices of detached, semi-detached or any other types of houses you choose.

Investigate the changes in house prices in your area over the past four years. Explain this trend in terms of supply and demand.

# chapter summary

❑ For the vast majority of goods and services, consumers will buy more of them as their price falls. This is known as a change in quantity demanded and produces a movement along the demand curve.

❑ A change in any of the determinants of demand leads to a shift of the whole demand curve, either to the left, or to the right. This is known as a change in demand.

❑ As the price of a good rises producers will increase their output of the good. This is known as an increase in quantity supplied and causes a movement along the supply curve.

❑ A change in any of the determinants of supply leads to a shift in the whole supply curve, either to the right, or to the left. This is known as a change in supply.

❑ The relationship between a change in the price of a good and the resulting change in quantity demanded/supplied is known as price elasticity of demand/supply.

❑ The equilibrium price of a good or service is determined by the interaction of the supply and demand curves.

❑ Changes in demand and supply will, all other things being equal, result in changes in the equilibrium price.

# 10 The market economy

## introduction

In this chapter we shall consider:

- how the forces of supply and demand can help to answer the fundamental basic economic questions that all societies face
- the advantages of economic systems that use market forces to decide how resources should be distributed
- how government intervention can help overcome the disadvantages of the market economy

## the fundamental economic questions

All societies need to answer three fundamental economic questions:

### what to produce and in what quantities?

In the UK millions of different goods and services are produced by thousands of different firms each year. These range from house bricks to aeroplanes, from window cleaning to financial advice. How does each firm decide what to produce and how do they know how much to produce in each colour and size?

### how should the goods and services be produced?

In deciding how a good or service should be produced a firm faces a wide variety of choices. It could rely heavily on vast numbers of workers (labour) and very little machinery (capital), alternatively it could use very few workers but make significant use of new technology in the form of highly complex computer controlled machinery. On what basis does a firm decide which method to employ?

### how should the goods and services produced be distributed?

In theory goods could be distributed equally to all families and individuals so that no one gained more that anyone else. In some societies the tribal elders may be entitled to the biggest share, or those who are related to the ruling elite. Which is the best system to choose?

# the price mechanism

Many societies use the *price mechanism* as the basis for answering these three economic questions. Such societies are sometimes called *free market, free enterprise*, or *capitalist* economies. In these societies the forces of supply and demand play an important role in deciding how limited resources should best be employed. More specifically the three fundamental questions are answered as follows:

### what to produce and in what quantities?

When someone buys a good or service they are creating a demand for it. If the demand for a particular product is high this is a sign that consumers want more of the good or service. As was shown in the previous chapter, an increase in demand, all other things being equal, will lead to an increase in price and this in turn will lead to an increase in firms' profits. The rise in profits is a signal for firms already in existence to produce more and for new firms to join the market. If too much of a product is being produced then the market price will fall. This leads to a fall in profits and in some cases losses will be made. Firms already in the industry will produce less and some firms will leave the industry altogether attracted by higher profits in other areas. It is through the price mechanism that consumers are able to send messages to firms about the goods and services they want them to produce.

### how should the goods and services that are wanted be produced?

The simple answer is that firms will tend to choose the cheapest method. A firm that fails to do this will discover that its costs of production are high and its profits low, or that it is even making a loss. Unless a firm in this position takes some positive action to reduce its costs it will eventually go out of business.

### how should the goods and services produced be distributed?

The price of a good in the market should be seen as a measure of its worth. If a consumer is willing to pay the market price then it is clear that s/he is placing an equivalent value on the good. If the value the consumer places on the good is less than the market price then s/he will not buy it. It would be irrational for a consumer to spend £12.99 on a CD if he or she did not derive at least £12.99's worth of enjoyment from it.

# the advantages of a market economy

### consumer sovereignty

The price mechanism helps to ensure that only the goods and services that are really wanted will be produced. This is the principle of *consumer sovereignty* and is possibly the most important advantage of a free market system – for who is better able to understand the needs of consumers than consumers themselves? If a firm produces goods and services that are not wanted then they will soon go out of business. Consumer sovereignty means that firms will endeavour to look after the needs of their customers. It explains why many firms today spend large amounts of money on *market research*. It also helps to ensure that valuable resources will not be wasted on the production of unwanted or shoddy goods and services.

### efficiency and profit

The need to choose the cheapest method of production means that consumers can obtain goods at the lowest possible prices, and at the same time producers can make sufficient profit to make their efforts worthwhile. The need to keep costs to a minimum encourages firms to eliminate waste and use the resources they are employing efficiently.

As consumers must pay the market price for goods and services, or go without, they too are encouraged to use their limited resources (*incomes*) as efficiently as possible. If goods were distributed equally amongst the population many people would end up with goods that they did not need while others would not be able to get enough of the goods that they really valued.

### environmental benefits

It can also be argued that the price mechanism helps to preserve the planet's scarce resources. Resources that are available in large quantities will tend to be relatively low in price compared to those that are in short supply which will tend to become relatively more expensive. Firms will, therefore, try to make greater use of resources that are plentiful and less use of those which are scarce.

# the disadvantages of a market economy

It would appear from the points made above that the market economy is the perfect system to produce an efficient distribution of resources. While many of the arguments stated here are widely recognised as being important benefits of a market economy some of the points made are only partial truths and as such they mask some serious problems. The disadvantages of the market economy are referred to by economists as *market failures,* and governments may need to intervene in the market to correct these failures. The main examples of market failure are:

### poverty

In a free market economy, goods are distributed to consumers on the basis of their willingness to pay the market price. Economists refer to this as the *exclusion principle*. It means that if consumers are unwilling to pay they will be excluded from consumption of a good. This is a principle that works well for most of the people most of the time, but does assume that all consumers have enough money to buy all the goods they need. In reality, of course, this is not the case. Some people are too ill to work, others are too young, too old, or unable to find a job. In a purely free market economy such people would have to rely on family and friends to support them, beg in the streets, or seek aid from charities. Most people regard such a situation as morally unacceptable. Governments intervene in the market to ensure that everyone has sufficient money to buy at least the basic necessities to lead a reasonably normal life.

Assistance is provided by government in the form of:
- old-age pensions
- unemployment benefit
- family income support
- child benefit
- free school meals and subsidised subscriptions

All these benefits are paid for from general taxation. The precise level of these benefits is highly controversial. Some would argue that if benefits are too high it encourages people to become lazy and not accept their responsibility to look after themselves and their families. Most would, however, accept that some level of support should be given to those who, through no fault of their own, are unable to earn enough money to support themselves and their families.

### the distribution of incomes and wealth

In a free market economy it is important that those people who are willing to work hard and accept the risks involved in setting up businesses, receive sufficient rewards to encourage their continued efforts. This inevitably means that some people will receive bigger incomes and accumulate more wealth than others. A distinction needs to be made between income and wealth.

*income is the benefits received, over a given period of time, from work, property and investments.*

The reward from work (selling one's labour) is wages; the reward from property (land) is rent and the reward from investments (capital) is interest.

*wealth is the stock of money and material possessions owned by an individual, institution or country.*

Wealth is most commonly held in the form of property, but can include shares, savings, or anything that has a monetary value.

Most people would agree that a certain degree of inequality of income and wealth is not only acceptable, but necessary in a dynamic economy. Most people would also accept that there comes a point where the gap between the most and the least affluent members of society is morally unacceptable and may even work against the operation of a smooth running and efficient economy. Very large differences in levels of incomes and wealth cause resentment and may result in some kind of social unrest. For these reasons governments frequently intervene to offset some of the most extreme inequalities that might otherwise occur.

In the table below households have been ranked in ascending order of *income*. The first column (original income) shows the distribution of income before any government intervention. Income is clearly very unevenly distributed with the poorest 20% of households receiving about 2.1% of household income and the top 10% receiving 32%. Column two (gross income) includes the effects of government cash benefits such as state retirement pensions, which makes the distribution of income more equal. The final column includes the effects of taxes and National Insurance.

**percentage shares of household income 1987**

| Group | Original income | Gross income | Disposable income |
|---|---|---|---|
| Bottom 10% | 0.8 | 3.3 | 3.5 |
| Bottom 20% | 2.1 | 7.5 | 8.2 |
| 2nd 20% | 7 | 11 | 12 |
| 3rd 20% | 16 | 16 | 16 |
| 4th 20% | 25 | 23 | 23 |
| Top 20% | 50 | 43 | 41 |
| Top 10% | 32 | 27 | 26 |

SOURCE: *Economic Review* 1991, reproduced by kind permission of Phillip Allan Publishing

The table below shows the distribution of *wealth* and also indicates a very uneven pattern. In 1987 the least wealthy 50% owned a mere 7% of the nation's wealth compared to 26% owned by the most wealthy 1%.

**distribution of marketable wealth 1987**

| % owned by | | 1976 | 1980 | 1987 |
|---|---|---|---|---|
| Least wealthy | 50% | 8 | 9 | 7 |
| Most wealthy | 50%` | 92 | 91 | 93 |
| | 25% | 71 | 73 | 75 |
| | 10% | 50 | 50 | 52 |
| | 5% | 38 | 36 | 38 |
| | 2% | 27 | 25 | 25 |
| | 1% | 21 | 19 | 18 |

SOURCE: *Economic Review* 1991, reproduced by kind permission of Phillip Allan Publishing

## the taxation of income and wealth

*Government intervention* in this area is normally through the *taxation* system.   Taxes can be classified as either *direct* or *indirect*.   Direct taxes are taxes on income;   the best of examples of direct taxes are:

• *income tax*, which is levied on the income of individuals

• *corporation tax*, charged on company profits

Indirect taxes are levied on expenditure;   they include Value Added Tax (VAT) and excise duties.

In the UK the income tax system is, for the most part, *progressive*. This means that those with the highest incomes pay a larger proportion of their income in taxes than those on the lowest incomes, who may not pay any tax at all.   Taxes on expenditure tend to be *regressive*, which means that those on the highest incomes tend to pay a smaller proportion of their income on taxes compared to those on lower incomes.   For example, if a person earning £200 a week buys a CD player that costs £100, they will have to pay VAT of 17.5%, ie £17.50 on their purchase.   This represents 8.75% of their income.   If a person earning £500 a week buys the same CD player, the VAT of £17.50 represents only 3.5% of their income.   VAT therefore tends to *increase* existing inequalities of income, rather than reduce them.

The greatest source of inequality in wealth comes from the inheritance system which allows individuals, on their death, to transfer the ownership of their wealth to their family and friends. When someone dies their estate (their wealth) may be liable for Inheritance Tax. The aim of inheritance taxes is to lessen this effect by taxing inherited wealth.   Land and property may need to be sold to pay for the taxes levied.   Only estates valued at more than £150,000 (for the tax year 1993/94) are liable and even then taxes can be avoided if wealth is given away seven years before death. Taxes raised in this way are often used to finance benefits paid to the least well off and to provide free services such as health and education.

---

**student activity 10.1 – investigating the UK taxation system**

Investigate and explain the main forms of taxation in the UK.  Classify them according to whether they are direct (taxes on income), or indirect (taxes on expenditure) and

(a)   explain how each type of tax operates

(b)   state whether each type of tax is direct or indirect

(c)   set out the current rates of taxation

(d)   state to what extent each tax helps to improve the distribution of incomes and wealth

---

## pollution – negative externalities

Another disdavantage of the market economy relates to the environment.   In order to make large profits, firms will attempt to minimize their costs of production. At first sight this seems to be a perfectly reasonable aim for businesses to pursue, but what if this involves inflicting costs (*negative externalities*) on others? For example, a chemical firm may find that it is cheaper for it to dump the waste products from its activities into a nearby river. Unfortunately the dumping of the waste leads to the death of thousands of fish. The water company further down stream can no longer extract water which in the past was used to process into drinking water. People who enjoy the river in their leisure time find that they are now unable to do so due to the appalling smell that comes from the polluted water. Although the external costs to society at large are considerable, the firm ignores them rather than spending money on installing a special filter that renders the waste harmless.

In this situation it is common for the authorities (on behalf of the government) to intervene in the market in order to reduce the level of pollution. Intervention could take several forms:

• *a tax could be imposed on the chemicals produced by the company*

   This would help to reduce the consumption of the chemicals and eventually reduce the pollution. The taxes raised could also be used to help pay for the costs of cleaning up the river and restocking it with fish.

• *limits and fines*

   A limit could be imposed on the amount of pollution that the company was allowed to dump into the river and a system of heavy fines imposed on firms which exceed this limit.

> ### student activity 10.2 – pollution solutions
> Individuals may also be responsible for pollution when, for example, someone smokes a cigarette or, when someone drives their car into the city centre or, on a congested road. Choose these, or TWO similar examples and explain how they give rise to negative externalities and what action governments might take to reduce or eliminate the problems created.

## under-consumption

Another disadvantage of the market economy is *under-consumption*. It may be that some goods, like those which are responsible for pollution, are being over-consumed, while others are being under-consumed. Consumers may not understand all the benefits, including those which might accrue to society at large *(positive externalities)*, that could arise from consuming a good, and so they do not buy enough of it.

Those who make occasional use of their local sports-centre to play squash may do so purely for pleasure. They may not be fully aware that their physical exertions help to improve their overall level of fitness and their chances of enjoying better health later in life. Even if they do understand the wide range of personal benefits, they are unlikely to appreciate some of the *positive externalities* that may be produced. By improving their own health and becoming less prone to serious illness they are indirectly reducing everyone's chances of becoming unwell in the future. One consequence would be that the NHS might spend less on health care, so that eventually taxes could be reduced.

Goods which have such characteristics are known as *merit goods* and it might be argued that they should be subsidised to help reduce their price and encourage consumers to buy more of them.

> ### student activity 10.3 – merit goods
> Think of TWO other examples of merit goods (apart from the leisure centre mentioned above). Explain the individual benefits and positive externalities that might be achieved if more of the goods were consumed, and how the government might increase the public's consumption of them.

## public goods

Some goods have characteristics that make them unlikely to be adequately provided in a free market economy. One such example is street lighting. A person may live in an area which is unlit at night and is very concerned about the safety of his or her family who often return home from work after dark. Despite these concerns, he or she is unlikely to visit the local branch of the DIY superstore, purchase a street light, install it and plug it in to their private electricity supply. Individual consumers will not behave in this way, as they will be only too well aware that they will be paying for a good that everyone else who lives in the same area will benefit from, and without paying anything towards its cost. This is known as the *free-rider* problem. Governments intervene in the market by providing goods like street lighting and then make everyone pay the cost through income taxes and VAT. Other examples of public goods include defence, roads and law and order.

## efficiency – regional inequalities

A further assumption of a market economy is that the price mechanism will ensure that resources will be used in the most efficient way. Resources that are plentiful will be relatively cheap and those that are scarce relatively expensive. Accordingly firms will try to use more of those resources that are plentiful and less of those that are scarce. A good example of this can be seen in the case of regional inequalities.

Some areas of a country might be relatively prosperous and characterised by high levels of business activity, low levels of unemployment, high wages and high land prices. Other areas might be relatively poor with low levels of business activity, high unemployment, low wages and land prices. In the prosperous area resources are being over-utilised, while in the poor area they are being under-utilised. Such a situation does not represent an efficient use of resources. Those who believe that the market economy will solve this problem argue that over time businesses will move from the prosperous area to the poor area. They will be attracted by low land and labour prices which help to reduce their costs. In the same way workers will move from the poor area to the prosperous area tempted by better employment prospects and higher wages. This argument is summarised in the diagram below.

**how the price mechanism resolves regional inequalities**

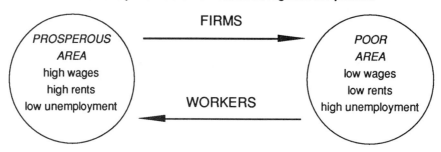

Regional inequalities in the UK have existed for some time, and the price mechanism has had ample opportunity to solve the problem of its own accord. Unfortunately a brief look at the unemployment figures for regions in the UK (see the table below "Unemployment in the Regions") shows that the price mechanism has failed to solve the problem. In reality many new firms have tended to locate in prosperous areas like the South East and moved away from poorer areas like the North. They are attracted, amongst other things, by the excellent communication links that exist in the South East and by the pool of skilled labour that can often be found there. Similarly, workers have often found that it is difficult to move to areas like the South East and that those who do move are the young and most highly skilled. There is a tendency for workers who remain in the poorer areas to be older and less skilled. As a result firms find such areas unattractive because they cannot always find the workers they need. In some senses the price mechanism has actually made the problem worse instead of better.

**unemployment in the regions**

| Region | 1965 | 1970 | 1975 | 1980 | 1985 | 1986 | 1987 | 1988 | 1989 | 1990 | 1991 |
|---|---|---|---|---|---|---|---|---|---|---|---|
| North | 2.4 | 4.5 | 4.2 | 7.7 | 15.6 | 15.4 | 14.3 | 12.1 | 10.1 | 8.7 | 10.2 |
| Yorks & Humberside | 1.0 | 2.8 | 2.8 | 5.1 | 12.0 | 12.5 | 11.5 | 9.5 | 7.5 | 6.7 | 8.5 |
| E Midlands | 0.8 | 2.2 | 2.5 | 4.2 | 9.9 | 10.0 | 9.2 | 7.3 | 5.5 | 5.0 | 7.0 |
| E Anglia | 1.2 | 2.1 | 2.5 | 3.6 | 8.1 | 8.5 | 7.5 | 5.4 | 3.6 | 3.6 | 5.6 |
| South East | 0.8 | 1.6 | 2.0 | 2.9 | 8.1 | 8.3 | 7.4 | 5.5 | 4.0 | 3.9 | 6.7 |
| South West | 1.5 | 2.8 | 3.3 | 4.3 | 9.3 | 9.5 | 8.3 | 6.4 | 4.6 | 4.2 | 6.8 |
| W Midlands | 0.6 | 1.9 | 2.9 | 5.2 | 12.8 | 12.9 | 11.7 | 9.1 | 6.7 | 5.8 | 8.4 |
| North West | 1.5 | 2.7 | 3.9 | 6.2 | 13.8 | 13.8 | 12.7 | 10.6 | 8.6 | 7.6 | 9.2 |
| Wales | 2.5 | 3.8 | 4.0 | 6.5 | 13.7 | 13.6 | 12.2 | 10.0 | 7.5 | 6.5 | 8.5 |
| Scotland | 2.8 | 4.1 | 3.6 | 6.8 | 12.9 | 13.3 | 13.2 | 11.3 | 9.5 | 8.2 | 8.6 |
| N Ireland | 5.9 | 6.6 | 5.4 | 9.1 | 16.0 | 17.1 | 17.1 | 15.7 | 14.7 | 13.5 | 13.7 |
| UK | 1.4 | 2.6 | 3.0 | 4.8 | 10.9 | 11.2 | 10.2 | 8.2 | 6.4 | 5.8 | 7.9 |

SOURCE: *Economic Review* 1992, reproduced by kind permission of Phillip Allan Publishing

### student activity 10.4 – regional inequalities

(a) What possible negative externalities (see page 104) might prosperous and poor areas of the UK experience as a result of the over-utilisation and under-utilisation of resources in these areas?

(b) Explain why unemployed workers do not always move to regions where job prospects are better. Classify your reasons under occupational and geographical headings.

## regional assistance

To try and overcome the problems associated with regional inequalities governments have often in the past intervened in the market by providing incentives for industry to move to areas like the North East and away from areas like the South East.   Similar incentives have been given to unemployed workers to accept jobs in other parts of the country.

The UK also receives regional assistance from the European Community.  EC regional policy came into operation with the establishment of a European Regional Development Fund (ERDF) in 1975. The ERDF accounts for about 8% of the Community's budget.   The UK, along with Italy, has benefited substantially from this fund.

---

**student activity 10.5 – government  regional assistance**

Investigate the forms of incentives offerered by the government to firms and workers, either in your locality or in an urban area of your choice which receives assistance.  How effective do you think these incentives are in reducing regional inequalities, and why?

*Sources of information include offices of the Department of Trade and Industry and local Enterprise Agencies.*

---

## monopolies

Supporters of free market economies have tended to assume that, for any given product, there are a large number of firms producing it and an equally large number of people willing to buy it. This is an important condition as, if it were true, would mean that all markets were highly competitive. In highly competitive markets it would be impossible for one firm to try to sell its product above the going (equilibrium) price as no one would buy it. Similarly if one firm were to produce goods that were of poor quality it would quickly go out of business as consumers would change to buying higher quality goods produced by other firms. In this way consumers can be certain of obtaining good quality products at the lowest possible prices.

In reality there are some markets that do come fairly close to the highly competitive conditions described above. Agriculture is often thought to be one possible example. There are so many growers of wheat that an individual farmer can only sell his output at the going price. If the wheat produced by one farmer is of inferior quality to that produced by the majority then it would be rejected. In the market for company shares (the stock market) there are so many buyers and sellers that it is virtually impossible for someone to be cheated by having to pay anything but the market price.

In the some cases, however, the market is far from competitive. It is possible for a market to be dominated by a few large companies known as *oligopolies* or, even by one company known as a *monopoly*. A monopoly has the potential to charge consumers very high prices and produce sub-standard goods in the knowledge that consumers cannot buy elsewhere as there is no alternative. If a monopolist were to behave in this way the consumer would be exploited and would be powerless to do anything about the situation.

An example of an *oligopolistic market* is in banking which is dominated by Barclays, Lloyds, National Westminster and the Midland. There are other banks in the same market such as the TSB and the Royal Bank of Scotland, but the big four banks dominate.

An example of a virtual *monopoly* is the telecommunications market, which is dominated by British Telecom (BT). Although there is another firm in the market,  BT is by far the most important supplier. It might, therefore, be possible for BT to take advantage of its market dominance and charge unreasonably high prices for telephone calls knowing that consumers are either forced to pay the price or go without.

---

**student activity 10.6 – oligopolies and monopolies**

Make a list of as many markets as you can think of, apart from those mentioned here, which are either *oligopolistic* (dominated by a few firms), or *monopolistic* (dominated by one large firm). Try to give the actual names of the companies involved in each case.

---

It would be a mistake to think that all oligopolies, or all monopolies exploit the consumer, but the important point is that they have the potential to do so. For this reason governments intervene in the market to protect the consumer from firms that might behave in a way considered to be against the public interest.

Government intervention can take many forms including:

- *nationalisation*
  In the past governments have taken over the running of certain industries such as coal, electricity, water, gas and the railways.   No government would exploit its own people by charging unreasonably high prices. Many of these industries have now been privatised – returned to the private sector.

- *the Monopolies and Mergers Commission (MMC)*
  The MMC may advise the government that a firm is charging unjustifiably high prices and recommend a reduction. They may also recommend that a proposed merger between two companies, that might lead to the creation of a monopoly, should not go ahead. Governments do not have to accept their recommendations.

- *the Restrictive Practices Court*
  This is a court that exists to investigate any form of business behaviour that could be against the public interest. If the court finds against the firm it would be forced to change its behaviour.

The UK is also covered by *EC regulations* dealing with anti-competition policies.  All agreements which prevent, restrict or distort competition in the EC, and extend over more than one country are prohibited.  Any abuse of a firm's monopoly power which affects trade between member states is also prohibited.

## the control of the economy

In addition to the activities described above governments also intervene in the economy to try and control:

- the level of prices
- the level of unemployment
- the balance of payments and the exchange rate
- the rate of economic growth

All of these issues will be discussed in more detail in Chapter 12.

## chapter summary

❑ All societies need to answer the three fundamental economic questions of what to produce, how to produce, and for whom.

❑ In a free market economy these questions are answered through the price mechanism where the consumer dictates what goods will be produced and in what quantities.

❑ The price system is an efficient mechanism for distributing resources in many respects, although free markets can have a number of serious failings, including:
  • poverty and the unequal distribution of income and wealth
  • lack of respect for the environment
  • under-consumption – lack of awareness of merit goods
  • the need for the provision of public goods
  • regional inequalities
  • monpolies and oligopolies

❑ Governments intervene in markets to try and correct these failures.

# 11 Planned and mixed economies

## introduction

In this chapter we shall begin by examining the main features of a *command* (centrally planned) economy and in particular consider:

- how the three fundamental economic questions discussed in the last chapter are resolved
- the advantages and disadvantages of a command economy

We shall go on to consider the nature of a *mixed* economy and explain:

- how the policy of nationalisation led to a significant increase in the share of national income spent by the state
- why, in more recent years, there has been an attempt to move the UK further towards a market economy
- how the UK's membership of the EC has affected the proportion of income controlled by the state

## the planned economy

The previous chapter (page 100) examined the way in which the three fundamental economic questions are answered in a market economy where there was no government intervention. The three questions are:

- what goods and services should be produced?
- how they are to be produced?
- for whom they are to be produced?

The *planned economy* or *command economy* lies at the opposite end of the spectrum and represents a situation where the majority of decisions regarding the allocation of resources are taken by the government of a country. The main characteristics of a planned economy are that:

- The main economic groups – consumers, workers, producers and government – are all willing to sacrifice their own selfish interests to work together for the good of the country as a whole.
- There is no private property. All the factors of production are owned by the state. The exception to this is labour – although workers may be asked to move to different jobs or, different parts of the country if this is regarded as being in the national interest.
- Resources are allocated through a planning process. The state decides what goods should be produced, and is responsible for ensuring that producers receive all the resources they need to carry out the plan.

## the advantages of a planned economy

It is argued that the state is in the best position to understand the needs of the nation as a whole and to allocate resources accordingly. One of the problems of allowing individual consumers to decide what goods and services to be produced is that this can result in the production of trivial or even harmful goods. Computer games machines, expensive perfumes and designer clothes are possible examples of goods that might be considered as unnecessary and wasteful of resources. Supporters of planned economies would argue that it is morally unjustifiable to permit the production of such goods when some of a nation's citizens are without adequate food and shelter. Similarly it might be argued that prostitution, gambling, alcohol and drugs are examples of goods commonly found in market economies that cause considerable physical and mental distress. In a planned economy the state might not allow such goods to be produced and thus be able to allocate more resource to health and education.

In a planned economy the state can take account of individuals needs as well as their ability to pay. In the case of housing the largest apartments might be allocated to the biggest families while those who live on their own might be given much smaller accommodation. In a market economy many large families have limited incomes and can only afford accommodation that is totally unsuitable in relation to their requirement.

The state may be in a good position to plan a long way ahead and allocate resources accordingly. In a market economy resources are allocated to the areas where the rewards (profits) are greatest and investors may tend to ignore long term needs in favour of quick returns. A country may need to put resources into the research of new sources of energy, but because the benefits may not be felt for thirty years or more, such projects may not be allocated sufficient resources.

## the planning process

In a planned economy the state has to take on the enormous burden of organising the entire economy. It is responsible for making literally millions of decisions about which goods and services need to be produced, ranging from nuts and bolts in their various sizes to the number of commercial airliners. Having decided upon *what* should be produced the state must then work out *how* they should be produced and ensure that all the resources needed to make them are available in the right place at the right time. Finally the state must determine how the economy's output should be shared out amongst its citizens.

Planners need to know, for example, the precise quantities of land, labour and capital required to mine the coal and iron ore needed to produce one tonne of steel. They can then work out how many resources are need to achieve the total planned output of steel. A similar exercise has to be carried out for all the planned activities of an economy in order to deduce the economy's maximum output and enable planners to decide what should be produced and which goods and services need to be sacrificed.

For the planning process to work well a number of assumptions must be made:
- planners must be able to gather accurate statistics about the economy
- they must be aware of the most efficient methods of production
- there must be no unexpected shocks such as poor weather which could disrupt production and transportation

In reality the complexity of the planning process is such that many of the smaller decisions are left to factory managers and individuals although they must operate within the limits set by the central planning authorities. In all planned economies workers are given wages and they have the freedom to spend their incomes as they see fit although in many areas such as health, education and housing, this freedom will be subject to some restrictions.

## the development of the Soviet System

Following the overthrow of the Russian monarchy in 1917 several key sectors of the economy including heavy industry, transportation, foreign trade and banking were controlled by the state. Gradually state control increased to include all industries that were regarded as being critical to the future growth of the economy. The idea of a *five year plan* was introduced which mapped out the course the economy should take over a five year period. Farms were organised into *collectives* where land and livestock were commonly owned – a system that has survived until relatively recently.

In the 1920s and 1930s the Russian economy grew impressively. A significant proportion of resources, however, were directed towards the production of investment goods. Unfortunately the large increase in the production of investment goods, combined with the marked increase in defence expenditure, meant that the average Soviet citizen did not benefit from the improved economic performance of the nation as a whole.

## the Soviet economy today

Until recently the central planning organisation of the Soviet economy was controlled by the Presidium which delegated authority to the Council of Ministers. The Council set broad economic goals regarding the proportion of resources to be allocated to consumer, investment and military goods. Once these goals were established the State Planning Commission (Gosplan) decided how the goals were to be achieved and set targets for each particular industry. It was then the responsibility of the regional planning councils in each of the republics to assign production targets and allocate resources to specific industries. Finally it was the responsibility of plant managers to see that the production targets were met.

In recent years there have been a number of significant changes including the independence of several of the republics that made up the former Soviet Union and the creation of the Russian Federation (CIS). There has also been an attempt to move the economy towards a market system, although at the time of writing, it is difficult to assess how far they have moved down this road or, how successful this policy has been.

## the problems of a command economy

It is easy to dismiss the planned economy system as a failure on the basis of the problems encountered by the Soviet Union and other Eastern European countries under communist control. While it is true that many of these countries failed to match the performance of other more liberal Western European countries, the problems faced by the USSR, Poland, East Germany and Rumania were political as well as economic and care must be taken not to confuse the two. There are a number of examples of command or partial command systems which have been much more successful. In China the problem of starvation which existed after the Second World War, was virtually eliminated when the communists under Mao Tse-Tung took control of the economy. China's real GNP per capita (the average output per worker after allowing for inflation) grew at about 5% per annum during the period 1949-79. Similarly in France, where state owned industries accounted for 23% of total output in 1984, real GDP per capita in the sixties and seventies grew at about 4% per annum. Despite these successes a number of valid criticisms can be made of command economies in general:

- *understanding consumers' needs*
  It is difficult for any central body to understand the needs of millions of individuals and although they act in what is considered to be the best interests of consumers it is not certain that the two views will coincide. This explains why scarce resources have sometimes been wasted through the production of unwanted goods.

- *shortages and black markets*
  In an attempt to give consumers some freedom in the way in which they spend their incomes markets exist for some goods and services such as food and clothing. As many goods are in short supply this often results in prices that are out of reach of all but the highest paid. To overcome the problem of high prices the central authorities tend to set maximum prices for many goods but this causes excess demand. This explains why many Russians are forced to endure long hours of queueing to obtain even the most basic items. The existence of maximum prices also explains the growth in illegal selling activities or *black markets*. Sellers can often obtain prices for goods such as petrol that are very much higher than official market prices and there is a considerable incentive for individuals to sell goods above official prices.

---

**student activity 11.1 – shortages and black markets**

Draw a hypothetical supply and demand curve for *petrol* and label clearly a maximum price for petrol that is below the equilibrium price. With the help of your diagram explain how the imposition of a maximum price gives rise to:

(a) a situation of excess demand

(b) the possibility of selling petrol illegally at prices that are well above the official price.

---

- *setting the levels of reward*
  Although both planned and market economies sometimes fail to set apprpropriate levels of reward (pay) it is probably true that there are fewer problems in the market system. Many politicians and other commentators have, for example, been critical of the large increases in salaries paid to the senior managers of UK utilities such as gas, water and electricity, upon the industries return to the private sector. In a command system it is the state which is responsible for setting the level of rewards, but there is no guarantee that they will be in a better position to make appropriate judgements. The common ownership of land introduced as part of the collectivisation of farming reduced the incentives of peasants to work, and as a result Soviet agricultural output actually fell.

- *production targets*
  The need for factory managers to meet production targets imposed by the state, rather than the more direct wishes of consumers can cause real difficulties. Quotas tend to be set in terms of the number of units produced, or by weight or volume. Factory managers have a great incentive to meet such targets but often at the expense of quality.

- *bureaucracy*
  The task faced by the central planners in a command economy is enormous and requires the development of a large and well organised administrative system or *bureaucracy*. Obviously all those who work in such an organisation need to be paid and thus a significant proportion of a nation's resources are allocated to a body that produces nothing. In a free market system the need for a central organisation body is eliminated avoiding what might be viewed as a considerable waste of resources.

- *the environment*
  Due to the tendency of market economies to consider only private costs and ignore externalities, problems such as pollution tend to arise. In a planned economy it should be easier for the central planning authorities to take environmental issues into account. In reality planners have been more interested in increasing output and the environmental record of planned economies is arguably much *worse* than that of market economies.

## student activity 11.2 – the spectrum of economic systems

The diagram below represents the *spectrum of economic systems*. On the extreme right-hand side there are the pure market or capitalist systems, and on the extreme left-hand side the pure command systems.

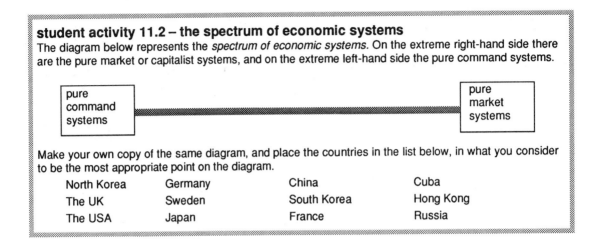

Make your own copy of the same diagram, and place the countries in the list below, in what you consider to be the most appropriate point on the diagram.

| | | | |
|---|---|---|---|
| North Korea | Germany | China | Cuba |
| The UK | Sweden | South Korea | Hong Kong |
| The USA | Japan | France | Russia |

# the mixed economy

In reality it is very difficult to find examples of economies that operate *purely* command, or *purely* market economic systems. The reason for this is that most countries employ a mixture of the command and free market systems, hence the term *mixed economy*. In the early 1990s a number of former planned economies have experienced both political and economic change and moved rather closer towards a market system, although one or two exceptions remain, such as Cuba and China.

One of the best examples of a mixed economy is the UK. This, however, has not always been the case. At the time of the Industrial Revolution (around 1750) there was very little government intervention in the economy, but over the years there has been widespread recognition of some of the failures of the market system and the government has gradually played a greater role in economic decision making. This culminated in the mid 1970s (see table below) to a point where the government was responsible for a little under 50% of UK Gross National Product (GNP). Since the election of a Conservative government in 1979 under the leadership of Margaret Thatcher, the pendulum has moved in the opposite direction and an attempt has been made to reduce the proportion of national income spent by the state. By 1990 this spending had declined to 38.9% of GNP.

### Central Government Expenditure as a Percentage of GDP, 1946-90

| year | Total Government Expenditure (%) |
|---|---|
| 1946 | 45.6 |
| 1950 | 34.6 |
| 1955 | 33.4 |
| 1960 | 34.7 |
| 1965 | 37.1 |
| 1970 | 40.5 |
| 1975 | 48.5 |
| 1980 | 45.1 |
| 1985 | 45.9 |
| 1986 | 42.8 |
| 1987 | 40.2 |
| 1988 | 38.1 |
| 1989 | 38.5 |
| 1990 | 38.9 |

# nationalisation

One of the main explanations for the increased share of the country's income spent by the state from 1945 can be found in the policies of the newly elected Labour government after the end of World War II. Under the leadership of Clement Atlee the new government took into full *public ownership* the Bank of England, the coal mines, railways, steel, civil aviation, broadcasting, gas and electricity. The reasons for such a massive programme of *nationalisation* were largely political and consistent with Clause four of the Labour Party's constitution which calls for "the public ownership of the means of production, distribution and exchange". Supporters of nationalisation claimed a number of possible benefits:

* *avoidance of the duplication of resources*
  If a number of competing gas or electricity companies are supplying a given town then this may result in several sets of pipes and cables being laid in every street, whereas only one of each may be needed. The wasteful duplication of resources of this kind is plainly inefficient and likely to result in increased gas and electricity prices to consumers.

* *economies of scale*
  Before nationalization many utilities were run by a number of smaller and separate regional companies. It was believed that by bringing each industry under the control of a unified management system a number of efficiency savings could be made which could reduce costs and prices.

* *control of the economy*
  It was argued that through state control of major industries, governments would have greater influence over the economy. For some years the steel industry in South Wales was intentionally over-manned as part of the government's policy of the maintenance of high employment.

* *control of monopolies*
  Where an industry is dominated by one very large company it has the potential to exploit the consumer by charging unjustifiably high prices for its goods and services (see Chapter xx). State ownership of monopolies thus protects consumers from such exploitation as the state is unlikely to intentionally act against the interests of consumers.

* *rescue of failing industries*
  In the 1970s both Labour and Conservative governments took control of industries that would otherwise have gone out of business because it was believed that their continued existence was in the national interest. One such example was Rolls Royce which was bought by the government in 1972 to save it from collapse. As a result of this action Rolls Royce was brought back into profitability and soon regained its reputation as one of the three world leading manufacturers of aero-engines.

## the problems of nationalised industries

Despite good intentions, governments encountered a number of practical problems in managing the industries under their control:

* *policy conflicts*
  At times managers of nationalised industries found that they were prevented from making decisions considered to be in the best interests of their industry because they conflicted with government national economic policy. For example, an industry might be prevented from raising prices in order to help the government's anti-inflationary policy.

* *profit*
  It was originally intended that through the control of utilities such as gas, water and electricity, such services could be made available to consumers at reasonable prices. In practice this meant that many industries were run either at a loss, or with a level of profit that was too low to finance new investment needed to improve the services. The management of British Rail has frequently complained of being deprived of sufficient funds to improve the quality of service in the South East.

- *the maintenance of loss making services*
  Nationalised industries were sometimes required to operate loss making services because they were in the wider social interest. BT, for example, made a loss from public telephone boxes as they were frequently vandalised. They were, however, unable to withdraw this facility as the government argued that those who were unable to afford a private telephone would be deprived of an important lifeline in times of emergency.

# privatisation

For the reasons given above, and many more besides, nationalised industries gained a reputation (not always justified) for inefficiency, incompetence and poor quality. It came, therefore, as little surprise when the Conservative government (elected in 1979), who were committed to a policy of reducing the role of the state in the economy, embarked on a programme of *privatisation* – the sale of previously nationalised industries to the private sector.

The table below lists:
- on the *left* – the nationalised industries in 1979
- on the *right* – the names of the companies that have been returned to the private sector together with the date the sale began

| nationalised industries (1979) | companies returned to the private sector | date sale begun |
|---|---|---|
| Electricity | British Petroleum | 1979 |
| British Telecom | British Aerospace | 1981 |
| British Gas | Cable and Wireless | 1981 |
| British Coal | British Telecom | 1984 |
| British Steel | British Gas | 1986 |
| British Aerospace | British Airways | 1987 |
| British Rail | Rolls Royce | 1987 |
| Post Office | British Airports Authority | 1987 |
| British Airways | British Petroleum | 1987 |
| British Airports Authority | | |
| Bank of England | | |
| Rover Group | | |
| Rolls Royce | | |
| Cable and Wireless | | |

## contracting-out and de-regulation

In some areas of government activity such as health and education it is not possible for the government to privatise the services provided. However, to try to extend the role of the market the government have introduced a policy of *contracting-out*. In the case of education, secondary schools and some of the larger primary schools have been encouraged to *opt-out* of local authority control. Schools which decide to opt-out receive their budgets directly from the government instead of the local authority. Some schools have decided to opt-out because they can then choose to run their institutions in the way in which they see fit instead of having to follow the policies laid down by their local education authority. There have been examples of opted-out schools re-introducing the selection of pupils by ability. The government would argue that by allowing schools to formulate their own policies they are giving parents *greater choice* when deciding which schools their children should attend. The principle of choice is one of the main features of a market economy and encourages the efficient use of resources.

*De-regulation* does not involve any kind of transfer of ownership or control as is true of privatisation and de-regulation. This policy involves the removal of some of the restrictions applied to businesses concerning the types of goods and services they provide. Until quite recently only solicitors were permitted to perform the service of conveyancing (the legal aspects of buying and selling property) but now other suitably qualified individuals and businesses are able to offer this service. This is another example of the way in which the government is attempting to extend the principle of choice.

---

**student activity 11.3. – the principle of consumer choice**

Discussion points:

(a)   Explain the importance of the principle of consumer choice in a market economy.

(b)   With the aid of an example explain the possible benefits of giving consumers greater choice.

**student activity 11.4 – 'contracting out'**

One of the effects of contracting-out is that many Colleges and schools have had to invite tenders from local businesses who are willing to provide cleaning and school meals services in these institutions.

Explain:

(a)   what is meant be "tendering" and,

(b)   investigate the possible costs and benefits to your school or College of having to invite tenders for some of the services offered.

---

# the size of the public sector

The 1979 Conservative party manifesto stated:

*" The state takes too much of the nation's income; its share must be steadily reduced. When it spends too much, taxes, prices and unemployment rise so that in the long run there is less wealth with which to improve our standard of living and our social services."*

The proportion of the country's income that is spent by the state is a matter of continued public debate and the table below reflects the differing attitudes of the seven major industrial nations. It is interesting to note that only in the UK did the percentage of GNP spent by the state decline between 1974-9 and 1980-9.

**Total Government Expenditure: Seven Industrial Countries (% of GDP, average figures)**

| Country | 1960-7 | 1968-73 | 1974-9 | 1980-9 |
|---|---|---|---|---|
| USA | 28.3 | 31.0 | 32.6 | 36.0 |
| Japan | 19.1 | 20.2 | 28.4 | 33.2 |
| West Germany | 35.7 | 39.8 | 47.5 | 47.6 |
| France | 37.4 | 39.0 | 43.7 | 50.3 |
| UK | 34.7 | 39.9 | 44.4 | 44.9 |
| Italy | 31.9 | 36.0 | 42.9 | 48.7 |
| Canada | 29.4 | 34.7 | 39.2 | 45.0 |

In addition to the policies of privatisation, contracting-out and de-regulation the decline in the role of the state in the UK can also be attributed to the government's acceptance of two further arguments:

- *taxation*
  In general higher levels of government expenditure also result in higher levels of taxation. When income tax rises beyond a certain level there is a danger that individuals may lose the incentive to work. Similarly high levels of taxes on companies (corporation tax) may deter businesses from investing and risk taking. As a result national output could decline leading to unemployment and lower standards of living.

- *crowding out*
  Some economists have argued that increased government spending *crowds out* private sector spending. This occurs because if governments spend more than they receive in the form of taxes they have to borrow the remainder. This in turn causes interest rates to rise and thus it becomes harder for private companies to invest.

## the European Community (EC)

It is important to appreciate that spending by the UK government is not the only form of state intervention in this country. As the UK is a member of the EC, a proportion of the money raised through UK taxation goes to the EC, and is then spent to further the interests of the community as a whole. The largest share of the community's income is accounted for by the *Common Agricultural Policy* (CAP) which, amongst other things, aims to ensure that all EC farmers receive reasonable incomes. This has largely been achieved through offering guaranteed prices for agricultural produce. The existence of minimum prices has encouraged the over-production of numerous products resulting in the notorious butter and wheat mountains and wine lakes. More recently a number of serious cases of fraud have been uncovered where unscrupulous farmers have attempted to claim subsidies to which they were not entitled. The degree of EC intervention is therefore, a further cause of controversy and the UK government has been active in trying to reduce the size of the community's budget.

## chapter summary

❑ In a command economy the three fundamental economic questions are resolved by the state.

❑ The command economy has a number of potential advantages over the market economy, although in practice such economies have not been as successful as many market or mixed economies.

❑ The recognition that both the command and market systems have their strengths and weaknesses has led to the development of the mixed economy, one of the best examples of which is the UK.

❑ In the UK the size of the public sector increased following a programme of nationalisation implemented after the end of World War II.

❑ The policies of privatisation, contracting-out and deregulation pursued in the 1980s and 1990s have led to a reduction in state intervention in the UK, although the proportion of a country's income spent by the state is a matter of continuing debate.

❑ Britain's membership of the EC has resulted in greater state intervention in the economy.

# 12 Government economic policy

## introduction

In this chapter we shall consider the main aims of government economic policy. We shall then go on to examine how governments might use the various means at their disposal to affect changes in each of the main policy targets and will explain why such policies have not been as successful as they might have hoped.

## the main aims of government economic policy

It is widely accepted that the four main aims of government economic policy are:
- low unemployment
- a low and stable rate of price increases
- balance of payments/exchange rate stability
- a high rate of economic growth

As was shown in Chapter 10 governments intervene in the economy for a number of other reasons, but such objectives are considered to be secondary to the four broad targets set out above. We shall deal with these in turn.

## the maintenance of a low rate of unemployment

### the background
The Great Depression of the 1920s and 1930s saw levels of unemployment rising to more than 13% of the labour force. Although some attempt was made by the state to supplement the incomes of the unemployed, the benefits they received were very small and the hardships they suffered were considerable. In the years immediately before the Second World War, and during the war itself, the

need to produce arms and defend the nation was such that unemployment virtually disappeared. After the war there was a strong feeling that the country should never return to the levels of unemployment that existed prior to 1936 and the maintenance of full employment became one of the main aims of the newly elected Labour Government in 1945.

## J M Keynes – fiscal policy and demand management

The possibility of achieving a low and stable rate of unemployment (a high and stable level of employment) was supported by the writings of J M Keynes who argued that governments could affect the rate of unemployment in the economy through *fiscal policy*, ie

*changes in the level of taxation and government expenditure*

It was his view that the main cause of the unprecedented levels of unemployment before the war was a low level of demand in the economy as a whole. This argument is presented in the diagram below which shows the supply and demand curves for goods and services in general.

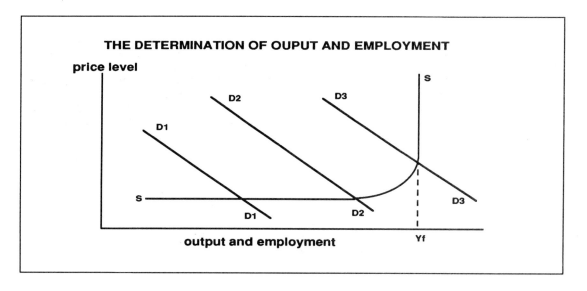

In the diagram SS represents the supply of goods and services. The point Yf is the maximum level of output and employment that can be achieved given existing resources and the current state of technology. Notice that at the full employment point the supply curve becomes vertical showing that output and employment cannot increase beyond this level. At levels of output below Yf the curve is mostly horizontal. Along this section output and employment can be increased. $D_1D_1 - D_3D_3$ represents the demand curves for goods and services. The current (equilibrium) level of output/employment and the level of prices is determined by the point of intersection of the two curves. Keynes argued that at the time of the Great Depression the level of demand in the economy $(D_1D_1)$ was too low, resulting in low levels of output and employment. In his view demand needed to be increased to $D_2D_2$ or $D_3D_3$ to achieve a higher level of output and employment.

The total, or *aggregate* level of demand in the economy is made up of:

* *consumption*: the amount of goods and services demanded by consumers
* *investment*: the amount of machinery demanded by firms
* *government demand*: the amount of goods and services demanded by the state
* *international trade*: the demand for exports minus the demand for imported goods and services

Keynes believed that by altering the level of taxation, governments could indirectly influence the level of consumption. A rise in taxes would leave consumers with less money to spend on consumption and a fall in taxes would lead to an increase in consumption. Similarly, raising and lowering government expenditure would have a direct influence on aggregate demand. Not surprisingly  government policy that is aimed at influencing the level of aggregate demand in the economy is also known as *demand management* policy.

---

### student activity 12.1 – demand management

(a)  Explain what fiscal adjustments a government could need to make to raise aggregate demand from $D_1D_1$ to $D_3D_3$ in the diagram on the previous page.

(b)  Suggest ways in which a government might influence the other components of aggregate demand to help bring about a higher level of output and employment.

---

### demand management policies in practice

Between 1945 and 1975 Labour and Conservative governments relied upon demand management policies in an attempt to achieve full employment although, as can be seen from the table below, the success of these policies tended to diminish over time. One possible explanation of the failure of governments to maintain a low level of unemployment in the 1970s has been offered by a second group of economists who are collectively known as *monetarists*. They argue that government attempts to control the economy through fiscal policy have merely led to higher prices and have had little real impact on unemployment. This argument is explained more fully in the section below on inflation.

**UK unemployment (%) 1950-1992**

| year | % | year | % | year | % |
|------|------|------|------|------|------|
| 1950 | 1.3 | 1975 | 3.0 | 1986 | 11.2 |
| 1955 | 10.9 | 1980 | 4.8 | 1989 | 6.4 |
| 1960 | 1.3 | 1985 | 10.9 | 1990 | 5.8 |
| 1965 | 1.4 | 1986 | 11.2 | 1991 | 7.9 |
| 1970 | 2.6 | 1987 | 10.2 | 1992 | 10.8 |

### other causes of unemployment

Apart from a low level of demand there are a number of other causes of unemployment that need to be considered (see also Chapter 26):

• *frictional unemployment*
  Even in the most successful of economies there will always be a certain number of people who are between jobs. It obviously takes time for someone who has lost a job to investigate all the possibilities open to them. They may even need to move house if there are no suitable opportunities in their local area.

• *structural unemployment*
  Sometimes an industry suffers from a permanent lack of demand and the jobs associated with an industry disappear. The coal industry is a good example of a sector of the economy that has experienced a permanent loss of demand for its products.

- *regional unemployment*
  As will be seen in Chapter 26, some regions of the UK have consistently suffered from levels of unemployment above the national average.

- *seasonal unemployment*
  Industries such as tourism, agriculture and construction are obviously adversely affected by the seasons and employment in these industries varies accordingly.

---

**student activity 12.2 – reducing unemployment**

Suggest what actions, if any, a government might take to reduce the levels of unemployment associated with each of the factors given above.

---

# a low and stable rate of price increases

In the mid 1970s and early 1980s the UK experienced levels of price increases (*inflation*) that had not previously been encountered.  High levels of inflation can have a number of damaging effects on an economy:

- *increase in borrowing*
  Goods will become more expensive in the future – consumers are likely to borrow to buy now.

- *reduced levels of saving*
  Inflation tends to reduce the value of people's savings, and thus people tend to spend more and save less. This may ultimately deprive businesses of the funds they need to invest.

- *a worsening balance of payments*
  If the prices of UK goods are rising faster than those of our international competitors there is a tendency for export volumes to fall and import volumes to rise – a situation that cannot be tolerated indefinitely (see below).  The reason for this is that UK exports will become more expensive abroad and UK imports will be cheaper at home

- *uncertainty*
  Inflation tends to make people lose confidence in their ability to plan for the future. Individuals and businesses tend to respond by reducing their expenditures and postpone investment decisions.

# the causes of inflation

### excess demand

It was shown above that if the level of aggregate demand in the economy was too low it could result in low levels of output and employment. Keynes also pointed out that if aggregate demand in the economy was too high – *excess demand* – then this could produce inflation (ie a sustained increase in the general level of prices)

In the diagram on the next page an increase in demand from $D_1D_1$ to $D_2D_2$ causes firms to try to increase their output. However, as there are no unemployed factors of production (land, labour and capital) firms can only attract these factors from other firms by increasing the level of rewards paid to these factors (rent, wages and interest). As all firms are finding that the demand for their products is increasing they will be keen to retain their workers and thus increase wage rates and other factor payments. The result of this bidding up of factor prices is higher prices of goods in the shops and ultimately inflation $P_1$ to $P_2$.

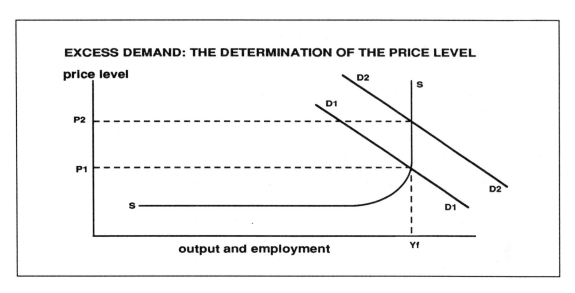

**EXCESS DEMAND: THE DETERMINATION OF THE PRICE LEVEL**

## excess monetary growth

Some economists reject the ideas of Keynes and argue that all inflation is caused by permitting the total supply of money in the economy to grow at too fast a rate. *Monetarists* argue that an increase in the money supply leads to an increase in aggregate demand (similar to that described in the diagram above) and, because the amount of goods and services produced in the economy cannot be increased, the inevitable consequence is inflation. It is important to appreciate that the money supply consists not only of notes and coin (cash) but also money held on deposit in banks and building societies.

The money supply can increase if individuals and businesses borrow more money from the banks, but the largest single borrower in the country can be the government. Governments need to borrow money if the income they receive in the form of taxes is less than their expenditure. This can happen when unemployment is high and the government needs to spend large amounts of money on unemployment benefit and other measures to help those on low incomes. Governments often finance this shortfall, or deficit, by borrowing from the banks, which is equivalent to instructing the Royal Mint to issue more cash. In either event monetarists argue that eventually the level of prices in the economy will rise. Between 1981 and 1987 Margaret Thatcher's government placed considerable faith in the monetarist view of inflation, and attempted to reduce it through monetary policy. Monetary policy involves changes in the supply and price of money though changes in interest rates.

### student activity 12.3 – controlling inflation

Suggest what policies a monetarist government might implement to reduce inflation in terms of

(a) the money supply

(b) interest rates

(c) government spending

Explain the reasons for the changes in each case.

## other causes of inflation

Apart from excess demand, inflation may also occur following increases in production costs. This is often referred to as *cost-push inflation* the two main causes of which are:

## unjustified wage increases

If workers are able to increase their productivity (the output per worker) by, for example, 10% they would be perfectly justified in asking for a 10% increase in their wages. Such a situation is not inflationary as the business will be able to finance their higher wage costs through the additional income generated from increased production. If, however, there had been no improvement in productivity the business would be forced to finance the additional costs by either reducing its profits, or by raising the prices of its goods. As firms are reluctant to accept lower profits the prices of their products are likely to rise. This can lead to an inflationary spiral as rising prices leads workers to demand yet higher wages which in turn leads to higher costs of production.

There is some evidence to suggest that trade union leaders, who negotiate wage claims on behalf of their members, have at times used the threat of industrial action, including strikes, to demand unjustified wage increases of employers. The notorious winter of 1978/79, named by some as the Winter of Discontent, is one such period.

The belief that trade unions were becoming too powerful and demanding unjustified wage increases led the government in the 1980s to pass several new pieces of legislation designed to make it more difficult for unions to behave unreasonably. The effects of this legislation have meant that:

- unions must conduct a secret ballot of their members before taking industrial action
- workers are only allowed to picket companies directly involved in a dispute
- unions cannot compel their members to take industrial action even though the majority have voted in favour of such action

In the past, governments have also employed *incomes policies* to limit the size of any wage increase that can be awarded to workers. This might sound like an effective remedy but in practice incomes policies tend to create more problems than they solve and they have not been part of official government policy for some time.

### raw material/imported inflation

The UK is forced to import a considerable proportion of the raw materials needed for its manufacturing industries, and is thus particularly susceptible to inflation caused by rising import prices. Unfortunately there is little that a government can do to prevent this type of inflation although the effects of rising import prices can be reduced by maintaining a high exchange rate (see below).

# balance of payments/exchange rate stability

The balance of payments is:

*a detailed account of one nation's transactions with the rest of the world*

The main components of the balance of payments are:

- exports and imports of goods      (visible trade)
- exports and imports of services    (invisible trade)
- inflows and outflows of funds      (the capital account)

If the total of exports plus capital inflows exceeds the total of imports plus capital outflows then a country is said to have a balance of payments *surplus*. If the opposite is true then a country is said to have a balance of payments *deficit*. In the same way that an individual cannot indefinitely continue to spend more than he or she earns, then a country cannot indefinitely continue to run a balance of payments deficit. To prevent this happening governments can intervene in a number of ways:

### tariffs

These are *taxes* on imports which have the effect of raising their price and reducing the quantity demanded. Similarly governments can impose *quotas* which restrict the value or quantity of goods that can be imported. The problem with restrictions of this kind is that they reduce the level of international trade which eventually reduces everyone's standard of living.  The *GATT* (General Agreement on Tariffs and Trade) has been set up specifically to reduce the level of trade restrictions between countries. It should be appreciated that as a member of the EC the UK and all other member countries, should have removed all internal trade restrictions from 1st January 1993.

## deflation

Governments can reduce imports by reducing the level of aggregate demand. By *deflating* the economy firms and consumers have less money to spend on imports. This can be achieved by one or a combination of the following measures:

- reducing government expenditure
- raising taxes
- restricting the growth of the money supply
- raising interest rates

### student activity 12.4 – deflation

Explain how each of the measures described above helps to reduce the level of aggregate demand and thus the level of imports.

## the exchange rate

The exchange rate may be defined as

*the price of one currency in terms of another*

In other words it refers to the amount of one currency that needs to be given up to obtain a given quantity of another currency, for example £1 = $2.00. The exchange rate is very important to businesses as changes in the rate have a direct effect on the prices of exports and imports.

A fall, or *depreciation* in the value of the pound sterling, from £1 = $2.00 to £1 = $1.50, causes a decrease in the price of exports and an increase in the price of imports. A rise, or *appreciation* of the exchange rate from £1 = $3.00, causes an increase in the price of exports and a decrease in the price of imports.

The actual exchange rate is determined, like the price of all goods and services, by the interaction of the relevant supply and demand curves. In the diagram below DD represents the demand curve for pounds and SS the supply curve for pounds. The exchange rate "E" (the price of pounds in dollars) is determined by the point of intersection of the two curves.

In general, a balance of payments deficit tends to cause a depreciation of a country's currency, while a balance of payments surplus has the opposite effect.

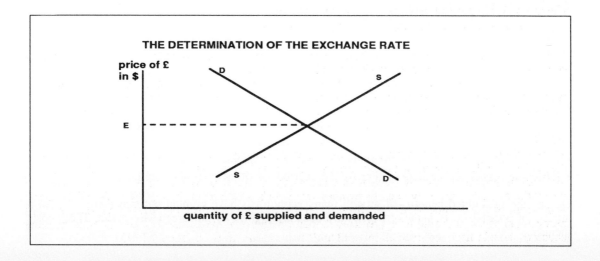

THE DETERMINATION OF THE EXCHANGE RATE

price of £ in $

E

quantity of £ supplied and demanded

Governments often intervene in the *foreign exchange markets* to maintain or change the value of their currency in what they consider to be the national interest. Intervention can take two main forms:

- buying or selling their currency
- changing domestic interest rates

In the case of the UK the government may *buy* pounds (thus shifting the demand curve for pounds to the right) to *raise* or stabilise the exchange rate. They can *lower* or stabilize the exchange rate by *selling* pounds (thus shifting the supply curve for pounds to the right).

If the government raises interest rates in the UK, foreigners will have a greater incentive to deposit their money in the UK, and the exchange rate will rise (the demand curve for pounds will shift to the right). The opposite will happen if UK interest rates are lowered.

---

### student activity 12.5 – exchange rate management
Draw a diagram similar to the one on the previous page and show how the following actions by the UK government would affect the exchange rate:

(a)   buying pounds on the foreign exchange market

(b)   selling pounds on the foreign exchange market

(c)   increasing domestic interest rates.

---

### the European Monetary System – Exchange Rate Mechanism (ERM)
From October 1990 to September 1992 the UK (like most other EC countries) was a member of the ERM, the basic aim of which is to maintain the value of each country's currency within fairly small limits or bands. The benefits of this system are argued to be that:

- it encourages trade between EC member countries
- it helps reduce inflation rates of member countries
- it helps reduce interest rates of member countries

The UK and Italy were forced to withdraw from the system in 1992, as both governments were unable to prevent the value of their currency from falling below its permitted level.

The ultimate aim of the ERM is to achieve European Monetary Union (EMU). This means that member states will operate either absolutely fixed exchange rates, or possibly a single European currency. Such proposals are highly controversial and subject to continuous debate.

# economic growth

Economic growth is:

*an increase in the real value of a nation's output over time*

Note that "real value" means value allowing for the effects of inflation. The benefits of economic growth for a nation are:

- its citizens can enjoy more consumption goods - cars and holidays abroad, for example
- the quality of essential services such as health and education can be improved
- the length of the working week might be reduced giving people more leisure time
- it becomes easier for the state to improve the distribution of incomes and wealth

Despite the undoubted benefits of growth many economists have pointed out that there are also a number of possible costs, some of which have been highlighted by the Green Movement. These costs include:

- increased pollution
- increased traffic congestion
- increased levels of stress, alcoholism and suicide
- the destruction of the countryside

## wealth v welfare
When considering the costs and benefits of economic growth, it is helpful to distinguish between *wealth* and *welfare*. The benefits of growth tend to result in improvements in *wealth* – the number of material possessions, while the costs of growth can lead to a reduction in *welfare* – the general level of well-being or happiness – which is not directly related to levels of material possessions.

## the causes of economic growth
There is considerable dispute amongst economists about which factors are the most important determinants of economic growth. However, most would accept that the list would include some of the following:

- a high level of investment in machinery
- a high level of research and development into new technologies
- an effective education system
- a large proportion of small businesses

A quick look at the data below shows that in recent years the UK has achieved a lower rate of economic growth than many of its international competitors.

**GDP average annual growth 1987 – 1991 (% per year)**

| country | % |
| --- | --- |
| UK | 1.1 |
| France | 2.1 |
| West Germany | 3.1 |
| Italy | 2.1 |
| Japan | 4.5 |
| USA | 1.6 |

SOURCE: Lloyds Bank Plc

## policies for economic growth
The UK government has, in recent years, implemented a number of policies designed to improve the rate of economic growth. As the aim of these measures is to shift the aggregate supply curve to the right economists often refer to them as supply side policies and include the following:

- *reduced taxation*
Under a Conservative government the basic rate of income tax was reduced from 33% in 1979 to 25% in 1987. The present government has also announced its intention to reduce the rate to 20% as soon as economic conditions allow. The reason for this reduction in income tax rates lies in the belief that individuals will have a greater incentive to work harder if they are allowed to retain a larger share of their earnings. There have been similar reductions in taxes on company profits in the hope that this will give them a greater incentive to invest and develop new products.

• *increased competition*

A number of measures have been taken to increase competition which, it is believed, helps keep costs and prices down and leads to better quality goods and services. The regulations governing the operation of buses have been relaxed to allow companies to compete to run services. School cleaning contracts and domestic refuse collection services are now awarded to businesses willing to undertake the work at the lowest price. The creation of a Single European Market following the removal of all trade barriers within the EC, and the acceptance of common standards for professional qualifications are both measures designed to encourage greater competition with the EC.

• *education and training*

The national curriculum, the Technical and Vocational Education Initiative (TVEI) and the Youth Training scheme (YT) are all examples of government initiatives designed to improve the skills and knowledge of the labour force and to make individuals more suited to the needs of industry.

• *the development of small businesses*

It is widely believed that the number of small businesses in a country is a good indicator of the health of an economy. The economic success of Japan has in part been attributed to the large proportion of small businesses there. The greater the number of small businesses the more intense the level of competition and the greater the degree of innovation. The government operates a number of schemes to help small business, directly through the Department of Trade and Industry and indirectly through the TECs (see Chapter 43).

• *anti-trade union legislation*

In the eighties many right-wing politicians expressed the view that employment law in the UK gave too much power to the trade unions. It was believed that trade unions were preventing managers from running their businesses in the most efficient way. The objections of the National Union of Railwaymen (NUR) to flexible rostering and union resistance to Sunday opening are two possible examples. In an attempt to reduce the power of the trade unions the government passed several significant pieces of legislation in the eighties which, amongst other things, effectively forced unions to conduct a secret postal ballot of its members before taking industrial action. It should be stressed that the introduction of new legislation with respect to trade unions was, and still is, a highly controversial matter. It is also ironic to note that some commentators on industrial relations have argued that the need to ballot union members has actually increased the power of the unions.

• *more effective markets*

Supporters of market economies argue that the price mechanism ensures the most efficient allocation of resources and that any restrictions on the operation of markets works against the best interests of the economy as a whole. The present government is considering the abolition of wage councils which set minimum wages in retailing and catering. The government argues that the existence of a minimum wage makes it impossible for some employers to afford the workers they need. This stifles the development of small businesses and leads to unemployment amongst the work force. Opponents of such a move argue that without minimum wages many employers would exploit their workers by paying wages that are already amongst the lowest in the country.

• *increased share ownership*

Through the privatisation programme and Personal Equity Plans (PEPs) the government has encouraged greater share ownership by individuals in the belief that people will become more sensitive to the needs of business.

## policy conflicts

When governments seem to have so many policy options open to them, it is tempting to ask why they have not been more successful in achieving the four broad aims of low inflation, low unemployment, balance of payments equilibrium and high growth? Part of the answer lies in the fact that in trying, for example, to address the problem of unemployment, aggregate demand may need to be raised. This increase might result in increased inflation and a worsening balance of payments. The task of government is to try and strike some kind of balance between the four goals, which is not as easy as it may sound.

# chapter summary

❑ The four main goals of government economic policy are low unemployment; low inflation; balance of payments equilibrium and a high rate of economic growth.

❑ According to Keynes the main cause of unemployment is a low level of aggregate demand. This type of unemployment can be reduced by raising the level of aggregate demand through increasing government expenditure and reducing taxation - fiscal policy. Monetarists however, reject this view and argue that increased government expenditure can only lead to inflation.

❑ High rates of inflation can cause considerable problems in an economy. One of the main causes of inflation is a high level of aggregate demand which can be reduced through a combination of fiscal and monetary policy.

❑ The other possible causes of inflation are unjustified wage increases and increases in the price of raw material imports. Governments have used incomes policies and anti-trade union legislation to control wage inflation. Governments can do little to combat imported inflation although its effects can be reduced by maintaining a high exchange rate.

❑ A country cannot run a balance of payments deficit indefinitely. To remedy a deficit a government can, in theory, protect its domestic industries by imposing tariffs, although as a member of the EC and the GATT this is not a realistic option for the UK. In practice governments have to remedy a deficit through deflation.

❑ A country's balance of payments and exchange rate are closely related. A balance of payments deficit tends to cause a depreciation of the exchange rate while a surplus has the opposite effect. Changes in the exchange rate directly affect the price of a country's exports and imports. Governments try to influence their exchange rate through buying and selling their currency and changing domestic interest rates.

❑ Economic growth can have good and bad effects, although a high rate of economic growth is an aim of most governments. There are a number of possible determinants of growth. In the UK the government has attempted to increase the rate of growth with the implementation of supply-side policies.

❑ In practice it is difficult for governments to pursue the four main economic goals simultaneously.

## EVIDENCE COLLECTION EXERCISE 4

# The products and purpose of business

| Element 1.1 | Explain the purposes and products of business |
|---|---|

Suggested Sources:
- public relations departments of businesses
- promotional material from businesses
- visits to businesses
- talks from representatives from business
- textbooks in libraries and resource centres

## INTRODUCTION

Choose a typical business, eg a public limited company or an organisation of a comparable size, from one of *each* of the following types of business:

- a major car manufacturer
- a major food supermarket chain
- a major public sector service industry, eg British Rail
- a charity, eg Oxfam, Mencap
- an oil company
- a computer manufacturer
- a business in the communications industry, eg British Telecom

## TASK 1

(a) State whether the businesses you have chosen can be classified as primary, secondary or tertiary. Check your findings with your teacher/lecturer before starting (b).

(b) Obtain a copy of the Annual Report and (if available) an environmental policy statement from one business from each of the three sectors of the economy. Identify the aims and objectives of the business (ie why they exist), eg to make profits, to help society, to save the environment.

(c) Explain in detail the nature and range of the product(s) of the three businesses, and, *if possible*, illustrate your findings with a catalogue/brochure and price list/tariff. State to what extent this or any other publicity material reflects the aims of each business.

## TASK 2

**either**

Explain *in detail* the factors that determine the demand for the products of the three chosen businesses. (Refer to Chapter 9 to check your understanding of the meaning and determinants of demand).

**or**

Choose a local business and investigate the factors that determine the demand for its product. It will be helpful to arrange (in consultation with your teacher/lecturer) a visit to the business concerned and to interview one of its senior managers to obtain the information you need.

## EVIDENCE COLLECTION EXERCISE 5

# *Management of economies*

| Element 1.2 | *Explain government influences on business* |

Suggested Sources:
- newspaper and periodical reports on the Exchange Rate Mechanism (ERM) and European Monetary Union (EMU)
- Chapter 12 of this book
- interest rate tables in back copies of the financial press
- *Social Trends* and *Economic Trends* (HMSO)

## TASK 1

Explain the main characteristics of *market*, *planned* and *mixed* economic systems, giving examples of each type of system.

## TASK 2

From October 1990 until September 1992 the UK was a member of the European Monetary System and a participant in the Exchange Rate System (ERM).

(a)  Briefly explain what the ERM is and how it operates.

(b)  Explain the possible benefits of membership of the ERM for UK businesses in general and, in particular, for a business that imports significant quantities of raw materials.

For the period of UK membership UK interest rates were maintained at a relatively high level compared to those of many other EC member states.

(c)  Investigate and draw a line graph of the interest rates of France, Germany and the UK over the period October 1990 to September 1992; use as a source the interest tables in the financial press.

(d)  Explain the likely effect of high interest rates on UK

 i  inflation

 ii  unemployment

 iii  economic growth

Illustrate your answer from sources such as *Social Trends* and *Economic Trends*, if they are available.

## TASK 3

(a)  Investigate a local manufacturing company and explain in detail how high interest rates in the UK might affect the business in terms of:

 i  their willingness to invest

 ii  the demand for their goods and services

The ultimate aim of the ERM is to achieve European Monetary Union (EMU) which would result in either absolutely fixed exchange rates or a common European currency.

(b)  Explain what is meant by:

 i  absolutely fixed exchange rates.

 ii  a common European currency.

(c)  What are the likely benefits to businesses within the EC of EMU?

# The supply of goods and services by business

| | |
|---|---|
| Element 1.3 | Investigate the supply of goods and services by business |

Suggested Sources: • Finance Officer of your school or college (via your tutor)
 • Report and Accounts of public limited companies
 • textbooks in libraries and resource centres

## TASK 1

From 1st April 1993 all Colleges of Further Education and all Sixth Form Colleges became *incorporated* (formed into limited companies). Following incorporation colleges now receive their income (budget) from Central Government rather than from the local authority. A further effect of this change is that colleges are regarded as businesses in their own right and as such they need to balance their income against their expenditure. Schools which have decided to *opt-out* of local authority control are in a similar position. By referring to your own school or college, or any other opted-out school/college with which you are familiar, complete the following activities:

(a) What do you understand to be the product/output of the institution?

(c) What are the possible benefits of incorporation to:

 i the institution itself

 ii the institution's teaching staff

 iii the institution's non-teaching staff (eg cleaners and caretakers)

 iv the local community

 iii the country as a whole

## TASK 2

(a) List the main sources of income for the school/college. (You will need to ask the person in charge of finance to supply you with this information)

(b) List the main areas of expenditure.

(c) Why is it difficult to measure the output of the business?

(d) Explain *in detail* how the business might try to measure its output and hence try to evaluate how successful it is.

## TASK 3

Obtain a copy of the most recent company Report and Accounts for any UK based public limited company (PLC) and answer the following questions (you could use the Report requested in Evidence Collection Exercise 5):

(a) Give the business' main sources of income and expenditure.

(b) Explain what factors the business might use to measure its performance.

(c) Evaluate the success of the business over the last year.

# SECTION

# 3

# marketing

## contents

In this Section we examine the marketing of consumer and industrial goods and services in the private sector and the public sector. In the last Section we looked at demand and supply in an *economic* sense; in this section we look at how customer needs are assessed and turned into products by a business.

The Section is divided into six chapters:

Chapter 13    This chapter looks at the functions of marketing – ie how it works in practice – and the need for a marketing plan (a theme developed in detail in Chapter 48).

Chapter 14    This chapter looks at marketing research – the way commercial and market information is gathered and analysed; it also examines market segments – different consumer groups.

Chapter 15    This chapter looks at consumer trends – how buying patterns are established and are related to external economic factors; it also explains how to predict future levels of sales using statistical techniques.

Chapter 16    The range of products a business produces is examined, and the product life cycle explained. The chapter concludes with a discussion of marketing policy – using market segmentation to advantage.

Chapter 17    This chapter explains the processes which determine how a product is priced.

Chapter 18    The final chapter in the Section explains the way in which a product is promoted, distributed and sold, and how this will differ, depending on the product and the type of market.

## linkage with Section 8 "Business Planning"

The final Section of this book concludes with Chapter 48 "The sales and marketing plan". This is included at the end of the book partly because it falls within GNVQ Unit 8, and also because certain elements of its content refer to material developed earlier in Sections 7 and 8. It should not, however, be viewed in isolation – it should be read as part of your study of "Marketing" (GNVQ Unit 3), to which it forms a natural conclusion.

# 13 The marketing process

## introduction

In Chapter 10 we examined the well-accepted economic theories of the twentieth century. You need now to appreciate how economic theory and marketing reality live together.

In this chapter we examine the following areas:

- objectives of marketing
- the ethics of marketing
- the marketing process
- the marketing plan
- the techniques which enable the marketing plan to be compiled – these include:
  - SWOT (Strengths, Weaknesses, Opportunities, Threats) analysis
  - the marketing mix (Product, Price, Promotion, Place)

## defining marketing objectives

At this stage, it is very useful to try to define the term 'marketing' so that the true scope and objectives of the subject can be appreciated. As you read through the following definitions, what common factors can you find?

> *"Marketing is the management function which organises and directs all those business activities involved in assessing customer needs and converting customer purchasing power into effective demand for a specific product or service, and in moving that product or service to the final consumer or user so as to achieve the profit target or other objective set by the company or other organisation."*

*"Marketing is human activity directed at satisfying needs and wants through exchange processes."* (Kotler).

*"Marketing is a total approach to business that puts the customer at the centre of things."* (Channel 4 and Yorkshire TV 'The Marketing Mix' )

or, on a lighter note:
*"Marketing is selling goods that don't come back, to people who do".*
(Baker)

Have you got the message?  By now you should be appreciating that businesses *do not* make products which they then try to sell to customers, but that they *research* what customers want, and then they try to make and market a range of those wants.  This is the difference between *production* orientation and *marketing* orientation.  The latter approach is *essential*.

## marketing objectives
There are therefore a number of objectives relating to marketing which a business may aim to achieve:
• to maximise sales, increase market share,  and be the market leader
• to saturate the market
• to maximise profit
• to dominate one region or country
• to be the technical leader in the product field
• to be the recognised innovator, always first with the new ideas
• to enhance product image by producing and selling the best *quality*  product(s), an objective aided by Quality Assurance (BS5750) certification, the kitemark of quality – see page 29
• to become the leader in 'social marketing', ie putting ethics and environmental considerations first
It must be stressed that this is a selection of objectives, many of which will be adopted at the same time.   Some objectives, as we will see later in the chapter, run counter to each other.  For example, it may not be possible to maximise profit and be a leader in 'social marketing', or saturate the market and produce the best 'quality' product.

## the marketing process

To consolidate your thoughts on what marketing is,  study carefully the many functions of marketing in the diagram shown on the next page.  The marketing process is continuous.  Many or all of these functions are occurring at the same time, especially where a product or service already exists.  Remember that this process applies equally to the marketing of a manufactured *product*, and also to a *service* which is supplied.

Note that the diagram is called 'The Marketing Cycle' because it shows a circular flow of activities in a clockwise direction:
• *Market and Product Research* – looking to see what the needs and wants of the consumer are, and looking to see what advances are possible with new technology;  the research stage leads to . . .
• *Product Launch and Sales* – following a controlled test of the new product in the market , and the decision to go ahead, the price is set,  promotion takes place, and distribution policy decided upon
• *Monitoring the Product and Analysing Sales* – once the product has been launched, its success (or lack of it) must be monitored, and the sales figures analysed – there may come a time when the decision may be taken to discontinue the product
Refer to this diagram from time-to-time when studying these marketing chapters, it summarises the whole of the process which we will be examining.

# THE MARKETING CYCLE – THE FUNCTIONS OF MARKETING

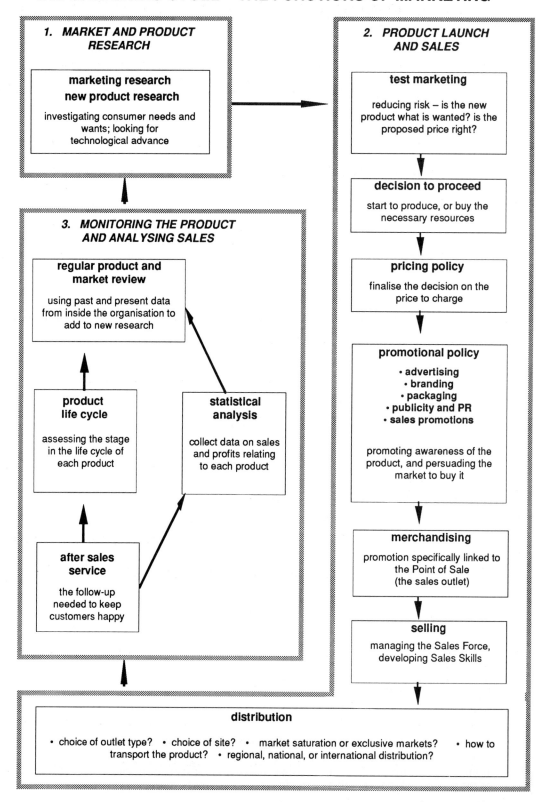

**1. MARKET AND PRODUCT RESEARCH**

**marketing research**
**new product research**

investigating consumer needs and wants; looking for technological advance

**2. PRODUCT LAUNCH AND SALES**

**test marketing**

reducing risk – is the new product what is wanted? is the proposed price right?

**decision to proceed**

start to produce, or buy the necessary resources

**pricing policy**

finalise the decision on the price to charge

**promotional policy**

- advertising
- branding
- packaging
- publicity and PR
- sales promotions

promoting awareness of the product, and persuading the market to buy it

**merchandising**

promotion specifically linked to the Point of Sale (the sales outlet)

**selling**

managing the Sales Force, developing Sales Skills

**3. MONITORING THE PRODUCT AND ANALYSING SALES**

**regular product and market review**

using past and present data from inside the organisation to add to new research

**product life cycle**

assessing the stage in the life cycle of each product

**statistical analysis**

collect data on sales and profits relating to each product

**after sales service**

the follow-up needed to keep customers happy

**distribution**

- choice of outlet type?   • choice of site?   • market saturation or exclusive markets?   • how to transport the product?   • regional, national, or international distribution?

# the ethics of marketing

There are many moral issues involved in the marketing of products and services. Marketing has a major impact on the conflicts between business and social issues, and it is important that people involved in marketing understand the criticisms that may be levelled against them. The problems originate from:

- the need to increase sales
- the demand that the sellers act ethically, socially correctly, and in an environmentally friendly manner

Some issues are the subject of specific legislation and are regulated by bodies such as the Trading Standards Department and the Advertising Standards Authority. These ethical issues can be seen as a negative force, but to the enterprising marketing person they should suggest new opportunities.

'Social marketing' is a key issue in the 1990s. The concept of materialism is being replaced by the need to care. 'Built in obsolescence' and 'the throw away society' are fading concepts. Quality of life and products, safety (especially of children and animals) and the preservation of finite resources are key consumer issues.

## student activity 13.1 – is marketing ethical?

Examine the following issues, and discuss whether you think each action is justifiable, and *why*.

*situations where an action may be wrong, but "it's good business"*

(a) The use of 'slush funds' to 'bribe' people who influence buying decisions, eg politicians, journalists, business people.

(b) Obtaining information about a competitor's products by 'industrial espionage'.

(c) Refusing to develop a revolutionary new *permanent* cure for dandruff.

(d) Selling the same product in different packaging and in different price categories in order to cover the whole market.

(e) Repackaging a product that has been on the market a long time, and calling it "new improved".

*situations where the end result is unsociable and unethical*

(f) The promotion of beer drinking as "manly" and "sociable" when it can lead to health problems and road accidents.

(g) E numbers (food additives and colourants) increase shelf life and visual appeal, but may adversely affect the health of consumers.

(h) Offering of easy terms (for borrowing) by financial institutions and retailers to low income families.

(i) Your production methods damage the environment (acid rain falling in another country)

(j) You carry out experiments on live dogs in the interests of medical research.

## marketing planning

For any organisation to function efficiently and effectively the Marketing Team (often a Marketing Department) must analyse past performance and present trends, and attempt to predict the future in the form of a *Marketing Plan*. This type of analysis can be undertaken in a variety of ways, all of which are effective if undertaken with care and an appreciation that forecasting is a hazardous business. A Marketing Plan must *not* be set in stone. It must be adaptable. Secondary plans of action must be prepared and adopted if circumstances change. However, the organisation that does not plan, and forecast, and anticipate, is unlikely to achieve long-term effectiveness.

The drawing up of a full-scale sales and marketing plan is covered in detail in Chapter 48 "The sales and marketing plan", and a sample plan is reproduced in a Case Study at the end of that chapter.

## constituents of a marketing plan

A typical Marketing Plan will contain the following elements:

1.  Clear statements on the current aims of the organisation, the markets being served and the product lines being offered to each market.

2.  Clear statements of the organisation's resources in terms of productive capacity, technical expertise, financial resources and marketing experience.

3.  Detailed analysis of the future opportunities for and threats to the organisation, eg economic, and social influences.

4.  The selection of one or more of the opportunities for future development.

5.  Action taken to neutralise the threats.

6.  Re-organisation of the company in view of the decisions made in 4 and 5 above.

7.  The recording of the above in a Marketing Plan, available to all management. The plan will detail:

    •   the organisation's long-term and short-term aims, for example market dominance, profitability

    •   product range – existing products to be updated or withdrawn, new products

    •   market segmentation – by age, location, industry type

    •   pricing – whether for long-term profitability or for short-term tactical gain

    •   promotional strategy – advertising, packaging, for example

    •   sales strategy – sales management and sales techniques

    •   distribution policy – choice of outlets

    •   budget statement – how much money is required, and how it will be used

    •   time schedule for implementation of the plan

## the planning process

Clearly a Marketing Plan is the result of much careful research, consultation and discussion. No organisation will plan in exactly the same way as another organisation. There are, however, a number of planning techniques and processes which have been successfully tried and tested over the years. These include:

• SWOT analysis
• the Marketing Mix

We will explain each of these in turn. It must be stressed that these are techniques which can be used singly, or, more commonly, in combination.

## SWOT analysis

SWOT stands for

> Strengths
> Weaknesses
> Opportunities
> Threats

SWOT analysis is a technique much used in many management as well as marketing scenarios. SWOT consists of examining the current activities of the organisation – its Strengths and Weaknesses – and then using this and external research data to set out the Opportunities and Threats that exist. The process is well illustrated by a practical example which you can undertake yourselves:

---

**student activity 13.2 – SWOT analysis of your school or college**

Take as an example the school or college where you are studying, and make suggestions for each of the four categories. Some points are already listed to get you started. Your lecturer/teacher/trainer could chair further discussion and add to the list. Decide what needs to be done.

*strengths*          large catchment area

*weaknesses*          old buildings, over-crowding

*opportunities*          self-financing/independence

*threats*          falling numbers of 16 year-olds

---

# the marketing mix

This approach appears in most marketing textbooks, and has been accepted for many years. It is based on the four Ps:

> Product
> Price
> Promotion
> Place

A SWOT analysis, of course, can be used to collect the data required to build the Marketing Mix plan. We will now introduce each if the four Ps in turn.

## product

'Product' is, in fact, the range of products (or services) that the organisation offers to the market(s). The decision areas concern quantities, timing, product variations, associated services, quality, style and even the packaging and branding. Most organisations have a range of products of different quality for the different market segments. Whatever quality is decided upon for whichever market segment, the quality should remain consistent. A 'brand name' is an indication of a known quality. The concept of Product is developed further in Chapter 16 "Product Policy" and Chapter 18 "Promotion and place".

## price

'Price' is a vitally important decision area because although it is a 'promotional' tool in many respects, it is the main source of income to the organisation. If prices are lowered for promotional purposes, the cash flow within the company, and its long-term profitability, could be seriously affected. As with products, there is normally a range of prices. These can vary according to the quantities bought, the importance of the customer, and the market segment. Pricing can be long-term (set at a level for sustained profit-making) and short-term (cut prices for tactical reasons, such as market penetration). Pricing can involve discounts, special offers, allowances, credit, and 'trade-ins.' It is vitally important to get price decisions right. The concept of Price is developed further in Chapter 17 'Pricing'.

## promotion

'Promotion' consists of a number of techniques which create awareness of the products and persuade the potential customer to make the buying decision. These techniques are advertising, branding, packaging, publicity/public relations, sales promotions and merchandising. Each differs from the others but all, or all of them thought relevant to the given situation, will be used to create a unified *product image* and an image for the organisation, the *corporate identity*. This means that if the market segment aimed at is at the premium (top price) end of the scale, then all promotional techniques used must be right for that set of customers.

A possible weakness of the Marketing Mix analysis approach is the inclusion of the *selling* activity in this sector. Selling is a *personal* activity, with physical or oral contact between buyer and seller. Promotional activity is *impersonal*, aimed generally at a market segment and with no personal contact. Perhaps the four Ps should be the five Ps, with Personal Selling being the fifth. This point is mentioned because of the different emphasis placed on these activities by different organisations. A simple example is the difference between promoting/selling an industrial machine and a chocolate bar. The machine needs expert demonstration by a salesperson. With the machine, marketing would split 80% selling effort, 20% back-up promotion. With the chocolate, 80% promotional effort would be backed by 20% selling, i.e. gaining retail/wholesale distribution. The concept of 'Promotion' is developed further in Chapter 18 "Promotion and place".

**place**

Through which outlets should we sell the product? How do we physically move the product to these chosen outlets? How far afield do we wish to operate (locally, nationally, or internationally)? Place, or distribution policy, is a massive, complex decision area that incorporates these three problems, and potentially more. See Chapter 18 'Promotion and place' for further explanation of this topic.

**the marketing mix – conclusion**

The Marketing Mix gives a plan by which to operate to influence and satisfy the buyer/consumer. The four Ps approach is not perfect, and is certainly not intended to cover all of marketing's activities, eg Marketing Research. Research, of course, is the provider of information for the decisions in all of the four P areas.

---

**student activity 13.3 – the marketing mix**

Divide into groups of three or four and take as an example, *either*

(a) the product or service you are promoting as part of your Young Enterprise or mini-business scheme, *or*

(b) a product decided on by the class as a whole, eg a car, a chocolate bar, a new magazine for a specific age or interest group

Work out a marketing strategy based on the Marketing Mix – Product, Price, Promotion, Place – and present your findings in a short oral report to the class.

Discuss any differences in approach.

---

# chapter summary

❑ The emphasis in marketing definitions is 'consumer orientation.'

❑ As was seen in the marketing diagram (page 136), the functions of marketing for *new* products can be given a specific order – market research, product launch and sales, product monitoring; for *existing* products many of these processes will be going on at the same time

❑ Planning for marketing can be organised in a variety of different ways to suit the person or organisation undertaking the planning; these methods are

  • SWOT analysis (Strengths, Weaknesses, Opportunities, Threats)

  • Marketing Mix (Product, Price, Promotion, Place)

❑ The Marketing Mix components will each be developed in later chapters

# 14 Marketing research

## introduction

This chapter sets out to explain the importance of gathering commercial information for use by the business for future decision making. 'Change' in the marketplace is inevitable, and all businesses have to recognise change when it occurs, or better still, they should anticipate it and be prepared.

In this chapter we examine the following areas:
- the terminology of marketing research
- the areas covered by research
- the sources of desk research
- the planning of field research, including data collection methods, sampling choices, and the design of a questionnaire
- market segmentation
- buyer types and behaviour

## the terminology of marketing research

In this section we will introduce some of the concepts of marketing research and explain the terminology used.

### marketing research
The chapter title used the term "marketing research" rather than "market research" a phrase which is commonly used. Why? "Marketing research" means not just the various estimates of market size and location, and consumer attitudes, it means also research into the *firm's* own pricing, advertising, selling methods and distribution policies. Marketing research involves an examination of the firm's environment and the success (or otherwise) of its use of its marketing functions in dealing with that environment. For example it will need to know if a price change was successful, which outlets sell most goods, which adverts appeal, and so on.

## secondary research and primary research

*Secondary (Desk) Research* is the gathering and analysis of already available information. This is a natural starting point because it is quicker and cheaper, and commercial organisations are always keen to save time and money. The problem is that information already available is already partly out of date. It may not be precisely what is required, either.

*Primary (Field or Original) Research* is the gathering of fresh information, specifically tailored to the business' own requirements. The problem here is the expense of the survey. Syndicated research is one answer: here the information seekers join together to conduct the research. Alternatively, established research agencies may undertake research and sell their findings to interested organisations.

Field and Desk Research are the most important classifications of marketing research, and the methods of carrying out the research will be covered in greater detail later in the chapter.

## quantitative and qualitative research

*Quantitative Research* collects numbers: the number of items bought, the price paid, the number of outlets stocking the product, and so on. In such numeric form the information is easy to collect and analyse, often by computer, a process known as *electronic monitoring*.

*Qualitative Research* examines opinions. As such it is the growth area of research, as consumer opinions are sought by product and service providers, politicians, town planners and virtually every organisation that exists. The key problem is that of information collation. Open ended questions collecting chatty responses tend to confuse, not assist, the opinion seekers. Therefore opinion research must be quantified. For the techniques used, see the section on questionnaire construction later in this chapter (pages 147 to 151).

## industrial and consumer research

*Industrial Research* studies data about industrial goods and services: items sold to the trade, not to the private individual. Industrial involves one organisation investigating other organisations.

*Consumer Research* investigates consumer goods and services. It looks at the different categories (segments) of the general public: quantities bought and consumer opinions. It does, of course, give valuable insight to organisations of competitor activity, ie market share and distribution patterns.

## overt and covert research

*Overt Research* is open and above board. *Covert Research* is not. This fascinating distinction emphasises the importance of information to commercial organisations. Covert research is in fact anything from posing as a customer or an official to gain information about a competitor, to stealing trade secrets (industrial espionage). It must be pointed out that certain areas of covert research are illegal, and are not to be recommended!

## ad hoc, continuous and omnibus research

*Ad hoc* means "one off", an activity which is undertaken once to provide information about a specific need, for example the local council research opinion for a new bypass, or new sports centre, a firm testing a new product. Most research is ad hoc.

*Continuous Research* can be conducted by individual organisations or by market research agencies. The same procedure/questionnaire is used at regular time intervals to provide an ongoing progress report on chosen question areas. This work is often syndicated (see above). It is conducted either within trades, ie industrial type research, or by consumer panels, or in omnibus surveys.

- trade research might include a *retail audit*, whereby sales from the same group of shops are monitored over a period of time, or an analysis by a panel (selected group) of *industrial* companies of their raw material consumption and production data
- consumer panels involve a representative sample of people (individuals or households) keeping a record of purchases, possibly in a special diary; the key link is that the membership of the panel stays the same, or as near as possible, to retain continuity and consistency

An *Omnibus survey* is a number of surveys combined in one. It provides a mix of questions on different subjects included on the same questionnaire. The reason for this type of survey is usually because the number of questions on any particular topic is small. Therefore the needs of several clients are satisfied by one survey. One disadvantage is that an omnibus survey can result in too many questions and too much of the respondent's time being taken up – a factor which may affect the care with which the later answers are treated.

In the rest of this chapter we deal with the practicalities of desk research and field research.

# desk research

Desk research is an essential starting point for any research work: if information is available already, it saves time and money. What a new organisation must do, even before it is set up, is to evaluate all available data about the market, from whatever source. Desk research combines:
- an examination of your own organisation's *internal* records
- a study of *external* publications, compiled by *experts* in various fields

## sources of internal data
Much data is available within an organisation which is already trading, for example:
- records of sales to customers: the number of items, frequency, how the goods were purchased (eg whether by mail order or through shops)
- accounts: the sales figures, costing and and profit figures for individual items
- regional sales trends
- an analysis of the types of customer
- the life cycle of individual items (how long they stay on the market)
- previous market research

From this data the organisation should be able to assess present trends and predict future trends (see Chapter 15).

If the organisation is newly established it will obviously lack these records, but it should set in motion a system to record all potentially useful data. It can turn instead to external data (which will, of course, also be used by established organisations).

## sources of external data – general and expert
### Government publications
An essential starting point is a copy of the free *Government Statistics, a Brief Guide to Sources* or the *Guide to Official Statistics,* found in reference libraries, and available from HMSO. These provide a guide to Government statistical publications including: Social Trends, Economic Trends, Annual Abstract of Statistics, Monthly Digest of Statistics, Business Monitor, Family Spending, Household Food Consumption and Expenditure, Censuses of Production Population and Distribution, Departmental journals, National Income Statistics, Import and Export Statistics.

### Commercial Organisations, Trade Associations and Professional Bodies
Much useful information can be gathered from organisations and societies which cater for the needs of businesses and particular trades and professions. These include the Confederation of British Industry (CBI), Chambers of Commerce - local and national, Business Clubs - local, the British Institute of Management, the Chartered Institute of Marketing, and Trade Associations.

### Other useful sources
- *Trade journals* – for a full list of what exists, consult *Willing's Press Guide*
- *Directories* – first consult the *Current British Directories* publications to see what exists; the main directories are Kompass, Kelly's and Sells, three excellent publications on products and organisations

- *newspapers* – some libraries have subject indices on CD, a very useful research resource
- *Universities and Business Schools* regularly undertake research and publish their findings
- *Research organisations* undertake surveys of chosen industries on a regular basis – always find out whether Mintel (Market Intelligence), Keynote and others have published recently on the required subject
- *Overseas Information:* Government Import and Export Statistics, International Marketing Data and Statistics, OECD publications

## research method

The list of information sources set out above may seem daunting, but it must be stressed that if you are undertaking desk research you will be very selective as to what you read. Desk research of this type may well form part of your project work in Business Studies, if for example you are studying a particular company or industry. It is a good idea before going to your reference library (your school/college library or a city centre commercial library) to make a list of the key areas you are researching, and check them with your lecturer. These details will comprise names and terms relating to your project, eg the names of the industry, the companies, the products and so on. You can then consult the index in the library and approach the reference librarian with your list. It is possible that the library has a computer index system which will then highlight the sources you need to consult. Always ask.

---

### student activity 14.1 – desk research

Identify the *sources* and *types* of information available in the following areas:

| specific search area | extended search area |
|---|---|
| mens shirts | the clothing industry |
| board games for children | the toy industry |
| local sports facilities | the leisure industry |

---

# field research

As we saw at the beginning of the chapter, the most valuable method of market research is the collection of primary or original data – *field research*. It is this area of investigation that the 'person in the street' normally identifies with market research.

Field research consists of six stages:

1. clarify the objectives of the research
2. choose a data collection method
3. construct a questionnaire
4. decide on the sampling techniques (the method of choosing the people to be questioned)
5. carry out a pilot survey
6. brief the interviewers for the main survey

## clarify the objectives of the research

Always ensure that you establish exactly what it is that the person who commissions the research wants to find out. They can all too easily ask for the wrong things and if this happens *you* will get the blame later. Talk it through! If you are undertaking school or college project work, this means discussing it with your teacher or lecturer.

## choose a data collection method

Firstly, *always* consider the possibility that the information is already available, ie undertake some desk research before launching a major survey. Secondly, consider the advantages and disadvantages of the many methods of data gathering set out below.

Before considering these methods, it is important to understand some of the statistical terminology used by market researchers:

| | | |
|---|---|---|
| *population* | = | *all of the items, eg people, being investigated* |
| *sample* | = | *a selection, random or otherwise, of the items being investigated* |
| *respondent* | = | *the person who answers the questions* |

### observation
The simplest method, ie merely recording numbers or events, eg counting cars passing a certain spot. No questionnaire is required, but an organised list of the variables most certainly is.  Plan in advance.

### telephone enquiry
Telephoning the respondent (the person answering the questions) is probably the second fastest method after 'observation'.  It is very useful in industrial research where the number of firms to be contacted is relatively small.  Its main advantage (to the questioner at least!) is that it is  intrusive and thus often fast and effective,  but can be costly and the 'interview' must be kept short.

### postal enquiry
This is a method often used in both consumer and industrial research.  Questionnaires are sent to respondents relatively cheaply, and a large geographical area can be covered.  Costs increase when pre-paid reply envelopes have to be included, plus reminders and gifts to persuade people to co-operate.  The major problem is one of poor response (20% is quite good in consumer research, with 30%-40% achievable after reminders).  The trouble is increased in that the sample gained is often unrepresentative of the total population – it will be comprised of the people who like replying, or who have the time to reply!  Further, no explanations about doubtful points in the questionnaire can be made.

### interviews
The personal interview is judged to be the best method overall;  it can take place in the street, or in the home. Speed is achieved with a street interview, and results quickly analysed; an interview in the home may take longer, but can produce detailed and well thought out answers.  In a personal interview queries about questions can be resolved; prompts (where people are forgetful) can be used and this reduces the number of "don't know" answers.  However, there are problems.  The presence of the interviewer may affect answers; filling quotas on a door-to-door basis can take time and prove expensive; interviewers need careful training; information may be wrongly recorded or the answer misheard.

## choosing the right method
All the above techniques are all useful and relevant under the right conditions.  The choices between types depend on the following requirements:
• total cost involved
• total time needed – ie the way in which the interviews are scheduled
• reliability of the answer (who fills it in?)
• thought time needed by the respondent
• the number of personal questions
• are there display cards or actual products to be shown to the respondent?
• length of the questionnaire
• type of sample
• size of sample
• location of respondents
• level of response required
• degree of explanation needed

# constructing and using a questionnaire

A questionnaire comprises a list of questions which can provide data including
- factual information
- opinions
- value judgements

The extent of the questionnaire will depend on the type of interview used, whether it is postal, face-to-face, or telephoned.  The *principles* of questionnaire construction will, however, remain the same.  In essence, it is a "garbage in, garbage out" situation – the quality of the answers and information gathered will reflect the quality of the questions asked.  An example of a well written questionnaire is illustrated on pages 149 to 151.

## structure of the questionnaire
- Start with the name of your firm (or invent an agency if you want your name to remain unknown) so that the respondent can see that it looks 'official'.  Do *not* use the name of your firm if this will bias the answers given.
- Give an introduction which greets the respondent and asks for his or her co-operation.  Sometimes an incentive (eg an entry into a free draw) may be given to the respondent.
- Explain the purpose of the exercise/research.
- Keep the questionnaire as short as possible, especially when interviewing in the street or on the telephone.  There is always the danger that the respondent will walk away (or put the telephone down).
- Thank the respondent for his or her time and in the case of a street interview record the name and address so that the validity of the interview can be checked out.

## construction of the questionnaire
- Include "Instructions to the interviewer or respondent", eg "tick the relevant boxes" so that answers are recorded accurately and consistently.  This is particularly important if the questionnaire is to be sent through the post.
- The layout and style of the questions asked are of paramount importance.
- Plan a logical sequence so that easy, confidence building questions come first, and the respondent can begin to take an interest.
- Record only as many *personal* details as are *essential* for your analysis.  If details like 'salary' are required, try leaving this until last and give 'ranges' for their answers.  Remember, personal details being asked for can result in the interview being terminated, so take care.  If ages are required, give a range and ask them to indicate the relevant one.  A common age range is: under 16, 16-24, 25 - 40, 41 - 60, over 60.
- Try to keep the boxes which record the response over to the right.  This allows for easy analysis, although the modern trend is for electronic reading (monitoring) of the completed questionnaires, so this point is not now so important.
- Boxes will be coded (ie given numbers) for easy and rapid analysis *after* the interview. (Look at the example questions on the next page and the specimen questionnaire).  The analyst records only those box numbers where a mark has been inserted.

## designing questions
- Keep the language simple.
- Avoid biased or 'loaded' questions.
- Questions should not be leading, ambiguous, too personal or misleading.
- Use closed questions, to which the answer is a clear "yes" or "no" rather than open questions, unless you are actively seeking an opinion.
- Create questions of a multi-choice nature, giving a good selection of responses without confusing the respondent.  These can be *factual* multiple choice, as shown on the next page.

---

4.  In what type of accommodation do you live?
    *(tick the relevant box)*

    (a)  lodgings/bedsit ☐ 15

    (b)  flat ☐ 16

    (c)  terrace/semi-detached house ☐ 17

    (d)  detached house ☐ 18

---

- Create questions of a multi-choice nature, even when asking for *opinions*. A common technique is to use the Likert scale which sets out a range of response, as in the example below:

---

5.  The local library is efficient
    *(tick the relevant box)*

    (a)  agree strongly ☐ 19

    (b)  agree ☐ 20

    (c)  neither agree nor disagree ☐ 21

    (d)  disagree ☐ 22

    (e)  disagree strongly ☐ 23

---

## other considerations

- Brief the interviewers (train them if necessary). Make sure they understand their areas of responsibility and the limits to which they can go with any prompts; the way to record half answers eg "did you watch programme x?", answer: "half of it". Ensure that the interviewers act honestly. Tell them "checks before cheques", meaning that a sample of respondents will be contacted to see if the interview really did take place. Give them a precise time deadline.

- Carry out a pilot survey, to check if the questionnaire works properly. Test the order of questions, identify any ambiguities, ensure that all the areas of information needed are being produced. Re-write the questions if there is *any* misunderstanding. Keep testing and altering until the questionnaire runs smoothly.

---

### student activity 14.2 – field research

Suggest a *best* and *second-best* method of data collection for the following circumstances:

(a)  opinions on new packaging styles – few questions, quick results

(b)  opinions from industrialists nationwide – detailed answers, no time constraints

(c)  political survey – a large number of interviewees with a balance between age groups and sexes, in a local area, today!

(d)  views on a technical subject – businesses to be questioned, London area, many questions

(e)  instant opinion of the general public on two topical issues for the local paper

(f)  facts from business people nationally, for a region by region analysis, requiring some confidential information

(g)  national survey into sex and alcohol related topics, full questionnaire, the general public

In each case use the list of possible data colllection methods set out on page 146.

# Customers First

At W H Smith we are committed to improving the service we offer you in our stores. This questionnaire is designed to let you say what you think of us so that we can make the improvements you want. When you have completed the questionnaire please fold it as indicated by the dotted lines and post it. Postage is paid so there is no need to use a stamp. All those returning questionnaires by 29.4.1992 will be entered into a free draw to win £500 worth of W H Smith vouchers. Please remember your answers are confidential, they will not be passed on to any third parties nor will they be used to sell you anything.

**Q 1**  Firstly, from which branch of W H Smith did you pick up this questionnaire?

**Please write in** _____  (1)
                                                                    (2)

**Q 2**  Overall how would you consider the service you received at W H Smith       (3)
on the occasion when you picked up this questionnaire?
**Please tick one box only(✓)**

| Excellent | Good | Neither good nor poor | Poor | Very poor | |
|-----------|------|-----------------------|------|-----------|---|
| ❑ | ❑ | ❑ | ❑ | ❑ | (4) |

**Q 3**  Thinking about the service you received from staff on this occasion, could you state all that you disliked about it, if anything?
**Please write in**




                                                                    (5)
                                                                    (6)

**Q 4**  And could you please state all that you liked about the service you received at W H Smith on this occasion.
**Please write in**




                                                                    (7)
                                                                    (8)

**Q**5   Below is a list of statements about service. Can you please indicate whether you strongly agree, agree, disagree or strongly disagree with each statement for this shopping occasion at W H Smith. If the comment is not applicable to this trip please tick the 'not applicable' box. **Please tick the box which applies to each statement (✓)**

| | Strongly Agree | Agree | Disagree | Strongly Disagree | Not Applicable | |
|---|---|---|---|---|---|---|
| Staff had time to help with my enquiry | ❑ | ❑ | ❑ | ❑ | ❑ | (9) |
| Staff were friendly | ❑ | ❑ | ❑ | ❑ | ❑ | (10) |
| Staff were approachable | ❑ | ❑ | ❑ | ❑ | ❑ | (11) |
| I did not have to queue to seek assistance | ❑ | ❑ | ❑ | ❑ | ❑ | (12) |
| Staff wanted to help me | ❑ | ❑ | ❑ | ❑ | ❑ | (13) |
| Staff were happy | ❑ | ❑ | ❑ | ❑ | ❑ | (14) |
| Staff were interested in serving me | ❑ | ❑ | ❑ | ❑ | ❑ | (15) |
| I did not have to queue too long to pay | ❑ | ❑ | ❑ | ❑ | ❑ | (16) |
| Staff were knowledgeable | ❑ | ❑ | ❑ | ❑ | ❑ | (17) |
| Staff were understanding | ❑ | ❑ | ❑ | ❑ | ❑ | (18) |
| Staff helped me make my decision | ❑ | ❑ | ❑ | ❑ | ❑ | (19) |
| I enjoyed shopping at W H Smith | ❑ | ❑ | ❑ | ❑ | ❑ | (20) |
| Staff were there if I needed them | ❑ | ❑ | ❑ | ❑ | ❑ | (21) |
| It was easy to find what I was looking for | ❑ | ❑ | ❑ | ❑ | ❑ | (22) |
| The shop is well laid out | ❑ | ❑ | ❑ | ❑ | ❑ | (23) |
| The signs helped me find my way around | ❑ | ❑ | ❑ | ❑ | ❑ | (24) |
| I could browse in peace | ❑ | ❑ | ❑ | ❑ | ❑ | (25) |
| It was fun to shop there | ❑ | ❑ | ❑ | ❑ | ❑ | (26) |
| I knew I could exchange goods easily | ❑ | ❑ | ❑ | ❑ | ❑ | (27) |

**Q** 6   Was there any member of staff you thought offered a very high level of service? Can you remember their name?

**Please write in** _____

*W H Smith – "Customer First" questionnaire*
Reproduced by kind permission of W H Smith Ltd and David Young & Associates

It would help us if you could give some background about the visit you made to W H Smith when you picked up this questionnaire.

**Q7** Listed below are areas or departments in W H Smith. In the FIRST column please indicate those that you planned to buy from, if any.
**Please tick as many boxes as apply (✓)**

**Q8** In the SECOND column please indicate those you actually bought from, if any.
**Please tick as many boxes as apply (✓)**

|  | Q7<br>Planned (✓) | Q8<br>Bought (✓) |  |
|---|---|---|---|
| Newspapers and Magazines | ❑ | ❑ | (28) |
| Books | ❑ | ❑ | |
| Music | ❑ | ❑ | |
| Videos | ❑ | ❑ | (31) |
| Stationery | ❑ | ❑ | |
| Calculators & typewriters | ❑ | ❑ | |
| Pens | ❑ | ❑ | |
| Computer games & software | ❑ | ❑ | |
| Greeting cards, giftwrap and<br>Christmas decorations | ❑ | ❑ | (36) |
| Film, developing & printing | ❑ | ❑ | |
| Games & toys | ❑ | ❑ | |

**Other (please write in)** Planned _____ (39)

Bought _____ (40)

**Q9** How much did you spend on this occasion, if anything, at W H Smith?

**Please write in £**_____ (41-44)

**Q10** How often do you buy something from this branch of W H Smith?
**Please tick one box only (✓)** (45)

| | |
|---|---|
| 2/3 times per week | ❑ |
| Once a week | ❑ |
| Once a fortnight | ❑ |
| Once a month | ❑ |
| Less often | ❑ |

*W H Smith – "Customer First" questionnaire*
Reproduced by kind permission of W H Smith Ltd and David Young & Associates

# sampling techniques

Samples are taken from a population (ie the people being investigated) to give a 'reasonable' assessment of some value about that population. Accuracy depends upon the choice of sample type, how well it represents the population, and its size. The main types of sample are set out below.

## random sampling and the sampling frame

If you were undertaking a survey in an ideal world, you would investigate the whole population, and by "population" we mean all of the items under consideration, and this could be people or things or firms. In the real world it is necessary to take a *sample* from this population, from a defined group known as a *sampling frame*. An example of a sampling frame is the Electoral Register, the list of people over 18 living in specific geographical areas. A sampling frame may be more local, for example all people running shops in Sheffield. From such information accurate samples can be constructed, and some firms actually compile and sell lists to Direct Mail firms. However, bias can creep into these listings. The Electoral Register is made up from those adults in residence in November, published in March, and in use until the following February – sixteen months after the data was collected. In that time many of the population will have moved and Direct Mailers using this list will have a substantial error factor.

## quasi-random sampling

Quasi-random sampling involves the use of some *control device* over the selection of the items within the sample. The techniques used are

- systematic sampling
- stratified sampling
- multi-stage sampling
- quota sampling
- cluster sampling

*Systematic Sampling:* choosing every 'nth' item from a list, but choosing the first item randomly, eg if a 5% sample is required, then every twentieth item on the list will be interviewed or recorded. However, the first item could be any between 1 and 20. Were this the fifth, then the sample would be made up of the fifth, the twentyfifth, the fortyfifth, and so on

*Stratified Sampling:* designed so that every type, age group, class, are part of the sample and in the correct weighting, eg if questioning, say, the student population as a whole and it is known that, say, 5% of all students are at university, then this is the percentage of interviews that must be held with this type of student. It may be necessary to go a stage further and form 'sub-strata', eg if it is known that 30% of such students are female, then to be accurate three out of every ten university interviews should be with females.

*Multi-Stage Sampling:* this is used when the population under review is widespread, as in a large but sparsely populated country like Australia. Here, areas within the total area are chosen, ensuring a fair spread of urban and rural, north and south. Within these areas, smaller areas are randomly chosen and the required interviews conducted. In a way, this is a stratified method of selection and certainly some form of stratification is usually used in the selection of respondents.

*Cluster Sampling:* where little information about the population is known, in, say, under-developed countries, areas – eg whole streets or neighbourhoods – are chosen at random and every single household is approached. This gains rapid results but suffers the disadvantage that all such households are probably very similar in, say, voting patterns and purchasing habits. Consequently many areas must be covered and a guess made at the likely types of people to be found in each, so that a reasonable cross section of the whole can be achieved. It is inevitably a compromise between receiving biased results and saving time and money.

*Quota Sampling:* the interviewer is given a number (or quota) of units to examine or interview, either with a free choice, or more often broken down in some considered manner, even where no real sampling frame data is available. Divisions may require so many of each sex, class, age group to be interviewed. This method requires a level of intelligence of the interviewers and a degree of honesty, as many interviews are conducted in the street and in bad weather it is tempting to ignore the quota and merely interview the willing. To avoid such dishonesty, names and addresses of respondents are usually collected so that checks can be made. Despite its shortcomings, the quota method is one of the most common, as it also one of the least expensive to operate.

## problems with sampling
There are many types of problem awaiting the would-be information gatherer. Note the following:

### sampling bias
This is caused by choosing the wrong type of sample. These 'types' were detailed in the last section. It is very easy to select a sample unrepresentative of the whole 'population', or to collect the information in a biased way, eg by telephone as opposed to street. Remember that the word "population" does not necessarily mean "people"; populations can be things, ages, measurements, ie whatever is being investigated in the survey.

### sampling error
Sample errors arise from *human* error in questionnaire construction:
- failure to ask the right questions; missing the relevant points
- asking personal questions, leading to dishonest replies
- asking ambiguous questions that respondents interpret in different ways
- asking misleading questions that gather the wrong information.
- asking too many open ended questions that are difficult to analyse
- asking questions out of sequence, so that the respondent cannot recall or remember the necessary facts at that moment of time.

### sample size
An error in sample size is an error in *selecting the size of sample;* choosing one too small to give the required level of 'significance' or 'confidence' in the results, or one too large to be acceptable on a cost basis. The size is calculated according to the level of confidence required.

---

### student activity 14.3 – sample types

Select one or two suitable sampling methods for the following situations:

(a) a large sample of the adult population of the UK for a brief telephone survey

(b) precise information on the opinions of males, by age groups, correctly weighted

(c) a swift street survey by age and sex

(d) a cross-country survey into regional characteristics

(e) a new product opinion survey to establish which socio-economic groups are likely to buy – swift reaction, short set-up time, local area

(f) a personal survey where refusals to take part may be high, but a balance of respondents must be maintained

# market segmentation

*Market segmentation is the process whereby the overall market is divided up into separate sets of customers (segments) which have separate identifiable product needs.*

*Industrial* market segments are categorised according to the type of industry, the location and size of of the target business, and the end-use of the product. If, for instance you were manufacturing household products, you would distinguish between selling to supermarkets and to corner shops (segment by size). If you manufactured fertilisers, you would sell well in rural areas, but would have limited success in city areas (segment by area).

There are a number of different ways of identifying *consumer* market segments:

• *social stratification*
A common way of segmenting the market is by social class. Each group will have its own product needs and pattern of income and expenditure. The UK social classes are divided into letter groupings (A to E) as follows:

| Social grouping | Social class | occupation type |
| --- | --- | --- |
| A | Upper/upper middle class | higher managerial, professional, eg director of a large company, partner in a firm of solicitor |
| B | Middle class | intermediate managerial, professional, eg commercial manager, salaried accountant, health service manager |
| C1 | Lower middle class | junior managerial and supervisory, eg insurance clerk, nurse, shop manager |
| C2 | Skilled working class | skilled manual workers, eg electrician, fitter |
| D | Working class | semi-skilled and unskilled workers, eg warehouseman, driver, shop assistant |
| E | Subsistence level | the lowest paid and the unemployed |

• *age groups*
The age grouping set out below is only one of many attempts to group the market into buying groups. You can probably think of some other or different subdivisions.

| age | buying group |
| --- | --- |
| 0 – 10 | child |
| 11 – 17 | teenager |
| 18 – 35 | young working person |
| 36 – 59 | mature working person |
| 60 – 100 | retired person |

• *regional groups* – different regions in the UK have different preferences: try selling tripe in Surrey and beer with a frothy head in London!

• *sex* – products for 'him' and 'her' are clearly different market segments

- *income groups* – this distinction sometimes overrides the social grouping set out above: lower income groups will look for a 'bargain', higher income groups will look for quality or self-consciously expensive products

- *ethnic groups* – many new religious and racial groups have appeared over the last thirty years, each requiring specilaised products and services.

## increases in market segmentation

Post-war production was geared to mass production techniques, which provided several relatively homogeneous products, each to a large market segment. In the 1980s and 1990s, however, as the Henley Forecasting Research team has pointed out, such mass marketing became less important. With greater affluence in the West, smaller market segments buying higher-priced specialist products began to grow in number. This has created additional problems for marketing people, but many more opportunities for product diversification.

# buyer types and behaviour

In order to appreciate the needs of each market segment, planners must understand *buyer behaviour,* an area which involves an element of psychology. The first consideration when looking at buyer behaviour is that there are two basic classifications of buyer: the *industrial* buyer (organisations buying plant, machinery, stock) and the *consumer* (the private purchaser).

## industrial buyers

*Industrial goods buyers* are usually more rational in their decision making, although never entirely so. The professional buyer's task is to buy the right materials and equipment for the organisation at the right time and at the right price. The buyer is a human being, however, and will still be affected by emotive considerations, eg the security or otherwise of the job, his or her personal life, ambition. One of the key considerations of selling to an industrial market is the possibility of finding not one buyer but a buying *group*, or what has been called a decision making *unit.* Identifying the key person, ie the one most likely to make the buying decision, is a constant problem for the seller. Imagine having an industrial machine to sell. The key person might be 'the buyer', but a greater likelihood would be the production manager, or the chief engineer, or the chief accountant, or the Board of Directors, or the Managing Director, or even an outsider if the firm employed a consultant. All of this depends on the internal organisation of the customer firm. The message is "do not assume, always research".

## consumers

*Consumer goods buyers* are the subject of regular market and motivational research as to what makes them buy or not buy. The key point to appreciate is that people do not buy products and services: they buy the *benefits* that such products or services offer to them. Think about this! Why *do* you buy a particular coat, or car, or chocolate? The reasons are many, but in all cases, they will be a combination of practical and emotive factors, some of which are set out below. Apply these factors to an item of clothing you want to buy.:

| practical factors | emotive factors |
|---|---|
| price/good value for money? | status (as fashion leader)? |
| hard wearing? | social acceptance (everyone else has one)? |
| suitable for work? | high price (to boast of wealth)? |
| easy to clean? | low price (to boast of bargaining skills)? |
| warmth? | sexual attraction? |

Psychologists have commented at length on buyer behaviour and marketing logic. They understand the basic needs and wants of individuals and groups.  Marketing's motivational researchers also seek to understand the reasoning that triggers the buying decision.  Research into buyer behaviour goes back a long way, mainly to Maslow's theory  – *The Hierarchy Of Needs* – published in "A Theory of Human Motivation" in 1943.  The "needs" are set out in order of importance, so that when the first category is satisfied, the individual moves to the next level.  Not all marketing people accept this order of things, but the importance of the five "needs" is not disputed, and forms the basis of advertising messages/reasons for buying to this day. The five, in order, are:

1    *Physiological* – the need to eat, drink, and stay alive

2    *Safety* – the desire to be secure and not to be hurt or disabled

3    *Love  and belonging* – the achievement of acceptance by the group

4    *Esteem* – the desire for confidence and to be thought of highly by others

5    *Self actualisation* – the satisfaction of creating something, realising ones full potential

## reference groups and opinion formers

Much of buyer behaviour relates to how others see us (love, esteem).  It is an accepted fact of market segmentation that 'groups' of consumers exist, and within those groups are 'opinion formers', the leaders of the groups.  Market research must identify both the groups and the opinion formers.  If these trend setters can be reached and persuaded towards your product a major sales success is likely. If a holiday venue is visited by a well known figure, the resort is likely to become more popular.

---

**student activity 14.4 – reference groups/opinion formers**

Identify organisations or individuals who can be used to influence your perception (and purchase) of:

(a)    a type of car                        (b)    a style of clothing

(c)    a Business Studies textbook    (d)    a charitable cause

(e)    a health drink                      (f)    a burglar alarm

---

# chapter summary

❑    Marketing research involves an investigation both into consumer needs and attitudes, and also into the firm's own pricing, advertising and selling methods.

❑    Secondary (desk) research examines  the data that is already available to organisations, internally and externally.

❑    Primary (field) research gathers fresh information, either for a 'one-off' decision, or a continuous basis.

❑    A sample survey consists of six stages: defining objectives, selecting a data collection method, selecting a sample type, designing a questionnaire, testing the questionnaire and briefing the interviewers.

❑    There are various sampling techniques, all of which try to ensure that a representative cross section of the target population is chosen.

❑    Market segmentation for *consumers* can be by social stratification, age groups, regional groups, sex,  income and ethnic groups; for *industrial* goods segmentation can be by type of industry, location of market,  size of target business and end-use of products.

❑    Organisations must be aware of buyer behaviour when formulating marketing policy: buyers respond to both practical and emotional stimuli.

EVIDENCE
COLLECTION
EXERCISE

# EVIDENCE COLLECTION EXERCISE

# 7

# *Market research – a local leisure centre?*

---

*Element 3.1*     *Analyse market research*

Suggested Sources:
- school/college and reference libraries – Government and other statistics on the lesiure industry
- Local Authority leisure department
- local leisure centres
- textbooks in libraries and resource centres

---

## INTRODUCTION

The local council (city or county) is investigating the need for a further  sports/leisure facility within its area. You are to research current availability and establish the views of the local population as to:

(a)   the need for a new facility

(b)   their attitude to public or private funding/ownership of this facility

(c)   their ideas as to the items/services to be provided

(d)   the site

Other relevant information areas may be added.

## TASK 1

Undertake secondary (desk) research into leisure activities, locally and nationally.  Draw up a list of information sources and state the types of information available about national activities.  Draw up an actual list of provisions locally, stating the sources of information.

## TASK 2

Recommend, with reasons, a data collection technique (eg postal) and a sampling type (eg systematic) best suited for a field survey.  State clearly which types/categories of respondents will be approached for this primary research.

## TASK 3

Create a questionnaire for use locally which examines the needs and opinions of the local population (see introduction above).  Once the questionnaire has been drawn up, *and approved by the tutor*, sampling can take place.  Results should, where possible, be input into a suitably drawn-up computer database for analysis.

## PRESENTATION OF EVIDENCE

A combination of written report and oral presentation is recommended, preferably in groups of three or four. Leaflets, brochures and  maps should be collected, and OHP material for the presentation would be expected.  Clear decisions on the type of data collection and sample type must be made and justified.  Note that if original research is undertaken, the class/group must agree on a questionaire for the task, to allow for the co-ordination and discussion of results.  Such original research is not necessary to satisfy this element, but does ensure an interesting and challenging exercise.

# 15 Consumer trends and sales forecasting

## introduction

This chapter looks at the statistics which are available for analysing consumer trends, and outlines the basic requirements of trend analysis and forecasting.

- it defines the consumer characteristics of culture, lifestyle, taste and conscience spending
- it shows how to calculate a trends
- it examines the trend pattern affected by seasonal, cyclical and random factors
- it gives a guide to the projection of trends in the short term (5 years)
- it explains the use of index numbers in business
- it gives examples of economic, social and business data, for trend analysis

## the characteristics of consumers

The different characteristics of consumers result in the *segmentation* of markets (See Chapter 14). We have seen in discussing buyer behaviour and reference groups that businesses need to be aware of changes in the ways that individuals and groups think. These patterns of behaviour are reflected in the changing pattern of purchases, as shown by trends in past and present sales.

### culture
Culture may be defined as the beliefs and traditions of a particular group. Immigration and emigration will affect the balance of cultural beliefs within a country. Marketing must monitor not just changes in demography but in ethnic movement as well.

### lifestyle
Lifestyle may be defined as the way in which various groups within society live. It may include the young (upwardly mobile) striving for social and material success; the elderly, with their desire for secure homes and leisurely pursuits; the family group, buying products for the expanding "nest".

## taste

Taste refers to the categories of likes and dislikes associated with the various cultures and lifestyles. Changes in taste will be noted by marketing people. The better organisation will *create* taste, eg in fashion, music, and thinking generally.

## conscience spending

Buyers are being increasingly subjected to social and technical information about the effects of our way of life on the human race, animals, and the environment. Clearly, business must respond to changing consumer ideologies and fashions by stressing their concern for them, eg healthy eating, reduction of CFC gases, experiments on animals, wasted resources (packaging).

## sources of information about consumer characteristics

Two key government publications detailing expenditure patterns are:

- *Household Food Consumption and Expenditure* (MAFF) which is the Annual Report of the National Food Survey Committee;
- *Family Spending*, which is a report on the Family Expenditure Survey. This gives details of the size and membership of families, and how they spend their money.

For other sources see the Desk Research section of the chapter on Marketing Research.

---

### student activity 15.1 – business response to consumer characteristics

Visit a local food supermarket and investigate

- the range of foods that are available
- promotional material within the store (eg leaflets at the entrance and checkouts)

Identify the different consumer characteristics that are responded to in terms of:

(a)  cultural groups (eg ethnic food)

(b)  different lifestyles (eg convenience foods)

(c)  different tastes (eg brands of drink)

(d)  conscience spending (eg organic vegetables)

Identify any consumer demands which you consider are *missing*.

---

# forecasting and decision making

## the importance of forecasting

*Forecasting is making an estimate of future events or values.* In business terms this can involve forecasting the likely future sales of a particular product. A business has to forecast demand for the next few time periods so that:

- Production Department can set up the machinery and employ the necessary labour
- Research and Development know what products and materials to test in full production
- Purchasing Department can order the necessary raw materials
- Accounts Department can construct a financial budget for the year

## forecasting techniques

Forecasting is normally achieved by examining past sales figures, assessing the present situation (with the help of market research) and then making a future forecast using statistical techniques. *Statistics* involves numerical techniques, including the use of averages, which will be explained in the next section. These techniques also develop the Core Skill of Application of Number.

## averages

Many business situations require the use of *one* value by which to summarise a whole set of data values.  For example:

- What are the average sales per week by area?
- What is the average cost of each product type?
- What are the average earnings on the shop floor, or of a salesperson?
- What is the average stock level of a particular product?

Only by  keeping control over areas such as these does the business increase efficiency and profitability.  Control is only possible when the precise answer to these questions is known.  It would be an easy option to reply "about" or "approximately" and give a rule of thumb answer.  The scientific and statistical approach is to calculate the *average*.  The problem is, however, that there are three types of average - the *arithmetic mean*, the *median* and the *mode* .

Let us take a series of numbers representing, say, the ages of eleven teachers/lecturers in a department:    20, 25, 29, 29, 29, 36, 37, 55, 60, 65, 65.

*The arithmetic mean is the sum of all the figures divided by the number of figures*

The sum of  20, 25, 29, 29, 29, 36, 37, 55, 60, 65, 65  =  450

The arithmetic mean    =    $\dfrac{450}{11}$    =    41.1  years

*The median is the value of the middle figure in a series of figures*

In this case the median is 20, 25, 29, 29, 29, **36**, 37, 55, 60, 65, 65    =    36 years

*The mode is the value that occurs most often in a series*

In this case the most common age is 29 years (3 members of staff), followed closely by 65 years (2 members of staff).  Note that these two ages are very widely dispersed.

## averages in statistics

In general practice and also in statistics it is the *arithmetic mean* which is seen to be the most reliable and the most commonly used average.  We will now examine statistical techniques used for forecasting, and as you will see, calculating averages plays an important role in establishing trends.

## statistical techniques used in forecasting

Forecasts in business are based on information about the way in which trends have established themselves in the past and are exhibiting themselves in the present.  It is then assumed that these trends will continue into the future, given that the economic and industrial conditions remain reasonably stable for the business in question.  If one takes a sales trend, for example,  established in the past, it is possible to predict a sales trend for the future using statistical techniques based on time series analysis.

There are four basic types of trend:

- the long term trend
- cyclical fluctuations superimposed on the long term trend
- seasonal fluctuations superimposed on the long term trend
- irregular fluctuations caused by external events

For example, if a business selling toys in the UK examines the option of  importing teddies from Taiwan, there may be a *long term trend* for the business to grow, *cyclical fluctuations* caused by the business cycle, *seasonal fluctuations* when sales are high before Christmas, and the possibility of *irregular fluctuations* caused by  the imposition of import tariffs.

## use of time series analysis: line graphs

By using time series analysis in line graph form (plotting the dependent variable being examined against the independent variable of time) it is possible to reduce these various distortions by using a number of techniques:

* *moving averages* to show the long term trend
* calculating *seasonal variations* to adjust and smooth out the trend line
* the use of *linear regression straight line graphs* to smooth out irregularities

It must be stressed that the use of these techniques by no means makes the forecasting of a future trend any more *certain;* it merely makes the trend more clear and comprehensible.

## moving averages

*The use of moving averages is the technique of repeatedly calculating a series of different arithmetic mean values for a dependent variable along a time series to produce a trend graph*

A moving average will move forward in time (the independent variable) step by step along the trend line, calculating a new average from the given data at each step, removing in the averaging process data which is literally "out of line" with the trend. Some data will be above the line, some below it; in the averaging process these fluctuations will offset each other to produce a smooth line. The following example shows the sales figures of a company, Arco plc, over 15 years.

| Year | Annual Sales £M | | 5 Year Moving Average £M |
|------|------|------|------|
| 1978 | 10 | | |
| 1979 | 4 | | |
| 1980 | 8 | 64 ÷ 5 = | 12.8 |
| 1981 | 18 | | 17.6 |
| 1982 | 24 | | 20.8 |
| 1983 | 34 | | 21.6 |
| 1984 | 20 | | 23.2 |
| 1985 | 12 | | 26.4 |
| 1986 | 26 | | 26.8 |
| 1987 | 40 | | 26.4 |
| 1988 | 36 | | 30.4 |
| 1989 | 18 | | 34.0 |
| 1990 | 32 | | 34.0 |
| 1991 | 44 | | |
| 1992 | 40 | | |

This chart has been produced as follows:

* the sales figures were plotted on a line graph (see next page)
* a *five yearly* fluctuating cycle was decided upon
* the sales figures for the first *five years* were added and divided by five to find the first of the moving averages: (i.e. $10 + 4 + 8 + 18 + 24 = 64$; $64 \div 5 = 12.8$)
* the *next* arithmetic mean is calculated over the five years 1979 to 1983, i.e. the average *moves* forward a year: $(4 + 8 + 18 + 24 + 34 = 88$; $88 \div 5 = 17.6)$
* the process is repeated for the following years until the data is exhausted
* the moving average line is plotted on the same axes as the annual sales (see next page)

### from moving average to sales forecast line

It is clear from the line graph below that the moving average smooths out the fluctuations, providing an upward moving sales trend line. This line could then be reasonably continued into the future, given that other conditions remained stable, to produce a *forecast of sales* for subsequent years. It is clearly a great deal more reliable than the erratic trend of the annual sales line. On the graph the forecast sales are indicated by the arrowed line.

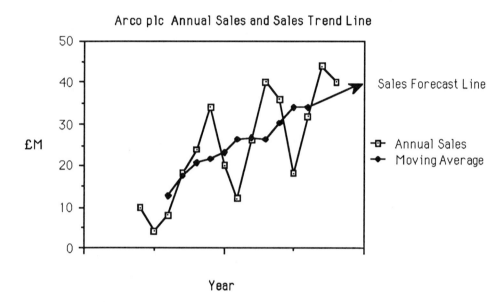

### seasonal adjustments

*Seasonally adjusted figures are used when reporting data on a quarterly or monthly basis when the actual figures are distorted by seasonal factors*

Seasonally adjusted figures are very useful in smoothing out seasonal fluctuations in data relating to past periods. They are useful also in forecasting because the seasonal variation figures worked out can be applied to estimates of future results (to the extended trend line) to produce a more reliable forecast.

### straight line graphs: linear regression

In addition to the moving average, which smooths out cyclical and seasonal fluctuations, it is useful when analysing data to be able to produce a simple straight line which smooths out all fluctuations. This is achieved by the use of linear regression.

The simplest linear regression is the production of a straight line plotted by points whose position is calculated by arithmetic mean averaging of the dependent variable over a time series. This technique is variously known as the three point, or semi-average, or Loveday method. It is essential to use a minimum of three plots, as this will show up errors of calculation should they occur, ie the regression line must pass through all three plots in a straight line.

If we take the sales figures for Arco PLC, seen earlier, it is possible to construct a straight line graph by linear regression technique to illustrate the upward trend.

This is achieved by plotting *three* points whose position is calculated by *arithmetic mean averaging*. The calculations are as follows (note that the £12M sales for 1985 – the middle year – is divided by 2 and £6M included in the 1978-85 average and £6M in the 1985-92 average):

**Arco plc Sales  1978 - 1992**

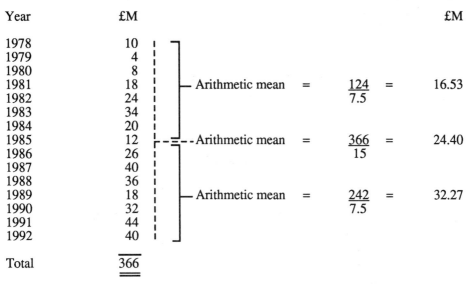

| Year | £M | | | £M |
|------|----|--|--|----|
| 1978 | 10 | | | |
| 1979 | 4 | | | |
| 1980 | 8 | | | |
| 1981 | 18 | Arithmetic mean = | $\dfrac{124}{7.5}$ = | 16.53 |
| 1982 | 24 | | | |
| 1983 | 34 | | | |
| 1984 | 20 | | | |
| 1985 | 12 | Arithmetic mean = | $\dfrac{366}{15}$ = | 24.40 |
| 1986 | 26 | | | |
| 1987 | 40 | | | |
| 1988 | 36 | | | |
| 1989 | 18 | Arithmetic mean = | $\dfrac{242}{7.5}$ = | 32.27 |
| 1990 | 32 | | | |
| 1991 | 44 | | | |
| 1992 | 40 | | | |
| Total | 366 | | | |

The three points are derived as follows, and are plotted on the graph below:
- the lower point is the arithmetic mean of the sales figures from 1978 to 1985*  =   £16.53M
- the middle point is the arithmetic mean of the whole series of sales figures      =   £24.40M
- the upper point is the arithmetic mean of the sales figures from 1985* to 1992  =   £32.27M
* note that the sales figure for 1985 has been halved in these calculations – if there were *no* middle year, this would be unnecessary.

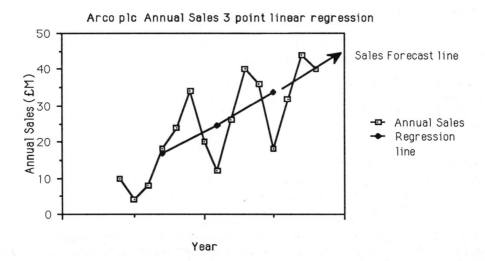

The straight line produced by the three point linear regression clearly shows the upward trend of sales, and could be extended (extrapolated), as in the graph above, to provide a forecast of further sales.

### use of linear regression lines in forecasting
The straight line produced by the three point linear regression clearly shows the upward trend of sales, and could be extended (extrapolated), as in the graph above, to provide a forecast of further sales.

### applications of forecasting

Statistical forecasting techniques are used not only in business, but also by economists in predicting national trends, including:

- economic information – GNP, employment levels, inflation, output
- demographic information on population size, age, sex, regional variations
- social trends – birth rates, health, migration
- consumer spending trends related to households, socio-economic groups

We will look at these forecasts in the student activities and Evidence Collection Exercises.

## index numbers and trend analysis

### index numbers

An index number is a statistic used to reduce a series of data to a common level so that we can make comparisons between items or groups of items over a specific time period.  Indices are used to describe changes in prices, output, income:

- price index numbers measure changes in price
- quantity index numbers measure changes in quantity
- value index numbers measure changes in the value of services, or activities, or goods

The particularly useful feature of index numbers is that they they enable different units of measurement to be compared over a time period, eg share prices, quantity of oil imported, by changing all values to a series of numbers *based on 100*.  The *base period* is the time (normally a year) to which comparisons are related.  Whatever the units involved, the data value at the base period will equal 100.

The formula for working out the index number is:

*Price in year 'x'   multiplied by  100*
    *Price in base year*

In the example below, UK annual output is compared. Look at the effect of the recession inn the early 1990s.

#### example:  GDP at factor cost – base year 1985

| Year | GDP (£bn )  1985 prices | Index |
| --- | --- | --- |
| 1985 | 307.9 | 100.0 |
| 1990 | 359.0 | 116.6 |
| 1991 | 350.2 | 113.8 |
| 1992 | 348.5 | 113.2 |

### index numbers and National Economic Statistics

Indices are commonly used by economists, and feature in the economic statistics mentioned and illustrated above. When dealing with total money values in these statistical tables, you must realise that the trends are affected by inflation.  Always look for a series that carries a statement such as 'at 1985 prices'.  This means that the effect of rising prices *has been removed,* leaving a much more accurate indicator of growth, ie actual output or sales.  National Income statistics – The *Annual Abstract of Statistics* and the *Monthly Digest of Statistics* – are prepared by the Central Statistical Office and published by HMSO.  If they are not available in your school or college library, you should find a copy in your nearest reference library.

**student activity 15.2 – predictions of sales trends**

The following figures represent the daily numbers of compact disc players sold at a local electrical store over the last 15 days:      2,5,10,7,4,9,12,10,6,12,14,11,7,13,18

(a)   Work out a moving average on these figures, using as a base for the average the number of figures which *you* think is appropriate.  Plot the original figures and the moving average figures on a line graph. What general trend do you predict on the basis of these figures?

(b)   Work out a three point linear regression line from the same data and plot it on the graph.  Is this more accurate than the moving average? If not, why not?

**student activity 15.3 – birth statistics**

Examine the births statistics for the UK as set out below (in 000's):

| 1960 | -     | 1970 | 904 | 1980 | 754 | 1990 | 799 |
|------|-------|------|-----|------|-----|------|-----|
| 1    | -     | 1    | 902 | 1    | 731 | 1    | 793 |
| 2    |       | 2    | 834 | 2    | 719 | 2    | 789 |
| 3    | 990   | 3    | 780 | 3    | 721 |      |     |
| 4    | 1,015 | 4    | 737 | 4    | 730 |      |     |
| 5    | 997   | 5    | 698 | 5    | 751 |      |     |
| 6    | 980   | 6    | 676 | 6    | 755 |      |     |
| 7    | 962   | 7    | 657 | 7    | 776 |      |     |
| 8    | 947   | 8    | 687 | 8    | 788 |      |     |
| 9    | 920   | 9    | 735 | 9    | 777 |      |     |

You are to:

(a)   Plot the data on graph paper.

(b)   Calculate and plot a five year moving average of this data series.  Comment on any trend.

(c)   List five organisations that should be monitoring this data and give their reasons for doing so.

**student activity 15.4 – vehicle buying trends**

Obtain a copy of the table showing new registrations of motor vehicles from the Transport section of the Monthly Digest of Statistics.  Examine it and state what evidence you can find of:

(a)   the business cycle (boom and slump)

(b)   seasonality of sales

(c)   lifestyle changes

# chapter summary

❑   Consumer characteristics include culture, lifestyle, taste and conscience spending.

❑   The average can be the mean, median or the mode.   The average used in statistical forecasting is the arithmetic mean.

❑   Methods of trend analysis include moving averages and linear regression.

❑   Using these techniques, future trends – eg sales – can be predicted.

❑   Index numbers can be used for comparing economic, social and business data.

❑   The index number series can be adjusted for inflation.

# EVIDENCE COLLECTION EXERCISE 8

## *Using consumer trends to forecast sales*

| Element 3.2 | *Use consumer trends to forecast sales* |
|---|---|

Suggested Sources:
- Social Trends, Economic Trends, Monthly Digest of Statistics and Annual Abstract of Statistics (all Government publications produced by the Central Statistical Office and published by HMSO).
- Statistical techniques explained in this chapter

## TASK 1

(a) Examine the Gross Domestic Product table (£million at 1985 market prices) set out below to establish trends in the key categories of expenditure by Consumer, Government (Central and Local combined), and Industry (gross domestic fixed capital formation), from 1983 to 1992 inclusive.

(b) Plot these three data sets, plus the total GDP. Why do you think that they change direction in different years?

(c) Explain why stocks decrease when recession approaches.

(d) What effects do changes in the import/export relationship have on UK industry?

---

### National income and expenditure

## 1.2 Gross domestic product: by category of expenditure
continued

| | | General government final consumption | | | | Value of physical | | | | | Statist- | |
| | Con- sumers' expend- iture | Central govern- ment | Local author- ities | Total | Gross domestic fixed capital formation | increase in stocks and work in progress[3] | Total domestic expend- iture | Exports of goods and services | Total final expend- iture | *less* Imports of goods and services | ical discrep- ancy (expend- iture)[4] | Gross domestic product |
|---|---|---|---|---|---|---|---|---|---|---|---|---|
| | CCBH | DJDK | DJDL | DJCZ | DFDM | DHBK | DIEL | DJCV | DJDA | DJCY | GIXS | CAOO |
| 1983 | 206 932 | 45 281 | 27 808 | 73 089 | 53 476 | 1 357 | 334 854 | 90 589 | 425 443 | 87 709 | −1 231 | 336 503 |
| 1984 | 210 959 | 45 741 | 28 051 | 73 792 | 58 034 | 1 084 | 343 869 | 96 525 | 440 394 | 96 394 | 348 | 344 348 |
| 1985 | 218 947 | 45 879 | 27 926 | 73 805 | 60 353 | 821 | 353 926 | 102 208 | 456 134 | 98 866 | − | 357 268 |
| 1986 | 232 996 | 46 684 | 28 422 | 75 106 | 61 813 | 737 | 370 652 | 107 052 | 477 704 | 105 662 | − | 372 042 |
| 1987 | 245 823 | 46 753 | 29 281 | 76 034 | 67 753 | 1 158 | 390 768 | 113 094 | 503 862 | 113 916 | − | 389 946 |
| | | | | | | | | | | | | |
| 1988 | 264 096 | 46 942 | 29 544 | 76 486 | 77 395 | 4 010 | 421 987 | 112 989 | 534 976 | 127 845 | − | 407 131 |
| 1989 | 272 917 | 47 365 | 29 819 | 77 184 | 82 997 | 2 657 | 435 755 | 117 256 | 553 011 | 137 281 | − | 415 730 |
| 1990 | 274 744 | 48 627 | 31 062 | 79 689 | 80 464 | −1 110 | 433 787 | 123 049 | 556 836 | 138 720 | −207 | 417 909 |
| 1991 | 269 083 | 50 229 | 32 053 | 82 282 | 72 529 | −3 418 | 420 476 | 123 265 | 543 741 | 134 436 | −748 | 408 557 |
| 1992 | 269 575 | 49 563 | 32 529 | 82 092 | 72 063 | −1 323 | 422 407 | 125 643 | 548 050 | 141 349 | −685 | 406 016 |

SOURCE: CSO Monthly Digest of Statistics

**TASK 2**

Examine the Consumers' Expenditure 'component categories' data in the table below (from Economic Trends, Table 6). This data is also at 1985 prices. Note that the column headed 'Total' matches the table in Task 1, column 1, headed 'Consumers expenditure'.

(a) Calculate and plot the five year moving average trend lines for Durable Goods and Food, for the period 1971 to 1991 and project these forward by eye to forecast ahead to 1996.

(b) Explain why durable goods represented 7% of total expenditure in 1971, 11% in 1989 but only 9% in 1991, whereas food represented 18% in 1971 but 12% in 1991. Relate this to lifestyle.

(c) Calculate the other growth percentages (1971 to 1991) and explain the huge variations. Identify the factors that affect each category, with particular reference to consumer characteristics.

# 6 Consumers' expenditure - component categories

£ million, 1985 prices

| | Durable goods | Food[1] | Alcoholic drink and tobacco | Clothing and footwear | Energy products | Other goods | Rent, rates and water charges | Other services[1,2] | Total[3] |
|---|---|---|---|---|---|---|---|---|---|
| 1968 | 9 350 | 28 587 | .. | 8 457 | 13 667 | 15 203 | 19 776 | 39 164 | 151 162 |
| 1969 | 8 763 | 28 700 | .. | 8 590 | 14 202 | 15 182 | 20 293 | 39 718 | 152 089 |
| 1970 | 9 491 | 29 107 | .. | 8 962 | 14 498 | 15 376 | 20 792 | 40 767 | 156 531 |
| 1971 | 11 252 | 29 203 | .. | 9 115 | 14 589 | 15 827 | 21 249 | 41 901 | 161 582 |
| 1972 | 13 675 | 29 247 | .. | 9 606 | 15 556 | 17.409 | 21 730 | 44 105 | 171 704 |
| 1973 | 14 421 | 29 629 | .. | 10 043 | 16 303 | 19 021 | 22 344 | 46 504 | 180 843 |
| 1974 | 12 633 | 29 121 | .. | 9 928 | 16 242 | 19 447 | 22 797 | 45 779 | 178 216 |
| 1975 | 12 847 | 29 126 | .. | 10 066 | 15 885 | 18 659 | 23 225 | 45 790 | 177 500 |
| 1976 | 13 481 | 29 436 | .. | 10 136 | 16 237 | 18 611 | 23 676 | 44 736 | 178 279 |
| 1977 | 12 538 | 29 175 | .. | 10 281 | 16 520 | 18 696 | 24 141 | 44 732 | 177 483 |
| 1978 | 14 337 | 29 714 | 24 312 | 11 247 | 16 912 | 19 992 | 24 586 | 47 691 | 187 510 |
| 1979 | 16 169 | 30 380 | 25 008 | 12 045 | 17 489 | 20 523 | 25 057 | 49 940 | 195 664 |
| 1980 | 15 417 | 30 419 | 24 087 | 11 903 | 17 259 | 20 036 | 25 432 | 52 405 | 195 825 |
| 1981 | 15 707 | 30 217 | 22 958 | 11 788 | 17 319 | 20 128 | 25 728 | 53 164 | 196 011 |
| 1982 | 16 504 | 30 299 | 22 002 | 12 227 | 17 410 | 20 586 | 26 134 | 53 476 | 197 980 |
| 1983 | 19 448 | 30 801 | 22 515 | 13 071 | 17 420 | 21 116 | 26 707 | 55 854 | 206 932 |
| 1984 | 19 261 | 30 276 | 22 564 | 13 767 | 17 755 | 21 988 | 27 033 | 58 315 | 210 959 |
| 1985 | 20 166 | 30 657 | 22 657 | 14 912 | 18 578 | 23 054 | 27 382 | 61 541 | 218 947 |
| 1986 | 22 100 | 31 541 | 22 512 | 16 220 | 19 299 | 25 068 | 27 771 | 68 485 | 232 996 |
| 1987 | 24 079 | 32 324 | 22 787 | 16 933 | 19 767 | 26 867 | 28 155 | 74 911 | 245 823 |
| 1988 | 27 488 | 33 125 | 23 181 | 17 621 | 20 352 | 29 325 | 28 533 | 84 471 | 264 096 |
| 1989 | 28 952 | 33 732 | 23 157 | 17 566 | 20 357 | 31 161 | 28 928 | 89 064 | 272 917 |
| 1990 | 27 564 | 33 337 | 23 073 | 17 616 | 20 616 | 31 211 | 29 342 | 91 985 | 274 744 |
| 1991 | 25 208 | 33 409 | 22 396 | 17 305 | 21 331 | 30 390 | 29 760 | 89 234 | 269 033 |

1 Before 1952 estimates for catering are included under Food; thereafter they are included under Other services.
2 Including the adjustments for international travel, etc. and final expenditure by private non-profit-making bodies.
3 For the years before 1983, totals may not equal the sum because of the method used in rebasing to 1985 prices.

SOURCE: CSO Economic Trends 1993

**TASK 3**

You work for a clothing firm in the UK, producing quality goods for socio-economic groups A and B (see page 154). Your own sales figures, since 1985, at 1985 prices, have been as follows:

| Year | Sales (£M) |
|---|---|
| 1985 | 1.30 |
| 1986 | 1.64 |
| 1987 | 1.72 |
| 1988 | 1.94 |
| 1989 | 2.00 |
| 1990 | 2.15 |
| 1991 | 2.29 |
| 1992 | 2.41 |

(a) Graph the clothing and footwear expenditure from the previous table and the sales figures above, and comment on the trends.

(b) Offer possible explanations why the firm's sales have not followed the national trend, ie consider the consumer characteristics.

(c) Calculate and draw a linear regression line and extend (extrapolate) this to 1997. Read off the likely sales values.

# 16 Product

## introduction

This chapter sets out to explain the importance of products and markets to an organisation. There must be a product or service sold in order to generate income. There must be a market for that product or service in order to provide that income. This chapter looks at both *product policy* and *market policy* as separate objectives, but it also emphasises the ways in which they are necessarily dependent on one another.

In this chapter we examine the following areas:
* the importance of product policy, product mix and product themes
* the concept of the product life cycle and recycling
* the special considerations of marketing a service
* the importance of market policy and strategy
* the product/market link

## product policy

### a product policy
The product policy of an organisation sets out the range of products – the product mix – that it will offer to its market(s). Its resources will be used to produce a type (or types) of product, and decisions will be made as to the timing and volume of that production. The range itself will change over a period of time, because markets for products and services are dynamic (constantly changing). An organisation is always researching the next step – tomorrow's needs!

### product themes
A successful way of combining a product mix is the development of product themes. This has become increasingly popular in the leisure industry, where theme parks such as 'The American

Adventure' present all of their entertainment under a single co-ordinated style. The Danish firm 'Lego' tries to introduce a new product theme each year to ensure continued sales to its regular customers. Such ideas are good for business and keep customer interest alive.

## complementary or competitive products
The product planners also have other factors to consider: some products are complementary to one another; others are competitive:

*Complementary products* sell together. The manufacturer of town clothes may also make leisurewear. Retailers stocking golf clubs would also hold golf gloves, shoes, balls and trolleys. Customers for one product might be persuaded to buy some of the other items. In fact, the customer would *expect* this range and may use only the manufacturer or shop that provides it.

*Competitive products,* as the name suggests, compete with each other for the buyers' attention. Competitive products may be produced by the same manufacturer. Why? There are several reasons: consumers have different requirements, so a range of soap powders or dog foods is at attempt to catch as many buyers as possible. For example the dogfoods Pal and Pedigree Chum are both made by Pedigree Petfoods Limited. If a purchaser of Pal did not buy Pedigree Chum, at least the sale went to Pedigree Petfoods Limited.

## updating the product range
An organisation will constantly prune and update its product range/mix. The extent of the mix is another important issue. If there are too *few* products, there is the danger that the obsolescence of one will seriously harm total sales. If there are too *many* products, the range becomes difficult to organise and will fragment production too much. Whatever the decision however, *never* be caught with just one product in just one market. The failure of one product or market would mean the failure of the organisation.

The product range of a firm is often limited by its area of expertise and by the limits imposed by its size and resources. Most firms adapt, the better ones by anticipating change, the others by reacting to it. Those that fail to adapt will fail to survive.

# product life cycle

*"In the long term we are all dead".* (J M Keynes)

Marketing people have accepted a slight variation of this principle when referring to each and every product or service ever placed before the consumer, i.e. "In the long term all of our existing products/services are dead". More concisely, "Nothing lasts for ever". An example of this is the replacement of the Ford Cortina (a highly successful car) by the Ford Sierra, and the replacement of the Sierra by the Ford Mondeo. Just as each of us humans is conceived, is born, grows, matures and dies, so in the commercial marketplace products and services are created, launched and withdrawn, in a process known as the *product life cycle*. The graph on the next page shows the product life cycle as a series of six stages. Its plots the money value of sales (the upper line) and the profit on those sales (the lower line) against the six stages, which we will explain in turn.

## Stage 1: development
No product or service is dreamed up on the Monday and produced and sold on the Tuesday. Each new product idea has to be researched, designed and tested. This may take a few weeks or, in the case of hi-tech products, many months or years. All of this requires funding, so it is important to calculate the extent of such costs when making the decision to develop a product. Costs include:

- *market research*, to establish whether the intended customers like the idea in this form
- *technical research,* to bring the product from the drawing board, through Research and Development, to test market condition

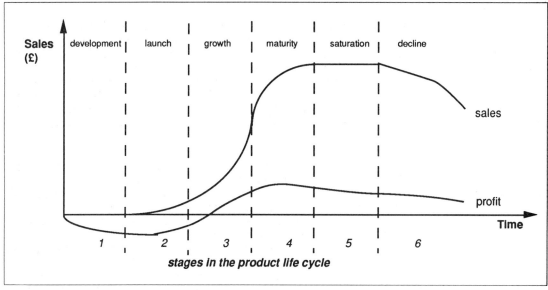

Fig. 16.1  the product life cycle

- *test market* (a limited trial run), where many aspects of the new product are tried out, but in particular the acceptability of the product itself and the price
- *executive time,* to co-ordinate the research work and make decisions on 'go ahead' or 'discontinue'

Note that the 'development' stage shows on the graph as a *loss* on the 'profits' line; this stresses the importance of a successful launch to recoup the development expenses.

### Stage 2:  the launch, or introduction

The go-ahead has been given and the new product is introduced to the market place.  This is a nerve-testing time in business.  The failure rate of new products is remarkably high, despite all of the research and testing undertaken.  Test markets often do well because consumers are curious people.  They will try anything once.  The real test for the new product is "will they buy it again, and again, and again?"

The diagram shows a slow sales uptake and an even deeper trough in the 'profits' curve – why? – think what costs a product launch entails:

- the product must be made available both to the trade and to the public;  the costs of distribution are high
- no-one is aware of the new product, so it must be promoted and sold to the trade and the public; promotional costs are high and sales teams are expensive

The timing of the product launch needs careful thought.  It also needs nerve if uptake is slower than expected, but herein lies the real problem.  Just *how* long can it be given?  How much more money can be risked to recoup the development costs?  There are *no* easy answers here.

### Stage 3:  growth

The launch is successful, consumers take to the product and sales take off.  An exciting time for the company, especially as the 'profits' line really does mean profits.  Depending upon the uniqueness and originality of the new product, profitability should be strong.  Here the management decisions relate to exclusivity or saturation.  Is it a mass market product aimed at all consumers, or is it to retain a certain exclusivity?  Will it be sold on a regional rather than national or international basis? Vigorous promotion and/or sales force activity will take the product into all the required outlets and sales to the final consumer will be influenced by the 'newness' factor.

### Stage 4: maturity

Inevitably, the fast rising sales curve will begin to level off as the new product excitement is lost and the competition reacts to your success. Sales continue to rise but new customers are harder to find. It is here also that the profits curve reaches its peak. Why should this be so if sales are still rising? The additional costs of promotion and sales force effort in keeping the sales curve rising may be large, especially in warding off your competitors' attack. Their own new or revamped products will be attracting attention and perhaps even taking your customers away. It may even be time to review your own 'new' product with a view to redesign, repositioning, and so on. Remember, nothing lasts for ever, and change is always influencing your market position. See 'Revamping' on page 173.

### Stage 5: saturation

This stage is more of a plateau than a curve, and its length varies from six months to six or sixty years. Once a product reaches this stage it is in the interests of the company to keep it there as long as profitably possible. Once distribution has been (expensively) achieved, the company will battle to maintain customer loyalty. The gimmick type product may last a few months, e.g. the hula hoop, the skate board, as a summer craze. Many small manufacturers of the skate board arrived on the scene too late, investing in production facilities as the demand died. Business can be brutal to the unplanned. Certain products seem to go on for ever, eg the Mars bar, although most have subtle variations of product or appearance to keep the customers interested, eg Coca Cola and Persil. Throughout this stage it is essential to watch the profitability level. Probably it will be in decline but it still represents the company's principal source of the revenue needed for new product development and the long-term suvival of the company. Products at this stage are often referred to as 'cash cows', being milked for the benefit of the company. See the next page for a full explanation of this term.

### Stage 6: decline

Inevitably the product or service will reach the end of its commercial usefulness. Sales will fall as newer, technically improved or more fashionable ideas appear in the market place. The decision to 'drop' a product is an extremely difficult one. Managements often argue, quite persuasively, for its retention. Are the newer products in the range established yet? Will important customers be upset by its removal from the range? Is the drop in sales purely temporary? Even emotive issues get into the argument, like "it was our first ever product". Usually, however, the decision to drop the product has to be made, for sound reasons: it makes the business appear out of date; another product is planned to take its place; it is not economical to produce in small production runs.

## the product portfolio

The product life cycle concept offers organisations a blueprint for the present and for the future. It is not enough for firms to say "we must have a range of products to offer the market(s)". They must have both a range of products *and* a range of time scales for product development, i.e. something in most of the stages of the product life cycle. This is known as the *product portfolio*, shown below.

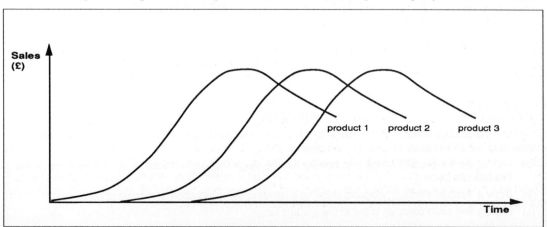

In the diagram on the previous page you will see how the product life cycles for individual products *overlap* in terms of time scale, providing the business with a steady source of income and profit.

## product portfolio – the Boston matrix

The Boston matrix, illustrated below, was devised in the USA by the Boston Consultancy Group, and is a useful way of looking at products in a product portfolio in respect of

- the *market share* of the product – how well is it selling in comparison with its competitors?
- the *market growth* of the product – how rapidly is the market for the product growing?

The consultancy group pointed out that the *faster* a market is growing, the *more cash* will be needed for products introduced in that market, the costs being the product development, heavy advertising and promotion necessary for a new product. The *ideal* position is therefore for a cycle to be set up whereby certain products in the portfolio are able to generate cash so that others can be developed and produce cash in the future.  The Boston Consultancy Group identified four types of product:

| | |
|---|---|
| *cash cows* | Products which have been on the market for a while, enjoying a high market share in a low growth market;  they are profitable, producing the cash which enables other products to be developed. |
| *stars* | Products which have a high market share in a high growth market;  they are profitable but need plenty of cash for development and promotion, but will hopefully become the 'cash cows' of the future. |
| *question marks* | Products with a low market share in a fast growing market;  they need much cash to increase market share, but their future may be in doubt, hence the name 'question marks';  they may be withdrawn if they do not increase market share and become 'stars'. |
| *dogs* | Products with low market share in  low growth markets are wasting time and resources, and are normally quickly withdrawn. |

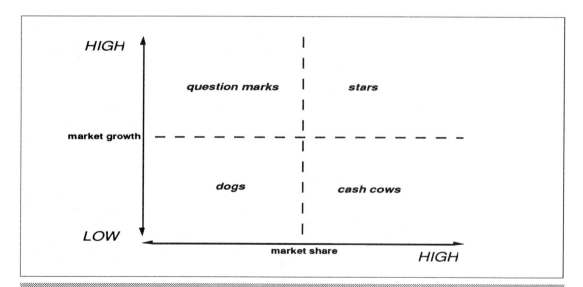

## student activity 16.1 – the product life cycle

Visit a local garage which sells a range of cars from one manufacturer. If possible, obtain from the manufacturer annual sales figures for individual models.

(a) Investigate the product range and identify the the stage that each model of car has reached in the Product Life Cycle.

(b) Draw a 'Product Portfolio' diagram showing a representative selection of models of cars.

(c) Identify any 'cash cows' or 'stars' in the product range.

## extension policies – revamping

It is often useful to try to stimulate the progress of a product during its own lifetime. This is called *extension policy* or *revamping* (or *recycling*). It can lead to the useful extension of the product's life. Set out below are two examples of revamping:

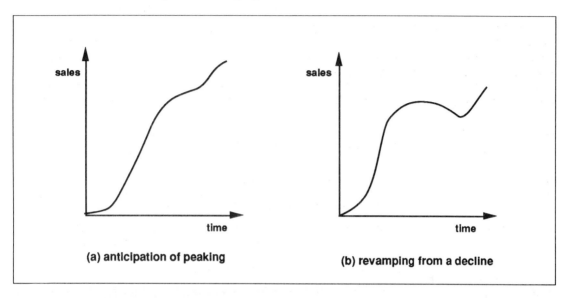

**(a) anticipation of peaking**       **(b) revamping from a decline**

Revamping has the advantage of building on an established product (name). The exercise carries with it less risk than would be taken if a brand new product was launched, but it is unlikely that a massive increase in sales and profits will occur. The success of revamping depends upon changes which can be made to the product or whether new market segments can be found. The recession of the early 1990s has made the successful launch of new products *less* likely, so revamping gained in popularity, e.g. 'new' this and 'repackaged' that.

### Diagram (a) – anticipation of peaking
This shows the product being given an extra boost as soon as growth appears to be levelling off. This has the advantage of retaining the early momentum of the product, and sometimes minor changes in quality or approach can be very significant. This stage is more likely to be *planned* as the preferred alternative to a new product.

### Diagram (b) – revamping from a decline
This shows the product's sales already in decline and so the probability of success is less. Revamping is often undertaken because something has gone wrong with the product development of a *replacement* product. It could be that the intended new product has failed at the test market or launch phase so that the expected growth and good profitability has not materialised. As a result, it becomes necessary to shore up the existing products because, amongst other things, of their important 'contribution' to fixed costs, until another *successful* addition can be made to the product 'mix'.

### student activity 16.2 – revamping
Examine the range of cars investigated in Activity 16.1:
(a) Identify examples of revamping of models which have been on the market for some years.
(b) State whether the revamping has been in anticipation of peaking, or from a decline.
(c) Identify any further models which you consider should be revamped. State your reasons.

# the marketing of services

When an organisation markets a service as opposed to a product, the functions of marketing are essentially the same, but there are some additional difficulties:    intangibility, heterogeneity, distribution and perishability.   We will explain each of these in turn.

### intangibility
Intangibility means something that cannot be touched.  A service cannot be picked up, examined or tried out before it is purchased.  Therefore, the reputation of the provider is very important.  It is possible to talk to earlier recipients of the service, i.e. a holiday, a bank loan, a visit to a museum, but there will always be an element of risk on the part of the purchaser.  This makes the marketing task of the seller that much more difficult.  This problem is intensified when we consider heterogeneity

### heterogeneity
Heterogeneity means being involved with items which cannot easily be compared.   In a manufacturing firm it can be reasonably assumed that each product coming off a production line will be the same as the last item, or last month's product.  To the buyer, the next Mars bar must surely be the same as the previous Mars bar.  With a service, however, no such guarantee can exist.  A visit to a museum may take place on a busy day or a hot day and be less enjoyable than it would be on a quiet or pleasantly cool day.  A show on a Monday may lack the atmosphere of a Saturday  evening. In other words, the 'same' service may not be the same at all.   Quality control and customer satisfaction cannot be guaranteed,  and there will be disappointments.

### distribution
*Distribution* (or *inseparability*) problems occur because the customer is required to travel to the service provider in many cases, eg the holiday hotel in Rhodes is in Rhodes, the NEC is in Birmingham, the Louvre is in Paris.  The customer must be persuaded to come to the seller.  Product manufacturers can make their products available as widely as they wish.  Obviously, some service providers can travel to the home of the buyer, e.g. the plumber, the dressmaker, but these examples are not the norm.  Note, however, how the travel and tourism industry works hard to make its products available for purchase, eg through travel agents and Teletext lists on the TV in the customer's own home.

### perishability
Consumer durables, such as TVs,  have a long shelf life.  If not sold today, they can be sold tomorrow.   Some food products do have a fairly limited life, but most services are instantly perishable.  If the show starts or the train leaves and a seat is empty, that sale is lost *for ever*.  The cost of putting on the service will remain the same, whether the theatre or the train is half full or full, but the revenue from that empty seat on that day is lost.  Note in this situation how last minute bargain prices become available.  Half price for the seat is better than no money at all.

# market policy and market strategy

### market policy
What is market policy?

*market policy decides the types of customers to whom you are selling, the types of outlets through which you are selling, and the various market segments you have identified and targeted*

Market policy is, in fact, about *market segmentation,* a subject covered in the last chapter. Whatever products the organisation chooses to produce and sell, no product is likely to appeal to all of industry, or all of the public.  Specific products will be designed for specific market segments.

## market strategies

There are therefore different *strategies* for approaching the different market segments.   If you are launching a product, do you aim at one segment, or do you aim at all of them? The choice will depend on the *size* of the business promoting its product(s).  A large concern can afford to promote a wide range of products to different segments;   many small businesses, on the other hand, have successfully exploited a gap in the market by what is known as *niche marketing* of a single product ('niche' means 'gap').   The traditional classification of strategies is:

*undifferentiated marketing*  This type of marketing (also known as mass marketing) is where a product is launched at *all* sectors. This strategy can be expensive and wasteful, but can be successful where the product suits all markets, eg Coca Cola, the Mars Bar

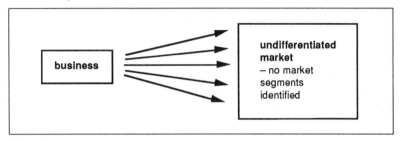

*concentrated marketing*  This is highly defined marketing, whereby a product is launched at a *specific* market segment, for example National Savings Childrens Bonds, 'singles' holidays;  this technique is useful for small businesses which rely on niche marketing (see above).  It should be noted that niche marketing has its dangers.  The problems arise when the business wants to diversify or expand: opportunities may not exist in the immediate business area, or may be blocked by the larger companies. The small firm is then left with no obvious escape routes and a market that may be dying.

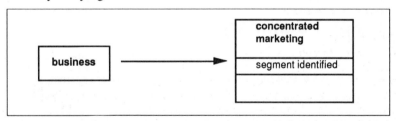

*differentiated marketing*  This form of market strategy promotes a range of different products, each designed specifically for a different market segment. It is costly in terms of promotion and production expenses, but it can be highly effective.   Examples include different types of bank account, and different types of car (compare the small family run-about with the four-wheel drive off-road vehicle.

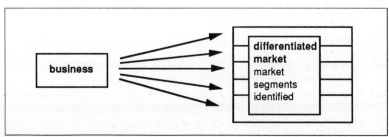

### conclusion – products for markets

The realisation by the producers of products or services that market segments exist means that the behavioural patterns and the needs of each group must be carefully investigated. Marketing is therefore concerned in creating an 'image' for the product or service which will appeal to one (or hopefully more) of the segments in the market for that particular type of product or service. The image will be accepted by the marketplace and will be extremely difficult to change, except over a longer period of time. To have products in different market segments is both feasible and usually desirable.

---

### student activity 16.3– marketing strategy

How would you extend the product portfolio for:

(a)   a manufacturer of men's town shoes

(b)   a manufacturer of traditional dining room tables and chairs

(c)   the management of a school which has a fully equipped sports hall

(d)   a cricket bat manufacturer

(e)   a coach company which services local schools

### student activity 16.4 – niche marketing

(a)   Make a list of businesses which satisfy a *niche* market.

(b)   What potential pitfalls do you see in this form of marketing, and how would you avoid those dangers?

---

# chapter summary

❏   An organisation must have a *range* of products or services.

❏   These products may be competitive or complimentary.

❏   No product or service lasts for ever.  The product life cycle traces a product through the six stages of development, launch, growth, maturity, saturation and decline.

❏   An organisation must have a *planned product portfolio,* a range of products which 'peak' at different times, ensuring a steady flow of income and profit.

❏   An organisation can use extension policies which involve revamping – putting new life into established products.

❏   The marketing of services brings particular problems: intangibility, heterogeneity, distribution and perishability.

❏   *Market policy* involves decisions based on market segmentation.

❏   Marketing strategies include undifferentiated marketing, concentrated marketing, and differentiated marketing.

# 17 Pricing

## introduction

*A price is the amount of money, or other consideration, that is agreed between a buyer and a seller, which enables the exchange of a product or service to take place.*

In this chapter we examine:
* the general factors which determine price
* the long-term objectives which determine price
* the short-term objectives which determine price
* break-even pricing decisions

## factors which determine price

The prices that an organisation charges are partly determined by the organisation itself and partly by outside influences. The factors, in general terms, are as follows:
* the state of the economy, both nationally and locally
* the demand for the product (see Chapter 9 which explains the concept of elasticity in relation to supply and demand)
* the costs that are incurred in making or purchasing and presenting the goods
* the competition that exists
* the product life cycle – is the product new and exciting and on its way in, or is it in decline?
* the environment – are there:
  - government rules and regulations
  - legal controls on price fixing
  - pollution prevention needs
  - packaging and waste disposal considerations
* the organisation's own objectives

# long-term pricing objectives

### the need to make a profit – cost plus and contribution pricing

As with overall Marketing Plan considerations (see Chapters 13 and 48), there are both long-term and short-term possibilities in pricing policy. In the *long-term,* the pricing structure must generate profits (or, in non-profit making organisations, revenue must cover costs and re-investment needs). Pricing *to cover costs* can therefore be:

- *cost plus*, ie the unit cost per item plus a profit margin – this works well in a small business which may only have one product or service to sell

- *contribution pricing*, ie analysing the different products in a product portfolio and allocating them with an appropriate share of the total costs of the business, so that the sales of the item will cover the variable costs of the product and *contribute* to the fixed costs – this works well in a larger business which has a variety of products

If you are not familiar with the terms "unit cost", "variable costs' and "fixed costs", they are covered in detail later in this chapter.

### long-term objectives

Long-term objectives will depend upon how the organisation wishes to position itself in the market place, or how it wishes to establish itself financially. Here are some examples:

- a certain return on total assets or investment (an accounting viewpoint, ie not too *low* a price)
- a price which will permanently discourage other organisations from entering the market (ie a *low* price)
- a price which will position the company at the quality end of the market (a *high* premium price)
- a stable price over long periods, to allow industrial and commercial customers to budget accurately; such stability will enable a business to retain its customers
- a price which will make the product a market leader and gain maximum sales (usually a *low* price)
- a price which will earn sufficient revenue to make the development of new products possible (*not* a *low* price)

All of these are long-term objectives. It is extremely difficult for an organisation to move from one long-term pricing policy to another. It is possible, however, for a single organisation to have a range of complementary products, in competition with each other, achieving different long-term objectives.

# short-term pricing objectives

In the *short-term* pricing can be used as a tactical weapon, as can promotional and selling activities. It must be remembered, however, that price represents revenue and there must always be sufficient funds flowing in to maintain a profitable organisation. Examples of short-term pricing are numerous:

### skimming/creaming the market

Entering the market at a high price, before competition exists, to regain development costs as soon as possible. As the competition arrives, so the price comes down.

### expansion or experience pricing

As demand increases to give economies of scale in production, the price is lowered in stages. It is possible for a firm to lower prices in anticipation of the increased demand.

### fraction below competition

This involves the constant adjustment of price in order to undercut the competitors. It is difficult to maintain and is sometimes irritating to customers. It is useful for retailers, however.

### penetration pricing

A low price is set to attempt to get into a market that is already established. Once market share has been taken, the initial low price may be increased.

### destroy the competition pricing

A concerted effort to price so low that the competition will be forced out. This is only possible if you are genuinely the lowest cost producer, or the competition is known to have cash flow problems.

### promotional pricing

This involves making 'special offers' to attract the attention of a wider market. It is important to take care to stay within the law regarding price reductions.

### loss leaders

A 'loss leader' involves offering a popular product at *below* cost price to attract attention, usually to get customers into a store. It is also used in, for example, photocopying – charging a very low rental for the photocopier but making a profit on the paper supplied and the machine's use. Again, beware the law. The loss leader must *not* be coupled to higher-than-average prices for the other products.

### psychological pricing

The psychologist investigates consumer/customer motivation. He wishes to find out how the price affects their perception of the product or service. We can all understand that setting a price too high may put the item out of the buyer's reach. What we may miss is that a higher price may result in the customer perceiving the product to be of a higher quality. Some buyers like to boast as to how *much* they paid. There are numerous examples of items failing in the market place, then being repackaged, renamed and relaunched at a higher price and succeeding. This brings us to the opposite factor, ie that we may price too low and risk the reaction "it can't be any good at that price!". Marketing must learn that keeping the price low is not necessarily the most desirable policy.

Another aspect of psychology in pricing is the effect of the appearance of the price. We are all used to seeing £0.99, £9.95, £99.95 etc. So why are they still used? Because they work! The eye is caught by the first figure(s). In the case of the above, these three are particularly special because they indicate a price level below a major price step up, ie under £1, under £10, under £100.

---

**student activity 17.1 –pricing policy**

Visit your local shopping centre and investigate a variety of shops including low cost and up-market

- clothing shops
- food shops
- electrical stores

Identify certain products found in a range of shops and list examples of

(a)   skimming pricing

(b)   penetration pricing

(c)   promotional pricing

(d)   fraction below competition pricing

Investigate in detail an up-market shop and a low cost clothing shop and

(e)   compare prices *and* qualities of comparable items

(f)   state why the more expensive shop is able to continue in business

# break-even pricing decisions

The decision as to what price to charge for a new product requires the marketing and accounting sections to liaise together to ensure long term profitability, whilst still taking advantage of market situations.   Once a price has been suggested, the organisation needs to know at what level of sales profitability will be achieved, ie the *break-even point*.  This figure is reached by means of a break-even calculation.

*Break-even is the point at which neither a profit nor a loss is made.*

An essential part of the break-even calculation is the estimation of the costs of producing an item. Costs may be:
- *fixed costs,* which are not affected (in the short-term at least) by the number of items produced; these are known as the overheads of the business, they include items such as rent, rates, advertising and power bills – all items which have to be paid, even if production ceases
- *variable costs,* which are affected by the number of items produced – these include the costs of raw materials and direct labour (labour used in the production process)

The case study set out below shows how a business manufacturing soft toys carries out the break-even calculation.

## Situation

A business manufactures soft toys, and is able to sell all that can be produced.  The variable costs (materials and direct labour) for producing each toy are £10 and the selling price is £20 each.  The fixed costs of running the business are £5,000 *per month.*  How many toys need to be produced and sold each month for the business to break-even?

## Solution

This problem can be solved by calculation, by constructing a table, or by means of a graph.

### ❏ calculation

| | |
|---|---|
| Selling price per unit | £20 |
| Less variable costs per unit | £10 |
| *Contribution* per unit | £10 |

Each toy sold gives a *contribution* (selling price, less variable costs) of £10.   This contributes towards the fixed costs and, in order to break-even, the business must have sufficient £10 'lots' to meet the fixed costs.  Thus, with fixed costs of £5,000 per month, this business must sell £5,000 ÷ £10 = 500 toys each month.  The break-even formula is:

$$\frac{Total\ fixed\ costs\ (£)}{Contribution\ per\ unit\ (£)} = Break\text{-}even\ point\ (number\ of\ units)$$

### ❏ table

| Units of production | Variable costs | Fixed cost | Total cost | Revenue | Profit/(loss) |
|---|---|---|---|---|---|
| | £ | £ | £ | £ | £ |
| 100 | 1,000 | 5,000 | 6,000 | 2,000 | (4,000) |
| 200 | 2,000 | 5,000 | 7,000 | 4,000 | (3,000) |
| 300 | 3,000 | 5,000 | 8,000 | 6,000 | (2 000) |
| 400 | 4,000 | 5,000 | 9,000 | 8,000 | (1,000) |
| 500 | 5,000 | 5,000 | 10,000 | 10,000 | nil |
| 600 | 6,000 | 5,000 | 11,000 | 12,000 | 1,000 |
| 700 | 7,000 | 5,000 | 12,000 | 14,000 | 2,000 |

## ❑ graph

A graphical presentation uses money amounts as the common denominator between fixed costs, variable costs, and sales revenue. The graph appears as follows

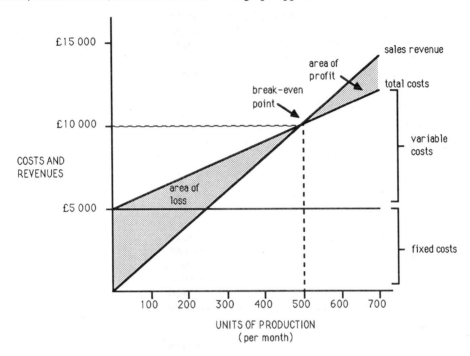

Note:
- With a break-even graph, it is usual for the vertical axis (the 'y' axis) to show money amounts; the horizontal axis ('x') shows units of production/sales.
- The fixed costs are unchanged at all levels of production, in this case they are £5,000.
- The variable costs commence, on the 'y' axis, *from the fixed costs amount,* not from 'zero'. This is because the cost of producing zero units is the fixed cost.
- The fixed costs *and* the variable costs form a *total costs line.*
- The point at which the total costs and sales revenue lines cross is the break-even point.
- Profit (or loss) for any given level of production may be found by measuring the distance between the sales revenue line and the total costs line. In the example given, profit at 650 units is £1,500, and profit at 700 units is £2,000.

## limitations of break-even analysis

The limitations of a break-even graph and break-even calculations can be summarised as follows:
- All costs and revenues are expressed on the graph in terms of straight lines. However, this may be misleading. Selling prices may vary if different quantities are sold; in a similar way, variable costs alter at different levels as a business takes advantage of lower prices to be gained from bulk buying, and/or more efficient production methods. As a result the lines will *not* always be straight.
- Fixed costs do not remain fixed at all levels of production: for example, a decision to double production is likely to increase the fixed costs.
- The profit or loss shown by the graph or calculations is probably only true for figures close to current production levels – the further away from current figures, the less accurate will be the projection of profit or loss shown.

## student activity 17.2 – Cuddly Toys Ltd: break-even calculations

Cuddly Toys Ltd. manufactures a popular children's teddy bear.  At present production is limited by the capacity of the factory to 50 bears each week.  The following information is available:

Wholesale price per teddy bear   £20

Raw materials per teddy bear   £4

Direct labour per teddy bear   £5

Weekly expenses:

- factory rent and rates   £100
- fuel and power   £20
- other costs   £34

(a)   You are to find the weekly break-even point
- by the graphical method
- check your answer by calculation

(b)   What would be your profit if you produced
- 20 toys a week?
- 50 toys a week?

(c)   Would you consider this calculation completely  reliable?  If not, why not?

(d   If you were introducing the teddies onto the market for the first time, what pricing strategies might you adopt, and why?

# chapter summary

❑   The prices that an organisation charges are determined by a combination of internal and external factors.

❑   Long-term pricing policy aims to keep the organisation profitable, or aims to achieve some other aim such as break-even or maximisation of revenue (as in the case of charities).

❑   Short-term pricing policies are usually tactical, and combine with promotional and selling activities to create interest and to influence potential purchasers.

❑   Break-even analysis can be carried out in respect of any given product or service.  It will show at what level of production money received from sales will equal and then exceed total costs.  Break-even analysis does have its limitations, and businesses should be aware of them.

# 18 Promotion and place

## introduction

Promotion – the third of the four "Ps" in the marketing mix – is the art of communicating the benefits of the product or service to the selected market segments of prospective customers. It aims to create awareness and stimulate interest.

In this chapter we examine the concept of *corporate image*: this is *the perception of the organisation in the eyes of the public*. The work of the promotional team of any organisation is to achieve the desired image, by the coordinated use of some or all of the following techniques:

• advertising planning and advertising control

• branding, packing/packaging

• publicity and public relations

• sales promotions

• merchandising

• selling and after-sales service

We conclude by looking at distribution – "place" – the final of the four "Ps" in the marketing mix.

## advertising

### what is advertising?

Advertising is defined by the Institute of the Practitioners in Advertising (the IPA) as

*The most persuasive possible selling message to the right prospects (markets) for the product or service at the lowest possible cost.*

Advertising has its critics and its supporters. It detractors would say that it is expensive and pushes up the price of the product, whereas its supporters claim that it increases demand, stimulates competition and lowers prices. Both points of view can be true.

### the ethics and control of advertising

There are many social criticisms associated with advertising, the main ones relating to the creation of wants in families of low incomes (in particular the offers of loans on 'easy' terms) and the encouragement of 'unnecessary' production and the wastage of finite raw materials. The *ethics* of marketing are covered in Chapter 13 (page 137).

*Control* of advertising is enforced by:

- the law – eg the Trade Descriptions Act states that goods for sale must be as described
- the Trading Standards (or Consumer Protection) Departments which enforce the Trade Descriptions Act
- the Advertising Standards Authority (ASA)
- the British Code of Advertising Practice – a voluntary agreement by advertisers supervised by the Advertising Standards Authority

# the advertising campaign

The consecutive stages in the campaign set out in numbered sections below are in a *recommended* order. Some organisations may adopt a different procedure. It should be obvious, however, that certain decisions must precede others. The campaign described is carried out by an advertising agency for a large organisation. A small business may not use an agency because of the expense, but nevertheless the *principles* described are still relevant for the smaller business.

### 1. identify the right markets

The advertiser *must* be aware which markets, or market segments, are being targeted. This is a straight-forward market segmentation exercise. With *consumer* goods, the choice might be age, sex, socio-economic grouping, occupation, race, religion, or region. With *industrial* goods, the choice might be the channel of distribution used, type of industry, the region, public or private sector.

### 2. how are you going to put the message across?

How would you best attract and influence the chosen target group(s) given the type of product or service? The following are typical of the questions that may well be asked:

*Is the cover to be local, regional or national?*  *Does the overall cost rule out any medium?*

*Which social group(s) does the medium reach?*  *How often should be message be put over?*

Many of these questions immediately suggest a particular medium such as TV or a newspaper. Most certainly, an agency's media executive would be fully aware of the above, and how they link with the different types of media set out in the next section.

### 3. identify the right media

The lists set out in boxes below have been drawn up in *categories* in order to help answer the questions asked above

| Television | National press | Leaflets – |
|---|---|---|
| Radio | Local press | • street handouts |
| Cinema | Advertising 'Free' papers | • door to door delivery |
| Video | Specialised magazines | • through the mail |
|  | General magazines | • inserted in other material |
|  | Trade journals |  |

In addition, the following media are fruitful areas of advertising: *direct reply* advertisements in the press with 'cut out' coupons; *catalogues* issued by manufacturers and retailers; *transport related* advertising – posters and hoardings, adverts on trains, buses, vans, cars; *directories* - Yellow Pages and Thompsons locally, trade directories and business directories, eg Kompass, nationally; *sponsorship* - of an individual, of a team, or of an event; *giveaways* - executive toys to business customers, diaries, calendars, carrier bags with retail purchases, pens, hats, T shirts to the general public; *exhibitions* - a stand at a relevant show.

### advertising cost
The key source of price information is BRAD, the 'British Rate and Data' publication which categorises all the media and the costs of usage. The directory is expensive, but your tutor may be able to obtain a copy discarded by an advertising agency (they replace them regularly).

### 4. create the right message - stress the benefits!
The 'right' message is one that appeals to the market segment identified, and suits the type of media chosen. Advertisers in particular, and the marketing team in general, are always searching for a USP – a Unique Selling Point or Proposition. Many messages work so well that they become part of the language, for example, *"I bet he drinks ...............".* They do not always work. You will no doubt have experienced an advert and then thought "What was all that about?"

What makes a successful message? Messages generally fall into one of two types, both of which set out the benefits to be gained by purchasing the product. The types are
• factual messages
• emotive messages
For example, we have a new car to advertise. What possible features might we stress? What benefits does it have? What advantages do we have over the competition?

| factual | emotive |
|---|---|
| price and value | status – must be rich or important to own one |
| economy of performance | sex appeal – attracting a partner? |
| acceleration | family comfort and safety – the caring parent |
| body strength (anti-rust) | personality – lost youth – sports car |
| safety record | comfort – arrive relaxed for the key meeting |
| reliability | health – of others – runs on lead-free petrol |

*psychological factors in the message*
When you consider the emotive content of a message you will see that there are certain basic drives which relate to and affect the behaviour of us all. The psychologists suggest that some of these drives can be taken advantage of:

| | |
|---|---|
| *need for basic necessities* | To breathe, to say alive, to eat and drink. Surely these are guaranteed in our society? But can we create doubts in the buyer's mind? Of course we can. |
| *fear of death* | Does our car have good tyres? Do we have adequate insurance? |
| *safe drink* | Is tap water safe? Perhaps bottled water is better? |
| *food* | Are we hungry? A chocolate bar will solve the problem. Is our food safe? Look at the additive content. |
| *sex* | The suggestion is that wearing this and smelling of that will enable us to attract the partner we want. |

**student activity 18.1 – the advertising message**
Watch (and video record if possible) the commercial TV breaks during the course of a day and answer the following questions:

(a) In what *other* media have you seen the product advertised? Are you aware of a specific advertising campaign?

(b) Do any of the products advertised offend on any ethical grounds? What could you do if they did?

(c) At which market segment(s) is the advertisement aimed?

(d) Is the timing of the advertisement (eg early evening, late evening) significant to the market sector?

(e) Is there a specific message? Does it work? It is mainly factual or mainly emotive?

(f) What psychological factors can you identify in the advertisement?

Note: this activity works best as a class exercise, ie the whole class sees, analyses, and discusses the advertisements as a group.

## 5. identify the right timing

Timing of the advertising is crucial. Too soon before the event, and the public forget; too late and the public has bought something else. Seasonal markets need careful timing.

## 6. calculate the cost of advertising

This area is one where marketing personnel and accountants sometimes disagree. Clearly the revenue from the sale of the product must cover advertising costs, but marketing personnel will want a boost to the advertising budget when sales fall, the accountant will want a reduction. Costs can be found in BRAD (British Rate and Data) – see page 185.

# branding

Branding is a method of identifying one product or service from another by creating a name, term, design or symbol (logo) which is unique to that product or service.

## advantages of branding

The establishment of a brand name will save on future advertising costs. The product has become 'known'. To the consumer a brand name represents a known quality of product, the next one bought being the same as the previous ones. To the manufacturer branding allows a range of different products to be offered, to different market segments. It also allows brand loyalty to be established, ie some consumers always specify and buy the same 'name'.

## types of brand

• *Individual Brands* are those which stand alone, with no reference to the maker's name, eg Persil, Mates

• *Family Brands* often carry the name of the company, eg Heinz, as a guarantee of quality. A family brand allows new products to be established more easily but should one product gain a bad reputation it may drag down all the rest.

• *Multibrand Strategy*. This involves the use of more than one brand in the same market segment to increase the chances of a company product being selected, eg different soap powders mnaufactured by the same firm

• *House branding* became commonplace in the 1960s with the growth of major retail chains around the country. Nowadays Marks & Spencer, Tesco, Sainsbury all have their own version of consumer goods made especially for them and they sell under the retailer's own name or a chosen alternative, eg Marks & Spencer's "St Michael". Once a house brand name has been established, it is customary to maintain the chosen quality image.

## packaging

Packaging may be defined as

*the protection of the product and the final selling appeal at the point of sale*

Packaging involves both *packing* (the materials protecting the product) and *packaging* (the way the product is presented to the consumer). One way to remember this distinction is "Packing is for Protection. Packaging is for Promotion". We will deal with both packing and packaging in turn.

### packing
Many factors are important to the design of effective product packing: ease of handling, strength, the ability to withstand contamination, avoidance of pilferage, safety factors, factors of size. Correct and intact packing must be seen as a *promotional* matter. Nothing detracts more from a retail sale than a damaged tin or torn box.

### packaging
Packaging involves portraying the right *image*, ie its appropriateness for the target market segment. Look at examples of packaging and consider the following factors:
* use of shape to attract attention or enhance usefulness.
* design features – graphics, photography
* colour effectiveness – the psychologists have identified the images of colour, eg red is warmth, black is sophisticated, white is pure, yellow (ignored for so long as harsh) represents hygiene/ cleanliness
* size – does it attract? does it deceive?
* ease of use – can you open it ?(eg milk cartons?); if you cannot, will you buy it again?
* security of use – medicine bottles
* environmental factors – 'Bio-degradable' matters
* re-use – selling the original product in a container that can be refilled from packs which are disposable and cheaper.

---

### student activity 18.2 – branding and packaging
Investigate your local stationery shop, examine the following range of products, and answer the questions set out below: roller ball pens, pads of A4 paper, birthday cards and special interest magazines:
(a) Into which category of branding do the products fall?
(b) How effective is the packing of each product? Can you suggest any improvements?
(c) How does the manufacturer make the packaging appeal? Refer to the list of factors on this page.
*Note: this activity could be extended if the students buy some of the products being discussed and bring them into class for comparison and discussion.*

---

## publicity, public relations and promotions

### publicity and public relations
*Publicity* is gained by being newsworthy. If something happens to the product or the company, the media may pick up th story and publish it. Gaining good publicity ranks very high on the agenda of most businesses. *Public relations,* on the other hand, is the function within the business which looks after its public image. If you are undertaking investigations into a business as part of your course of

studies, you may well have to get in touch with the Public Relations Department. *Publicity* has the advantage over public relations in that it is usually free and it has a greater impact because it comes from a third person. Of course, publicity may not always be good publicity!

## sales promotions

A sales promotion may be defined as *an attempt to create interest in and stimulate sales of a product or service by a non-standard activity for a limited period of time.* In many ways, a sales promotion is a link between advertising and direct selling. It gives the advertiser an extra benefit to draw to the consumers' attention and it allows the sales person to revitalise interest in the product by having something new to discuss or offer. There are two levels of sales promotion:

- *trade* promotion – the manufacturer promoting to the retailer or wholesaler
- *consumer* promotion – the manufacturer or retailer promoting to the consumer

## trade promotions

The object of a trade promotion is to get the retailer to stock a product, or more of a product or to stay loyal. Techniques used are:

- quantity discounts – order more than a stated number of items per period to gain a price discount
- holidays or other incentives for an achieved sales target
- tailor-made promotions linked to one major store

Many of the above are derived from consumer type offers. Most are related to a consumer offer that is running at the same time.

## consumer promotions

The object of a consumer promotion is for the retailer to lift the long-term level of sales. Techniques used include:

- money off this purchase
- money off the next purchase
- two for the price of one
- two related products sold together for the price of one
- coupons and/or samples through the door
- competitions – they generate much interest and provide publicity when winners are announced

# merchandising

In a retail outlet, the merchandiser is in charge of the display of the goods and the store generally. His or her job involves attracting the attention of the consumer.

If a simple distinction between advertising and merchandising is required, it would be fair to say that advertising moves the customer to the point of sale, ie the shop, whereas merchandising helps to persuade the customer to actually buy the goods. The distinction between selling and merchandising is equally precise – the salesman sells goods into the shop, whilst the merchandiser helps the retailer to sell them out to the consumer.

Modern merchandising leans heavily on the psychology of advertising in its research into what motivates the consumer. Factual and/or emotive messages, package design, brand names, publicity, short-term promotions all influence the consumer. It should be fairly obvious, therefore, that factors such as shop layout, lighting, outer and inner appearance, will also affect the buying decision.

Most people can recall an 'impulse' purchase. Why? Was it previously seen advertising? The known brand name? The appearance of the package? Or was it the general 'feel' of the shop that inspired the additional buy, or the change from the usual brand? If it was the latter, the merchandiser has been successful.

## selling

Selling may defined as

*A personal communication which attempts to 'make the sale'*

Selling is the culmination of all of the other marketing activities, particularly the promotional. It is the final requirement for the success of the business. All of the other 'promotional' activities are impersonal; they require no actual contact between seller and purchaser. The selling function, however, is direct contact, whether it be face to face or over the telephone, and as such requires special training and careful planning.

### sales planning

Sales planning is generally accepted as a four-stage activity. Most training manuals would list research, preparation, presentation and closing. The time period of operation for achieving a sale can be a few weeks or a few years, depending upon the complexity of the product type and of the buying operation.

### *1. research*

There is a vast amount of information required before a professional sales person can approach the customer. The following list assumes that that a manufacturer is selling to another business:

- the trade you are in: its seasonality, conventions, rules and regulations, laws
- the competition that exists and their product strengths and weaknesses
- your own firm's products and strengths and weaknesses
- the customer organisation – whom and when to contact, their needs
- the need for records of customers to be kept – the date of the last visit, what was purchased, any problems (computer databases are becoming increasingly common in this area)
- the need to acquire personal information about the buyer(s) so that a rapport be established – this, of course, is a major problem for the new sales person, although with luck the previous sales person can be contacted.
- your own firm's procedures and requirements – the paperwork and order processing, delivery times, prices and discounts

### *2. preparation*

The potential and existing customers have been identified. The visits must now be planned and appointments made. Assemble a sales package. This might include product samples, fact sheets, leaflets, order forms and even a portable video. Many products cannot be carried to the purchaser, but a video of them in action can. Practice the sales 'pitch'. The hotels of the world are reputed to be full of sales people practising in front of a mirror to see what they look like.

### *3. presentation*

The presentation is critical: the personal contact is the factor upon which everything depends. The salesperson must appear in a manner appropriate to the situation. This usually means wearing smart clothes, but not necessarily if, say, 'down on the farm', or at the market.

- Establish a suitable opening line. To a new customer this will be an attention-gaining remark, possibly indicating something that is new and will make his life easier. To an existing customer, a social remark based on your knowledge of him or his organisation
- Make the 'sales pitch,' emphasising the *benefits* of your product to his organisation. If he is a professional buyer, he needs to buy something from somebody. Make it you!
- Counter objections with additional benefits. Do not tell lies, nor refuse to accept genuine criticism, eg 'the product was late arriving last time!'. 'Yes, we're sorry but we've made positive delivery changes since, and can guarantee arrival in 10 days.' Make sure you can! Offer guarantees, from yourself or your company, as above.

- Make concessions, gradually.  You should know your bottom price, so let him or her argue you down a little.  Let him win the argument (on *your* terms)!
- Forget the planned approach if the unexpected happens.  Be flexible.
- Listen carefully to his requirements.  Don't just talk.

### 4 . Close the sale.
For some people this is the hardest stage of all, but if you don't achieve this, there is no point to all the rest of the marketing activity.

Learn to recognise a buying signal, ie when the buyer seems happy with the 'sell':

> *"Are you sure it could be here within seven days".*
> *"Is that price reduction agreed?"*
> *"That sounds an improvement on the earlier model"*

All these comments indicate a positive thought, even if some sound like doubts.  At this point, have a suitable closing response, eg to the first one above – *"I'm positive, if you could sign the order straight away!"*.

# after-sales service

We have already seen in Chapter 3 the importance of Customer Care.  After-sales service is an essential element of *customer service.*

After-sales service is the follow-up activity to selling, which ensures that the customer is satisfied with the purchase, and would be happy to buy again.  After-sales service may be part of the product promotion and the sales promise, which ensures that the customer has a reference point for any query on the product's quality, performance and appearance.  In such instances the business may set up a Customer Service Department to deal with such queries.

After-sales service may also be required under consumer protection legislation (see pages 26 and 27).  Any defective goods must either be repaired to the customer's satisfaction or replaced, according to what the customer requires.  Another aspect of after-sales service is the insurance contract, whereby for a initial payment, the purchaser 'buys' a service contract, eg for electrical goods for a period of five years.  It should be stressed that this contract does not affect a customer's rights under the law:  it is an additional longer-term safeguard.

So far we have confined discussion of after-sales service to *consumer* goods.  When selling industrial goods and services a business must ensure adequate back-up services to cover aspects such as spare parts, servicing, technical advice, replacement of faulty equipment, and so on.  Any business which does not offer this support will quickly lose out to the competition.

### student activity 18.3 – sales and after-sales
Compare the *selling methods* and the *after-sales service* offered by the following businesses.  Account for any differences.   In the case of (d) what additional pressure is there to maintain the quality of after-sales service?

(a)   a garage selling new cars from one manufacturer only

(b)   a second-hand car firm

(c)   an electrical equipment warehouse

(d)   a monopoly or virtual monopoly, eg British Gas, British Telecom

# "place"– distribution

*Place* is the term used in the 'Marketing Mix' to describe the function alternatively known as 'Distribution', ie getting the goods to the eventual comsumer.   An organisation's distribution policy will involve identifying the various factors which will influence how the goods are distributed to the eventual consumer and then the making of decisions on some or all of the following:

- selecting the type(s) of outlet(s) to be used
- calculating the number of outlets required
- choosing a suitable 'physical' distribution method
- choosing the best site or 'place' for  the business itself

As you will see from these factors, the distribution method is an important policy decision for an organisation.

### selecting the type of outlets

The channel of distribution for any organisation may be short (direct to customer) or long (using several intermediaries).  The various choices are shown in the diagram below, and then explained in the text set that follows.

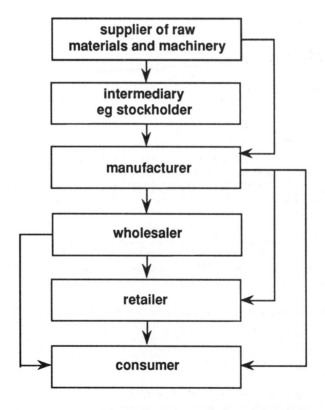

The supply routes are best examined by looking in turn at supplies received by:

- the manufacturer
- the retailer
- the consumer

*supply of raw materials and machinery to the manufacturer*
Many sales of raw materials, machinery and heavy plant are made *directly* to the manufacturer by the supplier. In other cases an *intermediary* ('middle-person') with expertise in a particular trade may be used. Intermediaries are given many different names, depending on the trade involved, for example: broker, dealer, factor, agent, stockholder, wholesaler, and so on.

*supply to the retailer*
The retailer (ie a shop) may be supplied by:

- a *wholesaler* (an intermediary who stocks goods and supplies a particular trade) or
- the manufacturer direct

Supply from a *wholesaler* is a traditional route, and is used where widespread distribution is required to a market which needs the product in relatively small quantities (eg a 'corner shop'). The wholesale function saves the manufacturer much time and money. Many large supermarket chains do not need wholesalers for many stock items: they buy in bulk from the manufacturers, and negotiate their own terms. They often negotiate low prices and "just in time" stock deliveries – ie they only take delivery of what they need in the near future, a common cost-saving policy.

*supply to the consumer*
The consumer has the best of all possible worlds. He or she can buy:

- from the *retailer*, 'shopping around' in the literal sense for the best price
- from *mail order firms* who buy direct from the manufacturer
- from the *wholesaler* – many of whom have managed to open their doors to the public without totally alienating their retailer customers. The admittance card that allows access to the wholesale establishment to the genuine 'trade' buyer is often made available to large local firms and other organisations, whose employees (consumers) use them.
- from the *manufacturer* direct – by direct mail and from factory shops
- through *agents* who buy direct from the manufacturer; their selling methods include door-to-door sales and "party" selling – ie throw a party, ask your friends, sell them something (eg Tupperware)

## intensity of distribution – how many outlets?
Another important decision area is related to the number of intermediaries (such as wholesalers) and outlets required. Clearly the greater the number, the higher the exposure of a product to the market, but this increase is not necessarily what is required for the organisation. Thus the question must be asked: "Maximum coverage or selectivity or exclusivity?" We will deal with each in turn.

*maximum (intensive) distribution*
This type of distribution relates to those products which are in very common use and have no *real* or *distinctive* character of their own. Most convenience goods like cigarettes, everyday foods, ordinary raw materials and so on, come into this category. The usual marketing strategy is to place them in every conceivable outlet, as sales depend on their availability when required.

*selective distribution*
This type of distribution means that the product is carried by more than one shop or dealer, but is not available everywhere. It is commonly used by new firms in the market to gain better distribution, offering as it does to the 'outlet' a degree of exclusivity whilst still allowing the manufacturer to 'grow' in the market. An example of selective distribution is the way car manufacturers limit their dealerships in a specific area.

*exclusive distribution*
This method of distribution tends to be a two-way agreement whereby the manufacturer gives the exclusive rights to sell his product in a particular region (eg the Midlands, Wales) to *one* dealer and in return that dealer agrees to sell only that product. Exclusive distribution obviously limits sales potential to the mass market but this is quite often the deliberate policy of the manufacturer to enhance the prestige of the product and to enable higher profts to be earned on each deal. Many luxury products sell *because* they are not generally available, eg Rolls Royce cars.

### choosing a distribution method
The main alternative methods of distribution are air, road, rail, and sea.

* *Air transport* is increasingly used because of its technical advances: the introduction of larger and faster planes. The major problems relate to high cost and limited airport availability. Major advantages are speed and security (although increased handling, ie road to air to road, may lessen this).

* *The road system* carries the majority of freight on a national and international basis. The problems with road transport are that even large juggernauts are limited in capacity, and stricter road regulations may further reduce road competitiveness, as will the cost factor of drivers and fuel. The major advantage is that of convenience, ie door to door delivery, even internationally, with the added advantages of security and safety (less handling).

* *Rail transport* has declined in the last few decades as the conveniences of road transport and road systems (motorways) have improved. The main advantages of rail are the large quantities that can be moved, and at speed. The major problem is the lack of convenient terminals. Some large organisations like coal and steel companies have their own link lines to the national network.

* *Sea transport* has the considerable advantage in that ships can carry large quantities of raw materials and products. The advent of container ships has dramatically improved the safety, security and speed factors. Container ownership is also common, the containers being loaded at the factory and transported to the docks by road or rail.

---

### student activity 18.4 – distribution
As producer of the following, make distribution policy decisions on the outlet type, number and siting of outlets, and transport needs:
(a) family cars
(b) market garden produce
(c) production raw materials for industry
(d) bread
(e) high priced fashion accessories

---

## chapter summary

❑ Promotion, the third of the four marketing mix "Ps" aims to communicate the benefits of the product to the selected market segment of prospective customers. It involves:
  * promoting a corporate image
  * planning an advertising campaign
  * branding, packing and packaging
  * merchandising
  * publicity, public relations and sales promotions
  * effective selling and after-sales service

❑ Place, the last of the four marketing mix "Ps" involves the distribution function:
  * the selection of intermediaries and outlets
  * the intensity of distribution, ie how many outlets?
  * choice of a distribution method, ie air, road, rail or sea
  *NOTE THAT THIS CHAPTER SHOULD BE STUDIED IN COMBINATION WITH CHAPTER 48 "THE SALES AND MARKETING PLAN'*

# 9 *The methods and ethics of marketing*

---

*Element 3.3*     *Investigate marketing activities*

Suggested Sources: • Businesses and market sectors under investigation: visits and promotional literature (Note: it is essential that students liaise with teachers/lectures in this activity in order that business organisations are not overwhelmed with enquiries)
• school/college and reference libraries – statistics on the markets being investigated, eg trade journals
• textbooks in libraries and resource centres

---

## TASK 1

Investigate products (manufactured items and services) which are currently being promoted and choose *two* that are directly competing, eg

• family estate cars, off-roaders, or fast hatchbacks
• special brands of strong lager and strong cider, Pepsi and Coca Cola
• local services, eg nightclubs, sports centres, fast food outlets

You can, of course make your own choice of the two products, in consultation with your teacher/lecturer as to their suitability. You should then compare them in terms of:

(a)    how they fit in with the product policy of the two businesses: their position in the product portfolio, their stage in the product life cycle, how they relate to the market policy of the business

(b)    the pricing policy of the two businesses – both short-term and long-term

(c)    the promotion and distribution policy of the two businesses – advertising, branding and packaging, publicity, sales promotions and techniques, after-sales service (if appropriate!) and distribution

Set out your findings in a formal written report.

Note: the exercise would be best carried out if the class divided into groups of two to four students who could then, after the completion of the comparison and the writing of the report, make an oral presentation (maximum fifteen minutes) to the whole class.

## TASK 2

Each student should look at the *range* of products from one of the businesses being investigated, or any *other* appropriate range of products, and draw up a diagram showing the stages of the product life cycle. The range of products should then be written onto the diagram to show what stage of the product life cycle each product has reached.

## TASK 3

Choose *two* products which raise questions of ethics, ie

• a products which can be harmful:  eg cigarettes, alcoholic drinks, and
• a product which can be beneficial:  eg organically grown food, condoms

Investigate the marketing techniques used in their promotion, and state in writing how the business avoids the issue (harmful products) and benefits from the issue (beneficial products).

SECTION

4

# human resources

## contents

In this Section we examine the implications to a business of *human resourcing*. "Human resources" are the employees of a business, and management decisions about the hiring, firing and treatment of staff are often crucial to its effectiveness and productivity.

The section is divided into four chapters:

| | |
|---|---|
| Chapter 19 | Human resource management involves a variety of roles – here we examine how employees are encouraged to stay with the business, how they can be dismissed, and the role of the trade unions. |
| Chapter 20 | We examine training for employees, the legal implications of employing staff, how employees can seek redress, and how human resource management can affect the productivity of a business. |
| Chapter 21 | We turn to the types of jobs that are available in a business, how those jobs are specified (job descriptions) and how the ideal candidate for the job can be defined (person specifications). |
| Chapter 22 | This major chapter looks at the recruitment process – how a job is advertised, how a person would apply for a job, and how the interview would be conducted. |

This section is of practical application to students in that it explains the "nuts and bolts" of employment and develops the job application skills – the completion of CVs, application forms and letters. The student activities and Evidence Collection Exercise reflect this practical bias.

## GNVQ Unit Coverage

Note: GNVQ Element 4.2 includes an investigation into a wide range of business organisations and their structures, eg sole trader, partnership and limited company. The writers consider these topics are best studied at the beginning of a business studies course, and they are therefore covered in detail in Chapters 1 and 2, to which students should refer.

# 19 Human resource management

## introduction

Human Resource Management is the management of the people who work in an organisation. Traditionally this was known as "personnel management", and it concentrated on *welfare* roles such as administering the pay system, holidays and the pension scheme, running the employees' medical service and organising social and sports facilities.

Nowadays the job of managing people is regarded as being more complicated and whereas the personnel manager's chief concern used to be how to look after the employees and keep them as satisfied as possible there is now much more involvement in how to get the *most value out of employees for the benefit of the organisation*. This means that human resource managers now work much more closely with other managers in production, marketing and finance areas.

In this chapter we will examine the following topics:
- the roles of human resource managers
- retention of employees
- appraisal of employees
- termination of employees' contracts
- employee representation and consultation

We will deal with the subject of recruitment in Chapter 22, and the areas of employee training and legal rights in Chapter 20.

## roles of human resource managers

The main roles of human resource managers are listed below. Obviously the amount of time devoted to each of these roles will vary according to the type of organisation, its size and its economic prospects, and whether its 'people management' function is still seen as 'welfare approach' *personnel management* or *human resource* management .

The main responsibilities are:

* *Recruitment and selection* – operating a well structured and effective recruitment system to ensure that the right people are selected to fill vacant posts.  This subject is covered in Chapter xx.
* *Health and Safety* – ensuring all employees work in a safe and healthy environment.
* *Employee consultation* – it is increasingly common for employers to seek the advice and help of their employees in a wide range of business decision matters.
* *Employee relations* – negotiations about pay and conditions of employees – this is usually, but not always, conducted between the employer and the trade unions who represent the employees.
* *Training and development of employees* – employees must be trained properly so that they can do their jobs effectively and safely; in addition they should be given the opportunity to develop by being given more responsibility in their work and by being given the chance to acquire extra qualifications.
* *Grievance and disciplinary matters* – all organisations need to operate effective and fair systems for dealing with employees who have complaints about how they are treated by the organisation (for example if they feel they have been unfairly passed over for promotion or if they feel they have been sexually or racially discriminated against). The organisation must also operate an effective and fair system of disciplining employees with proper procedures to ensure that the employee has the chance to improve the quality of his work (or of his behaviour) before he is faced with dismissal .
* *Redundancy procedures* – since the early 1980s it has become very common for employers to get rid of employees, either because of the need to become more efficient, or because the organisation (or part of it at least) is actually closing down.  It is necessary to have a proper system, believed to be fair by all the workforce, when choosing people to be made redundant. It should also be made as painless as possible through the use of generous redundancy payments and help in finding people other jobs (eg by giving paid time off to go for interviews).

## employee retention

Having recruited and inducted an employee – a subject covered in Chapter 22 – the most important issue is how to retain him or her,  assuming of course that the organisation is satisfied with the person's work.

We need therefore to examine why employees leave:

### the level of pay
The most common reason for leaving is pay.  If pay rates for the particular job are better in another organisation then it is quite likely the job holder will consider moving. Factors such as the convenience of the existing job and the existence of long working friendships will put some people off going elsewhere, but the cost of living and the need to provide the best possible life style for the employee's family will make a higher pay rate very attractive.

### lack of  promotion
Where there are few career progression opportunities people will leave. Some organisations prefer to recruit externally to fill more senior posts which means that anyone who wants to get on in their career has no choice but to leave. Luckily, most organisations take a more sensible view but even then cut backs due to economic recession or greater competition may still mean they can offer very few career prospects.

### lack of career development opportunities
Organisations which offer the chance to gain more qualifications and a wider variety of skills will retain people at least until the training is finished or the extra qualifications have been acquired. Organisations which do *not* offer these opportunities are less likely to retain their staff.

### poor working conditions

Working in unpleasant, dirty and unsafe conditions with poor canteen and social facilities will encourage people to leave if other organisations nearby offer something better. Nowadays legislation such as the Factories Act and the Health and Safety at Work Act makes bad working conditions much less common than 30 years ago.

### personal treatment – discrimination

If an employee is treated badly, either by management or by fellow employees, then he or she will be more likely to try to get a job elsewhere. The commonest examples of bad treatment are discrimination against employees on racial or on sexual grounds. Even if it is fellow employees who are responsible for such behaviour the *employer* is legally responsible. Although people are encouraged to take legal action against their employer for discrimination, in reality many people are frightened by legal matters and will not want to make any fuss.

### repetitive and uninteresting work

Boring work will encourage people to leave if there are more interesting alternatives elsewhere. Clearly, highly paid boring work is less unattractive than badly paid boring work. Nevertheless, there has been a sharp increase since the 1970s in the numbers of employees who will not put up with boring work since it does not provide any mental challenge at all.

---

**student activity 19.1 – conditions of work**
Examine critically the course of study you are on at the moment. Identify and write down individually the main aspects of the course which will affect whether you may stay on or leave. Then exchange your views with other people in your class and your teacher/lecturer.

---

## employee performance

### performance appraisal

At one time the assessment of an employee's performance took place irregularly, if at all, and was very rarely done in a professional manner. Employers were usually quite happy if the employee turned up for work every day, had as little time off for illness as possible and did his or her work satisfactorily. Today the regular and systematic assessment of a persons work performance is commonplace. Contrary to initial worries it is now welcomed both by managers and by employees so long as it is done fairly and the process is fully explained to the parties concerned.

The assessment of work performance is called *Performance Appraisal* and it is normally carried out by the job holder's immediate superior. This means that the chairman of the organisation (be it in the private or the public sectors) will appraise the Managing Director/General Manager. He/she then appraises the most senior level of managers. The senior managers appraise the junior managers who then appraise their supervisory staff (at foreman level for instance). Finally, supervisors will appraise the lowest grades of staff.

### the procedures and documentation of performance appraisal

In setting up an appraisal system, two practical issues have to be settled:

*How often does one get appraised ?*
Appraisals take up a lot of management time, so having them just once every year is quite common. However, this is unsatisfactory – once every six months is much more beneficial because it gives employees more regular feedback on performance, and managers can assess how far objectives laid down at the last appraisal have actually been achieved.

*What kind of documentation does one use?*

Basically there are three choices, or a mixture of all three:

- a blank sheet of paper – this gives the appraiser freedom to write what he or she likes but there are the dangers that key issues may be missed out, or that the appraiser may not like writing reports, nor be very good at writing reports
- a form with questions and spaces to complete – this directs but also limits the appraiser
- a rating form – for each heading the appraiser simply gives a mark out of, say, 10 or a grade (A to E) – this appears to give the appraisal a precision which it, in fact, lacks

The best choice is probably a mixture of all three. This means having a form with spaces to make brief comments in but with a larger space at the end for more detail. The spaces may also have boxes for grades or marks out of 10.

## appraisal interview format

Appraisals can be:

- *open* – this is where the appraisee can discuss the appraisal with the manager as the interview takes place. This means he/she can argue about the points made or add relevant information which might mean the appraisal needs changing.
- the old fashioned *closed* approach in which the manager simply delivers his appraisal presentation to the appraisee who may make no comment at all – this is clearly not desirable!
- *two-way* – some organisations ask the appraisee to do an appraisal of himself/herself. This means he/she fills an identical form to the appraiser's. The forms are then compared and where there are clear differences there must be more discussion (eg if the appraiser rates work effort at say 5 out of 10 and the appraisee rates it at 8 out of 10).

## the benefits of performance appraisal

There are many benefits gained from the process of assessing performance – for both employers and employees:

- It helps to identify *training needs* – if the appraiser identifies lack of competence in some aspect of a persons work, extra training can be arranged.
- It may reveal *other problems* – all kinds of things can cause poor quality work and these can be uncovered by an appraisal. For example, there may be workplace difficulties with other staff (eg it might be caused by sexual harassment) or perhaps money problems or family problems.
- It may untap useful *new skills* – the appraisal process may show that a person has skills or intellectual abilities which he is not using fully. He may then be given a new or redesigned job which uses more of his talents. The organisation will now get more value from him, and he will benefit from the greater challenge, a greater feeling of worth and, hopefully, more money.
- It helps identify *potential* – appraising performance in the job being done now has some bearing on the ability to perform in more senior jobs.
- It improves *communications* between employees and management: it gives managers the chance to sit down and talk seriously with their staff about their work and career prospects. The few words of encouragement and praise for doing a good job are often highly motivating. Even if the comments are critical an employee will value them if they come from a manager who takes an interest in him and suggests ways in which his work could be improved.
- They provide *disciplinary documentation* – if the employer needs to dismiss somebody the existence of thorough appraisal records which identify the person's inabilities or lack of effort will be very useful. This is especially true if the employee fights the dismissal in an Industrial Tribunal (to win compensation or to get his job back) when the employer will need proper records to show that he has acted fairly at all stages (see Chapter 20). The appraisal records should show that the employee was given several chances to improve his work effort or was offered extra training to help him to do his job more competently.
- It helps to fix *pay rises* – for senior managers in particular,the result of their appraisal by an even more senior manager will determine what their salary will be. Although for most staff pay levels are determined 'collectively' – through bargaining between the employer and the trade unions, in

the future more and more people will get performance related pay and the appraisal interview will become an essential part of pay determination for many more people.

### training to appraise

It is essential to provide managers and supervisors with proper training on how to appraise their staff. This is usually done by private training companies or consultants by means of a short course including some role playing by the participating managers who may be given a case study of an imaginary employee and then told to write up an appraisal of the person's work performance.

### the appraisal report

The essential features of an appraisal *report* will be as follows:
- A clear outline of what the employee is supposed to do in his/her job.
- A list of any *performance indicators* laid down in the job – eg a car salesman might have to sell a minimum number of motor cars per month. In many jobs outside the sales field it is far harder to identify performance indicators that are so specific, but general standards of performance can be devised for most jobs. One method is to set a series of objectives at the last appraisal and now check up to see if these objectives have actually been achieved.
- An examination of the *strengths* of the employee.
- An examination of the *weaknesses* of the employee.
- The advice given to the employee in relation to future performance. This should include:
  - praise for strengths
  - helpful criticisms of the weaknesses the manager has identified.
- An action plan for the next few months until the next appraisal. This will list the key objectives which the employee will be expected to have achieved by then. If extra training or experience or qualifications is believed necessary to help achieve these objectives then the organisation should (within reason) provide it.
- Advising the employee that if he/she is unhappy about the appraisal outcome he/she may formally appeal to senior management to have another interview.

All training for appraisals emphasises that it is not meant to be a 'trial' and that criticisms should always be made in a positive manner (ie "what can be done by both of us to sort these problems out?")   Nevertheless,the manager has to make it clear that if objectives fixed at an appraisal are not at least partly achieved then the appraisee (the person being appraised) may face disciplinary charges and eventually even dismissal.

---

### student activity 19.2 – performance appraisal

(a) Design an appraisal form which could be used to assess the performance of a student on a GNVQ level 3 programme of study.  Identify the key areas you would need to assess.

(b) Write a brief item for an organisation's internal staff newspaper from the point of view of management which will 'sell' the idea of appraisal to the staff. Stress the good points of appraisals and try to anticipate employee fears and anxieties.

---

# termination of employment

Termination of an employee's contract  – *dismissal* – can result because:
- the employee's work is not satisfactory for one of a number of reasons
- the employee's work is no longer required – redundancy

We will look at each of these in turn.

## dismissal – the employee's work is not satisfactory

Other than redundancy there are several reasons why a person can be *fairly* dismissed:

• *incapability in the job*

Before the dismissal occurs the employer must have shown the employee exactly what the job required, and the employer must have given the employee at least one chance to improve the standard of work. If the dismissed employee decided to go to an Industrial Tribunal to challenge the dismissal decision (to get compensation or his job back) it will be necessary for the employer to provide documentary evidence that he took all reasonable steps to help the employee become 'capable' in the job.

Incapability also includes prolonged illness. Where an employer can show that a person's prolonged illness is causing significant inconvenience to the organisation (and that there is medical evidence to show no real improvement in health is likely) then it is fair to dismiss. In such cases the employer must always be able to show that he discussed the problem with the sick employee and that all reasonable alternatives to dismissal were considered.

• *misconduct*

Any kind of bad behaviour at work such as hitting another employee or stealing may be classed as 'gross misconduct' which may lead to instant dismissal. If the offence is fairly minor an employer should only dismiss if it happens more than once (following severe warnings to the employee).

• *illegality*

Sometimes it may be illegal to employ an individual in a particular job. A common example is where somebody is dismissed following the loss of their driving licence because their job requires them to drive ( a salesperson for instance).

• *some other substantial reason*

This covers a wide range of possibilities. One of the best known is lack of 'care' – examples of cases in the past include failure to take proper care of the employer's samples or tools. Another reason commonly mentioned is 'bad faith' – all employees are expected to show 'good faith' in dealing with their employer so if an employee does something which harms that relationship it could mean dismissal. Examples of this include the use of employer's time and equipment or premises to do private work, working for a competitor in one's spare time and divulging confidential information about customers to outsiders.

## the employee's work is no longer required - redundancy

Since the late 1970s Britain has experienced two serious recessions – in 1980-82 and in 1990-92 – in which unemployment increased to over 3 million from about half that figure. Both of these caused structural changes in industry which forced employers to make many people redundant. Many businesses shut down completely, but most of the remainder went through serious job cuts. In both recessions, but particularly in the second one, the public sector also cut the number of jobs available, although large scale redundancies did not occur (people who left were just not replaced).

## the costs of redundancy

To both employees and employers there are significant costs. It is a commonly held view but a completely wrong one, to argue that employers are happy to get rid of staff, and that so long as the redundancy money is good employees are always happy to go. For employers and employees redundancy has many painful consequences. These include:

• *psychological effects on the individual*

Studies dating back to the economic slump of the early 1930s show that redundant employees are badly hurt by being rejected and, unless they soon get another job, they feel they are failures in all aspects of their lives.

• *economic effects on the individual*

Although some organisations, notably the coal and steel industries in the early 1980s, paid out very high sums of compensation, the majority of them now pay out far less. Some only pay the minimum laid down by the Redundancy Payments Act, ie one week's pay for each year of service up to a maximum of 20 years work (for under 21s it is half a week and for over 42s it is one and a half weeks).

* *loss of morale in the organisation*
Once redundancies are even threatened, morale of all employees drops sharply and even after the redundancies have occurred the lucky ones who keep their jobs may well feel that their turn will come very soon. Good employees may well leave as soon as they can find another job.

* *Trade union action*
Strikes and other industrial action may occur to prevent redundancies. This will hit employees and the employer – a classic example being the 1984-85 miners strike which caused immense damage to the coal industry and financially crippled many miners' families.

* *restructuring and rebuilding morale*
Much managerial time will have to be spent on reorganising the workforce, changing job descriptions, creating new work teams and negotiating it all with the trade unions. The rebuilding of morale will be far harder and will not come about until it is clear that the organisation is strong again and the remaining jobs are secure.

* *financial costs*
The trade unions will exert pressure to get the best deals for members made redundant and this will often mean a package well above the legal minimum. Two or even three weeks pay per year of service will be paid out and often for more than the statutory maximum number of years. This is not subsidised by the government and so all money will have to come from the company's own resources, and will affect the business' ability to plan for new investment or pay rises.

A hidden cost - but a very real one – is that organisations often agree to letting people volunteer for redundancy rather than upset the trade unions even more by forcing people to go who do not want to. The result is that many volunteers are young, able, well-qualified staff who can easily get other work but want the chance to pick up a 'nice redundancy bonus'. People who are less value to the organisation, and usually much older with less up-to-date skills, do not volunteer because they have a slimmer chance of getting a new job. This policy therefore reduces the organisation's overall efficiency .

---

**student activity 19.3 – redundancy**
Prepare a short written report for a personnel manager which will outline the key factors to be considered when selecting employees to be made redundant.

---

# dismissal procedures

For the two types of dismissal – unsatisfactory performance/misconduct and redundancy – the procedures will be entirely different:

### dismissal for unsatisfactory performance/misconduct
Almost all disciplinary procedures will have several stages and most of them follow the guidelines set out in the Code of Practice on Disciplinary Practice and Procedures published by the Advisory, Conciliation and Arbitration Service(ACAS).

The sequence, if taken to its full conclusion progresses through an *informal*, *formal* and *final* stage, as follows:

### informal stage
- counselling
- investigation
- informal action
- a review period

Very often the whole problem can be sorted out at the informal stage and no disciplinary action need be taken. If it is a misconduct matter such as an isolated case of lateness a quiet word with the offender may well be enough. Where the issue is unsatisfactory performance in the job, the manager can make a more specific request that the standard be improved and a statement that he will review performance again within one month. Again, this is best done in a friendly manner.

Suppose the lateness persists with no explanation or the performance does not improve? What happens then?

### formal stage
- investigation
- formal warnings
- a review period

At this stage the personnel manager will become involved, whereas at the informal stage the matter would probably be handled only by the employees own manager. The formal stage will involve detailed investigation of the problem with a series of interviews with the employee and other managers/supervisors. The personnel manager will then give the employee *a first written warning* which will fully detail what is wrong and give a time period (usually one month) to improve to the required standards.

If performance or conduct does improve then the matter will be dropped, but the written warning may be kept on file by the personnel department for perhaps six months in case the employee 'reoffends' after the fuss has died down. If there has been no improvement, what happens then ?

### final stage
- final written warning
- possible dismissal

The employee will be given a second and final written warning which threatens dismissal if there is no improvement to the required standard. There will usually be no more chances after this final stage. The next step, assuming that performance still is not up to the required standard, will be a formal interview. At this the employee may bring a friend, usually a Trade Union shop steward – this is a term for a spokesman elected by the other trade union members in the workplace. Most good employers encourage this to ensure that everything is open and fair. The interview will enable the management to give full detailed reasons for dismissal, and a copy of the statement must be given to the individual. All financial matters will be dealt with (eg paying any wages or salary still owed). Most importantly, the employee will be given an opportunity to give his/her side of the story, although by this stage few employers will be likely to give yet another chance.

Finally, employees should be advised that they may appeal against the dismissal and that they are also entitled to apply to an Industrial Tribunal (see Chapter 20) if they wish to (this must be done by them within 30 days of dismissal).

The general pattern outlined above does vary a little. Some organisations give more written warnings, and some would make the first 'informal stage' more formal than described here. Nevertheless the essentials will always basically be the same.

## redundancy dismissal

Under the Employee Protection (Consolidation) Act 1978 the main aspects of the redundancy dismissal procedure are:

- *Consultation*
  Consultation involves the employer telling the trade unions (or other employee representatives if there is no trade union) of his plans to declare jobs redundant. Do remember that it is a job which becomes redundant not a person. This can be very important indeed – an employer could declare 50 jobs redundant at the consultation stage but there may be enough vacancies in other areas of the organisation to mean that nobody need actually leave the workforce (see below).

  Consultation means that the employer must state why jobs must disappear, how many are to disappear, the methods for selecting people for redundancy and the time period over which they will occur. The trade unions must be given the chance to suggest alternatives which they consider are more acceptable, and if the employer rejects these he must explain why (in a written statement).

- *Compensation*
  The employer will have to pay at least the minimum under the 1965 Redundancy Payments Act but the trade unions will often persuade them to pay a good deal more (see page 215 for the actual rates). In addition employers must make reasonable arrangements for redundant employees to have time off (on full pay) to look for other jobs and a good employer will allow them to leave before notice expires if their new job requires an immediate start.

As we have seen above, the number of redundancies may far exceed the number of people who actually leave. After all, if an organisation can find people other jobs instead of getting rid of them it keeps the trade unions happy and saves on the redundancy bills. The law permits employers to offer suitable and reasonable alternative employment for which the employee must have a trial period of 4 weeks. After 4 weeks, if either the employer or the employee feels that the job is unsuitable the employee will be made redundant on the normal terms.

---

### student activity 19.4 – making people redundant
Draft a letter to employees in an imaginary organisation which outlines plans to make staff redundant. Give your reasons for those plans. From the last Student Activity (page 202) set out the main considerations you will have in mind when you are choosing which people are to be made redundant.

---

# employee representation and consultation

### negotiation by individuals

The relationship between the employee and his employer comes under the broad title of 'Employee Relations'. An employee has to negotiate conditions of service (rates of pay, holiday entitlements etc) with his employer. Not only does he have to do this when he starts working for somebody but he may have to do it again if he gets promoted. Every so often, usually every year, he will probably want a pay rise to enable him to maintain his standard of living.

If an employee is in a *strong* bargaining position he/she will be in a powerful position to negotiate all these issues. Top class footballers,TV, film and pop stars are all in such a position. Their rarity value and ability to make huge sums of money for their employers makes it easy for them to command very high incomes.

## negotiation by groups – Trade Unions

Of course most people are unlikely to have the bargaining power of  Paul Gascoigne, Robin Williams or Madonna. Most individuals will always find that they have much more strength if they bargain as a group.  As a group they can put pressure on an employer by threatening to stop work – which costs the employer money – whereas one employee's threat to stop work would not harm the employer very greatly. From this principle has developed trade unionism.

In the UK about 8 million people currently belong to recognised trade unions. A recognised trade union is defined in the Trade Unions and Labour Relations Act (TULRA) 1974 as an organisation which

*"consists wholly or mainly of workers, of one or more descriptions,whose principal purposes include regulation of relations between workers of that or those descriptions and employers or employers associations"*

We will look at the trade union structure in the UK, the system of employer associations, and will briefly examine the roles of trade unions with some emphasis on the issue of Employee Consultation. There are four types of trade union in the UK:

- *Craft Unions*
  In Britain, trades unions were first set up in the eighteenth century, the earliest examples being small organisations which brought together skilled employees in the newly-emerging industries such as the Cutlery Trades Union and the Lock Makers.  A modern example of a craft union is the Amalgamated Engineering and Electrical Union.

- *General Unions*
  General unions do not confine themselves to one skill or industry, but cover a wide area of activities.  The biggest are the Transport and General Workers' Union (the 'T & G') with over a million members; the General, Municipal & Boilermakers (the 'GMB') with slightly less, and Unison, a recently created public services union composed of three older unions in nursing services and local government with about 1.6 million members.

- *Non-manual unions*
  Traditionally, unions were set up to represent people in wage-earning manual jobs (where you earn a weekly income, often paid in banknotes given out in envelopes). These are known as 'blue collar' jobs and are often described as any kind of work where you would "get your hands dirty". However, there are now just as many union members in salary-earning jobs (where you get a monthly income paid into your bank account). These are often called 'white-collar' jobs and are generally in areas of work where you keep your hands fairly clean, eg local and central government, banks and insurance, medical work and teaching.

- *Occupational unions*
  In Germany employees belong to the union which represents their type of work  rather than their individual skills.  This means that if you work in the chemicals industry you join the Chemical Industry Union.  The biggest union in Germany - IG Metall - is also Europe's biggest with three and a half million members because it represents anybody who works in the metal-related sector (cars, trucks, machine tools,  ships etc.)  The only union in Britain like this is the National Union of Mineworkers since it includes all types of employee working in coal mines.

## new developments in UK trade unions

The two most important developments are both a result of the current decline of trade union membership and power:

- *the single union agreement*
  In this situation employers refuse to recognise  more than one trade union. A major reason for this is that more and more new jobs are created by Japanese businesses opening new  factories in the UK. The Japanese only have single unions (or no unions at all in some cases ) in their factories in Japan and they would not come to Britain without similar arrangements being guaranteed.

- *managing without unions*
  Increasingly one of the results of a weakened and smaller union movement is that more organisations are giving up recognition of trade unions altogether.  Employers are legally required to win the agreement of employees to 'derecognise' their unions. In return employers often offer improved pay and conditions. The best known example of this is the British division of  IBM which traditionally guarantees its employees a job for life together with one of the best pay and working conditions packages available.

---

### student activity 19.5 – trade unions

In consultation with your tutor devise a brief questionnaire to investigate the trade union membership among employees working at your school or college.  The areas to be covered could include:

(a)   Which different unions are represented in your institution?

(b)   What types of union are they?

(c)   What proportion of employees questioned belong to a union?

(d)   What benefits of belonging to a union are the employees aware of?

---

## the functions of trade unions

Most trade unions have basically the same roles, although the relative importance of each of them will vary. These are:

- *improvement in pay and conditions*
  Pay and conditions have steadily improved over many years and this is at least partly due to the actions of trade unions. Through industrial action of a variety of types they have forced employers to improve pay rates, holiday entitlements and actual working conditions (including Health and Safety).

- *job protection*
  A very important role traditionally but, as we noted earlier, circumstances have changed since the advent of high unemployment and the fast moving pace of new  technology. Unions are now more realistic about the economic situation and accept that jobs will steadily be replaced by new technology. They therefore usually fight to persuade employers to only make volunteers redundant and to pay those volunteers the most generous redundancy compensation possible.

- *a political role*
  The trade unions in the late nineteenth century helped to create the Labour Party and the links between them are still very close. The big general unions such as the T & G and the GMB are the most powerful influence because they give the Labour Party most of the money it needs to operate from day to day and for fighting General and Local Elections.

- *a consultative role*
  This is dealt with separately below.

The trade unions are represented in a national body, the *Trade Union Congress* (TUC), which aims to implement the functions outlined above.  The TUC is governed by a General Council.  Policy issues are discussed at the annual conference.

## employer associations

The principal aim of the associations is to represent the employers in negotiations with employees. The Trade Union and Labour Relations Act 1974 defines an employer association as an organisation which consists of:

*"employers or individual proprietors of one or more descriptions, whose principal purposes include the regulation of relations between employers of that description and workers or trade unions"*

For most industries there will be an Employers Association which represents the businesses in that industry. There is a big variety, of type and of size, ranging from the National Farmers Union which represents hundreds of thousands of farmers to the Newspaper Publishers Association representing about a dozen national newspapers.   Their main functions are:

- employers associations illustrate the principle of 'strength in numbers' – they present a united front by agreeing to offer the same basic pay and conditions to the unions
- most of them provide a comprehensive advisory service to member companies; this includes information on local labour market trends, wage rates, and the provision of professional legal advice
- they fight for the industry they represent to ensure it gets the best deal when dealing with the government and other national and local organisations; in this sense they act as pressure groups

The employers associations are represented in a national body, the *Confederation of British Industry* (CBI), which makes known the employers' viewpoint on policy matters to the Government, and is effectively the public mouthpiece of the employers.

## employee involvement and consultation

### the issues of employee involvement
'Employee Involvement' is a very broad term which covers the following areas:

- supplying information to employees on all issues of concern to them
- consulting with employees to get their views and ideas and opinions on matters relating to the workplace and its operations
- getting employees to be more committed to the organisation
- giving employees more information about the organisation to make them more aware of the financial and economic realities facing it

There are a number of mechanisms to assist organisations to ensure that they achieve these aims These are listed below.

### joint consultative committees (JCC)
These are made up of employee and management members and they originally concentrated upon day to day employee welfare type issues – sometimes referred to as "tea and toilets" topics. More managements now use them as a way of getting employee involvement on more crucial issues such as how to increase output, and changes in pay and conditions. In a unionised organisation the more serious areas are handled by negotiation with the union rather than through the JCCs, but where there are no unions the JCCs play a more prominent role.

### team briefings
The basic idea of team briefings is that  all employees belong to a *work team* and they are briefed every fortnight or so by their immediate superior. It operates on a cascade system in that the Managing Director briefs his senior managers, they brief junior managers, they brief supervisors and they brief everyone on the lowest grades (in a similar way to the operation of appraisal procedures mentioned in the Employee Performance section above). The target is to get everybody briefed within 48 hours so that the information passed down is not out-of-date.

### quality circles
Quality circles are an American idea which never really caught on in America but was adopted with great enthusiasm by Japanese companies after World War Two. Quality Circles are now becoming more common in Britain because of all the Japanese businesses that have become established in the UK.  The main idea is to get employees in their work teams to meet every week or two to examine the quality of what they are doing and to devise ways of improving quality further. One writer has said that Quality Circles are *the* reason for the Japanese economic miracle. They get everyone involved in their work, and this increases commitment as well as improving product quality. Many

adaptations to existing products are thought of in quality circles and this means that they are constantly being upgraded.

---

### student activity 19.6 – quality circles

Divide into groups of five or six students to form *quality circles* to monitor the quality of your own school or college course. Identify what factors you would want to assess and then think of ways each of these factors could be improved. Present your findings in the form of a memorandum to your teacher/lecturer.

---

### noticeboards

These may sound very old-fashioned, but nowadays they are becoming a sophisticated method of encouraging a two-way flow of information and ideas. Old style boards were *one way* – they simply delivered messages from management. Many organisations now have smart information display areas in factory or office complex entrances which give employees plenty of space to make their own contributions about all kinds of issues. Like team briefings they are a good way of passing on information about the organisation, its performance and the competitive economic environment in which it operates.

### suggestion schemes

Employees are asked to make suggestions about anything they can think of which would improve the organisation in any respect. It might be a sophisticated idea for a product improvement with complex technical drawings attached or it might be a general observation on canteen food or the state of the toilets. Employers will always acknowledge the suggestions, and will often reward good suggestions in the form of a money payment or benefit.

### industrial democracy

A further stage of employee involvement is getting employees to take a role in helping to run the organisation. There are two ways – one passive and one active.

* *Passive involvement* is where employees buy shares in their organisations. Business law permits private limited companies to sell shares to their employees. As far as public limited companies are concerned employees can buy shares in those in exactly the same way as anybody else can. However, in both types of business it is now common for management to actively encourage employees to buy shares. Often employees are offered special deals to buy them cheaply and they may get a small number as a free gift.
* *Active involvement* is when employees are elected, by their fellow employees, to be members of the board of directors of a company. It is European Community policy to get all public companies throughout the EC to reserve between one third and one half of all places on the Board of Directors for elected employees. This is not, as yet, a legal requirement in the UK

---

## chapter summary

❑ Organisations cannot assume that staff will stay with them forever. They must have positive policies to encourage them to stay.

❑ Appraisal systems are now extremely common and are very useful in motivating and retaining employees, provided that they are carried out in a professional and sensitive manner.

❑ Termination of an employment contract has to be carried out in a sensitive and efficient manner which reflects well on the organisation and complies fully with all employment legislation.

❑ Trade Unionism is still important in Britain but it is a far less powerful institution than twenty years ago because of legal changes, high unemployment and changes in the structure of industry.

# 20 Human resourcing – employee training and legal rights

## introduction

This chapter examines the following topics:
- the training and professional development of employees
- legal requirements in human resourcing
- legal redress for employees
- business performance and human resourcing

## training and professional development

Firstly we will examine the importance of *training* employees. Secondly we will look at how employees might be developed to increase job satisfaction and, consequently, become of more use to the organisation in the longer run.

### the changing need for training
A general definition of "training" is:

*"the acquisition of a body of knowledge and skills which can be applied to a particular job"*

Traditionally, young people left school and found a job which provided them with sufficient initial training to enable them to continue to do the same job indefinitely. This was true whether the job was unskilled/semi skilled, requiring only very basic training, or skilled where an "apprenticeship" of several years was required. It was not unusual to be given an apprenticeship in, for example, a shipyard, a coalmine or a newspaper printing works which would provide a steady, secure and well-paid job from the day of joining the company until the day of retirement fifty years later. The training provided in that apprenticeship would be expected to be sufficiently thorough to ensure that very little extra training would ever be required.

In the 1990s this picture now looks very strange. There are now very few traditional apprenticeships, and very few people can now assume that any job will be a "job for life". Even people who do keep the same job for a long time are required to update their skills regularly, or face redundancy because their old skills are rapidly made useless by the advance of new technology.

For most people it is now assumed that they will change their jobs several times in a lifetime, often switching to completely different types of work .

The significance of this is that *training* is much more central to peoples' lives as an *ongoing process* rather than just something they do at the start of their careers.

## training programmes

Most larger organisations employ professional training officers to run training programmes for employees. In a large manufacturing company, for example, the training manager will have teams of training instructors to teach all kinds of courses to employees.  Even in small businesses several types of training will still be necessary.  In all organisations there are several types of training required:

* *Initial training for new employees*
  This is to ensure that the job is done competently and safely.  All new employees must be given training immediately after the induction procedures have been carried out (see Chapter 22).

* *Updating training*
  Increasingly employees are required to learn new skills in place of skills that are becoming redundant, eg in the newspaper printing industry the traditional printing skills have virtually been replaced by completely different work requiring completely different skills.  Printers either had to learn the new skills or lose their jobs.   Most importantly there is now a "culture" of training in which employees are increasingly expected to update knowledge and skills on a regular basis.

* *Multi skilling training*
  Multi skilling means that employees are trained to do several jobs rather than just one.  Employers gain because:
  - an employee can do  the work of somebody who is *absent* through illness or holidays
  - employees are more *motivated* because doing several jobs is usually more interesting than doing just one; where an employee is able to do several jobs it increases his value to the organisation and makes him feel more appreciated and more secure; better motivation in the workforce cuts staff turnover which in turn saves money .
  - the flexibility gained from multi-skilling means the total number of employees can be cut down; for example "One person operated" buses meant that bus operators got rid of over 70,000 bus conductor jobs in the UK in the 1970s

* *Government  training schemes*
  High unemployment  in most of the 1980s meant that  many government schemes were set up to persuade employers to train more young people.  The main scheme was YTS - the Youth Training Scheme - now known as "YT ".  Organisations received financial subsidies to recruit young people for one year (later extended to two years) during which they would provide a proper training programme which would increase the young persons chances of finding permanent work .

  A big advantage of these schemes is that employers can take on trainees, and later offer them permanent jobs if the trainee has worked well.  On the other hand if they are not satisfied with the trainee they can 'say goodbye' to them at the end of the training contract.

## training courses

We will now examine briefly the main types of training course that organisations may run.

* *"In house"  training courses*
  This is where employers run courses inside their own organisation. Courses might be held in a room above the factory or in a smart training centre owned by the organisation.  Courses run "in house" will be ones where it is impractical and unrealistic to offer any other alternative – an obvious example would be the organisations induction programme.  Other examples include training staff  to use equipment which is  specific  to that organisation and   customer care programmes.

The main benefits of using in house courses are:
- they are fairly cheap – there is usually no need to employ outside trainers and lecturers
- course content is tailor-made for your organisation
- references and examples to highlight points can be related to your own organisation.
- everybody knows one another, so there is no time wasted in having to get to know people

- *External courses*
  Sometimes it is necessary to send staff to do courses elsewhere. This may be with another employer or at a specialist training centre or at the factory of an equipment supplier (when an organisation buys new equipment the supplier will usually run training programmes at its own factory to get employees accustomed to using it).

  The benefits of using external courses are:
  - they bring together specialist trainers/tutors who would never be available to an in house course chiefly because of the high cost
  - course members get together from several organisations, and this enables them to learn more about each other and how their respective organisations operate
  - trainers place great value on the benefits of being away from the workplace – the course members are in a comfortable and peaceful environment away from any distractions

  External courses are generally quite expensive because they include fairly luxurious accomodation in lavish surroundings and the guest speakers are highly paid. This means employers have to think very seriously about the value of such courses to the organisation and they have to carefully identify which staff would get the most personal benefit.

- *Vocational and professional courses*
  Internal and external courses often have to be reinforced by courses provided by local colleges and universities. These courses provide the essential knowledge to support what is learnt in the workplace and on internal courses. College courses include vocational courses and professional courses:
  - *vocational* courses provide training in job-related skills, eg office-skills; the National Council for Vocational Qualifications (NCVQ), established by the government, sets standards for workplace competences which can be assessed both in the workplace and at College by examining bodies such as BTEC, RSA and City and Guilds
  - *professional courses*: all the professions operate professional training schemes which enable people to acquire qualifications for their career development; these include the various Accountancy Institutes, the Law Society, and the Institute of Personnel Management; colleges are given permission to run these courses and the students sit exams which are usually set by the professional bodies

Employers are therefore faced with a very wide range of options to offer their staff. For example a school leaver starting work at 18 with 2 GCE A levels might be encouraged to do a BTEC Higher qualification by part-time study at College. After succesful completion (in two years) the employee could then be encouraged to do a professional qualification such as accountancy or personnel management (both taking 3 or 4 years to achieve).

---

**student activity 20.1**

Investigate the training opportunities open to a person starting a permanent job in an organisation, such as a firm of accountants or a retail store. This can be done through work experience, a part-time job, or by talking to a personnel manager in a local business. It can also be linked to career path exercises. Find out what opportunities there are for:

(a) internal vocational (job-related) training

(b) external vocational training

(c) professional training

## evaluation of training in the organisation

Good employers will continually evaluate the effectiveness of their training programmes to ensure that they are worthwhile. The key points to consider are:

- *How have trainees reacted to the training given them?*
  Typically training officers will have a review session at the end of a training course to assess what participants thought about it . A questionnaire asking for individual comments may also be used. It is important to stress that a training course might have been a lot of fun with a great deal of personal interaction between the participants, but in fact they may have learnt very little of direct use to their jobs.

- *What have they actually learnt /what skills have they acquired?*
  The simplest way of checking this is through a test. Trainers should stress that the test results are to assess the effectiveness of the training course not to assess how  particular individuals have performed.

- *How has their job performance improved?*
  Over the first  few months after the training the participants work performance could be monitored to see if there has been any improvement.

- *How has the training benefited the organisation as a whole?*
  Training is not done just for the employees' benefit. The organisation will aim to achieve specific benefits from running training courses, and if  those benefits are not achieved then the training needs looking at again.  A good example are  'customer care' programmes' – more and more organisations are training employees how to deal with customers in a more sensitive, helpful and friendly manner. This has obvious benefits in terms of increasing customer loyalty and increasing sales.

---

### student activity 20.2 – course evaluation

In groups of three or four, devise a series of questions which will help you assess the effectiveness so far of your own course of study (eg GNVQ Level 3). You will need to start by determining what you think "effectiveness" actually means.  Compare your list of questions with the other groups in a full class session. What overall conclusions do you reach?

---

# employee development

## identifying potential

Employee development may be defined as:

*"a course of action designed to enable the individual to realise his potential for growth in the organisation"*

In other words the employer does not just train people for *now*, but for the *future*.

How is this done? A good employer will have a system of identifying career potential in an employee. If there is no system to do this, the result will be that employees stay in 'dead end' jobs which may make them frustrated and bitter. Often they will leave for a better job where their potential is more likely to be recognised.  This means that the employer will lose people who could have been a very great  asset to the organisation, had their potential been realised.

A system to identify potential should include:

- *An appraisal system*  – as  explained and described earlier in the last chapter.

- *An analysis of employee performance*
This means that the employer should have recorded their employees' significant progress and achievements to date. Any evidence of achievement has a bearing on the ability to perform at a higher level. For instance, evidence of good ability at supervising a small team of people shows there is potential to supervise or manage larger numbers of people.

- *A system of assessment centres*
In simple terms this means that the employer identifies particular staff with potential, using previous work experience etc as a guide, and then arranges a series of practical tests to assess their ability to handle the kind of work which more senior jobs might involve. These tests might include a short period (a day or so) doing a higher level job under the supervision of a senior manager. Another commonly-used test is to get the employee to carry out an 'in tray' exercise. This involves giving him a series of letters, memos and reports, some urgent and some non urgent, to assess how he deals with them.

## methods of developing employees with potential

Several techniques can be used to help promising employees to develop their  abilities and give management a better idea of exactly where the employees' future may lie:

- *Job rotation* – giving people a range of jobs in rotation widens their experiences and increases their skills.
- *Job enlargement* – giving people extra tasks to do gives management a better idea of  the employees  true capacity, ability and stamina.
- *Job enrichment*  – adding  more interesting and more difficult tasks to the job. This might be done with a person of very great potential (often known as a 'high-flier') to see just how capable he or she really is.
- *Understudying* – this means that  an employee will be attached to a very senior manager to act as an assistant. This gives the employee  insight into what senior managers have to do, and is often used to groom very able people to move rapidly into a top job.
- *Project work* – giving a promising employee a specific investigative project  enables them to get to appreciate many aspects of the organisation and it enables them to get to know senior managers. A typical project might involve the employee devising ways of saving the organisation money by proposing redundancies or by restructuring the workforce. How the employee handles people in this sensitive area will give a accurate picture of his potential to take on a very senior post later in his career.
- *Internal and external courses* – potential managers will be sent on a wide range of courses to help them and the organisation to identify their potential and interests. Some courses will give them the detailed knowledge they will need to be able to take on more responsible jobs (eg courses in law and accountancy).  A special type of course,which is now extremely popular, is the 'survival weekend' in which a group of managers or potential managers (sometimes from several different organisations) are brought together and given tasks to perform in a hostile environment. Tasks might include building bridges across streams or rock climbing or canoeing – in most cases the aim is to get the participants to work together as a team and to develop leadership skills.
- *Studying for further qualifications* – many employers encourage able employees to study for advanced qualifications. This not only improves their knowledge for use at work, but it also demonstrates they possess the stamina to complete courses which may be one or two years long.

In the final analysis it is not very useful to encourage employees to carry out any of activities listed above unless it *does* lead on to improved career prospects.

---

**student activity 20.3 –**
You are working as a personnel manager in a large organisation.
(a) Write down a list of ways in which you could identify employees with potential for promotion to supervisory or management level.
(b) How would you develop those employees so that they can realise that potential?

# legal rights of the employee

All personnel work requires a basic knowledge of employment law . In this section we will examine the ways in which an employee may protect his or her interests through the legal system. We will start with a broad summary of the main rights of employees, and then examine how the employee can enforce any of those rights in an Industrial Tribunal.

The main employee rights are:

### to have equal pay
Since 1970 employees of both sexes have been entitled to equal pay. Before this it was legal for an employer to pay women less than men. The Equal Pay Act 1970 meant that, for example, a restaurant would have to pay all its waiters and waitresses exactly the same rate of pay.  Despite the Act, the gap between men and women's average pay did not narrow that much in the 1970s. This was because many jobs were predominantly held by men and others – the less well paid ones – were predominantly held by women. For example, most nursing jobs were held by women and were relatively poorly paid.

In I983 an Equal Value Amendment was added to the 1970 Act. This European Community ruling enabled women to improve their pay by comparing their jobs with particular 'mens jobs' and showing that their jobs are of 'equal value'.  This means that, for example, if shop assistants in a particular store chain can show their job is of equal value to that of better-paid warehousing staff then they all must get the same pay  (the actual assessment of the relative value of the jobs concerned must always be carried out by independent experts.)

### not to suffer from discrimination on grounds of sex, race or disability
The Sex Discrimination and Race Relations Acts in 1975 and 1976 made it illegal to discriminate on sexual or racial grounds when offering jobs, advertising for applicants for jobs, determining pay and conditions in jobs, and when promoting employees. The employer would also be liable if it let employees discriminate against other employees.

Both Acts include a small number of exceptions where discrimination can still occur but these only cover a small proportion of the workforce (for example, the Act includes a 'Chinese Restaurant clause' which enables ethnic restaurants to discriminate in favour of particular ethnic groups when filling jobs as waiters.)

In addition employers may not discriminate against people with registered physical or mental disabilities (under the 1944 and 1959 Disabled Persons Acts). Indeed, they are required to take positive steps to employ disabled people – at least 3% of all workforces should be people with registered disabilities (obviously certain organisations cannot employ disabled people for safety reasons and they are given exemption certificates). Government money is also available to help organisations to modify buildings and buy special equipment for the use of disabled employees.

### to have their jobs protected against unfair dismissal
The Employment Protection (Consolidation) Act 1978 sets out the framework for employees obtaining compensation or re-instatement if they are judged by an Industrial Tribunal (see next section) to have been *unfairly* dismissed.  The Act sets out situations where dismissal can be unfair. These are where an employee:
- decides not to join a trade union on religious grounds
- joins a trade union
- is unfairly selected for redundancy
- is pregnant, or is not allowed to come back again immediately after the pregnancy
- is dismissed for striking when other striking employees have stayed on

Compensation for unfair dismissal may be awarded by an Industrial Tribunal, as very often the employee may not want to return to the workplace. The current rates, for each year of employment (subject to a £5,200 maximum) are:

Employees between 18 and 21 years of age        half a week's pay

Employees between 22 and 41 years of age        a full week's pay

Employees between 42 years of age and retirement        one and a half's a week's pay

## to have safe and healthy working conditions

The Health and Safety at Work etc Act 1974 sets down the regulations for employers providing a safe working environment for their employees. The scope of the Act extends to premises, systems of work.To achieve this aim, employers should provide and maintain:

- safe and healthy plant and systems of work – and maintenance of the equipment
- safe and healthy working environment and adequate welfare facilities and arrangements
- safe and healthy premises with adequate amenities, access and exits
- safe methods for handling, storing and transporting materials
- adequate instruction and training for employees, and adequate supervision
- information to employees concerning health and safety

In addition, the employer must issue a written *safety policy* stating his intention to secure the health and safety of persons employed, and setting out the arrangements made for this purpose. The Act also makes provision for the appointment of safety representatives and states the employer's obligation to form a safety committee.

The area of health and safety at work is subject to constant review, particularly in terms of Directives issued by the EC, which are binding in the UK. The regulations relating to VDUs (computer screens) are a case in point.

---

### student activity 20.4 – employee rights

You are the union representative in a large organisation. You often get queries from employees about their rights. How would you deal with these?

(a) a VDU (computer) operator complains of constant headaches and backache

(b) a pregnant secretary is told that she will not be able to come back to her job after she has had her baby, as her "replacement will be settled down by then"

(c) a woman mechanic has been told that she cannot do a certain job because it is "too dangerous"

(d) a woman packer complains that she is paid less than than the warehouseman with whom she works

(e) an English bilingual secretary who has a working knowledge of Japanese complains that she has not been promoted to join a team to deal with Japanese customers; a Japanese secretary has been given the job

---

## legal redress

### Industrial Tribunals

If any employee considers that he or she is being denied any of the rights outlined above, they can pursue their case through an *Industrial Tribunal*. Industrial Tribunals were established by Act of Parliament as a form of informal court – a panel of experts – to offer employees the chance to get themselves quick, cheap and efficient justice, with none of the legalistic language and procedures which many people find rather offputting (and expensive). They operate in several large regional centres (eg Bristol, Birmingham, Manchester). A tribunal consists of one representative from the local branch of the Trades Union Congress and one from the local branch of the Confederation of British Industry. The chairman will be a full time post held by a barrister or a solicitor. Tribunals deal with actions taken under:

- Equal Pay Act 1970
- Sex Discrimination Act 1975
- Race Relations Act 1976
- Employment Protection (Consilidation) Act 1978

## taking a case to an Industrial Tribunal
### stage 1 – dismissal
Suppose Ivor Case, an employee of Firem Limited is dismissed because his work is of substandard quality. Before getting to the stage of actual dismissal the employer must go through a number of steps in accordance with the regulations laid down in the 1978 Employment Protection (Consolidation) Act and with the Code of Practice published by the Advisory, Conciliation and Arbitration Service (ACAS). Dismissal procedures are examined in the last chapter.

### stage 2 – has the employee got a case for taking the matter to a Tribunal? Is it worth it?
Assuming Ivor has been dismissed he will then have to decide if it is worth bringing an action against Firem Ltd. A number of factors need considering:

- *Does he have enough evidence* to make him feel that he really has a case ? For example, was he given a chance to improve the quality of his work? Was he offered extra training? When it came to the actual dismissal procedure was he given sufficient verbal and written warnings about the quality of his work? Did he get the chance to explain why his work was substandard to the employer (in the presence of a 'friend' such as an official of his own trade union?) Finally, was he given a written statement explaining in full detail why he was being dismissed, together with details of how he might appeal against the decision.

- *What remedy does he want?*   For unfair dismissal cases there are three choices:
  - you get your job back – reinstatement
  - you get another job in the same organisation – re-engagement
  - you get financial compensation based on the degree of personal 'injury' to your feelings and on your length of service with the employer

The employee also needs to bear in mind that:
- very few people ever get their job back, or even another job in the same organisation.
- levels of financial compensation are usually very low – the average is a little over £1,000
- only about 1 in 3 applicants ever win their cases in Tribunal hearings
- he will have to pay his own legal costs – even if he wins (although if he is a trade union member then he may get full financial support from them if his case is a strong one)

### stage 3 – taking the case to the Tribunal
*documentation*
If Ivor still decides it is worth going on he will need to fill in a form IT 1 which outlines his case against the employer. The form also asks him what remedy he prefers. The form then goes to the Headquarters of the Industrial Tribunal service. They send a copy of his IT 1 to Firem Ltd and ask them to fill in an IT 2 form which is a reply to the allegations made by the ex-employee.

*ACAS consultation*
At this stage both the ex-employee (called the *Applicant*) and the ex-employer (called the *Respondent*) will be visited by an official of *ACAS* who will try to get them to settle their differences without going to a Tribunal. The ACAS official is unbiased and will point out all the weak and strong points of both cases and make his recommendations. Where the employee's case looks hopeless he will say so to help him avoid embarrassment and legal costs at a later date.

*pre-hearing assessment*

The next stage is a *pre-hearing assessment*. This means that a Tribunal will look at all the relevant documents from both sides and see if the ex-employee has a fair chance of winning. If they feel his chances are not good they will issue a certificate stating that if he goes any further and does lose his case he will have to pay the legal costs of both sides. For a person with little money this is a big encouragement to drop out at this stage. Many people do.

*Tribunal hearing and decision*

The Tribunal hearing usually takes no longer than a day (often only half a day). As mentioned above the tribunal consists of a lawyer and representative from the TUC and the CBI. Both sides in the dispute will give their evidence – either in person or through representative lawyers – and both sides can bring along witnesses as in any court case. The Tribunal will ask many questions, most of these coming from the Chairman, since he or she has the most detailed legal knowledge. After the hearing the tribunal will adjourn for half an hour or so and then give their decision.

---

**student activity 20.5 – Industrial Tribunals**

A friend of yours has been dismissed for unsatisfactory performance in his job. He considers he has been unfairly dismissed because he was the only male operator on a production line, all the other operators being women, and more experienced at the job. He was also on holiday when the others had received training on a new method of working. He wants to take the matter to an Industrial Tribunal. He is a member of a trade union. How would you advise him

(a)  about the case he may have against his employer?

(b)  about the procedures for going to an Industrial Tribunal?

---

# business performance and human resourcing

The effective management of human resources has ultimately one key aim as far as the management of a business is concerned: the improvement of business performance. We will now look at some specific aspects of business performance.

## productivity and profitability

Better management of human resources should result in better productivity. Productivity is output per employee. It can be increased by:

- *Effective negotiation with the employee representatives.* Whenever employees are in a weak bargaining position (due to high levels of unemployment for example) this might enable an *unscrupulous employer* to force them to accept worse conditions of service and lower rates of pay. This would raise profits if wage cuts are significant and less money is allocated for holidays and social welfare facilities. By contrast, many *well intentioned employers* have preserved pay and conditions, and often improved them, but they have used their stronger power to force employees to accept redundancies (usually with quite generous levels of redundancy payments). This again should raise profits.
- Use of *employee participation* in its various forms (see pages 207 - 208).
- Use of *sustained programmes of high quality training and employee development*. To ensure that employees are able to work more productively requires thorough training which includes regular updating with knowledge of the newest approaches and techniques.

## resolving problems of absenteeism

It is clear that most of the factors listed above will also help to reduce the levels of absenteeism in any organisation. For example, whenever employee power is weakened by high unemployment, staff will be less likely to be off work without a good reason such as illness. It is easier to replace staff and therefore employees cannot afford to risk having time off for trivial reasons.

Employee participation and involvement in decision making increases morale and because employees are happier and more involved in their work, they are less likely to take time off. Finally, good training and development policies – especially the latter – demonstrate a caring approach by employers and this may also raise morale and reduce absenteeism.

### quality of service

The same factors will also improve the quality of service provided by an organisation. Any economic pressure – be it the fear of unemployment or the threat of privatisation in a state-owned organisation – will make employees attend more to customer-care. For example, the use of compulsory competitive tendering in local authorities for the supply of refuse collection services, street lighting maintenance and grass cutting, has forced both managers and employees to improve the quality of customer service to enable them to keep on winning the contract each time it is renewed. *Employee participation*, eg owning shares in the business, also improves service standards. Finally, good training and development policies lay great emphasis on customer care and service. Good employers put great stress on customer care in initial induction programmes and the message should continually be reinforced.

---

**student activity 20.6 – improving productivity through human resourcing**

A friend of yours runs a High Street travel agency business employing five staff, and is having a number of problems, which she is blaming on current economic conditions. You ask her to analyse the problems and she tells you the following:

(a)   holiday bookings are down 15% on last year

(b)   complaints are being received about poor customer service in the shop

(c)   staff absenteeism has increased by 20% over the last three months

What do you consider is her real problem, and how would you advise her to tackle it?

---

# chapter summary

❑   Training and professional development needs to be carried out to ensure that organisations are making the fullest use of their human resources in a manner which also helps to motivate their employees.

❑   Employees are protected in law in a number of areas including equal pay, discrimination (sex, race and disability) and unfair dismissal. Their working conditions are also protected by Health and Safety Regulations.

❑   Industrial Tribunals provide a cheap and convenient form of legal help for employees who consider they have been unfairly treated by their employers. The financial compensation paid to employees who win their cases, however, is usually quite small.

❑   Proper attention by an organisation to human resourcing issues usually results in an improved level of performance and productivity.

# EVIDENCE COLLECTION EXERCISE

# 10

# *Investigating human resource management*

---

Element 4.1        *Investigate human resourcing*

Suggested Sources:  • talks by personnel officers
• work experience
• works visits
• investigation into large public companies
• textbooks in libraries and resource centres

---

## INTRODUCTION

This activity is a major piece of research work which will require you to examine in detail the operations of one large business organisation.

This can be *either*

• a business in your neighbourhood with which your school or college has links (remember that the term "business" can include public sector organisations), *or*

• a large public limited company

Information about the public limited company can be obtained from a college or reference library, eg from the Stock Exchange Year Book and other suitable sources. Information will also be available from the company itself. In liaison with your teacher/lecturer, you should either write to or telephone the company and request this years' Report and Accounts together with any other published material available about the company. Most large companies operate 'corporate communications' departments or public relations departments, and are usually quite helpful, as long as you are polite. You may also have to get in touch with the Personnel Department, who may be able to provide a speaker.

Note: you may already have information such as a set of Report and Accounts from your investigations undertaken in Evidence Collection Exercise 4 "The products and purpose of business".

## TASKS

On the basis of the information you have collected you should then examine it in the light of what you have studied in the last two chapters. You should produce a written report which will:

(a) Examine how far the company operates a system of employee representation and involvement – what types of involvement are encouraged ?

(b) Examine the systems set up by the company to train and develop employees.

(c) Identify any evidence that the company appreciates the linkage between good human resource management and its business performance.

# 21 Job roles in organisations

## introduction

In this chapter we will examine the following:

- job roles in organisations – the different types of job in the hierarchy of a business
- job descriptions – how the duties and responsibilities of a job are defined
- person specifications – how a business will set standards for recruiting the ideal candidate for a job

## job roles in organisations

This section will look at the key roles held by people in a typical business organisation – a limited company – and examine their responsibilities and powers. It should be stressed that other 'businesses' including public sector bodies and charities have similar job roles and similar hierarchies – it is largely the terminology that differs. The limited company is chosen here as it is a common form of business. You should refer to Chapter 2 "Business structures and administration systems" for a full explanation of how the job roles fit into the actual structure of a business.

### the director

The Companies Act 1985 requires that private and public limited companies must have at least two directors to determine the policy of the organisation and to look after the interests of the shareholders who actually own the business. In the case of small companies the directors may themselves be the only shareholders. In most businesses there will be two types of director – *executive directors* and *non-executive directors*.

*Executive Directors* are those who actually work in the organisation. The Production Director or the Finance Director are examples. Executive Directors are usually highly paid and will probably own large numbers of shares in the organisation.

*Non-executive directors* are appointed on a part time basis to attend the board meetings and give perhaps one or two days a week of their time to the organisation. They are often appointed for their influence. For example, retired politicians are sometimes appointed to the boards of large companies because they have useful contacts and influence which can be very helpful to these businesses. Non-executive directors may also be elected by the shareholders to protect their interests by ensuring that the Executive Directors do not have too much power or make rash business decisions. A third type of non-executive director, becoming increasingly common, is the employee representative.

Together all the directors form the Board of Directors which will be headed by a Chairman, elected by the directors, and – to run the organisation from day to day – there will be a Managing Director. The chairman will usually be a non-executive role whereas the Managing Director will be an executive role.

## the manager
Managers in an organisation will be appointed by the board of directors to ensure that the business is run in an effective and efficient manner. They are required to carry out the policy of the board of directors, to ensure their own department works efficiently and to supervise the work of all of their departmental staff. Good managers will employ a range of  management techniques (outlined in Chapter 20) to ensure that their staff are not only effective but also highly motivated.

## the team member
A board of directors and its managers can only succeed if the team members  in every department are working effectively – a principle which can be extended to a football team and manager.  The business team will comprise the manager, supervisory staff and administrative, clerical and production staff.  Every department in an organisation is composed of a manager and his/her team. It is essential that the manager gets the very best out of the team. Every individual should know what his/her role is in the team, and they should be properly trained and developed so they can work effectively. Most importantly, they should realise that they are a 'team' and not just individuals (again, compare with a football team in action).  Building a group of employees into a team requires considerable management skill. As noted in the last chapter it is quite common nowadays to use outdoor 'activity weekends' to build up better working relationships between employees so that they are able to relate to one another more effectively in their jobs.  The team idea has also been exploited effectively by the Japanese who set up "cells" of approximately 80 staff to manage and be responsible for functional areas within a  business.

### student activity 21.1 – teamwork
Think of a series of exercises and activities you could use to get your own class at school or college to work as a team.  If you think it is already working well as a team,  identify the reasons why this is so.

## job descriptions

*A job description describes what  a job involves.*

What are the main tasks required in a job? More and more organisations have job descriptions for every job they have – from the caretaker to the managing director.

In drawing up a job description the personnel department has a number of alternatives. These are:
(a)  the department itself can draw up a description of what the job entails
(b)  the department can get the existing job holder to do it instead
(c)  the department can interview the job holder to find out what he or she does

In most cases it is probably best to combine approaches. Clearly approach (b) and (c) may produce a biased view of what the job involves. After all, most people are likely to exaggerate the importance of what they do and the effort and ability that is required to do it. On the other hand, approach (a) will probably miss out many little but important tasks which are not obvious unless you actually do the job yourself.

The aim of the exercise is to *itemise* all the tasks involved in a job and to try to allocate a proportion of the working week to each task. The list of tasks, and the relative importance of each one, is vitally important for several reasons:

- In carrying out *appraisals* (see Chapter 19) a manager cannot appraise his employees if he does not know what the job comprises
- When analysing the job for *training needs* (see Chapter 20) the manager must be able to see what tasks a job involves so that he can determine what training may be required.
- In *planning the size of the workforce* for the future, it will be necessary to know exactly what tasks each job involves in case the re-allocation of tasks between jobs is required, eg three people may be required to share the work of a fourth post which is being made redundant – this cannot be done fairly without a detailed knowledge of the tasks involved in the fourth post.
- *For pay determination* – many employers now rely upon sophisticated job-evaluation exercises to determine what work and responsibilities are involved in every job in the organisation. Having done this, the jobs can then be ranked and allocated a salary or wage level. A simple and common example is to give clerical jobs which include the responsibility of handling money a higher ranking than clerical jobs which do not. Clearly, none of this is possible without good quality detailed job descriptions.

## drafting the job description

From all the information collected, by whichever method is chosen, it will then be necessary to draw up the document itself. Most people applying for jobs will get a job description along with the application form and a person specification (explained below).

The main features of a job description are:

1. the job title
2. the location of the job
3. a brief outline of what the employing organisation does
4. the main purpose of the job
5. a detailed list of the main tasks required in the job
6. the standards that the job holder will be required to achieve
7. pay and other benefits
8. promotion prospects
9. the person to whom the job holder reports
10. the person(s) who report(s) to the job holder

Nowadays employees are expected to be more flexible and to be able to do a wider range of work. This means that job titles (point 1) tend to be broader than they used to be. Point 3 is important in that a go-ahead, successful, organisation will find it easier to attract applicants and of an above average quality. Points 4, 5 and 6 are the essentials of the job description, so that anyone interested in applying will know what they would be required to do if offered the job. Points 7 and 8 are needed as attractions to draw in good quality applicants. Finally, points 9 and 10 give the applicant a clear idea of the position of the job within the organisation.

In summary, the job description has a number of roles, not least of which is to turn enquiries from capable people into real job applications. Therefore, *presentation* of the job description is very important, although, regretably, often forgotten by many employers.

**JOB SPECIFICATION**

**Mereford County Council**

**County Secretary and Solicitor's Department**

**Trading Standards Section**

| | |
|---|---|
| Job Title | Technical Assistant |
| Post No. | 43/789 |
| Section | Trading Standards |
| The Employer | Mereford County Council is one of England's largest Shire Counties with a population of 1.7 million. The County Council employs 69,000 staff. |
| Grade | Scale 1 (spinal column pay points 1-10). Successful applicant will be placed on the point appropriate to his/her previous experience and qualifications. |
| Aim and purpose of the job | To assist generally in the enforcement activities of trading standards officers and enforcement officers. |
| Responsible to | The Divisional Trading Standards Officer |
| Duties | To assist Trading Standards Officers and Enforcement Officers in the performance of their indoor and outdoor duties arising under Trading Standards and Animal Health legislation. |
| | To assist in the testing of weighing and measuring equipment and the adjusting of weights. |
| | To assist in the testing of goods and services, the preparation of samples for testing, examination and analysis. |
| | To prepare notes and statements relating to investigations in which he/she has been involved and to give evidence in court where necessary. |
| | To maintain equipment belonging to the department in a clean and operational condition. |
| Job prospects | The department is a large one with ample career prospects for keen, enthusiastic and committed people who are willing to study for further professional qualifications. |

## student activity 21.2 – job specifications

What do you think about this job specification ? Identify its good points and any weak points. Do you think it will attract good quality candidates for the job ? How would you improve it? Carry out this task either singly or in small groups, and then discuss your analysis in class.

# person specifications

A *person specification* will be drawn up after the job description has been prepared. It identifies the kind of person who is needed to carry out that particular job, and will be invaluable in the recruitment process (see Chapter 22). The difference between a person specification and a job description is that *a person specification sets out the qualities of an ideal candidate, the job description defines the duties and responsibilities of the job.*

The best-known method of drawing up person specifications is called the *'seven-point plan'* originally devised by Alec Rodger. This bases the person specification upon seven separate groups of characteristics:

1. *Physique, health and appearance* – this includes grooming, looks, dress sense, voice, hearing and eyesight as well as general health matters.

2. *Attainments* – this includes educational qualifications such as GCSEs, GNVQs, A levels and degrees and vocational qualifications such as NVQs and job experience.

3. *General intelligence* – this is estimated by IQ tests and by assessment of general reasoning ability.

4. *Special aptitudes* – what special skills does a person have? These include skills with words, with numbers, with musical instruments, with artistic technique and with mechanical equipment.

5. *Interests* – are they intellectual or practical or social or a mixture of them all?

6. *Disposition* – this is an assessment of the person's acceptability by other people, leadership qualities, the person's emotional stability and self-reliance.

7. *Circumstances* – factors such as age, whether single or married, whether mobile or not.

The Rodgers Seven Point plan usually requires managers to distinguish between essential and desirable qualities under each of the seven headings. For example, five GCSE s at grade C or above might be an *essential* "Attainment" to do a particular job whereas two GCE 'A' levels might be *desirable* but not essential.

### student activity 21.3 – person specifications

Now have another look at the Job Specification for the Technical Assistant in the Trading Standards Department on the previous page. You also need to go to the library careers section and find out more about the work involved in a Trading Standards department. Check up on the qualifications and aptitudes that the job requires.

Having done all this you must prepare a 'person specification' for this job in which you will use the Rodgers seven point plan. Clearly identify what you think will be the essential and desirable qualities required in the job.

## chapter summary

❑ Job roles in a limited company business can be divided into three functions: director, manager and team member. These functions are also to be found in other types of business, but the terminology may differ.

❑ Job descriptions are drawn up to set out the responsibilities and duties of a particular job.

❑ Person specifications set out the attributes of an ideal candidate for the job.

# EVIDENCE COLLECTION EXERCISE

# 11

# *Job descriptions and person specifications*

| | |
|---|---|
| Element 4.2 | *Investigate job roles in organisational structures* |
| Suggested Sources: | • Chapter 21 |
| | • talks by personnel officers from public and private sector organisations |
| | • specimen job descriptions and person specifications |
| | • detailed investigation into the types of job involved here |
| | • textbooks in libraries and resource centres |

## TASK 1

Examine the Job Description set out on the next page. It is for a job as Personal Assistant to the Managing Director of Pharmatex Limited.

In preparation for interviewing candidates for the job, draft a *person specification* using the Rodgers 'seven point plan' for the Pharmatex Ltd job:

Remember to identify the *essential* and *desirable* features required in the job.

## TASK 2

Compare the Pharmatex job description with that for the Technical Assistant in Mereford County Council shown on page 223.

Set out your findings in writing, ensuring that you have answered the following questions:

• In what respects are they similar ?

• How do they differ ?

• How far does the Pharmatex example meet the key requirement which is to attract 'good quality' applicants?

• To what extent do the two job descriptions illustrate the differences between the way private sector and public sector organisations recruit staff ?

It would be useful to interview or be given a talk by personnel officers from the Local Authority and from a business comparable to Pharmatex Limited in order to help the comparison.

## PHARMATEX LIMITED

| | |
|---|---|
| **Job Title** | Personal Assistant/Secretary to the Managing Director |
| **Further information** | Sylvia Fordston, Personnel Officer (0675 453421 x 564) |
| **Responsible to** | The Managing Director, Andrew Johnson |
| **Responsible for** | Two junior clerical assistants |
| **Job location** | Pharmatex Ltd Head Office, 134 Sunderland Road, Durham  DH3 OHP |

**Duties**

- Acting as Secretary at  business meetings.
- Producing agenda and Minutes of meetings.
- Making travel arrangements for the Managing Director and for other Executive Directors.
- Accompanying Mr Johnson on business appointments in the UK and abroad.
- Organising hospitality/accommodation etc for business visitors to Pharmatex Ltd.
- Supervision of duties of the Clerical Assistants.

**Previous experience**

Good secretarial and P/A experience at a senior managerial level is essential.

**The Organisation**

Pharmatex Ltd is a medium-sized manufacturer of products for the retail pharmaceutical industry specialising in cough syrups, throat lozenges and paracetamol-based pain relief tablets. 30% of products are sold to the French and Spanish markets. Apart from two factories in Warrington and Durham there is also a small factory and distribution centre in Calais, France.

**Pay and Conditions**

Working hours 9 am to 5 pm Monday to Friday.

Salary is negotiable but substantial to reflect the importance of the job.

There is a generous company pension scheme.

Because the nature of the job involves a lot of foreign trips a generous travel allowance is paid.

**General comments**

This job calls for organisational abilities and personal qualities of a very high order and it is doubtful if it could be filled by anybody under the age of 25.

# 22 Recruitment, job applications and interviews

## introduction

Recruitment is the first part of the process of filling a vacancy for a job. The recruitment process includes:

- the examination of the vacancy itself
- consideration of the sources of suitable candidates
- making contact with potential candidates and attracting them to apply for a job with your organisation
- the job interview and the selection of the successful candidate

In this chapter, we will look at each stage of this process in turn . We will also look at other related processes, including:

- the writing of letters of application
- the drawing up of a curriculum vitae (CV)
- interviewer techniques
- techniques for candidates being interviewed

## the recruitment process

### the vacancy itself

If a vacancy for a job exists in an organisation it will be for one of several reasons:

- a *new job* is available because of the expansion of the organisation
- somebody in the organisation has *retired* – every year roughly one in forty of the workforce nationally will retire
- somebody has *gone elsewhere* – there is a steady turnover of staff due to people acquiring better jobs in other organisations or better jobs in other establishments of the same organisation ,or because they are following their partners/husbands/wives in their career moves
- somebody has been *promoted* - the vacancy arises because the previous holder has been given a better job either in the same establishment or the same organisation

- somebody has *died* – sadly there are many employees who die during their working lives and with increased stress and the growing incidence of heart disease this is becoming more common
- there is a *restructuring* of the business, which means there are gaps to be filled in the organisation

## alternatives to filling a vacancy

Personnel (or Human Resource) Management departments are under constant presssure to justify the filling of a vacancy since *not* to do so will save the organisation money. There are several alternatives to filling a vacancy, all with benefits and all with disadvantages:

- *overtime by the remaining employees*
  The remaining employees cover the work with overtime – employees like overtime because it earns them more money, usually at a higher rate of pay, but they do not want it all the time.Too much overtime causes tiredness and greater inefficiency and more likelihood of making mistakes.
- *restructuring of the work*
  The organisation of work could be restructured – it is quite common to find that a job or several jobs could be removed with very little damage.
- *employing part-time staff*
  Part-time staff can be employed when the business becomes busy and laid off at quieter times, thus producing a big cost saving . They have fewer employee rights than full-timers and less job security. The disadvantage is that they will have less commitment, and training costs will also be just as high as for full time staff.
- *more use of machinery/technology*
  In offices and in factories staff can easily be replaced with greater use of machines and new technology.  Post rooms, for example, used to employ large numbers of staff to fill and seal envelopes whereas nowadays two or three staff can manage with the aid of automatic filling, folding and sealing machines.

It is important that when considering the alternatives the Personnel Department looks critically at the *job description* and *person specification* for the vacancy (see Chapter 21). From these documents it will be possible to assess how practical it is to rely upon the use of overtime, part-time staff or machinery instead of filling the vacancy.

## filling the vacancy - finding the applicants

If the Personnel Department, after consideration of alternatives examined above, decides that the vacancy *will* need filling,  then the next stage will be where to look for candidates. There are basically only two sources of candidate – internal and external.

### internal candidates

Unless a vacancy is for the lowest grade job possible, there will be internal candidates who are interested in the vacancy as a promotion. The main benefits to the employer of internal appointments are:

- an organisation with a reputation for internal advancement will find it easier to motivate staff, whereas in organisations where internal advancement is rare, staff will be less committed to the work and may be preoccupied with external job applications
- the organisation will attract better candidates if they see there is a future career in it
- many candidates will be local people who have bought homes there, have children at local schools and husbands/wives in other local jobs
- internal candidates know the business and what will be expected of them,  and they can become effective in the new job very quickly
- although there is bound to be bitterness from other internal applicants who do not get the job, they will at least feel that there will be other career opportunities in the organisation and that their "turn" will come
- the organisation will not need to rely upon external references when choosing from internal applicants – accurate information will be available from departmental heads and other colleagues

The disadvantages of appointing internally are equally valid:

- the successful candidates may suffer *role conflict* in that they are now senior to people with whom they worked with as equals –there may be a problem for them in asserting their authority
- a person promoted internally may be expected to pick up the new job in an unreasonably short space of time
- filling a vacancy internally leaves another vacancy to fill, and so on
- if the promotion policy is based upon seniority (often called "filling dead mens shoes") young keen staff will leave, whereas a policy of promoting keen young people will demoralise and demotivate older staff who think they have no prospects at all

### external candidates

From the observations above it is easy to see that there are clear benefits from "going outside" to fill a vacancy. These benefits are :

- much wider range of people from which to choose
- newcomers to the organisation will bring in new ideas
- newcomers are not associated with the old policies of the organisation – for this reason it is always a good idea to bring in people from outside if a change in the organisational culture is planned
- newcomers are likely to be more mobile than existing staff and in a multi-site business this can be very useful to the organisation
- newcomers may bring skills and management techniques from their former employers which your organisation might also adopt

There are also disadvantages of filling a vacancy with an external candidate:

- it is more expensive than internal recruitment, and often much more so
- it takes time for a newcomer to get used to his or her new employer, and therefore the newcomer will not be performing effectively for the initial period
- people who move between jobs have a better idea of their market value than people who stay with the same organisation for a long time, and they make the best use they can of this by threatening to leave unless they get high pay rises or rapid promotion
- employers have to rely heavily on the references of other employers, and in reality these can be quite unreliable – people are sometimes given good references by their employers simply to help to get rid of them!
- if the newcomer leaves shortly after joining, it will have cost the organisation a great deal in terms of embarassment in the eyes of the existing staff and in terms of the actual recruitment costs (see later section)

## sources of external candidates

Assuming that the advantages of external recruitment are judged more important than the disadvantages, where would an organisation go to find external applicants ? It will depend on the type of job an employer is trying to fill. The main sources and the particular jobs they specialise in are as follows:

| *source of applicants* | *types of employee available* |
|---|---|
| *The School Careers Services* | school leavers for a wide range of jobs and traineeships such as Youth Training schemes |
| *Job Centres* | a wide range of jobs but chiefly semi-skilled, unskilled and clerical workers |
| *University Career Services* | graduates |

| | |
|---|---|
| *Employment Agencies* | many will find applicants in virtually all areas of work although their most important areas are clerical, secretarial and unskilled manual employees |
| *Employment Businesses* | this is a legal term for an agency which employs its own staff and hires them to organisations on a weekly fee basis – mainly for short term unskilled manual and clerical work |
| *Recruitment and Executive Consultants* | management and professional jobs |

In a typical organisation with a mixture of jobs, skilled and unskilled, secretarial and clerical, professional and managerial there will be a need to call on most of the above services at some time. They also need skilled and unskilled people from the job centres and clerical and secretarial staff from the agencies. Executive Search Consultants ("head-hunters") are used to find new managers or professionally qualified engineers and research staff. Agencies can find staff to fill short-term contracts and Agency 'Businesses' will supply ready-made work teams to organisations for as little as one week (or even one day) for a fixed weekly fee (this means the employees do not go onto the organisation's own payroll, thus saving administrative work).

All these services provide organisations with a more flexible workforce for as little inconvenience to them as possible. However, apart from the Careers Service and the Jobcentres, which are both free, the other services are quite expensive. Using an Executive Search Consultant to fill a senior management job can cost the equivalent of 20 to 30% of the first year salary for that manager. Agencies supplying short term labour will charge hourly rates two to three times more than the standard pay rates offered by an organisation. Convenience costs money!

In addition to these organisations the other sources available include factory gate notices, newspaper and radio advertising and word of mouth. Newspapers are a useful medium for advertising jobs but they attract a large number of unsuitable people and it takes a lot of departmental time to sift through them to find the few good applicants. Radio adverts get a similar level and quality of response.

## advertising the job

Unless an organisation pays a recruitment consultancy or an executive search consultant to find potential recruits, it will have to design its own advertisements to attract people. Specialist consultancies have sophisticated advertising departments which place large and expensive adverts in the 'quality' press such as 'The Times','The Guardian' the 'Sunday Times' and 'The Independent'. Most businesses, however, will not have such facilities and they will have to draft up their own advertisements. The newspaper will itself normally typeset the final version.

## writing the advertisement

Before writing the advertisement the employer must determine exactly what is wanted from the job being advertised. To ensure this the employer must look carefully at the *Person Specification* – what type of person is required – and the *Job Specification* – what the person will be required to do in the job – before writing the advert (see Chapter 21).

When drafting the advertisement the key points to consider are:

• *job specification*
  The advert should specify what the job requires the person to do. Obviously this can only be fairly general but the key duties need outlining.

• *type of person*
  The advert should then say what kind of person is required. It is illegal to specify a particular sex or someone of a particular racial origin, except in a few quite rare situations (eg you could advertise for a person of Chinese origin to work in a Chinese restaurant (see page 216). "What kind of person?" includes issues like experience and qualifications.

- *pay and conditions*
  Depending on the nature of the job, state what the pay and conditions are, eg holidays, hours and pension arrangements (where appropriate). As the government moves towards restricting rights to State-provided pensions the provision of good private pension schemes by employers becomes more and more attractive to job seekers. Flexible hours ("flexitime") is attractive to some people, whilst for others the opportunity to earn overtime pay will be very appealing.

  Obviously,what to stress most in the advert will vary from job to job – office work jobs might emphasise the good pension or the flexitime, whereas a factory job might stress the chance to earn money from overtime.

- *place of work*
  The job location should be made clear. Some organisations are multi-sited: for example most County and District Councils have offices and workshops all over a County or town, and the location of the job may be awkward for some potential applicants, eg if they have to deliver children to school before 9 am. The advert should also say if travel is required as part of the job (and if so, how it is dealt with financially – is a company car or a mileage allowance provided, or a travelcard for use on the buses?)

- *how to apply*
  The advertisement should say whether applicants should write in or telephone for an application form. It needs to be borne in mind that it will take up more staff time dealing with telephone requests than dealing with enquiry letters. Cost-conscious organisations might want a "S.A.E." (stamped addressed envelope) and may ignore requests not accompanied by a S.A.E.

- *depth of detail*
  An advertiser should not give too much irrelevant detail on the background of the organisation, although its "guiding principle" or "philosophy" could be mentioned if it helps to attract good candidates. For example, Body Shop Plc stresses its commitment to being environmentally friendly, and this will be an appealing feature to many people looking for work.

- *ethics and honesty*
  Be honest about the job being advertised – it is no use giving an over-attractive picture of a job in order to attract very good candidates, because if the job does not measure up to what they expect they will soon leave – remember that very good candidates can find other jobs quite easily, even in times of high unemployment.

- *placing the advertisement*
  Finally, where and when is the advert placed? This will depend on the type of job, how many vacancies there are, the budget available, and how quickly the job needs filling. For example the government advertises on the television to encourage recruits into the armed forces and into nursing. A factory with a sudden order may need extra people, so an advert in the local evening paper will be essential (and usually over two or three consecutive evenings). If a business needs a chief accountant or a personnel manager, an engineer or a solicitor, then the best place is a specialist magazine for that particular profession. Certain newspapers, notably 'The Guardian', run specialised job supplements on particular days of the week .

---

### student activity 22.1 – effective job adverts

Illustrated on the next page are two examples of poor quality advertisements from local newspapers.

(a) bearing in mind the points set out above, identify what is wrong with the advertisements

(b) redraft the text in a more effective way, making up any details which you consider that you need – if you have access to a good word processor or a Desk Top Publishing system, design the final versions which will be sent to the newspaper

**student activity 22.1 (continued)**

---

**RELIABLE AGENT WANTED**
For regular evening deliveries
in the Newtown area, 6 evenings
per week.
Must have own car and telephone.
please write to
**Wilfrid Owen,Dept.WR**
**72 Regent Road**
**Birmingham B1 2JP**

---

SITE MANAGER WANTED

Newtown shopping centre.
Morning shifts only
Experience necessary
£4.85p per hour

0334-6787896

---

## the selection process

Having attracted a number of candidates the next stage will be to reduce them to a small enough number to invite for an interview. For some jobs like the Managing Directorship of British Telecom Plc there will be very few serious candidates and so a lot of time can be spent on investigating all of them. For most jobs, depending on the general economic situation, there are many applicants and a simple quick process is needed to sort them out. The three main documents assessed in this sorting process are:

- the letter of application
- the curriculum vitae (CV)
- the application form

All organisations ask applicants to send in at least one of these documents. We will now examine all three in turn.

## the letter of application

This is simply a letter written or typed/word processed asking for the job and explaining why the applicant is suitable for it. The letter will be structured in any way the candidate thinks is appropriate, and this very fact makes it a useful selection method. If the letter is badly structured, poorly expressed and full of spelling mistakes, it could indicate that the applicant is not suitable for a clerical or administrative job which requires neat well-structured work and a "tidy mind". On the other hand, a poorly-structured letter which is nevertheless imaginative and interesting could indicate a very good applicant for certain types of job.

The disadvantages of letters of application as assessment method are that:

- the person taught to write letters well at school will stand out even though his/her other qualities might not be very special – this is even more so today since the art of letter writing is rarely taught in schools and is therefore highly valued by some employers
- the letter writer may miss out information which is important, and conversely the writer is likely to dwell on factors which make him/her look a more attractive applicant – the only way around this is to ask applicants to supply a curriculum vitae (which is discussed below)

Despite their shortcomings, letters of application are quite often used and increasingly it is specified by employers that they should be *handwritten*. The science of graphology (the assessment of a person's character by the analysis of his handwriting) is highly regarded in the USA, France and Germany because many personal characteristics are apparent from a close analysis of handwriting. It is less well regarded in the UK, but is becoming more commonly used by recruitment and executive search consultants in this country.

An advertisement, letter of application and curriculum vitae are illustrated on the next two pages.

---

**Dynatechic Limited**
# Accounts Clerk

A vacancy exists for a trainee Accounts Clerk in this engineering company to operate a computer book-keeping system.

*Salary based on age and experience. Please apply in writing with CV to:*

Mr N Farrant, Personnel Manager,
Dynatechnic Limited,
Unit 14, Oak Industrial Estate, Stourminster MR8 5TG.

---

*an advertisement for a job*

---

7, Mill Lane,
Broadwater
Mereford MR6 8JP

7 May 19–9

Mr. N Farrant, Personnel Manager,
Dynatechnic Limited,
Unit 14, Oak Industrial Estate,
Stourminster, MR8 5JG

Dear Mr Farrant,

I am writing in reply to the advertisement in "The Evening Echo" dated 5 May 19–9 for a vacancy for a trainee Accounts Clerk. I would like to apply for this post, and have pleasure in enclosing my curriculum vitae.

I am at present studying for a GNVQ Advanced Level Award in Business at Mereford College, and am very interested in working in the field of accounting. As you will see from my CV I have already spent three weeks on a work experience placement with MRC Electronics, working in their Accounts Department. At Mereford College I have been active in the student-run College Bookshop, helping with the accounts.

My course finishes in June of this year, and I would be free to start full-time employment from 1 July. I will be available to attend for interview at any time convenient to you.

Yours sincerely

*A. Peters*

Alice Peters (Miss)

---

*a letter of application for the job from Alice Peters*

CURRICULUM VITAE

Personal Details

Name                      Peters, Alice Joanne

Address                   7, Mill Lane, Broadwater, Mereford, MR6 8TP
Telephone                 0605 456729
Date of birth             20 January 1978
Nationality               British
Marital status            Single


Education

1989 - 1993               Henry Bulstrode High School, Mereford
                          GCSE's:  English Language (B); Mathematics (B);
                          French (C);  Geography (C); Home Economics (C).

1993 - 1995               Mereford College, Mereford
                          GNVQ Advanced Level course in Business
                          Final Assessment June 1995.


Positions of Responsibility

School                    Form captain and member of Under 11's netball team.

College                   Student representative on Course Liaison Committee.
                          Book-keeper to Student-run College Bookshop (a Young
                          Enterprise Scheme).


Work Experience

July - August 1994        Part-time assistant in the shop at Peters Garage, the
                          family business.

November 1994             Work placement (part of GNVQ course).  Three weeks
                          spent at MRC Electronics Limited, Mereford.  Work in
                          the Accounts Department, processing invoices for
                          payment, cash book and payroll.


Interests

Sports                    Canoeing , orienteering, swimming.
Leisure                   Jazz music, science fiction.

References

Employment                Mr George Bush, MRC Electronics Limited,
                          7 Cedar Court, Mereford MR3 4RT, Tel. 0605 827281

College                   Miss Jean Wilberforce, Department of Business,
                          Mereford College of Technology, Grantham Street,
                          Mereford MR1 2JF,  Tel 0605 723384

*the curriculum vitae drawn up by Alice Peters*

### the curriculum vitae

The *curriculum vitae* (the CV) – a formal description of an applicant's life and achievements – will normally accompany a letter of application as an alternative to the application form when the advert asks "please apply in writing".   See the previous page for an example.

### the design of a CV

Unfortunately many people who write their own CVs do it in an unprofessional and untidy manner which does little to impress a possible employer. Such CVs are badly typed (or even written) often on poor quality paper.   Nowadays there are plenty of specialist agencies who prepare CVs for people in a professional manner.   Many people now have their own home word processors which can also produce a well presented CV.  The next question is what you include in a CV?  The simplest rule is to try to include anything which would normally be asked for in an application form. The basics will therefore be:

1.   name and address
2.   telephone number (some people may miss this out for security reasons)
3.   date of birth
4.   marital status
5.   education & qualifications
6.   training (where appropriate)
7.   employment history (school and college leavers should include part-time employment)
8.   hobbies and interests
9.   references

### the application form

This is a far more commonly used method of selection.   Consultants devote hours to designing new and better forms which will extract even more accurate information from people.   A typical form will require details on addresses, next of kin, education, training, qualifications, work experience, non-work interests and, finally, names of references from whom the organisation can collect even more information.  See the next three pages for an example of an application form.

The main benefits to the employer of using application forms include:

- The personnel staff will have identified specific requirements from the job and person specifications. They can then compare these with the information on the forms.  They need only shortlist for interview those people who have met those requirements.   For example, if the personnel staff are told to remove all candidates who do not possess a particular qualification this will help to reduce the pile of forms very quickly indeed.
- The forms can act as a framework for the interviewer to use should the applicant get shortlisted. For example the interviewer can query gaps in the employment record, or ask about poor examination results, or about relevant non-work interests.
- The organisation can keep all the forms which are anywhere near suitable for the vacancy and draw on them again if another vacancy arises.
- The form from the successful applicant will become a very useful part of his/her initial personnel records.

### student activity 22.2 – effective application forms

(a)   Draw up a list of the main requirements that you believe a good application form should include.

(b)   Obtain, if possible, a sample application form and compare it with the example set out on the next three pages. How do they differ, and  why ?  Which is the more effective?

# BASSETT CONSTRUCTION LIMITED

## application for post of _____

### personal details

| surname | forename(s) |
|---|---|
| Mr/Mrs/Miss/Ms | date of birth |
| permanent address | |
| postcode | telephone number |
| nationality | marital status |

### education and training

| school/college/university | qualification | grade | date |
|---|---|---|---|
| | | | |

**employment history**

| employer | job held, duties and responsibilities | dates |
|---|---|---|
|  |  |  |

**additional information**

Describe your present state of health.
Please give details of any serious illnesses or operations over the last 10 years.

Do you have a criminal record or criminal charges pending?                    Yes/No

Do you hold a clean driving licence?                    Yes/No

Where did you hear of this vacancy?

When are you *not* available for interview?

**references**

Please give the names and addresses of two referees

| name | name |
|------|------|
| address | address |

**interests**

Please give details of your interests and hobbies, any positions of responsibility held, and any other information which you would like to support this application.

**DECLARATION**

I declare the information supplied by me in this form is, to the best of my knowledge, correct.

*signature of applicant*                    *date*

## student activity 22.3 – job applications

Set out below are the personal details of Sarah Maryhead, who is thinking of leaving her post as secretary to the Assistant Governor of Swindon Prison.

---

Sarah Louise Maryhead lives at 28 Fairfax Road, Swindon, Wiltshire SN5 7GF. Tel 0793 - 567453. She was born in Bath on 27 July 1954 and has a UK passport. She is divorced.

She was educated at Parkway Grammar School, Chippenham (1965-1970) and obtained GCE 'O' levels (ie GCSE equivalents) in English Language, English Literature, History, Maths, Chemistry, Biology and French.

She left school in 1970 and trained at Leeway Secretarial College in Swindon from 1970 to 1972 where she passed RSA Stage 2 certificates in Shorthand (100 words per minute), Typewriting (50 wpm), Audio typewriting and Secretarial Duties.

In 1990 she studied at Swindon Technical College on a part-time one year Word processing familiarisation course.

Her employment history is as follows:

Sept 72 - Oct 74  Ashfield Building Ltd, Swindon, Secretary to Production Director

Nov 74 - Oct 76  Ashfield Housing Ltd, Wootton Bassett, Wilts, Secretary to Managing Director. General P/A duties.

Nov 79- Oct 84  Smithfield Hanson Ltd, Calne, Wilts, Secretary to Personnel Director. General personnel administration work including organisation of all job interviews.

Oct 84 - July 89  Linway Smith (Electronics) Ltd, Wootton Bassett, Secretary to Production Manager, dealing with a wide range of secretarial duties and ordering of stationery and new office equipment.

Sept 89 -July 90  Part time shorthand typing tutor at Griffin Secretarial College, Calne, Wilts.

Sept 90 - now  H.M. Prison, Swindon, Secretary to the Assistant Governor

She is interested in drama, reading, aerobics, swimming and sailing.

She has a generally clean bill of health, but suffers from asthma. She has no criminal record, and has a clean driving licence. She is available for interview at any time.

Her references are:
Roger Purcell, Assistant Governor, HM Prison, Swindon, SN6 9UH

Anthony Fox, Managing Director, Ashfield Ltd, Badger Road, Swindon  SN3 6AT.

---

(a)  From the information set out above complete a CV for Sarah Maryhead. Set out the finished document with a word processor or typewriter.

(b)  Assume the role of Sarah Maryhead and fill in the application form set out on pages 236 to 238 (it may have to be photocopied) using the material in her CV. The job for which you will be applying is that of a Secretary to the Chief Accountant at Bassett Construction Limited, Green Park, Wootton Bassett, Wilts, SN8 6TY The job was advertised in the Swindon Herald last Friday, and applications should be sent to A Jackson, Personnel Manager.

(c)  To accompany the application form you have also been asked by Bassett Construction to provide a letter of application. Review the section above on letters of application and then draft one in your own handwriting. This is your chance to concentrate on the strongest points of your career to date but the letter must be legible, tidy and free of spelling errors.

### references

For most jobs it is usual for the prospective employer to take up *references* provided by the job applicant.   There are several types of reference:

- *A testimonial* – a letter, usually from a former employer or teacher which will say very positive and kind things about the applicant.  As the applicant has been given this letter it is unlikely that the writer will make anything other than positive helpful statements (clearly, if the writer did say something critical the applicant would tear the testimonial up and look around for someone else to write one!)

- *Reference letters* requested by the prospective employer – this is the most usual type of reference. The letters are confidential so that the referee can be completely honest without embarassment, but it may not tell the prospective employer all he needs to know.  Employers can learn to "read between the lines", and often the omission of information can be a telling factor.

- *Reference forms* – some organisations, the Civil Service being a good example, use a structured form which asks specific questions about the applicant. These include assessments of effort and ability, and opinions about their honesty and health.

- *Telephone references* – some organisations telephone the people given as referees. The main benefit is that the recruiter can assess the tone of voice of the referee, and this can often say far more about an applicant than a letter can.  They can also question the referee far more searchingly.

- *Medical references* – most employers will carry out some kind of medical check up even if it is only the completion of a form asking a few simple questions about health problems in the past. Such a check is necessary because:

  - the employer needs to safeguard the health of other employees
  - the job itself may require specific health standards (eg perfect colour vision for a train driver, because of the need to be able to distinguish railway signals).
  - if an employee is to join a company pensions scheme a medical check-up will be needed (again only the completion of a simple form may be required).

Medical matters of growing importance – notably the problem of AIDS – may mean that in the future medical checks will have to be far more rigorous, and include blood tests.

# interviewing

After all the preliminary matters examined above, the final selection stage will be an interview, and possibly some form of testing.  Interviews are arranged for almost every kind of job. The process of sifting through forms or letters and the examination of references will mean that only a few of the applicants for the job will be interviewed. This is because interviews take up the time of senior managers who have to carry them out, and this will be costly for the business.

### interviewing – the employer's viewpoint
Interviewing is sometimes done in a poorly thought out and badly structured manner which gives the organisation a bad image. To avoid this situation only requires the observation of a few simple rules:

#### planning the interview itself

- The interviewer must ask "what are my objectives ? what am I looking for ? how will I phrase the questions I am going to ask ?"  It may sound obvious, but one key objective is to fill in all the gaps which are left after all the information from the application forms, curricula vitarum and references have been assembled.  Another objective is to explore in detail and in depth some of the points raised in the application forms which you consider to be of importance.

- Decide if the vacancy requires just  one interviewer or two or even a panel of four or five. There are advantages and disadvantages in either approach. 'One to one' interviews put applicants at ease so that they will talk more naturally.  The problems are that one interviewer lacks the range and depth of knowledge of a panel of experts; secondly one interviewer is more likely to suffer from bias and can be highly prejudiced – against particular races, against women, against men, against the older or the younger.

- If there is more than one interviewer , the panel should ensure that there is a planning meeting beforehand to decide how the questioning will be shared out. Nothing gives a worse image to an interviewee than if the interviewers interrupt or contradict each other or repeat questions.

### *practical points for interviewers*

- Send very clear instructions to applicants with the precise time and venue for the interview. A map and a list of local hotels may be useful for those coming from far away.
- If possible the interviews should be planned so that applicants are interviewed soon after they have arrived and so that they can leave immediately afterwards.
- Decide if there is a need for a test as well. For example, more and more schools and colleges expect applicants to do a practice lesson to assess actual teaching ability. For secretarial posts a test in shorthand/typing/wordprocessing may be required. Where tests are needed extra administrative arrangements will have to be made.
- The facilities should be organised well in advance – an interview room and also a comfortable waiting room,with freely available tea and coffee, are important. If the interviews take all day applicants should also be given lunch.

### *carrying out the interview*

- As a general rule the "talking split" in a job interview should be around 20% for the interviewer and 80% for the interviewee. The interviewer learns far more from the applicant if he listens than if he talks! However, "listening" is not just "not talking" – listening is the art of conveying to the applicant that you are interested in what he/she is saying, together with an ability to make the occasional comment which encourages them to say a lot more.
- The interview should always begin with a few friendly questions to put the candidate at ease – ones about the journey or the weather – before asking more detailed questions. Most interviewers will ask a mixture of questions. Some will be about the application form itself, eg asking for more details about work experience or about qualifications. It is usual to then ask deeper questions such as how the candidate might handle a difficult situation at work.
- Finally, there should be a question asking the candidate for his/her questions.

## interviewing - the candidate's viewpoint

The candidate invited for interview should always ensure that he or she follows a number of basic rules:

### *preparation*

- If invited for interview by letter then the invitation must be acknowledged by the candidate, preferably by letter or if necessary by telephone.
- If the interview is some distance away then the candidate must plan the route well in advance (or make railway timetable enquiries) to ensure he/she has plenty of time to allow for traffic hold-ups or rail delays.
- If it is likely to be a long, rushed, hectic and tiring journey it is better to spend the previous night in a hotel so that one goes refreshed to the interview. Organisations will usually pay interviewees' travel and hotel expenses.
- Candidates should get to know about the organisation from leaflets and handbooks so that they can show some basic knowledge of it in the interview.
- The candidate should wear appropriate clothes. Even in the 1990s this will almost always mean a suit for a man or a skirt and blouse for a woman. Less suitable, but usually acceptable, would be a jacket and trousers for a man or a dress for a woman. It is certainly not acceptable to dress casually in interviews.

- The candidate should be there on time or not more than a few minutes early.
- Candidates may be called straight into the interview and leave the building immediately afterwards. In some cases, especially in public sector jobs, they may instead have to sit, for what will seem like ages, in a waiting room with three or four other candidates until the result is announced. If this is the case they should only exchange polite comments about the journey or the weather, with the other candidates. Discussing the job or one's own interview performance is unwise since this may help the other candidates and thus harm one's own chances.

### *the interview itself*
- When called into the interview room the candidate should introduce him/herself to the panel and shake hands with them if offered the opportunity.
- Although this has been said many times it is worth repeating here – most interviewers make their minds up about a candidate within a minute or two of meeting them. This might be very unfair but it is a fact of life. It means one needs to do everything possible to create a good impression within that first minute or two.
- The candidate should sit up in the chair in as relaxed a manner as possible, but not appear *too* comfortable. He/she should not fidget with hands or feet as it gives the impression that concentration is lacking.
- If it is a panel interview the candidate should look at all the members from time to time. A golden rule is that candidates who make poor eye contact with interviewers do badly because it makes them appear unconfident and, perhaps, 'shifty' looking.
- When asked questions it is wise for the candidate to hesitate a little before answering. This shows they have thought about the question and have not just jumped in without considering it properly.
- Candidates should always answer the question as briefly as possible. They should not wander into other issues which, they might feel, arise from the question asked. If the panel want a candidate to elaborate they will ask them to. Interviewers are working to a timetable and have only, say, half an hour to cover the key areas.
- It is not uncommon for interviewers to make mistakes and members of a panel may even contradict each other. Candidates should not attempt to correct such mistakes as it usually does not create a good impression with the interviewer(s).
- Interviewers always ask candidates if they have any questions at the end of the interview. Candidates should ask one or two questions (some of which have been prepared beforehand.)

### *ethical aspects*
- Remember that there are ethical obligations by which the candidate and the interviewers should abide. One should always be open and honest about one's background, qualifications and experience. If a candidate is dishonest (about experience, qualifications, trouble with the police) this could be a justified reason for dismissal if the employer subsequently found out. Employers should also act fairly by never discriminating on sexual or racial grounds and by ensuring that they have proper equal opportunities policies (eg for the employment of disabled people).

### the post-interview stage
After interviewing all candidates and carrying out whatever tests may be necessary the final stage is to select one or more of them. Interview panels often find it very hard to choose between the final two or three applicants. Clearly, if there are two or three vacancies, to fill this will be very convenient and very economical for the organisation.

Although applicants will need to know the outcome within a few days there should be a thorough analysis of all the information that has been collected on each of them . It is fairly easy to devise a list of the key points. These will include attainments, experience, disposition, personal circumstances, reference letters, results from the medical check up, results from any essential tests and, finally, comments from the interviewers. By comparing the information on each one with the job and person specifications it will be easier to do the selection.

It is important, for the image of the organisation, to be polite and constructive when advising unsuccessful applicants that they have failed to get the job. They may be very good people who may be suitable for different vacancies later on, and a polite, helpful letter may encourage them to apply for such positions. Reasonable expenses should also be paid to all interviewees, again to help create a good image for the organisation.

The successful applicant should be notified first of all. This is because he/she may be looking for other jobs and if you have thought the applicant suitable to employ there is every chance other organisations will too. It is wisest to wait a day or two before notifying the best of the unsuccessful candidates just in case the successful one does turn down the offer.

### the new recruit and induction

The successful applicant should be sent immediately all the details relating to the job. This should include joining instructions (the date of starting work, where to go and who to ask for on arrival) and some details of the social facilities such as canteens, sports clubs, medical care and pension provisions. They are also legally entitled to a "Written Statement" of the terms of their employment Details of this and of the Contract of Employment are outlined in Chapter 3, page 22.

*Induction* is the process of introducing new employees to the organisation and its way of life. What does an induction programme include?

• A *tour of the buildings* to show the newcomer all the important areas – the sick bay, the canteen, the pay office, toilets, car parking etc – and to introduce them to the important staff such as the pay and personnel clerks and the factory nurse.

• An introduction to their *new workplace* – the specific office or factory area or shop department – where they will be working.

• Some *background detail about the organisation* – the easiest and best way to do this is to show them a video.

---

### student activities – job applications and interviews
*Please note that the Evidence Collection Exercise which follows this chapter develops the material already set out in student activities 22.2 and 22.3. Together they fulfil the assessment requirements of Element 4.3 "Evaluate job applications and interviews".*

---

## chapter summary

❑ Employers are increasingly aware that there are often alternatives to filling the vacancies that arise.

❑ Advertising to fill vacancies has to be done in a considered scientific manner if it is to be worthwhile.

❑ Selecting candidates to interview to fill vacancies is a lengthy procedure and there are no short cuts if it is to be done properly.

❑ The interview process needs to be seen to be completely fair to all candidates in order to remain within the law and to ensure the organisation has a good reputation in the labour market.

❑ A proper system of induction for new employees is important to help to motivate them to work effectively .

## EVIDENCE COLLECTION EXERCISE 12

# Job applications and interviews

---

**Element 4.3**  *Evaluate job applications and interviews*

Suggested Sources:
- sample application forms, letters of application and CVs
- talks by personnel officers
- textbooks in libraries and resource centres

Note: Student Activity 22.3 on page 239 *must* be completed as part of this exercise.

---

## TASK 1

(a) Complete Student Activity 22.3 on page 239. Assume that you are Andrew (or Andrea) Jackson, personnel officer at Bassett Construction Ltd, and that you are going to interview Sarah Maryhead for the job. As background research you may need to find out more about what a Secretary's job involves from the careers library. Having done any research required, identify *ten* questions you might ask Sarah in order to assess if she is suitable to do this particular job.

(b) Pair up with a fellow student. Refer to the CV and completed application form of Sarah Maryhead, completed in Student Activity 22.3. Read the material carefully together with the ten questions produced for (a) above. Carry out a mock interview for the job advertised by Bassett Construction Ltd. You must between you play the roles of Sarah and Andrew/Andrea Jackson, the personnel officer. Remember that Jackson is interviewing Sarah for the job of Secretary to the Chief Accountant. He/she must use the questions devised in (a) above, plus any others felt to be relevant.
The rest of the class should watch the interview and make notes on its effectiveness. Afterwards there should be a review session which will provide useful feedback for the two participants (A video of the interview is also extremely helpful to the participants and to the rest of the class ).

(c) Having carried out the interview but *before* the review session you should write a brief appraisal of your own performance in the interview. List what you considered were the good points and the bad points of your performance. You will find the comparison between your own comments and those of other class members in the review session most helpful.

## TASK 2

*Prepare your own Curriculum Vitae.* Use the format shown in Chapter 22 if you want to, or design your own format if you think it might look better or have more impact. If possible you should do this on a word processor. Remember that a CV is a general document which you might want to send to a wide variety of potential employers. Never forget that it is your way of 'selling' yourself to one of them so its presentation must be good. Now pair off with another student and swap your CV with another member of your group. Offer honest but helpful comments on each others' work.

## TASK 3

Investigate Management Trainee posts in your locality – this is a typical job for a young person with good qualifications who wants a business career. (You may need to find out more about business careers from the guides in the careers section of your library). *Draft a letter of application for a typical management trainee post to accompany your CV* – write it out in longhand, and then key it onto a word processor. Swap the letter(s) with the letter(s) produced by your student colleague and comment on their strengths and weaknesses.

SECTION

# 5

# employment in the market economy

## contents

In the last Section we examined the implications to a business of *human resources* – the employees of a business, and management decisions about the hiring, firing and treatment of staff. In this section of the book we look at the *economic background* to the labour market.

The section is divided into five chapters:

## information sources

Data relating to this Section can be found in the following publications:

Social Trends (HMSO)

Economic Trends (HMSO)

Employment Gazette (HMSO)

Employment in Europe (European Commission)

Lloyds Bank Economic Profile of Great Britain (Lloyds Bank)

OECD Database (Lloyds Bank Headway Programme)

Prest and Coppock, *The UK Economy*, Weidenfeld & Nicolson

# 23 The background to the labour market

## introduction

In this chapter we shall explore the concepts of employment, labour and work in order to establish a clear understanding of their importance in economics and business. We shall start with an *historical* approach in order to see how the situation in which we find ourselves has arisen and how economists take account of a variety of technological, demographic (relating to population) and political factors.

The basic economic question which faces everyone no matter who they are or where they live is "How can I get the things I need in order to survive?" At the very least these things include food, clothing and shelter, but in many societies the list is very much longer. In the UK the most usual way of answering this question is to go out to work to earn money which can then be exchanged for goods and services. However, this has not always been the answer for the majority of people in Britain.

## back to basics

### earlier societies

If we looked at the most primitive societies we should find that people answered the basic economic question of "How can I get the things I need in order to survive?" by being self-sufficient. They literally "worked for themselves". All the tasks which were required to gather food, find shelter and provide clothing were done either individually or co-operatively in small groups. In either case there was no separation between the producer and the consumer. Any *division of labour* which existed was based around the biological necessity that women give birth and suckle their babies. Family groups would, therefore, co-operate in order to benefit from this biological specialisation. This form of economic arrangement is still in evidence today in some *primitive societies*.

Later developments from primitive societies included the system of *slavery*, which still persisted in America in the nineteenth century. Slaves were *owned* in the same way that animals were owned; they were a source of labour for their owners who gave them food and shelter. In the early Middle Ages the European system of *feudalism* enabled those who did not own land to farm it and so provide for themselves in return for military service under the command of the landowners.

## modern society

British society today is characterised by a high degree of *occupational specialisation*. Not only do we have specialists to teach young people, a task which traditionally was part of the role of parents with help perhaps from the church, but we have specialist teachers for different age groups and different subject areas. Not only do we have workers who make cars but within that industry there is a high degree of division of labour, so that workers specialise in a small part of the total production process. For example, some workers will shape body panels, another group will apply the paint, others build the engine and yet others fix the trim to the interior of the car. Even within those tasks there may be further division into smaller operations such as tightening a set of wheel nuts which someone else had already put onto the bolts. This specialisation and division of labour mean that the labour market as a whole is very complex, as we shall see later in this chapter.

The most significant developments in the labour market occurred in the period from the eighteenth century to the present day, and these will now be examined in detail.

# the industrial revolution and the growth of capitalism

## population growth

Gradually, during the eighteenth century *technological* and *demographic* (population) changes necessitated a greater degree of *specialisation*. Changes in farming methods, new crops and new technologies such as the use of fertilizers and drainage, brought about an improvement in the diet of many people, which led in turn to an increase in the UK population. It rose dramatically from 10.5 million in 1801 to 18.1 million in 1841. The trend continued into the twentieth century, as you will see from fig. 23.1. below.

**1.2**      **Population change: actual and projected**

*United Kingdom*              Thousands

| | Population at start of period | Live births | Deaths | Net natural change | Net civilian migration | Other adjustments[2] | Overall annual change |
|---|---|---|---|---|---|---|---|
| | | | | *Average annual change* | | | |
| **Census enumerated** | | | | | | | |
| 1901-1911 | 38,237 | 1,091 | 624 | 467 | -82 | . | 385 |
| 1911-1921 | 42,082 | 975 | 689 | 286 | -92 | . | 194 |
| 1921-1931 | 44,027 | 824 | 555 | 268 | -67 | . | 201 |
| 1931-1951 | 46,038 | 785 | 598 | 188 | 25 | . | 213 |
| **Mid-year estimates** | | | | | | | |
| 1951-1961 | 50,290 | 839 | 593 | 246 | -9 | 15 | 252 |
| 1961-1971 | 52,807 | 963 | 639 | 324 | -32 | 20 | 312 |
| 1971-1981 | 55,928 | 736 | 666 | 69 | -44 | 17 | 42 |
| 1981-1991 | 56,352 | 757 | 654 | 103 | 21 | 6 | 130 |
| **Mid-year projections** | | | | | | | |
| 1991-2001 | 57,561 | 800 | 639 | 161 | 0 | 0 | 161 |
| 2001-2011 | 59,174 | 736 | 650 | 86 | 0 | 0 | 86 |
| 2011-2021 | 60,033 | 750 | 679 | 71 | 0 | 0 | 71 |

*Fig 23.1 Population growth in the UK 1900 and beyond*
SOURCE CSO: Social Trends, 1993

## technological change – the Industrial Revolution

The invention of the steam engine in the eighteenth century, and its application to the production of cloth, iron and steel meant that large numbers of men and women were required to work in factories. These inventions led to increased demand for iron, steel, bricks and fuel to build machinery and factories. This increased demand for products meant more jobs in those industries and so the cycle of economic growth continued. The period after 1790 saw the emergence of large scale production processes. Previously, manufactured goods such as yarn and cloth had been produced in the homes of workers using simple machines which required only one person to operate them. These *cottage industries* were soon replaced by factories which could take advantage of economies of scale and produce larger quantities of the product at lower cost. These factories in turn required a supply of local labour and towns grew up around them.

The development of industrial towns and *mass production techniques* required an associated growth of the *economic infrastructure*. Changes took place in methods of road building, a canal system was built to link producers and markets and a railway network was established to transport both freight and passengers. More rapid methods of transport enabled the many people who lived in towns to buy the food which was being produced in the countryside and goods made in, say, Sheffield to be sold in Exeter. It also enabled trade with other parts of the country to take place more freely as business people could contact each other more easily.

All of these developments were inter-related: each depended on the demands being made by previous innovations and on the technological changes which made new solutions to old problems possible.

## the growth of specialisation

In this way occupational specialisation accelerated rapidly. There was a growing need for education and training and greater opportunity for entre-preneurship. Britain was changing from an agricultural country to an industrial one. Instead of growing their own food, building their own home and making their own clothes people were going to work in a factory, making enough clothes for thousands of people, taking home wages and buying the food that was being grown by others living miles away from the towns and the factories.

These changes required workers to acquire new skills and carry out new tasks. Many new jobs were being created which had not previously existed. There were no engine drivers before the railway engine was invented, no machine tool makers, no electrical engineers and so on. Not only did new technology provide the need for new skills and new jobs, but as firms became larger so management functions within firms became more specialised. A range of professional services were required, accountants, personnel sales and marketing managers, engineers each responsible for a part of the process of producing and selling goods.

## the political environment

The economic system which accompanied and made posible these changes (which we now know as the Agricultural and Industrial Revolutions) is called *Capitalism*. Under this arrangement labour is sold to the owners of the other factors of production (capital, land and entrepreneurship). The rewards to labour (wages) can then be used to purchase the goods and services which are produced. There is a separation between the producer and the consumer which is the consequence of the high degree of specialisation allowed by this system.

Previously, under the feudal system government's role was to manage the defence of the country and pursue foreign policy. It had little to do with economic affairs. Wars had to be paid for but revenue from import taxes were the main source of income. There was no need for the government to become involved in industry or commerce, or to worry about issues such as inflation, unemployment or the exchange rate. There was little they could do about a bad harvest, and the way people conducted their trading activities was "none of the government's business". This approach is known as "laissez-faire" which is a French phrase meaning to leave alone. Little was written about what we now call economics before Adam Smith wrote his book "The Wealth of Nations" in 1776 in which he argued that if individuals were allowed a free hand in economic affairs then all would be well.

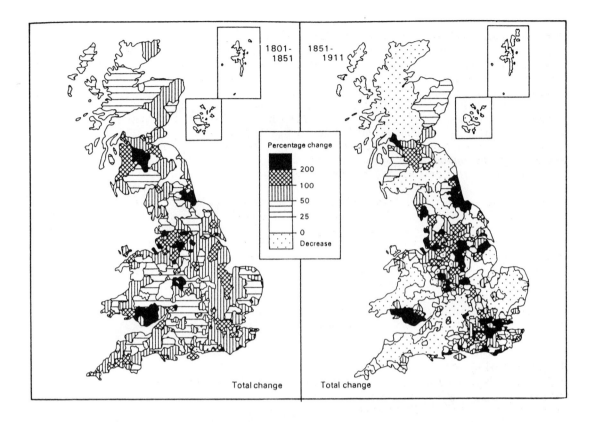

*Fig 23.2 Changes in population 1801 - 1911*

SOURCE: *Atlas of Industrialising Britain 1780 - 1914*, Ed. J Langton and R J Morris, Methuen

## student activity 23.1 – changes in population and industry

(a)  Draw a line graph showing the growth (actual and projected) in population in the UK from 1801 to 2011, using the figures quoted on page 247.

(b)  Find out from the reference library what the population of your local town or city was in 1801 and 1851 (census dates) and is at present. Does the trend follow that shown in (a) above? Comment on your findings.

(c)  Does this trend correspond with the percentage changes shown for your locality in the maps shown in fig. 23.2 above?

(d)  What was the *result* of the increase (or decrease) in population in the area in which you currently live? What effect did it have on the types of jobs made available? Did any particular type of industry flourish in your area?

(e)  What is the *current* pattern of labour in your own area? What types of industry and process are on the increase/decrease? Are they a continuation of previous trends, or are they a change or a reversal?

(f)  Using whatever data gathering technique is most convenient (interviewing elderly relatives or friends, visiting the local museum, enquiring at a local company which has been in the area for a long time, using local newspapers or the library) compile a project comparing aspects of working life in a period before 1960, with those of the present day. The exhibition could include pictures, tape recordings, products, statistics as well as written descriptions.

### student activity 23.2 – changes in labour methods

Study carefully the three photographs and the descriptive texts on this and the next page. They represent three stages in the way that labour methods have developed over time.

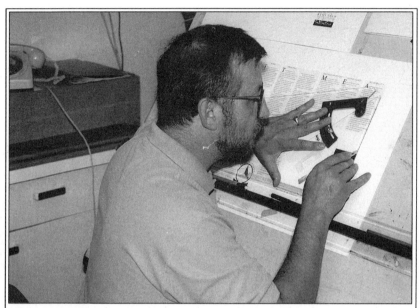

**Terry Symonds** is a freelance graphic designer who works from his studio at home in Malvern. He produces designs for product packaging, advertising material, business logos, and book covers for Osborne Books.

**Morgan Motor Company** produces handbuilt motor cars at its factory in Malvern. There is a long waiting list for this quality vehicle. The photograph shows the final process which includes the fitting of leather upholstery.

**Rover Group** produces cars for the mass production market. The photograph illustrates the Rover 200 Series facility at Longbridge and shows the robotic spot weld line in the body production process. (Photograph by courtesy of Rover Group).

Now answer the following questions:

(a) Which stage of the development of labour methods and production processes do these three businesses represent?

(b) All three products are highly successful in the modern economy because they fulfil consumer needs. Identify the needs of the consumer which are fulfilled in each case. In the case of the two car manufacturers, how are these needs different?

(c) Imagine you were working in each of the organisations shown in the photographs. What sort of *satisfaction* and *reward* would you expect from your work?

(d) Identify *two* other examples of each of the three types of process, but involving different products. Do the customers' needs in each case correspond with those identified in (b) above?

# the need for government intervention

## the need for government revenue

The growing complexity of the industrial and commercial world of the nineteenth and twentieth centuries required governments to take and increasingly important role. There had always been the need for governments, as mentioned above, to organise the defence of the country. As the technology of war became more sophisticated so the need for a larger defence budget became a central part of the government's economic policy. Income tax was originally introduced by prime minister Pitt at the end of the seventeenth century in order to fund war. It became a permanent feature of economic policy after 1842.

## the need for regulation of factories

The entrepreneurs who were responsible for establishing factories, managing the pits which produced coal to fuel the engines and running the companies which controlled the canal system were motivated by profit. They regarded labour as a cost of production just as managers do today. In 1800, however, there were no laws to restrict the ways in which they managed the work force, no limits on the age of the workers nor regulations about health and safety in the work place. The conditions faced by many workers were extremely dangerous and unhygienic, very young children worked in mines and factories and toxic chemicals were used in ways which seriously damaged the health of the workers involved.

The concentration of workers in factories, mines and docks coupled with the poor living conditions faced by many of the working class led to the conditions necessary for the formation of political pressure groups and trade unions. Towards the end of the nineteenth century, as many more workers were educated and thus able to organise themselves, these unions were able to influence the level of wages and working conditions and to force the government to pass Factory Acts which set out limits on the freedom of the employer. They also played a major role in the emergence of the Labour Party as a major political force committed to improving the lot of the working class.

## the growth of state benefits

Tax revenue began to be used as a means of redistributing income as the inevitable inequalities produced by capitalism grew to unacceptable limits. The government began to provide benefits such as pensions, sickness pay and family allowances as well as services such as free education for all children and free medical treatment. This commitment to general social welfare and the need to manage the economy in times of war by taking key industries such as the railways and coal into national ownership gave the government an unprecedented influence over the economy.

## the government's role in the economy – the late twentieth century

By the late 1950's the welfare state was in place and economists, influenced by the work of John Maynard Keynes, generally believed that the government was responsible for the performance of the economy in all its aspects. There was a clear commitment to *full employment* (a situation in which all those able and willing to work are in employment) which was effectively maintained until the late 1960's even at the considerable cost of periods of serious inflation and problems with the Balance of Payments.

Since 1979 the direct influence of the government in industry has been reduced by returning to private ownership key state monopolies such as gas, water, electricity and telephones in the hope of allowing them to become more efficient through the process of being exposed to competition. However, the government still takes approximately 40% of GDP (the total value of the annual output of the UK economy) in tax revenue. This figure shows how vital a role the government plays in the UK economy.

**student activity 23.3 – government influence on the labour market**

(a)   Using either a book or a pamphlet about how to start your own business, or an interview with a local employer, compile   a list of the ways in which the government is involved in the running of business.  The list could be organised under headings such as:  protecting the worker, protecting the consumer, raising funds, helping businesses.

(b)   Using newspaper cuttings (or CD ROM if avilable) and other sources (eg talking to local business people), evaluate the policy towards industry which the Chancellor of the Exchequer has set out in a recent budget speech.  What policies have been seen as most helpful, and which most criticised?

## conclusion

From this brief historical analysis it is clear that in our complex capitalist economy the method by which most people in the UK meet their economic needs is to sell their labour to an entrepreneur or to the government, although there is also a significant number of people who work for themselves either selling a service or the product of their labour directly to the consumer.  There is also a large number of people who do not work for payment.  This includes voluntary or unpaid workers, those who have not yet reached the age when they are allowed into the labour market and those who have reached the age where they no longer do paid work.  This group have their economic needs met by others, either directly through being cared for by their families or others, or by receiving benefits from the government.

The level of employment which the economy can sustain and the rewards which those who are in paid work (the *working population*) receive for their labour depends on a number of important and inter-related factors.  These include the level of taxation, the rate of interest, the level of government spending and the many regulations which are imposed on industry through health and safety and employment legislation.  The role of the government in managing the economy is crucial and the days of *laissez-faire* policies are gone.  However, governments may be able to do little about the two other key variables, the development and application of technology and the size and structure of the population.

## chapter summary

❑  The way in which the basic economic question is answered has changed from self-sufficiency to capitalism.

❑  This change was prompted by changes in technology and population size.

❑  The change from an agricultural to an industrial economy meant that there was an increase in specialisation and a greater diversity of occupations.

❑  Technological changes led to changes in production methods and the concentration of workers into towns and factories.

❑  The inequalities which developed as a result of the growth of capitalism required the government to play an increasing role in the management of the economy.

# 24 The present day labour market

## introduction

In this chapter we shall consider the current state of employment in the UK economy. The changes in population and in the demand for labour which have taken place since 1980 will be considered in detail.

We shall also consider what the government can do in order to manage the economy in a situation in which population and technological changes combined with trends in the world economy produce imbalances in the labour market.

## population size

The size of the population in a country will have major effects on both the productive capacity of the economy and the level of *aggregate demand*. If a country has a very small number of inhabitants then it may not require many goods and services, and will only have a small number of workers to produce them. This lack of people may be a factor which inhibits economic growth and keeps the standard of living in that country low. On the other hand a country with a very large population will have plenty of workers and high levels of demand but unless it has the necessary levels of technology and natural resources it may not be able to provide a high standard of living for its inhabitants.

There is, then, the idea of an *Optimum Population* for a country with a given level of natural resources and at a particular stage in its technological development. This is where an increase in population leads to no further rise in the *standard of living* of the inhabitants. This concept is illustrated in fig. 24.2 on the next page.

As you will see from the diagram, if the population grows beyond the optimum level there will be a *fall* in the standard of living. Countries can only support larger populations and increase the general standard of living if they increase the level of technology or bring more natural resources into productive use.

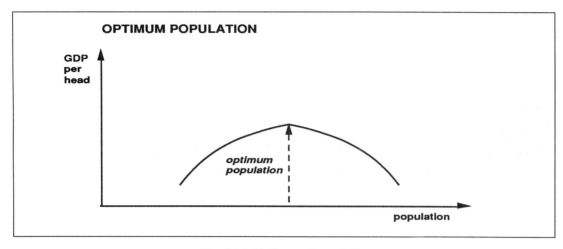

*Fig 24.1 Optimum Population*

# the structure of the population

## working and dependant population

Although the number of people in a country is very important because everyone has certain basic economic needs and wants which must be met, the age structure of the population is also of great significance to the productive capacity of the economy.  We must distinguish between the *working* population and the *dependant* population.  The *working population*  – the *economically active* – includes only those who are in paid work and thus contribute to the output of the economy as measured by Gross Domestic Product (GDP).  The *dependant population* are those who, although they may work very hard, are not being rewarded for their efforts directly by being paid wages.  Many of the dependant population may be capable of work and may be actively seeking work, however others may be too young, too old or not fit to be employed.  There are others who choose not to undertake paid employment.  The diagram in fig. 24.2 below shows how the proportion of the population which is economically active has changed.

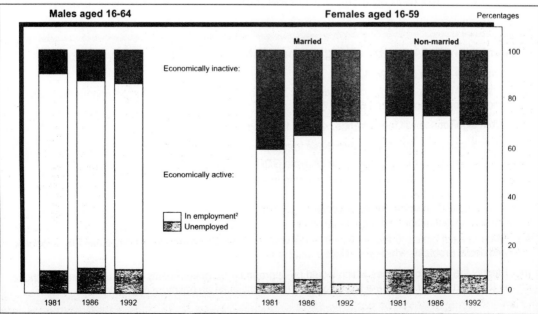

*Fig. 24.2 Population of working age: by sex and economic status*   SOURCE: CSO Social Trends, 1993

## age structure of the population

Not only is it significant to consider the structure of the population in terms of how many people are working and how many are dependant on their output, but it is also important to consider the number of people in each age group so that predictions about future needs can be made. After the second world war there was a "baby boom", a significant rise in the birth rate which lasted for a relatively short time. The effects of this will be that, at the end of this century, there will be very large numbers of people over the age of 60 who will need special housing and medical care and who will not (under present arrangements) be in paid work. This is shown in fig. 24.3 below.

### 1.3   Age and sex structure of the population[1]

*United Kingdom* — Percentages and millions

| | Under 16 | 16-39 | 40-64 | 65-79 | 80 and over | All ages (= 100%) (millions) |
|---|---|---|---|---|---|---|
| **Mid-year estimates** | | | | | | |
| 1951 | .. | .. | 31.6 | 9.5 | 1.4 | 50.3 |
| 1961 | 24.8 | 31.4 | 32.0 | 9.8 | 1.9 | 52.8 |
| 1971 | 25.6 | 31.3 | 29.9 | 10.9 | 2.3 | 55.9 |
| 1981 | 22.2 | 34.9 | 27.8 | 12.2 | 2.8 | 56.4 |
| 1991 | 20.3 | 35.2 | 28.7 | 12.0 | 3.7 | 57.6 |
| *Males* | 21.4 | 36.5 | 29.1 | 10.7 | 2.3 | 28.1 |
| *Females* | 19.3 | 34.0 | 28.3 | 13.3 | 5.1 | 29.5 |
| **Mid-year projections[2]** | | | | | | |
| 2001 | 21.3 | 32.6 | 30.5 | 11.4 | 4.2 | 59.2 |
| 2011 | 20.1 | 30.0 | 33.7 | 11.7 | 4.5 | 60.0 |
| 2021 | 19.5 | 30.5 | 31.9 | 13.6 | 4.5 | 60.7 |
| *Males* | 20.2 | 31.6 | 32.1 | 12.7 | 3.4 | 30.0 |
| *Females* | 18.7 | 29.5 | 31.6 | 14.5 | 5.7 | 30.7 |

1 See Appendix, Part 1: Population and population projections.
2 1989-based projections.

*Source: Office of Population Censuses and Surveys; General Register Office (Scotland); General Register Office (Northern Ireland); Government Actuary's Department*

*Fig 24.3  Age (and sex) structure of the population*   SOURCE: CSO Social Trends, 1993

### student activity 24.1 – the changing population

*Using the table shown in fig. 24.3 above*

(a) Draw line graphs showing the trends from 1961 to 2021 (projections) for the population under 16 and the population between 65 and 79.

(b) What significance will these trends have for the Government?

(c) What opportunities and threats will these trends pose for existing and new businesses?

*Refer to the figures on the opposite page showing GDP per head in a variety of countries, and*

(d) Provide examples of countries which seem to have:
   i   the population at an optimum level
   ii  the population below the optimum level
   iii the population above the optimum level

(e) State in each case the factors which made you choose these countries, and discuss any economic and social problems which you might expect to find there.

(f) Identify the kinds of policies which would be appropriate for governments in the countries you chose in (a ii) and (a iii) if they were trying to achieve and maintain an optimum population.

## student activity 24.1 – statistical table – changing population and output

| country | population (millions) | population density per km² | GNP (1989) (million US$) | GDP per person (US$) | annual rate of change % |
|---------|----------------------|---------------------------|--------------------------|----------------------|-------------------------|
| Belgium | 9.85 | 311 | 162,026 | 16,390 | + 1.7 |
| China | 1,139.10 | 122 | 393,006 | 360 | + 9.6 |
| Holland | 14.95 | 440 | 273,248 | 16,010 | + 1.8 |
| UK | 57.24 | 237 | 834,166 | 14,570 | + 3.1 |
| USA | 294.22 | 27 | 5,237,707 | 21,000 | + 3.2 |
| Zambia | 8.45 | 11 | 3,060 | 390 | – 0.2 |

# de-industrialisation

If we consider the major changes in the British economy since 1950 one of the most significant would be the reduction in employment in manufacturing industry and the growth of the service sector. Some economists use the term *de-industrialisation* to describe these trends in the employment patterns. Although there is not an agreed definition of this term it will be taken to mean a decline in the number of workers employed in the manufacturing sector of the economy. It may be that de-industrialisation is a positive feature of economic development if the output of the manufacturing sector increases using fewer workers then efficiency must have increased. This might be accompanied by an increase in leisure time without a reduction in the country's standard of living. On the other hand, de-industrialisation might mean that manufacturing industry has become uncompetitive and no longer needs workers because demand for its products has declined. In this case de-industrialisation would be a negative aspect of economic change.

We would also note the increased use of computer based technology in a wide range in industrial contexts. This has led to many tasks which were carried out by humans being mechanised and an associated increase in the demand for computers, software and the services of operators and maintenance workers.

The third major change is the increase in unemployment which has been consistently higher since 1980 than at any other time in the country's history. There seems to be little likelihood of unemployment returning to a level below 1 million, or that the country will reach *full employment* (a situation in which all those seeking work are able to find jobs) in the foreseeable future.

It is easy to link these last two points together and to say that it is computers which have put people out of work and that it is the fault of the new technology that we have so many unemployed people in the country. However, to say that computers cause the country's unemployment rate to rise is to oversimplify the situation. Technological developments create employment as well as making existing jobs redundant. What is certainly true is that new technology requires different sorts of jobs to be done and new skills to be present in the work force and so produces the need for appropriate education and training to be provided (see pages 258 to 259).

**student activity 24.2**

(a)   Look at the statistics in fig. 24.4 below and describe in detail the changes which have taken place. Which industries have decline the most, which the least?

(b)   Suggest as many reasons as you can to explain your findings.

(c)   What further information would you need in order to show whether your suggestions were true or not?

### employment trends by industrial sector

| industrial sector | employment in thousands | | | |
|---|---|---|---|---|
| | 1971 | 1980 | 1990 | 2000 |
| agriculture, forestry, fishing | 770 | 670 | 600 | 490 |
| energy and water | 800 | 720 | 450 | 370 |
| manufacturing | 8,190 | 7,070 | 5,460 | 4,430 |
| construction | 1,550 | 1,620 | 1,810 | 1,830 |
| distribution, hotels, repairs | 4,430 | 4,990 | 5,660 | 5,720 |
| transport and communications | 1,630 | 1,600 | 1,570 | 1,420 |
| banking, finance, insurance | 1,490 | 1,860 | 3,140 | 3,220 |
| public administration and defence | 1,810 | 1,900 | 1,800 | 1,980 |
| education and health | 2,370 | 2,980 | 3,290 | 3,950 |
| other services | 1,390 | 1,820 | 2,580 | 3,330 |
| all industries | 24,430 | 25,230 | 26,360 | 26,740 |

SOURCE: Prest and Coppock *The UK Economy*, 13th edition, Weidenfeld & Nicolson

Fig 24.4   Employment in UK manufacturing

## the role of the government

### the problems of negative de-industrialisation

It is clear from the figures quoted above and from reading the newspapers that British manufacturing industry has declined and is unlikely to employ such large numbers of workers in the future as it did in the past. It is also clear from the figures that the de-industrialisation which has taken place in the UK has been of the negative rather than the positive kind. So we should now consider what, if anything the government has done or could do to arrest, or at least slow down the process.

The main aim of the government policy in this respect is to increase the *supply side* of the economy – in other words to provide the conditions in which firms can produce goods and services as cheaply as possible. Supply side policies are targeted at those aspects of firms' costs over which the government has some influence. We shall now look at some of the supply side measures which a government can take.

### education and training

The Industrial Revolution precipitated the growth of primary education in the UK in the later part of the nineteenth century; compulsory secondary schooling for all was introduced in 1944 as Britain realised the need to maintain competitiveness with German industry.  The growth in Higher

Education has followed the spread of computer-based technology.  In 1993 the government announced its target to expand the numbers of young people between the ages of 16 and 19 in full time education by 25% over the following three years.  Some might see this as a way of dealing with high levels of unemployment by keeping young people out of the group seeking work, but it also an attempt to enable industry to have at its disposal a pool of skilled labour in order to maintain and increase efficiency.

One of the most important costs facing any firm is wages.  Every firm will try to gain the maximum output from its work force and keep labour costs to a minimum.  One of the factors affecting the productivity of labour is the level of skill which it possesses.  The government is responsible for the provision of education and training opportunities.  Clearly firms conduct their own training schemes and there are many private providers too, however the vast majority of young people are educated and trained in schools and colleges funded and regulated by the government.  Through the control of funding and standards the government can ensure that the curriculum is relevant to the needs of the economy and that adequate provision is made so that all young people can be educated and trained to as high a standard as possible.

## labour relations
One of the ways in which the costs of labour can be reduced is by making the market for labour more competitive.  In other words, if there were no restrictions to the supply of labour then the price would fall if supply exceeded demand.  In reality there are a number of factors which restrict the supply of labour.  Workers are not prepared to move from one part of the country to another nor are they mobile between different kinds of work because it is not easy to retrain.  The government can try to improve this situation by offering training schemes and relocation incentives.

One of the most important imperfections in the labour market has been the power of trade unions to restrict the supply of labour in a number of ways.  In the 1950s and 1960s when labour was relatively scarce unions negotiated agreements with management which ensured that only union members could do particular jobs in the firm.  These agreements ensured work for union members and bound management to pay levels agreed nationally without reference to local costs of living and the profitability of the individual firm.  Unions were able to call for strike action in support of a grievance without a formal ballot, and many believed that union leaders had too much power in key industries such as coal, electricity and engineering.

The Conservative government made it a high priority to reduce the power of the unions when they came to power in 1979.  A series of laws were passed relating to strike action, the political levy (the contribution made to Labour Party funds) and the balloting of members.  The Miners' Strike of 1982 saw the government determined to defeat the National Union of Mineworkers.  The teachers' unions were stripped of their power to negotiate at national level over pay and conditions by the abolition of the Burnham Committee which had been the forum in which unions employers and the government had decided teachers' pay.  The government has also removed Wages Councils which were responsible for suggesting wage rates in industries such as catering, where it very difficult for workers to form effective unions because of the small number of workers on each site and the fact that many work unsociable and irregular hours.

All of these measures were designed to free the labour market from the imperfections caused when a group of workers can push the price of labour above the local market equilibrium.  In this way the government hoped to allow firms to keep labour costs down and thus be more competitive.

## incentives to work
The Conservative government in the 1980s and early 1990s reduced the basic and higher rates of *income tax* significantly.  The justification for this was to encourage people to work harder by removing the disincentives which arise from high rates of tax particularly on those on large incomes.  It is argued that people will not feel that it is worthwhile working harder if a high proportion of the extra income they will earn is taken away by the government.

The government was also conscious of the need to ensure that the level of *benefits* paid to those who are not in employment is not so high that it acts as a disincentive to seek work.  If the wage a person could expect is not higher than the benefits that he or she is receiving whilst unemployed, then there is no incentive for that person to try to find a job. The benefit system acts as a kind of lower limit for wages, since wages need to be above the benefit level in order to attract people into work. The idea of "workfare" is used in America and John Major spoke publicly of its merits. It is a system whereby those claiming benefit are given work to do which is of benefit to local communities. This scheme would have the effect of giving those claiming benefits a sense of purpose and helping them to keep to a lifestyle which was based on regular work commitments.

### the encouragement of investment – interest rates

*Investment* is a key factor of the productive capacity of the economy. Firms can be offered incentives to invest through subsidies and tax allowances. One of the key determinants of investment is the interest rate. A government which has the objective of improving the supply side of the economy will try to keep interest rates low in order to stimulate investment. The government will also try to keep its own spending and borrowing as low as possible so that there is money available in the economy for private firms to use for investment. If government spending and borrowing are high there is the danger that private investment will be *"crowded out"*. Maintaining a low interest rate is not an easy thing to do particularly when there are inflationary pressures in the economy. The interest rate also has a direct effect on the country's exchange rate and the government is faced with a difficult balancing act if it wishes to maintain a strong currency, keep inflation down, and at the same time stimulate investment.

### the promotion of enterprise

One of the key successes of the Conservative government in the 1980s was to encourage many people to become entrepreneurs. Britain had very few small companies relative to its main industrial competitors and this was seen a reason why the economy was not producing as efficiently as it might. Through direct help from the Department of Trade and Industry, and through educational programmes in schools and colleges the government were able to develop an *"enterprise culture"* and as a result, the number of people starting their own business grew rapidly. Although many of these enterprises did not succeed in the long term many did grow to become successful businesses and make valuable contributions to the nation's output. The government continues to support small businesses through the tax system and by offering grants to new firms.

---

**student activity 24.3 – government intervention in the labour market**

(a)   Divide into groups of three or four and visit the Careers Centre and the local Jobcentre and gather data about schemes which are on offer to help school and college leavers and the unemployed.

(b)   Analyse the schemes in order to identify – who is eligible, what the intended outcome is, how attractive the scheme is to the target group, and how successful the scheme will be in reducing unemployment in the short-term and the long-term. Present your findings to the rest of the school/college in the form of a display or a ring-binder.

(c)   Find out what help is available locally from the government or government-funded bodies for people who want to start their own business. Your local Business Promotion Centre or Chamber of Commerce may be able to help you. Present your findings with (b) above.

---

## chapter summary

❑   The supply of labour depends on the size and structure of the population.

❑   The population can be divided into the working population and the dependant population.

❑   The proportion of the work-force of the UK working in manufacturing is declining and the proportion working in the service sector of the economy is increasing – this known as de-industrialisation.

❑   The government can adopt policies which will help to maintain high levels of employment. These include: improving education and training, improving labour relations, providing incentives to work, encouraging investment, promoting enterprise.

# 25 The cost of labour

## introduction

In this chapter we shall look at the decisions which affect the owners of businesses as they seek to produce the required level of output using the most appropriate combination of *labour* and *capital*.

By "labour" we mean the total activity of those in paid employment; its cost comprises wages and salaries paid. "Capital" means the machinery, buildings and equipment which are needed in the process of making and selling goods and services; its cost is the price paid for the item plus any interest paid on money borrowed to purchase it.

Part of this balancing act between capital and labour will be the decision about *how much to pay each worker*. We shall investigate in this chapter:

- how wage levels are determined and the factors which affect how much a particular worker is paid
- the labour market as a whole, and the role which trade unions, professional organisations and employers' organisations play in affecting wage levels

Finally we shall look at some of the *problems* with the labour market and try to evaluate some actions which could be taken by government, unions and employers in order to improve matters.

## the relationship between labour and capital

As we have seen in the previous chapters, many of the tasks which were once done by humans are now performed by machinery. Combine harvesters, tractors and other machinery reduced the level of employment in agriculture dramatically after the invention of the internal combustion engine. Car manufacture is now highly automated, making extensive use of computer controlled machines to carry out repetitive operations which do not require any decisions to be made as part of the process. It is not difficult to imagine many manufacturing processes being carried out by "robots" in the future.

It is possible to use a graph to show how labour and capital can be combined in order to produce a given level of output.

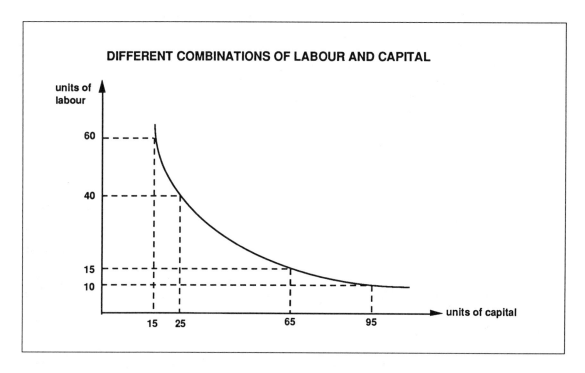

Fig 25.1.  *Different combinations of capital and labour*

This diagram shows all the combinations of labour and capital which are possible in order to achieve a given output.

Clearly it may not be possible to replace all labour with capital nor all capital with labour. However, within certain limits, which will be peculiar to each production process, there will be a range where *substitution* is possible.  What, then are the factors which would affect a decision to move to a different point on the curve?

The relative *cost* of the capital and the workers is obviously of prime importance.  This calculation will be based on certain key assumptions.  For example:
• how long the machine will last
• what its total output over the period of its life will be
• how reliable the machine will be
• what its installation, running and maintenance costs will be

Assumptions will be made about *labour costs* too:
• how wages and other non-salary costs will change over the life of the machine
• what the cost of training and staff replacement will be
• how reliable the workers will be
• the level of productivity that can be expected from workers in this situation

**student activity 25.1 – calculating the cost of labour**

The following figures refer to a firm planning to produce headphones for portable stereo systems.  Look at the figures and answer the questions which follow:

- weekly output is planned at 5,000 units.  There is no intention to alter this in the short run.
- the weekly wage is £100 per week for all production workers.
- the cost of renting the machines, which can be substituted for workers, is £120 per week
- there are three possible production methods which the firm is contemplating:

  *Method A* uses 7 units of capital and 7 workers

  *Method B* uses 12 units of capital and 2 workers

  *Method C* uses 4 units of capital and 10 workers

(a)  Calculate the total cost of production for each method.

(b)  Which method will the firm choose?

(c)  Suppose the wage rate rises to £120 per week which method will the firm choose?

(d)  What other factors would influence the firm's decision in cases where the difference in total costs was very small?

# how much are workers to be paid?

The labour market, like any other, is susceptible to the forces of demand and supply.  We can see the wage as the *price of labour* and use the same kind of analysis as set out in detail in Chapter 9 to determine the market or equilibrium price.  The supply curve will show how many hours of labour workers will be prepared to offer at a give rate of pay and the demand curve how many hours firms will be prepared to buy at each wage level.  The intersection of the two curves will show the equilibrium wage where there will neither be an excess of labour being offered, nor an excess demand for labour given the wage which is offered.

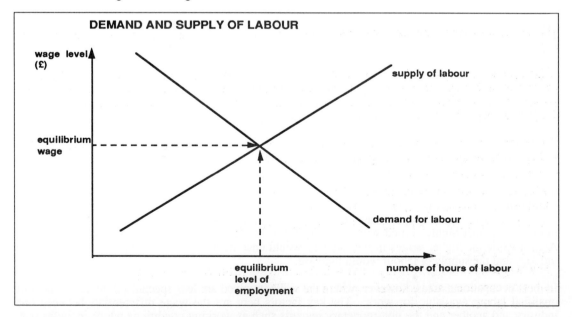

**DEMAND AND SUPPLY OF LABOUR**

*Fig. 25.2  The demand and supply of labour*

# the supply of labour

In considering the supply of labour it is important to distinguish the hours of labour which will be supplied by the individual and those that will be supplied by workers in general to an industry.

### the individual's supply of labour

It has been shown that an individual's supply curve for labour is the shape shown in fig. 25.3. below.

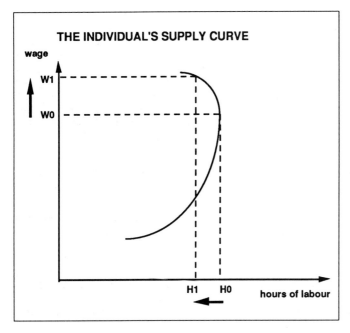

The curve begins by sloping upwards to the right as higher wages induce a worker to offer more hours of his/her time in order to increase the standard of living which he or she is able to enjoy. However, after a certain point ($W_0$ and $H_0$) a worker will choose to supply fewer hours of work ($H_1$) as the wage rate rises ($W_1$). He or she will be content with a certain level of income and choose leisure time in preference to work.

*Fig.25.3: The individual's supply of labour*

There will be a range of factors which affect how much time a person wishes to spend working which are separate from the wage rate itself. A person may have other income from a partner or family, he or she may have another job or source of earnings, or may have little need for material goods and choose a life-style which does not depend on a high degree of spending power.

### the supply of labour to an industry

In general, the supply of labour to an industry will be relatively elastic in the long run but inelastic in the short run. For example, it would not be possible for the supply of rocket engineers to be significantly increased quickly. There is a long training period and the skills required are highly specialised. The only way to increase recruitment to that industry, therefore, would be to raise wages in order to attract highly skilled workers away from their existing jobs and into rocket technology. After a while the higher wages in the industry would encourage more young people to train for the industry and the supply of labour would increase.

In most occupational areas, however, where the skills involved are less specialised, there is a pool of qualified labour available for work. The key factors here are the wage differentials between one industry and another and the non-monetary rewards such as working conditions which includes risk, unsociable hours, career structure and job security. Firms within the industry will compete for labour on wage levels but also on such staff benefits as pension schemes, sports facilities, creche provision, holiday entitlement, company cars and health schemes.  In occupational areas such as secretarial work, lorry driving, school teaching or carpentry there is a rate of pay which is generally accepted, known as the *going rate*.  In order to attract workers firms simply offer the going rate with minor variations to take account of local labour market conditions and the cost of living in the area.

It might be the case that if a larger firm were to move to an area and make larger demands on a particular pool of skilled labour it may "bid up" the wage rate in order to attract workers. However, it is unlikely that such a situation would last for long, particularly if there was local unemployment in other skill areas and appropriate training was available.

## the elasticity of supply of labour

The key determinant of the elasticity of labour is the skills required by the job.  The supply of operatic tenors or international tennis players is not going to be significantly increased in the short run by changes in the wages available to them.  Special skills or long periods of training will mean *inelastic* supply.  Conversely, where the job involves few specialist skills which can be learned very quickly the supply of workers to the industry can be quickly and significantly affected by a change in wage levels.  Other factors which affect elasticity of supply include the cost of entering the occupational group.  For example, entry to the legal profession requires expensive training and practical experience, dentists require expensive equipment, musicians need high quality instruments, all of which will mean that changes in the wages offered will not, in the short run at least, affect the number of workers making themselves available to these occupational groups.

---

**student activity 25.2 – the supply of labour**

(a)  List at least six different occupational groups which you would find working in a large hospital.  Rank the list in order of the elasticity of supply putting the least elastic first and the most elastic last.

(b)  Imagine that you are the managing director of a small, but rapidly expanding firm producing custom-made computer software for the printing industry.  The firm is located in Leominster, a small town near the Welsh border.  There is no pool of local labour with the skills which your firm requires.

What strategies would you adopt to recruit a team of specialist computer programmers, technical sales representatives and systems analysts to join the staff of your firm?

---

# the demand for labour

No firm will choose to employ workers unless it can justify the decision on the basis of its *output* – ie the number of items it makes and sells (or the volume of services it provides).  This means that a firm will take on *more* workers if it wishes to *increase* output and will *cut* its labour force if it can no longer *sell* all of its output.  The demand for workers is directly *derived* from the demand for the *product* itself.

## elasticity of demand for labour – demand for the product

The *elasticity of demand* for labour will depend on a number of factors most of them related to the elasticity of demand for the product.  If the demand for the product is relatively inelastic then the elasticity of demand for workers in the industry will also be inelastic, and vice versa.  For example, an increase in the wages of skilled engineers in the electricity industry is likely to be passed on to the consumer rather than lead to a change in the number of workers employed *because the demand for electricity is relatively inelastic* and so a rise in the price of electricity will not lead to a substantial drop in quantity demanded.

### elasticity of demand for labour – how significant are the labour costs?

The *proportion of the total cost of production which is taken up by the labour cost* will also have an effect on whether more or less labour is employed. If labour costs only form a very *small* part of the total cost, then demand for labour will be relatively *inelastic*. However, if the industry uses highly labour intensive methods  (ie the proportion of labour costs is high) then a small change in the price of labour could lead to substantial changes in the quantity demanded.  An example here would be production workers in firm making shirts.  A small rise in the wage rate could lead to a large rise in total costs.  The firm would therefore look at cheaper production techniques involving more capital rather than see its wage bill increase significantly, unless there were corresponding improvements in productivity.  This could lead to a cut in the number of workers employed by the firm.

### elasticity of demand for labour – demand for the skill

The degree to which it is possible for a firm to substitute capital for labour will also influence the elasticity of demand.  If we consider the demand for solicitors, police officers or nurses it is clear that there is no easy way of replacing these workers with machines.  Therefore the demand for their labour will be relatively inelastic.  On the other hand if there were to be a significant rise in the cost of employing a production worker in an engineering firm making screws, the management might well decide to reduce the workforce and buy a computer controlled machine to do the job instead.

---

### student activity 25.3 – the elasticity of demand for labour

(a) Show, using appropriate diagrams, how the wages of workers would be affected by the following changes in the market for the goods they produce.  Make sure that you show the correct elasticity of demand for labour in each case.

    i   a rise in the demand for wheat on the wages of farm labourers

    ii  a rise in the demand for hip replacements on the wages of orthopaedic surgeons

    iii a fall in the demand for novels by J Archer on the wages of J Archer.

    iv a rise in demand for CD players on the wages of those who produce Compact Discs

    v  a fall in the number of people moving house on the wages of solicitors

    vi a fall in the demand for chocolate bars on the wages of production workers in the chocolate factory

(b) Imagine that you are either a trade union representative or a director of a firm making building materials.  Your firm is considering buying a computer-controlled machine which will saw and plane timber to size ready for use in roof trusses.  The machine will mean that you can reduce the workforce by ten people making the firm less labour intensive. Make a list of questions which you would need to answer in order to make the case for or against buying the machine. (Note: it would not necessarily be the case that the director would end up in favour of the machine and the trade union official against.)  Put your list in order of priority with the most important question at the top.

---

# the marginal productivity theory of labour

From assumption made in the section above that demand for labour is *derived from the demand for the product* follows the *Marginal Productivity Theory of Labour*.  This suggests that a firm will go on hiring workers *until the value of the marginal product (the output of the extra worker) is equal to the wage rate for that worker*.

In other words, if a business pays £100 a week in wages for each worker, it will look for at least £100 extra weekly income from sales if it takes on that worker.  If the extra income received from taking on an extra worker is less than £100, it is not worthwhile hiring that extra person.

In the table set out on the next page you will see that as the business takes on more workers, so the total output *per worker* falls.  Look at the table carefully and then read the notes that follow. Remember that the marginal product *is the number of items produced by each extra worker*.

## the marginal product of labour

| workers employed | total weekly output (units) | marginal product (MP) (units) | marginal revenue product (MRP) (£) – based on a unit price of £5 |
|---|---|---|---|
| 1 | 30 | 30 | 150 |
| 2 | 57 | 27 | 135 |
| 3 | 82 | 25 | 125 |
| 4 | 102 | 20 | 120 |
| 5 | 117 | 15 | 105 |
| 6 | 127 | 10 | 50 |
| 7 | 132 | 5 | 25 |

The table set out above shows how total output changes as more workers are employed. The addition to total output made by each extra worker is known as the *marginal product* (MP); the law of diminishing returns tells us that this marginal product will decrease as more workers are employed. This is clearly shown in the figures: the first worker employed increases output by 30 units, the second by 27 units, but the seventh worker can only manage to increase total output by 5 units.

The final column shows the Marginal Revenue Product (MRP) which is calculated by multiplying the marginal product by the price of each unit of output – in this case the price is £5. The MRP shows the *value of the contribution of each additional worker,* ie the extra sales income the worker will bring in.

It is clearly not in the firm's interests in the long run to employ a worker who is not producing output at a value in excess of the wage he or she is receiving. In the short run it may be that workers will be employed even if they are not producing above the wage rate because of the costs of making workers redundant and of recruitment and training in the event of an upturn in demand. However, in the long run a rise in wages with no corresponding rise in the value of the marginal product will lead to fewer workers being employed.

### student activity 25.4 – the marginal product of labour

(a) Using the data in the table set out above, plot a graph showing MRP. Use the vertical axis for wage and revenue and the horizontal axis for the number of workers employed. Note that the revenue per unit is £5.

(b) How many workers would be employed if the wage was £120 per week?

(c) Suppose the wage rose to £125 per week how many workers would now be employed?

(d) Draw another MRP line to show the effect of a fall in the price of the product to £4.

(e) All other things being equal, how many workers would the firm now employ at a wage of £120 per week?

### problems with the marginal productivity theory

Marginal productivity is fine in theory, but there are a number of reasons why it does not provide a completely satisfactory explanation of wage levels and employment patterns. Firstly there are many workers whose marginal product is impossible to measure in money terms. For example, waiters, cleaning staff, shop assistants and managing directors all make valuable contributions to the efficient running of a firm yet their value is impossible to measure. Even a production worker is rarely solely responsible for a unit of output and therefore the value to the firm of employing an extra worker is very difficult to calculate precisely.

However, we can look at this in a slightly different way and show that the theory does have real merit. Look at fig. 25.4 below.

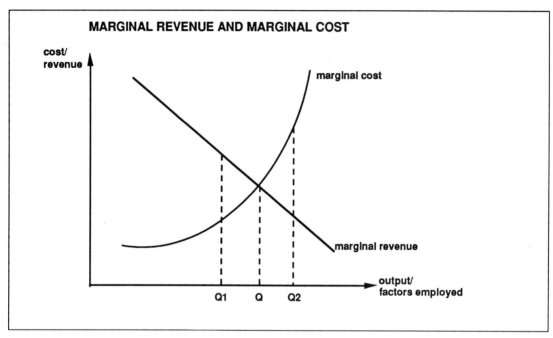

Fig. 25.4: Marginal revenue and marginal cost

Clearly no firm will increase its costs of production unless in so doing it can also increase its total revenue. So taking the situation overall, rather than trying to evaluate the value of the output of one extra worker, firms would look more broadly and see whether the marginal increase in cost is matched by the marginal increase in revenue.

### student activity 25.5 – marginal revenue and marginal cost

(a)   Look at fig. 25.4 and explain why a firm will try to produce at Q rather than at either Q1 or Q2.

(b)   Working in groups make a list of ways in which the firm producing luxury carpets could try to push its MRP of labour line to the right so that it could gain the same revenue product with fewer workers.

(c)   Consider the list which another group has made from the point of view of Trade Union representatives in the firm. Which of the measures listed would you support and which would you oppose? Give reasons for your answers.

# chapter summary

❑ The labour market is like other markets insofar as there is an equilibrium wage which is determined by the forces of supply and demand.

❑ Capital can be a substitute for labour and generally the trend is towards this substitution in industries where the production process involves repetitive and predictable tasks.

❑ Workers will supply more of their time as the wage rate increases up to the point where they are satisfied with their income. Beyond that point they will choose leisure time rather than a higher income as the wage rate rises. This produces a backward sloping supply curve for individual workers.

❑ The elasticity of supply of workers is determined by the speed and ease of entry into the occupational group.

❑ The demand for workers is derived from the demand for the product of their labour.

❑ The elasticity of demand will be linked to the elasticity of demand of the product and to the proportion of total costs which is taken up with labour costs.

❑ The number of workers which a firm will employ will be such that the marginal revenue product is equal to the wage, although this point may be very difficult to identify in practice.

# 26 Unemployment: cause and effect

## introduction

In this chapter we shall see why the labour market does not settle in an *equilibrium* – providing *all* workers with a job at a market-determined rate of pay – as was shown in the previous chapter. *Unemployment* has been an almost permanent feature of economic life in the UK since the early 1970s, and there were periods of high unemployment before that, notably in the Great Depression of the 1930s.

We shall consider how unemployment is measured, look at the different types of unemployment and their causes, and then consider what, if anything can be done to *reduce* high levels of unemployment.

## the measurement of unemployment

The unemployment figures are of great interest to politicians and to economists. No politician wishes to see high unemployment figures and most will argue that their policies are designed to reduce the number of jobless people. Since 1979 there have been several changes made to the way in which the figures are calculated and there is debate among the political parties about who should be included and who left out of the official totals. Most of the controversy hinges on whether to count only those who are actively seeking work and claiming benefit, or whether to include those who would accept work if it were available but who do not register for benefit. There are also some people who claim benefit and have some form of paid work and so may be counted in the jobless totals, although strictly speaking they should be left out.

The major significance of the unemployment trend is that it helps to indicate whether the economy is moving into, or out of, recession. A downward trend in the unemployment figure will not be the first sign that the economy is growing because of the time lag between firms experiencing increasing sales and taking on more staff. However if the jobless total begins to rise then this is a sign that the economy is slowing down and that other signs of reduced growth are likely to follow.

The unemployment figures also indicate how much the government is likely to have to pay out in benefits. The cost of unemployment to the Treasury is considerable, and will have a serious impact on the amount of money which can be spent on other government services such as health and education. It may also mean that the government will have to borrow large sums of money to pay for benefits, this in turn could push interest rates upwards as the demand for money increases.

## the natural rate of unemployment

Economists accept that a certain level of unemployment is inevitable. It is not possible for every person in the country who is of working age to be in paid employment. There is a *Natural Rate of Unemployment* which is the percentage of those of working age who are not fit to work or choose not to seek paid employment. This group includes:

- those with a handicap or illness
- those who decide to work unpaid in the home or in some form of voluntary capacity
- those who are not prepared to work at the prevailing wage rate – they may be fit for work and would be prepared to take a job if the pay was acceptable to them

We can refer to this latter group of people as being *Voluntarily Unemployed*. The remainder of those who are unemployed would be prepared to work at the prevailing wage rate and are experiencing *Involuntary Unemployment*.

## forms of involuntary unemployment

### frictional unemployment

Within the group of those who are willing to work at the wage being offered will be some who have left one job and are about to start another. There will also be students who have left school, college or university and will be starting a career after a vacation. They will be classed as unemployed in the economic sense, though they may not count in the statistics. This form of unemployment is called *Frictional Unemployment*. There is little that the government can do about this situation and it is not a major problem in the economy.

### seasonal unemployment

Many workers do one sort of job in the winter and another in the summer months. Many firms significantly alter their levels of production during certain times of the year to coincide with seasonal demand or supply. There are many more jobs in retailing available at Christmas, many agricultural workers will be unable to find work in winter time, but the holiday industry employs many more staff in the summer months. In order to allow for these variations in employment opportunities the official statistics are *seasonally adjusted*.

### structural unemployment

Of far greater importance in the economy is unemployment which arises because the structure of UK industry is undergoing significant change. Traditional UK manufacturing industries have shed large numbers of workers in the twentieth century. Coal mining, ship building, and steel making are prime examples of industries which have declined dramatically, causing structural changes in employment patterns in Britain. The resulting unemployment has meant high concentrations of redundant workers with specialist skills and experience in particular areas of the country. The effect of closing mines, shipyards and factories which may have employed the majority of the workers living in the locality has been to reduce demand for the goods and services required by these firms, the workers and their families. This has meant secondary unemployment in the area and a general decline in the local economy. Regions which were once prosperous become less so, workers move away in order to seek work and those who cannot afford to do so often remain unemployed for long periods of time. Examples of this structural unemployment are to be found in Tyneside, South Wales and Yorkshire.

### cyclical unemployment

The economist John Maynard Keynes put forward the theory that there was an inevitable cycle of boom and slump through which the economy would pass.

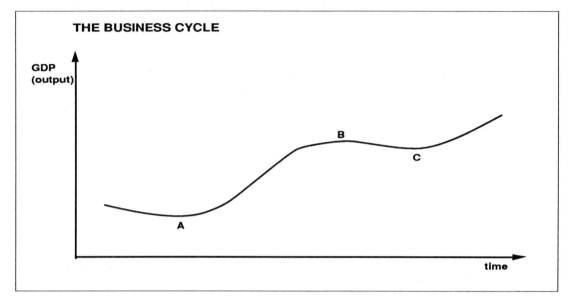

*Fig. 26.1: The Business Cycle*

The boom (between A and B in the diagram) could be caused by an increase in demand for UK goods, either at home or abroad, which would encourage producers of to invest in capital goods. The workers in these industries therefore have more money to spend and this in turn stimulates further demand for consumer goods. After a period of boom the demand for capital goods falls (between B and C in the diagram) reducing the earning power of those employed in industries such as construction and machine manufacturing. Their demand for goods is reduced and so other firms will cut production and the numbers in work will fall. The unemployment caused by the slump in demand and therefore output is known as *Cyclical Unemployment*. After a while demand will begin to increase and output and employment will increase once again (beyond point C in the diagram).

# explanations of involuntary unemployment

### is unemployment inevitable?

It was believed by early economists usually known as *'Classical Economists'* that there would be no *involuntary* unemployment. They argued that if workers were unemployed then wages would be driven down which would reduce the cost of production making goods cheaper. As the price fell, so demand for goods would rise and more workers would be required in order to increase production. Also, if workers were unemployed they would be prepared to accept work with lower wages rather than face poverty.

This 'Classical' theory was accepted and largely proved to be true until the depression of the 1930s when there were very high levels of unemployment which persisted for several years. By then the government was playing a very significant role in the economic life of the country. It took a large amount of GDP in taxes and controlled a number of key industries. Keynes rejected the classical theory and proposed that unemployment would arise because there was *insufficient demand* in the economy, in other words people did not have sufficient money to buy enough goods to keep everyone in work. He suggested that the government should increase its own spending in order to add to the total demand in the economy, as in fig. 26.2 below. If workers had money to spend they would buy goods which would require others to be employed. He argued that it was better to have people digging holes and others filling them in, rather than allow those people to remain unemployed.

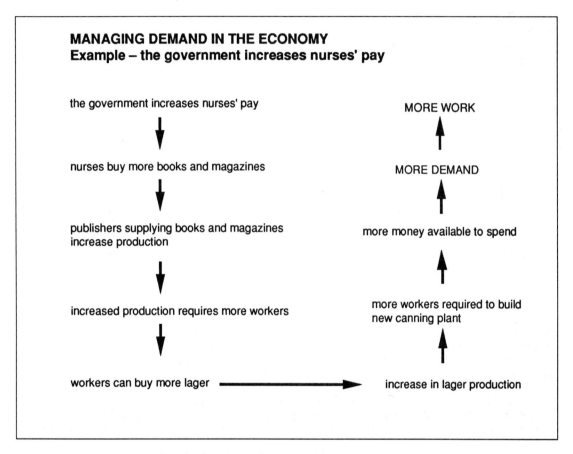

**MANAGING DEMAND IN THE ECONOMY**
**Example – the government increases nurses' pay**

the government increases nurses' pay

nurses buy more books and magazines

publishers supplying books and magazines increase production

increased production requires more workers

workers can buy more lager

increase in lager production

more workers required to build new canning plant

more money available to spend

MORE DEMAND

MORE WORK

*Fig. 26.2:  Managing demand in the economy*

**student activity 26.1 – the business cycle and demand management**

(a)    Look at fig. 26.1 on the previous page.  Write down as many situations as you can think of which might cause a boom to start, or to end?  Prepare a script (about 150 words) for a Chancellor of the Exchequer (of which ever party you prefer) announcing that a recession which has faced the UK for the past three years is coming to an end.  Make reference to as many economc indicators as you can to support your view.

(b)    Look at fig. 26.2 above.  Why might a policy such as raising the wages of public sector workers be harmful rather than helpful to the economy of the country?  In groups of three, debate the case for the government trying to increase demand in the economy so that unemployment is reduced.  One of you could play the role of a leader of one of the public sector unions (teachers, nurses, health workers, civil servants) and the other could play that of a Treasury official who does not want public spending to rise.  The third member of the group should listen carefully to what is being said and report back to the whole class on the strengths and weaknesses of the arguments put forward.

### the end of demand management – Monetarism

The idea that the government could control the level of demand in the economy in order to maintain full employment was accepted by economists until the mid 1970s when Milton Friedman and his colleagues developed the theories which we now know as *'Monetarism'*. Monetarists argue that the main aim of government should be to allow the labour market to stabilise itself and that it is not wise for a government to try to influence total demand. They suggest that *the control of inflation* ought to be the main aim of government policy. If governments try to boost employment beyond the level which current demand for goods allows it to reach, then there will be inflation. This will make British goods expensive abroad and will lead to a fall in total demand for UK output.

Rather than trying to increase demand for goods the government should aim its policies at the control of inflation and increasing the productive capacity of UK industry through the supply side measures which were discussed in the previous chapter.

## what makes the labour market different?

It seems from recent events as though the classicists and their followers the monetarists, as well as the Keynesians, have got it wrong. Despite the best efforts of governments of both right and left the UK has experienced periods when high numbers of people are involuntarily unemployed. Nor is this simply a British disease, unemployment has been a serious problem in USA and most of the European Community, as the table set out below shows.

**average annual unemployment figures (% of workforce)**

|      | UK   | USA | Japan | Germany | France | Italy |
|------|------|-----|-------|---------|--------|-------|
| 1983 | 12.4 | 9.4 | 2.6   | 8.0     | 8.3    | 8.9   |
| 1984 | 11.7 | 7.4 | 2.7   | 7.0     | 9.7    | 9.4   |
| 1985 | 11.2 | 7.1 | 2.6   | 7.1     | 10.2   | 9.6   |
| 1986 | 11.2 | 6.9 | 2.8   | 6.4     | 10.4   | 10.5  |
| 1987 | 10.3 | 6.1 | 2.9   | 6.2     | 10.5   | 10.9  |
| 1988 | 8.6  | 5.4 | 2.5   | 6.2     | 10.0   | 11.0  |
| 1989 | 7.1  | 5.2 | 2.2   | 5.6     | 9.4    | 10.9  |
| 1990 | 6.8  | 5.4 | 2.1   | 4.9     | 8.9    | 10.3  |
| 1991 | 8.9  | 6.6 | 2.1   | 4.3     | 9.4    | 9.9   |

SOURCE: Lloyds Bank Plc

### wages do not tend to fall

The labour market is different from the market for, say, eggs because the price of labour does not tend to fall over time. One of the main reasons for this is that it is relatively rare for workers to experience a fall in wages in the event of a fall in the demand for their product. This is partly because trade unions would oppose such a move but also because it would prove very de-motivating to the work force. Workers are likely to work harder if they feel that they are the lucky ones who still have a job rather than if they feel that they are worth less this week than they were last. Also it is often the case that a whole firm or a section of a firm becomes redundant when output is reduced. In such cases there is little point in trying to keep the workers who operated in that part of the firm in employment even on a reduced wage; they too, become redundant.

## barriers to entry in the labour market.

One of the assumptions which is made when the demand and supply curves are drawn for a particular product is that factors of production can be attracted into the industry in order to allow a rise in supply to take place. Conversely, factors of production can easily leave the industry if there is over-production. For example, a farmer can relatively easily reduce the number of fields on which he or she grazes cattle, and increase the acreage used for wheat production . A firm can easily buy a new machine, or it could quickly decrease the amount of capital it employs simply by not using a part of the factory or "moth-balling" a part of the plant. Changing the amount of labour which is employed is less easy. Workers cannot be laid off without certain procedures being followed and costs met (see Chapter 19). New workers cannot be employed without advertising, interviewing and training (see Chapter 22). There are, then, important costs which act as barriers to the free entry to and exit from the labour market.

## geographical immobility of labour– financial and domestic costs

Labour is not a particularly mobile factor of production: workers are reluctant to move to other parts of the country in order to seek work. This *geographical immobility* is due to a number of factors:

* the cost of moving house which can run into several thousands of pounds and would be too expensive for many workers
* the difference in the cost of housing in various parts of the country means that, for example, someone moving from a large house in a suburb of Liverpool to take up a job in London would find that they could only afford a much smaller house near London and might still face high travelling costs into the city
* the reluctance to move children away from schools and friends where they are happy and successful
* the reluctance to move away from family, friends and familiar surroundings.

## occupational immobility of labour – lack of skills and experience

Workers may be unable to change to another kind of work because they lack the necessary skills and experience. This is known as *occupational immobility* and is a key reason why structural unemployment may lead to high numbers of people being unemployed for very long periods of time, and why some workers who lose their job in an area dependant on traditional industries may not find work again.

*Occupational immobility* is particularly acute amongst workers who develop highly specialised skills in occupations where there are rapid changes in technology or where Britain has lost international competitiveness. Such industries include mining, ship building and machine tool making. In these industries Britain no longer produces competitively to the extent that it once did. Workers who may have considerable skill and experience find themselves redundant and unable to sell their skills to another employer. The skills that they have are not transferable to a different work place. The workers may not be suitable for retraining for jobs which are available in other parts of the country because they may not have the necessary aptitudes and may also be unwilling to relocate. The new industries based around computers which have grown up along the M4 corridor are not likely to recruit redundant steel workers from Ravenscraig or trawler crews from Hull.

# what can be done about unemployment?

The policies which can be used to deal with unemployment are all described in more detail elsewhere in this book (see Chapter 12). The government will try to provide an environment in which firms can be successful. This will require:

* a low and stable inflation rate
* low and stable interest rates

- a stable exchange rate
- high quality education and training opportunities linked to the needs of industry
- laws which will inhibit the power of trade unions and professional associations to distort the labour market
- a regional policy to encourage geographical mobility of labour
- control of public sector pay so that industry does not have to raise its wages in order to maintain differentials between the public and private sector
- benefits at a level which will not discourage the unemployed from seeking work and accepting jobs with low wages
- the avoidance of policies which will force up labour costs – these might include regulations relating to maternity leave, pension rights, sick pay, redundancy entitlement and health and safety rules

The problem with all of this is that there will be important moral and political considerations to be taken into account. There will always be a conflict between what free market economics dictates and what individual people are prepared to accept. The role of the government is to balance these competing interests so that society as a whole benefits both by having low unemployment and a work force which enjoys appropriate rights and is effectively protected from exploitation.

## student activity 26.2 – analysing the economic performance of the UK

Look at the statistical tables below and answer the questions set out on the next page.

### average change in industrial production (%)

|      | UK    | USA   | Japan | Germany | France | Italy |
|------|-------|-------|-------|---------|--------|-------|
| 1983 | 4.0   | 3.7   | 3.2   | 0.7     | 0.1    | - 2.0 |
| 1984 | 0.1   | 9.5   | 9.3   | 3.1     | 1.7    | 3.7   |
| 1985 | 5.6   | 1.7   | 3.7   | 4.9     | 0.7    | 1.1   |
| 1986 | 2.4   | 1.0   | - 0.2 | 1.9     | 1.1    | 4.0   |
| 1987 | 3.3   | 4.9   | 3.4   | 0.4     | 2.0    | 2.5   |
| 1988 | 3.8   | 5.4   | 9.3   | 3.6     | 4.1    | 7.4   |
| 1989 | 0.2   | 2.6   | 6.1   | 4.9     | 3.7    | 4.1   |
| 1990 | - 0.6 | 1.0   | 4.7   | 5.1     | 1.5    | - 0.5 |
| 1991 | - 3.0 | - 1.9 | 2.4   | 3.1     | 0.4    | - 2.5 |

### average change in GDP (%)

|      | UK    | USA   | Japan | Germany | France | Italy |
|------|-------|-------|-------|---------|--------|-------|
| 1983 | 3.8   | 3.6   | 2.8   | 1.9     | 0.7    | 1.2   |
| 1984 | 1.7   | 6.8   | 4.3   | 3.0     | 1.3    | 3.0   |
| 1985 | 3.6   | 3.3   | 5.1   | 2.1     | 1.9    | 2.6   |
| 1986 | 4.0   | 2.9   | 2.7   | 2.1     | 2.6    | 2.9   |
| 1987 | 4.6   | 3.1   | 4.3   | 1.4     | 2.2    | 3.2   |
| 1988 | 4.2   | 3.9   | 6.3   | 3.5     | 4.2    | 4.1   |
| 1989 | 2.3   | 2.5   | 4.8   | 3.9     | 3.9    | 3.0   |
| 1990 | 1.0   | 1.0   | 5.2   | 4.7     | 2.9    | 1.9   |
| 1991 | - 2.0 | - 0.7 | 4.4   | 3.2     | 1.1    | 1.6   |

SOURCE: Lloyds Bank Plc

**student activity 26.2 – continued**

Using the table on page 274 and the two tables on the previous page:

(a)    Plot a graph showing unemployment figures and changes in GDP for the UK over the period 1983 to 1991 (add later figures if you can find them). What correlations can you see?

(b)    Using the figures on unemployment, GDP and industrial output for all the countries shown in the three tables, evaluate the UK's economic performance relative to its competitors. What other information would you need in order to give a more complete picture?

# chapter summary

❑    There are a number of types of unemployment:
  • frictional
  • seasonal
  • cyclical
  • structural

❑    The main cause of unemployment can be summed up as a lack of demand for the output of the workers concerned. (The demand for labour is derived demand).

❑    Workers rarely experience a drop in wages and this means that the market will not adjust to a new equilibrium wage if demand falls, instead there will be unemployment.

❑    The labour market does not clear because labour is relatively immobile both geographically and occupationally.

❑    Keynesians believe that the government can control the level of demand within the economy such that full employment is maintained.

❑    Monetarists believe that the governments role is to pursue supply side policies in order to allow UK firms to be competitive in international markets.

# 27 Employment trends – present and future

## introduction

This chapter will focus on the present trends in employment, and from them we shall try to draw some conclusions about the way in which the structure of employment in the UK and in Europe is changing.   In particular we shall consider

- the increase in the role of women in the work-force
- the growth of part-time work
- the increase in self-employment.

We shall also consider the way  employment law affects the sort of jobs which are available, and how managers try to increase the productivity of the work force.

## women in employment in the UK

Women now make up a higher percentage of the workforce than at any other time in history.  During war time many of the jobs done by men were taken over by women including heavy factory work. However in peace time there has traditionally been an assumption that women should play the major role in home-making and child-rearing and that the main wage earner would be the man.  This has meant that where women have a paid job, this has been in addition to their role in the home.  Surveys have shown that women looking after children at home work on average 70 hours per week and various estimates have been made of the value in money terms of the work which they do.  These estimates suggest that women's unpaid work is worth many thousands of pounds per year in each household.  In the UK women now make up approximately 42% of the work force and the trend is towards a yet more even sex ratio in the total of those in employment, as the figures below show:

**men and women in employment**

|                                  | 1979 | 1992 |
|----------------------------------|------|------|
| men in employment (millions)     | 13.1 | 10.7 |
| women in employment (millions)   | 9.4  | 10.1 |
| total (millions)                 | 22.5 | 20.8 |

SOURCE: Department of Employment

Already in certain sectors there are more women employed than men. These tend to be the service sectors and retailing, and many of the jobs which women hold are part-time. Recent unemployment statistics show that unemployment among men has risen faster that among women.

**unemployment amongst men and women**

|  | 1986<br>(peak) | 1993<br>(January) |
|---|---|---|
| unemployment – women | 9.0% | 5.6% |
| unemployment – men | 13.5% | 14.1% |

The survey goes on to conclude that the trend towards more part-time work will continue, and will result in more women being employed. The reason suggested for this is that there will be a continuing decline in traditional manufacturing jobs and an increase in service occupations. See fig. 24.4 (page 258). These trends are illustrated on a regional basis in the table set out below.

### WHERE WOMEN WORKERS OUTNUMBER MEN
### (figures in thousands)

| County/Region | Full-time men | Part-time men | All men | Full-time women | Part-time women | All women |
|---|---|---|---|---|---|---|
| Essex: | 218.9 | 24.2 | 243.1 | 123.6 | 123.3 | 246.9 |
| Isle of Wight: | 17.7 | 2.7 | 20.4 | 9.4 | 11.6 | 21.0 |
| East Sussex: | 90.0 | 14.4 | 104.4 | 61.4 | 59.3 | 120.7 |
| West Sussex: | 116.6 | 14.8 | 131.4 | 73.3 | 64.1 | 137.4 |
| Cornwall/<br>Scilly Isles: | 55.9 | 9.5 | 65.4 | 33.5 | 40.2 | 73.8 |
| Devon: | 154.2 | 21.7 | 175.9 | 87.6 | 93.7 | 181.3 |
| Hereford<br>& Worcester: | 109.8 | 11.8 | 121.6 | 62.6 | 59.1 | 121.7 |
| Merseyside: | 210.9 | 19.2 | 230.1 | 128.6 | 117.5 | 246.1 |
| Mid Glamorgan: | 70.1 | 4.8 | 74.8 | 41.4 | 35.8 | 77.3 |
| Borders Region<br>(Scotland): | 17.1 | 1.6 | 18.7 | 10.4 | 8.6 | 19.0 |
| Lothian Region<br>(Scotland): | 155.7 | 13.9 | 169.6 | 101.1 | 69.6 | 170.7 |

*Source: 1991 Census of Employment, published in the Department of Employment Gazette, April 1993.*

SOURCE: The Independent

*Fig 27.1: Regional trends in the employment of men and women*

### the increase in part-time work

The figures also show clearly that women are out-numbering men in a number of areas of the country in part-time work by such a margin that they make up a greater proportion of the total work-force in those areas.

The explanation of these figures is not difficult to find. It has to do with the cost of employing someone on a part-time basis. The law which guarantees a worker certain statutory rights such as protection from unfair dismissal, maternity leave and redundancy pay does not apply to someone who is employed for less than 16 hours per week unless they have been in that job for more than five years. If the employer does not have to meet the costs of these entitlements in addition to the wage, then the total cost to the firm of employing a part-time worker will be much less than if they were employed on a full-time contract. Also, if someone is only working for, say, four hours per day they will not require a lunch break for which the employer would have to pay but would gain no production.

The kinds of work which are particularly easy to arrange on a part- time basis include shop work and cleaning where the tasks involved require a low level of skill and therefore little training. It would be quite wrong to suggest, however, that women are only employed in low skill jobs. Many jobs in health care and hospitality, for example, require considerable skill but are also divisible into small "parcels" of work which can form part-time contracts.

In such occupations it is easy to arrange for many workers to share the total hours of work required by the firm in such a way that no-one does more than 16 hours. This arrangement may well suit those who take up these jobs. Many women work in order to enhance the family income rather than to provide the main wage in the household and welcome the opportunity to be employed at such times that do not interfere with their unpaid work in the home.

The recent abolition of wages councils which fixed wages for the low paid will probably encourage the trend towards more part-time work for women. Women already make up 80% of the two million workers who are classed as low paid. Many of these workers are employed in firms which do not recognise any trade union and where the workers have little power in negotiating wage increases with their employer.

---

### student activity 27.1 – women in employment

(a) Find out from your local careers office about the trends in local employment for female school and college leavers. Include questions such as:

- what percentage of females stay on in full-time education beyond 16?
- what percentage go on to Higher Education?
- what percentage enter full-time employment?
- what percentage join government schemes?

*Show the results in graphical form using appropriate graphs or charts.*

(b) Look at the statistics published by UCAS (UCCA/PCAS) about subjects studied at university and identify those which are most popular amongst males and those which are most popular amongst females.

*Show the results in graphical form using appropriate graphs or charts.*

(c) What conclusions can be drawn from the data you have gathered in (a) and (b)? What policies would you recommend to reduce further the inequalities which you have identified?

---

# the European scene

Employment trends involve the analysis of data. On the next two pages are set out a number of statistical tables relating to employment figures for workers within the European Community (EC):

- Fig. 27.2 shows the numbers of workers in the three basic sectors of Agriculture, Industry and Services in the various member states of the European Community
- Fig. 27.3 shows the percentage of women and men in the EC member states who do part-time work.
- Fig 27.4 on the following page shows the women's earnings in the EC as a percentage of men's earnings

Study the figures carefully, see what trends and features you can identify, and then compare your findings with those set out on page 282.

*Note: the figures were compiled from sources showing the situation in 1988. Figures for Spain and Portugal are omitted in fig. 27.4.*

**EMPLOYMENT BY SECTOR IN THE EC (000'S)**

| | AGRICULTURE | | | INDUSTRY | | | SERVICES | | |
|---|---|---|---|---|---|---|---|---|---|
| | *male* | *female* | *total* | *male* | *female* | *total* | *male* | *female* | *total* |
| Belgium | 82 | 29 | 111 | 879 | 213 | 1092 | 1251 | 1030 | 2281 |
| Denmark | 117 | 27 | 154 | 532 | 191 | 723 | 806 | 985 | 1791 |
| Germany | 654 | 549 | 1203 | 8260 | 2682 | 10942 | 7541 | 7314 | 14855 |
| Greece | 537 | 435 | 972 | 715 | 213 | 928 | 1127 | 629 | 1756 |
| Spain | 1229 | 442 | 1671 | 3185 | 629 | 3814 | 3697 | 2527 | 6224 |
| France | 1014 | 533 | 1547 | 4858 | 1568 | 6426 | 6475 | 6961 | 13436 |
| Ireland | 156 | 15 | 171 | 245 | 66 | 311 | 337 | 268 | 605 |
| Italy | 1377 | 694 | 2071 | 5175 | 1621 | 6796 | 7491 | 4742 | 12233 |
| Luxembourg | 4 | 2 | 6 | 40 | 5 | 45 | 56 | 46 | 102 |
| Netherlands | 217 | 69 | 286 | 1324 | 239 | 1563 | 1283 | 1858 | 3141 |
| Portugal | 477 | 467 | 944 | 1080 | 460 | 1540 | 1050 | 911 | 1961 |
| UK | 471 | 131 | 602 | 6415 | 1946 | 8361 | 7770 | 8788 | 16558 |

*Fig. 27.2: Male and female employment in the EC*

**PERCENTAGE OF TOTAL WORKERS IN PART-TIME EMPLOYMENT**

| | AGRICULTURE | | INDUSTRY | | SERVICES | |
|---|---|---|---|---|---|---|
| | *male* | *female* | *male* | *female* | *male* | *female* |
| Belgium | 2 | 14 | 1 | 13 | 3 | 26 |
| Denmark | 11 | 41 | 1 | 29 | 11 | 44 |
| Germany | 8 | 34 | 1 | 24 | 3 | 33 |
| Greece | 6 | 14 | 2 | 5 | 2 | 10 |
| Spain | 4 | 11 | 1 | 9 | 3 | 14 |
| France | 6 | 33 | 1 | 14 | 5 | 26 |
| Ireland | 4 | 42 | 2 | 8 | 5 | 18 |
| Italy | 11 | 28 | 2 | 8 | 3 | 9 |
| Luxembourg | 5 | 31 | 2 | 15 | 2 | 14 |
| Netherlands | 14 | 71 | 9 | 44 | 18 | 59 |
| Portugal | 11 | 14 | 1 | 6 | 3 | 12 |
| UK | 8 | 51 | 2 | 27 | 8 | 48 |

*Fig. 27.3: Male and female part-time employment in the EC*

**WOMEN'S EARNINGS AND EMPLOYMENT IN THE EC**

|  | women's earnings as % of men's | women as percentage of labour force | women as percentage of officially unemployed |
|---|---|---|---|
| Belgium | 75 | 41 | 60 |
| Denmark | 84 | 46 | 55 |
| Germany | 73 | 39 | 48 |
| Greece | 79 | 36 | 51 |
| France | 81 | 43 | 54 |
| Ireland | 68 | 31 | 31 |
| Italy | 83 | 37 | 52 |
| Luxembourg | 63 | 34 | 39 |
| Netherlands | 76 | 35 | 38 |
| UK | 69 | 43 | 28 |

Fig. 27.4: Women's earnings and employment in the EC

## male and female employment trends

It is clear from fig. 27.2 that women make up a large proportion of the work-force in all the EC countries and in all of the sectors identified. The trend shown seems likely to continue as men are forced to change their attitude towards women in work, as women's expectations about work change and as better arrangements become available for women to combine paid work with family roles.

## full-time and part-time trends

Fig. 27.3 shows clearly that the tendency for women to take part-time employment is very pronounced, with significant regional variations

## women's pay

Despite the numbers of women now in work there is still a considerable discrepancy in the level of pay which they receive compared to men who do similar work as fig. 27.4 shows. It is difficult to separate the *economic* reasons for this from those which have to do with discrimination and prejudice. However, many employers would argue that employing a woman who chooses to take a break in her career to have children and bring up a family will cost a company more than employing a man who does not leave the company. The reason for this is that the firm will face costs of recruiting and training a replacement for the woman during her maternity leave and possible career break.

### student activity 27.2 – analysis of EC employment trends

Study the tables carefully and answer the following questions:

(a) In which two countries is the highest proportion of workers employed in agriculture?

(b) In which two countries is the highest proportion of workers employed in industry?

(c) In which two countries is the highest proportion of workers employed in services?

(d) In which four countries do women make up the greatest proportion of the work force overall?

(e) What reasons might there be for the difference between the number of part-time workers in services and the number in industry?

(f) What reasons might there be for the difference in the number of part-time workers in the Netherlands and the UK and countries such as Greece, Spain and Portugal?

(g) In which countries are women's wages most different from men's? What explanations might there be for this?

(h) Why do you think there are, on average, more men *officially* unemployed than women?

# equal opportunities policy

In the EC there are laws which prohibit discrimination against a worker on the grounds of sex, religion or race. In theory, then, workers should enjoy equal rights and equal pay. Despite this it is clear that many women face discrimination at work which can take a number of forms.

## male prejudice

Women may not be appointed to a job in the first place even though they have the necessary qualifications and experience to be able to perform all the tasks required as well as any man. Many men feel uncomfortable when women are in a position of authority over them; it threatens their assumptions about males being "naturally" dominant. Some men believe that women do not have the strength of personality to deal effectively with discipline or situations where conflict arises. The myth that women are the "weaker" sex still persists and for these reasons women may not be appointed to managerial positions in firms or government departments.

## career expectations

Some employers assume that women are not interested in long term careers; it is expected that they will work for a few years until they get married and have children. This assumption means that women may not be offered the opportunity for further training and development because it would not be seen as a worthwhile investment in the long term. If women return to work after a career break, they may find that their skills and knowledge are out of date. Employers may then believe that there will be an additional cost of employing a woman who will need to be retrained before she can make a full contribution to the firm. The employer may also take the view that the woman will not work as hard as a man because she will not be the main wage earner in the family and will want the job "just for pin money" and will not be keen to take on more responsibility or adapt to new challenges.

## sexual harrassment

Women may find that they face sexual harassment at work from male colleagues. Sexual harassment is any unwanted and repeated attention, and ranges from personal remarks and unwanted physical contact to the extreme cases of indecent assault and rape. There have been a number of successful cases brought against men who have been guilty of sexual harassment, but many women suffer physical and psychological discomfort at work because of the behaviour of their male colleagues.

## family commitments

Many would argue that few firms do enough to enable women to combine their role in the family with that of full time employee. There are insufficient creche and nursery facilities, and some employers are not sympathetic if women need time off to look after sick children. Although some large firms are now improving their provision, the UK in general lags behind many other countries in this regard.

## current changes in attitude

These reasons all combine to make it easy for men to find excuses for the continuing discrimination against women in the work situation. However, attitudes are changing. There are relatively few areas in which women have not been successful and many firms are adopting policies to ensure that discrimination is eliminated. Trade unions are very active in supporting women members as the need arises and will be quick to point out to management where improvements can and should be made.

It is also now illegal to advertise a job in such a way as to imply that a person of a particular sex would be preferred. Words such as "Fireman" and "Policeman" are being replaced by "Fire-fighter" and "Police officer" so as to ensure that the female members of fire brigades and police forces are not ignored. Language in general is becoming less sex specific so that the words used in everyday speech recognise more clearly the importance of people of both sexes and do not refer to all workers as if they were male.

### the responsibilities of education

It is still the case, despite campaigns to change matters, that relatively few girls study science subjects at school and relatively few boys study subjects which are particularly relevant to "caring " occupations. The assumptions which are made about girls being more suited to certain jobs and boys to others have a strong influence on subject choice at school, college and university. This inevitably leads on to career choices which help to perpetuate the higher concentrations of women in occupations such as nursing, secretarial work and primary school teaching, and men in areas such as road transport, engineering and construction.

---

### student activity 27.3 – equal opportunities

(a)   Obtain a copy of your school or college's equal opportunities policy. Read it carefully and identify ways in which the institution is living up to its own standards and ways (if any) in which it needs to improve.

(b)   Using a list of the staff employed at your school or college work out the extent to which the trends towards part-time work and greater female involvement at senior levels applies in your institution.

---

## self-employment

### an upward trend

One of the main features of the changes in employment patterns which have taken place since 1980 is the growth in self-employment. The figures below show this very clearly:

**SELF-EMPLOYED WORKERS IN THE UK – BY SEX AND INDUSTRY**

|  | 1986 000s | 1992 000s |
|---|---|---|
| all industries | 2,799 | 3,212 |
| subdivided into: |  |  |
| males | 2,109 | 2,422 |
| females | 690 | 791 |
| manufacturing industry | 257 | 348 |
| services | 1,694 | 1,871 |
| other | 844 | 981 |

SOURCE: Department of Employment

Not only has self employment grown in terms of the number of those who work for themselves but this group now represents a larger proportion of the workforce than ever before.

## economics of self-employment

The Conservative government led by Mrs Thatcher did a great deal to encourage self employment. Enterprise education became a part of the curriculum in many schools and there were grants for those, young and old, who wanted to start their own business. The advantages of self employment for the economy are as follows:

- self-employed people tend to be prepared to work very long hours for relatively low pay, especially in the early stages of setting up their own business – this means that the costs of producing the good or service are greatly reduced

- many very small firms use the labour of family members without paying them at all, this again reduces costs and increases competitiveness

- small firms are flexible and can respond quickly to changes in the market for their product

- people who set up their own firm have a great deal to lose because they may have needed to use their house as security against a loan to start their business; for this reason they will work very hard to ensure that their business survives

- self-employed people may be prepared to take opportunities and try new ventures which larger firms may consider not worth the risk

- many small businesses will provide a good or service to a large firm far more cheaply than the firm itself because they do not have expensive management and administrative overheads; small firms often operate from the owner's home and so do not have to pay expensive rents

- there may well be no economies of scale for a firm offering a service such as hair-dressing at home, advice about small office computer installation or plastering – in such cases the small firm will have no disadvantages over a larger one, only the advantages mentioned above

Inevitably many of the small firms which did start up failed in a very short time with distress and possible hardship to their owners. However, many did survive either to carry on as one person businesses or to grow and provide employment for others. Government policies, particularly in relation to VAT have developed with small firms very much in mind. Some would argue that the banks have not treated small firms well, charging too high a rate of interest and being too quick to call in debts if things are not going well. One remedy which has been proposed is to establish a National Enterprise Bank which would be backed by government money and would be responsible for lending money to those with sound business plans but without the necessary capital.

## the way ahead

### out-workers and information technology

The growth of self-employment has been encouraged by firms as well as government. Some large firms have offered some of their managers incentives to leave the company's pay-roll and work for themselves, often from home. The manager becomes free to take on work from other firms on a consultancy basis and may be guaranteed a certain amount of work from the firm. These "out-workers" provide the firm with the opportunity to pay only for the work they need doing, and also to reduce the amount it spends on office space, support staff and equipment for managers.

The growth in the use of information technology means that a manager can work at home yet be in contact with the firm's central computer via a personal computer and modem. The electronic transfer of data is now possible not only between offices but also to workers anywhere, as long as they have a portable telephone and the necessary computer hardware.

Many large firms are now choosing to relocate much of their administrative function to sites outside London where land and labour are cheaper and in more plentiful supply. Electronic communications make this a very attractive option to the firm and to those who are seeking work near to the new operation.

## flexibility and motivation

There has been much talk about Japanese management styles and techniques which have contributed to the enormous success of that country's economy since the last war. The main feature of this approach is the idea that everyone is *equally responsible* for the success of the company. All workers are equally important and everyone is encouraged to make suggestions about how production processes can be improved. Managers are expected to dress in the same way as all other workers so as to minimise the appearance of the differences between workers and management. Production workers are given more information about the running of the firm than would be usual in a more traditionally managed firm.

More flexible working practices are now the norm in many manufacturing firms. It is less common to find strict demarcations between the job of an engineer and that of an electrician or a welder. Workers need to have a range of skills and be prepared to contribute to the production process as the job demands rather than on the basis of their union membership or a narrowly defined job description.

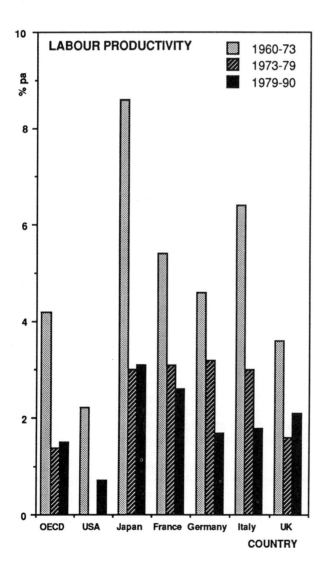

SOURCE: OECD

These changes are leading to an acceptance in many firms of the idea that everyone has a part to play in making the firm successful. This is in contrast to the view that managers were simply there to exploit the workers as much as they could, and that the workers were trying to get away with as little work as possible. This is not to say that there is no longer any conflict between management and workers or that firms now act like big happy families. However, there is evidence that managers are recognising the value of the workforce in more practical ways and that consultation and involvement is replacing some of the more confrontational management practices of the past.

The evidence of the benefit of this shift in management style and employee response can be found in the increase in labour productivity which is shown in the graph drawn on the left.

This graph indicates that the UK improved its productivity after 1979 faster than some of its main industrial competitors, though not as fast as Japan and France. This improvement came after many years when the UK performance was well behind other countries with the exception of USA.

**student activity 27.4 - productivity and the labour market**

(a)   Invite a manager of a local manufacturing firm in to talk to your group about productivity in her/his firm. Ask her/him to describe the ways in which the management has tried to increase productivity and the reaction to these changes from the workforce.

(b)   Conduct a survey among parents of your class in your school or college in order to find out
   • how many *men* and *women* are in work
   • how many are in part-time work
   • how many are self-employed or employed
   • whether they work in the manufacturing, services or 'other' sector

   Liaise with your teacher or lecturer to ensure that you are all collecting the same data. Collate and put the results onto a computer database, but ensure that anonymity of the data subject (ie the parent) is maintained – some of the data may be sensitive. Use the database to produce charts and graphs of your data. Compare your findings with the data in this chapter and account for any differences you discover.

   Note: if a computer database is not available, the data can be collated and analysed manually.

# chapter summary

❏   The number of women in employment is growing.

❏   The majority of part-time workers are women.

❏   The majority of low paid workers are women.

❏   Although women have reached high office in almost every sphere of work, there are still some occupations and institutions where women are seriously under-represented.

❏   The number of self-employed people has grown significantly since 1979.

❏   The self-employed often work very long hours and pay themselves low wages and so are able to produce goods and services more cheaply than large firms.

❏   Information technology means that many people can work effectively away from a firm's offices.

❏   UK productivity improved during the 1980's. Much of this came about because firms shed surplus labour and became "leaner and fitter".

❏   Trade Unions are weaker than they were, and new management styles mean that in some firms there is less confrontation and more co-operation between staff at different levels in the organisation.

# A study of employment in two business sectors

| Element 5.1 | Investigate employment in business sectors |
|---|---|
| Suggested Sources: | • Chapter 24, fig 24.4 (page 258), |
| | • Chapter 27, figs 27.2, 3 and 4 (pages 281 to 282) |
| | • school/college/reference libraries |
| | • Chambers of Commerce and lcoal businesses |
| | • textbooks and reference books generally (see page 245) |

## INTRODUCTION

The aim of this study is to consider in some detail the differences between the employment structure of two business sectors. These sectors will be organised differently in the UK and elsewhere in the EC, so there will be the opportunity to make international comparisons. You will need to complete each of the following tasks in order to produce a satisfactory outcome. The order here is a logical one, but you could go on to later tasks before completing earlier ones to avoid being held up whilst waiting for information.

## TASK 1

Identify the two business sectors you intend to study. There is a list on page 258. Some sectors will be quite similar across all the EC countries, the sector with the greatest contrast may well be agriculture. You should also decide on which countries you will look at in most detail.

Make a list of questions to which you want to find the answer. The following are suggestions to get you started; you need to think of six or so all together:

- What is the total number of workers in the sector?
- What proportion are women?
- What proportion are full-time?
- What is the size of the firms which exist in the sector?

Collecting the data will clearly be a major task. There are some data sets in this book but you are expected to use your initiative to collect more. The library in your school or college will help and your teacher or lecturer will be able to point you in the right direction. There are a number of European databases in print, and large Chambers of Commerce will have access to very detailed information about all aspects of business in the EC. The Department of Trade and Industry also provides data to businesses trading within Europe.

It may also be useful to identify a large local firm in your chosen business sector(s) which trades with Europe, and ask for information.

## TASK 2

Decide on a structure for the presentation of your findings – a formal written report is recommended. You should include an introduction showing some basic background information about employment generally in the countries you have chosen to focus on. Then you should go into detail using the questions you chose as a framework. You should try to draw out from the data some conclusions about the differences you have discovered and suggest possible explanations for them wherever you can.

Decide how you will present the statistics you use in your answers. If you have access to a spreadsheet package you will be able to use the graph facility to produce charts or graphs comparing various sets of data. If not, you will need to do this task manually. Remember that although presentation is important, the main aim of the project is to show that you understand about economics and business. You should also try to link the more general ideas of the labour market which are discussed in this section of the book to your findings.

# A study of external influences on the workforce of a business

| Element 5.2 | Analyse external influences relating to employment |
|---|---|

Suggested Sources:
- contact with personnel officers in local businesses
- work experience
- people you know who employ staff
- local trade unions
- textbooks and reference books generally (see page 245)

## INTRODUCTION

In this study you will focus on a single businesses and come to an understanding about the way in which it deals with external changes which affect the workforce. You will also consider critically the information which the business uses to help it take decisions relating to its management of the work force.

## TASK 1

The first task is to carry out your investigations into the business.

### primary sources of information

Ideally, the way to carry out this task is to make contact with a local business and ask to discuss your project with the manager responsible for personnel matters. From this discussion could come the opportunity to collect data from the business and the chance to talk to other managers and workers there. This approach might well be possible if you could combine it with work experience or if you already have a contact at a senior level in a local business. However, it may well be that the some firms are not willing to share information about their personnel policy because it relates to decisions which affect local people's lives in a very direct and serious way and therefore the information is regarded as confidential.

### secondary sources of information

If you are not able to do this project by direct contact then you will need to use newspaper and other reports. It may also be possible that a local trade union would be prepared to provide information which it has about local company policy regarding the workforce.

### schoolor college support

Your teacher/lecturer will help you to identify the most likely sources of local information and may well make some initial contacts on your behalf.

### dealing with local businesses

Remember that the business you study need not be a large firm. This project could be done using the local shop and its approach to its paper delivery staff, for example. When you are working with a business person asking questions and seeking information, do remember the following rules – which are no more than basic good manners – but will make all the difference to the recepetion that you and subsequent students will receive.

- Make sure the *arrangements* you make are clear and that you stick to them. Confirm appointments in writing if possible.
- Be *prepared*. You must know what questions you want to ask at the start of the interview. It would be a good idea to let the person you are meeting know what the questions are before you arrive so that he or she can prepare answers and information for you.
- Be *polite*. Remember a busy manager who gives up an hour of his or her time to talk to you is not doing the job they are being paid for and will have to catch up with their work in their own time. So make sure that they realise how helpful they have been and that you are grateful for their co-operation.

### the scope of the investigation.
The investigation could look at any of the following aspects of a business' personnel policy:

- an increase in the workforce as a result of an increase in demand for the product
- a decrease in the workforce by, for example, voluntary or compulsory redundancy, or by non-replacement of staff who leave, as a result of a declining market
- a change in the proportion of full-time and part-time workers
- a change in the working hours (eg Sunday opening, short-time working, increase in over-time)
- a change in the wage or salary
- a change in training policy
- a change in recruitment policy
- a change in staff benefits (eg creche, canteen or sports facilities or holiday entitlement)
- decisions taken as a result of trade union pressure
- changes in working practices as a result of recent legislation or regulations (eg EC directives on VDUs)
- changes in the structure of the workforce brought about by technological advances, or by the pressure of competing businesses

## TASK 2
The second task is to present your findings in the form of a case study.

It will be important to describe the decisions which the firm took in the context of the information it had at its disposal. You will need to look at this information carefully to see if it was complete and whether, in your opinion, other information would have been useful.

You could conclude by referring to other courses of action the business might have taken given the situation in which it found itself. You should also try to link to your findings the more general ideas of the labour market which are discussed in this section of the book.

# Workforce-related performance in two businesses

| Element 5.3 | Evaluate the workforce performance of business |
|---|---|

Suggested Sources:
- company records and reports
- trade union records and reports
- observation of the workplace
- interviews with the management of businesses
- interviews with employees of businesses

## INTRODUCTION

In this study you will consider the way in which the performance of the workforce of two different businesses is measured and evaluated. You will consider the information which a firm collects in order to assess performance and the conclusions which it draws from the data.

## TASK 1

This study needs to be carried out in the workplace if at all possible. You will need to choose two contrasting businesses, eg public sector and private sector, manufacturing and service business. A wide variety of data could be collected which could include all or some of the following:
- rates of pay for groups of workers
- hours worked
- output figures
- production overhead costs
- changes in capital employed in the production process
- workers' views on motivation and productivity
- managers' views on motivation and productivity

The method of data collection could include:
- using company records and reports
- using trade union records and reports
- taped interviews with managers and other members of the workforce
- observing and recording in writing in the workplace
- using written questionnaires
- video recordings in the workplace

All of these methods of data collection would require careful negotiation with the firm before permission was given. You must remember that many firms feel the need for a degree of secrecy about their operations and about personnel issues in particular. It is important to have the support of your teachers or lecturers when making contact with firms. It is suggested that the whole class compares the same two businesses.

## TASK 2

Present your findings in a way appropriate to the method of data collection. You should show clearly how each firm assesses productivity and how levels of productivity have changed. You should try to draw some conclusions about the factors which affect productivity in general based on your findings. You should also try to link the more general ideas of the labour market which are discussed in this section of the book to your findings.

# SECTION

# 6

# financial transactions and monitoring

## contents

Financial transactions are carried out by a business when it buys and sells goods, pays money into and out of the bank account, and pays wages.  Financial transactions involve *documents* such as invoices and payslips, and the use of documents requires *control* by the business.  The first four chapters of this Section cover this area:

Chapter 28     explains *why* financial transactions have to be recorded

Chapter 29     examines the *documents* involved in financial transactions

Chapter 30     examines the processes involved in *making payments*

Chapter 31     examines the processes involved in *receiving payments*

Financial documents form the basis for entries in the accounting system of the business.  From the accounting system are produced financial statements, eg the profit statement and the balance sheet (the final accounts), which are *monitored* so that the level of profit and the 'financial health' of the business can be assessed by the owner(s) and other interested parties, such as the bank.

In this Section of the book the authors depart from the GNVQ Unit divisions and explain the financial statements which are required in GNVQ Unit 7.4.  The reason for this is that financial statements *must* be understood if the process of monitoring them (GNVQ Unit 6.3) is to be fully appreciated.

The remainder of the Section is therefore divided as follows:

Chapter 32     looks at the recording of purchases and sales in day books

Chapter 33     examines how accounts are generated in the double-entry book-keeping system of the business

Chapter 34     looks at how accounts are balanced to produce the trial balance

Chapter 35     examines the final accounts (trading and profit and loss account and balance sheet) produced in the form of an extended trial balance

Chapter 36     examines the production of the final accounts in conventional format

Chapter 37     explains the final accounts of limited companies

Chapter 38     examines the format of the Cashflow Statement which analyses the flow of money in and out of a business over a period of time

Chapter 39     explains how the financial statements can be monitored to provide the owner(s) of the business and other interested parties with an indication of the performance of the business

# 28 Financial transactions

## introduction

Financial transactions are carried out by a business when it, for example:
- buys and sells goods and services – makes payments and receives payments
- transfers money in and out of the bank account
- pays wages

Financial transactions are supported by a variety of documents. In the next three chapters we will look in detail at these documents and the way in which they are used. In this chapter we look at the reasons for financial transactions and their documentation. These reasons include:
- keeping business records
- providing information for the accounting system of the business
- enabling the performance of the business to be monitored
- the fulfilment of legal requirements

## introduction to the accounting system

Businesses need to record financial transactions for very practical reasons:
- they need to quantify items such as sales, expenses and profit
- they need to present these figures in a meaningful way to monitor the performance of the business

Business financial records can be very complex, and one of the problems that you face as a student is having difficulty in relating what you are learning to the accounting system of the business as a whole. It is, of course, possible that your chosen course of studies does not include a study of accounting. Nevertheless if you are to appreciate why financial transactions are recorded and documents issued – and this is an area you *do* have to study – it is essential that you appreciate how they relate to the accounting system of a business.

In this chapter we will summarise how a typical business records and presents financial information in the form of accounts. The accounting system follows a number of distinct stages which are illustrated in the diagram below, and are explained in the text which follows.

> **documents**
> processing of documents relating to financial transactions, eg invoices, cheques

> **books of prime entry**
> initial recording of financial transactions in *summary* books (books of prime entry)

> **double-entry accounts system**
> regular transfer of figures from the books of prime entry into the double-entry book-keeping system of accounts contained in 'the ledger'

> **trial balance**
> extraction of figures (often monthly) from the double-entry accounts in the ledger to check their accuracy in the form of a list of figures known as the trial balance

> **final accounts**
> production from the double-entry accounts of a profit statement, and a balance sheet – the 'final accounts' – normally monthly or annually

# business documents

Financial transactions generate documents. In this section we will relate the documents to the type of transaction involved and also introduce other terminology which is important to your studies.

## purchase and sale of goods and services – the invoice
When a business purchases or sells goods or services the seller prepares a document known as an *invoice* stating:
- the amount owing
- when it should be paid
- details of the goods sold or service provided

An invoice is illustrated on page 305.

## the distinction between cash sales and credit sales – the receipt and the invoice
Sales can be *cash* sales or *credit* sales:
- *cash sales* – where payment is *immediate*, whether by cash or by cheque; note that not all cash sales will require an invoice to be prepared by the seller – shops and some businesses will issue a *receipt* for the amount paid
- *credit sales* – where payment is to be made *at a later date* (often 30 days later); an invoice is invariably issued for credit sales

Note that:

A *debtor* is a person who owes you money when you sell on credit.

A *creditor* is a person to whom you owe money when you buy on credit.

### return of goods – the credit note

If the buyer returns goods which are bought on credit (they may be faulty or incorrect) the seller will prepare a credit note (see page 307 for an example) which is sent to the buyer, reducing the amount of money owed. The credit note, like the invoice, states the money amount and the goods or services to which it relates.

### banking transactions – paying-in slip and cheque

Businesses, like anyone else with a bank account, need to pay in money, and draw out cash and make payments. Paying-in slips and cheques are used frequently in business as source documents for bank account transactions.

### petty cash vouchers

Businesses often carry a cash 'float' for reimbursing staff who make small cash purchases for the business, eg paying the window-cleaner, paying a client's taxi fare. Reimbursement is made after completion of a petty cash voucher. The amount recorded on the voucher will be recorded in the accounting system of the business as an expense, eg "premises maintenance" or "travel expenses". For a more detailed explanation of a petty cash voucher, see page 335.

### pay slips

Businesses issue a pay slip to each employee when the wages or salaries are paid. The amounts recorded on the pay slip are also recorded in the accounting system. For a more detailed explanation of a pay slip, see page 341.

# initial recording of transactions – books of prime entry

Many businesses issue and receive large quantities of invoices, credit notes and banking documents, and it is useful for them to list these in summary books, during the course of the working day. These summaries are known as books of *prime (or original) entry*.

These books include

- *sales day book* – a list of sales made, compiled from invoices issued
- *purchases day book* – a list of purchases made, compiled from invoices received
- *sales returns day book* – a list of 'returns in', ie goods returned by customers, compiled from credit notes issued
- *purchases returns day book* – a list of 'returns out', ie goods returned by the business to suppliers, compiled from credit notes received
- *cash book* – the business' record of the bank account and the amount of cash held, compiled from receipts, paying-in slips and cheques
- *petty cash book* – a record of small cash (notes and coin) purchases made by the business, compiled from petty cash vouchers
- *journal* – a record of non-regular transactions, ie all the items that are not recorded in any other book of prime entry.

Note:
If your course of studies includes an Accounting unit, it is likely that you will study these books of the business in some detail.

# double-entry accounts system

The basis of the accounting system is a method known as *double-entry book-keeping* which is embodied in a series of records known as the *ledger*. This is divided into a number of separate *accounts* for recording and categorising financial transactions, for example 'wages account' for wages, 'sales account' for sales made, and 'bank account' for keeping a record of banking transactions.

## double-entry book-keeping

Double-entry book-keeping involves making *two* entries in the accounts for each transaction: for instance, if you are paying wages by cheque you will make an entry in bank account and an entry in wages account. If you are operating a manual accounting system you will make the two entries by hand, if you are using computer accounting you will in most cases make one entry on the keyboard, but indicate to the computer where the other entry is to be made by means of a numerical code.

It must be stressed that your studies do *not* require you to be proficient in the mechanics of double entry book-keeping – unless, of course, you are taking an Accounting unit. It is nevertheless important to have a broad *understanding* of double-entry book-keeping, as it forms the 'nuts and bolts' of the accounting system.

## accounts

The books of prime entry provide the source for the entries you make in the double-entry system. The ledger into which you make the entries is normally a bound book (in a non-computerised system) divided into separate *accounts*. As we saw above, accounts record and categorise financial transactions; thus there will be a separate account for sales, purchases, each type of business expense, each debtor, each creditor, and so on. Each account will be given a specific name, and a number for reference purposes (or input code, if you use a computer system).

## division of the ledger

Because of the large number of accounts involved, the ledger has traditionally been divided into a number of sections. These same sections are used in computer accounting systems.

* *sales ledger* – personal accounts of debtors, ie customers to whom the business has sold on credit
* *purchases ledger* – personal accounts of creditors, ie suppliers to whom the business owes money
* *cash books* – a cash book comprising cash account and bank account, and a petty cash book for petty cash account (small purchases); note: the cash books are *also* books of prime entry
* *general (or nominal) ledger* – the remainder of the accounts: *nominal accounts*, eg sales, purchases, expenses, and *real accounts* for items owned by the business

# trial balance

Double-entry book-keeping, because it involves making two entries for each transaction, is open to error. What if the book-keeper writes in £45 in one account and £54 in another? The trial balance effectively checks the entries made over a given period and will pick up most errors. It sets out the *balances* of all the double-entry accounts, ie the amounts left in each account at the end of a particular period. It is, as well as being an arithmetic check, the source of valuable information which is used to help in the preparation of the *final accounts* of the business.

# final accounts

The final accounts of a business comprise the profit statement and the balance sheet.

## profit statement

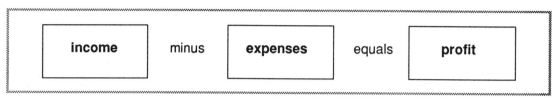

The profit statement of a business incorporates the *trading and profit and loss account.* The object of this statement is to calculate the profit due to the owner(s) of the business after certain expenses have been deducted from income. The figures for these calculations – sales, purchases, expenses of various kinds – are taken from the double-entry system. The profit statement shows the results of a business for a stated time period, often a year.

## balance sheet

The double-entry system also contains figures for:

*assets*                items the business *owns,* which can be
   • fixed assets – items bought for use in the business, eg premises, vehicles
   • current assets – items used in the everyday running of the business, eg stock of goods held for resale, debtors (money owed by customers), and money in the bank

*liabilities*           items that the business *owes,* eg bank loans and overdrafts, and creditors (money owed to suppliers)

*capital*               money or assets introduced by the owner(s) of the business – this figure shows how the business has been financed

The balance sheet is so called because it balances in numerical (money) terms:

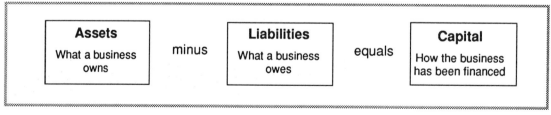

The balance sheet, which is often produced on an annual basis, shows the state of the business on a particular day. If you think about it, it will change every time a financial transaction takes place.

## the accounting equation

The balance sheet illustrates a concept important to accounting theory, known as *the accounting equation.* This equation is illustrated in the diagram above, namely

$$\text{Assets} - \text{Liabilities} = \text{Capital}$$

Every business transaction will change the balance sheet and the equation, as each transaction has a *dual effect* on the accounts. The equation, however, will always balance.

## the accounting system and business performance

The accounting system provides valuable information both to the owner and to outside bodies about the performance of the business:

### information for the owner(s)
The accounting system will be able to give information on:
- purchases of goods (for resale) to date
- sales (also known as 'turnover') to date
- expenses of different types to date
- debtors – both the total amount owed to the business, and also the names of individual debtors and the amount owed by each
- creditors – both the total owed by the business, and the amount owed to each creditor
- assets owned by the business
- liabilities owed by the business
- profit made by the business during a particular time period

### information for outside bodies
Other people interested in the accounts of a business include:
- the bank manager, if the business wants to borrow from the bank
- the Inland Revenue – the business will have to pay tax on its profits
- HM Customs and Excise (the VAT authorities) if the business is registered for Value Added Tax
- financial analysts who may be giving advice to investors in the business
- official bodies, eg Companies House, who need to see the final accounts of limited companies
- creditors, who wish to assess the likelihood of receiving payment
- employees and trade unions, who wish to check on the financial prospects of the business

Monitoring of the financial records of the business is therefore an important exercise both for the owner(s) and also for the outside bodies listed above.

## legal requirements of recording financial transactions

There are certain legal obligations on businesses to maintain financial records and issue correct documentation. Examples include:

*Companies Acts 1985 and 1989*
Limited companies must
- maintain records showing financial transactions
- send every year a copy of the profit and loss account and balance sheet together with a directors' and auditor's report to Companies House

*Employment Protection (Consolidation) Act 1978*
An employer must provide every employee with an itemised pay slip in writing.

In addition, all businesses – sole traders, partnerships and limited companies – are legally bound to keep accurate accounts so that they can provide information to
- the Inland Revenue – for tax liability
- HM Customs and Excise – for VAT purposes

The object here is to prevent businesses from evading tax. Both the Inland Revenue and HM Customs and Excise are legally empowered to inspect a business' financial records, and they do so from time-to-time.

## chapter summary

❑ Financial transactions of a business form the basis of the accounting system, the stages of which are
- processing of documents
- recording of documents in the books of prime entry
- recording of the transaction in the double-entry accounts system
- extraction of the trial balance – proving the accuracy of the system
- production of the final accounts – profit statement and balance sheet

❑ The financial records of a business must be monitored both by the owner(s) of the business and by outside bodies so that the performance of the business can be assessed and decisions taken accordingly.

❑ Businesses are legally bound to keep accurate financial records (in part for the tax authorities) and to provide pay slips for their employees. Limited companies are obliged to file annual accounts with Companies House.

 ## student activities

**28.1**    (a) List the five main stages of the accounting system.
        (b) Where are the financial transactions first recorded?
        (c) What does the trial balance prove?
        (d) What are the two statements which comprise the final accounts?

**28.2**    What is the difference between a creditor and a debtor?

**28.3**    What are the four divisions of the ledger?

**28.4**    What items does a balance sheet 'balance'?

**28.5**    (a) Why would the owner of a business want to monitor the financial records?
        (b) What outside bodies would be interested in the financial records?

**28.6**    What are the legal requirements for a business to maintain financial records?

# 29 Business documents

## introduction

When an organisation buys goods or services, it will eventually have to pay for them. Most goods and services are supplied *on credit:* the goods arrive or the service is supplied first, and payment is made later, often after thirty days.

The process involves a number of distinct stages – order, supply, request for payment, and payment. At each stage a *business document* is normally issued, the most well-known of which is the invoice; this tells the organisation buying the goods or services how much they cost, and what charges or discounts (if any) are applicable.

The business documents can either be produced manually or by computer on *paper* – the traditional and most common method, or as *electronic messages* between the supplier's and the buyer's computers, a system known as Electronic Data Interchange (EDI).

In this chapter we will look at the paper-based system of business documents, partly because it is the more common system, and partly because it forms the basis for EDI. We will also explain the basics of computer accounting and the EDI system. The financial documents to be examined are:

- purchase order
- delivery note
- invoice
- credit note
- goods received note
- statement and remittance advice

## the buying and paying process in the organisation

The size of an organisation largely determines who deals with the business documents. In a larger organisation there may be a *purchasing department* which deals with ordering goods, a *sales department* which sells the goods, and an *accounts department* which makes the payments. In a smaller organisation these functions may be left to individuals, eg the buyer and the accounts clerk. In a sole-trader business, the owner usually prepares the documents, or possibly employs somebody part-time to undertake the work.

# business documents

There are a number of business documents which you will need to understand when studying financial transactions. In this chapter we will look at the business documents set out below by means of a Case Study which follows the ordering of laser printer paper by Martley Machine Rental Limited, the delivery of the paper, the return of some of the paper, and the final settlement by cheque.

**purchase order**     the official order form which the buyer uses to order the goods required

**delivery note**     the document which accompanies the goods and gives details of the goods supplied – it is normally signed by the recipient when the goods are delivered

**goods received note**     the document which is completed by the warehouse staff of the buyer, setting out details of the supplier, the goods, the date of receipt and any shortages or damage to the goods

**invoice**     the document which is sent by the seller to the buyer stating how much is owed and when it has to be paid

**credit note**     a document sent by the seller to the buyer if the amount owing (as shown on the invoice) has to be reduced for any reason, for example

- the goods were damaged in transit
- some of the goods have been returned by the buyer
- not all of the goods were sent
- a higher price has been charged in error

**statement**     a document sent by the seller to the buyer, normally at the end of every month, giving details of invoices issued, credit notes issued and payments made (just as a bank sends a regular statement to its customers showing money paid in and money paid out)

**remittance advice**     a form which will be sent with the buyer's payment when the invoice(s) or statement is settled; a remittance advice may be a separate piece of paper prepared by the buyer, or it can be a tear-off slip sent with the supplier's statement

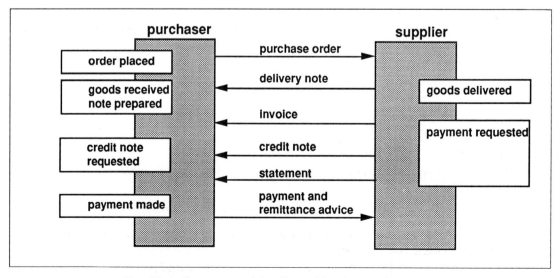

*Fig. 29.1  Summary of the flow of business documents*

## Case Study: business documents

# purchase order

In the this Case Study, Martley Machine Rental Limited are ordering some paper for their laser printer from Stourford Office Supplies. The purchasing department or buyer at Martley Machine Rental will post or fax the authorised purchase order shown below, which will have been typed out in the office, or produced on a computer accounting program. The details of the laser printer paper will have been obtained from Stourford Office Supplies' catalogue, or possibly by means of a written or telephoned enquiry.

---

### PURCHASE ORDER
#### MARTLEY MACHINE RENTAL LTD
67 Broadgreen Road
Martley  MR6 7TR
Tel 090655 6576 Fax 090655 6342

Stourford Office Supplies
Unit 12
Avon Industrial Estate
Stourford SF5 6TD

No          47700
Date        13 March 19-5
Delivery    to above address

| catalogue | quantity | description | price |
|---|---|---|---|
| 3564749 | 15 reams | 100gsm white Supalaser paper | £4.00 per ream |

**authorised**   signature....*C J Farmer*....................   date.*13 March 19-5*..........

---

*Note the following details:*
- each purchase order has a specific reference number – this is useful for filing, and quotation on later documents such as delivery notes, invoices and statements – here it is 47700
- the heading 'Delivery' enables the buyer to indicate if the goods are to be delivered to an address other than the address on the letterhead, eg to a warehouse or to a different office
- the catalogue number of the goods required is stated – this number can be obtained from the supplier's trade catalogue
- the quantity of the goods required is stated – here it is supplied in reams (packs of 500 sheets)
- the description of the goods is set out in full
- the price will have been obtained from Stourford Office Supplies' catalogue or from an enquiry
- the purchase order is signed by the buyer in the purchasing department, and dated – without this authorisation the supplier is unlikely to supply the goods.

# delivery note

The delivery note is prepared by the supplier of the goods, and is either typed in the supplier's office or produced on a computer printer if the supplier has a computer accounting program.

The delivery note travels with the goods, normally in the care of the van driver, in which case the person receiving the goods will be asked to sign the delivery note. If the goods are *posted*, the delivery note will be packed with the goods in the carton, or possibly in a transparent envelope on the ouside of the box containing the goods. If the goods are posted by letter post or parcel post, the signature of the recipient will not be needed, unless they are sent recorded delivery, registered post or datapost.

---

### ══ DELIVERY NOTE ══

### Stourford Office Supplies
Unit 12, Avon Industrial Estate, Stourford SF5 6TD
Tel 0807 765434 Fax 0807 765123

```
Martley Machine Rental Ltd        Delivery Note No   26754
67 Broadgreen Road                Date               26 March 19-5
Martley                           Your Order No      47700
MR6 7TR                           Delivery           Van
```

| product code | quantity | description |
|---|---|---|
| 3564749 | 15 reams | 100 gsm white Supalaser paper |

**received**
signature....*G Hughes*................name (capitals)..............*G HUGHES*.........
date..........*30 March 19-5*.............

---

*Note the following details:*

- the delivery note has a numerical reference, useful for filing and later reference if there is a query
- the delivery note quotes the purchase order number – this enables the buyer to 'tie up' the delivery with the original order
- the method of delivery is stated – here the delivery is by van
- the delivery note quotes the supplier's catalogue reference, the quantity supplied and the description of the goods – these details will be checked against
  - the goods themselves
  - the invoice when it is received
- no price is quoted on the delivery note
- the delivery note will be signed and dated by the person receiving the goods
- the person receiving the goods will also print his or her name – this is to enable the person to be identified later if there should be a query about the goods
- if the person receiving the goods does not have time to check them there and then – as is often the case – the phrase 'contents not inspected' can be written on the delivery note (not shown here)

# invoice

The invoice is the trading document which is sent by the seller to the buyer to advise how much is owed by the buyer for a particular delivery of goods. The invoice, like the delivery note, is prepared in the supplier's office, and is either typed or produced on a computer printer by a computer accounting program. Invoices produced by different organisations will vary to some extent in terms of detail, but their basic layout will always be the same. The invoice illustrated below is typical of a modern typed or computer printed document. Look at it carefully and then read the notes.

---

### INVOICE

**Stourford Office Supplies**
Unit 12, Avon Industrial Estate, Stourford SF5 6TD
Tel 0807 765434 Fax 0807 765123
VAT Reg 0745 4672 76

**invoice to**

| Martley Machine Rental Ltd | Invoice No | 652771 |
| 67 Broadgreen Road | Account | MAR435 |
| Martley | Date/tax point | 26 March 19-5 |
| MR6 7TR | Your Reference | 47700 |

**deliver to**

as above

| product code | description | quantity | price | unit | total | disc % | net |
|---|---|---|---|---|---|---|---|
| 3564749 | 100 gsm white Supalaser | 15 | 4.00 | ream | 60.00 | 0 | 60.00 |

**Terms**
Net monthly
Carriage paid
E & OE

| | |
|---|---|
| GOODS TOTAL | 60.00 |
| CASH DISCOUNT | 00.00 |
| SUBTOTAL | 60.00 |
| VAT | 10.50 |
| TOTAL | 70.50 |

---

*Note the following details:*

**addresses**      The invoice shows the address:
- of the seller/supplier of the goods – Stourford Office Supplies
- where the invoice should be sent – to Martley Machine Rental Ltd
- where the goods were sent – if different from the invoice address

**references**

There are a number of important references on the invoice:

- the numerical reference of the invoice itself – 652771
- the account number allocated to Martley Machine Rental Ltd by the seller – MAR435 – possibly for use in the seller's computer accounting program
- the original reference number on the purchase order sent by Martley Machine Rental Ltd – 47700 – which will enable the buyer to 'tie up' the invoice with the original order

**date**

The date on the invoice is important because the payment date (here one month) is calculated from it. The date is often described as the 'tax point' because it is the transaction date as far as VAT calculations are concerned, ie it is when the sale took place and the VAT was charged. Note: VAT (Value Added Tax) is a tax on the supply of goods and services; at the time of writing the rate is 17.5%.

**the goods**

As the invoice is a statement of the amount owing, it must specify accurately the goods supplied. The details – set out in columns in the body of the invoice – include:

- *product code* – this is the catalogue number which appeared on the original purchase order and on the delivery note
- *description* – the goods must be specified precisely
- *quantity* – this should agree with the quantity ordered
- *price* – this is the price of each unit shown in the next column
- *unit* is the way in which the unit is counted and charged for, eg
  – reams of paper (packs of 500 sheets)
  – boxes of ballpoint pens (100 in a box, for instance)
  – items of furniture (eg individual desks and chairs)
- *total* is the unit price multiplied by the number of units
- *discount %* is the percentage allowance (known as trade discount) given to customers who regularly deal with the supplier ie they receive a certain percentage (eg 20%) deducted from their bill
- *net* is the amount due to the seller after deduction of trade discount, and before VAT is added on

**cash discount and VAT**

Further calculations are made in the box at the bottom of the invoice:

- *Goods Total* is the net amount due to the seller (the total of the net column)
- *Cash Discount* is a percentage of the Goods Total (often a 2.5% discount) which the buyer can deduct if he or she pays straightaway rather than waiting the month allowed on the invoice – there is no cash discount in this example
- *Value Added Tax* (VAT), here calculated as 17.5% of the total after deduction of any cash discount is added to produce the invoice total

**terms**

The terms for payment are stated on the invoice. In this case these include:

- *Net monthly* – this means that full payment of the invoice (without cash discount) should be made within a month of the invoice date
- *Carriage paid* means that the price of the goods includes delivery
- *E & OE* stands for 'errors and omissions excepted' which means that if there is a error or something left off the invoice by mistake, resulting in an incorrect final price, the supplier has the right to rectify the mistake and demand the correct amount

# credit note

A credit note is a document issed by the supplier which reduces the amount owed by the buyer. The document is prepared by the supplier and sent to the buyer. This could happen when:

• the goods have been damaged, lost in transit or are faulty
• not all the goods have been sent – a situation referred to as 'shortages'
• the unit price on the invoice may be too high
• the buyer may not want some or all of the goods, and the supplier agrees to accept them back

A credit note is often prepared by the seller following the receipt of a *returns note* (sent with returned goods) or a *debit note* (issued, for example, when the buyer has been overcharged).

In the case of the credit note below, Martley Machine Rental has only received 10 reams of paper instead of 15; they are short by 5 reams and are therefore receiving a credit for £23.50.

---

## CREDIT NOTE

**Stourford Office Supplies**
Unit 12, Avon Industrial Estate, Stourford SF5 6TD
Tel 0807 765434 Fax 0807 765123
VAT Reg 0745 4672 76

to

Martley Machine Rental Ltd
67 Broadgreen Road
Martley
MR6 7TR

| | |
|---|---|
| Credit Note No | 552793 |
| Account | MAR435 |
| Date/tax point | 2 April 19–5 |
| Your Reference | D/N 8974 |
| Our invoice | 652771 |

| product code | description | quantity | price | unit | total | disc % | net |
|---|---|---|---|---|---|---|---|
| 3564749 | 100 gsm white Supalaser | 5 | 4.00 | ream | 20.00 | 0 | 20.00 |

**Reason for credit**
shortages –
only 10 reams of paper delivered, 15 ordered

| | |
|---|---|
| GOODS TOTAL | 20.00 |
| CASH DISCOUNT | 00.00 |
| SUBTOTAL | 20.00 |
| VAT | 3.50 |
| TOTAL | 23.50 |

---

*Note the following details:*
• the invoice number of the original consignment is quoted
• the reason for the issue of the credit note is stated at the bottom of the credit note – here 'shortages'
• the details are otherwise exactly the same as on an invoice

# goods received note

A goods received note (GRN) is prepared by the warehouse staff of the buyer.  Not all businesses use GRNs, but when used they act as a useful 'checklist' that the goods received tally with the goods ordered.  It is often printed in multiple copy form (three copies normally).  When the goods have been checked on arrival, the form is completed and the three copies will be distributed to:

• the purchasing department to notify receipt of the goods (it is attached to the original order)
• the accounts department (so that the invoice may be paid when due)
• the warehouse/stockroom (so that the stock records can be updated).

If there are any problems with the goods, a *credit note* may be requested from the supplier, or a *debit note* issued to the supplier (see previous page).

---

## GOODS RECEIVED NOTE
### MARTLEY MACHINE RENTAL LTD

**Supplier**

| | |
|---|---|
| Stourford Office Supplies<br>Unit 12<br>Avon Industrial Estate<br>Stourford SF5 6TD | GRN No.     6524<br>Date        30 March 19–5 |

| quantity | description | order number |
|---|---|---|
| 10 reams | 100 gsm white Supalaser paper | 47700 |

| **carrier** | Express Parcels Ltd     consignment ref.     6378378 |
|---|---|

| **received by** | *G Hughes* | checked by   *R Amphlett* |
|---|---|---|

| **condition of goods** | good condition ✓<br>damaged<br>shortages    *5 reams missing* | **copies to**<br>Purchasing<br>Accounts ✓<br>Stockroom |
|---|---|---|

---

*Note the following details:*

• as the document is an internal one, it does not have an address printed on it
• details of the goods are noted, together with the order number (which will be on the delivery note)
• the details of the carrier are noted, the consignment reference is the carrier's reference
• the signatures of the person receiving the goods, and also that of the checker
• the condition of the goods and the shortages are recorded
• the distribution of the document is indicated – this is the Accounts Department copy

# statement and remittance advice

A supplier will not normally expect a buyer to pay each individual invoice as soon as it is received: this could result in the buyer having to write a number of cheques during the month. Instead, a *statement of account* is sent by the supplier to the buyer at the end of the month. This statement, which can be typed out, or printed by the seller's computer accounting program, will show exactly what is owed by the buyer to the seller. It contains details of:

- invoices issued for goods supplied – the full amount due, including VAT
- refunds made on *credit notes*
- payments received from the buyer

The statement issued by Stourford Office Supplies to Martley Machine Rental Ltd for the transactions described on the previous pages is illustrated below. It lists

- the date of each transaction
- the invoice (abbreviated to 'inv') for the 15 reams of paper
- the credit note (abbreviated to 'CN') for the 5 reams that were short – note that the money amount is followed by the letters "CR" which stand for "credit"
- the outstanding amounts – ie what is actually owed on each invoice – here £70.50 less the £23.50 refund = £47.00

You will see that the statement has a tear-off slip attached on the right. This is known as a *remittance advice*. The buyer can detach this, tick the invoice(s) being paid in the far right-hand column, and send it with the cheque to the supplier. Some organisations will prepare their own remittance advice to send with the cheque (see next page). If the organisation has a computer accounting program, the computer will probably print out the remittance advice, and in some cases the cheque as well.

| **statement** | | | | | | **remittance advice** | | |
|---|---|---|---|---|---|---|---|---|
| **Stourford Office Supplies** Unit 12, Avon Industrial Estate, Stourford SF5 6TD Tel 0807 765434 Fax 0807 765123 VAT Reg 0745 4672 76 | | | | | | **Stourford Office Supplies** Unit 12, Avon Industrial Estate, Stourford SF5 6TD | | |
| Account MAR435  Date 31 March 19-5 | | | | | | Account MAR 435 | | |
| Martley Machine Rental Ltd 67 Broadgreen Road Martley MR6 7TR | | | | | | *please indicate items you are paying (✔) and return this advice with your remittance* | | |
| date | type | reference | value | outstanding | | ref | outstanding | ✔ |
| 26/03/-5 02/04/-5 | INV CN | 652771 552793 | 70.50 23.50CR | 47.00 | | 652771 | 47.00 | |
| | | | TOTAL | 47.00 | | TOTAL | 47.00 | |

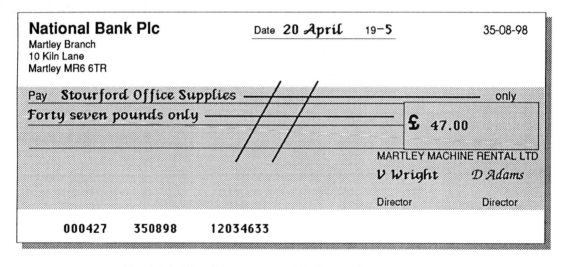

**REMITTANCE ADVICE**
**MARTLEY MACHINE RENTAL LTD**
67 Broadgreen Road Martley  MR6 7TR

| Stourford Office Supplies | Cheque No | 000427 |
| Unit 12 | Date | 20 April 19-5 |
| Avon Industrial Estate | Account | ST0006 |
| Stourford SF5 6TD | | |

| date | our ref . | your ref. | amount | payment |
|------|-----------|-----------|--------|---------|
| 20/04/-5 | 47700 | 652771 | 47.00 | 47.00 |

cheque value    £  47.00

*Fig. 29.2  A separate remittance advice sent with the payment*

**National Bank Plc**    Date **20 April**    19-5    35-08-98
Martley Branch
10 Kiln Lane
Martley MR6 6TR

Pay   **Stourford Office Supplies**                       only
**Forty seven pounds only**                       £  47.00

MARTLEY MACHINE RENTAL LTD
**V Wright**        **D Adams**
Director        Director

000427    350898    12034633

*Fig. 29.3  The cheque sent with the remittance advice*

### BACS payments

An increasing number of businesses, instead of sending payment by cheque, obtain the banking details of *regular* suppliers, and send the money through the banking system to the bank account of the supplier. This transfer is usually made by the banks through a computer-based system known as BACS (Bankers Automated Clearing Services), explained in detail on page 338.

When the BACS settlement system is used, an advice of payment containing all the details that would normally appear on a remittance advice, is posted by the buyer to the supplier so that the supplier can update the appropriate accounting records.

# authorisation of payments

It is important that invoices must be checked carefully before being authorised and paid by the Accounts Department, or the person who deals with Accounts.

### what to do with incorrect invoices

Clearly only correct invoices can be paid and authorised. Invoices with errors will need to be queried with the seller. If the error relates to the goods sent, the seller's Sales Department should be contacted, if the error is in the calculation of the invoice, the seller's Accounts Department should be advised. A fax or a letter could be sent; often a telephone call will quickly sort out any problem.

### authorising correct documentation

When an invoice is checked and found to be correct, the person carrying out the check will usually initial and date the document and pass it forward for payment. Payment then has to be authorised, usually at supervisor level. The authorisation process will vary from business to business, but it will generally take the following form:

- the relevant documentation – purchase order, delivery note, invoice, goods received note (if used) – is collated together, and checked to make sure that there are no problems which might delay payment, eg missing goods, delayed goods, returned goods
- the organisation often has a special rubber stamp, which acts as an authorisation, placed on the invoice – see fig 29.4 below
- alternatively the goods received note can act as a checklist – when it has been satisfactorily completed, it will show the supervisor that the invoice can be paid

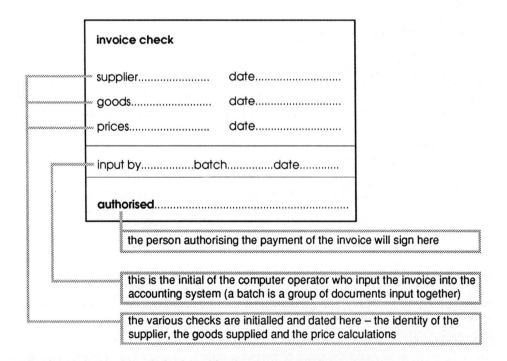

*Fig. 29.4 Authorisation stamp placed on an invoice received for checking*

# business documents and computers

Many organisations now use computers to produce the business documents described in this chapter. If an organisation does not have a large mainframe computer, it can use a PC (personal computer) to print purchase orders, delivery notes, invoices, credit notes, statements and remittance advices, and in some cases, cheques. Once all the preliminary information is input into the computer (names and addresses of customers, product details, prices etc), the transaction details are input according to instructions given on the screen. All that is required is an inexpensive computer program and the necessary hardware.

There are many advantages of using computers to produce financial documents:

* *accuracy* – as long as the information input is correct, all the calculations, including the VAT, are performed automatically and accurately
* *speed* – the typist is spared the lengthy and repetitive production of individual documents
* *efficiency* – all statements can be sent out to customers on time: the computer will print them automatically at a given command
* *availability of information* – as all the information about sales and purchases is stored on computer file, it is a simple matter to call up on screen how much is owed by customers and how much is owed to suppliers

The type of computer accounting program described above is fast and efficient, but it relies on a paper-based system: the documents are posted (or faxed) to their destination and are checked manually. A recent development, Electronic Data Interchange, commonly known as EDI and described in detail below, does away with the paper documents.

# Electronic Data Interchange (EDI)

As you will have found in your study of business systems, computers in different organisations can 'talk' to each other. Telephone links can be set up and computer data – word-processed files, databases and other types of data – can be transmitted, often at night when the telephone rates are cheaper. If you bought this book at a bookshop, the order may have been processed on a computer behind the counter, and the order data sent off that evening to Osborne Books via a computer link.

Systems now exist whereby all the business documents described in this chapter are generated on computer file and the data sent between the computers of the buyer and the seller. This system, known as *Electronic Data Interchange (EDI)*, is extensively used in the UK, particularly by large retailing organisations which need to renew stock frequently. You will have seen how the tills in large chains of shops operate by scanning bar codes with a light pen. Each branch is linked to a central computer, so that each time an item is sold, the data is recorded by the light pen, transmitted to the main computer, updating the stock records of the shop. When a certain minimum stock level is reached, an order for new stock is automatically triggered by the computer and sent to the computer of the supplier. The supplier then delivers new stock. No paper is involved.

How does EDI work in practical terms?

**definition**      EDI is a system which transfers commercial and administrative instructions between computers using agreed formats for the messages.

**EDI standards**   The two parties involved agree a format for the electronic messages which take the place of purchase orders, delivery instructions, invoices, credit notes and statements. In the UK the standard retail transfer system is *Tradacoms*, and internationally the United Nations is sponsoring a worldwide EDI standard known as *UN-EDIFACT*.

**EDI transfers**    The transfer is normally sent from one computer to another via a third party known as a VAN (value added network). A value added network operates like an electronic post office: you deposit your information electronically in your 'post box' and the value added network transfers it to the 'postbox' of your trading partner (see fig 29.5 below).

**EDI benefits**    The benefits of EDI include
- reduced handling costs
- reduced postage costs
- reduced paper storage costs
- fewer errors (there is less re-keying of existing computer data)
- faster payment

**'just in time' retailing**    Holding stock costs organisations money and therefore the larger retailers – Tesco and Marks & Spencer for example – operate a 'just-in-time' ordering policy whereby stock is ordered as late as possible. Some food chains order from only two to five days before the goods are needed. This is useful for the retailers, but can cause headaches for the suppliers. One of the advantages of EDI is that *estimates* of future orders can be sent to suppliers so that they can produce approximately the correct quantity of goods in time for the expected orders.

**EDI payments**    In the normal course of paper-based trading (ie using paper invoices and other business documents), settlement is usually made by cheque which is posted to the supplier or by BACS (an inter-bank computer transfer system). The banks are now introducing a system – NatWest's BankLine for example – whereby the buyer can use the EDI system for authorising his bank to make payment to the supplier's bank. As the buyer's computer system already has details of each trade transaction – the parties involved and the amounts – it is a simple matter to add the banking details of the supplier, so that settlement can be made on the due date (see fig 29.5 below).

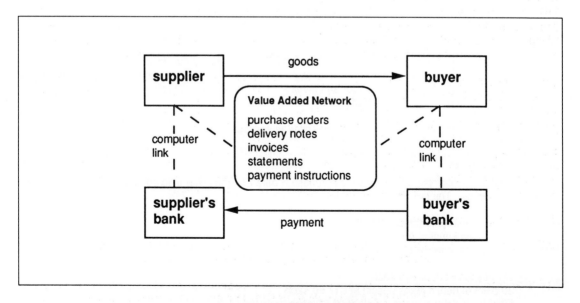

*Fig. 29.5 The EDI system*

# chapter summary

❑ All organisations use commercially accepted business documents to carry out trading transactions. The most commonly used business documents are
  • purchase order
  • delivery note
  • invoice
  • credit note
  • goods received note
  • statement
  • remittance advice

❑ Organisations will either prepare business documents manually, or use a computer program; the standard format and terminology remaining the same whichever method is used.

❑ Some organisations are now using a paperless system known as EDI (Electronic Data Interchange) whereby the details normally found on paper business documents are sent as electronic messages beteeen the computers of the buyer and the seller.

In the next chapter we look at the documents involved when an organisation or an individual receives a payment.

 **student activities**

*Some of the activities set out below involve the use of a number of different business documents. You can either use the specimen photcopiable blank forms available from Osborne Books, or you can design your own documents, using as a guide business documents encountered in your work or work experience. If you have access to a suitable computer accounting package, this can be used to produce the documents involved.*

**29.1** If you are studying in a group you should divide into pairs and play the roles of buyer and seller. The buyer is a clothes shop and the seller a clothes wholesaler. You will need copies of two blank business documents: purchase order and invoice. You can use the current date and VAT rate but will need to make up the following details:

  • the names and addresses of buyer and seller as appropriate to your locality
  • catalogue numbers
  • order numbers and invoice numbers

The buyer is to complete two separate purchase orders and the seller is to complete a separate invoice for each order. The orders are as follows:

(a) 100 pairs of tights (black) at £1.25
   25 woollen jumpers (green) at £15 each
   50 nighties (pink) at £8.50 each

(b) 25 dresses (red) at £15 each
   30 pairs of denim jeans (black) at £17.50 each
   50 pairs of tights (fishnet black) at £1.30 each

Assume that there is no trade discount available to the buyer. Add VAT at the current rate.

29.2 Look at the invoice shown below and explain what is meant by

(a) deliver to

(b) account

(c) date/tax point

(d) your reference

(e) product code

(f) unit

(g) carriage paid

(h) net

(i) net monthly

(j) E & OE

---

## INVOICE

### Stourford Office Supplies
Unit 12, Avon Industrial Estate, Stourford SF5 6TD
Tel 0807 765434 Fax 0807 765123
VAT Reg 0745 4672 76

invoice to

```
Martley Machine Rental Ltd
67 Broadgreen Road
Martley
MR6 7TR
```

| | |
|---|---|
| Invoice No | 652771 |
| Account | MAR435 |
| Date/tax point | 30 March 19-5 |
| Your Reference | 47700 |

deliver to

```
as above
```

| product code | description | quantity | price | unit | total | disc % | net |
|---|---|---|---|---|---|---|---|
| 3564749 | 100 gsm white Supalaser | 15 | 4.00 | ream | 60.00 | 0 | 60.00 |

**Terms**
Net monthly
Carriage paid
E & OE

| | |
|---|---|
| GOODS TOTAL | 60.00 |
| CASH DISCOUNT | 00.00 |
| SUBTOTAL | 60.00 |
| VAT | 10.50 |
| TOTAL | 70.50 |

---

29.3 A new accounts clerk at Martley Machine Rental Limited telephones querying the invoice shown above, saying that he does not understand why 'discount' appears twice – in a vertical column and also as 'cash discount' further down on the document. He asks how his organisation can qualify for each type of discount. What would you tell him?

**29.4** You work in the Accounts Departments of Mercia Building Supplies, Unit 3 Severnside Industrial Estate, Stourminster WR4 3TH.  Your financial records show the following details about your customer N Patel:

| | |
|---|---|
| 1 Mar. | Balance due, £145 |
| 3 Mar. | Goods sold to N Patel, £210 (including VAT), invoice number 8119 |
| 10 Mar. | Cheque received from N Patel, £145 |
| 23 Mar. | Goods returned by N Patel, £50 (including VAT), credit note number 7345 issued. |
| 28 Mar. | Goods sold to N Patel, £180 (including VAT), invoice number 8245 |

You are to prepare the statement of account to be sent to the customer at his address at 45 Archway Avenue, Stourminster WR2 5RT on 31 March 19-5.  This should show clearly the balance due at the month-end.

**29.5** You work for Deansway Trading Company, a wholesaler of office stationery, which trades from The Modern Office, 79 Deansway, Stourminster WR1 2EJ.  A customer, The Card Shop of 126 The Crescent, Marshall Green, WR4 5TX, orders the following on order number 9516:

5 boxes of assorted rubbers at £5 per box, catalogue no 26537
100 shorthand notebooks at £4 for a pack of 10, catalogue no 72625
250 ring binders at 50p each, catalogue no 72698

Value Added Tax is to be charged at the current rate on all items, and a 2.5 per cent cash discount is offered for full settlement within 14 days.  Prepare invoice number 8234, under today's date, to be sent to the customer.

**29.6**

# GOODS RECEIVED NOTE
### MARTLEY MACHINE RENTAL LTD

**Supplier**

| | | |
|---|---|---|
| Grantham Motor Spares<br>23 Tunnel Hill<br>Mereford<br>MR3 8NC | GRN No.<br>Date | 6600<br>30 April 19-5 |

| quantity | description | order number |
|---|---|---|
| 5 | 50 cm Sharpness Hedge Trimmers | 47765 |

| **carrier** | Speedy Parcels | consignment ref. | 83728 |
|---|---|---|---|

| **received by** | *G Hughes* | checked by | *R Amphlett* |
|---|---|---|---|

| **condition of goods** | good condition | **copies to** |
|---|---|---|
| | damaged ✓   *2 with damaged blades* | Purchasing |
| | shortages | Accounts ✓ |
| | | Stockroom |

Examine the Goods Received Note illustrated above.

(a) identify the parties involved, the goods supplied and the procedure involved when the goods arrive

(b) identify the problem

(c) what action should be taken, and by whom?

Note: the trimmers cost £85.00 each , excluding VAT (which is payable).

# 30 Receiving payments

## introduction

Businesses can receive payment in a number of different ways:
- in cash, by cheque or by credit or debit card over the counter
- by cheque for goods and services supplied (as in the last chapter)

They then pay these payments into the bank, and keep track of what is in the bank account by means of the bank statement.

Your course in business studies requires you to understand the *format* of a number of documents, but it does *not* require you to acquire the practical skills of a cashier. In this chapter we therefore look at
- the issue of receipts for cash (or cheque)
- the format of the cheque
- credit cards and debit cards
- the paying-in slip
- the bank statement

## cash

Cash is used for most small transactions, and we are still nowhere near the 'cashless society' which is often talked about. For the purchaser, cash is a convenient and fast method of paying small money amounts but, for larger amounts, it is unsuitable because it is bulky to carry, liable to be lost, and a temptation to thieves. As far as the organisation accepting payments in cash is concerned, the main disadvantage of cash is the security problem, both in terms of internal security, and also because of the increasing risk of armed robbery.

### receiving payment in cash

For a business receiving sums of money in the form of cash it is necessary for a member of staff to count the cash received and check it against the amount due. Change will need to be given when the exact amount is not tendered (given). For example:

| | |
|---|---|
| Sale | £3.64 |
| Amount tendered (given) by customer | £10.00 |
| Change to be given | £6.36 |

The amount of change is the difference between the amount tendered and the amount of the sale. When a cash till is in use, modern types of till will indicate the amount of change to be given after the amount tendered has been entered through the keyboard. You will know, from having bought items in shops, that many cashiers count out the change starting with the amount of the sale and working to the amount tendered. From the above example this would be done as follows:

| Sale | | £3.64 | |
|------|--|-------|--|
| Change given: | 1p coin | £3.65 | |
| | 5p coin | £3.70 | |
| | 10p coin | £3.80 | |
| | 20p coin | £4.00 | |
| | £1 coin | £5.00 | |
| | £5 note | £10.00 | Amount tendered |
| | £6.36 | | |

Often when payment is made in cash, a receipt is given: this can take the form of a machine-produced receipt, such as is given in a shop, or a handwritten receipt (examples of both are shown in fig. 30.1 below).

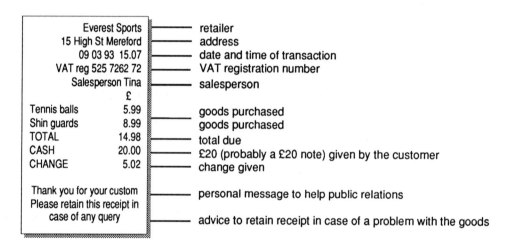

Fig. 30.1  *Machine-produced receipt (top) and handwritten receipt (below)*

## cheques

Cheques are issued by banks to their personal and business *current account* customers. Building societies also issue cheques on current accounts – their customers are mainly personal. Payment by cheque is one of the most common methods of payment for all but the smallest amounts. A specimen cheque is shown below in fig. 30.2.

### what is a cheque?

A cheque, as used in normal business practice, may be defined as

*a written order to the bank signed by its customer (known as the 'drawer') to pay a specified amount to a specified person (known as the 'payee')*

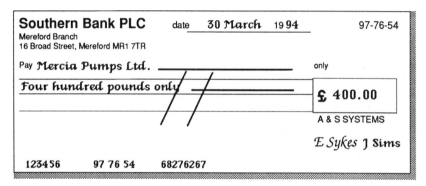

*Fig. 30.2   A specimen cheque*

Businesses will normally receive cheques
- through the post with remitttance advices in settlement for goods or services supplied on credit (see previous chapter)
- over the counter for goods or services supplied

Some businesses – large retail stores, for example – have machines which print out their customers' cheques at the till. A large number of cheques, however, are still written by hand, and great care must be taken both when writing out cheques and also when receiving cheques in payment. The cheques must be examined to ensure that all the details and signatures are correct. The details that must be looked at when receiving a cheque in payment are:
- is the cheque signed? – it is completely invalid if it is not
- is the payee's name correct? – it should be changed and initialled by the drawer if it is not
- is the cheque in date? – a cheque becomes out of date and invalid after six months; note that if the date is missing, it may be written in
- do the words and figures agree? – the cheque may be returned by the drawer's (issuer's) bank to the payee if they do not

If the business accepting payment by cheque is inefficient and does not carry out these precautions, the cheque(s) may be returned to the business' bank after it has been paid in, and the amount of the cheque deducted from the business' bank account. This may happen if the cheque is received through the post. If the cheque is issued with a cheque card, different conditions apply (see page 321).

### cheque crossings

Cheques may, as in the example shown above, be *crossed*, that is, they are printed with two parallel lines across the face of the cheque. If a cheque is not crossed, it is an *open* cheque. A *crossed* cheque may only be paid into a bank account; it cannot be cashed (ie exchanged for cash) by the payee (the person to whom the cheque is made payable). An *open* cheque, on the other hand, can be cashed by the payee at the bank branch named on the cheque. The payee in the case of an open cheque does not have to have a bank account. As you will appreciate, crossed cheques are much safer then open cheques, which if lost or stolen could be cashed by any person impersonating the payee!

## endorsements

In law the payee of a cheque is entitled to sign it on the back – *endorse* it – so that it can be passed on to another person who can pay it into a bank account and receive payment. This is common practice if a person who is given a crossed cheque has no bank account – the cheque can be endorsed and passed to someone who *does* have a bank account who can then reimburse the payee with the amount of the cheque. This signature on the back – the endorsement – should read as follows:

> *Pay Ivor Brown*
> *James Smith*

In the above example James Smith, the payee, is endorsing the cheque over to Ivor Brown who will pay it into his bank account. He has actually written "Pay Ivor Brown" above his signature. If he just signs the back of the cheque he may run into problems. The cheque in this case technically becomes a *bearer* cheque, which like a bank note (which says "pay bearer" on the front) can be paid in by *any* person who is in possession of it. This type of endorsement – the plain signature – is therefore not recommended, as the cheque could be lost or stolen, and then paid into anyone's bank account!

## payee "only" cheques

An increasing number of cheques are being printed with "only" after the space where the payee's name is written (see Fig. 30.2 on the previous page). These cheques cannot be endorsed over to another person, they can only be paid into the payee's account (if they are crossed) or cashed by the payee (if they are open). This practice has become widespread since the passing of the Cheques Act 1992.

## crossings and endorsements

Sometimes there is wording written or printed between the two lines of the crossing which may affect the ability of the payee to endorse the cheque and pass it on to another person.

| *crossing* | *effect* |
|---|---|
| *not negotiable* | The cheque can still be endorsed over, although if the cheque has been stolen and passed on, the person who pays it into his bank account may lose his money if the cheque has been 'stopped' by the person who wrote it out. |
| *account payee* | Following the passing of The Cheques Act 1992 the "account payee" crossing effectively prevents the cheque from being endorsed, as it can only be paid into the account of the payee. You will sometimes see variations to the "account payee" wording, for example "account payee only" or "a/c payee" or "a/c payee only". These all have the same effect. |
| *Midland Bank Pershore* | This type of crossing – known a *special* crossing – means that the cheque may only be paid in at Midland Bank, Pershore. If it is paid in at another bank, payment may be refused. |

## cheque cards and payment cards

### cheque cards

In order to encourage shops and other businesses to accept cheques more readily, banks and some building societies issue cheque cards to suitable personal and business customers (but not to limited companies). This plastic 'card' acts as a guarantee that cheques up to and including a stated limit (normally £50, sometimes £100 or £200) will be paid as long as certain conditions are fulfilled.

The rules for the use of a cheque card may be found on the reverse of the card, or they may be made available separately by the bank. The following is an example of the wording:

> XYZ Bank plc guarantees in any single transaction the payment of one cheque taken from one of its own cheque books for up to £50 provided the cheque is not drawn on the account of a Limited Company, and
> (1) The cheque bears the same name and code number as this card.
> (2) It is signed, before the expiry of the card, in the United Kingdom of Great Britain and Northern Ireland, the Channel Islands or the Isle of Man in the presence of the payee by the person whose signature appears on this card.
> (3) The card number is written on the back of the cheque by the payee.
> (4) The card has not been altered or defaced.

### receiving payment by cheque and cheque guarantee card

You will appreciate from the cheque card conditions set out above that when a business accepts payment by cheque and guarantee card it must take great care that all the conditions are met, eg that the cheque is signed in the presence of the payee. If the conditions are not met, the cheque may be returned unpaid by the purchaser's bank, and the business will lose the money. Also, because of the large number of stolen cards in circulation, businesses must be on their guard against suspicious-looking cards and customers.

### payment cards

Whereas a cheque card will only guarantee payment of cheques, many banks now issue 'payment cards' which combine the functions of
* *cheque guarantee* – guaranteeing single cheques up to a set limit
* *cash card* – enabling the holder to withdraw cash from cash machines – ATMs (automated teller machines)
* *debit card* – enabling the holder to make payment for goods and services from a bank account without writing out a cheque – examples include Switch cards and Barclay's Delta card

## credit cards and debit cards

### credit cards

Credit cards provide a means of obtaining goods and services immediately, but paying for them later. The commonest credit cards used in the UK use the names Visa, Access, Mastercard, Eurocard. The cards are issued, upon application, to customers of banks, building societies, and retail groups. A credit limit is set on each cardholder's credit card account (which is entirely separate from his or her normal bank account). Goods and services can be obtained at shops and other outlets having computer terminals or the special machine (imprinter) for preparing sales vouchers to record the transaction. Credit cards can also be used for mail order and telephone order sales. Retailers pay to the credit card company a set percentage (usually between 2% and 5%) of each transaction amount for the use of the credit card facility.

Each month a cardholder is sent a statement of the purchases made and can choose to pay off the balance of the account, or to pay part only (subject to a certain minimum amount), carrying forward the remaining balance to next month. Interest is charged on balances owing to the credit card company. An annual flat fee is normally charged to the cardholder for the use of the card.

### debit cards

Debit cards are issued to personal customers by banks and building societies to enable their customers to make payments from their bank accounts by Electronic Funds Transfer – see below. Examples of debit cards are Barclays' Visa 'Delta' and Midland's 'Switch' cards. Such cards are issued to selected customers of the bank; they enable a payment to be made from the person's bank account, subject to having sufficient money in the account, without the need to write out a cheque.

From a seller's point of view, when a customer wishes to pay by debit card *in person*, the transaction is handled in a similar way to a credit card. As mentioned earlier, some banks have combined the functions of a debit card with that of cheque guarantee card and cash card (ATM card).

### Electronic Funds Transfer

Credit cards and debit cards can be used to make electronic payments by means of a system called Electronic Funds Transfer at Point Of Sale (EFTPOS). This is a system which allows a shop to debit the bank account or credit card account of the purchaser at the point of sale and, at the same time, to credit the retailer's bank account. Besides removing the need to carry a lot of cash, the system reduces the paperwork of writing out cheques or filling in credit card vouchers.

EFTPOS is operated by means of plastic cards – either *debit cards* issued by banks/building societies, or by *credit cards*. When goods are to be paid for using this method, the retailer 'swipes' the card through a card reader (as with a credit card) and the total amount is entered into an electronic checkout till. The till prints a sales slip which is signed by the customer to authenticate the transaction. The retailer checks that the signature on the sales slip is the same as that shown on the card. Details of the transaction are transmitted electronically by means of a computer link to a central computer, either immediately or later in the day. Sometimes a telephone call has to be made to authorise the transaction. The cost of the goods being purchased is checked against the amount available in the card holder's bank or building society account, or the available credit in the credit card account. If everything is in order, the customer's account is debited and the retailer's account is credited with the appropriate amount.

The benefits of EFTPOS to a retail business are:
- greater efficiency, with less time taken by customers to make payment, and reduced queuing time
- less cash to handle (giving fewer security risks)
- guaranteed payment once acceptance has been made

## paying-in slips

Business customers are generally issued by their bank with a paying-in book containing paying-in slips. These can be used for paying in cash, cheques, credit card and debit card vouchers. The details (see figs 30.3 and 30.4 on the next page) to be completed are:
- the name of the bank and branch where the account is held (these details are normally pre-printed)
- the name of the account to be credited, together with the account number (normally pre-printed)
- a summary of the different categories of notes or coins being paid in, the amount of each category being entered on the slip
- amounts and details of cheques being paid in, usually entered on the reverse of the slip, with the total entered on the front
- the cash and cheques being paid in are totalled to give the amount being paid in
- the counterfoil is completed
- the person paying-in will sign the slip

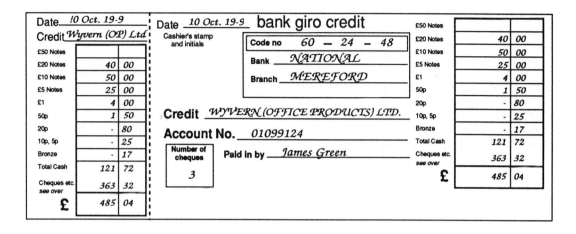

*Fig. 30.3 The front of a completed paying-in slip, including counterfoil (on left)*

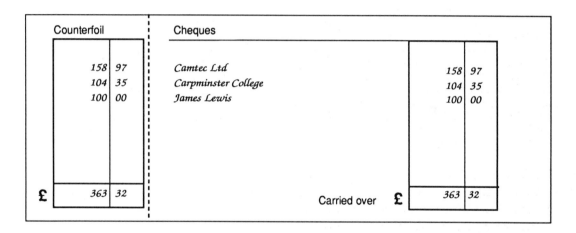

*Fig. 30.4 The back of a completed paying-in slip, including counterfoil (on left)*

## procedures for paying in

### preparing the cash

The notes should be counted, checked and sorted so that they all face the same way, usually with the Queen's head to the right of the note. Notes from Scotland and Northern Ireland are normally accepted by banks, but should be kept separate. Similarly, defaced (damaged) notes are usually accepted by the banks (it is surprising how many notes go in the washing machine). Coins should normally be sorted and placed in separate denominations in bags as follows:

| denomination | amount in bag |
|---|---|
| £1 | £20 |
| 50p | £10 |
| 20p | £10 |
| 10p | £5 |
| 5p | £5 |
| 2p | £1 |
| 1p | £1 |

## preparing the cheques

The cheques must first be examined carefully for any irregularities, such as

- *signatures* – has the drawer signed the cheque?
- *endorsements* – if the name on the payee line is not the same as the name of the account into which it is being paid, has it been suitably endorsed?
- *crossings* – if the cheque has the "account payee" wording in the crossing and your organisation is not the payee, it will not be possible to pay it in, even if it has been endorsed
- *date* – is it out of date (over six months old)? is it post-dated? – if so, it cannot be paid in
- *words and figures* – do they agree?

The details of the cheques – the amounts and the customer names – may then be listed on the back of the paying-in slip, as in fig. 30.4 on the previous page. If the volume of cheques paid in is very large, there will not be room on the paying-in slip, so the cheque details may be listed on a separate schedule. Some banks accept instead a calculator tally-roll listing the amounts, the number of cheques, and the total money amount transferred to the front of the paying-in slip. The important point is that the organisation paying in the cheques must keep a record of the cheque details in case of future queries, and in the event of any of the cheques being returned unpaid ('bounced').

## paying in at the bank

At the bank the completed paying-in book is handed to the bank cashier together with the notes, coins, and cheques. The cashier counts the cash, ticks off the cheques and, if everything is correct, stamps and initials the paying-in slip and counterfoil. The slip is retained by the bank for the amount to be credited to the account-holder, while the paying-in book is handed back, complete with the receipted counterfoil. A business paying-in book is sometimes larger than the paying-in slip illustrated, and sometimes there is a carbon copy behind the business paying-in slip which acts as a counterfoil.

Care must be taken when taking large amounts of cash to the bank. If possible two staff members should visit the bank. If the amount is very large, for instance the takings from a department store, a security firm may be employed to carry the cash. If the cash is received by an organisation over the weekend or, late in the day, it may be placed in a special wallet and lodged in the bank's *night safe* – a small lockable door in the wall of the bank leading to a safe.

## credit card voucher clearing

As we saw earlier in the chapter, the sales voucher is the basic document normally produced when a credit card transaction takes place. The sales voucher may be produced as a result of an 'over the counter' sale or from a mail order or telephone sale. The details recorded on it will enable the credit card company to charge the amount to their customer. The voucher, like a cheque, is paid in at the bank and sent off to the credit card company and 'cleared'.

Although there are a number of different credit card companies – Access and Visa for example – the normal practice is for the organisation accepting payment to sign an agreement with a *separate* company which will accept *all* vouchers from cards issued by different companies. For example, a customer of The Royal Bank of Scotland may sign an agreement with a company called Roynet (owned by the Royal Bank of Scotland) and accept payment by Access and Visa and other nominated cards. The customer will pay in *all* credit card (and debit card) vouchers on one paying-in slip and schedule at The Royal Bank of Scotland. The bank will pass them to Roynet, which will then process them by sending them to the issuing card company (eg Access or Visa). Roynet is only one of a number of companies which will process credit card sales vouchers.

The business paying in the vouchers is charged a set percentage fee – usually between 2% and 5% – of the total sales amount. This charge is automatically deducted from the business' bank account by computer transfer (known as a direct debit) and a statement of charges is sent to the customer by post.

# bank statements

At regular intervals the bank sends out statements of account to its customers. A business current account with many items passing through it may have weekly statements, a less active account or a deposit (interest bearing) account may have monthly or even quarterly statements.

A bank statement is a summary showing
- the balance at the beginning of the statement – 'balance brought forward'
- amounts paid into (credited to) the account
- amounts paid out of (debited to) the account – eg cheques issued, cheques returned 'unpaid' ('bounced'), bank charges and standing orders and direct debits (automatic computer payments – see the next chapter for an explanation of these).

The balance of the account is shown after each transaction. A specimen bank statement is shown in fig. 30.5 below.

---

IN ACCOUNT WITH

# National Bank plc

**Branch**....Mereford.........

TITLE OF ACCOUNT........Osborne Electronics Ltd.

ACCOUNT NUMBER......01099124.........................          STATEMENT NUMBER  96

| DATE | PARTICULARS | PAYMENTS | RECEIPTS | BALANCE |
|------|-------------|----------|----------|---------|
| 19-9 | | £ | £ | £ |
| 1 Oct. | Balance brought forward | | | 625.50 CR |
| 9 Oct. | Cheque 352817 | 179.30 | | 446.20 CR |
| 10 Oct. | Credit | | 485.04 | 931.24 CR |
| 17 Oct. | Cheque 352818 | 169.33 | | 761.91 CR |
| 23 Oct. | Credit | | 62.30 | 824.21 CR |
| 24 Oct. | Credit | | 100.00 | 924.21 CR |
| 26 Oct. | Cheque 352819 | 821.80 | | 102.41 CR |
| 26 Oct. | Unpaid cheque | 250.00 | | 147.59 DR |
| 28 Oct. | Credit | | 108.00 | 39.59 DR |
| 31 Oct. | Bank charges | 25.00 | | 64.59 DR |

*Fig. 30.5 A specimen bank statement*

---

You will see from the specimen bank statement that the balance of the account is indicated each time by the abbreviation 'CR' or 'DR'; the first of these means that the customer has a credit balance, ie has money in the bank, while 'DR' indicates a debit balance to show an overdraft, ie the customer owes the bank money. The bank charges referred to can either be calculated on an item basis (ie the number of items passing through the account) or on a turnover basis (ie the money total of all the items paid out of the account). In addition, interest will be charged on overdrawn balances.

When a bank statement is received it should be checked against the firm's record of bank receipts and payments – the cash book.

# chapter summary

❑ Businesses receiving payment in cash will normally issue a receipt – either a till receipt or a handwritten receipt form.

❑ Businesses receiving cheques in payment must inspect the cheque carefully for any irregularities or omissions. If a cheque card (or payment card) is used to back the cheque, the business must take care the card is not being used fraudulently.

❑ Debit cards and credit cards are becoming popular as means of making payment, particularly as many retail outlets now operate EFTPOS (Electronic Funds Transfer at Point Of Sale) tills.

❑ Once payment has been received, whether it be cash, cheque or plastic card payment, a paying-in slip must be prepared so that the money can be paid into the bank.

❑ A business will receive a regular statement from its bank so that it can check money paid in and money paid out with the transactions recorded in the business cash book.

 **student activities**

**30.1** You work as a shop counter assistant at New Era Lighting. You make a number of sales during the day (use today's date) which require the completion of a handwritten receipt. Complete the receipts set out below. Include VAT on all purchases at the current rate. All prices quoted here are catalogue prices and exclude VAT.

(a) 2 flexilamps @ £13.99, 2 60W candlelight bulbs @ 85p, to Mr George Meredith

**NEW ERA LIGHTING**                                      977
17 High Street Mereford MR1 2TF
VAT reg 141 7645 23

**CASH RECEIPT**

Customer...................................................date...........................

|  |  |
|---|---|
|  |  |
|  |  |
| VAT |  |
| TOTAL |  |

**(b)** 1 standard lamp @
£149.95,
1 3 amp plug @ 99p,
to Mr Alex Bell

**NEW ERA LIGHTING**     **978**
17 High Street Mereford MR1 2TF
VAT reg 141 7645 23

**CASH RECEIPT**

Customer.................................................date...........................

|  |  |
|  |  |
| VAT |  |
| TOTAL |  |

**(c)** 2 external Georgian
lamps @ £35.99,
to Miss S Fox

**NEW ERA LIGHTING**     **979**
17 High Street Mereford MR1 2TF
VAT reg 141 7645 23

**CASH RECEIPT**

Customer.................................................date...........................

|  |  |
|  |  |
| VAT |  |
| TOTAL |  |

**30.2** You work as an accounts clerk in the Accounts Department of Mercia Pumps Ltd, Unit 13, Severn Trading Estate, Mereford MR3 4GF. Today is 3 April 1994. In the morning's post are a number of cheques enclosed with remittance advices. These cheques are illustrated on the next page. Examine the cheques carefully, and identify any problems, and state what action (if any) you will take, and why. Draft letters *where appropriate* for your Manager's (Mrs D Strong) signature. You note from the remittance advices that the addresses are as follows:

(a) The Accounts Department, A & S Systems, 5 High Street, Mereford MR1 2JF

(b) Mrs P Thorne, Hillside Cottage, Mintfield, MR4 9HG

(c) The Accounts Department, C Darwin Ltd, 89 Baker Street, Mereford MR2 6RG

(d) Mr I M A King, 56 Beaconsfield Drive, Pershore MR7 5GF

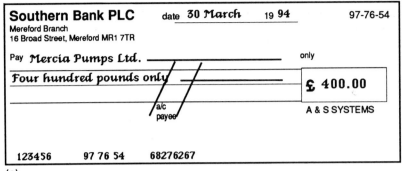

(a)

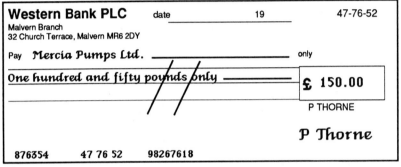

(b)

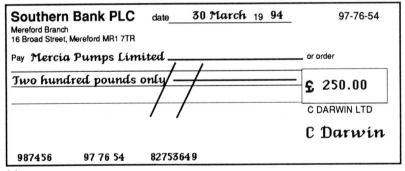

(c)

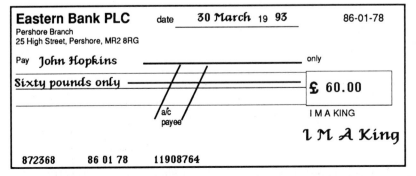

(d) John Hopkins, the Sales Director of Mercia Pumps Ltd, who has been dealing with Mr King, offers to endorse this cheque.

**30.3** You work as a cashier at Cripplegate DIY store. Today is 30 March 1994, and you deal with a number of customers who wish to make payment using a cheque and a cheque card. What action would you take in the following circumstances?

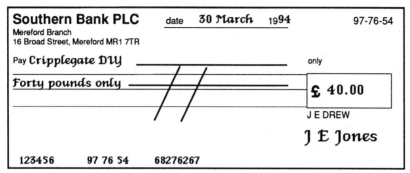

(a) Card limit £50, expiry 30 June1995, code 97-76-54. The name on the card is J E Drew. The lady explains that she has just got married, and Drew is her maiden name.

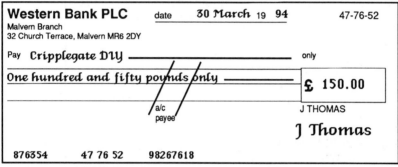

(b) Card limit £100, expiry 31 May 1994, code 47-76-52.

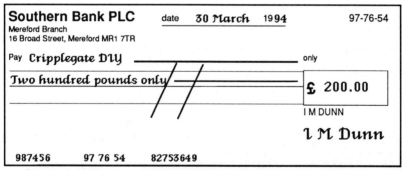

(c) Card limit £200, expiry 30 April 1995, code 97-76-54. The cheque has been made out and signed in advance. The cheque card is handed to you in a plastic wallet.

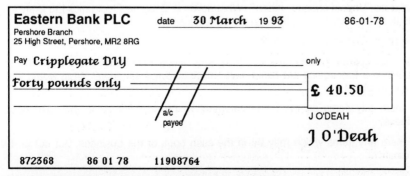

(d) Card limit £50, expiry 30 June 1995, code 86-01-78.

**30.4**   Make out the following paying-in slip and counterfoil for your own bank current account. (Assume that you bank at the Southern Bank, Carpminster branch, sort code no. 40-21-15; your account no. is 77078330). Use today's date. The items to be banked are:

|  |  |
|---|---|
| Cash | two £10 notes |
|  | two £5 notes |
|  | five £1 coins |
|  | six 50p coins |
| Cheques | £25.00 |
|  | £10.00 |

*Note:  assume the cheques have been listed and totalled on the reverse of the credit.*

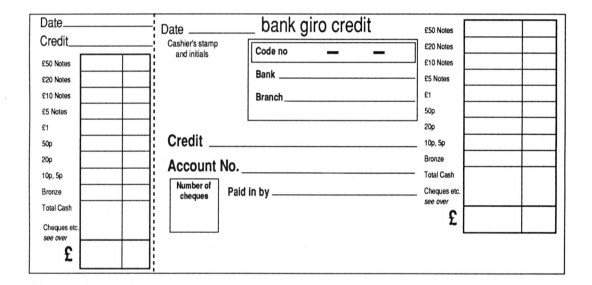

**30.5**   Look at the bank statement illustrated on page 325, and answer the following questions:

(a)   What does "Balance brought forward" mean?

(b)   What do the numbers following the description "Cheque" represent?

(c)   What does "Unpaid cheque" mean?  What action is Osborne Electronics Ltd likely to take as a result of this item passing through the bank account?

(d)   What does "CR" and "DR" mean?

(e)   What has happened to the balance of the bank account in October, and why?  Do you think that Osborne Electronics Ltd could have anticipated this situation? What would you advise them to do about it?

(f)   Are there any items on the bank statement which may not be in the cash book of the business?

(g)   Are there any items which may be in the cash book of the business, but not on the bank statement?

# 31 Making payments

## introduction

Businesses make payment in various forms:

- cash payments
- cheque payments
- bank giro payments
- bank computer payments (standing orders and direct debits)

Businesses make payment for many different purposes:

- paying suppliers
- buying large 'one-off' items such as machinery and equipment
- paying bills, eg electricity, business rates
- reimbursing employees for expenditure incurred
- paying wages and salaries to employees

In this chapter we will look at the *forms* and *purposes* of payment, and also examine the systems for *authorising* payment and the signing of cheques.

## paying trade suppliers by cheque

We have already seen in Chapter 29 that a supplier of goods and services is paid when the documents relating to the transaction have been checked and payment is authorised. If you are paying a supplier you should attach the cheque to a *remittance advice*. This may be a tear-off slip attached to the supplier's statement of account (see page 309), or it may be a standard form used within your organisation. An example of the latter, together with the cheque issued, is illustrated in fig. 31.1 on the next page. You should note that the following details are shown:

- the date of the payment
- the amount of the cheque
- the details – ie the reference number ('your ref') and date – of the invoice(s) being paid
- the amount of any cash discount deducted for early settlement (there is none in the illustration)

In addition the remittance advice may show further details such as the cheque number, the account number of the buyer's organisation, and the buyer's order number ('our ref'). The remittance advice may also show a *deduction* made from the payment for a credit note issued by the supplier. The details will be recorded on the remittance advice in the normal way, as for an invoice.

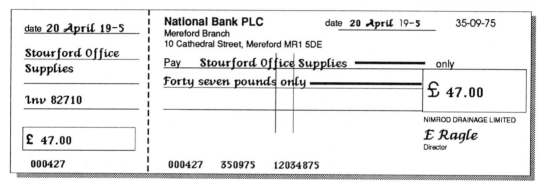

**REMITTANCE ADVICE**
**NIMROD DRAINAGE LIMITED**
UNIT 6 Riverside Industrial Park Mereford MR4 5TF
Tel 0605 675187 Fax 0605 415181 Vat Reg 63 6252 27

Stourford Office Supplies
Unit 12, Avon Industrial Estate
Stourford SF5 6TD

| Cheque No | 000427 |
| Date | 20 April 19-5 |
| Account | 9873 |

| date | our ref | your ref | amount | discount | payment |
|---|---|---|---|---|---|
| 18 02 -5 | 47621 | 82710 | 47.00 | 00.00 | 47.00 |

cheque value     £   47.00

date **20 April 19-5**

**Stourford Office Supplies**

**Inv 82710**

£ 47.00

000427

**National Bank PLC**
Mereford Branch
10 Cathedral Street, Mereford MR1 5DE

date **20 April 19-5**     35-09-75

Pay     **Stourford Office Supplies** ———————— only

**Forty seven pounds only** ————————

**£ 47.00**

NIMROD DRAINAGE LIMITED
**E Ragle**
Director

000427   350975   12034875

*Fig 31.1 Remittance advice and cheque with counterfoil*

## issuing cheques

Suppliers are normally paid monthly on the basis of the monthly statement issued rather than in response to individual invoices. A statement issued at, say, the end of March will show all the outstanding invoices; if an organisation normally pays invoices after *thirty* days, it will pay all the *February* invoices and any dated earlier than February on receipt of the statement. It will ignore any March invoices, which will be paid at the end of April. The person in a business preparing cheques and remittance advices will probably have a list of payments to make, with the payment amount already decided upon and authorised by a supervisor.

When writing (using ink, not pencil) or typing out the cheque you should take care to complete the
• date
• name of the payee (person receiving the money)
• amount in words
• amount in figures
• authorised signature (it may be your signature, it may be that of a more senior individual)
• counterfoil (date, amount, payee)

No room should be left for possible fraudulent additions or alterations; any blank spaces should be ruled through. If any errors are made when you are writing out the cheque, they should be corrected and an authorised signature placed close to the alteration in order to tell the bank that it is an approved correction. Large companies often, instead of writing out each cheque by hand, use cheque writing machines or computers. Clearly such a machine or computer needs to be kept under strict supervision.

## paying for 'one-off' items – cheque requisition forms

So far we have looked at the payment of trade suppliers who supply on a regular basis for the normal activities of an organisation, eg merchants who supply potatoes for crisps manufacturers. The procedure for the issue of cheques in this case is reasonably straightforward. There will be times, however, when a cheque is needed for a 'one-off' purpose, for example:

- purchase of an item of equipment, authorised by the organisation
- reimbursement of 'out-of-pocket' expenses incurred by an employee
- payment of a proforma invoice (a proforma invoice is a request for payment to be made *before* the supply of the goods or services – contrast this with a normal invoice when payment *follows* supply)

The normal procedure in these cases is the completion of a cheque requisition form by the person who needs the cheque. An example is illustrated below in fig. 31.2.

---

**Mercia Pumps Limited**
**CHEQUE REQUISITION FORM** ──────────────────

required by.......*Tom Paget*......................Dept...................*Marketing*......

CHEQUE DETAILS ──────────────────────

date.....*30 March 19–5*...........................................

payable to.....*Media Promotions Ltd*......................................

amount £......*45.00*...........................................

despatch to (if applicable).......*Media Promotions Ltd., 145 High Street,*
*Mereford, MR1 3TF*
...........................................

reason.....*Advert in business journal*.............nominal ledger.....*7556*......

DOCUMENTATION ──────────────────────

invoice attached/~~to follow~~.....*invoice 24516 dated 23 March 19–5*......

receipt attached/to follow...........................................

other...........................................

AUTHORISATION.....*Andrew Wimbush, Marketing Director*......................

---

*Fig. 31.2 Cheque requisition form*

*Note the following details:*
- the cheque has been ordered by Tom Paget, but is to be sent direct to Media Promotions Ltd
- the requisition is authorised by Andrew Wimbush, the Marketing Director
- the invoice is attached
- the nominal ledger code is included – this is the category of expense for which an account is maintained in the computer accounting system of the business – 7556 is the computer account number for advertising account; if the business did not have a computer accounting system the name of the nominal account – "advertising" – would be written here

# control and authorisation of payments

## spending limits

In order to avoid fraud or unchecked spending within an organisation, all payments must be controlled and authorised. We have seen that incoming invoices must normally be stamped, and signed or initialled by an authorised person before being passed for payment. This is part of an overall system whereby no payment can be made without the necessary authority. The system will vary from organisation to organisation, but the following elements will be usually be found:

- the larger the payment, the more senior the person who needs to give it authority; often each level of management has a money limit imposed – for example a new vehicle costing £25,000 will be authorised at senior management level, a supplier's invoice for £250 will be paid at supervisory level

- when an item of expenditure is authorised, the person giving the authority will sign or initial and date the supporting document, eg an invoice, a cheque requisition form

## cheque signatures

While an organisation will have an *internal* system of signing for and authorising expenditure, it will also have a written agreement with the bank – a *bank mandate* – which will set out who can sign cheques. A limited company or partnership may, for example, allow one director or partner to sign cheques up to £5,000, but will require two to sign cheques in excess of £5,000. It is common to have a number of different signatories to allow for partners and directors going on holiday, going sick and being otherwise unavailable for signing cheques.

# petty cash

## petty cash system

Petty cash is a cash 'float' used by a business to make small cash payments for expenses incurred, which do not warrant the issue of a cheque. Examples of the type of payments made from petty cash include:

- stationery items
- casual wages
- window cleaning
- bus, rail and taxi fares (incurred on behalf of the business)
- meals (incurred on behalf of the business)
- postages
- tips and donations

In order to operate a petty cash system, an appointed 'petty cashier' needs the following:

- a *petty cash book* in which to record transactions
- a lockable *petty cash box* in which to keep the money
- a stock of blank *petty cash vouchers* (see fig. 31.3 on the next page) for claims on petty cash to be made
- a *lockable desk drawer* in which to keep these items

The petty cashier, who is likely also to have other tasks within the organisation, is responsible for control of the petty cash, making cash payments when appropriate, keeping records of payments made, and keeping the petty cash book up-to-date.

## petty cash vouchers

Payments out of petty cash are made only against correct documentation – usually a petty cash voucher (see Fig. 31.3 below). Petty cash vouchers are completed as follows:

- details and amount of expenditure
- signature of the person making the claim and receiving the money
- signature of the person authorising the payment to be made
- additionally, most petty cash vouchers are numbered, so that they can be controlled, the number being entered in the petty cash book
- any relevant documentation, eg invoice or receipt, should be attached to the petty cash voucher

<table>
<tr><td colspan="3"></td><td>No <u>807</u></td><td></td></tr>
<tr><td colspan="5">Petty Cash Voucher</td></tr>
<tr><td colspan="3"></td><td>Date</td><td>11 May 19-1</td></tr>
<tr><td></td><td></td><td colspan="3">AMOUNT</td></tr>
<tr><td>For what required</td><td></td><td></td><td>£</td><td>p</td></tr>
<tr><td>Envelopes</td><td></td><td></td><td>1</td><td>55</td></tr>
<tr><td>10 Floppy disks</td><td></td><td></td><td>6</td><td>10</td></tr>
<tr><td></td><td></td><td></td><td>7</td><td>65</td></tr>
<tr><td>Signature</td><td colspan="4">T. Harris</td></tr>
<tr><td>Passed by</td><td colspan="4">D. Adams</td></tr>
</table>

*Fig. 31.3  An example of a petty cash voucher*

## procedure for obtaining petty cash - a typical transaction

*you are asked to purchase a business magazine for use in your office*

*you go to the local newsagent and buy the magazine; you make sure that you retain the receipt (for £3.50) which you hand to the petty cashier on your return to the office*

*a supervisor authorises a petty cash voucher which sets out details of the purchase*

*the petty cashier gives you £3.50 in cash*

*the petty cashier attaches the receipt to the petty cash voucher and enters the details in the petty cash book*

## petty cash and VAT

Value Added Tax is charged by VAT-registered businesses on the goods and services which they supply. Therefore, there will often be VAT included as part of the expense paid out of petty cash. However, not all expenses are subject to VAT, and if you are dealing with a petty cash voucher you will need to establish whether or not VAT is included in that item of expense. There are a number of possible situations:

*VAT has been charged*
- the expense item *includes* VAT at the standard rate, but it may not *show* the VAT amount

*VAT has not been charged*
- VAT has not been charged because the supplier is not VAT-registered
- the *zero* rate of VAT applies, eg food and drink (but not meals, which are standard-rated), books, newspapers, transport (but not taxis and hire cars)
- the supplies are *exempt* from VAT (eg financial services, postal services)

Often the indication of the supplier's VAT registration number on a receipt or invoice will tell you that VAT has been charged at the standard rate. Where VAT has been charged, the amount of tax might be indicated separately on the receipt or invoice. However, for small money amounts it is quite usual for a total to be shown *without* indicating the amount of VAT. To calculate the VAT amount, with VAT at a rate of 17½%, the full amount of the receipt or invoice is multiplied by 17.5 and divided by 117.5. For example:

| | |
|---|---|
| Amount of receipt | £4.70 |
| Therefore VAT is $17.5/117.5$ of £4.70 | = £0.70 |
| Amount, net of VAT | = £4.00 |

## bank giro credits

We have already seen in the last chapter how money can be paid into a bank account by means of a bank paying-in slip or *bank giro credit*.  So far we have looked at a business which pays in at its own branch, and receives the money on the account on the same day.  The banking system also allows for a *bank giro credit* – also known as a *credit transfer* – to be paid in at one branch and sent through a three day clearing system (like the cheque clearing system) to another bank or branch, sometimes by computer link.  This bank giro credit can, of course, be made out to a person or business other than the organisation making the payment.   This bank credit clearing system is used widely for

- paying wages
- paying bills (electricity, gas, telephone)

Clearly payment can be made either to one bank account (eg gas bill) or to a number of bank accounts (eg paying wages).

## procedure for paying by bank giro credit

You may well be familiar as a personal bank customer with paying a bill by bank giro credit;  the procedure for an business is exactly the same. The person or business making payment (or payments) prepares a cheque for the total amount to be paid (payment by cash would be very unusual for a business) and completes a bank giro credit, or a number of credits if more than one bank account is to receive payment.  If more than one credit is to be completed – for example if wages are being paid – it is usual to list and total the credits on a separate schedule for the benefit of the bank.

If you are using a *blank* giro credit (see fig. 31.4 below) the details that need to be completed are:
- the name of the bank where the beneficiary's account is held (the beneficiary is the person receiving the money)
- the bank, branch and sort code where the beneficiary's account is held. *Note:* the sort code is a system of numbering each bank branch  (the sort code of a bank branch appears in the top right hand corner of a cheque)
- the name and account number of the beneficiary
- the sender's name and reference
- the amount and date of the payment
- the counterfoil

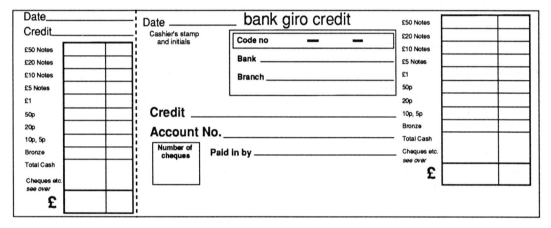

Fig. 31.4  *Bank giro credit to be completed by hand*

If you are using a *preprinted* bank giro credit (to pay a bill, for example), all you need to do is complete the amount, the date, and the name of the person paying the bill (see fig 31.5 below).

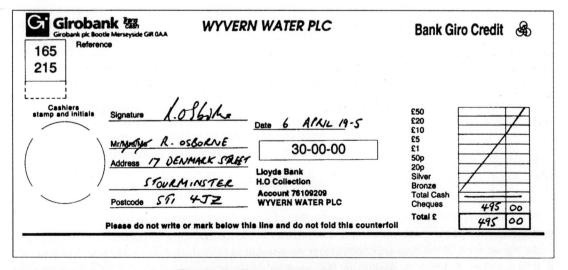

Fig. 31.5  *Preprinted bank giro credit*

# BACS: standing orders and direct debits

While bank giro credits are useful for making payments through the banking system for variable amounts, for example telephone bills, the procedure is time-consuming because you need to visit the bank each time. To avoid this problem the banks have established an interbank computer transfer system (also used by building societies) called BACS (Bankers Automated Clearing Services). With this system the transfer of money is made by computer link between banks and building societies. Payment can take a number of forms:

**standing order**
The bank customer who needs to make regular payments completes a written authority (a mandate) instructing the bank what payments to make, to whom, and when. The bank then sets up the instructions on its computer, and the payments are made automatically by computer link on the due dates. Standing orders are useful for businesses making regular fixed payments such hire purchase repayments and rental payments. Personal customers use them for making payments such as mortgage repayments.

**direct debit**
Whilst direct debits can be used for regular payments they differ from standing orders in two ways:

- direct debits can be used for either fixed and variable amounts and/or where the time intervals between payments vary
- it is the receiver (beneficiary) of the payment who prepares the computer instructions that request the payer's bank account for payment through the banking system – a direct debit may be seen as a standing order operating backwards

The direct debit system is useful for organisations such as insurance companies and credit card companies which receive a large number of variable payments. The normal procedure is for the customer making payment to complete and sign a written authority (mandate) prepared by the beneficiary (eg insurance company); this is then returned to the beneficiary, the payment details are given to the beneficiary's bank so that the computer instructions can be set up, and the original form returned to the payer's bank.

**'autopay' systems**
For customers who need to make regular payments of variable amounts (eg wages, payments to established suppliers) the banks have established a system whereby they set up standing orders to the regular beneficiaries. All the customer has to do each time payment is to be made is to complete and give to the bank a schedule setting out the date, beneficiaries and amounts. The bank will then input these details direct into its computer system, and payments will be made automatically via the BACS system.

For all BACS payments – standing orders, direct debits and autopay – the bank needs a signed authorisation form (a mandate) from the customer before the amounts can be deducted from the account. The details needed by the bank – some of which may be preprinted – are:

- the name of organisation or person which is to receive the money, eg insurance company, hire purchase company, etc
- the details of recipient's bank, ie bank, branch, sort code number, and bank account number
- the reference number to be quoted
- the amount (unless it is not fixed, as in the case of some direct debits and autopay)
- the frequency of payment (unless it is not fixed, as in the case of some direct debits and autopay)
- the signature(s) of the customer authorising the amount to be deducted from the bank account

If it is a business which is setting up the standing order or direct debit, it is important that the mandate form is signed by a person authorised to do so – it will often be the person(s) authorised to sign cheques. See the next page for examples of a standing order and a direct debit mandate.

**STANDING ORDER MANDATE** ───────────────

TO _____ BANK

ADDRESS _____

**PLEASE PAY TO**
BANK _____ BRANCH _____ SORT CODE [ ][ ][ ]

BENEFICIARY _____ ACCOUNT NUMBER [_____]

THE SUM OF £[_____] AMOUNTS IN WORDS _____

_____

DATE OF FIRST PAYMENT _____ FREQUENCY OF PAYMENT _____

UNTIL _____ REFERENCE _____

ACCOUNT TO BE DEBITED [_____] NUMBER [_____]

SPECIAL INSTRUCTIONS _____

SIGNATURE(S)..............................................................DATE..................

..........................................................................

*Fig. 31.6  Bank standing order mandate*

───────────── **direct debit instruction** ─────────────

**Tradesure Insurance Company**
PO Box 134, Helliford, HL9 6TY

Originator's Identification Number 914208

Reference (to be completed by Tradesure Insurance)...........................................

*Please complete the details and return this form to Tradesure Insurance*

name and address of bank/building society

instructions to bank/building society

- I instruct you to pay direct debits from my account at the request of Tradesure Insurance Company
- The amounts are variable and may be debited on various dates
- I understand that Tradesure Insurance Company may change the amounts and dates only after giving me prior notice
- I will inform the bank/building society if I wish to cancel this instruction
- I understand that if any direct debit is paid which breaks the terms of this instruction, the bank/building society will make a refund.

account name

account number        sort code                signature(s)                date

*Fig. 31.7  Direct debit mandate*

# payslip

It is a legal requirement for an employer to provide each of its employees with a written payslip. If you have been in a job you will know that you will be given a payslip showing:
* *gross pay* (pay before deductions) plus any overtime, bonus or commission
* *deductions* in the form of
    - Income Tax (a tax to fund Government spending)
    - National Insurance Contributions (money paid to the State to fund pensions and State benefits)
    - pensions payments (if you contribute to a pension scheme)
    - payments to charity
* *tax code* – a three digit number followed by a letter which indicates your level of personal allowance – ie the amount you can earn which is not liable to tax (see the explanatory note below)
* *net pay* – the amount you will receive
* *the method of payment* – whether by cash or to a bank account

We will now explain some of these terms in more detail.

## income tax

*Income tax is a tax on income received by an individual.*

'Income' for tax purposes includes pay, tips, bonuses, and benefits in kind (eg company car, cheap loans), pensions, most State benefits, and interest and dividends from investments. If you are in employment the Income Tax on your pay, together with National Insurance Contributions, is deducted by the employer from your gross pay by means of a scheme known as PAYE (Pay As You Earn). This scheme, as its title suggests, enables you to spread out your taxation evenly over the year instead of having to pay it in one amount.

## taxable income:  the Personal Allowance

*Income which is liable to tax is known as taxable income.*

*Taxable income is calculated by deducting the personal allowance from gross income.*

You do not, fortunately, have to pay tax on all your income. In order to help the lower paid, the Government gives to all wage earners a *Personal Allowance*, an amount which you can earn during the tax year (6 April – 5 April), on which no tax is paid at all. The personal allowance, which is set by the Chancellor of the Exchequer in the Budget, is normally increased in line with inflation, and is fixed for each tax year. The amount of the personal allowance varies, depending on factors such as whether you are single or married, or over a certain age. The allowance may be increased for specified expenses incurred in employment, eg work clothing, and subscriptions to professional bodies.

## calculation of the tax code

How does the employer know what allowances have been given to the employee and how much tax to deduct under the PAYE scheme?  The Inland Revenue gives each employee a *tax code,* a number which is used by the employer to calculate the taxable pay. The tax code incorporates *all* the tax allowances, including the personal allowance. The code itself is a three digit number. The Inland Revenue totals up the allowances, and then removes the *last* digit to produce the tax code. It also then adds a letter to the code. Common letters include L (the single person's allowance) and H (the married person's allowance).

## payroll processing

Employers may pay wages:
* direct to the employee in the form of cash or by cheque
* direct to the employee's bank or building society account by means of bank giro credits or BACS

Many businesses now use computer payroll packages to calculate wages, produce payslips, and in some cases to send payments through the BACS payment system.

# Case Study – the payslip

Dora Penny is a senior accounts clerk who is starting work for the first time in the Treasurer's Department of the Local Authority. She is employed full-time by the Local Authority and will receive her salary direct into her bank account from Wyvern County Council. Her personal situation is as follows:

- her annual gross salary is £14,400
- she receives a personal allowance of £3,445
- National Insurance is paid at the not contracted-out rate
- 6% of her gross salary is paid into a pension scheme
- she pays £40 subscription to her professional association each year (direct from her bank account)

Illustrated below is the payslip she received in her second month at work.

| *WCC* **Wyvern County Council** | | **Pay Statement** May 1993 | |
|---|---|---|---|
| | **£** | | **£** |
| **Pay** | 1200.00 | **Tax (Code 348L)** | 216.09 |
| **Overtime** | 0.00 | **N.I. Non-Contr Out** | 91.08 |
| | | **Superannuation** | 72.00 |
| **TOTAL GROSS PAY** | 1200.00 | | |
| | | **TOTAL DEDUCTIONS** | 379.17 |
| | | **NET PAY** | 820.83 |
| **CUMULATIVES** | | **EMPLOYEE DETAILS** | |
| **Taxable earnings to date** | 1818.50 | | |
| **Tax to date** | 433.66 | Miss D Penny | |
| **NI to date** | 182.16 | Staff No 0178653425 | |
| **Superannuation to date** | 144.00 | NI No YT 77 77 01 A | |
| | | Tax Ref 792/W1 | |
| **NET PAY TO DATE** | 1640.18 | Payment via BACS | |

*Note the following details:*

- the Net Pay box on the right shows the amount received by Dora Penny in May
- the left hand side of the payslip (upper half) shows the gross amount earned in May
- the right hand side of the payslip (upper half) shows the income tax and National Insurance Contributions for May
- the superannuation payment is 6% of Dora's gross salary
- the tax code shown (348L) is calculated by the Inland revenue as follows:

| | |
|---|---|
| personal allowance | £3,445 |
| professional subscription | £40 |
| total allowances | £3,485 |

- the final digit of 3485 is removed and the letter 'L' added to give a code of 348L
- the 'cumulatives' section sets out for Dora the running totals of taxable earnings and deductions in the current tax year
- Dora's staff number, National Insurance number and reference number from the local tax office and means of payment are shown in the Employee Details section
- figures for Income Tax and National Insurance are produced by a computer payroll package

# chapter summary

❑ Businesses make payments in a variety of different ways, depending on the circumstances involved.

❑ Suppliers are generally paid by cheque accompanied by a remittance advice after the buyer has received a monthly statement.

❑ Cheques for 'one-off' items are usually issued when a cheque requisition form has been completed and authorised.

❑ Employees making small cash purchases and payments may reclaim their out-of-pocket expenses after completion and authorisation of a petty cash voucher.

❑ Businesses making payments direct to the bank account of the beneficiary may do so
   • by completing a bank giro credit manually
   • by setting up a standing order or completing a direct debit, which will allow the payments to be processed by the BACS computer payment system.

❑ Businesses pay wages to their employees, setting out all the details of the payments and deductions on a payslip issued to each employee.

 **student activities**

**31.1**   You work in the Accounts Department of Nimrod Drainage Limited.  Part of your day's work is the preparation of remittance advices and cheques for payments to suppliers.  You are not required to sign the cheques.  On 5 April 19-9  you are handed three payments to prepare:

**(a)**   Statement from Mereford Cleaning Services, 78 Friary Park, Mereford MR4 3BJ, with a note from your Supervisor indicating the following invoices to be paid:
Invoice 1982 dated 15 February 19-9, your order number 5541, for £243.50
Invoice 2019 dated 17 March 19-9, your order number 5783, for £1,245.60

There is no cash discount.  Complete the remittance advice and cheque set out below.

**REMITTANCE ADVICE**
**NIMROD DRAINAGE LIMITED**
UNIT 6 Riverside Industrial Park Mereford MR4 5TF
Tel 0605 675187 Fax 0605 415181 Vat Reg 63 6252 27

|  |  | Cheque No |
|  |  | Date |
|  |  | Account |

| date | our ref | your ref | amount | discount | payment |
|---|---|---|---|---|---|
|  |  |  |  |  |  |
|  |  |  |  |  |  |
|  |  |  |  |  |  |

| | cheque value | £ |

date _____

_____

_____

£ _____

000450

**National Bank PLC**
Mereford Branch
10 Cathedral Street, Mereford MR1 5DE

date _____ 19 _____         35-09-75

Pay _____ only

_____

£

NIMROD DRAINAGE LIMITED

Director

000450   350975   12034875

---

**(b)** Statement from Mercia Wholesalers, Unit 12 Riverside Industrial Park, Mereford MR2 7GH, with a note from your Supervisor indicating the following invoices to be paid, and a credit note to be set off against payment:

Invoice 8765 dated 12 February 19-9, your order number 5517, for £765.25
Invoice 8823 dated 19 March 19-9, your order number 5792, for £3,567.80
Credit note CN3420 dated 25 March 19-9 (your ref R/N 5168), for £250.00

There is no cash discount. Complete the remittance advice and cheque set out below. Note that the total of the credit note should be shown in the money column *in brackets*, indicating that it is a deduction from the payment. You are not required to sign the cheque.

### REMITTANCE ADVICE
**NIMROD DRAINAGE LIMITED**
UNIT 6 Riverside Industrial Park Mereford MR4 5TF
Tel 0605 675187 Fax 0605 415181 Vat Reg 63 6252 27

Cheque No
Date
Account

| date | our ref | your ref | amount | discount | payment |
|------|---------|----------|--------|----------|---------|
|      |         |          |        |          |         |
|      |         |          |        |          |         |
|      |         |          |        |          |         |

cheque value   £

---

date _____

_____

_____

£ _____

000451

**National Bank PLC**
Mereford Branch
10 Cathedral Street, Mereford MR1 5DE

date _____ 19 _____         35-09-75

Pay _____ only

_____

£

NIMROD DRAINAGE LIMITED

Director

000451   350975   12034875

**31.2** You work in the Accounts Department of Nimrod Drainage Limited. It is 5 April 19-5. Your supervisor, Ivor Cash, hands you an invoice and asks you to prepare a cheque requisition form for the purchase of a computer, for which the company has to pay immediately. The details are :

Cheque amount £4,545.50, payee Wyvern Micros Limited on their invoice 626 dated 1 April 19-9. Reason: purchase of Intertel PC6000 workstation. Nominal account to be debited 7600.

As the amount is a large one, Ivor asks you to prepare the requisition in his name, and to send it with a covering memorandum to John Flint, Finance Director, for authorisation. The requisition should be returned to Ivor who will then process and despatch the cheque.

---

**Nimrod Drainage Limited**
**CHEQUE REQUISITION FORM** ━━━━━━━━━━━━━━━━━━━━━

required by...................................................................Dept....................................

CHEQUE DETAILS ━━━━━━━━━━━━━━━━━━━━━━━━━━━━━━━━━━━

date........................................................................................................

payable to................................................................................................

amount £..................................................................................................

despatch to (if applicable)............................................................................

...............................................................................................................

reason.....................................................................nominal ledger.....................

DOCUMENTATION ━━━━━━━━━━━━━━━━━━━━━━━━━━━━━━━━━

invoice attached/to follow..............................................................................

receipt attached/to follow..............................................................................

other.......................................................................................................

AUTHORISATION............................................................................................

---

**31.3** *Note: for this exercise you will need to obtain some blank petty cash vouchers from your teacher or lecturer, or a commercial stationer, or you may design your own.*

You work in the Accounts Department of Enigma Promotions Limited, where you are in charge of petty cash, and are allowed to authorise and sign the petty cash vouchers. It is 5 April 19-5. A number of staff members bring in receipts and ask for reimbursement.

(a) Derek Heffer has bought a jar of coffee for the staff rest room – receipt for £4.50 (no VAT shown)

(b) Jim Taylor has bought stamps at the Post Office – receipt for £15.00 (no VAT shown)

(c) Donna Everard has bought a box of envelopes – receipt for £4.70 (including 70p VAT)

(d) Tom Greenaway has bought two reams of coloured photocopy paper – receipt for £7.05 (no VAT shown)

You are to make out petty cash vouchers for these four transactions, making a note on the voucher of any VAT involved, in which case the amount charged before VAT should also be shown.

**31.4**   You work in the Accounts Department of Nimrod Drainage Limited. The date is 5 April 19-5. Your supervisor, Ivor Cash, has received a memorandum from the Personnel Department stating that a new member of staff requires a refund for incidental expenses to be made direct to her bank account. The authorisation is in order, and the details are as follows:

| | |
|---|---|
| Beneficiary | J Patel |
| Bank | Midland Bank, Stourford Branch, sort code 40 99 87, account 87875231 |
| Payment | cheque |
| Amount | £78.50 |

You are to complete the bank giro credit shown below.

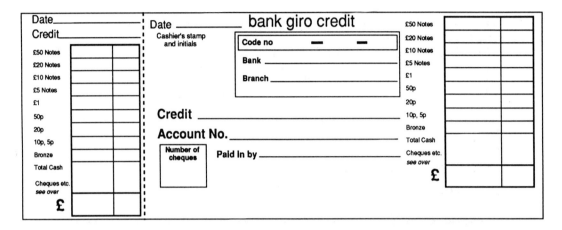

**31.5**   You work in the Accounts Department of Nimrod Drainage Limited. You work at a clerical grade and cannot sign cheques or other payment instructions. The date is 5 April 19-5. Your supervisor, Ivor Cash, hands you the two documents set out on the next page:

- a blank standing order form provided by the bank
- a direct debit instruction received from Tradesure Insurance Company

He is in rather a rush and asks you to process the two documents, and to return them to the appropriate address with a compliments slip. He also leaves you a piece of paper with written instructions:

> *Hire Purchase Payments*
> *12 monthly instalments of £350 to Broadbent Finance from 1 May 19-5, under reference BE/6637.*
> *Bank details Barclays, Eveshore, 30 98 15, Account 72627161.*
> *Debit our Account 12034875*

You are to
(a)   complete the forms as required (look at a Nimrod Drainage cheque for your banking details)
(b)   state to which address you will send them
(c)   comment on any other procedure which you may have to carry out before sending off the forms

**31.6**   You are asked by your Personnel Department to draft an A5 leaflet (A4 folded in half) to be given to new members of staff joining the company direct from school or college. The leaflet is to explain the payslip they will receive from their employer. The leaflet should be illustrated with a sample payslip and should set out clearly what the individual items on the payslip signify. If you have a Desk Top Publishing (DTP) program within your school or college, you should use it if possible.

## STANDING ORDER MANDATE ━━━━━━━━━━━━━━━

TO _____ BANK

ADDRESS _____

**PLEASE PAY TO**

BANK _____ BRANCH _____ SORT CODE [ ][ ][ ]

BENEFICIARY _____ ACCOUNT NUMBER [ ]

THE SUM OF [£ ] AMOUNTS IN WORDS _____

_____

DATE OF FIRST PAYMENT _____ FREQUENCY OF PAYMENT _____

UNTIL _____ REFERENCE _____

ACCOUNT TO BE DEBITED [ ] NUMBER [ ]

SPECIAL INSTRUCTIONS _____

SIGNATURE(S)...................................................................DATE...................

...................................................................

---

## ━━━━━━━━ direct debit instruction ━━━━━━━━

### Tradesure Insurance Company
PO Box 134, Helliford, HL9 6TY

Originator's Identification Number  914208

Reference (to be completed by Tradesure Insurance)......................................................

*Please complete the details <u>and return this form to Tradesure Insurance</u>*

name and address of bank/building society | instructions to bank/building society

- I instruct you to pay direct debits from my account at the request of Tradesure Insurance Company
- The amounts are variable and may be debited on various dates
- I understand that Tradesure Insurance Company may change the amounts and dates only after giving me prior notice
- I will inform the bank/building society if I wish to cancel this instruction
- I understand that if any direct debit is paid which breaks the terms of this instruction, the bank/building society will make a refund.

account name

account number | sort code | signature(s) | date

# Explaining the financial transactions and documents

| Element 6.1 | Explain financial transactions and supporting documents. |
|---|---|

Suggested Sources:
- work experience – examing the financial records and documents used by a business (with permission from the business)
- talks by accounts staff from a business, or interviews with them
- practical observation as a customer of a business and in shops
- textbooks in libraries and resource centres

## TASK 1
What documents will be used in the processes listed below? In each case give a brief description of the document(s) and their purpose.
(a) a business orders goods from another business
(b) the warehouse assistant of a business accepts a delivery of goods
(c) the seller of goods sold on credit asks for payment for the goods
(d) the seller of goods sold on credit gives a refund for faulty goods
(e) a business makes a payment through the post in settlement for goods purchased on credit
(f) a business makes regular payments direct to the bank account of a local authority for business rates
(g) a business pays wages direct to its employees' bank and building society accounts
(h) a business pays in money over the counter at the bank
(i) a customer buys goods from a business over the counter, and pays using cash

## TASK 2
Outline for a new member of staff joining an Accounts Department the documents that will be used when ordering goods on credit. Illustrate your explanation with a diagram of the' flow' of documents between buyer and seller.

## TASK 3
What procedures would you follow in the situations listed below, and what documents would you use? In each case ensure that you explain any security and authorisation procedures that may be involved in the process.
(a) obtaining a cheque within a business for a large purchase, eg a photocopier costing £1,800
(b) reimbursing a member of staff for a small cash purchase for a business, eg £5 spent on postage stamps
(c) checking that the items on a statement received from a supplier can be paid
(d) ordering a consignment of goods from a supplier

## TASK 4

Set out below are the final accounts – the profit statement and balance sheet – of a small printing business owned by John Brown.  Look at the figures, and then answer the questions underneath.

---

**PROFIT STATEMENT OF JOHN BROWN  FOR THE YEAR ENDED 30 JUNE 19-1**

|  | £ |
|---|---|
| Sales | 100,000 |
| *less* purchases of goods (cost of sales) | 50,000 |
|  | 50,000 |
|  |  |
| *less* expenses | 25,000 |
| **Net profit** | 25,000 |

---

**BALANCE SHEET OF JOHN BROWN AS AT 30 JUNE 19-1**

| Fixed Assets | £ | £ |
|---|---|---|
| Premises |  | 200,000 |
| Machinery |  | 50,000 |
|  |  | 250,000 |
| **Current Assets** |  |  |
| Stock | 10,000 |  |
| Debtors | 25,000 |  |
| Bank | 5,000 |  |
|  | 40,000 |  |
| *less* **Current Liabilities** |  |  |
| Creditors | 20,000 |  |
|  |  | 20,000 |
| **NET ASSETS** |  | 270,000 |
| FINANCED BY |  |  |
| **CAPITAL** |  | 270,000 |

---

State the figures from these final accounts for:

(a)   sales for the year
(b)   purchases for the year
(c)   expenses incurred during the year
(d)   profit due to John Brown
(e)   the amount the business owes to its suppliers
(f)   the amount the business is owed by its customers
(g)   John Brown's capital
(h)   how much money the business has in its bank account

In your answers for (a), (b), (c), (e), (f), (h), state what *documents* will have *originally* been used to provide the figures for entering the transactions into the accounting system of the business.

## TASK 5

Outline the stages involved in the accounting process from the original documents to the final accounts set out above.

## TASK 6

What other parties, apart from the owner, may be interested in the final accounts, and why?

## EVIDENCE COLLECTION EXERCISE

# 17

# *Completing business documents*

| | |
|---|---|
| **Element 6.2** | *Complete documents for financial transactions* |
| Suggested Sources: | • work experience – examing the documents used by a business (with permission from the business) |
| | • talks by accounts staff from a business, or interviews with them |
| | • local banks |
| | • textbooks in libraries and resource centres |

## TASK 1

You work for Stourford Office Supplies, and on 15 March 19-5 receive a purchase order from Osborne Micros Limited for 100 computer printer ribbons. The purchase order is illustrated below.

---

### PURCHASE ORDER
### OSBORNE MICROS LIMITED
Unit 1B, Severnside Industrial Estate
Mereford MR1 2TR
Tel 0906 226576 Fax 0906 226342

| Stourford Office Supplies<br>Unit 12<br>Avon Industrial Estate<br>Stourford SF5 6TD | No       6372<br>Date    13 March 19-5<br>Delivery  to above address |
|---|---|

| catalogue | quantity | description | price |
|---|---|---|---|
| 726261 | 100 | OKISONIC Macroline 276<br>computer printer ribbon | £4.50 each<br>(less our<br>usual 10%<br>discount) |

**authorised**    signature...Richard J Osborne..............    date.13 March 19-5.........

---

You are to complete on 15 March 19-5 the invoice and delivery note set out on the next page:

- *delivery note:* number 26755, delivery method Parceline
- *invoice:* number 652772, account OSB 002, catalogue price £4.50, customer discount 10%, VAT at the current rate

## DELIVERY NOTE

### Stourford Office Supplies
Unit 12, Avon Industrial Estate, Stourford SF5 6TD
Tel 0807 765434 Fax 0807 765123

Delivery Note No
Date
Your Order No
Delivery

| product code | quantity | description |
|---|---|---|
| | | |
| | | |

*received*

signature...................................................name (capitals)..............................................

date...........................................

## INVOICE

### Stourford Office Supplies
Unit 12, Avon Industrial Estate, Stourford SF5 6TD
Tel 0807 765434 Fax 0807 765123
VAT Reg 0745 4672 76

invoice to

Invoice No
Account
Date/tax point
Your Reference

| product code | description | quantity | price | unit | total | disc % | net |
|---|---|---|---|---|---|---|---|
| | | | | | | | |
| | | | | | | | |
| | | | | | | | |

**Terms**
Net monthly
Carriage paid
E & OE

| | |
|---|---|
| GOODS TOTAL | |
| CASH DISCOUNT | |
| SUBTOTAL | |
| VAT | |
| TOTAL | |

On 22 March 19-5 you receive a telephone call from Osborne Micros Limited pointing out that ten of the ribbons supplied on invoice 652772 are faulty. You reply that you will issue them with an adjusting credit note.

You are to complete the credit note set out below. The details are:

- credit note number 2167
- date 22 March 19-5
- customer discount and VAT rate as on the invoice

---

## CREDIT NOTE

### Stourford Office Supplies
Unit 12, Avon Industrial Estate, Stourford SF5 6TD
Tel 0807 765434 Fax 0807 765123
VAT Reg 0745 4672 76

to

Credit Note No
Account
Date/tax point
Your Reference
Our invoice

| product code | description | quantity | price | unit | total | disc % | net |
|---|---|---|---|---|---|---|---|
| | | | | | | | |
| | | | | | | | |

**Reason for credit**

| | |
|---|---|
| GOODS TOTAL | |
| CASH DISCOUNT | |
| SUBTOTAL | |
| VAT | |
| TOTAL | |

---

On 30 April 19-5 you are preparing statements to send to all your customers to show the balance outstanding on each account at 31 March.

You are to prepare the statement for Osborne Micros Limited using the document set out on the next page.

*Note that in addition to the invoice and credit note already completed:*

- an invoice 652213 for £450.00 was issued on 20 January
- a cheque for £450.00 was received on 12 March (cheque number 228181) in settlement of invoice 652213
- no further payments were received during March or April
- invoice 652801 for £456.75 was issued on 14 April

**statement** ──────────────────── | **remittance advice**

**Stourford Office Supplies**
Unit 12, Avon Industrial Estate, Stourford SF5 6TD
Tel 0807 765434 Fax 0807 765123
VAT Reg 0745 4672 76

| **Stourford Office Supplies**
| Unit 12, Avon Industrial
| Estate, Stourford SF5 6TD

| Account        Date | | **Account** |
| --- | --- | --- |
| | | *please indicate items you are paying (✔) and return this advice with your remittance* |

| date | type | reference | value | outstanding | ref | outstanding | ✔ |
| --- | --- | --- | --- | --- | --- | --- | --- |
| | | | | | | | |
| | | | TOTAL | | TOTAL | | |

## TASK 2

You now put yourself in the position of the employee of Osborne Micros Limited who will be dealing with the transaction in Task 1 above.   You are to complete:

(a)   the goods received note set out on the next page, the details being

   • goods received note number 72837, date 22 March 19-5

   • carrier Parceline, consignment 298298

   • goods in good condition (no damages or shortages), Accounts Department copy

(b)   the remittance advice on the statement illustrated above (assuming that you only pay items which have been outstanding for more than 30 days)

(c)   the cheque set out below with the appropriate amount payable and dated 5 May 19-5

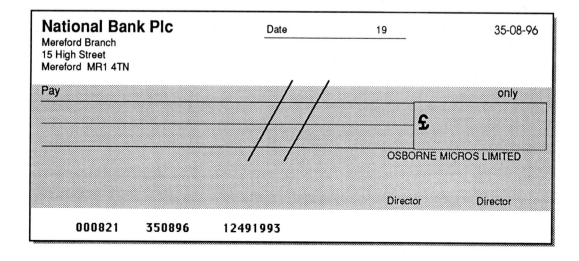

**National Bank Plc**
Mereford Branch
15 High Street
Mereford  MR1 4TN

Date                19                    35-08-96

Pay                                                                    only

£

OSBORNE MICROS LIMITED

Director        Director

000821      350896      12491993

# GOODS RECEIVED NOTE
## OSBORNE MICROS LIMITED

**Supplier**

GRN No.
Date

| quantity | description | order number |
|----------|-------------|--------------|
|          |             |              |

**carrier**          consignment ref.

**received by**          checked by

**condition of goods**    good condition        **copies to**
                       damaged                 Purchasing
                       shortages               Accounts
                                                  Stockroom

## TASK 3

It is obviously important that documents should be completed accurately and correctly. The situations set out below are examples of things that can go wrong. Read through the six situations and then in each case:

- identify the problems that have arisen
- suggest practical solutions which could be adopted by the business concerned
- state what might happen if the problem is not dealt with

(a) a business selling goods receives a purchase order where the catalogue number quoted and the description of the goods ordered do not tally

(b) an invoice is received from a supplier and the addition is incorrect – as a result you have been overcharged

(c) a business receives a statement of account (from a supplier) which does not show a cheque which you have sent to the supplier; you telephone your bank and are told that the cheque has been paid in and deducted from your bank account

(d) the person checking the delivery note against a consignment of goods fails to record a shortage (ie not enough goods sent) in a delivery received from a supplier

(e) you receive a cheque from a customer; the cheque has not been signed

(f) you receive a cheque from a customer; the cheque is not dated at all

# 32 Recording purchases and sales – day books

## introduction

In Chapter 29 we have seen how documents are used by organisations for the purchase and sale of goods. These documents are then used as a means of recording transactions in the accounting system.

The two most common types of accounting transactions recorded are:
* *the purchase of goods* with the intention that they should be resold at a profit, eg a plumbers' merchant buying bath taps from the manufacturer
* the *sale of goods* in which the business trades, eg a plumbers' merchant selling bath taps to plumbers and other customers

In this chapter we will examine how these transactions are recorded in the accounting system of the business in *day books*. As these books are the first books in which the transactions are recorded, they are also known as *books of prime entry* or *books of original entry*.

## purchases day book

The purchases day book is a collection point for accounting information on the credit purchases of a business and it takes the following form (with sample entries shown):

**Purchases Day Book**

| Date | Details | Invoice No | Folio | Net | VAT* | Gross |
|------|---------|-----------|-------|-----|------|-------|
| 19-1 | | | | £ | £ | £ |
| 2 Jan. | P Bond Ltd | 1234 | PL 125 | 80.00 | 14.00 | 94.00 |
| 11 Jan. | D Webster | A373 | PL 730 | 120.00 | 21.00 | 141.00 |
| 16 Jan. | P Bond Ltd | 1247 | PL 125 | 40.00 | 7.00 | 47.00 |
| 20 Jan. | Sanders & Sons | 5691 | PL 495 | 160.00 | 28.00 | 188.00 |
| | | | | | | |
| 31 Jan. | Totals for month | | | 400.00 | 70.00 | 470.00 |

* VAT = 17½ per cent

*Notes:*

• The purchases day book is prepared from invoices received from suppliers.

• It is totalled at intervals – daily, weekly or monthly, to suit the needs of the business – and the total (of the *net* column) will tell the business the amount of purchases for the period.

• The *gross* column records the full amount of each invoice, ie after VAT has been included.

• We will see in Chapter 33 how the amounts from the day book are recorded in the business' book-keeping system.

• The *folio* column is used for cross-referencing transactions to the book-keeping system: it will be explained in Chapter 33.

## sales day book

The sales day book works in the same way as the purchases day book but, as its name suggests, it lists the sales made by a business. In its simplest form the total sales recorded by a shop till for the day, week or month acts as a sales day 'book'. For a business that sells on credit terms, with the issue of an invoice for each transaction, the sales day book, which is prepared from the invoices, takes the following form (with sample entries shown):

**Sales Day Book**

| Date | Details | Invoice No | Folio | Net | VAT | Gross |
|------|---------|-----------|-------|-----|-----|-------|
| 19-1 | | | | £ | £ | £ |
| 3 Jan. | Doyle & Co Ltd | 901 | SL 58 | 120.00 | 21.00 | 141.00 |
| 8 Jan. | Sparkes & Sons Ltd | 902 | SL 127 | 160.00 | 28.00 | 188.00 |
| 12 Jan. | T Young | 903 | SL 179 | 80.00 | 14.00 | 94.00 |
| 15 Jan. | A-Z Supplies Ltd | 904 | SL 3 | 200.00 | 35.00 | 235.00 |
| 18 Jan. | Sparkes & Sons | 905 | SL 127 | 120.00 | 21.00 | 141.00 |
| 31 Jan. | Totals for month | | | 680.00 | 119.00 | 799.00 |

*Notes:*

• The sales day book is prepared from invoices issued to customers.

• The total of the net column of the day book tells the business the amount of sales for the period.

• The gross column includes VAT.

• In Chapter 33 we will see how the amounts from the day book are recorded in the book-keeping system; the use of the folio column will also be explained.

## Case Study: Mr I Lewis

### Situation

Mr I Lewis runs an engineering business, which is registered for VAT. All his purchases and sales are on credit terms. He employs a clerk on a part-time basis to keep his accounting data up-to-date. Unfortunately the clerk was taken ill last week and Mr Lewis, knowing nothing about finance, asks if you can help. On investigation you find an 'in-tray' with last week's invoices received from suppliers of goods, together with copies of invoices sent out to customers by Mr Lewis' typist. The list is as follows:

19-1

8 Dec.  Invoice no 1234 received from MPF Metals for £108.75 + VAT* of £19.03

8 Dec.  Invoice no A 340 sent to Johnson Bros for £220.00 + VAT of £38.50

9 Dec.  Invoice no X 678 received from A Osborne for £85.50 +VAT of £14.96

9 Dec.  Invoice no A 341 sent to McGee's Metals for £180.25 + VAT of £31.54

10 Dec.  Invoice no A 342 sent to Wilson Trading Co for £112.40 + VAT of £19.67

10 Dec.  Invoice no P 41 received from Murray Ltd for £115.00 + VAT of £20.12

11 Dec.  Invoice no 1256 received from MPF Metals for £111.50 + VAT of £19.51

12 Dec.  Invoice no A 343 sent to Johnson Bros for £121.00 + VAT of £21.17

* VAT = 17½ per cent (note that fractions of a penny are ignored, ie VAT is rounded down to the nearest penny)

You are asked to enter these transactions in the appropriate day books (leave the folio column blank).

## Solution

**Purchases Day Book**

| Date | Details | Invoice No | Folio | Net | VAT | Gross |
|------|---------|-----------|-------|-----|-----|-------|
| 19-1 | | | | £ | £ | £ |
| 8 Dec. | MPF Metals Ltd | 1234 | | 108.75 | 19.03 | 127.78 |
| 9 Dec. | A Osborne | X678 | | 85.50 | 14.96 | 100.46 |
| 10 Dec. | Murray Ltd | P41 | | 115.00 | 20.12 | 135.12 |
| 11 Dec. | MFP Metals Ltd | 1256 | | 111.50 | 19.51 | 131.01 |
| 12 Dec. | Totals for week | | | 420.75 | 73.62 | 494.37 |

**Sales Day Book**

| Date | Details | Invoice No | Folio | Net | VAT | Gross |
|------|---------|-----------|-------|-----|-----|-------|
| 19-1 | | | | £ | £ | £ |
| 8 Dec. | Johnson Bros Ltd | A340 | | 220.00 | 38.50 | 258.50 |
| 9 Dec. | McGee's Metals | A341 | | 180.25 | 31.54 | 211.79 |
| 10 Dec. | Wilson Trading Co Ltd | A342 | | 112.40 | 19.67 | 132.07 |
| 12 Dec. | Johnson Bros Ltd | A343 | | 121.00 | 21.17 | 142.17 |
| 12 Dec. | Totals for week | | | 633.65 | 110.88 | 744.53 |

## day books and Value Added Tax

Many businesses and other organisations are registered for Value Added Tax (VAT). This means that:

- VAT is charged on invoices issued to customers
- VAT charged on invoices received from VAT-registered suppliers can be either reclaimed from HM Customs and Excise (the VAT authority), or set off against VAT charged on invoices issued

When writing up day books you should always check to see if VAT should be charged on invoices issued to suppliers, or has been charged on invoices received from suppliers; if so, the amount is entered in the VAT column of the day book, with the total amount of the invoice in the gross column, and the amount of the invoice before VAT in the net column.

When a business is not registered for VAT, it cannot charge VAT on invoices issued and it cannot reclaim VAT charged on invoices received from suppliers. In such circumstances the total amount of the invoice is recorded in both the net and gross columns; a dash may be inserted in the VAT column. In Chapter 33 we shall see how the VAT columns from the day books are entered into the book-keeping system.

## returns day books

Whenever goods are bought and sold there are, inevitably, a number of occasions when they have to be returned. It might be that the wrong goods have been supplied, the wrong size or colour, or perhaps the goods are faulty. There are two aspects of returned goods to consider:

- *purchases returns* (also known as returns outwards) – goods which have been bought by the business are returned *by* the business to the supplier
- *sales returns* (also known as returns inwards) – here goods which have been sold by the business to a customer are returned *to* the business

Those businesses or organisations that have a reasonable number of returns transactions will use *returns day books,* one to record purchases returns and the other to record sales returns:

- *purchases returns day book* is prepared from credit notes received
- *sales returns day book* is prepared from credit notes issued

Returns books use the same layout as purchases day book and sales day book – the only difference is that the appropriate credit note number is recorded instead of the invoice number.

## chapter summary

❑ Day books are used as listing devices for the credit transactions of purchases, sales, purchases returns and sales returns.

❑ Day books are books of prime entry because transactions are recorded in them first before being recorded in the book-keeping system.

In the next chapter we shall look at the principles of double-entry book-keeping and see how the information collected by the day books is used in the book-keeping system.

**Student Activities**

- *In these Activities the rate of Value Added Tax is to be calculated at the current rate (17½% at the time of writing). When calculating VAT amounts, you should ignore fractions of a penny, ie round down to a whole penny.*
- *Leave the folio column blank.*

**32.1**   You are working for Wyvern Wholesalers and are required to enter up the purchases day book from the following details:

19-1
2 Apr.  Bought goods from Severn Supplies £250 + VAT, their invoice no. 6789
4 Apr.  Bought goods from I Johnstone £210 + VAT, her invoice no. A241
10 Apr.  Bought goods from L Murphy £185 + VAT, his invoice no. 2456
12 Apr.  Bought goods from Mercia Manufacturing £180 + VAT, their invoice no. X457
18 Apr.  Bought goods from AMC Enterprises £345 + VAT, their invoice no. AMC 456
24 Apr.  Bought goods from S Green £395 + VAT, her invoice no. 2846

After entering the above, total the purchases day book at 30 April.

**32.2**   The following details are to be entered in the sales day book of Wyvern Wholesalers:

19-1
2 Apr.  Sold goods to Malvern Stores £55 + VAT, invoice no. 4578
4 Apr.  Sold goods to Pershore Retailers £65 + VAT, invoice no. 4579
7 Apr.  Sold goods to E Grainger £28 + VAT, invoice no. 4580
10 Apr.  Sold goods to P Wilson £58 + VAT, invoice no. 4581
12 Apr.  Sold goods to M Kershaw £76 + VAT, invoice no. 4582
14 Apr.  Sold goods to D Lloyd £66 + VAT, invoice no. 4583
18 Apr.  Sold goods to A Cox £33 + VAT, invoice no. 4584
22 Apr.  Sold goods to Dines Stores £102 + VAT, invoice no. 4585
24 Apr.  Sold goods to Malvern Stores £47 + VAT, invoice no. 4586
27 Apr.  Sold goods to P Wilson £35 + VAT, invoice no. 4587
29 Apr.  Sold goods to A Cox £82 + VAT, invoice no. 4588

After entering the above, total the sales day book at 30 April.

**32.3**   The following transactions are to be entered in the *appropriate* day books of Wyvern Wholesalers for the month of May; total the day books at the month-end:

19-1
2 May   Bought goods from S Green £180 + VAT, her invoice no. 2901
3 May   Sold goods to P Wilson £48 + VAT, invoice no. 4589
6 May   Bought goods from Mercia Manufacturing £211 + VAT, their invoice no. X495
8 May   Sold goods to Dines Stores £105 + VAT, invoice no. 4590
10 May   Some of the goods, value £50 + VAT, bought from S Green are unsatisfactory and are returned to her; she issues credit note no. 221
12 May   Sold goods to D Lloyd £105 + VAT, invoice no. 4591
14 May   P Wilson returns goods £18 + VAT, we issue credit note no. CN989
17 May   Sold goods to M Kershaw £85 + VAT, invoice no. 4592
20 May   We return goods £35 + VAT to Mercia Manufacturing; credit note no. 811 received
22 May   Bought goods from AMC Enterprises £55 + VAT, their invoice no. AMC 612
24 May   D Lloyd returns goods £22 + VAT, we issue credit note no. CN990
26 May   Sold goods to Pershore Retailers £75 + VAT, invoice no. 4593

# 33 Generating accounts – the double-entry system

## introduction

Having looked at the different financial documents (Chapter 29) and the way in which these documents are recorded in day books (Chapter 32), we now turn our attention to the further recording of financial transactions in the accounting system by means of *double-entry book-keeping*. Your course does not require you to become book-keepers, but it does require you to appreciate how financial transactions recorded in business documents and daybooks *generate accounts*, either on paper or by input into a computer accounting program. It is from these accounts that the *trial balance* and the *financial statements* of the business are prepared (see Chapters 34 to 36).

## the use of accounts

The accounting system is organised on the basis of a number of *accounts* which record the money amounts of financial transactions: collectively these accounts are known as 'the ledger'. Accounts are maintained in the names of customers and of suppliers of the organisation, and also for other transactions such as the receipt and payment of money for various purposes. Accounts can be maintained on paper or on a computer system. In a handwritten system, accounts are entered either in a bound book or a series of separate sheets of paper – each account occupying a separate page. The business can set up its own manual system, or can buy one ready-made from a business supplies shop. In a computerised system each account is held as data in a computer file. Whether a handwritten or computerised system is being used, the principles remain the same. A handwritten system can either use specially ruled accounting paper – known as ledger paper – which can be purchased from a business supplies shop, or a suitable layout can be ruled as follows:

| Debit | | | Name of Account, eg Purchases Account | | Credit | |
|---|---|---|---|---|---|---|
| Date | Details | £  p | Date | Details | £  p |
| ↑ of trans-action | ↑ name of other account | ↑ amount of trans-action | | | |

Note the following points about the layout of this account:
- the name of the account is written at the top
- the account is divided into two identical halves, separated by a central double vertical line
- the left-hand side is called the 'debit' side ('debit' is abbreviated to 'Dr.' – short for DebitoR)
- the right-hand side is called the 'credit' (or 'Cr.') side
- the date, details and amount of the transaction are entered in the account
- in the 'details' column is entered the name of the other account involved in the book-keeping transaction

In practice, each account would occupy a whole page in a handwritten book-keeping system but, to save space when doing exercises, it is usual to put several accounts on a page. In future, in this book, the account layout will be simplified to give more clarity as follows:

| Dr. | Purchases Account | Cr. |
|---|---|---|
| 19-1 | £ | 19-1 | £ |

This layout is often known in accounting jargon as a 'T' account; it is used to illustrate accounts because it separates in a simple way the two sides – debit and credit – of the account. An alternative style of account has three money columns: debit, credit and balance. This type of account is commonly used for bank statements, building society passbooks and computer accounting statements. Because the balance of the account is calculated after every transaction, it is known as a *running balance account*.

## debits and credits

The principle of double-entry book-keeping is that for every financial transaction:
- one account is debited, and
- one account is credited

The principle is often known as the *dual aspect* of book-keeping, ie each transaction has a dual effect on the accounts – one account gains while another account gives value by recording a payment or a liability.

Debit entries are on the left-hand side of the appropriate account, while credit entries are on the right. The rules for debits and credits are:
- *debit entry* – the account which gains value, or records an asset, or an overhead
- *credit entry* – the account which gives value, or records a liability, or an income item

This is illustrated as follows:

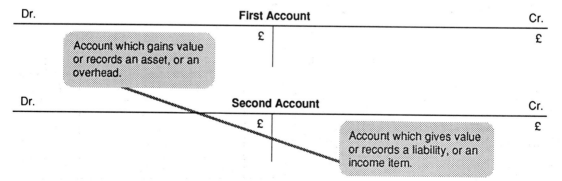

When one entry has been identified as a debit or credit, the other entry will be on the *opposite* side of the other account.

## division of the ledger

Accounts, as mentioned above, are normally written on separate pages of a book known as 'the ledger'. In practice, several separate ledgers are kept, each containing different classes of accounts:

* *sales ledger*, containing the accounts of a firm's debtors (customers)
* *purchases ledger*, containing the accounts of a firm's creditors (suppliers)
* *cash book*, containing the bank account and cash account records of the business
* *general ledger* (often known as *nominal ledger*) containing all other accounts, such as income, overheads, fixed assets, owner's capital, etc.

## computer accounting

When computers are used for accounting, the physical ledger books do not exist, but the term 'ledgers' is used and will appear on computer menus. The actual input of transactions into the computer is by means of one entry only into the accounts. The second (double) entry is automatically entered into the second account by means of a code input by the computer operator.

# purchases and sales

In finance the terms purchases and sales have specific meanings:
* *purchases* – the purchase of goods with the intention that they should be resold at a profit
* *sales* – the sale of goods in which the business or organisation trades

Thus an office stationery supplies business buying goods from a manufacturer records the transaction in *purchases account*. When office supplies are sold to customers, the transactions are recorded in *sales account*. Other items purchased in connection with the running of the busines – eg buildings, equipment, vehicles – are recorded in suitably named accounts, ie buildings account, equipment account, vehicles account, etc. The following accounts are used in connection with purchases and sales:

* *purchases account* – to record the purchase of goods, whether bought on credit or for cash
* *sales account* – to record the sale of goods, whether sold on credit or for cash
* *purchases returns account* – to record the return of goods to the supplier
* *sales returns account* – to record the return of goods by the customer
* *Value Added Tax account* – to record the VAT amount of purchases, sales and returns

## double-entry book-keeping for purchases

Invoices received from suppliers form the prime documents for the preparation of the purchases day book (see Chapter 32). After the day book, the double-entry book-keeping accounts are written up. The example purchases day book (already seen on page 354) is reproduced for reference:

**Purchases Day Book**

| Date | Details | Invoice No | Folio | Net | VAT* | Gross |
|------|---------|-----------|-------|-----|------|-------|
| 19-1 | | | | £ | £ | £ |
| 2 Jan. | P Bond Ltd | 1234 | PL 125 | 80.00 | 14.00 | 94.00 |
| 11 Jan. | D Webster | A373 | PL 730 | 120.00 | 21.00 | 141.00 |
| 16 Jan. | P Bond Ltd | 1247 | PL 125 | 40.00 | 7.00 | 47.00 |
| 20 Jan. | Sanders & Sons | 5691 | PL 495 | 160.00 | 28.00 | 188.00 |
| 31 Jan. | Totals for month | | | 400.00 | 70.00 | 470.00 |

* VAT = 17½ per cent

The accounts in the purchases ledger and general ledger to record the above transactions are:

## PURCHASES LEDGER

| Dr. | | P Bond  (account no 125) | | | Cr. |
|---|---|---|---|---|---|
| 19-1 | | £ | 19-1 | | £ |
| | | | 2 Jan. | Purchases | 94 |
| | | | 16 Jan. | Purchases | 47 |

| Dr. | | Sanders & Sons  (account no 495) | | | Cr. |
|---|---|---|---|---|---|
| 19-1 | | £ | 19-1 | | £ |
| | | | 20 Jan. | Purchases | 188 |

| Dr. | | D Webster  (account no 730) | | | Cr. |
|---|---|---|---|---|---|
| 19-1 | | £ | 19-1 | | £ |
| | | | 11 Jan. | Purchases | 141 |

## GENERAL LEDGER

| Dr. | | Purchases Account | | Cr. |
|---|---|---|---|---|
| 19-1 | | £ | 19-1 | £ |
| 31 Jan. | Purchases Day Book | 400 | | |

| Dr. | | Value Added Tax Account | | Cr. |
|---|---|---|---|---|
| 19-1 | | £ | 19-1 | £ |
| 31 Jan. | Purchases Day Book | 70 | | |

Note that from the purchases day book:

- the total of the net column, £400, has been debited to purchases account (ie the account which has gained value)
- the total of the VAT column, £70, has been debited to VAT account (which has gained value)
- the amounts from the gross column *for each separate purchase* have been credited to the accounts of the suppliers, ie the business owes to each creditor the amounts shown
- the purchases day book incorporates a folio column which cross-references each transaction to the personal account of each creditor in the purchases ledger (PL); this enables a particular transaction to be traced from prime document (invoice received), through the book of prime entry (purchases day book), to the creditor's ledger account

## double-entry book-keeping for sales

Invoices issued by a business form the prime documents used in the preparation of the sales day book (see Chapter 32). After the day book, the double-entry book-keeping accounts are written up.

The example sales day book (see also page 355) is shown below:

### Sales Day Book

| Date | Details | Invoice No | Folio | Net | VAT | Gross |
|------|---------|-----------|-------|-----|-----|-------|
| 19-1 | | | | £ | £ | £ |
| 3 Jan. | Doyle & Co Ltd | 901 | SL 58 | 120.00 | 21.00 | 141.00 |
| 8 Jan. | Sparkes & Sons Ltd | 902 | SL 127 | 160.00 | 28.00 | 188.00 |
| 12 Jan. | T Young | 903 | SL 179 | 80.00 | 14.00 | 94.00 |
| 15 Jan. | A-Z Supplies Ltd | 904 | SL 3 | 200.00 | 35.00 | 235.00 |
| 18 Jan. | Sparkes & Sons | 905 | SL 127 | 120.00 | 21.00 | 141.00 |
| 31 Jan. | Totals for month | | | 680.00 | 119.00 | 799.00 |

The accounts in the sales ledger and general ledger to record the above transactions are:

### SALES LEDGER

| Dr. | | **A-Z Supplies Ltd**   (account no 3) | | | Cr. |
|-----|---|---------------------------------------|---|---|-----|
| 19-1 | | £ | 19-1 | | £ |
| 15 Jan. | Sales | 235 | | | |

| Dr. | | **Doyle & Co Ltd**   (account no 58) | | | Cr. |
|-----|---|--------------------------------------|---|---|-----|
| 19-1 | | £ | 19-1 | | £ |
| 3 Jan. | Sales | 141 | | | |

| Dr. | | **Sparkes & Sons Ltd**   (account no 127) | | | Cr. |
|-----|---|-------------------------------------------|---|---|-----|
| 19-1 | | £ | 19-1 | | £ |
| 8 Jan. | Sales | 188 | | | |
| 18 Jan. | Sales | 141 | | | |

| Dr. | | **T Young**   (account no 179) | | | Cr. |
|-----|---|--------------------------------|---|---|-----|
| 19-1 | | £ | 19-1 | | £ |
| 12 Jan. | Sales | 94 | | | |

## GENERAL LEDGER

| Dr. | | Sales Account | | Cr. |
|---|---|---|---|---|
| 19-1 | | £ | 19-1 | £ |
| | | | 31 Jan.   Sales Day Book | 680 |

| Dr. | | Value Added Tax Account | | Cr. |
|---|---|---|---|---|
| 19-1 | | £ | 19-1 | £ |
| 31 Jan.   Purchases Day Book | | 70* | 31 Jan.   Sales Day Book | 119 |

\* Amount already entered from purchases day book.

Note that from the sales day book:
- the total of the net column, £680, has been credited to sales account (ie the account which has given value)
- the total of the VAT column, £119, has been credited to VAT account (which has given value)
- the amounts from the gross column *for each separate sale* have been debited to the accounts of the customers, ie the business has a debtor for the amounts shown
- the folio column gives a cross-reference to the debtors' accounts in the sales ledger (SL)

## double-entry book-keeping for returned goods

Returns transactions make use of two accounts:
- *purchases returns account* – to record the return of goods to the supplier
- *sales returns account* – to record the return of goods by the customer.

The double-entry book-keeping transactions to record returns are:

- Sales returns: credit note issued to customer
  - *debit* sales returns account, with amount of credit note before VAT is added
  - *debit* VAT account, with amount of VAT on credit note
  - *credit* debtor's account, with total amount of credit note, including VAT

- Purchases returns: credit note received from supplier
  - *debit* creditor's account, with total amount of credit note, including VAT
  - *credit* purchases returns account, with amount of credit note before VAT is added
  - *credit* VAT account, with amount of VAT on credit note

## recording credit transactions and returns: a summary

The diagram (Fig. 33.1) on the next page summarises the procedures for recording the transactions in the accounting system
- for purchases and purchases returns
- for sales and sales returns

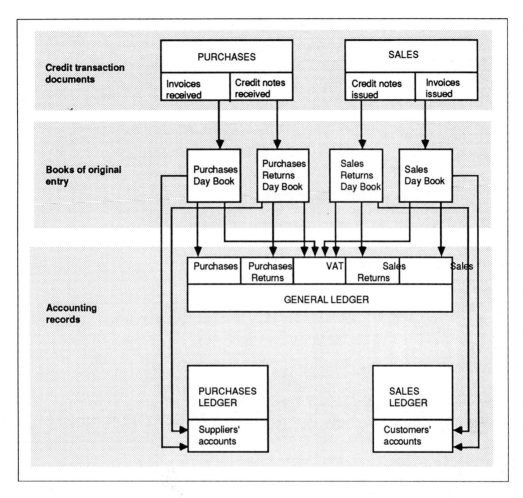

*Fig. 33.1 Recording transactions in the accounting system of a business*

When payment is received from customers or made to suppliers, the method of payment is usually either by cheque or in cash. While separate accounts are kept for bank (ie cheque) transactions and for cash transactions, most organisations bring these two accounts together in a division of the ledger called *cash book*.

### payment received from debtors (customers)

When debtors pay for goods that have been sold to them, the double-entry book-keeping entries are:

* payment received by cheque
  - *debit* bank account
  - *credit* debtor's account

* payment received in cash
  - *debit* cash account
  - *credit* debtor's account

### payment made to creditors (suppliers)

Payment for purchases is recorded by the following double-entry book-keeping entries:

- payment made by cheque
  - *debit* creditor's account
  - *credit* bank account

- payment made in cash
  - *debit* creditor's account
  - *credit* cash account

## cash sales and cash purchases

If sales or purchases are made with immediate payment at the time of the transaction (called a 'cash sale' or 'cash purchase' – when payment is made in cash *and* by cheque), debtors' and creditors' accounts are not used. Instead the book-keeping transactions are:

- Cash sales
  - *debit* bank account (cheque), or cash account (cash) with total amount, including VAT
  - *credit* sales account with amount of invoice before VAT is added
  - *credit* VAT account with amount of VAT on invoice

- Cash purchases
  - *debit* purchases account with amount of invoice before VAT is added
  - *debit* VAT account with amount of VAT on invoice
  - *credit* bank account (cheque), or cash account (cash) with total amount, including VAT

## chapter summary

❑　The accounting system comprises a number of specific stages of recording and presenting financial transactions:
- documents
- books of prime entry
- double-entry book-keeping
- trial balance
- final accounts

❑　Financial transactions are recorded in accounts using double-entry principles.

❑　The rules for debit and credit entries in accounts are:
- *debit entries* – the account which gains value
- *credit entries* – the account which gives value

❑　Division of the ledger divides the accounts contained in the accounting system between four sections:
- *sales ledger* – containing the accounts of debtors
- *purchases ledger* – containing the accounts of creditors
- *cash book* – containing the bank account and cash account
- *general (or nominal) ledger* – containing all other accounts

In the next chapter we see how 'T' accounts are balanced at the end of each month, and a trial balance is extracted.

# ✍ Student Activities

**33.1** James Scriven started in business as a furniture wholesaler on 1 February 19-2. He has registered for Value Added Tax. During the first month of business, the following credit transactions took place.

19-2
1 Feb.  Bought furniture for resale and received invoice no 961 from Softseat Ltd, £320 + VAT*
2 Feb.  Bought furniture for resale and received invoice no 068 from PRK Ltd, £80 + VAT
8 Feb.  Sold furniture and issued invoice no 001 to High Street Stores, £440 + VAT
14 Feb. Sold furniture and issued invoice no 002 to Peter Lounds Ltd, £120 + VAT
15 Feb. Bought furniture for resale and received invoice no 529 from Quality Furnishings, £160 + VAT
18 Feb. Sold furniture and issued invoice no 003 to Carpminster College, £320 + VAT
19 Feb. Bought furniture for resale and received invoice no 984 from Softseat Ltd, £160 + VAT
25 Feb. Sold furniture and issued invoice no 004 to High Street Stores, £200 + VAT

* VAT = 17½%

**You are to:**

(a)  enter the above transactions in James Scrivens' purchases day book and sales day book

(b)  record the accounting entries in James Scrivens' purchases ledger, sales ledger and general ledger

**33.2** Anne Green owns a shop selling paint and decorating materials; she is registered for Value Added Tax. She has two suppliers, Wyper Ltd (account no 301) and M Roper & Sons (account no 302). During the month of May 19-2 Anne received the following business documents from her suppliers:

19-2
2 May   Invoice no 562 from M Roper & Sons for £190 + VAT*
4 May   Invoice no 82 from Wyper Ltd for £200 + VAT
10 May  Invoice no 86 from Wyper Ltd for £210 + VAT
18 May  Invoice no 580 from M Roper & Sons for £180 + VAT
18 May  Credit note no 82 from M Roper & Sons for £30 + VAT
21 May  Invoice no 91 from Wyper Ltd for £240 + VAT
23 May  Credit note no 6 from Wyper Ltd for £40 + VAT
25 May  Invoice no 589 from M Roper & Sons for £98 + VAT
28 May  Credit note no 84 from M Roper & Sons for £38 + VAT

* VAT = 17½%

**You are to:**

(a)  enter the above transactions in the appropriate day books which are to be totalled at the end of May

(b)  enter the transactions in the appropriate accounts in Anne Green's ledgers. (The credit balances of M Roper & Sons and Wyper Ltd at the beginning of the month were £85 and £100 respectively.)

**33.3** A local company, Sidbury Trading Co Ltd, has asked your advice about computerising their accounts. At present, the company operates a manual double-entry book-keeping system.

Using professional computer magazines, investigate hardware and software suitable for accounting from reviews and advertisements; send away for details if necessary. Prepare a report for the company, listing a suitable machine (or machines) and appropriate software. Bear in mind the considerations of value for money and reliability. Present your findings in a report addressed to Sid Bury, Managing Director, Sidbury Trading Co Ltd, 55 Newtown Road, Rowcester RW5 2JA.

# 34 Balancing accounts – the trial balance

## introduction

With the 'traditional' form of account (the 'T' account) that we have used to record business transactions, it is necessary to calculate the balance of each account from time-to-time – often at the end of each month – and at the end of the financial year. The balance of an account is the total of that account to date, eg the amount of sales made, the amount of wages paid. In this chapter we shall see how this *balancing of accounts* is carried out.

We shall then use the balances from each account in order to check the double-entry book-keeping by extracting a *trial balance,* which is a list of the balances of every account in the accounting system.

## balancing the accounts

The balance of an account is the money amount of transactions remaining on the account. Accounts are balanced at regular intervals – often at the end of each month – in order to show the amount:
- owing to each creditor
- owing by each debtor
- of sales
- of purchases
- of sales returns (returns in)
- of purchases returns (returns out)
- of money – in the bank (or a bank overdraft) and in cash
- of overheads incurred by the business
- of fixed assets, eg premises, machinery, etc owned by the business
- of capital and drawings of the owner of the business
- of other liabilities, eg loans

# method of balancing accounts

The following is an example of a 'T' account, taken from the sales ledger, which has been balanced at the month-end (the balancing figure is shown with a shaded background for illustrative purposes):

| Dr. | | | **J Smith** | | Cr. |
|---|---|---|---|---|---|
| 19-1 | | £ | 19-1 | | £ |
| 5 Sep. | Sales | 250 | 12 Sep. | Sales returns | 50 |
| 25 Sep. | Sales | 140 | 18 Sep. | Bank | 200 |
| | | ___ | 30 Sep. | Balance c/d | 140 |
| | | 390 | | | 390 |
| 1 Oct. | Balance b/d | 140 | | | |

The steps involved in balancing accounts are:

*Step 1*
The entries in the debit and credit money columns are totalled; these totals are not recorded in ink on the account at this stage, but can be recorded either as sub-totals in pencil on the account, or noted on a separate piece of paper. In the example above, the debit side totals £390, while the credit side is £250.

*Step 2*
The difference between the two totals is the balance of the account and this is entered on the account:
- on the side of the smaller total
- on the next available line
- with the date of balancing (often the last day of the month)
- with the description 'balance c/d', or 'balance carried down'

In the account above, the balance carried down is £390 – £250 = £140, entered in the credit column.

*Step 3*
Both sides of the account are now totalled, including the balance which has just been entered, and the totals (the same on both sides) are entered *on the same line* in the appropriate column, and double underlined. The double underline indicates that the account has been balanced at this point using the figures above the total: the figures above the underline should not be added in to anything below the underline.

In the account above, the totals on each side of the account are £390.

*Step 4*
As we are using double-entry book-keeping, there must be an opposite entry to the 'balance c/d' calculated in Step 2. The same money amount is entered on the *other side of the account* below the double-underlined totals entered in Step 3. We have now completed both the debit and credit entry. The date is usually recorded as the next day after 'balance c/d', ie often the first day of the following month, and the description can be 'balance b/d' or 'balance brought down'.

In the example above, the balance brought down on J Smith's account on 1 October 19-1 is £140 debit; this means that J Smith owes the business £140.

*A practical point*
When balancing accounts, use a pen and not a pencil. If any errors are made, cross them through neatly with a single line, and write the corrected version on the line below. Do *not* use correcting fluid: at best it conceals errors, at worst it conceals fraudulent transactions.

# extracting a trial balance

The book-keeper uses the balances from accounts to extract a trial balance in order to check the arithmetical accuracy of the double-entry book-keeping, ie that the debit entries equal the credit entries.

*A trial balance is a list of the balances of every account in the accounting system, distinguishing between those accounts which have debit balances and those which have credit balances.*

A trial balance is extracted at regular intervals – often at the end of each month.

## example of a trial balance

### Trial balance of John Smith as at 31 December 19-1

| Name of account | Dr. £ | Cr. £ |
|---|---|---|
| Stock at 1 January 19-1 | 12,500 | |
| Purchases | 105,000 | |
| Sales | | 155,000 |
| Administration | 6,200 | |
| Wages | 20,500 | |
| Rent paid | 3,750 | |
| Telephone | 500 | |
| Interest paid | 4,500 | |
| Travel expenses | 550 | |
| Premises | 100,000 | |
| Machinery | 20,000 | |
| Debtors | 15,500 | |
| Bank | 450 | |
| Cash | 50 | |
| Capital | | 75,000 |
| Drawings | 7,000 | |
| Loan from bank | | 50,000 |
| Creditors | | 16,500 |
| | 296,500 | 296,500 |

*notes:*
• The debit and credit columns have been totalled and are the same amount. Thus the trial balance proves that the accounts are arithmetically correct. (A trial balance does *not* prove the *complete* accuracy of the accounting records.)

• The heading for a trial balance gives the name of the business whose accounts have been listed and the date it was extracted, ie the end of the accounting period.

• The balance for each account transferred to the trial balance is the figure brought down after the accounts have been balanced.

• As well as the name of each account, it is quite usual to show in the trial balance the account number. Most accounting systems give numbers to accounts and these can be listed in a separate 'folio' or 'reference' column (not shown here).

## debit and credit balances – guidelines

Certain accounts always have a debit balance, while others always have a credit balance. The lists set out below will act as a guide, and will also help in your understanding of trial balances.

*Debit balances* include:
* cash account
* purchases account
* sales returns account (returns in)
* fixed asset accounts, eg premises, motor vehicles, machinery, office equipment, etc
* overhead accounts, eg administration, wages, rent paid
* drawings account (which records the amount of money taken out of the business by the owner for his/her own use)
* debtors' accounts (often, for the purposes of a trial balance, the balances of individual debtors' accounts are totalled, and the total is entered in the trial balance as 'debtors')

*Credit balances* include:
* sales account
* purchases returns account (returns out)
* capital account (which records the amount invested in the business by the owner)
* loan account (loans made to the business by banks and others)
* creditors' accounts (often a total is entered in the trial balance, rather than the individual balances of each account)

*Note:* bank account can be either debit or credit – it will be debit when the business has money in the bank, and credit when it is overdrawn.

## single column trial balance

The conventional trial balance, as we have just seen, lists the balances of accounts in two columns: debit and credit. A further method of listing account balances is in the form of a *single column trial balance*. Here, all the balances are listed in one column, with debit balances being added, and credit balances being shown in brackets and deducted. Proof that the trial balance 'balances' is given by the fact that the 'total' is zero.

It should be noted that the two column trial balance is the more common format, and is generally favoured by practising accountants.

### example of a single column trial balance
This example uses the same figures extracted from the accounting records as the conventional trial balance shown earlier on page 370.

**Trial balance of John Smith as at 31 December 19-1**

| Name of account | £ |
|---|---|
| Stock at 1 January 19-1 | 12,500 |
| Purchases | 105,000 |
| Sales | (155,000) |
| Administration | 6,200 |
| Wages | 20,500 |
| Rent | 3,750 |
| Telephone | 500 |
| Interest paid | 4,500 |
| Travel expenses | 550 |
| Premises | 100,000 |
| Machinery | 20,000 |
| Debtors | 15,500 |
| Bank | 450 |
| Cash | 50 |
| Capital | (75,000) |
| Drawings | 7,000 |
| Loan from bank | (50,000) |
| Creditors | (16,500) |
| | zero |

*notes:*
* Debit balances are added.
* Credit balances are shown in brackets and deducted.
* The trial balance 'balances' when the 'total' is zero.

## importance of the trial balance

A business will extract a trial balance on a regular basis to check the arithmetic accuracy of the book-keeping. However, the trial balance is also used as the starting point in the production of the year-end or *final accounts*. These final accounts, which are produced once a year (and sometimes more frequently), comprise:
* trading and profit and loss account
* balance sheet

## chapter summary

❑   'T' accounts need to be balanced at regular intervals – often at the end of each month.

❑   When each account has been balanced, a trial balance can be extracted.

❑   A trial balance is a list of the balances of every account in the accounting system, distinguishing between those accounts which have debit balances and those which have credit balances.

❑   A single column trial balance lists debit and credit balances in one column; credit balances are shown in brackets and are deducted. The trial balance 'balances' when the 'total' is zero.

In the next chapter we see how the trial balance is used as the starting point for the preparation of the year-end or final accounts.

**student activities**

**34.1** The following balances have been extracted from the accounting records of James Green as at 30 June 19-2:

|  | £ |
|---|---|
| Purchases | 11,925 |
| Sales | 20,515 |
| Sales returns | 210 |
| Purchases returns | 85 |
| Bank overdraft | 695 |
| Cash | 50 |
| Debtors | 3,240 |
| Creditors | 2,935 |
| Motor vehicle | 5,500 |
| Office equipment | 1,220 |
| Wages | 4,620 |
| Administration | 2,840 |
| Capital | ? |

**You are to:**

(a) produce a conventional trial balance with columns for debit and credit balances

(b) produce a single column trial balance

*Note:* In both trial balances capital needs to be inserted as the balancing figure.

**34.2** The following balances have been extracted from the accounting records of Lorna Fox at 31 December 19-3:

|  | £ |
|---|---|
| Stock at 1 January 19-3 | 8,500 |
| Purchases | 96,250 |
| Sales | 146,390 |
| Administration | 10,240 |
| Wages | 28,980 |
| Rent paid | 1,340 |
| Telephone | 1,680 |
| Interest paid | 2,350 |
| Travel expenses | 1,045 |
| Premises | 125,000 |
| Office equipment | 15,000 |
| Motor vehicles | 24,000 |
| Debtors | 10,340 |
| Cash | 150 |
| Creditors | 12,495 |
| Loan from bank | 20,000 |
| Drawings | 9,450 |
| Capital | ? |

**You are to:**

(a) produce a conventional trial balance with columns for debit and credit balances

(b) produce a single column trial balance

*Note:* In both trial balances capital needs to be inserted as the balancing figure.

# 35 Final accounts – extended trial balance format

## introduction

For most businesses the final accounts, or financial statements, that are produced at the end of each financial year comprise:

- trading account
- profit and loss account
- balance sheet

Collectively these three are usually referred to as the 'final accounts' of a business, although correctly only the first two are accounts – in the sense that they form part of the double-entry book-keeping system. The third – the balance sheet – is a list of all accounts which remain open at the end of the financial year.

Each of the final accounts can be produced more often than once a year in order to give information to the owner(s) on how the business is progressing, eg if the business uses a computer accounting package they may be produced as a 'monthly report'. However, it is customary to produce annual accounts for the benefit of the Inland Revenue, bank manager, and other interested parties. Limited companies also have a legal responsibility to report to their shareholders each year (see Chapter 37).

In this chapter we will explain how final accounts can be produced from the trial balance (see Chapter 34) of a sole trader business.

## final accounts and the trial balance

The trial balance is on the borderline between book-keeping and accountancy. The book-keeper's role is to record day-to-day transactions by means of handwritten or computer systems. Every so often, the book-keeper will prove the accuracy of the work by extracting a trial balance of all the accounts in the books. The accountant's role is to take the trial balance and prepare the final accounts – the accountant will also be involved in interpreting the final accounts for the owner of the business and negotiating with the Inland Revenue on taxation matters.

We will use, as the starting point in the preparation of final accounts, the trial balance already seen in Chapter 34. For ease of reference the trial balance is shown again below:

**Trial balance of John Smith as at 31 December 19-1**

| Name of account | Dr. £ | Cr. £ |
|---|---|---|
| Stock at 1 January 19-1 | 12,500 | |
| Purchases | 105,000 | |
| Sales | | 155,000 |
| Administration | 6,200 | |
| Wages | 20,500 | |
| Rent paid | 3,750 | |
| Telephone | 500 | |
| Interest paid | 4,500 | |
| Travel expenses | 550 | |
| Premises | 100,000 | |
| Machinery | 20,000 | |
| Debtors | 15,500 | |
| Bank | 450 | |
| Cash | 50 | |
| Capital | | 75,000 |
| Drawings | 7,000 | |
| Loan from bank | | 50,000 |
| Creditors | | 16,500 |
| | 296,500 | 296,500 |

*note:* Stock at 31 December 19-1 was valued at £10,500.

As we have seen in the previous chapter, the trial balance is produced more often than once a year in order to 'prove' the arithmetical accuracy of the transactions recorded by the book-keeper. It is also produced at the end of a financial year (as is the above trial balance) in order that the year-end final accounts can be prepared.

### debit balances

These comprise *assets* of the business, and *costs* representing the total of purchases made and the cost of overheads for the year. Thus the debit money column indicates that this business has made purchases of goods at a cost of £105,000 during the year, while wages is an overhead, a cost to the business of £20,500. The balances for premises, machinery, stock, debtors, cash and bank indicate, in money terms, an asset of the business. The debtors' figure includes the individual balances of all the firm's debtors, ie those customers who owe money to the firm.

### credit balances

These comprise *liabilities* of the business, and *revenue* amounts, including the total of sales made. For example, the sales figure shows the total amount of goods that has been sold by the business during the year. The figures for capital, loan from the bank and the creditors shows the amount of the liability at the trial balance date. The creditors figure includes all the individual balances of the business' creditors, ie those suppliers to whom the business owes money.

### treatment of stock

You will see that the trial balance includes the stock value at the start of the year, while the end-of-year valuation is noted after the trial balance. For the purposes of financial accounting, the stock of goods for resale is valued by the business (and often verified by the auditor) at the end of each financial year, and the valuation is entered into the book-keeping system.

We will now look in more detail at the final accounts and see how they are prepared using, firstly, the extended trial balance method.

# final accounts and the extended trial balance

As we have noted earlier in this chapter, the final accounts comprise:
• trading account
• profit and loss account
• balance sheet

Fig. 35.1 shows how the final accounts are prepared using the *extended trial balance* method. Here the trial balance is listed and then each balance is allocated (see *allocation* column) to one of the three final accounts which appear in the next three columns and are explained in more detail below.

## trading account

The main activity of a trading business is to buy goods at one price and then to sell the same goods at a higher price. The difference between the two prices represents a profit known as *gross profit*, a figure which is not shown in the trial balance but which has to be calculated. Instead of calculating the gross profit on each item bought or sold, we use the accounting system to record the total of purchases and sales for the year in purchases account and sales account. At the end of the year, the totals of purchases and sales accounts are used in the trading account, together with a note of the amount of stock of goods for resale at the beginning and end of the year.

From fig. 35.1, you will see that the trading account column of John Smith's extended trial balance uses:
• the value of stock at 1 January 19-1 (known as the opening stock)
• the figure for purchases for the year
• the figure for sales for the year
• the value of stock at 31 December 19-1 (known as closing stock) – the amount is given as a note to the trial balance and is obtained by valuation of the stock

Gross profit is calculated as the difference between the debit and credit amounts:

*total of credit entries – total of debit entries = gross profit*

In John Smith's case, the credit entries are sales £155,000 and closing stock £10,500 = £165,500; the debit entries are opening stock £12,500 and purchases £105,000 = £117,500. Gross profit is £165,500 – £117,500 = £48,000, ie the balancing item which makes both sides come to the same total.

Gross profit is then transferred to the *credit* side of profit and loss account (see below) because, in double-entry book-keeping terms, we are debiting trading account and crediting profit and loss account.

## profit and loss account

The profit and loss account lists the various overheads (or *revenue expenditure*) of the business. The total of overheads is deducted from gross profit to give *net profit* for the year.

Fig. 35.1 shows how the profit and loss account column of John Smith's extended trial balance uses:
• the figures for overheads for the year, ie administration, wages, rent paid, telephone, interest paid, travel expenses
• the gross profit transferred from trading account

Net profit is calculated as:

*gross profit – overheads for the year  =  net profit*

## JOHN SMITH: final accounts for the year-ended 31 December 19-1

| | Allocation* | Trial balance as at 31 December 19-1 | | Trading account | | Profit and loss account | | Balance sheet | |
|---|---|---|---|---|---|---|---|---|---|
| | | Dr £ | Cr £ | Dr £ | Cr £ | Dr £ | Cr £ | Assets Dr £ | Liabilities and Capital Cr £ |
| Stock at 1 January 19-1 | T | 12,500 | | 12,500 | | | | | |
| Purchases | T | 105,000 | | 105,000 | | | | | |
| Sales | T | | 155,000 | | 155,000 | | | | |
| Administration | P & L | 6,200 | | | | 6,200 | | | |
| Wages | P & L | 20,500 | | | | 20,500 | | | |
| Rent paid | P & L | 3,750 | | | | 3,750 | | | |
| Telephone | P & L | 500 | | | | 500 | | | |
| Interest paid | P & L | 4,500 | | | | 4,500 | | | |
| Travel expenses | P & L | 550 | | | | 550 | | | |
| Premises | BS | 100,000 | | | | | | 100,000 | |
| Machinery | BS | 20,000 | | | | | | 20,000 | |
| Debtors | BS | 15,500 | | | | | | 15,500 | |
| Bank | BS | 450 | | | | | | 450 | |
| Cash | BS | 50 | | | | | | 50 | |
| Capital | BS | | 75,000 | | | | | | 75,000 |
| Drawings | BS | 7,000 | | | | | | 7,000 | |
| Loan from bank | BS | | 50,000 | | | | | | 50,000 |
| Creditors | BS | | 16,500 | | | | | | 16,500 |
| | | 296,500 | 296,500 | | | | | | |
| Stock at 31 December 19-1 | T and BS | | | | 10,500 | | | 10,500 | |
| Gross profit | T and P & L | | | 48,000 | | | 48,000 | | |
| Net profit | P & L and BS | | | | | 12,000 | | | 12,000 |
| | | | | 165,500 | 165,500 | 48,000 | 48,000 | 153,500 | 153,500 |

*Fig. 35.1  Final accounts produced using an extended trial balance*
*(* T = trading account,  P & L = profit and loss account,  BS = balance sheet)*

In John Smith's case, gross profit is £48,000. The overheads are administration £6,200, wages £20,500, rent paid £3,750, telephone £500, interest paid £4,500, travel expenses £550, totalling £36,000. Gross profit is £48,000 – £36,000 = £12,000, ie the balancing item which makes both sides come to the same total.

Net profit belongs to the owner(s) of the business and is transferred to the credit side of the balance sheet (see below), which is the final column of the extended trial balance. In double-entry book-keeping terms we are debiting profit and loss account and crediting the owner with the net profit.

### balance sheet

A balance sheet is a different type of financial statement from the trading account and profit and loss account, which show two types of profit – gross profit and net profit respectively – *for the financial year* (or such other time period as may be chosen by the business). A balance sheet, on the other hand, shows the state of the business *at one moment in time*. It lists the *assets* (amounts owned by the business) and the *liabilities* and *capital* (amounts owed by the business) at a particular date, and can be described as a 'snapshot' of a business.

In fig. 35.1, the final column of the extended trial balance shows the balance sheet of John Smith. This uses the remaining balances from the trial balance, together with:
• closing stock (at 31 December 19-1) from the trading account
• net profit, calculated in the profit and loss account

You will note that the balance sheet 'balances', ie the debit (asset) column and the credit (liabilities and capital) column have the same total, so proving the arithmetic accuracy of the extended trial balance.

---

## chapter summary

❏   The final accounts of a business comprise:
   • *trading account,* which shows gross profit for the year
   • *profit and loss account,* which shows net profit for the year
   • *balance sheet,* which shows the assets, liabilities and capital of the business at the year-end

❏   The extended trial balance method of preparing final accounts starts with the trial balance and then allocates each account balance to one of the final accounts.

❏   Each item from the trial balance is entered into the final accounts once only; the additional items of closing stock, gross profit and net profit are listed in two separate final accounts – this ensures that the double-entry book-keeping rules of one debit and one credit for each transaction are maintained.

❏   The extended trial balance method gives us an understanding of the principles of final accounts. It is a method often used by accountancy firms as a first step towards preparing year-end accounts for their clients.

❏   The extended trial balance method uses a spreadsheet approach and you may well be asked to set it up in the format of a computer spreadsheet.

In the next chapter we will look further at final accounts and see how they are presented in a more conventional format used by accountants.

## student activities

The student activities in this chapter all require the preparation of final accounts, using the extended trial balance method. This is an appropriate use for a computer spreadsheet and you may be asked to set up a spreadsheet mask.

**35.1**   The following trial balance has been extracted by the book-keeper of Nick Johnson at 31 December 19-1:

### Trial balance of John Smith as at 31 December 19-1

| Name of account | Dr.<br>£ | Cr.<br>£ |
|---|---:|---:|
| Stock at 1 January 19-1 | 25,000 | |
| Purchases | 210,000 | |
| Sales | | 310,000 |
| Administration | 12,400 | |
| Wages | 41,000 | |
| Rent paid | 7,500 | |
| Telephone | 1,000 | |
| Interest paid | 9,000 | |
| Travel expenses | 1,100 | |
| Premises | 200,000 | |
| Machinery | 40,000 | |
| Debtors | 31,000 | |
| Bank | 900 | |
| Cash | 100 | |
| Capital | | 150,000 |
| Drawings | 14,000 | |
| Loan from bank | | 100,000 |
| Creditors | | 33,000 |
| | 593,000 | 593,000 |

*note:* Stock at 31 December 19-1 was valued at £21,000.

**You are to** prepare the final accounts of Nick Johnson for the year ended 31 December 19-1, using the extended trial balance method.

**35.2**   The following trial balance has been extracted by the book-keeper of John Adams at 31 December 19-8:

| Name of account | Dr. £ | Cr. £ |
|---|---|---|
| Stock at 1 January 19-8 | 14,350 | |
| Purchases | 114,472 | |
| Sales | | 259,688 |
| Administration | 23,968 | |
| Wages | 42,540 | |
| Rent paid | 4,500 | |
| Telephone | 2,272 | |
| Interest paid | 3,500 | |
| Travel expenses | 4,250 | |
| Premises | 100,000 | |
| Office equipment | 29,500 | |
| Debtors | 23,854 | |
| Bank | 1,235 | |
| Cash | 125 | |
| Capital | | 62,500 |
| Drawings | 12,358 | |
| Loan from bank | | 35,000 |
| Creditors | | 19,736 |
| | 376,924 | 376,924 |

*note:* Stock at 31 December 19-8 was valued at £16,280.

**You are to** prepare the final accounts of John Adams for the year ended 31 December 19-8, using the extended trial balance method.

**35.3**   The following trial balance has been extracted by the book-keeper of Clare Lewis at 31 December 19-4:

| Name of account | Dr. £ | Cr. £ |
|---|---|---|
| Debtors | 18,600 | |
| Creditors | | 13,350 |
| Bank overdraft | | 4,610 |
| Capital | | 25,250 |
| Sales | | 144,810 |
| Purchases | 96,318 | |
| Stock at 1 January 19-4 | 16,010 | |
| Administration | 1,820 | |
| Wages | 18,465 | |
| Rent paid | 5,647 | |
| Telephone | 940 | |
| Interest paid | 734 | |
| Travel expenses | 855 | |
| Motor vehicles | 9,820 | |
| Office equipment | 5,500 | |
| Drawings | 13,311 | |
| | 188,020 | 188,020 |

*note:* Stock at 31 December 19-4 was valued at £13,735.

**You are to** prepare the final accounts of Clare Lewis for the year ended 31 December 19-4, using the extended trial balance method.

# 36 Final accounts – conventional format

## introduction

In the previous chapter we saw how the final accounts – trading account, profit and loss account, and balance sheet – are prepared in the form of an extended trial balance.

In this chapter we continue our studies of final accounts by adapting the extended trial balance and presenting the accounts in the conventional format customarily used by accountants. For the example in this chapter we shall continue to use the accounts of John Smith (from the previous chapter) for the year ended 31 December 19-1. The same figures are used and the same profit – both gross profit and net profit – is calculated: it is the format that is different.

## preparation of final accounts from a trial balance

The trial balance contains the basic figures necessary to prepare the final accounts and is a suitable summary from which to prepare the final accounts in the conventional format. The information needed for the preparation of each of the final accounts needs to be picked out from the trial balance; you will find the following guidelines helpful:

* go through the trial balance and write against the items the final account in which each appears
* 'tick' each figure as it is used – each item from the trial balance appears in the final accounts *once only*
* the year-end (closing) stock figure is not listed in the trial balance, but is shown as a note; the closing stock appears *twice* in the final accounts – firstly in the trading account, and secondly in the balance sheet (as a current asset).

If this routine is followed with the trial balance of John Smith, it will then appear as shown in the illustration below:

**Trial balance of John Smith as at 31 December 19-1**

| Name of account | Dr. £ | Cr. £ | | | |
|---|---|---|---|---|---|
| Stock at 1 January 19-1 | 12,500 | | T | | ✓ |
| Purchases | 105,000 | | T | | ✓ |
| Sales | | 155,000 | T | | ✓ |
| Administration | 6,200 | | P & L | (overhead) | ✓ |
| Wages | 20,500 | | P & L | (overhead) | ✓ |
| Rent paid | 3,750 | | P & L | (overhead) | ✓ |
| Telephone | 500 | | P & L | (overhead) | ✓ |
| Interest paid | 4,500 | | P & L | (overhead) | ✓ |
| Travel expenses | 550 | | P & L | (overhead) | ✓ |
| Premises | 100,000 | | BS | (fixed asset) | ✓ |
| Machinery | 20,000 | | BS | (fixed asset) | ✓ |
| Debtors | 15,500 | | BS | (current asset) | ✓ |
| Bank | 450 | | BS | (current asset) | ✓ |
| Cash | 50 | | BS | (current asset) | ✓ |
| Capital | | 75,000 | BS | (capital) | ✓ |
| Drawings | 7,000 | | BS | (capital) | ✓ |
| Loan from bank | | 50,000 | BS | (long-term liability) | ✓ |
| Creditors | | 16,500 | BS | (current liability) | ✓ |
| | 296,500 | 296,500 | | | |

| | | | | |
|---|---|---|---|---|
| Stock at 31 December 19-1 was valued at £10,500 | | { T | | ✓ |
| | | { BS | (current asset) | ✓ |

*Note:* T = trading account; P & L = profit and loss account; BS = balance sheet

# trading and profit and loss account

You should note that businesses which buy and sell goods, eg shops, garages, wholesalers, builders, restaurants, use both a trading account and a profit and loss account. By contrast, businesses that provide a service, eg solicitors, estate agents, hairdressers, dentists, secretarial agencies, use a profit and loss account. With service businesses there is no gross profit; in profit and loss account the amount of income from clients or customers is recorded. Overheads are listed in the same way as we have already seen in the previous chapter, and both types of business will prepare a balance sheet.

When both trading account and profit and loss account are used, it is usual to show them in a combined *trading and profit and loss account*. This is presented in the following way using the figures from John Smith's trial balance:

**Trading and profit and loss account
of John Smith for the year ended 31 December 19-1**

| | £ | £ |
|---|---:|---:|
| Sales | | 155,000 |
| Opening stock (1 January 19-1) | 12,500 | |
| Purchases | 105,000 | |
| | 117,500 | |
| Less Closing stock (31 December 19-1) | 10,500 | |
| Cost of Sales | | 107,000 |
| **Gross profit** | | 48,000 |
| | | |
| Less overheads: | | |
|   Administration | 6,200 | |
|   Wages | 20,500 | |
|   Rent paid | 3,750 | |
|   Telephone | 500 | |
|   Interest paid | 4,500 | |
|   Travel expenses | 550 | |
| | | 36,000 |
| **Net profit** | | 12,000 |

*notes:*
- The account is presented in a vertical format, ie the figures run down the page.

- The trading account forms the first half of the account as far as gross profit, while the profit and loss account is the second half of the account.

- Sales and purchases only include items in which the business trades – items bought for use in the business, such as machinery, are not included in sales and purchases but are classified as fixed assets and shown in the balance sheet.

- Adjustments are made for the value of stock in the store or warehouse at the beginning and end of the financial year. The opening stock is added to purchases because it is a cost brought in from the previous year. The closing stock is deducted from purchases because it has not yet been sold; it will form the opening stock for the next financial year, when it will be added as a cost to next year's figure for purchases.

- The figure for *cost of sales* (often written as *cost of goods sold*) represents the cost to the business of the goods which have been sold in this financial year. Cost of sales is:

  > opening stock
  > + purchases
  > – closing stock
  > = cost of goods sold

- Gross profit is calculated as:

  > sales
  > – cost of sales
  > = gross profit

  If cost of sales is greater than net sales, the business has made a *gross loss*.

- The overheads of the business are listed and sub-totalled and deducted from gross profit.

- If the total of overheads is less than gross profit, the business has made a *net profit*; if the total of overheads is more than gross profit, the business has made a *net loss*.

- The net profit is the amount the business earned for the owner(s) during the year; it is important to note that this is *not* the amount by which the cash/bank balance has increased during the year. The reason for this is that some transactions have no effect on profit, but do affect the cash/bank balance, eg owner's drawings, purchase of fixed assets.

- Net profit is added to the owner's capital in the balance sheet (a net loss is deducted).

- Drawings by the owner(s) are *not* listed as an overhead in profit and loss account – instead they are deducted from capital (see balance sheet below).

# balance sheet

A balance sheet shows the assets, liabilities and capital of a business at one moment in time. The conventional vertical presentation of a balance sheet is as follows:

**Balance sheet of John Smith as at 31 December 19-1**

|  | £ | £ |
|---|---|---|
| **Fixed Assets** | | |
| Premises | | 100,000 |
| Machinery | | 20,000 |
| | | 120,000 |
| **Current Assets** | | |
| Stock | 10,500 | |
| Debtors | 15,500 | |
| Bank | 450 | |
| Cash | 50 | |
| | 26,500 | |
| **Less Current Liabilities** | | |
| Creditors | 16,500 | |
| **Working Capital** | | 10,000 |
| | | 130,000 |
| **Less Long-term Liabilities** | | |
| Loan from bank | | 50,000 |
| **NET ASSETS** | | 80,000 |
| **FINANCED BY** | | |
| **Capital** | | |
| Opening capital | | 75,000 |
| Add net profit | | 12,000 |
| | | 87,000 |
| Less drawings | | 7,000 |
| | | 80,000 |

*notes:*

## fixed assets

*Fixed assets* comprise the long-term items owned by a business which are not bought with the intention of early resale, eg premises, machinery, motor vehicles, office equipment, fixtures and fittings, etc. When a business buys new fixed assets, such expenditure is called *capital expenditure* (in contrast to *revenue expenditure* which is the cost of the business' overheads charged to profit and loss account).

## current assets

*Current assets* comprise short-term assets which change regularly, eg stocks, debtors (amounts owed to the business by customers), bank balances and cash. Each one of these items will alter as the business trades, eg stocks will be sold, or more will be bought; debtors will make payment to the business, or sales on credit will be made; the cash and bank balances will alter with the flow of money paid into the bank account, or as withdrawals are made.

By tradition, fixed and current assets are listed starting with the most permanent, ie premises, and working through to the most liquid, ie nearest to cash: either cash itself, or the balance at the bank.

## current liabilities

These are liabilities which are due for repayment *within twelve months* of the date of the balance sheet, eg creditors (amounts owed by the business to suppliers), and bank overdraft (which is technically repayable on demand, unlike a bank loan which is negotiated for a particular time period).

## working capital

This is the excess of current assets over current liabilities, ie current assets – current liabilities = working capital. Without adequate working capital, a business cannot continue to operate.

## long-term liabilities

Such liabilities are where repayment is due *in more than one year* from the date of the balance sheet; they are often described as 'bank loan', 'long-term loan', or 'mortgage'.

## net assets

This shows the net amount of assets used by the business, ie fixed and current assets, less current and long-term liabilities. The net assets are financed by the owner(s) of the business, in the form of capital. The total of the net assets therefore equals the total of the 'Financed by' section, ie the balance sheet 'balances'.

## capital

Capital is the owner(s) investment, and is a liability of a business, ie it is what the business owes the owner. It is important to realise that the assets and liabilities of a business are treated separately from the *personal* assets and liabilities of the owner(s) of the business. For example, if a group of people decided to set up in business they would each agree to put in a certain amount of capital to start the business. As individuals they regard their capital as an investment, ie an asset which may, at some time, be repaid to them. From the point of view of the business, the capital is a liability, because it is owed to the owner(s). In practice, it is unlikely to be repaid as it is the permanent capital of the business.

To the owner(s)' capital is added net profit for the year, while *drawings*, the amount withdrawn by the owner(s) during the year, is deducted. (Note: drawings must *not* be included amongst the overheads in the profit and loss account.) This calculation leaves a closing capital at the balance sheet date which balances (agrees) with the net assets figure.

## significance of the balance sheet

The balance sheet shows the assets used by the business and how they have been financed. The concept may be expressed as a formula:

> Fixed assets
> + Working capital
> – Long-term liabilities
> = Net assets
> = Capital

Thus it can be seen that the vertical presentation balance sheet agrees the figure for net assets (£80,000, in the example), with capital.

# depreciation of fixed assets

Fixed assets, for example machinery and vehicles, reduce in value as time goes by, largely as a result of wear and tear. In this section we will see how depreciation is shown in the final accounts of a business. While we are concerned with depreciation of fixed assets owned by businesses, the same principles apply to items that are owned by individuals. You may be thinking of buying a car in the next year or so, and people will be quick to tell you that you are spending your money on a 'depreciating asset'.

*Depreciation is the estimate of the amount of the loss in value of fixed assets over a specified time period.*

As the amount of depreciation is an estimate, rather than the actual amount, it is referred to as a *provision for depreciation.*

## recording depreciation in final accounts
To provide an accurate view of the financial state of a business we record depreciation of fixed assets in the final accounts as follows:

- include the amount of depreciation for the year as an overhead in profit and loss account; the effect of this is to reduce the net profit
- the value of fixed assets shown in the balance sheet is *reduced* to reflect the amount that they have depreciated

The reason for making these adjustments for depreciation is because the business has had the use of the fixed assets during the year: the estimated fall in value of the assets is recorded in profit and loss account, which now shows a more accurate profit figure while, in the balance sheet, fixed assets are reduced in value to indicate their approximate 'true' value.

## example of depreciation in final accounts
John Smith tells you that he wishes you to show £2,000 for depreciation of machinery in his final accounts for 19-1.

The effect of this on his final accounts is:

- profit and loss account – to include an overhead for *provision for depreciation: machinery* £2,000
- balance sheet – reduce the value of machinery by £2,000

The relevant extracts from his accounts now appear as:

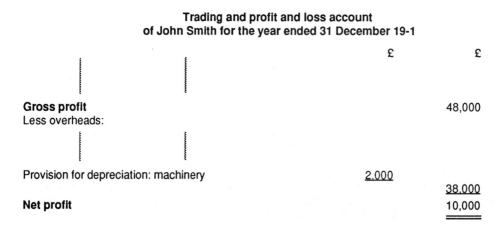

**Trading and profit and loss account
of John Smith for the year ended 31 December 19-1**

|  | £ | £ |
|---|---|---|
| **Gross profit** |  | 48,000 |
| Less overheads: |  |  |
| Provision for depreciation: machinery | 2,000 |  |
|  |  | 38,000 |
| **Net profit** |  | 10,000 |

**Balance sheet of John Smith as at 31 December 19-1**

| Fixed Assets | £<br>Cost | £<br>Depreciation<br>to date | £<br>Net |
|---|---|---|---|
| Premises | 100,000 | – | 100,000 |
| Machinery | 20,000 | 2,000 | 18,000 |
| | 120,000 | 2,000 | 118,000 |
| | | | |
| NET ASSETS | | | 78,000 |

| FINANCED BY | |
|---|---|
| **Capital** | |
| Opening capital | 75,000 |
| Add net profit | 10,000 |
| | 85,000 |
| Less drawings | 7,000 |
| | 78,000 |

*notes:*
- Only the relevant extracts from John Smith's final accounts are shown – other figures remain unchanged.
- Net profit is reduced by £2,000 because of the additional overhead for depreciation.
- In the fixed asset section of the balance sheet, further columns have been included so that, for each class of fixed asset, there is shown:
    - cost price
    - depreciation to date
    - net value of each class of fixed asset
- In the 'financed by' section of the balance sheet, net profit has been shown at the reduced figure from profit and loss account.

## further years' depreciation

If John Smith continues to depreciate his machinery at £2,000, then in each year's final accounts:
- in the profit and loss account, £2,000 will be shown as an overhead for provision for depreciation
- in the balance sheet the depreciation to date figure will increase by the amount of depreciation, ie it will be this year's depreciation, plus depreciation from previous years

For example, the fixed asset section of John Smith's balance sheet at the end of 19-2 will be:

| Fixed Assets | £<br>Cost | £<br>Depreciation<br>to date | £<br>Net |
|---|---|---|---|
| Premises | 100,000 | – | 100,000 |
| Machinery | 20,000 | 4,000 | 16,000 |
| | 120,000 | 4,000 | 116,000 |

In this way, depreciation to date increases with the addition of each further year's depreciation. At the same time, the net figure reduces – it is this net figure (or *net book value*) which is added to the other fixed assets to give a sub-total for this section of the balance sheet. The amount of depreciation to date gives an approximate indication of the loss in value of the asset.

# chapter summary

❑ The conventional layout of the trading and profit and loss account is presented in vertical format and shows cost of sales and the sub-total of overheads.

❑ The conventional layout of the balance sheet is presented in vertical format and shows:
  - fixed assets
  - current assets
  - current liabilities
  - working capital
  - long-term liabilities
  - net assets
  - capital

❑ Depreciation is an estimate, in money terms, of the fall in value of fixed assets.

❑ The depreciation amount for each class of fixed assets is
  - included as an overhead in profit and loss account
  - deducted from the value of the fixed asset in the balance sheet

❑ Net profit is reduced by the amount of depreciation.

In the next chapter we continue with final accounts by looking at limited company final accounts.

# student activities

**36.1**   Refer to the trial balance from question 35.1 (page 379)

   **You are to** prepare the final accounts of Nick Johnson for the year ended 31 December 19-1, in conventional format.

**36.2**   Refer to the trial balance from question 35.2 (page 380)

   **You are to** prepare the final accounts of John Adams for the year ended 31 December 19-8, in conventional format.

**36.3**   Refer to the trial balance from question 35.3 (page 380)

   **You are to** prepare the final accounts of Clare Lewis for the year ended 31 December 19-4, in conventional format.

**36.4** The trial balance of Alan Harris, who runs a bookshop, has been prepared at the end of his first year in business on 30 June 19-6, as follows:

| | Dr. | Cr. |
|---|---|---|
| *Name of account* | £ | £ |
| Capital | | 60,000 |
| Premises | 65,000 | |
| Fixtures and fittings | 1,000 | |
| Motor vehicle | 7,500 | |
| Purchases | 55,000 | |
| Sales | | 85,500 |
| Administration | 850 | |
| Wages | 9,220 | |
| Telephone | 680 | |
| Interest paid | 120 | |
| Travel expenses | 330 | |
| Rates | 1,200 | |
| Debtors | 1,350 | |
| Creditors | | 7,550 |
| Bank | 2,100 | |
| Cash | 600 | |
| Drawings | 8,100 | |
| | 153,050 | 153,050 |

*notes:*
- Stock at 30 June 19-6 was valued at £8,100
- Provision for depreciation for the year is: fixtures and fittings £250, motor vehicle £2,000

**You are to** prepare the final accounts of Alan Harris for the year ended 30 June 19-6, in conventional format.

**36.5** The trial balance of Jane Richardson, who runs a secretarial agency, has been prepared at 31 December 19-2, as follows:

| | Dr. | Cr. |
|---|---|---|
| *Name of account* | £ | £ |
| Capital | | 20,000 |
| Office equipment at cost | 20,000 | |
| Provision for depreciation on office equipment at 1 January 19-2 | | 5,000 |
| Income from clients | | 55,450 |
| Administration | 3,280 | |
| Wages | 27,145 | |
| Rent paid | 6,031 | |
| Telephone | 1,287 | |
| Interest paid | 147 | |
| Travel expenses | 779 | |
| Rates | 2,355 | |
| Debtors | 3,698 | |
| Creditors | | 1,074 |
| Bank | 3,971 | |
| Cash | 241 | |
| Drawings | 12,590 | |
| | 81,524 | 81,524 |

*note:* Provision for depreciation for the year on office equipment is £2,500

**You are to** prepare the final accounts of Jane Richardson for the year ended 31 December 19-2, in conventional format.

# *J Simpson –*
# *profit and loss statements*
# *and balance sheets*

| Element 7.4 | Produce and explain profit and loss statements and balance sheets. |
|---|---|
| Suggested Sources: | • work experience – examining the profit and loss statements and balance sheets used by a business (with permission from the business) |
| | • talks by accounts staff from a business, or interviews with them |
| | • obtaining a set of year-end accounts from a company, eg public limited company |
| | • textbooks in libraries and resource centres |

## INTRODUCTION

A year ago, on 1 October 19-3, your friend, John (or Jane) Simpson, set up in business as a self-employed decorator with capital of £2,500. The business has developed well and now includes a number of regular contract clients. During the year you have acted as the book-keeper and, at the end of the first financial year, on 30 September 19-4, the following are the balances of the accounts:

|  | £ |
|---|---|
| Stock at 1 October 19-3 | nil |
| Purchases | 15,500 |
| Sales | 32,900 |
| Administration | 2,400 |
| Wages | 3,500 |
| Rent paid | 1,250 |
| Telephone | 490 |
| Interest paid | 995 |
| Travel expenses | 685 |
| Equipment | 750 |
| Motor vehicle | 7,500 |
| Debtors | 2,540 |
| Bank overdraft | 790 |
| Cash | 25 |
| Capital | 2,500 |
| Drawings | 6,850 |
| Loan from bank | 4,250 |
| Creditors | 2,045 |

## TASK 1
Extract a single column trial balance as at 30 September 19-4 from the list of balances, and total it to zero.

## TASK 2
Prepare an extended trial balance, if possible using a computer spreadsheet. The extended trial balance should:
- indicate to which account balances are allocated:
  - trading account
  - profit and loss account
  - balance sheet
- take note of the fact that you have valued the closing stock on 30 September 19-4 at £745
- show the gross profit and net profit for the year to 30 September 19-4, together with a balance sheet at that date

## TASK 3
Rewrite the extended trial balance in conventional format.

## TASK 4
Explain to your friend, John (or Jane) Simpson, who doesn't understand finance, what the various year-end statements show, and to whom they would be of interest.

# 37 Limited company accounts

## introduction

In this chapter we will examine the year-end final accounts of limited companies. These statements broadly follow the layout of those prepared for sole-traders. The Companies Act 1985 (amended by the Companies Act 1989) stipulates that certain annual final accounts must be filed with the Registrar of Companies and copies have to be sent to each shareholder. Such 'published accounts', as they are known, will not be discussed in this chapter: it may be that you will study these in detail as part of later accounting courses. You may also have to obtain the 'Report and Accounts' of public limited companies as part of your investigations for your Portfolio of Evidence .

In this chapter we will concentrate on the basic form of company final accounts. Before we examine the final accounts in detail we will first look at the principal way in which a company raises finance: shares. There are different types of shares which appear in the company balance sheet as a capital item.

## shares and debentures issued by limited companies

A clause contained in the Memorandum of Association (the document setting out the powers and objects of a company) states the share capital of that company and its division into shares of a fixed amount. This is known as the *authorised share capital,* ie the share capital that the company is allowed to issue. The authorised share capital may not be the same as the amount that the company has actually issued – this is known as the *issued share capital*. The latter can never exceed the former: if a company which has issued the full extent of its authorised share capital wishes to make an increase, it must first pass the appropriate resolution at a general meeting of the shareholders.

The authorised and issued share capital may be divided into a number of classes or types of share, the principal of which are *ordinary shares* and *preference shares*. Each share has a nominal or face value which is entered in the accounts. Shares may be issued with nominal values of 5p, 10p, 25p, 50p or £1, or indeed for any amount. Thus a company with an authorised share capital of £100,000 might state in its Memorandum of Association that this is divided up into:

| | |
|---|---|
| 100,000 ordinary shares of 50p each | £50,000 |
| 50,000 seven per cent preference shares of £1 each | £50,000 |
| | £100,000 |

The nominal value of a share often bears little relationship to its true value. It is easy to find out the value of shares in a public limited company – if they are quoted on the Stock Exchange, the price may well be listed in the *Financial Times*. Shareholders receive *dividends* on their shares, being a distribution of a part of the company's earnings for a year or half-year.

### ordinary (equity) shares

These are the most commonly issued class of share. They take a share of the profits available for distribution after allowance has been made for all overheads of the business, including loan interest, taxation, and after preference dividends (if any). When a company makes large profits, it will have the ability to pay higher dividends to the ordinary shareholders; when profits are low or losses are made, the ordinary shareholders may receive a smaller or even no dividend.

### preference shares

Such shares. which are less common, usually carry a fixed rate of dividend – 7% for example, based on the nominal share value – which, as their name suggests, is paid in preference to the ordinary shareholders; but it is only paid if the company makes profits.

### loans and debentures

In addition to money provided by shareholders, who are the owners of the company, further funds can be obtained by borrowing in the form of loans or debentures, for example, from a bank. The term 'debenture' usually refers to a formal certificate issued by a company acknowledging that a sum of money is owing to a specified person. Interest is normally payable on debentures; this must be paid, just like other overheads, whether a company makes profits or not.

## limited companies: trading and profit and loss account

A limited company uses the same type of year-end final accounts as a sole trader. However, there are two items commonly found in the profit and loss account of a limited company that are not found in those of other forms of business:

- *Directors' remuneration* ie amounts paid to directors. As directors are employed by the company, their *pay* appears amongst the overheads of the company.
- *Debenture and loan interest* as already noted, when debentures are issued and loans are raised by companies, the interest is shown as an overhead in the profit and loss account

A limited company follows the profit and loss account with an *appropriation section* (often described as an appropriation account) to show how the net profit has been divided amongst the owners of the business – the shareholders. Here is an example of a simple appropriation account:

|  | £ |
|---|---|
| **Net profit for year** | 100,000 |
| Less corporation tax | 25,000 |
| Profit after taxation | 75,000 |
| Less proposed ordinary dividend | 50,000 |
| Retained profit for year | 25,000 |
| Add balance of retained profits at beginning of year | 35,000 |
| Balance of retained profits at end of year | 60,000 |

### notes:

- The company has recorded a net profit of £100,000 in its profit and loss account – this is brought into the appropriation section.
- Corporation tax – the tax that a company has to pay on its profits, is shown in the appropriation account.
- The company proposes to distribute £50,000 to the ordinary shareholders as a dividend. This will be paid in the early part of the next financial year.

- Added to net profit is a balance of £35,000. This represents profits of the company from previous years that are undistributed, ie they have not been paid to the shareholders in the form of dividends. Unlike a sole trader, where all profits are added to owner's capital, a company will rarely distribute all its profits. You will note that this appropriation account shows a balance of retained profits at the year-end of £60,000. Such retained profits form a *revenue reserve* of the company. It is usual for a company to keep back some part of its profits in the form of reserves, to help the company build for the future.

- It should be noted that reserves are *not* a cash fund to be used whenever the company needs money, but are in fact represented by assets shown on the balance sheet. These assets may, or may not be realisable. The reserves recognise the fact that the assets belong to the shareholders (via the company).

- Besides the balance of retained profits – sometimes described as profit and loss account balance – companies often have several different revenue reserve accounts, eg general reserve or, for a specific purpose, reserve for the replacement of machinery. Transfers to or from these revenue reserve accounts are made in the appropriation section of the profit and loss account.

A more comprehensive appropriation account is shown below.

**APPROPRIATION ACCOUNT OF ORION LTD
FOR THE YEAR ENDED 31 DECEMBER 19-4**

|  | £ | £ |
|---|---|---|
| **Net profit for year before taxation** |  | 43,000 |
| Less corporation tax |  | 15,000 |
| Profit for year after taxation |  | 28,000 |
|  |  |  |
| Less:  interim dividends paid |  |  |
|    ordinary shares | 5,000 |  |
|    preference shares | 2,000 |  |
|    final dividends proposed |  |  |
|    ordinary shares | 10,000 |  |
|    preference shares | 2,000 |  |
|  |  | 19,000 |
|  |  | 9,000 |
| Less transfer to general reserve |  | 5,000 |
| Retained profit for year |  | 4,000 |
| Add balance of retained profits at beginning of year |  | 16,000 |
| Balance of retained profits at end of year |  | 20,000 |

# limited companies: balance sheet

The *balance sheet* of a limited company follows the same layout as that of a sole trader but the capital section is more complex because of the different classes of shares that may be issued, and the various reserves.

Fig. 37.1 on the next page shows the balance sheet of Orion Ltd. as an example.

**BALANCE SHEET OF ORION LTD AS AT 31 DECEMBER 19-4**

| **Fixed Assets** | Cost | Dep'n to date | Net |
|---|---|---|---|
| | £ | £ | £ |
| Freehold land and buildings | 180,000 | 20,000 | 160,000 |
| Machinery | 280,000 | 110,000 | 170,000 |
| Fixtures and fittings | 100,000 | 25,000 | 75,000 |
| | 560,000 | 155,000 | 405,000 |

| **Current Assets** | | | |
|---|---|---|---|
| Stock | | 50,000 | |
| Debtors | | 38,000 | |
| Bank | | 22,000 | |
| Cash | | 2,000 | |
| | | 112,000 | |

| **Less Current Liabilities** | | | |
|---|---|---|---|
| Creditors | 30,000 | | |
| Proposed dividends | 12,000 | | |
| Corporation tax | 15,000 | | |
| | | 57,000 | |
| **Working Capital** | | | 55,000 |
| | | | 460,000 |
| **Less long-term Liabilities** | | | |
| 12% debentures | | | 60,000 |
| **NET ASSETS** | | | 400,000 |

| **FINANCED BY** | | |
|---|---|---|
| **Authorised Share Capital** | | |
| 100,000 10% preference shares of £1 each | | 100,000 |
| 600,000 ordinary shares of £1 each | | 600,000 |
| | | 700,000 |

| **Issued Share Capital** | | |
|---|---|---|
| 40,000 10% preference shares of £1 each, fully paid | | 40,000 |
| 300,000 ordinary shares of £1 each, fully paid | | 300,000 |
| | | 340,000 |

| **Capital Reserve** | | |
|---|---|---|
| Share premium account | | 10,000 |

| **Revenue Reserves** | | |
|---|---|---|
| General reserve* | 30,000 | |
| Profit and loss account | 20,000 | |
| | | 50,000 |
| **SHAREHOLDERS' FUNDS** | | 400,000 |

* including transfer of £5,000 (see appropriation account on page 394)

*Fig. 37.1  An example of a limited company balance sheet*

A word of explanation about some of the items appearing in company balance sheets is appropriate at this point.

## fixed assets

Like other balance sheets, this section comprises those items that do not change daily and are likely to be retained for use in the business for some time to come. It is usual for fixed assets, with the possible exception of freehold land, to be depreciated over a period of time or with use. The headings used for fixed assets in a balance sheet read: *cost, depreciation to date* and *net* (see fig. 37.1).

## current assets

The usual current assets will be included, ie stocks, debtors, balance at bank, and cash in hand.

## current liabilities

As with the balance sheets of sole traders and partnerships, this section contains those liabilities that are normally due to be paid within twelve months from the date of the balance sheet, eg creditors, bank overdraft. For limited companies, this section also contains the amount of proposed dividends and the amount of corporation tax to be paid within the next twelve months. Both of these amounts are also included in the appropriation account.

## long-term liabilities

These are generally considered to be liabilities that are due to be repaid more than twelve months from the date of the balance sheet, eg loans and debentures.

## authorised share capital

As already explained, this is the share capital of the company and its division into shares of a fixed amount as authorised by the company's Memorandum of Association. It is included on the balance sheet 'for information', but is not added into the balance sheet total, as it may not be the same amount as the issued share capital.

## issued share capital

Here are detailed the classes and number of shares that have been isued. As stated earlier the issued share capital cannot exceed the amount authorised. In the balance sheet of Orion Ltd., the shares are described as being *fully paid,* meaning that the company has received the full amount of the value of each share from the shareholders. Sometimes shares will be *partly paid*, eg ordinary shares of £1, but 75p paid. This means that the company can make a *call* on the shareholders to pay the additional 25p to make the shares fully paid. Companies often issue partly paid shares and then make calls at certain times: for example, a company that is issuing shares to raise the finance for a new factory may wish to receive the proceeds of issue at different stages of the building and equipment of the factory. For the purpose of entering the amount of issued share capital in the balance sheet, always multiply the number of shares by the amount paid on them, eg 100,000 ordinary shares of £1 each, 75p paid = £75,000 (the other £25,000 will be called by the company at a later date).

## capital reserves

A capital reserve is created as a result of a non-trading profit. Examples are:

• *Revaluation reserve.* This occurs when a fixed asset, most probably property, is revalued in the balance sheet. The amount of the revaluation is placed in a revaluation reserve where it increases the value of the shareholders' investment in the company. Note, however, that this is purely a 'book' adjustment, no cash has changed hands and the reserve cannot be used to fund the payment of dividends.

- *Share premium account.* An established company may well issue additional shares to the public at a higher amount than the nominal value. For example, Orion Ltd (fig. 37.1) may seek finance for further expansion by issuing additional ordinary shares. Although the shares have a nominal value of £1 each, because Orion is a well-established company, the shares are issued at £1.50 each. Of this amount, £1 is recorded in the issued share capital section, and the extra 50p is the share premium.

A capital reserve cannot be used to fund the payment of dividends: one of its few uses is the issue of bonus (or 'free') shares.

### revenue reserves
The reserves from profits are the amounts which the directors of the company have retained in the business. Examples of revenue reserves include *general reserve, profit and loss account,* and more specific reserves such as *debenture redemption reserve.*

### shareholders' funds
This total represents the stake of the shareholders in the company. It comprises share capital (ordinary and preference shares), plus reserves (capital and revenue reserves).

# chapter summary

❑ A limited company, unlike a sole trader or a partnership, has a separate legal entity from its owners.

❑ A company is regulated by the Companies Act 1985 (as amended by the Companies Act 1989), and is owned by shareholders and managed by directors.

❑ The main types of shares issued by companies are ordinary shares and preference shares.

❑ Borrowings in the form of loans and debentures are a further source of finance.

❑ The year-end accounts of a company include an appropriation section, which follows the profit and loss account.

❑ The balance sheet of a limited company is similar to that of a sole trader, but the shareholders' funds section reflects the ownership of the company by its shareholders:
   – a statement of the authorised and issued share capital
   – details of capital reserves and revenue reserves

## ✍️ Student Activities

**37.1** (a) Broadheath Ltd, a music publishing company, has an authorised share capital of £500,000 divided into 100,000 8 per cent preference shares of £1 each and 400,000 ordinary shares of £1 each. All the preference shares are issued and fully paid; 200,000 ordinary shares are issued and fully paid.

On 31 December 19-2 the company's reserves were £60,000; current liabilities £35,000; current assets £125,500; fixed assets (at cost) £350,000 and provisions for depreciation on fixed assets £80,500.

Prepare a summarised balance sheet as at 31 December 19-2 to display this information.

(b) Explain to a potential shareholder the difference between ordinary shares and preference shares.

**37.2** Mason Motors Limited is a second-hand car business. The following information is available for the year ended 31 December 19-1:

- balance of retained profits from previous years stands at £100,000
- net profit for the year was £75,000
- it has been agreed that a transfer to a general reserve of £20,000 is to be made
- corporation tax of £20,050 is to be paid on the year's profit
- it has been agreed that a dividend of 10% is to be paid on the issued share capital of £100,000

(a) Set out the appropriation account for Mason Motors Limited for the year ended 31 December 19-1.

(b) One of the directors of the company asks if the £20,000 being transferred to general reserve could be used to rebuild the garage forecourt. How would you reply?

**37.3** You are a trainee accountant working for Rossiter and Rossiter, a local firm of Chartered Accountants. The senior partner, Mrs Rossiter, hands you the following trial balance at 31 December 19-2, of Sidbury Trading Co Ltd, a local stationery supplies firm:

| | Dr £ | Cr £ |
|---|---|---|
| Share capital | | 200,000 |
| Freehold land and buildings at cost | 142,000 | |
| Motor vans at cost | 55,000 | |
| Provision for depreciation on motor vans at 1 January 19-2 | | 22,000 |
| Purchases and sales | 189,273 | 297,462 |
| Administration | 13,050 | |
| Wages | 38,502 | |
| Telephone | 1,850 | |
| Interest paid | 1,695 | |
| Travel expenses | 3,455 | |
| Directors' remuneration | 25,000 | |
| Debtors and creditors | 26,482 | 16,974 |
| Retained profits at 1 January 19-2 | | 18,397 |
| Stock at 1 January 19-2 | 42,618 | |
| Bank | 15,908 | |
| | 554,833 | 554,833 |

You are given the following additional information:
- the authorised share capital is 300,000 ordinary shares of £1 each; all the shares which have been issued are fully paid
- stock at 31 December 19-2 is valued at £47,288
- it is proposed to pay a dividend of £8,000 for 19-2
- provision for depreciation on motor vans for the year is £11,000

You are to prepare in conventional format the trading and profit and loss accounts of Sidbury Trading Co Ltd for the year ended 31 December 19-2, together with a balance sheet at that date.

# 38 Cashflow statements

## introduction

A balance sheet shows the financial state of a business at a particular date and is usually only prepared once a year. While it is possible to obtain a great deal of information on the progress of the business by comparing one year's balance sheet with that of the next year, it is more difficult to see what has gone on during the period between the two balance sheet dates.

*A cashflow statement uses information from the accounting records (including profit and loss account) and balance sheet, and shows an overall view of money flowing in and out of a business during an accounting period.*

Such a statement concentrates on the liquidity of a business and explains to the owner or shareholders why, after a year of good profits for example, there is a reduced balance at the bank or a larger bank overdraft, at the year-end than there was at the beginning of the year.

Cashflow statements are especially important because they deal with flows of money. It is invariably a shortage of money that causes most businesses to fail, rather than a poor quality product or service. The importance of the cashflow statement is such that all but the smallest companies are required to include this statement as a part of their accounts which they publish and send to shareholders. For sole traders and partnerships, the information that the statement contains is of considerable interest to the owner(s) and to a lender, such as a bank.

A cashflow statement can look either at what has gone on in a past accounting period (normally a year), or it can, based on a forecast trading and profit and loss account and balance sheet, demonstrate the effect on cashflow of future alternative courses of action.

## cashflows

Cashflow statements are divided into five sections:
1. Operating activities
2. Returns on investments and servicing of finance
3. Taxation
4. Investing activities
5. Financing

The cashflows for the year affecting each of these main areas of business activity are shown in the statement.

## 1 operating activities

The main source of cashflow for a business is usually that which is generated from the operating (or trading) activities of the business.

The *net cash inflow from operating activities* is calculated by using figures from the profit and loss account for the year and the balance sheet at the beginning and the end of the year:
- net profit (before interest and tax)
- *add* depreciation for the year*
- *add* decrease in debtors, or *deduct* increase in debtors
- *add* increase in creditors, or *deduct* decrease in creditors
- *add* decrease in stock, or *deduct* increase in stock

*Depreciation is added to net profit because depreciation is a *non-cash expense,* that is, no money is paid out by the business in respect of depreciation charged to profit and loss account.

Note that changes in the main working capital items of stock, debtors and creditors have an effect on cash balances. For example, an increase in stock reduces cash, while a decrease in debtors increases cash.

## 2 returns on investments and servicing of finance

This section of the cashflow statement shows the cashflows relating to receipts and payments of interest and dividends, eg
- interest received
- interest paid
- dividends received
- dividends paid (drawings – for a sole trader or partnership business)

## 3 taxation

Here is shown the tax paid during the year (companies only)

## 4 investing activities

This section of the cashflow statement shows the cashflows relating to the purchase or sale of fixed assets, eg
- purchase or sale of plant and machinery
- purchase or sale of investments

## 5 financing

The financing section of the statement shows the cashflows in respect of shares and loans, eg

*cash inflows*
- increase in capital/share capital
- raising/increase of medium/long-term loans

*cash outflows*
- repayment of capital/share capital
- repayment of medium/long-term loans

Note that the change in cash/bank balances is not included in this section.

### increase or decrease in cash

The subtotals from the five main areas of business activity are totalled to give the *increase/ (decrease) in cash* for the year. There then follows a reconciliation of the cash at the start of the year, plus the increase, or minus the decrease, for the year (as above), which then equals the balance of cash at the end of the year. Note that 'cash' includes cash itself and the balance at bank.

# layout of a cashflow statement

A cashflow statement uses a common layout which can be amended to suit the particular needs of the business for which it is being prepared. The following layout is commonly used (specimen figures have been included):

### CASHFLOW STATEMENT OF ABC LTD FOR THE YEAR-ENDED 31 DECEMBER 19-1

|  | £ | £ |
|---|---|---|
| **Operating activities:** | | |
| Net profit (before tax and interest) | 75,000 | |
| Depreciation | 10,000 | |
| Decrease in stocks | 2,000 | |
| Increase in debtors | (5,000) | |
| Increase in creditors | 7,000 | |
| *Net cash inflow from operating activities* | | 89,000 |
| **Returns on investments and servicing of finance:** | | |
| Interest received | 10,000 | |
| Interest paid | (5,000) | |
| Dividends paid (note: amount *paid* during year) | (22,000) | |
| *Net cash outflow from returns on investments and servicing of finance* | | (17,000) |
| **Taxation:** | | |
| Corporation tax paid (note: amount *paid* during year) | (6,000) | |
| *Tax paid* | | (6,000) |
| **Investing activities:** | | |
| Payments to acquire fixed assets | (125,000) | |
| Receipts from sales of fixed assets | 15,000 | |
| *Net cash outflow from investing activities* | | (110,000) |
| Net cash outflow before financing | | (44,000) |
| **Financing:** | | |
| Issue of share capital | 225,000 | |
| Repayment of capital/share capital | – | |
| Increase in loans | – | |
| Repayment of loans | (90,000) | |
| *Net cash inflow from financing* | | 135,000 |
| Increase in cash | | 91,000* |
| **Analysis of changes in cash during the year:** | | |
| Balance at start of year | | (8,000) |
| Net cash inflow | | 91,000* |
| Balance at end of year | | 83,000 |

*These two figures are the same: they represent the change in cash (ie cash and bank balance) for the year.

**Important note:**
Money amounts shown in brackets indicate a deduction, or where the figure is a subtotal, a negative figure.

# Case Study: Mrs Green – a sole trader

## Situation

Mrs Green runs a children's clothes shop in rented premises in a small market town. Her balance sheets for the last two years are as follows:

### BALANCE SHEET AS AT 31 DECEMBER

| | 19-1 £ Cost | 19-1 £ Dep'n | 19-1 £ Net | 19-2 £ Cost | 19-2 £ Dep'n | 19-2 £ Net |
|---|---|---|---|---|---|---|
| **Fixed Assets** | | | | | | |
| Shop fittings | 1,500 | 500 | 1,000 | 2,000 | 750 | 1,250 |
| **Current Assets** | | | | | | |
| Stocks | | 3,750 | | | 4,850 | |
| Debtors | | 625 | | | 1,040 | |
| Bank | | 220 | | | - | |
| | | 4,595 | | | 5,890 | |
| **Less Current Liabilities** | | | | | | |
| Creditors | 2,020 | | | 4,360 | | |
| Bank | - | | | 725 | | |
| | | 2,020 | | | 5,085 | |
| **Working Capital** | | | 2,575 | | | 805 |
| | | | 3,575 | | | 2,055 |
| **Less Long-term Liabilities** | | | | | | |
| Loan from husband | | | - | | | 1,000 |
| **NET ASSETS** | | | 3,575 | | | 1,055 |
| | | | | | | |
| ***FINANCED BY*** | | | | | | |
| **Capital** | | | 3,300 | | | 3,575 |
| Add  Net profit for year | | | 5,450 | | | 4,080 |
| | | | 8,750 | | | 7,655 |
| Less  Drawings | | | 5,175 | | | 6,600 |
| | | | 3,575 | | | 1,055 |

*Note:* Loan and overdraft interest paid in 19-2 was £450.

Mrs Green says to you: "I cannot understand why I am overdrawn at the bank on 31 December 19-2 when I made a profit of £4,080 during the year". She asks you to explain.

# Solution

A cashflow statement will give Mrs Green the answer.

**CASHFLOW STATEMENT OF MRS GREEN FOR THE YEAR-ENDED 31 DECEMBER 19-2**

|  | £ | £ |
|---|---|---|
| **Operating activities:** | | |
| Net profit (before interest) | 4,530 | |
| Depreciation for year | 250 | |
| Increase in stock | (1,100) | |
| Increase in debtors | (415) | |
| Increase in creditors | <u>2,340</u> | |
| *Net cash inflow from operating activities* | | 5,605 |
| | | |
| **Returns on investments and servicing of finance** | | |
| Interest paid | (450) | |
| Drawings paid | <u>(6,600)</u> | |
| *Net cash outflow from returns on investments* | | |
| *and servicing of finance* | | (7,050) |
| | | |
| **Taxation:** | | |
| *Tax paid* | | – |
| | | |
| **Investing activities:** | | |
| Purchase of fixed assets | (500) | |
| *Net cash outflow from investing activities* | | <u>(500)</u> |
| Net cash outflow before financing | | (1,945) |
| | | |
| **Financing:** | | |
| Loan from husband | <u>1,000</u> | |
| *Net cash inflow from financing* | | <u>1,000</u> |
| Decrease in cash | | (945) |
| | | |
| | | |
| **Analysis of changes in cash during the year:** | | |
| Bank balance at start of year | | 220 |
| Net cash outflow | | <u>(945)</u> |
| Balance at end of year | | (725) |

*Notes:*

- Net profit for the year (before interest) is calculated as: net profit for 19-2 £4,080 *add* interest for 19-2 £450 *equals* £4,530
- Depreciation for the year of £250 is the amount of the increase in depreciation to date shown on the balance sheets, that is, £750 minus £500.
- In this example there is no tax paid (because Mrs Green is a sole trader who will be taxed as an individual, unlike a company which pays tax on its profits); however, the place where tax would appear is indicated on the cashflow statement.
- An increase in stock and debtors reduces the cash available to the business (because stock is being bought, debtors are being allowed more time to pay). In contrast, an increase in creditors gives an increase in cash (because creditors are allowing Mrs Green more time to pay).
- The change in the bank balance is summarised at the end of the cashflow statement: from £220 in the bank to an overdraft of £725 is a 'swing' in the bank of minus £945, which is the amount of the decrease in cash shown by the cashflow statement.

### explanation to Mrs Green

In this example, the statement highlights the following points for the owner of the business:

- net cashflow inflow from operating activities is £5,605, whereas owner's drawings are £6,600; this state of affairs cannot continue for long
- fixed assets costing £500 have been purchased
- a long-term loan of £1,000 has been raised from her husband
- over the year there has been a decrease in cash of £945, this trend cannot be continued for long
- by the end of 19-2 the business has an overdraft of £725, caused mainly by the excessive drawings of the owner
- in conclusion, the position of this business has deteriorated over the two years, and corrective action will be necessary

## Case Study: a limited company cashflow statement

### Situation

The balance sheets of Newtown Trading Company Limited for 19-8 and 19-9 are as set out below. You are asked to prepare a cashflow statement for the year ended 31 December 19-9.

**BALANCE SHEET AS AT 31 DECEMBER**

|  | 19-8 | | | 19-9 | | |
|---|---|---|---|---|---|---|
|  | £ Cost | £ Dep'n | £ Net | £ Cost | £ Dep'n | £ Net |
| **Fixed Assets** | 47,200 | 6,200 | 41,000 | 64,000 | 8,900 | 55,100 |
| **Current Assets** | | | | | | |
| Stocks | | 7,000 | | | 11,000 | |
| Debtors | | 5,000 | | | 3,900 | |
| Bank | | 1,000 | | | 300 | |
| | | 13,000 | | | 15,200 | |
| **Less CurrentLiabilities** | | | | | | |
| Creditors | 3,500 | | | 4,800 | | |
| Proposed dividends | 2,000 | | | 2,500 | | |
| Corporation tax | 1,000 | | | 1,500 | | |
| | | 6,500 | | | 8,800 | |
| **Working Capital** | | | 6,500 | | | 6,400 |
| | | | 47,500 | | | 61,500 |
| **Less Long-term Liabilities** | | | | | | |
| Debentures | | | 5,000 | | | 3,000 |
| **NET ASSETS** | | | 42,500 | | | 58,500 |
| | | | | | | |
| *FINANCED BY* | | | | | | |
| Ordinary share capital | | | 30,000 | | | 40,000 |
| Share premium account | | | 1,500 | | | 2,500 |
| Retained profits | | | 11,000 | | | 16,000 |
| **SHAREHOLDERS' FUNDS** | | | 42,500 | | | 58,500 |

*Note:* Loan interest paid in 19-9 was £400.

# Solution

**NEWTOWN TRADING COMPANY LTD**
**CASHFLOW STATEMENT FOR THE YEAR-ENDED 31 DECEMBER 19-9**

|  | £ | £ |
|---|---:|---:|
| **Operating activities:** | | |
| Net profit (before interest) * | 9,400 | |
| Depreciation for year § | 2,700 | |
| Increase in stock | (4,000) | |
| Decrease in debtors | 1,100 | |
| Increase in creditors | <u>1,300</u> | |
| *Net cash inflow from operating activities* | | 10,500 |
| | | |
| **Returns on investments and servicing of finance:** | | |
| Interest paid | (400) | |
| Drawings paid | <u>(2,000)</u> | |
| *Net cash outflow from returns on investments* | | |
| *and servicing of finance* | | (2,400) |
| | | |
| **Taxation:** | | |
| Corporation tax paid | <u>(1,000)</u> | |
| *Tax paid* | | (1,000) |
| | | |
| **Investing activities:** | | |
| Payments to acquire fixed assets | <u>(16,800)</u> | |
| *Net cash outflow from investing activities* | | <u>(16,800)</u> |
| | | |
| Net cash outflow before financing | | (9,700) |
| | | |
| **Financing:** | | |
| Issue of ordinary shares at a premium £10,000 + £1,000 | 11,000 | |
| Repayment of debentures | <u>(2,000)</u> | |
| *Net cash inflow from financing* | | <u>9,000</u> |
| | | |
| Decrease in cash | | (700) |
| | | |
| | | |
| **Analysis of changes in cash during the year:** | | |
| Bank balance at start of year | | 1,000 |
| Net cash outflow | | <u>(700)</u> |
| | | |
| Bank balance at end of year | | 300 |

*Notes:*
* Calculation of the net profit for 19-9 before interest, tax and dividends:

| | £ |
|---|---:|
| increase in retained profits | 5,000 |
| interest paid in 19-9 | 400 |
| proposed dividends, 19-9 | 2,500 |
| corporation tax, 19-9 | <u>1,500</u> |
| net profit before interest, tax and dividends | 9,400 |

§ Depreciation charged: £8,900 – £6,200 = £2,700

Proposed dividends and corporation tax, which are current liabilities at 31 December 19-8, are paid in 19-9. Likewise, the current liabilities for dividends and tax at 31 December 19-9 will be paid in 19-0.

## how useful is the statement?

The following points are highlighted by the statement:
- cashflow from operating activities is £10,500
- a purchase of fixed assets of £16,800 has been made, financed partly by operating activities, and partly by financing activities with an issue of shares at a premium
- the bank balance during the year has fallen by £700
- in conclusion, the picture shown by the cashflow statement is that of a business that is generating cash from its operating activities and using them to build for the future

# chapter summary

❑   The objective of a cashflow statement is to show an overall view of money flowing in and out of a business during an accounting period.

❑   A cashflow statement is divided into five sections:
- operating activities
- returns on investments and servicing of finance
- taxation
- investing activities
- financing

❑   Most limited companies are required to include a cashflow statement as a part of their published accounts. They are also useful statements for sole traders and partnerships.

 **Student Activities**

**38.1**  John Smith has been in business for two years. He is puzzled by his balance sheets because, although they show a profit for each year, his bank balance has fallen and is now an overdraft. He asks for your assistance to explain what has happened. The balance sheets are as follows:

### BALANCE SHEET AS AT 31 DECEMBER

|  | 19-1 £ Cost | 19-1 £ Dep'n | 19-1 £ Net | 19-2 £ Cost | 19-2 £ Dep'n | 19-2 £ Net |
|---|---|---|---|---|---|---|
| **Fixed Assets** |  |  |  |  |  |  |
| Fixtures and fittings | 3,000 | 600 | 2,400 | 5,000 | 1,600 | 3,400 |
| **Current Assets** |  |  |  |  |  |  |
| Stocks |  | 5,500 |  |  | 9,000 |  |
| Debtors |  | 750 |  |  | 1,550 |  |
| Bank |  | 850 |  |  | - |  |
|  |  | 7,100 |  |  | 10,550 |  |
|  |  |  |  |  |  |  |
| **Current Liabilities** |  |  |  |  |  |  |
| Creditors | 2,500 |  |  | 2,750 |  |  |
| Bank overdraft | - |  |  | 2,200 |  |  |
|  |  | 2,500 |  |  | 4,950 |  |
| **Working Capital** |  |  | 4,600 |  |  | 5,600 |
| **NET ASSETS** |  |  | 7,000 |  |  | 9,000 |

| FINANCED BY | 19-1 | | 19-2 |
|---|---|---|---|
| **Capital** | 5,000 | | 7,000 |
| Add Net profit for year | _8,750_ | | _11,000_ |
| | 13,750 | | 18,000 |
| Less Drawings | _6,750_ | | _9,000_ |
| | 7,000 | | 9,000 |

*Note:* Interest paid in 19-2 was £250.

**You are to** prepare a cashflow statement for the year-ended 31 December 19-2. Explain to John Smith the reason for the change in the bank balance.

**38.2** Richard Williams runs a stationery supplies shop; his balance sheets for the last two years are:

### BALANCE SHEET AS AT 30 SEPTEMBER

| | 19-5 | | | 19-6 | | |
|---|---|---|---|---|---|---|
| | £ | £ | £ | £ | £ | £ |
| | Cost | Dep'n | Net | Cost | Dep'n | Net |
| **Fixed Assets** | 60,000 | 12,000 | 48,000 | 70,000 | 23,600 | 46,400 |
| **Current Assets** | | | | | | |
| Stocks | | 9,800 | | | 13,600 | |
| Debtors | | _10,800_ | | | _15,000_ | |
| | | 20,600 | | | 28,600 | |
| **Less Current Liabilities** | | | | | | |
| Creditors | 7,200 | | | 14,600 | | |
| Bank overdraft | _1,000_ | | | _4,700_ | | |
| | | 8,200 | | | 19,300 | |
| **Working Capital** | | | _12,400_ | | | _9,300_ |
| | | | 60,400 | | | 55,700 |
| **Less Long-term Liabilities** | | | | | | |
| Bank loan | | | _10,000_ | | | _15,000_ |
| **NET ASSETS** | | | 50,400 | | | 40,700 |
| | | | | | | |
| FINANCED BY | | | | | | |
| **Capital** | | | 50,000 | | | 50,400 |
| Add Net profit/(loss) | | | _10,800_ | | | _(1,500)_ |
| | | | 60,800 | | | 48,900 |
| Less Drawings | | | _10,400_ | | | _8,200_ |
| | | | 50,400 | | | 40,700 |

*Note:* Loan and overdraft interest paid in 19-6 was £2,200.

**You are to** prepare a cashflow statement for the year-ended 30 September 19-6. As his accountant, use the cashflow statement to write a reply to Richard Williams (address: The Stationery Shop, 32 Bank Street, Redgrove RD1 7GT) who says: "I don't know what has gone wrong – I have worked very hard to build up the business so that I can earn profits to repay the bank".

**38.3** Martin Jackson is a shareholder in Retail News Ltd, a company that operates a chain of newsagents throughout the West Midlands. Martin comments that, whilst the company is making reasonable profits, the bank balance has fallen quite considerably. He provides you with the following information for Retail News Ltd:

### BALANCE SHEET AS AT 31 DECEMBER

| | 19-4 £000 | 19-4 £000 | 19-5 £000 | 19-5 £000 | 19-6 £000 | 19-6 £000 |
|---|---|---|---|---|---|---|
| **Fixed Assets** at cost | | 252 | | 274 | | 298 |
| Add Additions during year | | 22 | | 24 | | 26 |
| | | 274 | | 298 | | 324 |
| Less Depreciation to date | | 74 | | 98 | | 118 |
| | | 200 | | 200 | | 206 |
| **Current Assets** | | | | | | |
| Stock | 50 | | 64 | | 70 | |
| Debtors | 80 | | 120 | | 160 | |
| Bank | 10 | | - | | - | |
| | 140 | | 184 | | 230 | |
| **Less Current Liabilities** | | | | | | |
| Creditors | 56 | | 72 | | 78 | |
| Bank | - | | 10 | | 46 | |
| Proposed dividends | 16 | | 20 | | 16 | |
| Corporation tax | 4 | | 5 | | 8 | |
| | 76 | | 107 | | 148 | |
| **Working Capital** | | 64 | | 77 | | 82 |
| **NET ASSETS** | | 264 | | 277 | | 288 |
| | | | | | | |
| **FINANCED BY** | | | | | | |
| Ordinary share capital | | 200 | | 210 | | 210 |
| Retained profits | | 64 | | 67 | | 78 |
| | | 264 | | 277 | | 288 |

*Note:* Interest paid was: £3,000 in 19-5, and £15,000 in 19-6.

**You are to** prepare a cashflow statement for the years ended for 19-5 and 19-6. Explain the reason for the change in the bank balance.

# 39 Monitoring business performance

## introduction

The ability to monitor and interpret financial information is an important function in a business. Questions which need to be be answered include:

*Did the business perform better this year than last year?*

*Is the business performing as well as expected?*

*How efficiently is the business managing its resources?*

The financial statements which are used in the monitoring process, and which we consider in this chapter are

* the profit and loss statement
* the balance sheet
* aged debtor and creditor schedules

## the monitoring process

Monitoring and interpretation are carried out (in the case of the profit and loss statement and balance sheet) by calculating accounting ratios and percentages, and then using the results to draw relevant conclusions. A number of the more important ratios, and percentages are considered in this chapter. It is important to note that interpretation consists of far more than mechnaically calculating a series of ratios and percentages; appropriate conclusions need to be drawn and decisions taken. To help in the task of interpretation, we will consider the calculations under five headings:

* *profitability* – the amount of profit the organisation makes
* *capital strength* – the amount of money invested by the owner(s) in comparison with outside borrowing (this is also known as *gearing)*
* *liquidity* – the availability of cash, or near cash, in an organisation
* *activity* – the control of stocks, debtors and creditors
* *investment ratios* – indicators to investors as to how profitable a business is, and what rate of return it gives on money invested

## reasons for monitoring performance

A number of parties are interested in the financial state of the business and the accounting ratios calculated from financial statements. The figures and ratios they will examine will differ and the reasons for their interest can be very different:

**the management**   The management of a business will want to know the current financial state of the business and the controls needed as the business develops. Management will therefore look at:

- *liquidity* – the ability of the company to meet its everyday running expenses and debt obligations, in other words, the *solvency* of a business
- *activity* – indicators of how well stock levels are being controlled, how efficiently customer debts are chased up, and how promptly suppliers are paid
- *profitability* – the management will be responsible to the owners of the business (they may *be* the owners of the business) and will need to ensure that profitability is maintained wherever possible
- *tax liability* – a business pays tax to the Inland Revenue on its profits – a sole trader pays income tax, a limited company pays corporation tax – the level of profitability will dictate the amount of tax that will have to be paid
- *ability to raise finance* – the management will want to be sure that the business has sufficient capital resources and future income to be able to raise and repay finance – see "the bank" below

**the bank**   The bank manager will want to be reassured that any money lent to the business will be repaid when due. The bank will be particularly interested in:

- *capital strength* – how dependent is the business on outside borrowing?
- *profitability* – what are the prospects of borrowing being repaid in the future?
- *liquidity* – what are the prospects of short-term borrowing being repaid in the present? is the business solvent?

**the investor**   A person investing in a business – a private individual or a specialised investment company – will be particularly interested in the return that will be received:

- *profitability* – what profits are being made ?
- *investment ratios* – what is the level of return given to the investor, and how does it compare with that of similar businesses?

**the employee**   The employer will want to motivate the employee and instil loyalty by showing that the business is doing well, particularly in terms of:

- *profitability* – the employee may receive a part of the profit in a 'profit-sharing' scheme
- *capital strength* – the employee will be reassured to know the extent of the total Net Assets of a business, as shown on the balance sheet

We will first look at how these ratios and percentages are calculated, and will then apply a number of them to a Case Study of a sole trader business: 'Financial Statements of J Brown' .

## profitability

### gross profit percentage

$\dfrac{\textit{Gross profit for year}}{\textit{Sales for year}} \times \dfrac{100}{1} = \textit{Gross profit/sales percentage}$

This expresses, as a percentage, the gross profit in relation to sales. For example, a gross profit percentage of 20 per cent means that for every £100 of sales made, the gross profit is £20.

The gross profit percentage should be similar from year-to-year for the same organisation. It will vary between organisations in different areas of business, eg the gross profit percentage on jewellery is considerably higher than that on basic items of food. A significant change from one year to the next, particularly a fall in the percentage, needs further investigation.

### net profit percentage

$\dfrac{\textit{Net profit for year}}{\textit{Sales for year}} \times \dfrac{100}{1} = \textit{Net profit/sales percentage}$

As with gross profit percentage, the net profit percentage should be similar from year-to-year for the same business, and should also be comparable with other firms in the same line of business. Ideally the net profit percentage should show a slight increase, which indicates that the profit and loss account costs are being kept under control. Any significant fall should be investigated to see if it has been caused by an increase in one particular expense, eg wages and salaries, advertising, etc.

A large expense item can always be expressed as a percentage of sales, eg

$\dfrac{\textit{Specified expense}}{\textit{Sales for year}} \times \dfrac{100}{1} = \textit{Expense/sales percentage}$

For example, the relationship between advertising and sales might be found to be 10 per cent in one year, but 20 per cent the next year. This would probably indicate that an increase in advertising had failed to produce a proportionate increase in sales.

### return on capital employed

$\dfrac{\textit{Net profit for year}}{\textit{Capital employed at start of year}} \times \dfrac{100}{1} = \textit{Percentage return on capital employed}$

This expresses the net profit of the business in relation to the owner's capital. For this calculation, the capital at the start of the year should, ideally, be used but, if this is not known, the year-end figure can be used. The percentage return is best thought of in relation to other investments, eg a building society might offer a return of eight per cent, or a bank might offer five per cent on a deposit account. A person running a business is investing a sum of money in that business, and the net profit is the return that is achieved on that investment. However, it should be noted that the risks in running a business are considerably greater than depositing the money with a building society or bank, and an additional return to compensate for the extra risk is needed.

The calculation of return on capital employed can be varied to consider not only the owner's capital, but also to include any long-term loans, because they are a part of the semi-permanent capital of the organisation.

# capital strength - gearing

It is useful to be able to see to what extent an organisation relies on outside borrowing and to what extent it is financed by the owner(s)' capital and accumulated profit. The relationship between these two figures demonstrates the *capital strength* of the organisation – the *gearing* as it is commonly known. The gearing percentage is usually calculated as follows:

$$\frac{\textit{Outside borrowing (eg bank loans)}}{\textit{Capital}} \; x \; 100 \; = \; \textit{gearing percentage}$$

If the percentage is over 100% it means that the organisation is borrowing *more* than the amount of the owner's capital, a vulnerable situation, if, say, the borrowing had to be repaid in a short space of time. High gearing also means that the business will be paying substantial amounts in interest. Note: gearing can also be expressed as a ratio (ie outside borrowing : capital).

# liquidity

### working capital ratio/current ratio

$$\frac{\textit{Current assets}}{\textit{Current liabilities}} \; = \; \textit{Working capital ratio (also known as the current ratio )}$$

Using figures from the balance sheet, this ratio measures the relationship between current assets and current liabilities. Working capital (calculated as *current assets minus current liabilities* ) is needed by all organisations in order to finance day-to-day trading activities.  Sufficient working capital enables an organisation to hold adequate stocks, allow a measure of credit to its customers (debtors), and to pay its suppliers (creditors) as payments fall due.

Although there is no ideal working capital ratio, an often accepted ratio is about 2:1, ie £2 of current assets to every £1 of current liabilities.  However, an organisation in the retail trade may be able to work with a lower ratio, eg 1.5:1 or even less, because it deals mainly in sales for cash and so does not have a large figure for debtors.  A working capital ratio can be *too* high: if it is above 3:1 an investigation of the make-up of current assets is needed: eg the organisation may have too much stock, too many debtors, or too much cash at the bank, or even too few creditors.

### liquid capital ratio

$$\frac{\textit{(Current assets - stock)}}{\textit{Current liabilities}} \; = \; \textit{Liquid capital ratio (also known as the acid test )}$$

This ratio (also known as the *quick ratio* or *acid test ratio*) includes the current assets and current liabilities from the balance sheet, but stock is omitted. This is because stock is the most illiquid current asset: it has to be sold, turned into debtors, and then the cash has to be collected from the debtors.  Also, some of the stock included in the balance sheet figure may be unsaleable or obsolete.

The balance between liquid assets, that is debtors and cash/bank, and current liabilities should, ideally, be about 1:1, ie £1 of liquid assets to each £1 of current liabilities.  At this ratio an organisation is expected to be able to pay its current liabilities from its liquid assets, a figure below 1:1, eg 0.75:1, indicates that the organisation would have difficulty in meeting pressing demands from creditors. However, as with the working capital ratio, certain types of organisation are able to operate with a lower liquid capital ratio than others.

With both the working capital and the liquid capital ratios, trends from one year to the next need to be considered, or comparisons made with similar organisations.

# activity

## stock turnover

$$\frac{Average\ stock}{Cost\ of\ goods\ sold}\ x\ 365\ days = Stock\ turnover\ (in\ days)$$

This calculation uses information from the trading account: average stock is usually found by taking the average of the opening and closing stocks, ie (opening stock + closing stock) ÷ 2; cost of goods sold is the figure before gross profit is ascertained. Stock turnover is the average number of days in the financial year that the stock is held by the business. For example, a market trader selling fresh flowers who finishes each day when sold out will have a stock turnover of one day. By contrast a furniture shop may have a stock turnover of 90 days, the average length of time for which an item of furniture is held in the shop before being sold. The lower the stock turnover, the more efficient the organisation, for the same *type* of business.

## debtors' collection period

$$\frac{Debtors}{Credit\ sales\ for\ year}\ x\ 365\ days = Debtors'\ collection\ time\ (in\ days)$$

This calculation shows how long, on average, debtors take to pay for goods sold to them by the organisation. The figure of *credit sales for the year* may not be disclosed in the trading account, in which case the sales figure should be used. Some organisations make the majority of their sales on credit but others, such as shops, will have a considerably lower proportion of credit sales. The debtors collection period can be compared with that for the previous year, or with that of a similar organisation. In the UK, most debtors should make payment within 30 to 60 days; however, sales made abroad will take longer for the proceeds to be received. A comparison from year-to-year of the collection period is a measure of the organisation's efficiency at collecting the money that is due to it.

## credit control – aged debtors schedule

The system set up to collect debts within the given credit period is known as *credit control*. It involves sending regular statements to customers, chasing up debts by telephone and letter, and threatening and taking legal action for the recovery of the debt where necessary. Good credit control is an important ingredient for successful trading: it enables money to be collected which can then be used in the business. An 'aged debtors schedule' is a list of individual debtors (buyers), the amounts they owe, and the period of time the debts have been outstanding. This schedule (which can be printed out by traders with computer accounting systems) will enable a business to follow up overdue amounts, and recover money which might otherwise be lost. An example of an aged debtors schedule is illustrated below.

```
JR CATERING LTD          SALES LEDGER – AGED DEBTORS SCHEDULE


A /C  Account  Name      Turnover Credit Limit  Balance  Current  30 Days  60 Days  Older
----  --------------     -------- -----------   -------- -------- -------  -------  ------
201   Merrion & Co         370.00    1000.00     164.50   164.50    0.00     0.00    0.00
202   Kingfisher Ltd       320.00     750.00     376.00   376.00    0.00     0.00    0.00
204   I Marcos         *  1730.00    1000.00    1632.75   799.00    0.00   833.75    0.00
205   Compusoft Ltd       2025.00    2000.00    1926.88  1880.00   46.88     0.00    0.00
208   R Weinberger         425.00     750.00     499.38   499.38    0.00     0.00    0.00

                         -------- -----------   -------- -------- -------  ------ - ------
              Totals :   4870.00    5500.00     4599.51  3718.88   46.88   833.75    0.00
```

Note the following details from the aged debtors schedule on the previous page:

- 'turnover' is the total amount of sales to the customer during the accounting period (usually a year)
- 'credit limit' is the maximum amount that the business is willing to allow a customer to owe at any one time (this is the same principle as a bank overdraft)
- the 'balance' is the amount owing by a customer at the date of the schedule – note that the asterisk marks an account over its credit limit
- the remaining columns show how the 'balance' is made up: '30 days' means 'over 30 days', '60 days' means 'over 60 days', and so on; clearly if 30 days' credit terms are given, anything over 30 days (possibly) or 60 days (definitely) would need chasing up

## creditors' payment period

$$\frac{Creditors}{Credit\ Purchases} \times 365\ days = Creditors'\ payment\ time\ (in\ days)$$

This calculation is the 'other side of the coin' to that of debtors: here we are measuring the speed it takes a business to pay creditors. While creditors can be a useful temporary source of finance, delaying payment too long may cause problems, as suppliers may 'stop' the account and refuse to supply further goods on credit. Paying at the last minute provides a business with interest-free money for 30 to 60 days. Large businesses sometimes exploit this opportunity by negotiating long periods of credit from 'small' suppliers, or simply by not paying until long after the due date. There is little the 'small' supplier can do!

### aged creditors' schedule

An aged creditor schedule may be drawn up, or printed out by the computer accounting system, on a monthly basis. It is based on the same principles as an aged debtor schedule and shows essentially what debts are due to whom, and when. It will ensure that debts are not paid before time, and at the same time it will prevent a due date from passing by unnoticed. A schedule is illustrated below.

```
JR CATERING LTD          PURCHASES LEDGER - AGED CREDITORS SCHEDULE


A /C   Account  Name     Turnover Credit Limit  Balance  Current  30 Days 60 Days  Older
----   --------------    -------- ------------  -------- --------  ------- -------  ------
601    Alpha Foods        1200.00    1000.00     164.50   164.50     0.00    0.00    0.00
602    Nova Meats Ltd     4562.50    3000.00     350.00   350.00     0.00    0.00    0.00
604    Tuscany Wines       750.75    1000.00     124.75     0.00   124.75    0.00    0.00
605    Bennets            2025.00    2000.00     345.26     0.00    45.26  300.00    0.00
608    Zeta Supplies       425.00     750.00       0.00     0.00     0.00    0.00    0.00
                         -------- ------------  -------- --------  ------- -------- ------
            Totals :      8963.25    7750.00     984.51   514.50   170.01  300.00    0.00
```

## investment ratios

Investment ratios are useful indicators for investors who intend to buy holdings of shares in limited companies. These ratios are also of interest to people who already own shares and who receive the annual report of the company. It must be stressed that the list of ratios set out below is by no means exhaustive; it does however include the main indicators to be found in the annual reports of companies and in the financial pages of the daily press. You will note that the word 'ratios' is applied in a loose sense; many of the indicators are expressed in terms of pence or percentages.

## dividend per share

$$\frac{Dividends\ for\ year}{Number\ of\ shares\ issued} = Dividend\ per\ share\ (pence)$$

Investors receive a return on their investment in the form of dividend payments, often twice a year: the *interim* dividend and the *final* dividend. The money amount of the dividends is calculated as a number of *pence* per share (the price of shares is always expressed in pence). Investors will clearly be interested in this figure as it represents what they will be receiving before deduction of tax.

## earnings per share

$$\frac{Net\ profit,\ after\ corporation\ tax\ and\ preference\ dividends}{Number\ of\ issued\ ordinary\ shares} = Earnings\ per\ share\ (pence)$$

Earnings per share (or EPS) measures the amount of profit *earned* by each share, after corporation tax and preference dividends. Comparisons can be made with previous years to provide a basis for assessing the company's performance. It must be borne in mind that profit per share is not the same as dividend per share. The profit per share will not be paid out in full as dividends, some of the profit will be retained in the company for reinvestment and expansion.

## dividend cover

$$\frac{Net\ profit,\ after\ corporation\ tax\ and\ preference\ dividends}{Ordinary\ dividends} = Dividend\ cover$$

This figure shows the margin of safety between the amount of profit a company makes and the amount paid out in dividends. The figure must be greater than 1 if the company is not to use past retained profits to fund the current dividend. For example, a figure of 5 as dividend cover indicates that profit exceeds dividend by five times – a healthy sign. The share price pages in the financial press quote the dividend cover figure under the column headed 'cover' or its abbreviation 'cvr'.

## price/earnings ratio

$$\frac{Market\ price\ of\ ordinary\ share\ (in\ pence)}{Earnings\ per\ ordinary\ share\ (in\ pence)} = Price/earnings\ ratio$$

The price/earnings ratio (or P/E ratio, as it is often abbreviated) compares the current market price of a share and the earnings (after corporation tax) of that share. For example, if a particular share has a market price of £3, and the earnings per share in the current year are 30p, then the P/E ratio is 10. This simply means that a person buying the share for £3 is paying ten times the last reported earnings of that share. Investors make use of the P/E ratio to help them make decisions as to the 'expensiveness' of a share.

## other indicators
Other figures of interest to investors and highlighted in the annual report of a company will include
- profit before taxation
- total assets
- shareholders' funds, ie the capital position of the company

# Case Study: financial statements of J. Brown

## Situation

The accounts of J. Brown have been submitted to you for analysis.

### TRADING AND PROFIT AND LOSS ACCOUNTS
### FOR THE YEAR ENDED 31 DECEMBER 19-1

|  | £ | £ |
|---|---:|---:|
| Sales | | 150,000 |
| Opening stock | 10,000 | |
| Purchases | 66.000 | |
| | 76,000 | |
| Less closing stock | 16.000 | |
| Cost of goods sold | | 60.000 |
| **Gross profit** | | 90,000 |
| | | |
| Less: | | |
| Wages and salaries | 60,000 | |
| Advertising | 15,000 | |
| Sundry expenses | 5.000 | |
| | | 80.000 |
| **Net profit** | | 10,000 |

### BALANCE SHEET AS AT 31 DECEMBER 19-1

|  | £ | £ | £ |
|---|---:|---:|---:|
| **Fixed assets** | | | |
| Premises | | | 70,000 |
| Machinery | | | 30.000 |
| | | | 100,000 |
| **Current assets** | | | |
| Stock | | 16,000 | |
| Debtors | | 12.500 | |
| | | 28,500 | |
| | | | |
| **Less Current liabilities** | | | |
| Creditors | 11,000 | | |
| Bank overdraft | 24.500 | | |
| | | 35.500 | |
| **Working capital** | | | (7.000) |
| **NET ASSETS** | | | 93.000 |
| | | | |
| *FINANCED BY* | | | |
| **Capital** | | | |
| Opening capital | | | 90,000 |
| Add net profit | | | 10.000 |
| | | | 100,000 |
| Less drawings | | | 7.000 |
| | | | 93,000 |

# Solution

## Calculations

### PROFITABILITY

Gross profit/sales percentage $= \dfrac{£90,000}{£150,000} \times \dfrac{100}{1}$ $= 60\%$

Net profit/sales percentage $= \dfrac{£10,000}{£150,000} \times \dfrac{100}{1}$ $= 6.7\%$

Wages and salaries/sales $= \dfrac{£60,000}{£150,000} \times \dfrac{100}{1}$ $= 40\%$

Advertising/sales $= \dfrac{£15,000}{£150,000} \times \dfrac{100}{1}$ $= 10\%$

Return on capital employed $= \dfrac{£10,000}{£90,000} \times \dfrac{100}{1}$ $= 11.1\%$

### CAPITAL STRENGTH/GEARING

Overdraft/Capital $= \dfrac{£24,500}{£93,000} \times \dfrac{100}{1}$ $= 26\%$

### LIQUIDITY

Working capital ratio $= \dfrac{£28,500}{£35,500}$ $= 0.8:1$

Liquid capital ratio $= \dfrac{£12,500}{£35,500}$ $= 0.35:1$

### ACTIVITY

Stock turnover $= \dfrac{£13,000}{£60,000} \times 365$ $= 79$ days

Debtors' collection time $= \dfrac{£12,500}{£150,000} \times 365$ $= 30$ days

Creditors' payment time $= \dfrac{£11,000}{£66,000} \times 365$ $= 61$ days

## Comments

### PROFITABILITY

This business has a product with a high gross profit percentage of 60% (comparisons with the previous year/similar firms need to be made). Unfortunately the high gross profit percentage is not fully reflected in the fairly low net profit percentage. Wages form 40% of the selling cost and an investigation should be made by the owner of the business to see if savings can be made here; similarly the advertising percentage appears to be quite high. Nevertheless, the business has provided a satisfactory return on the owner's capital.

## CAPITAL STRENGTH/GEARING

The size of the owner's capital (£93,000) is in excess of the overdraft (£24,500), which is the only external borrowing of the business, although as we will see, there may be a problem with this bank borrowing. The gearing percentage of 26% is nevertheless very satisfactory: the business should not be vulnerable to the withdrawal of loans.

## LIQUIDITY

Both the working capital and the liquid capital indicators are extremely low. The problems here seem to stem from the high bank overdraft, and the reasons for this need investigating. The business is technically solvent in that assets nominally exceed liabilities, but the danger is that the bulk of the assets are premises and machinery – possibly charged (mortgaged) to the bank to cover the borrowing – and therefore not available to pay pressing bills. The

## ACTIVITY

The stock turnover is 79 days, and comparisons need to be made to see if this is satisfactory for the type of business.

The debtors' collection time is satisfactory, indicating good control procedures. The aged debtor's schedule (see below) supports this conclusion. On the other hand, the creditors' payment time is twice as long, and the aged creditors' schedule (see below) contains one or two large bills that are overdue. It may be that the bank has refused to pay any more cheques and this has resulted in the lengthy period of credit being taken: these are very real danger signals to the owner of the business and, of course, to the bank.

| | SALES LEDGER - AGED DEBTORS SCHEDULE | | | | 31 Dec 19-1 | | |
|---|---|---|---|---|---|---|---|
| A/C  Account Name | Turnover | Credit Limit | Balance | Current | 30 days | 60 days | over 90 |
| 201  Caithness & Co | 35000 | 10000 | 4150 | 4150 | 0 | 0 | 0 |
| 202  Mereford College | 10500 | 2000 | 1750 | 0 | 1750 | 0 | 0 |
| 204  Avon Publishers | 67500 | 40000 | 6000 | 4000 | 2000 | 0 | 0 |
| 205  Farrow Designs | 25000 | 1000 | 100 | 100 | 0 | 0 | 0 |
| 208  A J Taylor Ltd | 12000 | 1000 | 500 | 300 | 200 | 0 | 0 |
| Totals : | 150000 | 54000 | 12500 | 8550 | 3950 | 0 | 0 |

| | PURCHASES LEDGER - AGED CREDITORS SCHEDULE | | | | 31 Dec 19-1 | | |
|---|---|---|---|---|---|---|---|
| A/C  Account Name | Turnover | Credit Limit | Balance | Current | 30 days | 60 days | over 90 |
| 601  Berwick Paper | 50000 | 30000 | 8000 | 0 | 0 | 3000 | 5000 |
| 602  Litho Supplies | 4000 | 2000 | 750 | 0 | 750 | 0 | 0 |
| 604  Mentor Group | 1000 | 2000 | 500 | 0 | 0 | 500 | 0 |
| 605  Barlow Paper | 7000 | 5000 | 1000 | 0 | 0 | 0 | 1000 |
| 606  Mereford Agency | 4000 | 1000 | 750 | 0 | 200 | 0 | 550 |
| Totals : | 66000 | 40000 | 11000 | 0 | 950 | 3500 | 6550 |

## conclusion

This appears to be a profitable business on the face of it , although there may be scope for cutting down somewhat on the profit and loss account expenses of wages and salaries, and advertising. The business offers a reasonable return on capital, and the gearing is low. However, the business badly needs a fresh injection of capital in order to reduce the bank overdraft and to pay pressing creditors: this would help to restore the working capital and liquid ratios to more acceptable levels. It might be that the owner of the business should consider taking on a partner who may be able to inject more cash and thus help the liquidity problem. In the meantime, however, the position is precarious, and care should be taken to placate creditors in order to enable the business to continue trading.

## problems of interpretation

It is important to appreciate that there are a number of problems which can make interpretation of financial statements more difficult:

* The financial statements record what has gone on in the past and are not a certain guide to what will happen in the future. Therefore decisions made on the basis of last year's financial statements may be invalid on the basis of changed circumstances – for example, consider the international price fluctuations of a barrel of oil and the effect this has on companies (and not just oil companies), or the effect of exchange rate fluctuations on companies which trade abroad.

* The balance sheet shows the assets and liabilities at one particular date, but may not be representative of the year as a whole – it may have been *window-dressed* for the financial year-end, or the business may be seasonal in nature.

* Inflation may have an effect on the year-to-year comparison of figures such as turnover and sales: the higher the rate of inflation, the greater the problem.

## chapter summary

❏ Monitoring financial information is an important function within a business. Conclusions can be drawn from financial statements which will be of use to the management of the business, the bank, the investor and employees.

❏ The financial statements monitored include the profit and loss statement, the balance sheet and aged debtors and aged creditors schedules.

❏ Monitoring of financial information involves the calculation of accounting ratios and percentages which can be used to measure
* profitability
* capital strength
* liquidity
* activity
* investment potential

❏ Comparisons need to be made with previous financial statements, or those of similar organisations.

❏ A number of limitations should be borne in mind when drawing conclusions from ratios. These include problems of changing circumtances, unrepresentative accounts and the effects of inflation

## Student Activities

**39.1**   You are working as a trainee accountant and come across, in your firm's files, the following information relating to two businesses, A and B.

|  | BUSINESS A | | BUSINESS B | |
| --- | --- | --- | --- | --- |
|  | £000s | £000s | £000s | £000s |
| **PROFIT AND LOSS ACCOUNT EXTRACTS** | | | | |
| Sales | | 3,057 | | 1,628 |
| Cost of goods sold | | 2,647 | | 911 |
| **Gross Profit** | | 410 | | 717 |
| Expenses | | 366 | | 648 |
| **Net Profit** | | 44 | | 69 |
| | | | | |
| **SUMMARISED BALANCE SHEETS** | | | | |
| **Fixed Assets** | | 344 | | 555 |
| **Current Assets** | | | | |
| Stock | 242 | | 237 | |
| Debtors | 6 | | 269 | |
| Bank/cash | 3 | | 1 | |
| | 251 | | 507 | |
| **Less Current Liabilities** | 195 | | 212 | |
| **Working Capital** | | 56 | | 295 |
| **NET ASSETS** | | 400 | | 850 |
| | | | | |
| **FINANCED BY** | | | | |
| | | | | |
| Capital | | 400 | | 850 |

One business operates a chain of grocery supermarkets; the other is a heavy engineering company.

As a training exercise your boss asks you to:

• Calculate the following accounting ratios for both businesses:

   (a)   gross profit percentage

   (b)   net profit percentage

   (c)   stock turnover (use balance sheet figure as *average* stock)

   (d)   working capital (current) ratio

   (e)   liquid capital ratio

   (f)   debtors' collection period

   (g)   return on capital employed

• Indicate which company you believe to be the grocery supermarket chain and which the heavy engineering business.  Briefly explain the reasons for your choice based on the ratios calculated and the accounting information.

Present your findings in the form of a memorandum.  Your boss is Gareth Davies, Senior Partner in Davies, Davies and Lloyd.  Use your own name and today's date.

**39.2** You work in the Accounts Department of Thomsons Sports Limited, a sports equipment wholesaler. Your department has recently been computerised and one of the programs provided is a spreadsheet. Your boss asks you to set up a spreadsheet for analysing the business' financial statements. He says that the management are particularly interested in

(a) return on capital employed
(b) gearing
(c) gross profit percentage
(d) net profit percentage
(e) current ratio
(f) liquid capital ratio
(g) debtor payment period (days)
(h) creditor payment period (days
(i) stock turnover (days)

Extracts from the figures for the last two years trading are as follows:

| | 19-8 | 19-9 |
|---|---|---|
| | £ | £ |
| Sales | 240,000 | 400,000 |
| Cost of sales | 160,000 | 300,000 |
| Purchases | 160,000 | 318,000 |
| Gross profit | 80,000 | 100,000 |
| Net profit | 60,000 | 70,000 |
| | | |
| Fixed assets | 70,000 | 75,000 |
| Stock | 14,000 | 32,000 |
| Debtors | 24,000 | 40,000 |
| Bank (<u>not</u> overdraft) | 2,000 | 3,000 |
| Creditors | 20,000 | 40,000 |
| Long-term bank loan | 20,000 | 20,000 |
| Share capital and reserves | 70,000 | 90,000 |

You are to

(a) set up a spreadsheet model into which you can enter the figures set out above and extract by means of formulas the various accounting ratios and indicators

(b) write a report addressed to the Finance Director, Jim Thompson, setting out the accounting ratios in a table, including graphs and charts where appropriate, and commenting on the strengths and weaknesses of the figures.

*Note: the use of computer spreadsheets is explained in Chapter 7.*

EVIDENCE
COLLECTION
EXERCISE

# 19

# *Monitoring business performance – Toscano Wines*

| Element 6.3 | *Identify and explain data to monitor business performance* |
|---|---|
| Suggested Sources: | • work experience – examing the financial statements used by a business  (with permission from the business)<br>• practical advice from accountants, bank lending officers and management consultants<br>• textbooks in libraries and resource centres |

## INTRODUCTION

Toscano Wines is a sole trader business operated by Luigi Costello.  He imports wine from the Italian wine growing area of Tuscany, and sells it on credit to large catering companies, hotels and restaurants.  He does not sell to the general public.  He holds the stocks of wine in a warehouse, which he owns, on the outskirts of Mereford (address Unit 1a, Severnside Industrial Estate, Mereford MR3 6TF).  He is proud of the quality of his products:  he has recently invested in a new temperature control system costing £5,000, funded by a loan from a finance company.

You are his accountant, Leslie Bell of 67 Sterling Chambers, Mereford MR4 9TP.  You have just been drawing up financial statements for his business for 19-2 (see the next two pages).  Although Luigi has operated profitably for a number of years, 19-2 saw his profits decline sharply, and you are concerned to identify what the underlying problems are.  You decide to call him in for a meeting.

Before you can discuss the financial position you need to analyse his financial statements by undertaking the tasks set out below, and *writing an informal report (including recommendations) to Luigi Costello incorporating your analysis.  The report is to be sent to  Mr Costello with a covering letter.  Use the date 28 February 19-3.*

## TASK 1
Extract accounting ratios relating to profitability, gearing, liquidity and activity for the two financial years 19-1 and 19-2.  Include in your report a comparison of the indicators for the two years.  Ensure that you *analyse* the figures;  do not just reproduce a list of percentages and ratios.

## TASK 2
*Analyse* the trends shown in the Cashflow statement.  Include in your analysis an explanation of what the statement shows.

## TASK 3
*Analyse* the aged debtors schedule, pointing out any particular weaknesses.

**BALANCE SHEET OF TOSCANO WINES (as at 31 December)**

|  | 19-1 | | | 19-2 | | |
|---|---|---|---|---|---|---|
|  | £ | £ | £ | £ | £ | £ |
|  | Cost | Dep'n | Net | Cost | Dep'n | Net |
| **Fixed Assets** | | | | | | |
| Premises | 75,000 | - | 75,000 | 75,000 | - | 75,000 |
| Fittings | 5,000 | 1,000 | 4,000 | 10,000 | 3,000 | 7,000 |
|  | 80,000 | 1,000 | 79,000 | 85,000 | 3,000 | 82,000 |
| **Current Assets** | | | | | | |
| Stock | | 7,000 | | | 15,000 | |
| Debtors | | 6,000 | | | 8,000 | |
| Bank | | 550 | | | - | |
|  | | 13,550 | | | 23,000 | |
| **Less Current Liabilities** | | | | | | |
| Creditors | 7,020 | | | 10,720 | | |
| Bank | - | | | 10,500 | | |
|  | | 7,020 | | | 21,220 | |
| **Working Capital** | | | 6,530 | | | 1,780 |
|  | | | 85,530 | | | 83,780 |
| **Less Long-term Liabilities** | | | | | | |
| Loan from finance company | | | - | | | 5,000 |
| **NET ASSETS** | | | 85,530 | | | 78,780 |
| | | | | | | |
| **FINANCED BY** | | | | | | |
| **Capital** | | | 75,000 | | | 85,530 |
| Add net profit for year | | | 20,530 | | | 10,250 |
|  | | | 95,530 | | | 95,780 |
| Less drawings | | | 10,000 | | | 17,000 |
|  | | | 85,530 | | | 78,780 |

**TOSCANO WINES: PROFIT AND LOSS ACCOUNT EXTRACTS (for year ended 31 December)**

|  | 19-1 | 19-2 |
|---|---|---|
|  | £ | £ |
| Sales (all on credit) | 200,000 | 175,000 |
| Cost of sales | 150,000 | 130,000 |
| Gross profit | 50,000 | 45,000 |
| | | |
| Net profit | 20,530 | 10,250 |
| | | |
| *Overheads included in the profit and loss account:* | | |
| Interest | 130 | 1,500 |
| Depreciation | 750 | 2,000 |
| Advertising | 1,545 | 3,575 |
| | | |
| *Drawings:* | 10,000 | 17,000 |

Note: the stock figure as at 31 December 19-0 was £5,500

**CASHFLOW STATEMENT OF TOSCANO WINES (for the year-ended 31 December 19-2)**

|  | £ | £ |
|---|---:|---:|
| **Operating activities:** | | |
| Net profit (before interest) | 11,750 | |
| Depreciation for year | 2,000 | |
| Increase in stock | (8,000) | |
| Increase in debtors | (2,000) | |
| Increase in creditors | <u>3,700</u> | |
| *Net cash inflow from operating activities* | | 7,450 |
| | | |
| **Returns on investments and servicing of finance** | | |
| Interest paid | (1,500) | |
| Drawings paid | <u>(17,000)</u> | |
| *Net cash outflow from returns on investments* | | |
| *and servicing of finance* | | (18,500) |
| | | |
| **Taxation:** | | |
| *Tax paid\** | | – |
| | | |
| **Investing activities:** | | |
| Purchase of fixed assets | (5,000) | |
| *Net cash outflow from investing activities* | | <u>(5,000)</u> |
| | | |
| Net cash outflow before financing | | (16,050) |
| | | |
| **Financing:** | | |
| Loan from finance company | <u>5,000</u> | |
| *Net cash inflow from financing* | | <u>5,000</u> |
| | | |
| Decrease in cash | | (11,050) |
| | | |
| **Analysis of changes in cash during the year:** | | |
| Bank balance at start of year | | 550 |
| Net cash outflow | | <u>(11,050)</u> |
| | | |
| Balance at end of year | | (10,500) |

\*Note: as Toscano Wines is a sole trader business, the owner is assessed for tax by the Inland Revenue on a *personal* basis, and therefore tax is not included here.

**AGED DEBTORS ANALYSIS OF TOSCANO WINES (accounts outstanding at 31 December 19-2)**

| TOSCANO WINES | SALES LEDGER - AGED DEBTORS SCHEDULE | | | | | DATE: 30 12 -2 | | |
|---|---|---:|---:|---:|---:|---:|---:|---:|
| A/C | Account Name | Turnover | Credit Limit | Balance | Current | 30 days | 60 days | over 90 |
| 251 | BULLIER LTD | 40000 | 3000 | 3500 | 0 | 0 | 500 | 3000 |
| 252 | CRAVEN HOTEL | 5000 | 1500 | 2000 | 0 | 1500 | 0 | 500 |
| 254 | HEATON FOODS | 3000 | 1000 | 500 | 100 | 200 | 100 | 100 |
| 255 | COX CATERING | 20000 | 3000 | 1500 | 1500 | 0 | 0 | 0 |
| 258 | TAMMADGE & CO | 7000 | 1000 | 500 | 0 | 200 | 300 | 0 |
| | Totals : | 75000 | 8500 | 8000 | 1600 | 1900 | 900 | 3600 |

**SECTION**

# financial resources

## contents

Financial resources are essential to a business. They comprise:

- sources of external finance – from banks and investors
- resources within the business itself – net assets and the ability of the business to generate profit

In the previous Section of the book – "Financial Transactions and Monitoring" – we looked at how a business constructs financial statements and measures its *past* performance. In this Section we examine the processes of a business assessing present and potential financial resources and making projections of those needs and *future* performance. These are dealt with as follows:

In the next Section of the book – "Business Planning" – we see how a number of these financial projections are combined in the *business plan*, a document which "sells" the business idea to an outside party, such as a bank, which is being approached with a request to provide financial resources.

## unit covereage

As already noted (see page 293) GNVQ Element 7.4 "Produce and explain profit and loss statements and balance sheets" is covered in Section 6 of this book, as the subject matter logically falls between a study of financial transactions and investigations into the monitoring of business performance: it is clearly necessary to study financial statements before becoming competent in analysing them. You should note that in order to fulfil the requirements of GNVQ Unit 7, it will be necessary to study Chapters 35 to 37 in Section 6 of this book, and provide the appropriate evidence for assessment.

# 40 Budgeting – the cash flow forecast

## introduction

Budgeting is a planning process which is carried out by everybody. If you want to go out in the evening, you decide where you are going, you work out how much money you are going to need, you look to see how much money you have got, and if you are short you borrow the money from your family. If you cannot raise the money you probably stay at home and watch a video!

This, in principle, is essentially the same financial planning process which an efficient business undertakes as a matter of course:

- management decides what resources are needed for the business
- the costs are calculated
- money is raised from outside if the owner does not have the resources
- if the money cannot be raised, or if the costs are too high, you do not proceed with the planned business activity – you plan something else instead

The budgeting process is not an activity which *only* takes place when a business is starting up for the first time, or is expanding its activities, budgeting is carried out as an ongoing activity, an aid to the management of the business.

In this chapter we will look specifically at a specific short-term budget, the *cash flow forecast,* also known as the cash budget, which projects cash received and cash spent month-by-month, and forecasts the likely bank balance at the end of each month

We examine the way the cash flow forecast is constructed and show how a computer spreadsheet can be used to speed up the process and provide flexibility when figures in the cash flow forecast need to be changed.

We will also examine the *variances* which affect the budget figures – factors such as a fall in sales, a fall in costs, a rise in interest rates (the cost of borrowing) – and see how a business adapts to these changes.

# budgets and the business plan

*A budget is a planning and control tool relevant to the management of an organisation*

The main purposes of budgeting are:
* to assist in the assessment and evaluation of different *courses of action*
* to create motivation by expressing a proposed plan of action in terms of *targets*
* to monitor the effectiveness of performance being accomplished against the budget, and to report *variances*

Budgets are usually prepared for a period of a year, and are usually broken down into shorter time periods, commonly monthly. This enables control to be exercised over the budget: as time passes by, the business' actual results can be compared to those projected in the budget, and discrepancies between the two can be investigated.

## subsidiary budgets and the master budget

Depending on the size and sophistication of the organisation, a number of different subsidiary budgets can be drawn up, for example
* sales budget
* purchases budget
* production budget
* overheads budget
* cash budget (the cash flow forecast)

These individual budgets are then combined in the production of a *master budget* which takes the form of budgeted *operating statements:* a profit and loss account forecast and a projected balance sheet. You will already be familiar with the format of these statements; we will deal with the method of *forecasting* them in the next chapter.

## business plan

The forecast profit and loss forecast and forecast balance sheet, together with the cash flow forecast (the subject of this chapter) are useful to the management of a business as they stand. They are *also* essential documents which form the basis of the financial section of what is known as a *busines plan*. A business plan is a formal written plan setting what the business is, what it aims to achieve, and how it intends to achieve it. Chapter 47 covers the compilation of a business plan in detail. Although there is no set format for a business plan, it is often set out in five sections:
* the *objectives* of the business - its aims and short-term and long-term targets
* the *marketing plan* of thebusiness – the market it is selling in, and how the business will approach that market
* the *production plan* (if the business is manufacturing or processing)
* the *resources* the business will need – premises, machinery, raw materials, and finance for these
* the *financial* projections, setting out how the finance will be repaid – cash flow forecast, profit and loss forecast and projected balance

A business plan will be produced when
* a business is starting up for the first time
* an existing business is expanding it operations
* an existing business is reviewing its operations

The business plan is both a useful exercise for the management in analysing the way the business is progressing (or not, as the case may be) and also an essential document a business will present to a potential lender, such as the bank, when it wants to borrow money.

We will now examine the way in which a cash flow forecast is constructed.

# cash flow forecast

*The purpose of a cash flow forecast is to detail the expected cash/bank receipts and payments, usually on a month-by-month basis, usually for the next six or twelve months, in order to show the estimated bank balance at the end of each month throughout the period.*

From the cash flow forecast, the managers of a business can decide what action to take when a surplus of cash is shown to be available or, as is more likely, when a bank overdraft needs to be arranged. A simplified format of a cash budget, with sample figures, is set out below.

Name ....................................................Cash Flow Forecast for the .................. months ending ...........

|  | Jan £000 | Feb £000 | Mar £000 | etc. £000 |
|---|---|---|---|---|
| **Receipts** | | | | |
| eg   sales receipts | 150 | 150 | 161 | 170 |
|       other receipts (loans, capital, interest) | 70 | 80 | 75 | 80 |
| Total receipts for month (A) | 220 | 230 | 236 | 250 |
| **Payments** | | | | |
| eg   to creditors | 160 | 165 | 170 | 170 |
|       expenses | 50 | 50 | 50 | 60 |
|       fixed assets | | 50 | | |
| Total payments for month (B) | 210 | 265 | 220 | 230 |
| Net cashflow (Receipts less Payments, ie A-B) | 10 | (35) | 16 | 20 |
| Add bank balance at beginning of month | 10 | 20 | (15) | 1 |
| Bank balance (overdraft) at end of month | 20 | (15) | 1 | 21 |

As you can see, a the cash flow forecast (cash budget) consists of three main sections:
- receipts for the month
- payments for the month
- summary of bank account

*Receipts* are analysed to show the amount that is expected to be received from sources such as cash sales, receipts from customers supplied on credit, sale of fixed assets, loans, capital introduced and any interest or other income received.

*Payments* will show how much is expected to be paid for cash purchases, to creditors (suppliers), running expenses, purchases of fixed assets, repayment of capital and loans, interest paid and VAT paid.

*Bank summary* at the bottom of the budget shows *net cashflow* (total receipts less total payments) added to the bank balance at the beginning of the month, resulting in the estimated closing bank balance at the end of the month. An overdrawn bank balance is shown in brackets.

*Important Note:* The main difficulty in the preparation of cash flow forecasts lies in the *timing* of receipts and payments – for example, debtors (customers given credit terms) may pay two months after the date of sale, or suppliers may be paid one month after date of purchase: the information given in each case should be studied carefully to ensure that such receipts and payments are correctly recorded. Note too that the cash flow forecast, as its name suggests, deals only in *cash* – any surplus in the bank does *not* equal profit  On the next page we look at a practical example in the form of a Case Study.

## Countrycraft – construction of a cash flow forecast

### the business

Countrycraft is a manufacturer of traditional style pine furniture, its main product being kitchen tables. It is operated as a sole trader business by its owner Tim Chipping in a leased converted mill three miles outside Mereford. Tim runs a van in which he delivers his furniture. Countrycraft sells mainly on credit to furniture stores in the area, although it does sell some goods for cash from the premises. It is New Year and Tim plans to expand the business: he wants to buy some new machinery for £5,000 in March, and is hoping for a loan for this amount from the bank. He is putting in £2,000 of new capital himself in January to help support the expansion. He has therefore with the help of his accountant drawn up a cash flow forecast to include in a business plan which he will submit to the bank.

### the figures

The construction of a cash flow forecast can be a complex operation, particularly when the *timing* element of cash receipts and payments is taken into account. Tim has talked through the figures with his accountant, and has produced the following information which he will use in the forecast (shown on page 431):

### receipts

| | |
|---|---|
| *cash sales* | Tim reckons on taking £500 a month from cash sales on the premises. |
| *from debtors* | Sales on credit are paid for two months after the issue of the invoice, thus sales of £2,000 invoiced in the previous November will be paid for in January. The remaining figures are |

- December sales of £5,000 received February
- January sales of £3,000 received March
- February sales of £4,000 received April
- March sales of £4,500 received May
- April sales of £4,000 received June

| | |
|---|---|
| *capital* | Tim is introducing £2,000 of new capital in January. |
| *loans* | Tim is anticipating raising a bank loan of £5,000 in March. |

### payments

| | |
|---|---|
| *cash purchases* | Tim's cash purchases (materials paid for straightaway) will be January £400, February £200, March £400, April £300, May £400, June £400. |
| *credit purchases* | Tim pays for purchases of timber two months after the month of invoice, ie he will pay for November purchases of £2,000 at the end of January. The other purchases figures are |

- December purchases of £2,500 paid for in February
- January purchases of £3,000 paid for in March
- February purchases of £2,000 paid for in April
- March purchases of £2,000 paid for in May
- April purchases of £1,000 paid for in June

| | |
|---|---|
| *capital items* | Tim plans to buy new machinery for £5,000 in March. |
| *wages* | The wage bill comes to £500 per month. |
| *rent/rates* | The rental and business rates amount to £3,000 and are payable in March. |
| *insurance* | Comprehensive premises insurance of £550 is due in February. |

| | |
|---|---|
| *electricity* | Tim calculates a quarterly electricity bill of £240 will be due in March. |
| *telephone* | Tim calculates a quarterly telephone bill of £300 will be due in April. |
| *VAT* | Tim calculates that he will have to pay VAT of £500 in March and in June (this represents VAT collected from his sales of furniture *less* any VAT paid on his purchases and expenses). |
| *vehicle expenses* | Tim runs a delivery van on the business; he calculates that he will pay £50 a month in petrol, plus road tax of £125 in March and insurance of £300 in May. |
| *stationery* | Tim calculates stationery will cost him about £50 a month. |
| *postages* | Tim calculates postages will be £50 a month, with an extra £150 in March when his catalogue goes out. |
| *bank charges* | These are likely to be £145, charged in March. |
| *interest* | The interest charges for bank borrowing on overdraft will be approximately £35 in March and £25 in June |
| *loan repayments* | It is anticipated that the first repayment of the bank loan (to include interest) will be £500 in June. |
| *advertising* | Tim calculates a cost of £50 per month, with an extra £825 for his catalogue in March. |
| *sundries* | Tim calculates a cost of £50 per month for 'one-off' expenses. |

## bank position

When the figures have been entered in the appropriate columns, and if a computer spreadsheet is *not* being used, the following totals should be calculated:

- the totals for each category of receipt or expense in the far right-hand column (total up each row)
- total receipts (A) for each month, and the far right-hand column, ie work down the columns
- total payments (B) for each month, and the far right-hand column, ie work down the columns
- the total of all the 'totals' (A) and (B) in the far right-hand column, as a cross check
- lastly, total payments (B) should be subtracted from total receipts (A) for each month and the figure entered in the row marked 'Net Cash Flow A – B); a positive figure indicates that money has flowed *into* the business during the month, a negative figure (shown in brackets) indicates that money has flowed *out* of the business during the month

The bank position can then be calculated

| | |
|---|---|
| *opening bank balance* | Insert the bank balance at the beginning of January in the row marked 'Opening bank balance', ie £100 in Tim' case, a figure he will have obtained from his financial records. |
| *closing bank balance* | This is the total of 'Net Cash Flow (A – B)' and opening bank; in Tim's case this is £1,350 plus £100 = £1,450. *This figure should then also be written in as February's 'Opening Bank Balance'* The process is then repeated for February, ie £1,500 plus £1,450 = £2,950 (which is also March's opening balance). |

The bottom line of the cash flow forecast shows the all-important figure of the closing bank balance (the balance at the end of the month). A figure in brackets indicates an overdraft – ie the business will be borrowing from the bank on its current account. In this case Tim will be borrowing on overdraft in March (£2,720), April (£1,570) and May (£20). At the end of June the bank account will be back in credit, at an estimated £1,305.

*Note*

The cash flow forecast will normally be for twelve months' trading, but for the sake of clarity only six months' figures are shown on the cash flow forecast for Countrycraft on the next page.

# Cash flow forecast

name....**Countrycraft**................................................period .....**January – June 19-9**................

| | January £ | February £ | March £ | April £ | May £ | June £ | TOTAL £ |
|---|---|---|---|---|---|---|---|
| **RECEIPTS** | | | | | | | |
| Cash sales | 500 | 500 | 500 | 500 | 500 | 500 | 3,000 |
| From debtors | 2,000 | 5,000 | 3,000 | 4,000 | 4,500 | 4,000 | 22,500 |
| Capital | 2,000 | | | | | | 2,000 |
| Loans | | | 5,000 | | | | 5,000 |
| Interest | | | | | | | |
| **TOTAL RECEIPTS (A)** | 4,500 | 5,500 | 8,500 | 4,500 | 5,000 | 4,500 | 32,500 |
| **PAYMENTS** | | | | | | | |
| Cash purchases | 400 | 200 | 400 | 300 | 400 | 400 | 2,100 |
| Credit purchases | 2,000 | 2,500 | 3,000 | 2,000 | 2,000 | 1,000 | 12,500 |
| Capital items | | | 5,000 | | | | 5,000 |
| Wages | 500 | 500 | 500 | 500 | 500 | 500 | 3,000 |
| Rent/Rates | | | 3,000 | | | | 3,000 |
| Insurance | | 550 | | | | | 550 |
| Electricity | | | 240 | | | | 240 |
| Telephone | | | | 300 | | | 300 |
| VAT | | | 500 | | | 500 | 1,000 |
| Vehicle expenses | 50 | 50 | 175 | 50 | 350 | 50 | 725 |
| Stationery | 50 | 50 | 50 | 50 | 50 | 50 | 300 |
| Postages | 50 | 50 | 200 | 50 | 50 | 50 | 450 |
| Bank charges | | | 145 | | | | 145 |
| Interest charges | | | 35 | | | 25 | 60 |
| Loan repayments | | | | | | 500 | 500 |
| Advertising | 50 | 50 | 875 | 50 | 50 | 50 | 1125 |
| Sundries | 50 | 50 | 50 | 50 | 50 | 50 | 300 |
| **TOTAL PAYMENTS (B)** | 3,150 | 4,000 | 14,170 | 3,350 | 3,450 | 3,175 | 31,295 |
| **NET CASH FLOW (A-B)** | 1,350 | 1,500 | (5,670) | 1,150 | 1,550 | 1,325 | 1,205 |
| **OPENING BANK BALANCE** | 100 | 1,450 | 2,950 | (2,720) | (1,570) | (20) | 100 |
| **CLOSING BANK BALANCE** | 1,450 | 2,950 | (2,720) | (1,570) | (20) | 1305 | 1305 |

# problems with cash flow forecasts

## limitations

While a cash flow forecast is a very useful guide, it is only as good as the estimates on which it is based. A cash flow forecast which is based on optimistic sales for the next six or twelve months will show an equally optimistic picture of the bank balance; a forecast that looks too far into the future will probably prove to be inaccurate in later months.  As with all budgets it is necessary to make comparisons between actual and budget figures: variances need to be investigated. Indeed, many cash budget and cash flow forms have columns for both *projected* and *actual* figures.

## problems with incorrect forecasting

It must be appreciated that cash flow forecasts are only informed estimates of what the cash position of a business *may* be over a given period.  If a business seriously *over*estimates the inflow of cash, it could have serious problems when that cash does not materialise.  The major problem is depletion of working capital.  As we have seen, working capital is the lifeblood of a business, being the excess of current assets (money in hand and due in the short-term) over current liabilities (debts which have to be paid in the short-term).   In basic terms, the business will have cash flow problems and may become insolvent (bankrupt) – the definition of insolvency being the inability to pay debts as they fall due.  A worst view scenario might run along the following lines:

* cash due from debtors does not come in – a major debtor may have become bankrupt
* there is pressure on the bank account as important creditors and wages have to be paid – the bank manager is distinctly unhappy as the overdraft rises above the limit set by the bank, even though the borrowing is secured by a charge (mortgage) over the business premises
* the bank refuses to pay a cheque to a major supplier to whom the business owes money – the supplier refuses to supply any further goods on which the business depends for its production
* the business is unable to fulfil some important orders, so sales income falls further
* employees find that their wages are not being paid
* the bank decides that it is unlikely to be repaid and so it appoints an Administrative Receiver under its mortgage
* the business is closed down by the Receiver and the premises sold off to repay the bank overdraft
* the employees lose their jobs

This is an extreme situation, although regretably it is all too common.  The point here is not that if you make a mistake with your cash flow forecast you are likely to become bankrupt, but rather that an appreciation of the cash flow position is critical for the management of any business.

## a solution – the computer spreadsheet

Often the managers of a business will wish to change the assumptions on which the cash budget is based by saying 'what if?'  For example:

* *What if* half our debtors take two months to pay?
* *What if* one of our major customers becomes bankrupt?
* *What if* we buy a new machine three months earlier than planned?

Each of these examples will change the cash budget substantially, and any two of the three, or all three together, is likely to have a considerable effect on a previously calculated budget, and may lead to an increased bank overdraft requirement.

To answer *'what if?'* questions, the whole cash budget has to be re-worked on the basis of the new assumptions.  The reason for this is that, as the estimates of receipts and payments change each month, so the estimated closing month-end bank balance changes.  This is where a *computer spreadsheet* is ideal for the preparation of cash budgets: each change can be put in, and the computer can be used to re-work all the calculations.  A printout can be taken of each assumption and then passed to the interested parties for their consideration.  On pages 433 to 435 we look at how a cash flow forecast can be input into a computer spreadsheet, using Countrycraft as an example.

## the cash flow forecast on a computer spreadsheet

*If you are unfamiliar with computer spreadsheets you are advised to study Chapter 7 before reading the next three pages.*

The calculations on a cash flow forecast are not particularly difficult, but they do take a long time if you are tackling the task with only pen, paper and calculator. Imagine the situation if you finish the forecast and then find that you have to revise the sales figures: you will have to re-calculate the Total Receipts line, the Net Cash Flow line and all the bank balances. The task is, of course, made simple when you have input the worksheet onto a computer spreadsheet program. You will be able to change any figure, and the computer will do all the recalculations automatically, for example:

• projections of different levels of sales – optimistic, realistic and pessimistic
• projections of different levels of expenditure
• the effect of buying an asset at different times

In each case you will be able to see the effect on the critical figure of the closing bank balance which indicates the amount of money the business may have to borrow.

On the next two pages we set out a six-month cash flow forecast for Countrycraft based on the forecast illustrated on page 431. The second of the forecasts shows the effect of a 25% fall in receipts from debtors. Look at the effect on the bank account – the 'bottom line'. Note also the decrease in VAT payable as the level of sales falls.

### notes on completion of the spreadsheet

• Row 1 includes the name of the business and the heading 'Cash Flow Forecast'
• Row 2 shows the period involved, eg January – June 19-3
• Rows 3, 11, 13, 14, 33, 34 and 36 are left blank to make the presentation clearer
• Column A is used for labels
• Columns B to G show the six months of the forecast
• Column H shows the totals

### use of formulas in the spreadsheet – column C

Extensive use is made here of the addition of a range of cells. You will need to check your computer manual to find the formula to use. The formula used here is *=Sum(C7:C11)* where all the cells between C7 and C11 are added together. Column C is used below for illustrative purposes. The formulas are as follows:

| | |
|---|---|
| • Row 12 – Total Receipts | *=Sum(C7:C11)* |
| • Row 35 – Total Payments | *=Sum(C16:C32)* |
| • Row 37 – Net Cash Flow | *=C12 - C35* |
| • Row 38 – Opening Bank | *=B39* – ie the closing bank balance of the *previous* month. Note that B38 is a value cell into which is entered the opening bank balance for the period. |
| • Row 39 – Closing Bank | *=C37+C38* |
| • Column H – Total column | Each row is totalled, eg cell H7 is *=Sum(B7:G7)*. Column H is also totalled vertically, in the same way as the other columns, except that cell H38 is *=B38* and cell H39 is *=G39* |
| • Row 29 – Interest | This figure may be estimated and entered as a value, or can be approximated by formula. If interest for January is charged at the end of the month, the formula in cell B29 will be *=(B39\*K2/100)/12*. K2 (column K row 2) is the reference of a value cell into which can be entered the current interest rate. |

| | A | B | C | D | E | F | G | H | |
|---|---|---|---|---|---|---|---|---|---|
| 1 | Name of Business: Countrycraft | | | | | | | | |
| 2 | Period:   January - June 19-9 | | | | | | | | |
| 3 | | | | | | | | | |
| 4 | | Jan | Feb | Mar | Apl | May | Jun | Total | |
| 5 | | £ | £ | £ | £ | £ | £ | £ | |
| 6 | RECEIPTS | | | | | | | | |
| 7 | Cash sales | 500 | 500 | 500 | 500 | 500 | 500 | 3000 | |
| 8 | Cash from debtors | 2000 | 5000 | 3000 | 4000 | 4500 | 4000 | 22500 | |
| 9 | Capital | 2000 | | | | | | 2000 | |
| 10 | Loans | | | 5000 | | | | 5000 | |
| 11 | Interest | | | | | | | | |
| 12 | TOTAL RECEIPTS | 4500 | 5500 | 8500 | 4500 | 5000 | 4500 | 32500 | |
| 13 | | | | | | | | | |
| 14 | | | | | | | | | |
| 15 | PAYMENTS | | | | | | | | |
| 16 | Cash purchases | 400 | 200 | 400 | 300 | 400 | 400 | 2100 | |
| 17 | Credit purchases | 2000 | 2500 | 3000 | 2000 | 2000 | 1000 | 12500 | |
| 18 | Capital items | 0 | 0 | 5000 | 0 | 0 | 0 | 5000 | |
| 19 | Wages | 500 | 500 | 500 | 500 | 500 | 500 | 3000 | |
| 20 | Rent/rates | 0 | 0 | 3000 | 0 | 0 | 0 | 3000 | |
| 21 | Insurance | 0 | 550 | 0 | 0 | 0 | 0 | 550 | |
| 22 | Electricity | 0 | 0 | 240 | 0 | 0 | 0 | 240 | |
| 23 | Telephone | 0 | 0 | 0 | 300 | 0 | 0 | 300 | |
| 24 | VAT | 0 | 0 | 500 | 0 | 0 | 500 | 1000 | |
| 25 | Vehicle expenses | 50 | 50 | 175 | 50 | 350 | 50 | 725 | |
| 26 | Stationery | 50 | 50 | 50 | 50 | 50 | 50 | 300 | |
| 27 | Postages | 50 | 50 | 200 | 50 | 50 | 50 | 450 | |
| 28 | Bank charges | 0 | 0 | 145 | 0 | 0 | 0 | 145 | |
| 29 | Interest | 0 | 0 | 35 | 0 | 0 | 25 | 60 | |
| 30 | Loan repayments | 0 | 0 | 0 | 0 | 0 | 500 | 500 | |
| 31 | Advertising | 50 | 50 | 875 | 50 | 50 | 50 | 1125 | |
| 32 | Sundries | 50 | 50 | 50 | 50 | 50 | 50 | 300 | |
| 33 | | | | | | | | | |
| 34 | | | | | | | | | |
| 35 | TOTAL PAYMENTS | 3150 | 4000 | 14170 | 3350 | 3450 | 3175 | 31295 | |
| 36 | | | | | | | | | |
| 37 | NET CASHFLOW | 1350 | 1500 | -5670 | 1150 | 1550 | 1325 | 1205 | |
| 38 | OPENING BANK | 100 | 1450 | 2950 | -2720 | -1570 | -20 | 100 | |
| 39 | CLOSING BANK | 1450 | 2950 | -2720 | -1570 | -20 | 1305 | 1305 | |
| 40 | | | | | | | | | |
| 41 | | | | | | | | | |
| 42 | | | | | | | | | |

*Fig. 40.1  Countrycraft's cash flow forecast on a computer spreadsheet*

| | A | B | C | D | E | F | G | H |
|---|---|---|---|---|---|---|---|---|
| 1 | Name of Business: Countrycraft Designs | | | | | | | |
| 2 | Period:    January - June 19-9 | | | | | | | |
| 3 | | | | | | | | |
| 4 | | Jan | Feb | Mar | Apl | May | Jun | Total |
| 5 | | £ | £ | £ | £ | £ | £ | £ |
| 6 | RECEIPTS | | | | | | | |
| 7 | Cash sales | 500 | 500 | 500 | 500 | 500 | 500 | 3000 |
| 8 | Cash from debtors | 1500 | 3750 | 2250 | 3000 | 3375 | 3000 | 16875 |
| 9 | Capital | 2000 | | | | | | 2000 |
| 10 | Loans | | | 5000 | | | | 5000 |
| 11 | Interest | | | | | | | |
| 12 | TOTAL RECEIPTS | 4000 | 4250 | 7750 | 3500 | 3875 | 3500 | 26875 |
| 13 | | | | | | | | |
| 14 | | | | | | | | |
| 15 | PAYMENTS | | | | | | | |
| 16 | Cash purchases | 400 | 200 | 400 | 300 | 400 | 400 | 2100 |
| 17 | Credit purchases | 2000 | 2500 | 3000 | 2000 | 2000 | 1000 | 12500 |
| 18 | Capital items | 0 | 0 | 5000 | 0 | 0 | 0 | 5000 |
| 19 | Wages | 500 | 500 | 500 | 500 | 500 | 500 | 3000 |
| 20 | Rent/rates | 0 | 0 | 3000 | 0 | 0 | 0 | 3000 |
| 21 | Insurance | 0 | 550 | 0 | 0 | 0 | 0 | 550 |
| 22 | Electricity | 0 | 0 | 240 | 0 | 0 | 0 | 240 |
| 23 | Telephone | 0 | 0 | 0 | 300 | 0 | 0 | 300 |
| 24 | VAT | 0 | 0 | 400 | 0 | 0 | 400 | 800 |
| 25 | Vehicle expenses | 50 | 50 | 175 | 50 | 350 | 50 | 725 |
| 26 | Stationery | 50 | 50 | 50 | 50 | 50 | 50 | 300 |
| 27 | Postages | 50 | 50 | 200 | 50 | 50 | 50 | 450 |
| 28 | Bank charges | 0 | 0 | 145 | 0 | 0 | 0 | 145 |
| 29 | Interest | 0 | 0 | 50 | 0 | 0 | 100 | 150 |
| 30 | Loan repayments | 0 | 0 | 0 | 0 | 0 | 500 | 500 |
| 31 | Advertising | 50 | 50 | 875 | 50 | 50 | 50 | 1125 |
| 32 | Sundries | 50 | 50 | 50 | 50 | 50 | 50 | 300 |
| 33 | | | | | | | | |
| 34 | | | | | | | | |
| 35 | TOTAL PAYMENTS | 3150 | 4000 | 14085 | 3350 | 3450 | 3150 | 31185 |
| 36 | | | | | | | | |
| 37 | NET CASHFLOW | 850 | 250 | -6335 | 150 | 425 | 350 | -4310 |
| 38 | OPENING BANK | 100 | 950 | 1200 | -5135 | -4985 | -4560 | 100 |
| 39 | CLOSING BANK | 950 | 1200 | -5135 | -4985 | -4560 | -4210 | -4210 |
| 40 | | | | | | | | |
| 41 | | | | | | | | |
| 42 | | | | | | | | |

*Fig. 40.2   Countrycraft's cash flow showing a 25% reduction in receipts from debtors*

# dealing with variances

## variances

We have seen when compiling the cash flow forecast that the projected figures are only estimates. It is common for the forecast to present two columns for each month: the *projected* figures are entered in the left-hand column and the *actual* figures are entered next to them in the right-hand column as the months pass. Thus the projected and actual figures can be directly compared. The differences betwen the projected and the actual figures are known as *variances*. There are two types of variance

- *favourable (positive) variances* – results are better than expected – commonly abbreviated to "f"
- *adverse (negative) variances* – results are worse than expected – commonly abbreviated to "a"

Sometimes the variances are not large or significant, in which case no action need be taken. Sometimes the variances can be substantial, in which case action needs to be taken, and particularly if the variances are adverse. As we have seen, businesses often use computer spreadsheet programs – as demonstrated on the previous three pages – to construct budgets by building in different variables, eg levels of sales. We will now look at the different variables.

## changes in sales income

The sales income of business is the number of items sold (or services provided) multiplied by the price of the item. The sales income can therefore vary according to the number of items sold and also as a result of the price charged.

*A rise in sales income* is clearly desirable. If a business has a number of different products, the successful product(s) should be identified and production increased.

*A fall in sales income* needs to be investigated quickly and action taken, eg:

- overpricing – if the item is priced too high when compared with the competition, the price may be reduced to stimulate demand
- slack consumer demand – if the level of spending in the economy is low, or the cost of borrowing high, consumer demand could be stimulated by promotional offers

## changes in costs

Costs involve both direct selling costs (raw materials, labour, production-related costs) and overhead costs (administration, rent and rates, telephone).

*A fall in costs* should result in a favourable variance – a better than expected cash position; the only exception to this would be the unfortunate situation if sales income fell more than costs.

*A rise in costs* can arise from a number of factors:

- a rise in the cost of raw materials from market fluctuations – eg petrol prices for transport firms, grain prices for bakeries
- a rise in the cost of imported materials following exchange rate fluctuations – for example electronics firms dependent on imported silicon chips priced in US Dollars and Japanese Yen, both of which can rise against the pound

## changes in interest rates

Interest rates, as we saw in Chapter 12, are used by the Government to affect the level of demand in the economy. High interest rates help control inflation but they also dampen borrowing by businesses because interest – the cost of borrowing – will be higher. There is not a lot businesses can do about the level of interest rates in the short-term, but a rise in interest rates will affect their budgeting:

- a business with substantial investments will benefit, because the interest income will increase as interest rates rise
- a business with substantial borrowing will suffer because the interest charge will increase

A computer spreadsheet program will be very useful in showing the effect of a change in interest rates. The cash flow forecast format shown on page 434 enables the user to input any given interest rate; the amount of interest will be calculated automatically and the monthly bank balance adjusted accordingly.

# chapter summary

❑ A budget is a planning and control tool used in the management of a business.

❑ In a fully developed budgeting system, subsidiary budgets will contribute to the master budget which comprises a profit and loss forecast and a projected balance sheet.

❑ In most business plans emphasis is placed on he *cash flow forecast* and *profit and loss forecast*. The cash flow forecast shows actual cash amounts received and spent (including VAT), and projects a monthly bank balance. The profit and loss forecast, on the other hand, shows the expected income and expenditure and resultant profit incurred during the period.

❑ Incorrect forecasting can lead to problems with a business' working capital position, to cash flow problems and even to insolvency.

❑ Many businesses find a computer spreadsheet a useful method of calculating and presenting these forecasts. A spreadsheet will enable a business to appreciate the effect on cash flow of a fall in income (or a rise in costs).

❑ Cash flow forecasts are only estimates, and it is normal to compare the actual figures against the projections. The differences between the two are known as variances, and appropriate action should be taken if the variances are significant.

❑ Variances can be caused by a number fluctuations including income, expenditure, interest rates, and exchange rates.

 **student activities**

**40.1**   You are an accountant, Gareth Davies, of Davies, Davies and Lloyd, 4 Bank Chambers, High Street, Stourminster, ST6 7TY. A financially unsophisticated client, Basil Edwards of 10 Springfield Avenue, Stourmnster, ST3 8HY, is raising money to start a business manufacturing wooden toys. He is concerned about the need for budgeting.

  (a)   Draft a letter telling him, in brief, what budget statements he will need in his business plan, and what the differences are between them.

  (b)   He telephones on receipt of your letter, saying that he cannot see how the figures can be accurate. State what you would tell him about the factors which would cause budget figures to vary. What budgeting system could he adopt to solve some of these problems?

**40.2**   Jane Merton is setting up a business selling perfume. She intends to rent a small shop unit in Stourminster for cash sales. The bulk of her sales, however, will be on credit to a network of agents she has already established in the area. The agents sell from door-to-door, and she allows them 30 days' credit.

  As she will need financing she has been advised by her accountant to draw up a cash flow forecast for the first six months of trading, which she can present to the bank, along with her business plan. The projected figures are as follows on the next page:

*income – cash in*

| | |
|---|---|
| Cash sales | £1,000 per month |
| Receipts from debtors | £5,000 Jan - Mar;  £6,000 April;  £7,000 May and June |
| Capital introduced | £5,000 in January |
| Loan from father | £5,000 in March (no repayments or interest for a year) |

*payments - cash out*

| | |
|---|---|
| Purchases | £6,000 for cash in January - a 'one-off' payment |
| | £4,000 monthly for credit purchases (first payment in February) |
| Wages | £750 per month |
| Rent and rates | £4900 lease payment in January, business rates £100 per month (from January) |
| Insurance | £650 to be paid in January |
| Electricity | £240 quarterly (from March) |
| Telephone | £300 in April |
| VAT due | Jane estimates the first quarter's VAT payment (due in April) will be £1,400 |
| Stationery & postages | £50 each monthly |
| Bank | Charges of £150 and interest of £100 due in March |
| Advertising | £50 monthly |

(a) You are to draw up a cash flow forecast for Jane Merton, using a computer spreadsheet, if available, for the period January to June 19-9.  You should start with a nil bank balance.

(b) Estimate the amount Jane will need to borrow  from the bank.  Is the bank likely to lend this to her? If there were objections, are there any other solutions to the financing problem?

40.3 Andrew Page is starting up a business consultancy, which will give advice to existing businesses and help new businesses to get started.  He and his colleague Henry Hardy plan to operate from a small office in Mereford.  They will bill their clients monthly, and will ask for payment within 28 days of the invoice date.  As their consultancy is a 'service' business, they will not have 'purchases' of materials or stock;  their main expense is in fact their salary of £1,500 each monthly.  Their projected income and expenses are as follows:

*income – cash in*

| | |
|---|---|
| Receipts from clients | £4,000 February to April;  £5,000 May;  £7,000 June |
| Capital introduced | £10,000 in January |

*payments – cash out*

| | |
|---|---|
| Office equipment | £2,500 in January |
| Salary | £3,000 per month (ie £1,500 each) |
| Lease payment | £2,900 in January |
| Rates | £100 per month |
| Insurance | £650 in January |
| Electricity | £200 quarterly from March |
| Telephone | £400 in April |
| VAT | Estimate of £1,400 for first quarter (due in April) |
| Stationery | £100 per month |
| Postages | £50 per month |
| Bank | Estimate of £200 charges and £75 interest due in March |
| Vehicle expenses | £350 per month |
| Advertising | £1,500 for business launch in January, theerafter £100 per month |

You are to draw up a cash flow forecast for the first six months (January to June 19-9), assuming a nil bank balance at the beginning of January.

**EVIDENCE
COLLECTION
EXERCISE**

**20**

# *Cash flow forecast  on a computer spreadsheet – Pronto Alarms*

| Element 7.2 | *Produce and explain a projected cash flow for a single product business* |
|---|---|

Suggested Sources:
- "How to start a business" booklets issued by banks
- computer spreadsheet programs
- contact with local accountants and business consultants
- textbooks in libraries and resource centres

## INTRODUCTION

Mereford is an area which has a rising crime rate: there has been a 45% increase in burglaries to domestic and commercial premises in the area over the last twelve months.

John Oak is a local electrical contractor who is has seen the need for security alarm systems.  He plans to set up a business, Pronto Alarms, which will operate from a small shop unit, selling alarm systems both on a cash basis to the general public, and also on credit to commercial customers.

The alarm system itself, which John will buy in from an outside supplier,  is a revolutionary battery-operated 'stand-alone' device which uses infra-red sensors, and does not need wiring up, and can therefore be installed by the owner.  John anticipates keen demand from customers who will call at the shop, and also from the business community.  He plans to advertise in the local press and to circulate leaflets among local businesses.

### financial data

John plans to start trading at the beginning of January 19-9.  He already has £10,000 to invest himself in the business and the offer of a £7,500 interest free loan from an an associate who wants to help in the business and take a share in the profit.  The associate can make the money available in January, but wants the first £1,000 repayment of the loan to be made the following December.

John needs to buy a van and office equipment for £10,000 in January.  He also needs £8,000 in cash in January to buy the initial stock of alarms.  He will pay for subsequent purchases made on credit at £4,000 a month, starting in February.

He realises that he will need financial assistance in the form of an overdraft from the bank to start up, and on the advice of his accountant, he draws up a cash flow forecast for the first twelve months of trading to include in his business plan.  He has a computer spreadsheet program for calculating the cash flow figures. He discusses the likely cash income and expenditure with his accountant, and produces the following figures:

*income: cash in*

| | |
|---|---|
| Cash sales | £1,500 per month January to December |
| Credit sales | £6,000 per month – first receipts in February |
| Capital | £10,000 invested in January |
| Loan | £7,500 received in January |
| Interest on long-term bank deposit | £50 per quarter, starting in March |

*payments: cash out*

| | |
|---|---|
| Cash purchases of alarms | £8,000 in January |
| Credit purchases | £4,000 per month, starting in February |
| Purchase of van and equipment | £10,000 in January |
| Wages | £1,500 per month |
| Lease payment on office | £4,900 due in January |
| Rates | £100, starting in January |
| Insurance | £650 due in January |
| Electricity | £240 quarterly, first payment in March |
| Telephone | £300 quarterly, first payment April |
| VAT | £1,360 net quarterly payment, first payment April |
| Vehicle expenses | £100 monthly, starting in January |
| Stationery | £50 monthly, starting in January |
| Postages | £50 monthly, starting in January |
| Bank charges | £150 quarterly, starting in March |
| Bank interest | £250 in March and June, £120 in September and December |
| Loan repayment | £1,000 in December |
| Advertising | £50 per month, starting in January |

## TASK 1

Draw up a cash flow forecast for thre first twelve months trading of Pronto Alarms.  Use a computer spreadsheet if possible (see page 434 for a model format).  Assume a starting bank balance of nil.

## TASK 2

(a)  State the amount of finance that John Oak will need from the bank.

(b)  What is the amount that John Oak is investing himself?  Is the bank likely to consider it sufficient?

## TASK 3

John Oak asks the questions set out below.  What would you answers be?

(a)  "If my sales for January are £7,500, and my investment of £10,000 and the loan of £7,500 are  paid into the bank in January, why will I have  such a big overdraft at the end of the month?"

(b)  "How can I increase the amount of money in the bank account at the end of the year – it looks a rather disappointingly low amount?"

## TASK 4

A  friend of John, also in the electrical trade,  is very dubious about his projection of sales of £6,000 a month to commercial customers. "You'll be lucky if you make three-quarters of that!"  he says.

(a)  Rework the cash flow forecast showing a 25% reduction in monthly credit sales (ignore effect on VAT).

(b)  What effect does this have on John's case to the bank?

(c)  What problems will it cause for the business?

# 41 Projected profit statement and balance sheet

## introduction

In the last chapter we examined how a cash flow forecast is constructed, ready for inclusion in the business plan. An equally important financial statement in the business plan is the *profit and loss forecast* – the operating budget – which is normally constructed as a twelve month projection, which can be monitored month-by-month as the business trades.

From the cash flow forecast and the profit and loss forecast may be constructed the forecast *balance sheet* showing the assets and liabilities of the business as they *might* stand at the end of the twelve month period. This is also an important financial statement which supports the business plan.

In this chapter we therefore look at
• the method of drawing up a projected profit and loss account
• the method of drawing up a projected balance sheet

## profit and loss statement

Before examining the profit and loss *forecast* it is important to be able to reproduce the format of a profit and loss *statement,* a subject covered in Chapter 36  As you will recall, most businesses produce annual *financial statements* at the end of the financial year.  A financial year need not coincide with a calendar year:  common financial year-ends are 30 June, 31 March, and 31 December.  The financial statements usually comprise
• a *balance sheet*
• a *profit and loss statement*
• a *cashflow statement* (see Chapter 38 – this is *not* the same as a cash flow forecast)
A simplified format of the profit and loss statement is set out in the diagram on the next page.

---

## profit and loss statement _____

**sales**
ie number of items sold x unit cost

*less*

**cost of sales**
ie purchases of raw materials or goods for resale

*equals*

**gross profit**

*less*

**other expenses**
ie overheads such as administration expenses, wages, advertising

*equals*

**net profit**

---

*Fig. 41.1  Profit and loss statement format*

### the significance of the profit and loss statement
The profit and loss statement  normally covers a year of trading and is an indication of the level of activity and profitability of the business.    The terms used in the statement are

**sales**
This is a record of the money amount received (or due to be received) for goods sold, or services provided

**cost of sales**
This is the total of purchases for the year, adjusted for any change in stock level if goods are involved (the calculation is: opening stock *plus* purchases *less* closing stock).  In basic terms, *cost of sales is what you have paid (or are due to pay) for what you have sold.*

**gross profit**
Gross profit is *trading* profit, ie profit before any dedutions are made for overhead expenses.  It is common to express gross profit as a percentage of sales.  The formula is

$$\frac{gross\ profit \times 100}{sales} \quad = \quad gross\ profit\ percentage$$

**other expenses**
These include expenses, eg wages, rent and rates, services (electricity and telephone), vehicle expenses, financial costs, advertising, insurance and depreciation.

**net profit**
Net profit is the final profit after deduction of all expenses which will be due to the owner(s) of the business, hence the expression it has coined: "the bottom line". Net profit is often expressed as a percentage of sales to provide an indicator of the profitability of a business.  The formula is

$$\frac{net\ profit \times 100}{sales} \quad = \quad net\ profit\ percentage$$

### preparing figures for the profit and loss forecast
On the next two pages are a profit and loss forecast  for an existing business, R & S Engineering Limited, together with explanatory notes explaining how the figures are derived. For the sake of clarity, only six months' figures are shown, rather than the usual twelve months' figures. Following this is a Case Study showing how a business draws up a cash flow forecast, a profit and loss forecast, and then extracts a projected balance sheet from these figures.

# Profit and loss forecast

name.......R & S Engineering Limited.........period...January – June 19–9........

| | January £ | February £ | March £ | April £ | May £ | June £ | TOTAL £ |
|---|---|---|---|---|---|---|---|
| **Sales** | 5,000 | 5,000 | 6,000 | 5,000 | 5,000 | 5,000 | 31,000 |
| Less: Cost of Sales | 2,500 | 2,500 | 3,500 | 2,500 | 2,500 | 2,500 | 16,000 |
| **Gross Profit** | 2,500 | 2,500 | 2,500 | 2,500 | 2,500 | 2,500 | 15,000 |
| **Gross Profit %** | 50 | 50 | 42 | 50 | 50 | 50 | 48 |
| **Expenses** | | | | | | | |
| Wages | 500 | 500 | 500 | 500 | 500 | 500 | 3,000 |
| Rent/Rates | 150 | 150 | 150 | 150 | 150 | 150 | 900 |
| Insurance | 40 | 40 | 40 | 40 | 40 | 40 | 240 |
| Electricity | 25 | 25 | 25 | 25 | 25 | 25 | 150 |
| Telephone | 35 | 35 | 35 | 35 | 35 | 35 | 210 |
| Other services | 55 | 55 | 55 | 55 | 55 | 55 | 330 |
| Vehicle expenses | 50 | 50 | 50 | 50 | 50 | 50 | 300 |
| Stationery | 10 | 10 | 10 | 10 | 10 | 10 | 60 |
| Postages | 55 | 55 | 55 | 55 | 55 | 55 | 330 |
| Bank charges | | | | | | | |
| Interest charges | | | | | | | |
| Professional fees | | | | | | 100 | 100 |
| Advertising | 50 | 50 | 50 | 50 | 50 | 50 | 300 |
| Sundries | 35 | 35 | 35 | 35 | 35 | 35 | 210 |
| Depreciation | 100 | 100 | 100 | 100 | 100 | 100 | 600 |
| **Total Expenses** | 1,105 | 1,105 | 1,105 | 1,105 | 1,105 | 1,205 | 6,730 |
| **Net Profit/ (Loss)** | 1,395 | 1,395 | 1,395 | 1,395 | 1,395 | 1,295 | 8,270 |

# completing the profit and loss forecast

**definition**

*A profit and loss forecast is a budgeted projection of expected sales, expected costs and expected profit on a monthly basis over a specific period of time* – here six months.  Because sales and purchases are made on credit (they are paid for later) the forecast shows the profit position rather than the cash position of the business.

**time period**

The time period shown is normally twelve months;  six months' figures are shown here for the sake of clarity.  The vertical columns show the figures for each month with a total figure for the time period on the right.  Some profit and loss forecast forms have two columns for each month:  one for the projected figures and one for the actual figures, so that the projections and actual figures can be compared during the time period.  For the sake of simplicity the budgeted figures only are shown in the illustration here.

**sales**

Sales is the *invoiced* value of the sales during the month.  It is *not* the amount of money received for sales during the month.  It does *not* include VAT (for VAT–registered businesses)

**cost of sales**

*Cost of sales* (also known as *cost of goods sold*) is the direct cost of what has been sold during the month.  The figure is normally based on the purchases adjusted for opening and closing stock (add opening stock, deduct closing stock). This figure obviously does not include capital items – such as machinery purchased – but only the cost of the normal stock-in-trade. It does *not* include VAT (where the business is registered for VAT).

**gross profit**

Gross profit is calculated by deducting cost of sales (cost of goods sold) from sales.  It is useful (as here) to calculate the gross profit percentage to show the margin achieved by the business.  The formula is

$$\frac{gross\,profit}{sales} \times 100 = gross\,profit\,\%$$

**expenses**

The figures entered in the expenses section represent the monthly cost of the expenses incurred, whether or not the bills have actually been paid.  You will see from the example that some items, electricity for example, are averaged out over the six month period, even if they are paid for quarterly.  VAT is not included in the expenses figures.

**depreciation**

As you will have seen when studying financial statements, depreciation is a non-cash expense.  It must, however, be included on the profit and loss forecast as it represents the cost to the business of the wear and tear of the fixed assets over their useful lives.

**total expenses**

The total expenses figure is the total of all the items below the gross profit calculation.  It must be stressed again that this figure does *not* represent cash paid out – it is the total of the expenses *incurred* during the month, and in all probability paid for later.

**net profit/(loss)**

The net profit is calculated as follows:

*gross profit minus total expenses  =  net profit*

A negative figure represents a net *loss* and will be shown in brackets.

# Case Study: Ian Phillips – financial projections

## Situation

Ian Phillips is an expert in computer software. He has worked until recently for a leading British software house which made him redundant four months ago. He has £10,000 available from his redundancy money and savings to invest as capital, and wishes to set up a computer software retail outlet in a new shopping arcade, which is offering units at preferential rates. He has named his venture 'Software Stores'. It will open on 1 January 19-9. His customers will include the general public and also local businesses who need expert guidance on the setting up of business packages. He wishes to raise finance from the bank but is not sure how much he needs. He therefore approaches, on a friend's recommendation, Jim Stoner, a local accountant, who is known to specialise in small business finance.

Jim Stoner extracts the following information from his client.

### income

- Ian Phillips has capital of £10,000 in the building society to introduce into the business
- expected cash sales from callers at the shop are £3,000 per month
- expected credit sales from business software are £1,000 per month on 60 days' credit (ie sales made in January will be paid for in March)

### expenditure

- initial purchase of stock of £5,000 is to be paid for immediately by cheque (stock will be reduced to a level of £3,250 at the end of each month, following estimated sales of £1,750 [at cost] of stock each month); the 'closing stock' figure for the profit and loss forecast and for the balance sheet will therefore be £3,250
- after January stock purchases are to be £1,750 each month:
  - (a) in February and March paid for immediately by cheque
  - (b) April onwards, all purchases on 30 days' credit (eg April's purchases will be paid for in the month following purchase, ie in May)

  The reason for (a) and (b) is that credit will often only be granted by suppliers *after* the business has shown that it is creditworthy, usually after a few months' trading
- equipment purchases (fixed assets) £4,500, to be paid for in January
- the telephone, bought in January will cost £135 (a fixed asset); the monthly running cost will be £15
- he buys shop fixtures and fittings (fixed assets) £5,250, to be paid for in February
- monthly payments the business will have to make are:

  rent and rates £575, insurance £50, electricity £25, stationery £10, postages £15, drawings £750
- advertising will cost £150 in January and £30 in subsequent months
- bank charges: arrangement fee of £100 and quarterly charges of £75 in March and June
- he estimates that bank overdraft interest of £65 will be payable in March
- depreciation of fixed assets is to be charged (in the profit and loss account) at £750 (£125 per month); depreciation is for office equipment £350, fixtures and fittings £400;

  *NOTE: as depreciation is a non-cash item it does not appear in the cash flow forecast*

### processing of the figures

Jim Stoner helps Ian to draw up a cash flow forecast and a forecast profit and loss account (illustrated on the following pages). Ian uses his spreadsheet program to calculate the cash flow forecast. Jim recommends that Ian does not register for VAT until the level of sales justifies it. It is therefore ignored for the present in the calculations.

# Cash flow forecast

name..**Software Stores**...............................................period.**January - June 19-9**

| | January £ | February £ | March £ | April £ | May £ | June £ | TOTAL £ |
|---|---|---|---|---|---|---|---|
| **RECEIPTS** | | | | | | | |
| Cash sales | 3,000 | 3,000 | 3,000 | 3,000 | 3,000 | 3,000 | 18,000 |
| Cash from debtors | | | 1,000 | 1,000 | 1,000 | 1,000 | 4,000 |
| Capital | 10,000 | | | | | | 10,000 |
| Loans | | | | | | | |
| **TOTAL RECEIPTS (A)** | 13,000 | 3,000 | 4,000 | 4,000 | 4,000 | 4,000 | 32,000 |
| **PAYMENTS** | | | | | | | |
| Cash purchases | 5,000 | 1,750 | 1,750 | | | | 8,500 |
| Credit purchases | | | | | 1,750 | 1,750 | 3,500 |
| Capital items | 4,635 | 5,250 | | | | | 9,885 |
| Wages | | | | | | | |
| Rent/Rates | 575 | 575 | 575 | 575 | 575 | 575 | 3,450 |
| Insurance | 50 | 50 | 50 | 50 | 50 | 50 | 300 |
| Electricity | 25 | 25 | 25 | 25 | 25 | 25 | 150 |
| Telephone | 15 | 15 | 15 | 15 | 15 | 15 | 90 |
| VAT | | | | | | | |
| Vehicle expenses | | | | | | | |
| Stationery | 10 | 10 | 10 | 10 | 10 | 10 | 60 |
| Postages | 15 | 15 | 15 | 15 | 15 | 15 | 90 |
| Bank charges | 100 | | 75 | | | 75 | 250 |
| Interest charges | | | 65 | | | | 65 |
| Professional fees | | | | | | | |
| Advertising | 150 | 30 | 30 | 30 | 30 | 30 | 300 |
| Drawings | 750 | 750 | 750 | 750 | 750 | 750 | 4,500 |
| **TOTAL PAYMENTS (B)** | 11,325 | 8,470 | 3,360 | 1,470 | 3,220 | 3,295 | 31,140 |
| **NET CASHFLOW (A-B)** | 1,675 | (5,470) | 640 | 2,530 | 780 | 705 | 860 |
| **OPENING BANK BALANCE** | 0 | 1,675 | (3,795) | (3,155) | (625) | 155 | 0 |
| **CLOSING BANK BALANCE** | 1,675 | (3,795) | (3,155) | (625) | 155 | 860 | 860 |

# Profit and loss forecast

name...... Software Stores ..........................................**period** January – June 19–9

| | January £ | February £ | March £ | April £ | May £ | June £ | TOTAL £ |
|---|---|---|---|---|---|---|---|
| **Sales** | 4,000 | 4,000 | 4,000 | 4,000 | 4,000 | 4,000 | 24,000 |
| Less: Cost of Sales | 1,750 | 1,750 | 1,750 | 1,750 | 1,750 | 1,750 | 10,500 |
| **Gross Profit** | 2,250 | 2,250 | 2,250 | 2,250 | 2,250 | 2,250 | 13,500 |
| **Gross Profit %** | 56 | 56 | 56 | 56 | 56 | 56 | 56 |
| **Expenses** | | | | | | | |
| Wages | | | | | | | |
| Rent/Rates | 575 | 575 | 575 | 575 | 575 | 575 | 3,450 |
| Insurance | 50 | 50 | 50 | 50 | 50 | 50 | 300 |
| Electricity | 25 | 25 | 25 | 25 | 25 | 25 | 150 |
| Telephone | 15 | 15 | 15 | 15 | 15 | 15 | 90 |
| Other services | | | | | | | |
| Vehicle expenses | | | | | | | |
| Stationery | 10 | 10 | 10 | 10 | 10 | 10 | 60 |
| Postages | 15 | 15 | 15 | 15 | 15 | 15 | 90 |
| Bank charges | 100 | | 75 | | | 75 | 250 |
| Interest charges | | | 65 | | | | 65 |
| Professional fees | | | | | | | |
| Advertising | 150 | 30 | 30 | 30 | 30 | 30 | 300 |
| Sundries | | | | | | | |
| Depreciation | 125 | 125 | 125 | 125 | 125 | 125 | 750 |
| **Total Expenses** | 1,065 | 845 | 985 | 845 | 845 | 920 | 5,505 |
| **Net Profit (Loss)** | 1,185 | 1,405 | 1,265 | 1,405 | 1,405 | 1,330 | 7,995 |

## notes on completion of the profit and loss forecast

**sales**
Total monthly sales of £4,000 comprise cash sales of £3,000 and invoiced credit sales of £1,000.   Note that these figure represent sales as they are made and *not* – in the case of credit sales – the money that is received.

**cost of sales**
The monthly cost of sales is the cost of the stock actually sold, here £1,750 per month.  The formula is:

*cost of sales = opening stock  + purchases  – closing stock*

The calculation for January is therefore

*cost of sales = 0  +  £5,000  –  £3,750 = £1,750*

The calculation for February and subsequent months is

*cost of sales = £3,750 + £1,750 – £3,750 = £1,750*

Remember that closing stock for one month is the opening stock for the following month.

**gross profit**
This figure is the difference between sales and cost of sales.  Sometimes (as here)  a profit and loss forecast will show the gross profit percentage.

**wages**
There is no entry here because Ian's drawings do not feature in the profit and loss account, but are deducted in the capital section of the balance sheet (see below).

**expenses**
The expenses are generally averaged out over the six month period and allocated to each month.

**telephone**
The cost of £135 becomes a fixed asset and only the running costs (£15 per month) are shown in the profit and loss account.  The cost of the machine is a capital item which will appear in the cash flow forecast (cash spent) and in the balance sheet (see on the next page).  The purchase price of capital items cannot be set off against profit.

**interest**
The estimated bank account interest is shown in the March column as it is a charge for the January – March quarter.

**depreciation**
The depreciation – wear and tear on the assets – is shown as a monthly charge of £125.  Note that this will never appear in the cash flow forecast, as it is not a cash expense, but an indication in the accounts of the fall in value of an asset, and therefore an expense to the business.

**net profit**
Net profit is calculated as

*gross profit less total expenses*

Net profit is the profit due to the owner of the business.  It is, of course, subject to tax, which in the case of Ian Phillips will be charged in an income tax assessment issued by the Inland Revenue.  It is also available for drawings (money taken out of the business by the owner), an item which appears in the cash flow forecast but not in the profit and loss forecast.

## completion of the balance sheet

Jim Stoner now shows Ian the source of all the figures for the projected balance sheet (shown below):

| *item* | *source* | *details* |
|---|---|---|
| **fixed assets** | cash flow | office equipment of £4,635 (including the telephone costing £135) and shop fixtures and fittings are capital items, recorded in January and February respectively |
| **depreciation** | profit & loss | depreciation (abbreviated to 'Dep'n) is the last expense item in the profit and loss forecast – the split between £400 and £350 will have been supplied by Ian Phillips |
| **stock** | profit & loss | stock in the current assets is always the *closing* stock figure from the cost of sales calculation |
| **debtors** | profit & loss | debtors is the total of *credit* sales not yet paid for, in this case, two months' sales £1,000 plus £1,000 = £2,000 |
| **bank** | cash flow | bank in the current assets is the closing bank balance from the cash flow forecast (bottom right-hand figure); a negative figure, an overdraft, would be a current liability |
| **creditors** | profit & loss | this figure represents one month's purchases not yet paid for (ie the cost of sales £1,750); note that if the business was given two months' credit, the figure would be doubled |
| **capital** | cash flow | £10,000 is introduced in January (receipts section) |
| **net profit** | profit & loss | the bottom right-hand figure from the profit and loss forecast – the total net profit for the period |
| **drawings** | cash flow | the last expense item in the cash flow forecast |

**PROJECTED BALANCE SHEET OF IAN PHILLIPS TRADING AS SOFTWARE STORES AS AT 30 JUNE 19-9**

| | Cost £ | Dep'n £ | Net £ |
|---|---|---|---|
| **Fixed Assets** | | | |
| Office equipment | 4,635 | 350 | 4,285 |
| Fixtures and fittings | 5,250 | 400 | 4,850 |
| | 9,885 | 750 | 9,135 |
| | | | |
| **Current Assets** | | | |
| Stock | | 3,250 | |
| Debtors | | 2,000 | |
| Bank | | 860 | |
| | | 6,110 | |
| | | | |
| **Less Current Liabilities** | | | |
| Creditors | | 1,750 | |
| | | | |
| **Working Capital** | | | 4,360 |
| **NET ASSETS** | | | 13,495 |
| | | | |
| *FINANCED BY* | | | |
| Capital | | | 10,000 |
| Add net profit | | | 7,995 |
| | | | 17,995 |
| Less drawings | | | 4,500 |
| | | | 13,495 |

## completion of the business plan

Ian, now that he has completed his financial projections, will compile the business plan. The sections will include:

- personal details of himself, his experience and qualifications
- a description of the business and the type of software he is proposing to sell
- an analysis of the market, and his pricing strategy
- his financial requirements – the bottom line of the cash flow forecast shows that he needs an overdraft of approximately £4,000 in February which will be repaid out of sales receipts by the end of May
- his financial projections – the profit and loss forecast, cash flow forecast and his projected balance sheet
- assets he has available for bank security – a £10,000 life policy and his house (already mortgaged to the Abbeyfax Building Society)

He arranges an interview with his bank manager to whom he sends a copy of the Business Plan, so that the bank manager can study it before the interview. The manager will look carefully at the financial forecasts and see from the bottom line of the cash flow forecast that the borrowing can be repaid. The manager will also see from the forecast profit and loss statement that the business should trade profitably.

## the interview with the bank

Ian visits the bank with his accountant and they are interviewed together by one of the bank's business managers who has a number of questions to ask:

*Do you know the software market well enough to be able to know what to stock in your shop? How will you keep up-to-date?  Is the market steady, or might you be left with a lot of out-of-date stock?*

*Is your projected level of sales realistic?  What would happen to your proposed overdraft if your sales were 10% lower than anticipated?  Have you got any orders or customers lined up?*

*Have you estimated the costs of running the shop realistically?  Is your figure for business rates up-to-date?*

*Can you live on your proposed drawings of £750 a month?  Could you make do with less if the business did not do as well as expected?  Is your wife earning and contributing to the household expenses?*

Ian, helped by his accountant, is able to give satisfactory answers to these questions and the bank manager, who has already looked at the business plan,  makes an offer:

- an overdraft limit of £4,000 for the six months January to June
- an interest charge of bank base rate plus 5%
- an arrangement fee of £100
- a charge over Ian's life policy as security for the borrowing (the house is not required as security because the proposed business borrowing is only short-term)

## conclusion

The offer is accepted and the bank manager then outlines other ways in which the bank can help: arranging insurance, pensions, and a variety of banking facilities. The interview is typical of a business lending situation.  One point remains very clear:  without the presentation of the business and the financial planning that went into the Business Plan, the bank manager would have had a more difficult decision to make.  The Business Plan gives both the owner and the bank greater confidence in the venture.

# chapter summary

❏   In order to be able to monitor its future performance, a business will often draw up financial projections over a six or twelve month period. These include:
  • the cash flow forecast (explained in the last chapter)
  • the projected profit and loss statement
  • the projected balance sheet as at the end of the period

❏   As the business trades it will compare its actual performance with the projections.

❏   Whereas a cash flow forecast projects the cash position of a business by calculating its monthly bank balance, a profit and loss forecast projects expected sales, expenses and profit.

❏   A cash flow forecast will include VAT. A profit and loss forecast will not include VAT.

❏   The projected balance sheet is compiled from figures contained in both the cash flow forecast and the forecast profit and loss statement.

❏   It must be remembered that these statements are only *projections*, and produced for guidance; they cannot be relied upon to be entirely accurate.

 **student activities**

**41.1**   You are planning to set up in business at the beginning of the year 19-8. Your enterprise is a small bookshop which you will call 'Anne's Bookshop'.

You plan to introduce capital of £6,000 in January. You also intend to purchase for cash an initial stock of books costing £5,000, together with fixtures and fittings costing £3,750, also to be paid for in January. You hope to start trading in January 19-8 and you have estimated sales for the first six months as follows:

January £3,000; February £2,400; March £3,600; April £4,500; May £4,200; June £3,900. All sales will be for cash. You plan to work to a gross profit margin of one-third of the selling price. Towards the end of each month you will replenish the stock to ensure that, at the month-end, it will be restored to £5,000. Your suppliers for book purchases, excluding the initial cash stock purchase, will allow one month's credit (eg purchases made in January will be paid for in February).

You estimate the monthly overheads of the shop will be rent and rates £250, wages £280, heat/light/telephone £95. You plan to withdraw for your own use drawings of £500 per month. Your accountant has advised you to depreciate fixtures and fittings at the rate of 20% per annum (straight line method).

Your accountant also advises you to prepare, for the six months ending 30 June 19-8:

• a cash flow forecast (using a spreadsheet if it is available)
• a profit and loss forecast
• a projected balance sheet as at 30 June 19-8

These documents will form part of the Business Plan which you will submit to the bank as part of your application for the finance, which your accountant suspects you will need. Prepare the documents and pass them to your accountant for checking.

**41.2** You are an accountant in the firm of Price Charterhouse, 67 Brewers Walk, Stourford, ST6 9UT, and have been asked to advise a client, John Carr.

John Carr has been unemployed for 12 months and intends to set up a mail order holiday guide business. He used to work in a travel agency, and knows the travel business well. He plans to sell an A4 format holiday resort guide giving invaluable information about all the popular resorts in the Mediterranean area. The guide and the business will be given the name 'Medfact'. John Carr will operate under the local TEC Enterprise Allowance Scheme which will pay him £40 a week for the first year of operation. He has £2,500 of his own in a building society account, saved when he was in employment.

You have talked through the figures with him and he has produced the following estimates for his first six months' trading (1 January to 30 June 19-8):
- he will introduce capital on 1 January of £2,500
- opening stocks of Medfact guides will cost £2,000 and be paid for by cheque
- estimated sales for the first six months (based on a peak month of May) are:

   January £1,000; February £1,600; March £1,800; April £2,000; May £4,000; June £2,400

- most sales are for cash, but he does expect to sell 25% of his guides through travel agents, and will have to wait a month for payment from them
- his Medfact guides cost 50% of his selling price; stocks of guides will be replaced each month so that the closing stock value will always be £2,000; January's stock purchases of guides will therefore be £1,000 (sales figure) x 50% = £500
- purchases will be made from his suppliers who allow 1 month's credit (apart from the initial cash purchase of stock)

*his expenses (which are paid for as they are incurred) are:*
- advertising £500 per month, except for April when he will spend £800
- post and packing £200 for January, February and March, £300 for April, May and June
- sundry expenses will be £10 per month, except for April when they will be £40
- you should ignore interest costs

*also*
- he wishes to buy office equipment for £1,000 by cheque in January; the equipment is expected to last for five years
- drawings from the bank account will be £180 per month (the Enterprise Allowance £40 per week will *not* be passed through the business) – his wife is a qualified teacher and her salary will subsidise him while the business is starting up
- John Carr suspects that he will have to approach the bank for finance in the early months of operation of the business. You realise that a Business Plan will have to drawn up, and you therefore advise him accordingly.

*You are to:*

(a) Construct a cash flow forecast for the first six months of operation of the business. Use a spreadsheet program if it is available.

(b) Draw up a forecast profit and loss account for the six months to 30 June 19-8, and a projected balance sheet as at 30 June 19-8.

(c) State how much he will have to borrow from the bank, and when. What form of finance do you think would be appropriate? (Refer to Chapter 43 "Sources of business finance" if you have not covered this topic).

# 42 The cost of goods and services

## introduction

We now turn to an area of accounting which helps the owner of a business to calculate the cost of manufacturing a product or of providing a service – this type of accounting is called *cost accounting*. In the chapter we will look at the principles involved and will then follow a Case Study which involves the costing of goods and a service.

For any business, whether manufacturing a product or providing a service, it is important to identify the appropriate unit of goods or service for that business. Examples are:

| *business* | *unit of goods or service* |
| --- | --- |
| • house builder | houses |
| • car manufacturer | cars |
| • solicitor | client hour |

Once the unit of goods or service is established, we then need to consider the elements of cost which go to make up a product or service.

## elements of cost

For any product or service there are always three elements of cost:
* materials
* labour
* expenses

Each element of cost can be categorised into:
* *direct costs* – those costs that can be identified with each unit made or service provided
* *indirect costs* – all other costs

The elements of cost now appear as:

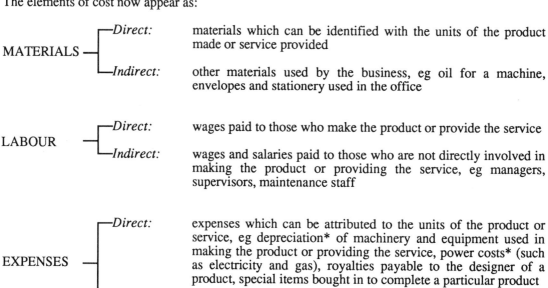

MATERIALS

*Direct:* materials which can be identified with the units of the product made or service provided

*Indirect:* other materials used by the business, eg oil for a machine, envelopes and stationery used in the office

LABOUR

*Direct:* wages paid to those who make the product or provide the service

*Indirect:* wages and salaries paid to those who are not directly involved in making the product or providing the service, eg managers, supervisors, maintenance staff

EXPENSES

*Direct:* expenses which can be attributed to the units of the product or service, eg depreciation\* of machinery and equipment used in making the product or providing the service, power costs\* (such as electricity and gas), royalties payable to the designer of a product, special items bought in to complete a particular product

*Indirect:* running expenses, such as administration, rent paid, telephone, travel expenses, etc, which cannot be attributed directly to each unit of the product or service, and marketing costs

*\* note that some businesses will classify depreciation and power costs as indirect expenses where there is no direct link between number of cost units and the expenses incurred*

### overheads
The indirect costs of materials, labour and expenses form the *overheads* of the business:

*indirect materials + indirect labour + indirect expenses = total overheads*

## calculating the cost of goods and services

Fig. 42.1 (on the next page) shows the steps to be followed when calculating the cost of goods and services. These steps are explained in more detail below.

### unit of goods or service
For both a manufacturing business and a provider of services it is essential to:
* identify the unit of goods or service
* calculate the number of units of goods or service provided in a particular time period (such as a day, week, month or year)

Only when these two tasks have been carried out is the business able to calculate the costs involved with each unit and then to establish the selling price. To help in establishing the correct costs for a unit of output we need to identify *cost units* and *cost centres:*

*Cost units are units of goods or service to which costs can be charged.* Thus a cost unit can be a *unit of goods* manufactured, eg a car, an item of furniture, etc, or it can be a *unit of service*, eg a passenger-mile on a bus, a transaction on a bank statement, an attendance at a swimming pool, an operation in a hospital, etc.

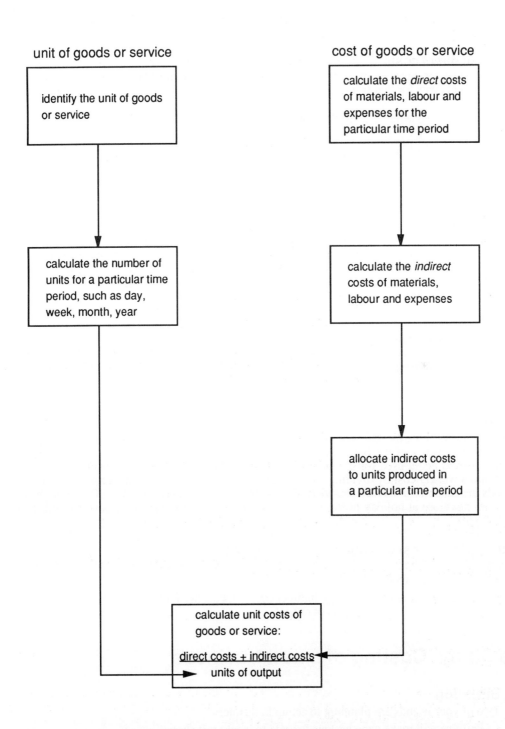

*Fig. 42.1 Calculating the cost of goods and services*

*Cost centres are sections of a business to which costs can be charged.* In manufacturing business a cost centre is a particular department of a factory, even a whole factory, or a particular stage in the production process. In a service business examples of cost centres are a ward or a unit of a hospital, a department of a college, etc.

### calculation of direct costs

Having established the number of units of output for a particular time period, the next task is to calculate the direct costs for that time period. As we have seen earlier, the direct costs comprise three elements:

*   direct materials – identifiable with the goods or service
*   direct labour     – wages cost of making the product or providing the service
*   direct expenses – attributable to the goods or service

The total of these gives the direct costs of the goods or service for the particular time period.

### calculation of indirect costs

The indirect costs, or overheads, of a business must be calculated; indirect costs comprise three elements:

*   indirect materials – materials used by the business not directly identifiable with the goods or service
*   indirect labour     – wages and salaries paid to those not directly involved with making the product or providing the service
*   indirect expenses – general running expenses of the business

### allocation of indirect costs to output

Once the indirect costs have been calculated, we must then ensure that their total cost is included in – or *allocated* to – the units of goods or service for a particular time period. Only by including indirect costs in the total cost of the output can a business recover their cost from the sales made.

Often indirect costs do not fall neatly into the time period we wish to use when calculating costs. For example, rent might be payable every month; insurance premiums every year; electricity, gas and telephone bills every three months; other expenses, such as office stationery and marketing expenses, as incurred by the owner of the business. In these circumstances, it is necessary to convert the cost into the time period being used for the units of goods or service. For example, an annual cost can be converted into a weekly cost by dividing, not necessarily by 52, but by the number of *working weeks* when goods are made or a service provided: this is likely to be between 48 and 50, although if the business does not close at holiday times, then the divisor (number by which the cost is divided) will be 52.

### calculation of total cost of a unit of goods or service

Once the direct and indirect costs for a time period are known, the total cost of a unit of goods or service can be calculated, as follows:

$$\frac{\text{direct costs} + \text{indirect costs}}{\text{units of output}} = \text{cost per unit}$$

## Case Study: Costing of a new business

### Situation

Two of your friends are planning to set up in business:

*   Philippa will make cane baskets for sale to local craft shops
*   James will offer a computer service providing word processing, desk top publishing and other facilities

They approach you for assistance in the costing of goods and services.

*Philippa's business*

Making cane baskets has been a hobby of Philippa's for a number of years. She already sells some of her goods to local shops and, now that she has left college, intends to see if she can turn her hobby into a full-time job. If things go well, she plans, in the longer term, to employ 'home workers' who will make the baskets for her, while she will attend to the marketing and administration of the business. For the moment, she will work from her parents' house but, if business develops, she will need to rent a small craft workshop.

*James' business*

James has always been interested in computers and, in recent years, has set himself up with a business computer system with software for word processing, database management (mailshots), payroll, and desk top publishing (publicity leaflets). Now that he has left college, he wants to develop a computer bureau so that he can make a living from his hobby. At present the computer system occupies a spare room in his parents' house. He realises that, if business develops, he will need to rent office premises in the town centre.

## Solution

We will follow Philippa and James' businesses and cost the goods and services provided by them using the steps outlined in the earlier part of this chapter.

*Note:* As both of these are small businesses run by the owner with no employees, the expected drawings of the owners have been treated as a cost: thus the cost per unit includes drawings. In larger businesses, the owner would take out drawings after calculating net profit.

### unit of goods and service

How do we go about identifying the unit of goods or service in the businesses planned by Philippa and James?

Philippa's business will be to make a product – cane baskets, all of the same size. Therefore the unit is each basket – this is the cost unit. If Philippa were to make other products from cane, each unit of output would be a cost unit.

James will provide a service – as a computer bureau. His unit of service is best costed on a time basis – eg each hour of computer time is a cost unit.

The next task is to calculate the number of units of goods and service provided in a time period. We will calculate for the two businesses for each week, although different time periods could be used.

Philippa tells us that she will work in the business for 35 hours each week. As she is the only person involved in the business, she will not only make the baskets but will also be involved in marketing and administration. She plans to spend 25 hours each week on making baskets, five hours each on marketing and administration. When making baskets she can complete one each hour. Therefore she will have 25 units of output each week.

James will work 40 hours each week. He will spend 30 hours working for customers, 4 hours on marketing and 6 hours on administration (which will include developing his skills in the use of new software). Therefore he will have 30 units of service each week.

### calculation of direct costs

Philippa gives you the expected direct costs of her business each week:

- *direct materials* – cane and bases for the 25 baskets she plans to make each week will cost £40.00
- *direct labour* – Philippa hopes to draw £140.00 each week from the business for a 35-hour week; as she plans that 25 hours will be spent each week on making baskets, the direct labour cost will be £140 x $\frac{25}{35}$ = £100.00

- *direct expenses* – at present Philippa doesn't anticipate any direct expenses; however, if she makes any special orders she may well need to hire a machine especially for this extra work

   *The total of direct costs each week is:* £40.00 (materials) + £100.00 (labour) = £140.00

For James' business, the expected direct costs each week are:

- *direct materials* – each week he expects to buy for use on customers' work, two boxes of floppy disks, one box of printout paper, and one box of labels, at a total cost of £35.00

- *direct labour* – he plans to draw £150.00 for his 40-hour week; of this time, 30 hours will be spent on customers' work, so his direct labour cost will be $£150.00 \times \dfrac{30}{40} = £112.50$

- *direct expenses* – his main direct expense will be the purchase of new and up-dated computer software, and depreciation of the hardware, ie computers and printers; in total he estimates these to be £45.00 each week

   *The total of direct costs each week is:*

   £35.00 (materials) + £112.50 (labour) + £45.00 (expenses) = £192.50

## calculation of indirect costs

Philippa gives you the expected indirect costs of her business:

- *indirect materials* – she has budgeted that she will spent £500.00 each year on office stationery, advertising leaflets, and other indirect materials

- *indirect labur* – as the only person working in the business we have already seen that Philippa will spend 25 hours each week in making baskets, ie direct labour; the other 10 hours spent each week on marketing and administration are indirect labour, the cost of which will be $£140.00 \times \dfrac{10}{35} = £40.00$ per week

- *indirect expenses* – for Philippa, these are costs such as electricity for heating and lighting, telephone, travel expenses, etc, which she has budgeted at £600.00 for the first year (if she moves the business from her parents' house to a craft workshop, there will be additional costs of rent paid, business rates, repairs and maintenance, etc)

For James' business, the expected indirect costs are:

- *indirect materials* – stationery, computer disks for his own use, printer ribbons, computer manuals and other indirect materials are budgeted at £800.00 for the year

- *indirect labour* – of James' 40-hour working week, he will spend 10 hours on marketing and administration, the cost of which will be $£150.00 \times \dfrac{10}{40} = £37.50$ per week

- *indirect expenses* – James expects to have similar types of expenses as Philippa, and he budgets the amount at £750.00 for the first year

## allocation of indirect costs to output

The indirect costs of Philippa's business (see above) are expected to be:

- indirect materials £500.00 each year
- indirect labour £40.00 per week
- indirect expenses £600.00 each year

Philippa plans to take 2 weeks' holiday each year, so the weekly indirect costs will be:

- indirect materials £500.00 ÷ 50 weeks             = £10.00
- indirect labour                                   = £40.00
- indirect expenses £600.00 ÷ 50 weeks          = £12.00
- *total of indirect costs* each week             = £62.00

James' business is expected to have the following indirect costs (see above):
- indirect materials £800.00 each year
- indirect labour £37.50 per week
- indirect expenses £750.00 each year

James plans to take 4 weeks' holiday each year so, as he will be working for 48 weeks, the weekly indirect costs will be:

| | |
|---|---|
| • indirect materials £800.00 ÷ 48 weeks | = £16.67 |
| • indirect labour | = £37.50 |
| • indirect expenses £750.00 ÷ 48 weeks | = £15.63 |
| *total of indirect costs* each week | = £69.80 |

## calculation of total cost of a unit of goods and service

Philippa intends to make 25 baskets each week. The costs already calculated are:

| | |
|---|---|
| • total of direct costs each week | = £140.00 |
| • total of indirect costs each week | = £ 62.00 |
| *total costs each week* | = £202.00 |

The cost per basket is:

$$\frac{£202.00}{25 \text{ baskets}} = £8.08 \text{ per basket}$$

As Philippa has included the amount she wishes to draw from the business each week in the costings, this means that she needs to sell baskets for a minimum average price of £8.08 each. Clearly some baskets will be sold to shops who will wish to buy at a trade price, while others will be sold direct to customers – probably at higher prices – who are buying for themselves. However, Philippa needs to recognise that, in order to cover her costs, she must sell all her production of baskets at a minimum average price of £8.08. Note that we have assumed that the baskets made by Philippa are all of the same size: if she decides to make them in a range of sizes, this would have to be allowed for in the costings.

James plans to spend 30 hours each week on customers' work. The costs already calculated are:

| | |
|---|---|
| • total of direct costs each week | = £192.50 |
| • total of indirect costs each week | = £ 69.80 |
| *total costs each week* | = £262.30 |

The cost per hour of service to customers is:

$$\frac{£262.30}{30 \text{ hours}} = £8.74 \text{ per hour}$$

James has also included the amount that he wishes to draw from the business in his costings. For him, he must charge a minimum of £8.74 per hour for each hour that he provides a service to his customers.

# chapter summary

❏   All businesses need to calculate the cost of goods and services.

❏   The three main elements of cost are:
   – materials
   – labour
   – expenses

❏   Each of the elements of cost comprises two categories:
   – direct costs, identified with each unit made or service provided
   – indirect costs, all other costs

❏   The unit of goods (eg cane basket) or service (eg hour of computer time) needs to be identified, and then the number of units in a particular time period (eg a week) can be calculated.

❏   The direct and indirect costs are then calculated for the time period.

❏   The unit cost of goods or service is then calculated: this represents the minimum price that must be charged for each unit of output.

 **student activities**

**42.1**   Select one business from each of the lists:

*goods*
- cake making
- ice cream making
- dried flower arrangements
- picture framing
- jewellery manufacture
- growing mushrooms

*service*
- car tuning
- household cleaning service
- golf lessons
- window cleaning
- car valet
- taxi service

(Alternatively, agree different goods and services with your teacher or lecturer.)

For each business selected, you are to investigate the likely costs of providing the goods or service. In particular you should:
- identify the unit of goods or service
- calculate the number of units for a particular time period
- calculate the direct costs for the particular time period
- calculate the indirect costs
- allocate indirect costs to units produced in the particular time period
- calculate the unit cost of the goods or service

# Calculating the cost of goods and services

| Element 7.3 | Calculate the cost of goods or service. |
|---|---|

Suggested Sources:
- work experience – examining (with permission) the costs of providing goods or service
- practical research into costs
- textbooks in libraries and resource centres

## INTRODUCTION

Two friends are planning to set up separate businesses: Tony will make wooden garden seats, while Karen will offer a gardening service. They each seek your advice as to the cost of goods and service. From discussion with them you have found out the following accounting information:

*Tony: Garden seat manufacture*

- wood and other materials will cost £11.50 per garden seat

- each seat will take four hours to make

- a friend will deliver seats sold locally; for more distant deliveries, a carrier will be used: both methods of delivery are expected to cost £5 per seat

- Tony will work in the business for 40 hours each week which will be spent as follows: 28 hours on manufacturing, 5 hours on administration and 7 hours on marketing the finished product; nobody else will be employed at present

- Tony plans to draw £120 per week as wages from the business

- he will take two weeks' holiday each year

- rent of a small factory unit and office will cost £4,160 per year; business rates will cost £1,040 per year

- a specialist machine will need to be purchased at a cost of £650 – it is expected to last for two years (104 weeks, less two weeks' holiday each year = 100 weeks' usage) at the planned level of production, after which it will be sold for scrap at an estimated value of £50

- other running expenses and insurance are expected to be £780 per year

**Karen:** *Gardening service*

- in the spring, summer and early autumn Karen will offer a grasscutting service for 30 weeks, and, in the late autumn and winter, a digging service, using a mechanical rotovator, will be offered for 20 weeks; she will take two weeks' holiday each year
- a heavy duty petrol lawnmower will be purchased at a cost of £1,000; it is expected to last for 300 weeks' use, after which it will be sold for an estimated £100
- a rotovator will be purchased at a cost of £600; it is expected to last for 100 weeks' use, after which it will be sold for an estimated £100
- Karen will buy a secondhand van to transport the gardening equipment: the cost of this will be £2,500 – it is expected to last for three years, after which it will be sold for an estimated £700
- van running costs are estimated at £1,040 per year
- both the lawnmower and rotovator will use £1.50 of petrol per hour; both will need an annual service costing £100 each; spare parts are estimated at £80 per year for the lawnmower, and £100 for the rotovator
- Karen will work a 40-hour week which will be spent as follows:

  20 hours working for customers, ie using the mechanical equipment, lawnmower or rotovator, 10 hours travelling to customers, 5 hours on administration and 5 hours on marketing (eg meeting new customers)
- she plans to draw £160 per week as wages from the business
- the van and all gardening equipment will be kept in a lock-up garage which will cost £10 a week for rent and £104 per year for business rates
- other running expenses and insurance are expected to be £1,300 per year

**Taking each business in turn, you are to undertake the following tasks:**

## TASK 1
Identify the direct and indirect costs under the headings of
- materials
- labour
- expenses

## TASK 2
Identify the unit of goods and service, justifying your choice.

## TASK 3
Calculate the number of units of the goods and service provided in a week.

## TASK 4
Calculate the direct costs of the goods and service each week.

## TASK 5
Calculate the indirect costs of the goods and service.

## TASK 6
Calculate the allocation of indirect costs to weekly output.

## TASK 7
Calculate the total cost of a unit of the goods and service.

*notes:*
- assume that each business will operate for 50 weeks each year
- no wages will be drawn during the two weeks' holiday taken each year
- rent paid, business rates, and other running expenses (including van depreciation and running costs) will apply for the whole year, but must be allocated using the 50 weeks that the businesses are operating
- for Karen's business, do not calculate separate unit costs for grasscutting and rotovating – instead, calculate an overall unit cost

# 43 Sources of business finance

## introduction

When preparing for the business plan (which we look at in detail in Chapter 47) it is essential to establish what physical resources the business will need:

* *assets* such as premises, machinery, office equipment
* *working capital* – short term funds which enable a business to operate from day-to-day: eg paying suppliers for materials purchased, paying wages

A business must also investigate the sources of finance for these differing resource requirements. These sources may include:

* bank finance – overdrafts, loans
* finance companies – leasing and hire purchase
* funds from private investors – individuals and venture capital companies
* government grants

In this chapter we will therefore

* identify the different types of resource requirement, distinguishing between fixed assets and working capital
* explain the different types of financial assistance available for funding these resources

We will examine by means of a Case Study how a business assesses its need for external finance and financial services when it is starting up, and also when it is expanding.

## resources planning

### fixed assets
You will recall from your study of the balance sheet of a business (Chapter 36) that fixed assets are

*long-term items owned by a business*

If for example, you consider a manufacturing business, its fixed assets may include items such as:

- land and buildings including the factory, the storage facilities, the car park and access roads
- production machinery
- vehicles – delivery vehicles and cars owned by the sales staff and directors
- office equipment – computers, photocopiers, switchboards, telephones, faxes
- fixtures and fittings – storage facilities, furniture, heating and lighting equipment

The list can be very long. Whether you are starting a business for real, or taking part in a Young Enterprise or mini-business scheme, you will have to sit down with your management and make a resources 'shopping list' and then come to the decision of what resources are *essential*, and whether you can afford them. One alternative to purchasing which we will consider later is leasing, an arrangement whereby you effectively 'rent' an item of equipment, eg a photocopier or a car. You do not own the asset (so it does not appear on your balance sheet), but have long-term use of it in return for a regular payment to the *leasing company* which owns it.

## working capital

You will also need to plan for short-term resources *for which you will need cash*. If, for example, you are a manufacturing business, you will need to

- buy stocks of raw materials which you will process into a finished product
- finance semi-finished products (known as work-in-progress) and stocks of finished products
- pay wages
- pay running expenses as they fall due: business rates, electricity, gas, water, insurance, advertising

If you fail to plan for these – and do not use a cash flow forecast – you are in danger of running out of cash: you will encounter 'cash flow problems', a situation which in the worst case can lead to bankruptcy.

It is essential therefore to plan for sufficient *working capital*. What is working capital? Working capital is the amount of money or potential money you have in the short-term, either in the form of cash or bank balances, money owed, or in stock which can be sold, *less* all the bills you have to meet in the short-term and any bank overdraft. It is essentially a cash or near-cash 'cushion'. In accounting terms the formula for calculating working capital is

*working capital equals current assets less current liabilities*

Look at the extract from a balance sheet shown below.

| | £ | £ |
|---|---|---|
| **Current assets** | | |
| Stocks – raw materials, work-in-progress and finished goods | 20,000 | |
| Debtors – money owed you in the short-term | 29,000 | |
| Cash – money held by the business | 1,000 | |
| | | 50,000 |
| **Less current liabilities** | | |
| Creditors – money you owe to suppliers and for bills | 22,000 | |
| Bank overdraft – money you owe to the bank | 3,000 | |
| | | 25,000 |
| **Working capital** | | 25,000 |

In this example, the total of current assets is £50,000. After the current liabilities of £25,000 have been deducted, working capital of £25,000 is left, a sufficient 'cushion' of short-term finance which is available should the business need it. If, for example, the business increased its purchases of stock and the creditors figure went up by £10,000, the business will still be able to pay them off. If there was no working capital, this would not be possible.

All businesses therefore need a certain minimum amount of working capital, and the amount required will vary from business to business, depending on the *nature of the business* (for example, a shop is likely to need less working capital than an engineering business), and on the *size of the business*.

# applying for finance

A number of institutions provide finance for fixed assets *and* for working capital. In this chapter we will therefore look at he institutions individually, at the same time drawing the distinction between *asset* finance and *working capital* finance.

Another distinction to be drawn is that between *external* finance provided by a lender and *internal* finance provided by the owner(s) of the business.

## how much external finance ?
There are a number of situations where external finance may be needed. These include:
• starting up a new business
• buying a business
• expanding an existing business

Some people do not like relying on external finance. One sometimes hears the old-fashioned notion that there is something *wrong* with borrowing. It must be stressed that *sensible* borrowing is essential to business growth. Without outside finance many good ideas would never have got off the ground. What, however, is *sensible* borrowing? A provider of external finance – such as a bank – will need reassuring about the owner's commitment to the business, and will not want to lend more than the owner is contributing. The lender will ask the potential borrower:

*What percentage of the total finance needed by the business are you putting in yourself?*

*If you are putting in less than 50%, is it possible for you to raise more from your private sources?*

If the business is a *new* one, the provider of finance will rarely lend more than half of the start-up cost, unless it will be repaid quickly. If the owner puts in less than 50%, a lender may quite rightly ask the question: "whose business is it?" If the finance is needed for expanding an *existing* business, the lender will not normally want to see outside borrowing (including the new borrowing) exceed the capital of the owner(s).

## the business plan
It is normal, if you are applying to an outside body for finance – a bank for example – to prepare a written plan, normally referred to as a *business plan*. This is explained in full in Chapter 47. The business plan sets out your product, expertise, market, your pricing policy and, most important of all, your *financial* requirements – ie how much you want to borrow. The *cash flow forecast* is used by the business to forecast expected 'cash in' and expected 'cash out' on a monthly basis. If there is a cash shortfall, particularly in the early months of operations when substantial costs are incurred, then this difference is the amount of external finance required by the business.

## matching the finance to the assets
Lenders will normally want to match the period of any lending to the expected life of the asset financed. There are *three* generally accepted timescales for finance, although you may find definitions which will vary from these:

| | | |
|---|---|---|
| *short-term* | 1 to 2 years | short-term requirements, ie working capital needs |
| *medium-term* | 3 to 10 years | purchase of fixed assets, eg machinery |
| *long-term* | 11 to 25 years | purchase of land and premises |

As you will see, the longer the life of the asset purchased, the longer the loan that will be made available. A lender will obviously be unwilling to lend money over 25 years to finance an ice cream salesman for his summer stocks, but will provide funds over that period to enable a company to purchase a factory unit. In short, the period for repayment of the finance should *match* the expected life of the asset. The next section examines the different *types* of finance available to businesses, and the *sources* of that finance.

# bank finance

We will now consider the various types and sources of finance. It should be noted that some of the sources listed here only provide finance to limited companies: this will be made clear in the text. The banks (which include some building societies registered as banks) are the largest providers of finance to *all* types of businesses. Forms of lending vary from bank to bank, and you should make your own investigations into the timespans of individual bank facilities. A bank will be able to arrange, by itself, or through specialised companies which it owns:

- overdraft
- short and medium-term loans ('business loans')
- commercial mortgage
- leasing for equipment purchase
- factoring services
- venture capital

Before looking at each of these forms of financing in turn, it is important to appreciate how *interest rates* are set, and also what *security* is required for lending.

## interest rates

The cost of borrowing usually involves two separate expenses:

- an *arrangement fee* – charged when the finance is arranged, and in some cases when it is renewed
- *interest* – a specific charge calculated as a percentage of the amount borrowed

Banks generally set their interest rates at a set percentage (which varies according to the risk element in the lending) *above* the prevailing Base Rate. Base Rate is an advertised fixed rate, set and varied periodically by the major banks, who use it as a *base* for working out interest rates for borrowers. No-one ever borrows at Base Rate. Base Rate is varied in line with interest rates in the economy. In this respect business borrowing differs from most *personal* borrowing – eg a car loan – which is charged at a *fixed* rate expressed in terms of an APR (Annual Percentage Rate) which the law requires be quoted to the borrower. Interest is normally charged to the bank account of the borrower on a monthly or quarterly basis.

## security for lending

Lending to businesses is seen by the financial institutions as being risky, because statistically businesses become bankrupt more often than do personal borrowers. Whereas a bank may lend £2,000 to a private individual for a new kitchen and not require any security cover, business borrowers will nearly always be asked to provide some security. Security can be in the form of:

- a *mortgage* – a legal document which the borrower signs stating in effect that, if the finance is not repaid, the lender can sell whatever is being 'mortgaged' . The items mortgaged can include the house of the borrower (the most common form of security) or investments with a market value, such as stocks and shares and insurance policies
- a *guarantee* – a legal document signed by an individual (the 'guarantor') stating that, if the borrower fails to repay when asked to, then the guarantor will pay up; limited companies are often guaranteed by their directors in this way

Security for business borrowing is normally

| | |
|---|---|
| *sole trader* | a mortgage over the home or any marketable investments |
| *partnership* | a mortgage over the homes or any marketable investments belonging to the partners |
| *limited company* | a mortgage over the assets of the company (this document is known as a 'debenture' or a 'fixed and floating charge') and/or the guarantees of the directors |

## bank fixed asset finance

**business loan** This is a fixed medium-term loan, typically for between 3 and 10 years, to cover the purchase of capital items such as machinery or equipment. Interest is normally 2% to 3% over base rate, and repayments are by instalments. Sometimes repayment of principal (the full amount borrowed) can be postponed during the first two years of the loan (a 'repayment holiday') when only interest payments are made.

**commercial mortgage** If you are buying premises for your business you can arrange to borrow long-term by means of a commercial mortgage, typically up to 80% of the value of the property, repayable over a period of up to 25 years. Your premises will be taken as security for the loan: if the business fails, the premises will be sold.

## bank working capital finance

**overdraft** An overdraft is short-term borrowing on bank current account. It is relatively cheap: the banks charge typically 4% to 6% over Base Rate for a new business, 2.5% to 5% over Base Rate for an existing business. Interest is normally charged quarterly, but you only pay interest on what you actually borrow. A 'limit' up to which you can borrow will be granted by the bank, and reviewed annually, when it can be increased, decreased or renewed at the same level. A renewal fee is payable for this service.

An overdraft is the most common form of finance for *working capital*. It provides the finance when a business needs to pay creditors or meet other short-term bills. It is not a 'bottomless pit' however, and if a bank becomes nervous about the ability of a business to repay, it can ask for the overdraft to be repaid *on demand*. This can have a catastrophic effect on the cash position of a business.

# finance arranged through bank-owned companies

## fixed asset finance

*Finance Houses*, specialist companies owned in the main by the major banks, offer alternative ways of obtaining assets:

**hire purchase** An HP agreement from a finance house enables a business to acquire an asset on the payment of a deposit and to pay back the cost plus interest over a set period, at the end of which ownership of the asset passes to the borrower. Hire purchase is often used to finance vehicles and machinery.

**leasing** Leasing arrangements are also provided by finance houses. With a leasing agreement, the business has use of assets bought by the finance house, and the business pays a regular 'rental' payment, normally over a lease period of two to seven years. Ownership of the goods never passes to the business. A common form of lease is a *pay back lease* or *finance lease* in which the business will pay back the cost of the item plus finance costs over the period of the lease. Clearly a lease is not a loan, but it can substantially reduce a business' financial requirements when it needs to make a capital purchase. Computer equipment and fleets of company cars are often leased.

## working capital finance

**factoring**   Many banks also provide *factoring services* through specialist factoring companies. A business may have valuable financial resources tied up because its customers owe it money and have not yet paid. A factoring company will effectively 'buy' these debts by providing a number of services:

- it will lend up to 80% of outstanding customer debts
- it will deal with all the paperwork of collecting customer debts
- it will insure against non-payment of debts

Factoring *frees* money due to the business and allows the business to use it in its general operations and expansion plans. It is therefore a valuable source of short-term finance.

## finance for limited companies: venture capital

Many banks own *merchant banks,* specialist banks which offer advice and financial assistance to limited companies. This financial assistance takes the form of loans and *venture capital* which provides finance for fixed assets and for working capital. Ownership of a limited company is in the form of shares, known as equity capital, held by the investors. Merchant banks may view such companies as ripe for investment and will inject money either in the form of loans or by the purchase of shares, or both. In return, they may expect an element of control over the company and will possibly insist on having a director on the board of the company. A merchant bank considering investing in a limited company will look for a business with a good profit record, strong management and a viable product range.

The funds introduced by the merchant bank could be used for:

- financing an expansion or launching a new product
- acquisition of another company
- the management of the company 'buying out' control of the company
- financing the employees 'buying out' control of the company
- providing working capital

Other financial institutions active in the venture capital market include *venture capital companies,* non-banking commercial organisations which attract money from private investors and re-invest in limited companies. Their financial assistance includes loans and investment in share capital. They often require a substantial element of control over the borrowing company.

## financing from creditors and landlords

### finance from creditors

Many businesses rely on their creditors as a form of short-term financing. If a business needs short-term funds and finds that there is not sufficient money in the bank or within the overdraft limit, it can *delay* payments to creditors, or obtain longer credit periods. The business effectively thus obtains an interest-free loan at the expense of its creditors.

It is the small business which often suffers at the hands of the larger business because of this practice:

- if large suppliers are not paid on time by small businesses, credit can be cut off entirely
- if the small business supplies a large business (usually a retail chain), the large business can more or less hold the small business to ransom by delaying payments (over six months in some cases) and threatening to stop buying if the small business does not accept long credit terms

As a consequence many small supplier businesses end up by helping to finance the large retailers.

## landlord finance

Businesses which lease premises sometimes obtain finance from their landlord. The most common example of this is where a Local Authority owns business "starter" units, and offers either deferred rental payments or low interest rate loans. The object of this form of "subsidy" financing is to encourage the growth of small businesses. This form of financing is clearly not often provided by commercial landlords!

# financial assistance from the Government

The Government offers considerable assistance in the way of grants, subsidies and training. These are made available directly and indirectly to new and established businesses.

### regional aid – the Department of Trade and Industry (DTI) 'Enterprise Initiative'

The Government offers considerable assistance in the way of grants, subsidies and training. These are made available directly and indirectly to new and established businesses.

The Department of Trade and Industry (DTI) has divided the UK into different types of area (illustrated in the map on the next page). The type of area in which a business operates or plans to operate will dictate the level of regional aid that will be made available. The types of area are:

* *Assisted Areas*

  - development areas: these areas are those which have the greatest unemployment and greatest deprivation

  - intermediate areas: these are less deprived than the development areas, and are usually to be found on the fringes of development areas

  - urban programme areas: specific inner city areas which are in need of direct and indirect government support

* *non-assisted Areas* – the rest of the country, where a limited amount of assistance is available

The schemes currently available include:

* *Assisted Areas*

  - *Regional Selective Assistance* (all Assisted Areas): discretionary grants for companies creating new jobs; the amount made available will depend on the cost of the project and the number of jobs that will be created

  - *Regional Enterprise Grants* for firms with under 25 employees (all Development Areas and a limited number of Intermediate Areas): 15% of cost of equipment up to a maximum of £15,000, and 'innovation' grants of 50% of the cost of new development up to a maximum of £25,000

  - *Consultancy grants*: two-thirds of the cost of approved business consultancy in the Assisted Areas and the Urban Programme Areas.

* *Non-Assisted Areas – Consultancy grants*: half of the cost of approved business consultancy

* *other assistance for all areas*

  - 'Managing into the 90's' Programme: information and advice on the management of product design, quality manufacture, purchasing and sales

  - Research and Technology Initiative: training sessions and grants towards research projects

* *Inner City 'Task Forces'*

  Task Forces are advisory bodies which operate in Inner City areas. They provide advice, training and financial assistance for new and growing businesses. The Task Force Development Funds (TFDFs) provide last resort loans and grants through the Local Enterprise Agencies.

### The Rural Development Commission

The Rural Development Commission provides businesses in rural areas with free advice and technical support. In development areas (see above) loans and grants are available.

## The Department of Employment: Loan Guarantee Scheme

The government offers a guarantee for 85% of a bank medium-term loan (2 to 7 years) up to £250,000. This security enables banks and other financial institutions to lend money for projects which would be too risky by normal criteria.   Borrowing under this scheme is charged to the borrower at a premium of 0.5% p.a  on the guaranteed amount of a *fixed* rate loan (1.5% for a *variable* rate loan).   The scheme, which until 1993 charged a higher premium, has been very successful, and has enabled many businesses to expand, Waterstones Bookshops in its early days, for example.

## Training and Enterprise Councils (TECs) – Enterprise Allowance Scheme

The Enterprise Allowance Scheme, also known as the  Business Start-up Scheme, is run by the local TECs (Training and Enterprise Councils) and provides financial assistance and training to selected previously unemployed people wanting to set up a *new* business.  The schemes are tailor-made by each local TEC and vary from area to area.  An applicant would typically:

- have been unemployed for six weeks
- be able to contribute £1,000 (from savings, or bank overdraft, or loan)
- attend an introductory training course
- write (with help provided by the TEC) a Business Plan which has to be approved by the TEC

If *accepted* by the local TEC the applicant would be paid a regular living wage for a year, be given a free place on a 'Business Skills Seminar' and be able to take advantage of advisory services and other training courses provided by the local TEC.

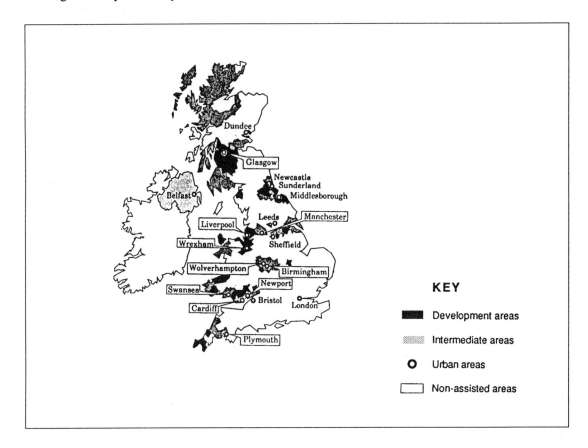

*Fig 43.1  The Enterprise Initiative:  The Assisted Areas*

## the cost of bank finance

It is essential when carrying out financial planning that the *cost* of finance is considered. As we saw earlier in the chapter, bank finance involves two types of charge – fees and interest:

**fees**          *arrangement fees* are charged when the finance is arranged
                  *renewal fees* are charged when the finance is renewed (eg every year for an overdraft)
                  *security fees* are charged when security is taken to cover the borrowing

**interest**      Interest – the basic cost of borrowing – is charged monthly or quarterly. For example, if a business borrows £100,000 to purchase fixed assets, and the interest rate is 16% p.a., the business will have to pay

$$£100,000 \quad x \quad \frac{16}{100} = £16,000 \text{ interest per year}$$

The charges made by the banks vary from bank to bank, but most institutions now publish their business tariff in booklet form, available from the branches. A person starting up a business would be well advised to 'shop around' for the best deal. Some banks offer special terms for new business start-ups; these are well worth investigating. The table set out below shows some *typical* charges for bank facilities of £50,000. It must be remembered that interest rates will vary as base rate changes, and more risky customers will be charged higher rates than less risky customers. The figures set out below are for general guidance only.

| typical cost of bank finance of £50,000 (assuming a base rate of 10%) | | |
|---|---|---|
| **type of finance** | **interest payable** | **fees payable** |
| **overdraft** of £50,000 for day-to-day needs (working capital) | Base Rate + 4% 10% + 4% = 14% amount = £7,000 p.a. | arrangement fee of 1.25% of amount = £625 renewal fee of 0.75% of amount = £375 security fee = £500 |
| **business loan** or **commercial mortgage** of £50,000 for purchase of fixed assets | Base Rate + 3% 10% + 3% = 13% amount = £6,500 p.a. | arrangement fee of 1.25% of amount = £625 no renewal fee security fee = £500 |

## conclusions

You will see from the table that the interest costs for an overdraft appear higher, but in fact they will probably be lower, because for an overdraft *you are only charged interest for what you borrow on a day-to-day basis.* As the balance of the account fluctuates from being overdrawn to being in credit, your interest charge will be calculated accordingly. The balances on a business loan and commercial mortgage on the other hand remain fairly constant, at a high level, and interest will be charged on the full amount. This is the reason why the overdraft is often referred to as the cheapest form of borrowing.

The fees payable on the different types of bank finance do not differ significantly. In the long run the overdraft will incur more fees because, unlike a business loan or commercial mortgage, it is usually renewed on a yearly basis, and an additional renewal fee will then become payable.

## Case Study:
## Capability Landscapes – financing a business

### Situation 1 – raising the finance

James Brown is a qualified landscape gardener who has been working for a large firm of gardening contractors for five years. His aim has been to gain experience of the trade so that he can eventually set up on his own as an independent landscape gardener. He has chosen the name 'Capability Landscapes' for his business. James intends to work from home, so he will not need premises. He will however need a pickup truck and equipment, including a lawnmower and cultivator. He has saved hard and has accumulated £5,000 in a building society account. In addition, his uncle has promised to lend him £5,000 over five years to help him get established. His uncle has also promised to guarantee any borrowing from the bank.

The question is, how much is it all going to cost, and will James need to borrow?

James is not experienced in financial matters, so he contacts his local Business Promotion Centre which puts him in touch with an accountant who specialises in helping small businesses.

### Solution

The accountant asks him to set out on paper what items he will need for the business, and how much they are likely to cost – these items will be his *assets*. His accountant asks him to distinguish between items which he will need permanently in the business – *fixed assets* – and items which he will on a day-to-day basis – *current assets*. James produces the following figures:

|  | £ | £ |
|---|---|---|
| **fixed assets required** | | |
| pickup truck, secondhand | 8,000 | |
| lawnmower and cultivator | 900 | |
| gardening tools | <u>350</u> | |
| *total of fixed assets* | | 9,250 |
| | | |
| **current assets required** | | |
| initial stock of plants and seed | 1,500 | |
| fertilisers | 150 | |
| cash in hand | <u>100</u> | |
| *total of current assets* | | 1,750 |
| | | |
| *TOTAL ASSETS REQUIRED* | | 11,000 |

The accountant then asks James to look at how much finance he has available. He asks him to distinguish between *capital* (the amount he is putting in himself) and *liabilities* (any borrowing from other sources). James produces the following figures:

|  | £ |
|---|---|
| **capital** | |
| building society savings | 5,000 |
| | |
| **liabilities** | |
| loan (long-term) from uncle | 5,000 |
| | |
| *TOTAL FINANCE AVAILABLE* | 10,000 |

## how much finance is needed?

The accountant points out that James needs finance of £1,000 on the basis of his calculations: he needs £11,000 of assets and has only £10,000 available.

The accountant recommends that James approaches his bank for an overdraft of £1,000, which can be guaranteed by his uncle. He says that an overdraft is the best solution because it is short-term (for financing working capital) and it is also the cheapest form of borrowing.

The accountant promises to draw up this proposal in a formal *business plan* for submission to the bank. The plan will include the projected balance sheet set out below. This shows clearly what assets are required and *how they are to be financed.*

---

### BALANCE SHEET OF JAMES BROWN TRADING AS CAPABILITY LANDSCAPES
(PROJECTED AS AT 31 DECEMBER 19-5)

| | £ | £ |
|---|---|---|
| **Fixed Assets** | | |
| Vehicle | | 8,000 |
| Equipment | | 900 |
| Gardening tools | | 350 |
| | | 9,250 |
| **Current Assets** | | |
| Gardening stock | 1,500 | |
| Fertilisers | 150 | |
| Cash | 100 | |
| | 1,750 | |
| **Less Current Liabilities** | | |
| Bank overdraft | 1,000 | |
| **Working Capital** | | 750 |
| | | 10,000 |
| **Less Long-term Liabilities** | | |
| Long-term loan from uncle | | 5,000 |
| **NET ASSETS** | | 5,000 |
| | | |
| *FINANCED BY* | | |
| | | |
| **Capital** | | |
| Owner's capital | | 5,000 |

---

## the business plan

It must be appreciated that the projected balance sheet will form only part of the business plan. The document will also include a description of the business, the qualifications and experience of the owner and other important financial projections, the cash flow forecast, and the profit and loss forecast, both dealt with in depth in Chapters 40 and 41.

### the interview with the bank

James and his accountant are interviewed by the bank manager who has been sent a copy of the business plan in advance. He readily agrees to James' request for finance. The bank manager hands him a booklet setting out the bank charges and terms for operating the account. He states that James will be charged as follows

| | |
|---|---|
| *overdraft interest* | base rate (say 10%) + 5%  = 15% |
| *arrangement fee* | £50 |
| *security fee (for the uncle's guarantee)* | £100 |

James calculates that his interest cost for the first year - assuming that he will utilise the overdraft to the full will be  £1,000  x  15%   = £150.  His first year's finance costs will therefore be

| | |
|---|---|
| interest | £150 |
| arrangement fee | £50 |
| security fee | £100 |
| TOTAL COST | £300 |

## Situation 2 – making the most of bank finance

James Brown has been trading successfully for three years. His business has expanded rapidly and his annual fee income is now £350,000. His balance sheet as at the end of the third year is illustrated below.

**BALANCE SHEET OF JAMES BROWN TRADING AS CAPABILITY LANDSCAPES**
(END OF YEAR 3)

| | £ | £ |
|---|---|---|
| **Fixed Assets** | | |
| Vehicles | | 15,000 |
| Equipment | | 2,500 |
| Gardening tools | | 500 |
| | | 18,000 |
| **Current Assets** | | |
| Gardening stock and chemicals | 5,000 | |
| Debtors | 50,000 | |
| Cash in till | 200 | |
| | 55,200 | |
| **Less Current Liabilities** | | |
| Bank overdraft | 10,000 | |
| **Working Capital** | | 45,200 |
| **NET ASSETS** | | 63,200 |
| *FINANCED BY* | | |
| **Capital** | | |
| Owner's capital (including profits) | | 63,200 |

The balance sheet shows that he has now built up a capital (his investment plus profits for the three years) of £63,200. His bank overdraft has been increased to £10,000 to cover his day-to-day trading requirements, he has bought another truck and some equipment, and his uncle's loan has been repaid.

## the problems

He employs ten people, rents a small workshop and yard and has to hire his equipment from a local machine hire firm. He is feeling the need to expand and reorganise his business. He again approaches his accountant who helps him to analyse his needs:

| | |
|---|---|
| *premises* | he wants to buy a workshop and yard for £75,000 |
| *equipment* | he wants to acquire more machinery at a cost of £50,000 |
| *debt chasing* | he is finding it increasingly difficult to collect money he is owed by his customers – his debtors owe him a total of £50,000 |

His basic problem is not having the cash to be able to invest – it is all tied up in amounts due to him from debtors. He is also rather ambitious in his spending plans: he wants to buy premises for £75,000 and equipment for £50,000 – a total of £125,000 and approximately twice his own capital of £63,200. No lender would be willing to lend more than James Brown's own capital of £63,200. The bank is already lending £10,000 on overdraft.

# Solution

His accountant and bank manager suggest:

| | |
|---|---|
| *factoring* | the bank's factoring company will manage his debtors, lending him 80% of the £50,000 owing, thus releasing £40,000 which he can use in the business straightaway |
| *commercial mortgage* | the bank will lend him £40,000 for his new premises against a mortgage of the property; he will contribute the remaining £35,000 |
| *leasing* | the bank's leasing company will buy the equipment he needs and lease it to him for a monthly rental |

## how much will it cost?

James will need to ensure that his business can afford these financial costs:

*factoring*
- an annual charge of 2% of the annual total of debts collected, here 2% x £350,000 = £7,000, <u>plus</u>
- interest on amounts borrowed, say an annual average of £40,000 at base rate (10%) + 4% = 14% = £5,600

*commercial mortgage*
- interest at Base Rate (10%) + 3% = 13%; the annual cost will be £40,000 x 13% = £5,200, plus any repayments
- arrangement fee 1.25% x £40,000 = £500
- security fee = £350

*leasing*
monthly rental payments to cover the financial cost of the lease, say twice the capital value of the assets (2 x £50,000) spread over 5 years (60 months):

$$\frac{£100,000}{60 \text{ months}} = £1,666 \text{ per month or } £20,000 \text{ per year}$$

# chapter summary

❑ When a business examines its needs for physical resources it will distinguish between fixed asset and working capital requirements.

❑ When applying for external finance you should prepare a full business plan which sets out your product or service, your market, your financial details and your financial needs.

❑ The most common source of finance is the banks. They can offer overdrafts, business loans and commercial mortgages, usually against security put down by the borrower or other individuals.

❑ The banks also provide financial assistance through their finance houses (HP and leasing), factoring companies and merchant banks (venture capital funding).

❑ The Government also provides financial assistance and advice through the Department of Trade and Industry's 'Enterprise Initiative', the Loan Guarantee Scheme and the TECs' Enterprise Allowance

❑ Banks charge the borrower for the provision of finance, both in the form of fees and also in interest charges. This expense should be budgeted for by the borrower.

❑ In conclusion it can be seen that the sources of business finance are as follows:

| *fixed asset finance* | *working capital finance* |
|---|---|
| owner's funds | owner's funds |
| equity finance | equity finance |
| funding from creditors | funding from creditors |
| Government grant | Government grant |
| commercial mortgage | overdraft |
| business loan | factoring |
| leasing | |
| hire purchase | |

# ✍️ Student Activities

Please note that there is no specific Evidence Collection Exercise for Element 7.1. We recommend that the Evidence required is submitted along with the Business Plan required in Unit 8.

**43.1** You work in the lending department of the National Bank plc,124 High Street, Stourminster, ST1 2JF and receive a number of enquiries during the week from customers wanting finance. What form of finance would you recommend in the situations set out below? In each case write a letter to the customer explaining:

- the type of finance appropriate to the situation
- how the finance will be repaid
- the likely cost to the customer in terms of interest and fees
- the bank's likely security requirements

When writing the letters use your own name, the title of Lending Officer, and today's date. You are not required to investigate whether the bank will or will not lend – your task is to explain the type of finance available.

Your bank's fee and interest tariff for existing businesses is:

*Overdraft:* interest 4% over base rate, arrangement fee 1.25% (minimum £75)

*Business Loan:* interest 3% over base rate, arrangement fee 1.25% (minimum £100)

*Commercial Mortgage:* interest 3% over base rate, arrangement fee 1.5% (minimum £150)

*Security fee (average):* limited companies £350, other borrowers £250

(a) Tony Page of 47 Rydale Villas, Stourminster, WR4 5TY, a sole trader builder, is expanding his business. He has got all that he wants in the way of vehicles and equipment, but he needs more money – £5,000 he reckons – to buy building materials and to deal with day-to-day trading requirements. Mr Page owns his house in Rydale Villas.

(b) Beattie Gold of "Glendale", Mill Street, Stourminster, WR4 5TH, runs a successful and profitable catering business as a sole trader. She owns a bakery and shop in town; they are worth £125,000. She wants to expand by installing more ovens and modernising the bakery; the cost will be £25,000.

(c) Barbourne Sofware Supplies Limited is a mail-order computer software supplier operating from a small warehouse which it owns (Unit 1B Severnside Industrial Estate, Stourminster, WR2 5TF). The business is expanding rapidly and the company wants to purchase an adjacent warehouse (Unit 1A) which has recently become vacant following a bankruptcy. The price of the unit is £175,000, and the company will additionally need to purchase more equipment costing £12,500.

(d) Jim Steinitz of The Hop Kiln, Rushworth Common, Rushworth, WR7 7CS, has formed a company (British Vintage Limited) to export British Wine to the USA and EC countries. He needs to raise £100,000. He realises that his venture is risky, and mentions that he has heard that the Government sometimes guarantees bank borrowing.

**43.2** You work as an adviser in the local Enterprise Agency. In the course of a working day you encounter a number of queries relating to financial problems and the raising of finance. Write down how you would deal with the problems set out below. In each case:

- identify the problem

- recommend a particular scheme which would solve the problem

- state where the scheme is made available, and whom the client should approach in the first instance

(a) Brian Richards was made redundant six months ago, and has since then been drawing Unemployment Benefit. He has £2,000 redundancy money left, and wishes to start up in business restoring antique furniture, a hobby he has practised for some time. He knows there is a market for his work, as he can sell to the local antique shops, making a good profit.

(b) Neeta Patel runs a clothing manufacturing business which sold more than £500,000 worth of goods last year. One problem she finds is that her customers are increasingly unwilling to pay up on time. As a result she is always short of money in the bank and cannot always pay *her* suppliers when she wants to.

(c) William Moss runs a computer consultancy service. He owns a number of computers which he bought eighteen months ago, but now finds that they are out-of-date. He is wary of buying new computers: in the first place he cannot afford them, in the second place they get out-of-date very quickly, and he does not want to be left with expensive obsolete equipment in a couple of years' time.

(d) Orchard Fruits Limited makes jam from fruit purchased in the local fruit growing area. It has recently been approached with the opportunity of buying Eveshore Fruiterers Limited, a major fruit growing company. The directors of Eveshore Fruiterers are retiring and want to sell their profitable company for £750,000. Orchard Fruits Limited are very interested in the proposed purchase as it will enable them to grow their own fruit. Their directors, however, are unable to raise the necessary capital for buying Evershore Fruiterers Limited.

# business planning

## contents

In this Section we examine the processes that are involved in business planning and the compilation of a business plan:

As mentioned in a number of places in the text of this book, it may be that you will be writing a business plan as part of a Young Enterprise or mini-business scheme within your school or college. The writing of a business plan is central to an understanding of business, and it is the firm belief of the authors that your Portfolio of Evidence should contain one.

# 44 Starting a business

## introduction

Starting a business 'for real' may well form a major part of your studies. Your school or college may run a Young Enterprise Scheme, or your studies may revolve around a long-term assignment based on setting up a business to manufacture a product or provide a service. Whatever the situation you should have the opportunity to

- decide on the type of business you are going to set up
- write a business plan
- appreciate the complexity of running a business
- discover the advantages and disdvantages of working with other people

When studying business, there is no substitute for actually *doing* it.

In this chapter we will look at what you need to do to *choose* the type of business you want to set up. If you are taking part in a school or college enterprise, the choice may surprisingly be *more* difficult than if you are starting for real: the choice will be wider, and the people involved in making the choice may have less of a common purpose. In this chapter we therefore look at:

- different business opportunities
- the personal factor – are you suited to it? – what role will you adopt?
- getting advice

## business opportunities

If you walk down your local main street you will see evidence of a wide variety of business organisations in operation: bus services, telephones, the Post Office, shops, banks, newspaper sellers and even the market research lady with a clipboard who always detains you with detailed questions when you are in a hurry to get somewhere else.

We have seen earlier in this book that organisations are either *public* sector (State owned and controlled), or in the *private* sector. *Private sector organisations* are owned by private individuals in the form of companies, partnerships, sole trader businesses, cooperatives and franchises.

Examples range from well-known names such as Marks and Spencer and W H Smith to your local corner shop. Business opportunities are therefore most often found within the *private* sector.

Before looking at the different options that are open to enterprising entrepreneurs, it is important to appreciate that the guidelines for planning a business laid down in this chapter apply equally to *new* businesses and also to the *expansion* of an existing business.

We mentioned in the introduction to this chapter that your course in business studies may be structured around a practical exercise in running a business, such as a Young Enterprise scheme. If this is the case, you should read this and the following chapters in the context of the literature relating to your 'mini enterprise'. Not all the options described in this book will be open to you, but you should appreciate that they will be available to a person setting up business outside the school or college context.

# what sort of business?

People who start in business normally do so for one of a number of possible reasons. They may be out of a job and want to 'get going' again, they may be in a job and thoroughly bored with it, or they may be 'self-starters' who have great ambitions. They may be students on Young Enterprise schemes. Whatever the situation the most important factor to be borne in mind is the *type* of business chosen. The person who wants to start or expand a business has a number of options open:

## what type of industry?

The term 'industry' is loosely applied to a variety of businesses; some produce goods, some sell goods, others provide services. Industry is normally classified under the following sector headings:

*primary*         Primary industry produces the raw materials used by other businesses. Examples include oil, gas, mining, agriculture and fishing.

*secondary*       The secondary stage of production processes the raw materials into finished products. Examples include the aircraft and pharmaceutical industries at one end of the spectrum, and joiners and metal workers at the other.

*tertiary*        Tertiary industries are service industries; they do not produce manufactured items but provide services such as transport, financial services (banking and insurance), and tourism.

Your choice here will depend on your resources and your experience. An agriculturalist could enter primary production with organic food production, a craftsman could undertake secondary production with a craft workshop, a computer programmer could set up a consultancy in the tertiary service sector. The most essential factor is to consider the *demand* for you product or service: is it an expanding or a contracting market?

## a new business or an existing business?

A number of choices exist:

• *to start a new business*

'Starting from scratch' – involves the highest degree of risk: you are unknown, you will have to to research and penetrate your market, the financial risks are high, and you cannot afford to make any mistakes (for example over the location of the business). The rewards can also be high.

• *to buy an existing business*
This is an easier but more expensive option.  If you buy an existing business you will have to pay for the 'name' of the business and its trading relationship with its customers – this is known as *goodwill*. Because a business is already in operation, it does not mean that it is doing everything that it should do:  the processses of analysis and planning set out in this and later chapters are of prime importance.

• *to take up a franchise*
A franchise is the situation where a successful business sells its name and methods to individuals prepared to pay the necessary investment costs.  An example of a franchise is Kentucky Fried Chicken.  A franchise is a low-risk venture, and banks are generally happy to lend to help set them up.  A franchise can also be a low-return venture, because the franchisor (owner of the name) usually requires a substantial cut of the profits.

• *expanding and diversify an existing business*
The same principles of planning and analysis apply to a business which wishes to expand and diversify.  An example of expansion is a shop-owner who wishes to open a second shop;  this can be a very successful way of increasing business, it can also be a very dangerous way of spreading out resources.   An example of diversification is a farmer opening a farm shop;   this is often very successful because selling fruit to the public is more profitable than selling fruit to supermarket chains.

---

### student activity 44.1 – what type of business? – a brainstorming session

If you are taking part in a Young Enterprise or mini-business project you will need to decide what type of business you are going to set up, whether it be primary (unlikely), secondary or tertiary.

Divide up the whole class (or the students who are forming an individual business) into smaller groups of approximately four students.  Elect a secretary and a spokesperson for each small group.  Conduct a "brainstorming session" for ideas for products or services which the eventual mini-business could provide.  Combine this with a SWOT analysis.  The secretary should record the suggestions, and the group should select the best three ideas.  When the groups have come to the end of their discussions (or arguments!) the class should re-assemble and the spokesperson from each small group should present the ideas.  The class as a whole can then debate the suggestions and vote on a democratic basis for the type of business that they are going to set up.

### student activity 44.2 – what type of business? – your locality

Undertake a survey of your local main street and select thirty businesses.  Classify  them into the following categories:
• public sector/private sector
• primary/secondary/tertiary
• sole trader/partnership/limited company
• independent business/franchise (if you can tell!)

---

# the aims and objectives of the business

The choice of business will also depend on the *aims* of the individual going into business.  Most people go into business to make money.  The *profit* motive remains the most important goal of any business organisation.  There are, as was explained in Chapter 8, other goals.  Generally speaking the larger the organisation, the more developed are the aims.  Examine any large company and you find that, as well as the profit motive, it has very specific policies related to
• improving the environment by way of 'green' initiatives
• benefiting society by sponsorship of sport and the Arts
The aims of business may be summarised as follows:

**break-even/subsidy**   Businesses aim to break-even, ie to cover their costs.  This is obviously the first law of survival.  As we will see when we look at the business plan, a business must be financially viable if it is to continue trading.  The only exceptions to this is where a *subsidy* is involved.  This could either be:
- a government subsidy to an assisted area, where the aim is to create employment and encourage technicological innovation
- in a large business, eg a pharmaceuticals company where a group company developing a new drug is subsidised by the parent company's successful sales of registered drugs

**profit making**   Profitability means success and wealth creation for the owners of the business, and indirectly for the employees.  But the drive for profitability also has its downside; it inevitably means a cutting of costs, which could affect the workforce or the environment:
- buying cheaper machinery or equipment which is less user-friendly for staff and less reliable
- purchasing cheaper materials which are less environmentally friendly than the more expensive options (eg buying non-degradeable packaging )

**power and influence**   One aim of a business may be to achieve power and influence in its market sector.  This, unlike the profit motive, will result in an upgrading of physical resources   and will affect profit *adversely*, for example if it has smart, high-profile premises in a prominent business area where the nature of the business does not warrant it (eg a mail order business).

**social responsibility**   Socially responsible businesses have to provide facilities and manufacture goods to fulfil their social objectives:
- the provision of welfare facilities for the staff at the workplace
- the provision of creche facilities (eg in shops and factories)
- manufacture of socially responsible products (eg child safety seats)

You will see from these examples that businesses which have a sense of social responsibility may well *increase* their sales because these features figure high in consumers' spending preferences.  You should also note that businesses are legally bound by Health and Safety and Employer Protection legislation in respect of the workplace.

**customer care**   Businesses need to look after their customers if they are to avoid losing them.  Customer care can have a dramatic effect on the physical resources needed by businesses, simply in the way that the premises are equipped and laid out.  Look, for example, at the way in which banks and railway stations are changing their rather old-fashioned image to bright, customer-friendly environments.

**the environment**   The need for a business to plan its physical resources around environmental factors is becoming increasingly important.  Examples of the influence of the environmental lobby include:
- ozone depletion – the use of products which do not contain CFCs (chlorofluorocarbons) which damage the ozone layer may add to the expenses of a business in the choice of an environmentally friendly but more expensive product
- waste disposal – it may be cheaper to dispose of waste in the local river, but it will pollute the water, kill the fish, and possibly result in a prosecution under anti-pollution legislation
- use of heating systems which, although expensive in terms of capital outlay, are energy-efficient and low in emissions into the atmosphere
- packaging – as noted above, bio-degradeable packaging may be more expensive, but the fact that it rots away makes it environmentally desirable

### business objectives – the mission statement

We have already discussed business *aims*; these are *general* policies such as profitability, care of the environment, social awareness. If you are starting or expanding a business you should also have *objectives*; these are specific targets which you hope to achieve. These objectives can be short-term and long-term. The current phrase for a summary of these objectives is the "Mission Statement". For example, the owner of Express Pasta, an Italian fast-food store, might have the following short-term objectives:

> *"In the next twelve months I intend Express Pasta*
>
> > *- to offer the best standard of customer care in Stourminster High Street*
> >
> > *- to turn over £100,000 of business*
> >
> > *- to achieve a profit after all expenses and deductions of £15,000*

This might be summed up in a mission statement:

> *"Express Pasta will provide the best quality Pasta, offer the best service, and be the most profitable fast food outlet in Stourminster High Street."*

A long term objective might be:

> *"Within three years, I intend  Express Pasta*
>
> > *- to open a further two branches in St Martins and in Wimbury*
> >
> > *- to increase annual turnover to £300,000*

In Chapter 47 we will look at how these objectives are set out in the business plan.

---

### student  activity 44.3 – what are the business objectives ?

If you are setting up a business in your school or college,

(a)  discuss in your class the *aims* of your business in terms of the factors outlined in this chapter

(b)  produce a written statement of your business aims

(c)  draft a mission statement for your business – bear in mind that it may have to be amended when you have produced the final draft of your business plan

Note: if you are not taking part in a mini-business scheme, but are doing work experience or a part-time job,

(d)   identify the aims of the business or organisation in which you work

(e)  produce a written statement of those aims, and discuss it with your adviser in the workplace.

---

# starting up a business -the personal factor

Starting a business involves personal factors:

• you will probably have to work with others

• you will have to work with *yourself!*

If you are starrting up or expanding a business you should take account of your own personality and experience.  You should preferably chose an area with which you are familiar, either through a previous job, or through an interest – restoring classic cars, for example.

Size up *yourself* to see if you are suited to running a business. Are you hardworking, healthy, determined, willing to work long hours with few holidays, a risk-taker and able to communicate with people? If you are, you will probably survive and succeed in business, but if you have doubts, you may be better off in paid employment.

---

**student activity 44.4 – practical self-analysis**
Try to give honest answers to the following 'yes/no' questions.

- are you self-disciplined?
- are you determined?
- do you have specific objectives for your business?
- are you able to change course and take advice if things go wrong?
- are you healthy?
- can you work seven days a week, ten hours a day?
- can you cope with stress?
- do you enjoy working with other people?
- are you a risk taker?

The more positive answers you give, the more you are suited to going into business.

---

## choosing a job role

If you are taking part in a school or college mini-business scheme, you have no choice in the matter – you will have to assume a role in the business. You will need to look at your interests and abilities and choose an area to which you are suited, eg:

- management
- finance and book-keeping
- production
- sales and marketing

In a larger 'real' business these roles will already be allocated, and the sections of the business plan, which we look at in Chapter 47, correspond with these areas of responsibility.

# where can you get advice?

You cannot be expected to know everything. The decisions, procedures and paperwork involved in starting a business can often assume nightmare proportions if you do not seek proper advice. If you are engaged in a Young Enterprise project, much of the paperwork will be explained in your Company Kit, and advice will be freely given by the Advisers. If you are starting a business to earn a living, there are a number of sources of information: some are free, and some will cost you money.

**the professionals**    You will probably need to take professional advice from an accountant, and possibly also from a solicitor. The accountant will help you establish your accounting system and advise on taxation and setting up a system for paying the wages. The accountant or solicitor will help by advising on the legal aspects of your business – the form of the business, employment of staff, maintenance of premises. Solicitors and accountants charge for their services, and you should be prepared for this! It may be useful to establish links with an accountant at this early stage because you will need one later on to help with the books, financial statements and tax calculations for the business.  The major banks, too, offer specialist advice to new businesses;  some may charge for the service, a fact you should establish before using a bank.

**TECs**
*Training and Enterprise Councils (TECs)* are government sponsored independent regional bodies – there are over eighty in number - which provide training and advice to all types of business.  They run the *Enterprise Allowance*, a scheme which provides financial assistance and training to selected unemployed people who want to start their own business.

**Enterprise Agencies**
Most cities and large towns run *Enterprise Agencies* which offer small businesses free advice, run training schemes and introduce businesses to sources of finance such as the Local Authority.

**Chambers of Commerce**
The membership of the Chambers of Commerce is made up of owners of local businesses.  They are useful sources of advice and many run 'business clubs'  in which local business people exchange ideas and are happy to help new entrepreneurs

If you want advice you should be prepared to go and 'shop around'.  You will be able to find a solicitor or accountant in the 'Yellow Pages', but best of all is a recommendation from someone you know who already has dealings with a good solicitor or accountant.  You will find the telephone numbers of TECs and Enterprise Agencies in the local phone book and at the Jobcentre.

Whatever you do, you must seek advice.  Even the most elementary point can be overlooked if a business is established without proper care and consultation.  There are some horror stories about businesses that have failed because they did not know of the need to register for VAT (ie they should have added VAT to the prices of the goods they sold).  When the VAT authorities (HM Customs and Excise) eventually caught up with them some time later, they were faced with bills for VAT which bankrupted them.  Ignorance of the law is no excuse!

# chapter summary

❑ Starting a business involves a number of choices:
  • the type of business – product or service?
  • to 'start from scratch', to buy a business, to take up a franchise

❑ Starting a business involves establishing a number of aims and objectives: these might include:
  • maximising profit
  • customer care
  • being socially and environmentally responsible

❑ The principal statement of business objectives is known as the "mission statement".

❑ Starting a business should also involves a searching analysis of your own capabilities – are you up to it? what role should you assume?

❑ Starting a business involves obtaining professional advice:  from a bank, a solicitor, or probably best of all, from an accountant.

❑ Advice is also available from Government run and sponsored agencies such as the Enterprise Agencies and the TECs.

# 45 Starting a business – the law and insurance

## introduction

If you are starting a business, as we saw in the last chapter, you will first decide upon the *type* of business and define its *objectives*. There then remains the question of the legal and insurance implications of your decisions. The type of questions that a person starting a busines will ask are:

- can the proposed business function in the premises we have in mind?
- do we need to issue contracts of employment to our staff?
- can we employ sixth-formers as casual workers?
- do we need a first aid officer?
- what guarantee will our customers have if our goods are faulty?
- what insurance do we need to cover our premises?

These areas can be a potential minefield to the unwary business owner, and it is essential that professional advice is sought before trading starts. Help can be given by Enterprise Agencies, solicitors, accountants and insurance brokers.

In this chapter we will look at:

*legal implications*

- the legal form a business can take – sole trader, partnership, limited company
- the name a business adopts
- the legal implications of taking on premises
- the legal implications of employing staff
- the legal implications of providing goods
- the need to keep accurate records

*insurance implications*

- insuring premises, machinery and stocks
- insuring against accidents which happen to employees and the general public on your premises
- insuring your product

# the legal form of the business

You will have to ask yourself a number of important questions when starting a business:

*What legal form will my business take: sole trader, partnership or limited company?*

We will look at all three types of business formation – sole trader, partnership and limited company. If you are taking part in a Young Enterprise scheme, the decision is made for you – you form a limited company.

## sole trader

*A sole trader is an individual trading in his or her name, or under a suitable trading name.*

If you set up in business, you may do so for a number of reasons: redundancy, dissatisfaction with your present job, or developing a hobby or interest into a business. The majority of people setting up in this way do so on their own. If you decide to do so, you become a *sole trader*. You can use your own name, or adopt a trading name. You do not have to register a trading name, but you may find yourself in court if you use someone else's name or a name connected with royalty. You cannot, for instance open a shop and call it 'Marks and Spencer' or 'Royal Designs'.

There are a number of *advantages* of being a sole trader:

- freedom – you are your own boss
- simplicity – there is less form-filling than there is,  for instance, for limited companies, and the book-keeping should be less complex
- saving on fees – there are none of the legal costs of drawing up partnership agreements or limited company documentation

There are also *disadvantages:*

- risk – you are on your own with no-one to share the responsibilities of running the business
- time – you will need to work long hours to meet tight deadlines
- expertise – you may have limited skills in areas such as finance and marketing

It is clear that setting up in business as a sole trader involves total commitment in terms of your capital, your time, your home, and the risk involved. If you are starting your business with other people or need to raise substantial capital, you may consider establishing a partnership or a limited company. The question is, which form of business is the better in your circumstances?

## partnership

*A partnership is a group of individuals working together in business with a view to making a profit.*

A *partnership* is simple to establish and involves two or more people running a business together. The partners *are* the business.  Examples of partnerships include groups of doctors, dentists, accountants, and solicitors.   A partnership – often known as a 'firm' – can either trade in the name of the partners or under a suitable trading name.  For example if M Smith & G Jones set up a glazing business, they could call themselves 'Smith and Jones & Co.' or adopt a more catchy name such as 'Classy Glass Merchants'. You should note that the '& Co.' does *not* mean that the partnership is a limited company.  Sometimes there may be a "sleeping partner" who contributes capital and shares in the profits, but who does not take any active part in running the business.

A partnership does not have to be registered anywhere but it is often advisable for partners to have a *partnership agreement* drawn up by a solicitor. This will state what money is being invested by each partner, how profits are split, and what will happen if there is a dispute. It is an unfortunate fact that partners can argue, and if you are entering into a partnership you will have to make sure that you can get on with and trust your co-partners – they may be spending your money and running up business debts for which you will be liable.

## limited company

*A limited company is a separate legal body, owned by shareholders, run by directors.*

A *limited company* is quite different from a sole trader in that it has a legal identity separate from its owners. If you are taking part in a Young Enterprise scheme you will be well aware of how a limited company is set up. The owners – the shareholders – are not personally liable for the business debts (the company's debts) but can be made so if they are asked by a lender to provide security (eg their homes) or give a guarantee (an undertaking to pay up if the company fails to repay its debts).

A company is managed by directors appointed by the shareholders (also known as members). In the case of many small companies the shareholders *are* the directors. A company must be registered at a central office known as Companies House, which will issue to the directors a Certificate of Incorporation, the 'birth certificate' of a company. An annual return and financial statement must be sent each year to Companies House by the directors. The rules for running the company must be set out in documents known as the 'Memorandum and Articles of Association' which must also be sent to Companies House. As you will see there is much paperwork and 'red tape' involved in establishing and running a limited company. Paperwork and 'red tape' clearly means extra expense.

If you want to start up a limited company called, for example, Dodgy Enterprises Limited, you are advised to approach a professional such as an accountant who will take one of two courses of action:

*   he will either draw up the necessary documentation (including a draft Memorandum and Articles) and apply to Companies House for the formation of a new company called "Dodgy Enterprises Limited", or
*   he will arrange to *buy* an existing dormant (not-operating) company "off the shelf" from a firm that specialises in selling them (for, say, £500) and then change the name of that company to "Dodgy Enterprises Limited" by sending a form to Companies House

The second course of action is often a quicker and cheaper way of setting up a limited company.

It should be noted that a limited company can be referred to as either

*   a *private limited company* (abbreviated to *Ltd*), or
*   a *public limited company* (abbreviated to *plc*)

Most small or medium-sized businesses which decide to incorporate (form a company) become private limited companies. If, however, they are larger, with a share capital of over £50,000, they can become public limited companies. A plc *can* be quoted on the Stock Markets, but not all take this step.

---

### student activity 45.1 – choosing the form of business

State the legal form business you would expect to be chosen by:

(a)   a plumber

(b)   a practice of dentists

(c)   a business employing 150 staff, manufacturing components for the car industry

State in your answer *why* this legal form has been chosen, and outline its advantages and disadvantages to the owner(s) of the business

# the legal implications of premises

If a business plans to operate from premises, there are a number of legal obligations that the owner(s) of the business must consider.  These include:

### planning permission
There must be *planning permission* for the type of business carried on at the premises – for example, you could not open up a retail outlet on an industrial estate, or set up a 'heavy' industrial process in a unit given 'light' industrial usage.  If you are using your own house for your business, planning permission may be required, depending on the use.  You are unlikely to be given permission to operate a second-hand car business from home.  Operating a business from home may also mean that your 'office' will be liable for business rates.

### licences
Certain types of business need a licence to trade; these include: restaurants, food manufacturers, ice cream and mobile food stalls, sellers of alcohol and tobacco, nursing homes, child nurseries and scrap metal dealers.

### covenants and restrictions
You must also check (with the help of a solicitor) to see if there are any covenants (restrictions which apply to the property) or local by-laws which might restrict what you are planning to do.

### checking the lease
If you are taking on a lease (ie renting the property for a set period of time rather than buying it), have you checked any restrictive terms and conditions in the lease?  Have you checked how long the lease has to run and how often the lease payments can be reviewed (ie increased), eg every five or seven years?

### environmental restrictions
The law places strict controls on the emissions which a business can make into the atmosphere, into drainage systems, into rivers and streams.  Offenders can (and are) prosecuted for breaking these regulations.

---

### student activity 45.2 – planning for premises

What legal implications relating to your premises would be involved if you set up:

(a)  a graphic design consultancy operating from home – a sole trader who designs publicity leaflets, brochures, packaging, book jackets and so on, using a computer and a drawing board in a spare bedroom

(b)  a car mechanic who decides to operate an engine tuning service from the garage in his house

(c)  an ice cream salesman who plans to operate a "Mr Creamy" van in the main shopping street in the town

(d)  a scrap metal dealer who wants to buy an old redundant school building and use the playground as a scrap metal yard

(e)  a printer who wants to move into a leased building on an out-of-town industrial estate

(f)  a skip rental firm which wants to take over an old quarry in which it plans to dump waste

# legal implications of employing staff

The legal implications of employing staff are dealt with in Chapter 3. For the purposes of this chapter you should note the following points:

## age limits
The normal minimum age for an employee in industry is 16, and there are restrictions on the part-time working hours for the under-16s in other occupations. The normal retirement age is 60 for women and 65 for men, although it has been proposed that the retirement age for everyone should be 65. There is nothing, of course, to prevent a person from retiring early or working beyond normal retirement age; the legal restrictions apply to those *under* age and aim to protect young people from exploitation.

## contracts of employment
By law all employees working sixteen or more hours a week must be given within thirteen weeks a written statement of the terms of employment. This *may* take the form of a formal written contract, but it does not need to. The statement must include
* the name of the employer
* the date when the job starts
* the name, job title and job description of the employee
* the hours of work
* holiday entitlement (and pay where appropriate)
* details of pay and when it is paid
* grievance, sickness and injury procedures (ie whom to go and see)
* pension schemes
* length of notice required for termination of employment

## discrimination
It is illegal for an employer (or an employer advertising for a job) to discriminate against any person on the grounds of race, sex or religion: eg "Required for work in bar: white girl. No Roman Catholics". The only exception would be if the nature of the business demanded discrimination (eg wet nurses).

## Health and Safety at Work
Health and Safety at Work is becoming an increasingly complex area of regulation, particularly with the influence of EC directives. A person starting a business would be well advised to approach the local Environmental Health Office which will be able to provide literature and advice about Health and Safety in the workplace. The Health and Safety Executive publish through HMSO an excellent and inexpensive booklet "Essentials of Health and Safety at Work". The main legislation affecting the workplace is the Health and Safety at Work etc Act 1974. This Act requires an employer to look after the health and safety of employees and people visiting the premises. It states specifically that the employer must provide
* safe machinery and equipment – and maintenance of that machinery and equipment
* safe operating systems for the machinery and equipment
* safe and healthy methods of using, handling, storing and transporting of items and substances: these can include solids, liquids and gases which may be harmful to health
* information, instruction and training in safety procedures
* supervision of employees
* safe and healthy premises – adequate toilets, canteen facilities, heating, lighting and ventilation
* safe access to the premises
* a safe environment for visitors to the premises, eg maintenance contractors, sales representatives

If the employer employs more than five people, he or she should issue a written *Statement of Policy* to the employees, giving details of the safety procedures in force on the premises. This policy may be given to the employees personally, or it may be placed where it can be read – on the notice board, for example.

Other Acts of Parliament relating to Health and Safety at Work include the Factories Act 1961, and the Offices Shops and Railway Premises Act 1963.

### payroll

An employer must by law deduct income tax and National Insurance Contributions from employees on its payroll who earn over a certain amount. This PAYE (Pay As You Earn) system requires the employer to pay these deductions to the Inland Revenue, together with a contribution from the employer for National Insurance.

It is a requirement that an employer must keep accurate and full records of pay and deductions, and make an annual return to the tax office. An employer is also obliged to isue each employee with a detailed pay slip. If an employer takes on a new employee, the tax office must be informed. Full details of the PAYE system are set out in Chapter 3, and a pay slip is illustrated on page 341.

---

### student activity 45.3 – planning for employing staff

What would be the legal implications for your planned business if:

(a) a girl replied to a job advert and quoted her age on the application form as 15?

(b) a man replied to a job advert and quoted his age on the application form as 66?

(d) a person interviewed by you stated "I *must* have a written contract of employment."

(e) you were opening a Chinese restaurant and asked in the job advert for "waiters, preferably Chinese."

(f) you decided that you did not want (or did not have time) to issue a written Statement of Policy relating to Health and Safety at Work.

(g) a new recruit told you that he wanted to be paid "in cash, because you won't have to pay any National Insurance ".

---

# the legal implications of providing goods

The subject of consumer law will be covered in detail if you take the "Business Law" option unit. For the purposes of business planning you should appreciate that manufacturing and selling a product (or in some circumstances providing a service) brings with it three basic legal obligations:

### 1. faulty products

If a product is faulty a customer will have a right to a refund or a replacement. There are no grounds for a manufacturer or a retailer disclaiming responsibility or putting up a notice stating "no refunds". The consumer's right is enshrined in law.

## 2. products as described

Products must be sold as described in advertising material, and must as far as is reasonably possible fulfil the claims made for them. A "waterproof jacket" should withstand a shower of rain, but the manufacturer could dispute a claim, if, for example the jacket were worn in a tropical storm and let in water. If goods are labelled with a false description (eg a gold-plated ring advertised as "solid gold"), a criminal prosecution could result.

## 3. safety standards

Products must meet with safety standards. The children's toys market, for example, is subject each Christmas to the usual influx of highly dangerous cheap foreign imports: teddy's eyes with come off and are swallowed, poisonous paint, and so on. Products which do not meet with the safety standards can result in prosecution for the business concerned. Manufacturers normally take out *product liability insurance* to safeguard against claims as a result of faulty goods (see next section on insurance).

## accounting records for the sale of products

An employer is also obliged to keep accurate accounting records of products that it sells, together with records of other transactions such as purchases and expenses. The reason for this is that it must account to the Inland Revenue for profits made, and to H M Customs and Excise for VAT collected from its customers (if it is registered for VAT) and paid on its purchases and expenses. Anyone starting up in business should plan carefully for the type of accounting records it will set up: a manual system may be sufficient, or a computer system may be installed. An accountant would be able to advise.

---

### student activity 45.4 – selling a product

What would be the legal implications relating to the sale of the products of your planned business when:

(a)  you are planning your after-sales service to deal with customer complaints

(b)  you are planning your publicity material

(c)  you are considering importing goods from abroad

(d)  you are setting up the record keeping systems of the business

---

# insurance needs of a business

## the need for sufficient insurance

Another aspect of business planning is the provision of sufficient insurance. Insurance costs have been rising well in advance of inflation in recent years and there is the temptation (followed by many home-owners) to under-insure. This, for a business, is a dangerous policy: whereas a *household* burglary or fire can result in personal loss and inconvenience, a warehouse fire or a computer theft can force a business to stop trading, lose its customers and even result in a trading loss.

## what type of policy?

A business would normally approach a firm of insurance brokers which would be able to obtain quotations from a number of insurers, and so provide the 'best deal'. It is possible to obtain different types of cover, eg fire cover and computer insurance, from different insurers, but it is becoming increasingly common to obtain a 'combined' insurance policy to cover all the appropriate risks from a single insurance company. These policies often operate on a 'pick and mix' basis – you pick the cover you need to cover your particular needs.

## what type of cover?

The list below sets out the most common types of cover.  Clearly not all businesses will want all types of cover:  the insurance broker will be able to advise.

## asset insurance – insurance of the business assets, eg premises, stock, money

*fire cover*

This type of cover insures premises and its contents against damage by fire and other disasters such as lightning, explosions, aircraft, riots, vandalism, earthquake, storms, floods.  The premises are normally insured for their rebuilding cost.

*theft*

This insurance covers the removable assets of the business, eg machinery, computers, office machines, stock, money.  The cover is normally for assets both on the premises and also off the premises, eg goods in transit, money being taken to the bank. These assets are normally insured for their replacement value and not  their value in the books of the business.

*business interruption*

Another form of cover related to asset insurance is business interruption cover.  This reimburses financial loss which happens as a result of the business coming to a halt following a fire or any of the other disasters covered under fire insurance.  This cover can be extended to insure against problems caused by a failure of the utilities, eg a long-term power cut, or contamination of the water supply.

*all risks*

This type of cover is available for accidental loss, damage or destruction of specified items anywhere in the UK (for UK businesses).  The insurance will be for the replacement value of the assets.

## employer's liability insurance – insurance of employees and other individuals

*employer's liability*

This type of cover insures the employer against claims from employees who have been injured at work.  'Employee' includes a person on the payroll, self-employed people contracted to work for the business (eg a consultant brought in for a specific job) and, in some instances, students on work experience!

*public liability*

This type of cover insures against claims from members of the public who may be injured as a result of something which happens in connection with the business, eg a person who visits a workshop and is injured by a machine which topples over.  The cover also extends to assets of the public, eg a parked car which is damaged by a falling roof tile from the business premises.  If you have access to your home insurance policy, you will see that household insurance also normally includes public liability cover.

## product liability insurance

*product liability*

An extension of public liability cover is insurance against claims arising from people who have suffered injury or damage from faulty products which they have purchased.  This type of insurance will cover legal costs in defending claims made under consumer protection law.

---

**student activity 45.5 – assessing insurance needs**

What would be the likely insurance needs if you were planning to start

(a)   a mobile ice cream van business?

(b)   an estate agency in leased premises in the town, employing 10 staff?

(c)   a firm employing 50 staff in a leased workshop manufacturing kitchen furniture?

What type of cover would you need to insure for the following risks:

(d)   your warehouse roof blowing off in a storm?

(e)   theft of your computer workstations from your office?

(f)   your employee being mugged on the way back from the bank, and the wages cash being stolen?

(g)   a loose coping stone falling off your office building and damaging a car parked nearby?

(h)   an employee's foot being crushed by a fork-lift truck?

(i)   a customer suing you after being electrocuted by a faulty hair dryer you have manufactured?

(j)   your business being put out of action by a fire at the factory, resulting in a financial loss from lost income?

---

# chapter summary

❏   The first legal implication of starting a business is the form the business should take: sole trader, partnership or limited company.

❏   Moving into premises also involves legal factors:
  •   getting planning permission and/or a licence where appropriate
  •   checking the lease, any covenants, by-laws and environmental restrictions

❏   Employing staff involves being aware of age limits, terms of employment, discrimination, Health and Safety at Work, and payroll requirements.

❏   Selling a product involves consumer law:
  •   dealing with faulty products
  •   ensuring publicity material is accurate
  •   ensuring the product meets safety standards
  Accurate records must also be maintained for the accounting system of the business.

❏   The insurance needs of a business will depend on the type of business involved. The normal insurance needs are:
  •   asset insurance: cover for fire, theft, interruption of business, all risks
  •   employer's liability: cover for accidents and injuries to employees
  •   public liability: cover for accidents, injury and damage to members of the public and their assets
  •   product liability: cover for injury suffered as a result of a faulty product

# 46 Resources planning

## introduction

Business planning when starting or expanding a business involves:
- quantifying short-term and long-term objectives, eg return on capital
- assessing the resources you have
- estimating the resources you need
- planning how you are going to achieve those objectives in the form of a business plan
- optimising the use of resources to minimise the effects of constraints such as size of premises, machine capacity

We will look at the format and construction of the business plan in detail in Chapter 47. In this chapter we will look specifically at the resources needed in business:
- *human resources* – ie the experience of management and the calibre of staff that will be needed to carry the plan through, and the back-up that will be necessary to support management and staff
- *physical resources* – the premises, machinery, computing equipment, stock, and materials that a business may need to acquire
- *financial resources* – the capital that the owners of the business are able to contribute, and the sources of finance that they may need to call upon

Another important resource is that of *time* – you only have a limited amount of time to achieve objectives. Careful planning is necessary so that all activities are co-ordinated so that the business can start up on schedule. In this chapter we will look at how a *flow chart* can be constructed to plan for this process.

If you are taking part in a Young Enterprise or mini-business scheme, all these processes may be formalised in the documentation you have been given. If this is the case, you should read these chapters in the light of your documentation.

## the business plan

In this section we will introduce the *format* of the business plan which is the final product of all the planning processes covered in this and the next chapter. The detail of the presentation of the plan will be dealt with in Chapter 47. The reason why the format is being explained here is so that you can appreciate the direction in which the planning processes are taking you.

## format of the business plan

The business plan illustrated in this book is divided into five sections. Not all business plans are identical in format, but most will contain these elements.

**1. business and objectives** We saw in Chapter 44 that all businesses should define their short-term and long-term objectives. These set out in the business plan, together with a description of the business and the personnel needed.

**2. marketing plan** We have already seen in the marketing section of this book that marketing planning is an essential part of succesful business practice. The *full-length* marketing plan of a business (which we cover in Chapter 48) will normally be condensed for the purposes of inclusion in the business plan. It will contain

- a description and pricing of the new product
- sales projections
- an analysis of the existing market – the competition
- where the proposed new product fits into the market
- promotion of the new product, with timing details
- distribution and sales
- marketing budget

**3. production plan** This sets out in practical terms what will be needed to produce the product (or service) in terms of design and development, premises, machinery and raw materials, and labour required.

**4. resource requirements** What will be needed in terms of physical assets, how much they will cost, and how they will be financed.

**5. financial support data** This is the crucial section for any prospective lender of funds to the business. It will set out:

- *projections*: a twelve month cash flow, profit and loss forecast, and projected balance sheet
- *past* financial statements (for an existing business): three years' profit and loss accounts, balance sheets and cashflow statements

The business plan is a key document. It will enable the businesss to define its objectives, resources and requirements, and it will enable a prospective lender such as a bank to assess the proposition rapidly and on the basis of accurate information. Further details and an example of a business plan are to be found in the next chapter.

# planning for human resources

## long-term planning

Planning for human resources involves the decision to choose and use people in a way which will maximise:

- the output and productivity of the business
- the profit of the business
- the motivation and job satisfaction of the people working in the business

These objectives may not always be achievable concurrently: for example, one way to maximise profit is to cut down on labour costs by making staff redundant – this may have the effect of demotivating the staff and reducing output. The best managed businesses combine all three objectives by means of encouraging teamwork and staff motivation.

## short-term planning – specialist skill areas

A business start-up will involve one or more entrepreneurs who have to provide skills in a number of areas:

- administration and management
- marketing and selling
- finance/book-keeping/payroll skills
- production and operations
- research and development – the "ideas" person

It may be that the sole trader has all these talents, or the partners/directors share these abilities between them. It is more likely, however, that the business starting up will have to "buy in" help in one or more of these areas. This can be done by:

- bringing in a new partner/director with a particular skill who may be willing also to put in capital and share in the success of the business
- using self-employed specialists (eg for accountancy services or marketing) on a contract basis
- employing temporary staff from an agency
- employing one or more general assistants ("Jack(s) of all trades") who can be on the permanent payroll of the business

Clearly the first option (new partner/director) can be a risky proposition. The personal factor may be a problem: can the new director get on with the existing management? Employing self-employed specialists or agency staff can be expensive, but it is also flexible: a business only pays for what it wants done, and no employer's National Insurance is payable. A general assistant may cost less in terms of £'s per hour, but there is little flexiblity in terms of hours worked, and the employees may need training.

## short-term planning – production staff

A business that manufactures a product will have to take on production line staff and support staff – packers, drivers and so on. The requirements of a new business will have to be carefully planned and costed.

## other human resources implications

In the human resources section of this book (Chapter 19) we looked in detail at the responsibilities of a personnel manager. As far as business planning is concerned, the owner(s) of a new or expanding business ought to bear in mind:

- manpower planning – what are the future staffing requirements likely to be?
- what training provision needs to be made?
- what industrial relations implications are there? will the new employees be joining a Union?
- what facilities will need to be made available for staff welfare? – is there a rest room?
- have the wages levels been fixed?
- have Health and Safety requirements been planned out?

---

### student activity 46.1 – human resource planning

You are starting up a new business as a sole trader making picture frames. You are giving some thought to human resource planning:

(a) What would be your main objectives in human resource planning?

(b) You are very good at making picture frames but have had less experience in financial matters and in selling. What options are open to you in solving this problem? State what option you would choose, and *why*.

(c) You are moving into a small workshop owned and subsdised by the local authority. What practical human resource planning will be necessary, bearing in mind that you may be employing other people to work on the premises?

# physical resources planning

Planning for physical resources is essential when starting up or expanding a business, and much of the detailed analysis of physical resource planning will be included in the business plan. In this chapter we deal with in turn:

- planning for premises
- acquiring machinery and equipment
- buying and planning for stock and raw materials

We also look at the principles of purchasing – how to buy wisely and get a good deal.

# premises

Choosing a location for your business can be a difficult process. It can be helped by thinking through the answers to a number of questions:

## can I work from home?

Many small businesses operate very successfully from home. These businesses are mainly sole traders who either provide a service to the public by travelling away from home, or who deal with the public over the telephone. Examples include electricians, photographers, designers, and insurance sales representatives. Business people who use the home as a base can charge a proportion of their expenses (telephone, electricity, heating) to their business – ie the business will pay rather than the expense falling on the household budget. This has the useful effect of reducing the business tax bill. The major disadvantage of using the home for business use is that the rooms used will be subject to Non Domestic Rate, a tax on business property collected by the Local Authority. Another practical disadvantage is keeping the business and private life separate: the problems of confidentiality and preventing small children from answering the telephone or disabling the fax machine!

## should I buy or lease the premises?

If the business needs to deal with the public face-to-face as part of its everyday operations, it needs premises – commercial property. Information about premises can be obtained from

- local Enterprise Agencies (some produce registers of vacant premises)
- the commercial property offices of estate agents
- the commercial property pages in the local press

You will see when you look at this information that premises can be classified in a terms of office space and warehousing and production space. This distinction is self-explanatory: certain businesses will only need offices, others will need a combination of office space and warehousing.

The principal concern when choosing premises will be whether you wish to *buy* or *lease* the property. If you have the capital you may wish to buy the premises, possibly with the help of a commercial mortgage. If, as is more likely, you do not have much spare money to invest, you will plan to *lease* a property, ie pay a 'rental' to the owner of the property.

*the buy option*        You will see from the estate agents' particulars that some property is *freehold*. This means that you can buy it outright: *freehold* is a legal term which denotes that your right to the property is absolute, and you can do what you want with it, subject only to legislation (eg planning Acts) and compulsory purchase orders (if you unfortunately buy premises on the route of the a new bypass). The term *freehold* can equally apply to domestic property.

*the lease option*

If a person owns freehold property, such as a warehouse or an office block, as an investment, the property can be *leased* out for a specific period of time, according to the terms of a document known as a *lease*. The person who takes on the property, and pays a regular rental, takes it as *leasehold* property. That person has right of occupation, but has to comply with terms of the lease. These normally include

- the *term* of the lease – the number of years it will run, eg ten years
- the *option to renew* the lease when it runs out – if there is no option, the business may have to move out at the end of the lease period
- the amount of the rental, and the periodic right of the owner to review the rent (ie increase it!)
- an undertaking by the *leaseholder* (the business in occupation)to insure and repair the property

Also, if a business takes over a lease which is already running (eg seven years left of a ten year lease) a one-off lease *premium* fee may be payable.

## what are the other considerations when taking on premises?

Other considerations include:

*Non-Domestic Rate*

Central Government taxes business premises and property by means of the *Non-Domestic Rate*. All business property has been valued for taxation purposes by the Inland Revenue and given a *rateable value* expressed in £s. Rateable value is a hypothetical annual rental value; it is *not* the market value of the property. A small factory unit purchased for £100,000, for instance, may be given a rateable value of £5,000. The tax due to Central Government is calculated by applying a standard multiplier (the Non-Domestic Rating Multiplier) to the rateable value. This multiplier is raised annually in line with inflation. If the multiplier is, say, 45p in the £, the rates due on the factory unit will be:

*£5,000 (rateable value) x 45p (Non-Domestic Rating Multiplier)  = £2,250 p.a.*

The Non-Domestic Rate is collected by the Local Authorities, and is often paid by ten monthly instalments (£225 per month in the above example.)

*valuation and survey*

It is important when taking on premises to make sure you are not paying too much, either in terms of purchase price (the buy option) or in monthly rental (lease option). A Chartered Surveyor will (for a fee) undertake a valuation of the property and also look at it for structural problems. If you are borrowing money, on commercial mortgage for example, the lender will want to see the survey and valuation report. The surveyor will also assess a fair rent, if you are taking on a lease. The surveyor's fee is therefore money well spent.

*insurance*

The cost of insuring business premises can be high (eg £3,000 per year for a £100,000 warehouse) because, as we saw in the last chapter, there are many risks against which to insure:

- fire insurance
- theft
- loss of profit if the business has to stop because of a fire or other disaster
- employer's liability – insurance against claims from employees for incidents such as accidents at work

- public liability – insurance against claims from the public for accidents (eg a builder falling off an unsafe roof) or for faulty products

*location*      A number of questions need to be answered:
- Can your staff and clients get to you easily? Is there sufficient parking?
- Do delivery and collection vehicles have clear access?
- Do you have sufficient office space?
- Do you have sufficient warehousing for the future?

All these considerations can appear overwhelming if you are starting up in business for the first time. It is therefore essential that you obtain professional advice:
- a *Chartered Surveyor* for valuation of property and help with negotiating a lease (if you are leasing a property)
- a *solicitor* for conveyancing (carrying out the enquiries and paperwork when a purchase is made)
- an *accountant* for the financial aspects – helping with the business plan and approaching the bank with a request for finance
- an *insurance broker* for a competitive quotation for the required insurance (no fee charged in this case)

Professional advice is not cheap, but your local Enterprise Agency should be able help with giving advice and introducing you to professionals who are used to dealing with business start-ups, and who may charge a lower rate.

---

### student activity 46.2 – planning for premises

(a)   You run a business which is looking for a 2,500 square feet warehouse with office facilities. Obtain through your lecturer details of up to five suitable vacant premises in your locality. Assess each of them in terms of
- price per square foot (if they are freehold)
- annual rental per square foot (if they are leasehold)
- accessibility and parking facilities
- the annual Non Domestic Rate (if you can find this out – you may not be able to)
- general condition (from an external inspection, if this is possible)

Note: be guided by your lecturer in what you can and cannot assess.

Write a brief report comparing the alternatives and giving your recommendation – with reasons – as to which warehouse is the best.

(b)   Carry out the same exercise as in (a) above, but this time looking for an office of 1,500 square feet for an insurance broker.

---

# machinery, equipment and vehicles

We have seen in Chapter 36 that premises, machinery, equipment and vehicles constitute what are known in accounting terms as *fixed assets:* the business owns them, and intends to keep them for at least a year. They will appear on the balance sheet, unlike rented or leased assets, which of course do not belong to the business.

When a business acquires machinery or equipment or vehicles – which we will for convenience call "equipment" –a number of critical decisions will have to be made:

- should the equipment be acquired now?
- should the equipment be bought or leased?
- which supplier should be chosen?

Other factors include affecting the choice will be payment terms (ie when payment can be made), after-sales service, and (possibly) environmental considerations.

The equipment which a business may need includes a wide range of items including telephones, computers and photocopiers, vehicles, and machinery used in the production process. Clearly every business has its own particluar needs, but the same principles apply in the decision-making process. We will now consider these principles in detail.

## should the equipment be acquired now?

When a business starts up for the first time, or expands, a certain amount of controlled chaos exists, caused by a small number of people being faced with a large number of decisions. It is easy to fall into the trap of creating a 'shopping list' for physical resources, assuming that they all have to be acquired at once. This is not always the case, and great care should be taken in the planning process. A business will have to list all the items it wants to acquire, cost them, compare them with the available financial resources, and decide

- which items have to be acquired immediately – eg telephones, delivery van
- which items can wait – eg updated replacement photocopier, a new car for the Managing Director

## should the items be bought or leased?

You will be aware that if you have a telephone line installed in your house or premises, you can choose either to rent a handset (and be charged regularly on your bill), or to go to a retail outlet such as Dixons or Boots and buy a plain or Mickey Mouse handset, and pay immediately. The same choice exists for a wide range of business assets – computers, photocopiers, machinery, cars and vans for example – buy now and pay up front, or pay regularly over a period of time. The term "lease" is often used when a piece of equipment is rented: payments are made by the business using the asset, but ownership always remains with the firm 'leasing' it out.

There are a number of factors which will be involved in the decision to buy or to lease. The most crucial of these is the availability of capital or finance. If neither of these is available, the business cannot buy the asset, and the decision to lease is made. If capital is available, the choice is normally based on financial considerations – whether more tax can be saved by:

- *leasing*, where the cost of leasing is charged to the profit and loss account of the business, and thus reduces the tax bill (less profit = lower tax bill)
- *buying*, where the depreciation (or 'capital allowance') on the asset is charged to the profit and loss account of the business, and thus reduces the tax bill

The Government, in order to encourage investment by businesses, sometimes increases the capital allowance, ie the percentage of the cost price of the asset which can be written off in the profit and loss account. Clearly the higher the percentage, the more tax can be saved (the tax being on the profit) and the greater the advantage to the business of buying rather than leasing.

## student activity 46.3 – replacing your van

Your bakery business owns an six year-old Ford Transit van, which is used for delivering bread and cakes. It is still running satisfactorily, but it is beginning to show its age. What considerations will you bear in mind about replacing this van? Set out in writing the alternative courses of action, having investigated the financial implications of your possible choices – eg value of existing van, the cost of a new van. Refer to the new and used vehicle prices published in specialist magazines; contact your local dealer (in consultation with your teacher/lecturer) Note that you do not have to buy a new van, or buy a Ford!

# purchasing stock

Purchasing has traditionally been defined as

*buying goods and services
of the right quality, in the right quantity, at the right time, from the right supplier, at the right price*

This may seem all very well in theory, but as most people in business will tell you, purchasing often gets a low priority in comparison, say, with selling. The task may be easier for the larger business which has a purchasing department and senior purchasing staff, but for the smaller concern or sole trader, purchasing very often means choosing the supplier that sends you a brochure, or always choosing the *same* supplier, a far from ideal situation.

When you are starting a business, there are so many decisions to be made that planning for purchasing often gets a low priority, and wrongly, as the example below shows.

## the right price – the importance of efficient purchasing
The price of materials and stock purchased is a crucial determining factor for a business which aims to make a profit. Achieving a price cut for raw materials and stock can have a dramatic effect on profitability : " a penny saved is a profit made", as the saying goes. Look at the following example taken from a business which is already trading:

A manufacturing company makes garden gnomes. The financial details are as follows:

| | |
|---|---|
| Annual sales | £500,000 |
| Annual spending on materials | £250,000 |
| Other expenses | £200,000 |
| Net profit | £50,000 |

The management want to increase profit by £5,000. How can they achieve this? There are two alternatives:

1. Increase sales by £50,000 – the business makes £5,000 profit from £50,000 of sales

2. Reduce costs by £5,000 – this will bring about an increase in profit without the need for an increase in sales

The second alternative appears by far the more attractive. If they spend £250,000 a year on materials, a saving of £5,000 is only a 2% reduction in material costs. To achieve the same increase in profit by increasing sales will require a 10% increase in sales. An increase in profitability is clearly more easily achieved by 'shopping around' for cheaper materials (a cut of only 2%) than by trying to increase sales of gnomes by 10%. £50,000 saved is a £50,000 increase in profit.

## methods of obtaining lower prices
How are these lower prices to be found? Various suppliers must be approached, and prices obtained from price lists, telephone enquiries and written requests for prices. If suppliers realise that a business is 'shopping around' it may be prepared to drop a price to gain a customer. Businesses must also be aware of discounts offered for
- early payment (cash discount), often 2.5% of the purchase price
- large quantity orders
- trade customers (trade discount) – this is discount given to customers 'in the trade' who are likely to give repeat orders

A new business must 'shop around' as a matter of course, and exisiting businesses should do so on a regular basis; it is all too easy for an established business to fall into a state of inertia when buying, and always buy from the same supplier, regardless of price.

## the right enquiries

A business should choose its suppliers carefully.   What procedures should a new or existing business adopt?   When assessing a supplier, a buyer should, in an ideal world

- obtain an idea of the supplier's reputation by talking to people in the trade – buyers and sales representatives – and by asking for references from other customers
- assess the financial soundness of the supplier – the supplier's bank will normally supply on request a reference to the buyer's bank
- assess the level of customer service – this can be done by seeing how promptly and courteously telephone and written enquiries are answered
- visit the supplier and look at the manufacturing process to see if it is  well-managed, efficient and manned by a well-motivated workforce
- enquire if there is any quality certification, eg BS 5750/ISO 9000:1987 (see page 29)
- request a sample,  analyse it and try it out

This is clearly the ideal situation, and not all businesses have the time or the resources to make these enquiries. Two important factors in the purchasng decision are quality of product and timing of delivery.  We will look at both of these in turn.

## quality

The quality of an item means in very basic terms "how good is it for the job?".   For example a "poor quality" audio tape means that it gets chewed up in the car stereo and wobbles in pitch – it is inadequate for the job.  If an item is described as a "quality" item, it should do its job well:  in fact the term "quality" is often used in advertsing to attract the customer to a product.

As far a business is concerned, purchasing for quality means balancing cost and performance:  the item must do the job well, but at the lowest obtainable cost (see above).  There is no point buying a superior brand of cement powder for making garden gnomes when a standard brand achieves the desired result – hardness, frost resistance, and so on.

A business must be prepared to balance quality and cost:  there is no point accepting the lowest quotation and then finding that five per cent of the goods have to be rejected because they are not up to standard.

## timing

A supplier must be able to keep to specified schedules. Any unreliability in supply could lose valuable sales for the buyer:  for example, a shop which is let down by a wholesaler and runs out of a popular item, or a manufacturer which is unable to obtain a vital component because the supplier has failed to deliver.  A buyer must take careful note of

- the time it takes for an order to be processed by the supplier
- the delivery time
- the re-order time for an item used frequently

This applies not only when a buyer is assessing a supplier for the first time, but also in an ongoing situation when a supplier's performance and reliability must be monitored.

A mention must be made here of *Just In Time (JIT)* ordering, a Japanese technique which involves ordering the materials and stock only *as and when they are needed*.  This system is used to effect by large retailing chains and by some manufacturers.   The object is to reduce stockholding to an absolute minimum, and to cut costs.

## methods of stock control

### stock - a dead investment
The planning of purchases and the control of stock is critical to the efficiency of a business.  By stock we mean
* *materials and components* held by a manufacturing business
* *goods for resale* held by a retailing or wholesale business

Stock held is a current asset, and has to be financed, possibly on an expensive overdraft.  Stock is a dead investment: it provides no return on capital until it is sold – it pays no interest.  If stock levels are reduced, money is released which can be used elsewhere and profitably in the business.

### methods of stock control and purchasing
There are a number of methods of stock control and purchasing.  The method adopted will depend on the size and sophistication of the business.  The important point is that a business must know *how much* stock it has at any time, either by taking a physical stock count, or by keeping a computer record, and it must know *when* it will have to order new stock.  The methods used include:

*guesswork*          Some small businesses do not keep much stock, and the owner may even *guess* the quantity and timing of stock purchases.  This is not a recommended method for a well managed business.

*'two bin' system*    The principle here is to keep two 'bins' of a stock unit.  When the first bin has run out, fresh stock is ordered and will be supplied before the second'bin' runs out.  The term 'bin' is used loosely, and can apply to any measure of stock.  This is a very basic principle, and it works well in many situations.

*perpetual inventory*   This system records issue and receipt of stock as the items pass in and out of the business, and reorders accordingly.  Records of stock are kept manually, or more commonly now on computer file activated by reading of bar codes.  Many supermarkets work on this basis, and order on a "Just in Time" basis.

*formulas*          Businesses need to calculate *when* to order stock, and *how much* stock to order.  There are various formulas that can be used.  These are explained below.

### goods for resale:  re-order level method of stock control
If you take the example of shop, it should
* keep the number of stock lines to a minimum compatible with customer demand
* know how long it takes for new stock to come in when ordered (the 'lead time')
* know the appropriate re-order amount
* know the minimum stock level – the lowest level stock should fall to before the new order from the supplier comes in
* know the maximum level of stock it can hold – this will largely be determined by physical constraints such as warehouse size

Many businesses run manual or computer  stock control systems which keep a running record of the amount of an item held in stock, the 'lead time' for re-ordering (how long it takes to come), and the minimum stock level.  The re-order system is illustrated in fig. 46.1 on the next page.

The critical factor for a business is to know when stock is to be re-ordered, ie when the *re-order level* is reached.

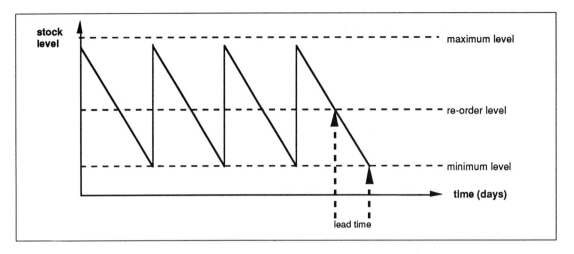

*Fig. 46.1 The re-order system of stock control*

## goods for resale – Economic Order Quantity (EOQ) method of stock control

It is clear that the re-order amount is critical to the stock-holding of a business :

- if re-order amounts are *too large,* too much stock will be held, which will be an expense to the business
- if re-order amounts are *too small,* the expense of constantly re-ordering will outweigh any cost savings on low stock levels, and there will the danger that the item might 'run out'

The most economic re-order quantity – the *economic order quantity* – can be calculated by a mathematical formula which involves a number of different costs and other figures:

- *processing cost* – the paperwork and administration cost involved in each order
- *unit cost* – the cost of the stock unit itself
- *stockholding cost* – the cost to the business of keeping the stock on the shelves expressed as a percentage of the average stock value for the year
- *annual usage* – the number of stock units used per year

The formula is:

$$Economic\ Order\ Quantity\ (EOQ) = \sqrt{\left(\frac{2 \times annual\ usage \times processing\ cost}{unit\ cost \times stockholding\ cost}\right)}$$

If you have a calculator with a square root function, this formula can easily be worked out.   Work out the figures in the brackets first, and then press the square root button ($\sqrt{}$).

If, for example, a stock item costs £10, the processing cost is £15, the stockholding cost is 20% of average stock value, and annual usage is 2,000 units, the EOQ formula will be applied as follows:

$$Economic\ Order\ Quantity\ (EOQ) = \sqrt{\left(\frac{2 \times 2,000 \times £15}{£10 \times 20/100}\right)} = \sqrt{30,000} = 173$$

The usual result of using EOQ is that high usage items are ordered more frequently, and low-usage items are ordered less frequently.  It results in a higher stock turnover rate.  You will recall that stock turnover is the number of times per year a stock item is replaced on the shelves:  a high stock turnover rate is a sign of efficiency and low stock holding.

---

### student activity 46.4 – planning for stock purchases

You are starting up a business:

(a)   Which is the more efficient way of increasing profit – increasing sales or reducing the cost of your purchases? Illustrate your answer with a numerical example.

(b)   What factors would you have in mind when choosing suppliers for your new business?

### student activity 46.5 – stock control

Which method of stock control would your recommend out of

• two bin system
• re-order method
• "Just in Time"

for the following businesses

(a)   a food supermarket
(b)   a wholesale stationer
(c)   a sweet shop

Give reasons for your decision and state the advantages for the business in each case.

---

## planning for design

### product design

The designing of a product requires resources:

• Research and Development (R&D) facilities – staff time and office space will be needed so that existing products can be improved and new products developed

• Computer equipment may be needed in the design process: Computer Aided Design (CAD) is a fast-growing area.

• Materials used – careful planning must take place as part of *cost benefit analysis*, ie balancing the benefits of savings on material costs against any fall-off in quality, eg should a car manufacturer use real wood or plastic veneer in its car facia panels?

• Labour force – does the business have the skilled labour which it needs for the processes required by a particular product design?

### workplace design

The business must also design the layout of its workplace carefully, both with regard to Health & Safety at Work requirements and also by providing the most efficient production layout.

## planning financial resources

This topic was covered fully in Chapter 43 "Sources of business finance". If you have not studied this chapter, you should do so before planning out or writing your business plan. If you have read Chapter 43, you will recall the basic principles it propounded:

• financial resources are needed both for fixed assets and also for working capital

• fixed assets are normally financed by long-term finance and working capital by short-term finance such as bank overdraft

• finance should be provided by the owner(s) of the business and is also often borrowed from outside sources such as banks, finance houses and specialist investment companies

The financial content of a business plan is explained and illustrated in full in the next chapter.

## planning methods

We will now look at some specific techniques used when a business is undertaking a project which involves planning to acquire physical resources in the form of fixed assets, eg premises, plant and machinery and current assets eg stock and materials.  Examples of this type of situation are the business start-up, relocation of a business, and expansion of an existing business. These techniques are based on two types of flow chart:

• critical path analysis
• bar charts known as Gannt charts

It should be stressed that these will form part of the *operations plan* of a business, and will not form part of the *business plan* as described in earlier chapters.  The *results* obtained from the planning process – for example how long it will take to complete a project – will contribute to the business plan.  The prospective lender who reads  a business plan will be interested in *when* a project becomes operational rather than *how* it is completed.

### critical path analysis

Critical path analysis is a technique for working out the minimum time a project is likely to take.  It is a form of what is termed 'network analysis'.  Critical path analysis operates by examining all the individual actions which contribute to the project, eg ordering, constructing, testing, and determining the *minimum* time the project will take.  The process can be very complex, and may be introduced by looking at a simple operation such as making a cup of instant coffee, eg "Take the kettle, fill it up, plug it in, take a cup" . . . and so on.

This form of analysis is presented in visual form by a network of arrows.  Each arrow represents an individual activity, and is normally labelled with the activity and the time it takes (in, say, weeks) to carry out the activity, for example:

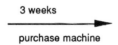

Arrows start and finish in circles known as *events* or nodes.  Activities shown by arrows pointing into a circle (event) must be completed before before any activity shown on an arrow coming out of an event can be started.  For example:

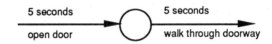

Here the door has to be opened before someone can walk through the doorway; to attempt to walk though the doorway before the door is opened would clearly not be advisable.

It is common for a number of activities to take place *simultaneously*. In the example above, if you are making a cup of coffee, the kettle will be boiling while you are getting a spoon and putting the instant coffee in the cup.  In this case the there will be arrows denoting these parallel activities, and these arrows will converge on the event which marks the pouring of the water into the cup.

It is important to note that all activities on the converging arrows must be completed before any activity on any arrow leaving the circle can be started.

### the critical path

You will know that if you are making a cup of coffee that you will have to wait for the kettle to boil before you can make a decent cupful. You therefore have to wait the *longest* time of the two alternative arrows before completing the event – the steaming cupful of coffee. In critical path analysis the activities which take the *longest* time to complete are known as *critical* activities, and are shown with a thicker arrow.

In an analysis of a complex project, the *quickest* time the project will take to complete will be the sum of the time taken for the critical activities in sequence. In visual terms there will be a thick black line runing through the network of activities: this will be the *critical path,* shown in the illustration below.

### labelling the network

In critical path analysis, there are certain labelling conventions:

- The *circle* (event) is often annotated with numbers to show the stage in the project which has been reached. The number is the event number.
- The *arrows* (activities) are also given abbreviated labels:
  - the time taken for the activity is shown a a simple number which could stand for minutes, days, weeks as is appropriate
  - the activity itself may be given a letter which is explained in a separate list (this would give clarity to the network when the activity descriptions re long and involved)

A critical path analysis is illustrated below. Note how the sum of the numbers on the critical path (the thicker arrows) indicates the activities which take the longest time – a total of 13 as opposed to the other route, which totals 8.

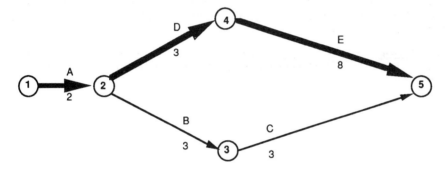

Now read the following Case Study which sets out how critical path analysis can be used by a business planning to relocate its premises.

## Case Study:  Hermes Bureau – relocation of premises

### situation

You run a computer bureau – Hermes Bureau – which provides accounting, payroll and other computer services to a wide range of commercial customers. You are planning to relocate your premises shortly, and have taken a lease on a new and larger office in the town, and will be able to move in six months' time.

You are taking the opportunity when moving to update your computer hardware and software (program) systems. There are a number of important tasks to carry out before you move, and after consultation with your colleagues you have made the list set out below. Your software needs updating and customising for your bureau by programmers, and this will be the task which will take the most time. You see that all the tasks will have to be completed before you can become operational, and the obvious fact that the ordering of software and hardware can only take place after full assessment. You allow yourself a clear two weeek planning period before starting the process. You are very busy at the moment. When should you start planning?

| Task A | time available for detailed planning | 2 weeks |
| Task B | assessment of computer hardware | 2 weeks |
| Task C | ordering new computers | 2 weeks |
| Task D | assessment of new software | 4 weeks |
| Task E | ordering software | 10 weeks |
| Task F | obtaining quotes from removal firm | 3 weeks |
| Task G | ordering the removal van | 3 weeks |

## solution

The planning process can be carried out using critical path analysis, which will set out the different activities in the form of a network and will determine the maximum time, and thus the project time. The procedure is as follows

*step one*
List the activities and the times which they will take, and give them a code letter. This has already been done (see above)

*step two*
Draw a sketch setting out the different activities in the forms of arrows, starting on the left, making sure that
- the arrows are annotated with the activity coding and the time taken (in weeks)
- all activities follow Task A – the planning process
- C follows B, E follows D, G follows F

*step three*
Set out the 'events' which mark the completion of activities in the form of circles, and give them consecutive numbers

*step four*
Add up the time taken by each alternative route taken by the arrows. This produces the result:
- planning and ordering software 16 weeks  (2 + 4 + 10)
- planning and ordering new computers 6 weeks  (2 + 2 +2)
- planning and arranging removal van 8 weeks  (2 + 3 + 3)

*step five*
Draw up a final neat copy of the network, marking in the critical path – the 16 week software upgrading – in heavy ink. The final version appears below.

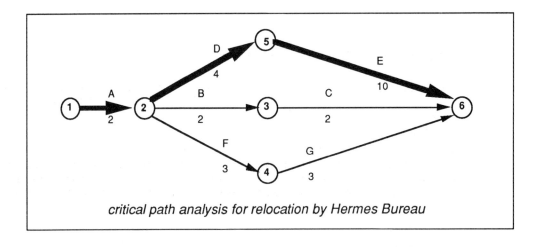

*critical path analysis for relocation by Hermes Bureau*

### using a Gannt chart

Your colleagues are impressed by this planning technique, but say that they cannot easily 'work' from the diagram. You therefore set out the activities on planning bar chart, known as a *Gannt chart*.

This chart shows

- the activities on a weekly schedule (the weeks are numbered across the top)
- the *critical* activities as black bars
- the activities which are *not* on the critical path as grey bars
- *float times* for non-critical activities, ie times during which a delay can occur which will not hold up the project

This chart is useful because each week it can be consulted to see what is due to start, to finish or to continue. Note that the chart shows the activity letters allocated to the critical

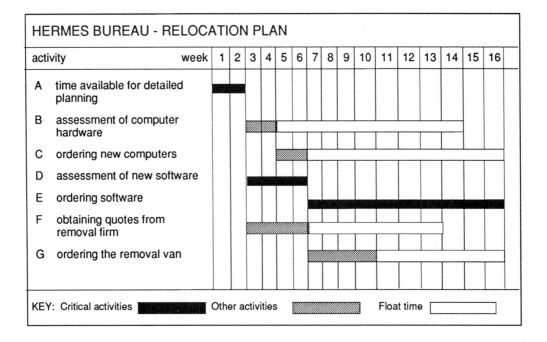

HERMES BUREAU - RELOCATION PLAN

| activity | week |
|---|---|
| A time available for detailed planning | |
| B assessment of computer hardware | |
| C ordering new computers | |
| D assessment of new software | |
| E ordering software | |
| F obtaining quotes from removal firm | |
| G ordering the removal van | |

KEY: Critical activities ████████  Other activities ▨▨▨▨▨▨  Float time ▭

### student activity 46.5 – Gannt chart planning

A friend of yours runs a small printing shop in Stourminster. He has decided to expand his operations into computer typesetting and colour copying. He works from a small shop in the city centre, and considers that he has room for

- a new desktop computer
- a colour photocopier which will also scan and print customers' colour pictures

He is concerned, however, that the introduction of the new machinery and the need to move an old printing machine to a new position will disrupt his everyday work-flow. He is anxious to reduce the disruption to a minimum. He wants to open for business with all his new equipment up and running on 1 November.

You question him and establish the following facts:
- he wants to spend one whole day planning what equipment he is going to buy, and also thinking up a new name for the business
- the new machinery will be delivered 10 days after order and will take one day to instal
- the owner will be given 3 days training on the new equipment after installation and before 1 November
- he will need paper and toner for the new machinery – delivery time is 7 days
- he will need new invoices and stationery as he is changing his business name – delivery time 14 days
- he will also need a new sign for the shopfront – delivery time is 7 days after order, installation time is one day
- the old machine will take one day to move and two days to refit
- everything must be finished by 1 November!

**You are to** produce for him a Gannt chart (as shown in the Case Study in this chapter) to help him work out the minimum time needed for the introduction of the new equipment, and for moving the old equipment.

# chapter summary

❑ Planning for a new or expanding business involves human resource planning: defining objectives for human resource planning, ensuring that there is the necessary expertise and manpower and making sure that that all the necesssary arrangements have been made for aspects such as training,  staff welfare, and Health and Safety

❑ Suitable premises must be chosen.  The choices to be made include:
- does the business operate from home or away from home?
- should the premises be leased or purchased?
The owner of the business must be clear about the position relating to
- business rates, valuation, insurance and choice of location

❑ Planning for a machinery and equipment involves the decisions of whether the assets are needed immediately and whether the assets should be purchased or leased

❑ Purchasing stock and raw materials for the business involves the selection of one or more suppliers who can supply at the right price, in the right quantity, in the right quality and at the right time.

❑ Ordering stock relies on an efficient method of stock control.  Methods include re-order method and Economic Order  Quantity (EOQ)

❑ Planning for a new or expanding business also involves financial resource planning:
- identifying the need  for fixed assets and working capital
- providing finance from within the business and from outside borrowing

❑ Planning for business also involves the efficient use of time;  planning techniques include the use of critical path analysis and are illustrated by Gannt charts.

# Sonic Deco Limited – preparing for the business plan

| Element 8.1 | Prepare work and collect data for a business plan |
|---|---|

Suggested Sources: • Case Study "Sonic Deco Limited" in Chapter 47
• talks by solicitors and insurance brokers
• talks from bank lending officers
• local Enterprise Agencies and Chambers of Commerce
• textbooks in libraries and resource centres

## INTRODUCTION

Form into groups of at least four students. Read and discuss the Case Study "Sonic Deco Limited" in Chapter 47 , and then carry out the following tasks as *advisers* to the company.

## TASK 1

Assess the legal and insurance implications of the proposed new venture, eg employing staff, taking on premises, manufacturing and selling a product.

## TASK 2

Set out a schedule listing the resource requirements of the proposed business, including:

(a)   the cost of the assets required

(b)   the annual cost of employing the directors and staff

(c)   the sources of finance for the proposed expenditure in (a) and (b)

## TASK 3

Draw up a Gannt chart scheduling the activities that will have to take place before full production can start. The chart should show 'critical' activities, 'other' activities and float times. The following data is known:

• production must start on 1 January 19-1, following a one week trial run with all staff and equipment
• advertising and promotion will start 10 weeks before production officially starts
• suitable premises have been found and will be occupied at the start of the ninth week before I January
• finance must be arranged 4 weeks before occupying the premises and ordering machinery

The following *must* be completed before the one week trial run:

• renovating and equipping the premises, which will take 6 weeks
• recruiting staff, which will take 5 weeks
• ordering and delivery of raw materials, which will take 4 weeks
• ordering and delivery of machinery, which will take 5 weeks; the machinery *must* be ordered in the same week as the premises are occupied
• installing the machinery, which will take 3 weeks
• arranging insurance, which will take 2 weeks and must be completed before the premises are occupied

# 47 Writing the business plan

## introduction

This chapter looks at the *practicalities* of writing a *business plan*. In this book so far we have looked at the preparatory work in terms of defining objectives, financial planning, resource and production planning, market research and marketing planning. All these processes culminate in the business plan, a written document – often in ring binder or similar format – which will be presented to any potential lender of money or investor in the business. The object of the plan is to convince the reader, who may know nothing about the business, that the proposition is viable and that money invested in it will be safe and will grow.

It is dangerous to assume that there is a *set format* for a business plan. The structure and contents of a plan may vary widely from business to business, depending on the nature and size of the project and the expertise of the writer. If you are undertaking a Young Enterprise or mini-business scheme, there may well be a specified format for you to follow.

In this chapter, having looked at the purposes of a business plan, we will set out the format and an example of a five-part plan, which is a fairly typical structure. The business is Sonic Deco Limited, a loudspeaker manufacturer. The five sections, which we will deal with in turn, are as follows:

- setting of objectives
- marketing plan
- production plan
- resource requirements
- financial support data

You will see that much of this material has been covered in earlier chapters. We will refer to the earlier text where appropriate and concentrate here on the practicalities of selecting the appropriate information and presenting it in a persuasive way. As we mentioned above, a business plan is about *selling a business idea*. The effective use of communication skills is vital to the plan's success.

# purposes of a business plan

## when should a plan be written?

The writing of a business plan is essential in a number of circumstances:

*a business start-up*   A business plan enables the owner(s) of a start-up business to establish:
- the financial and physical resources that are already available
- the financial and physical resources that are needed
- the market need for the product or service
- the price of the product or service
- the ability to repay any borrowing

*a business expansion*   If the owner(s) of a business plans to expand operations, either by diversifying into different areas or by increasing production of an existing line or service, a business plan will be required.  The processes will be the same as for a start-up, although much of the data – eg financial statements and forecasts – will already be to hand, and it may be a case of updating an earlier plan.

*"where do we go now?"*   A business plan should be written at regular intervals by existing businesses so that the owner(s) can take time out from the day-to-day decision making, and see how the business should progress in the future. Too often businesses only see to the end of the week rather than planning effectively for the future by looking at new markets, new products and services, at opportunities and threats.

## how should a plan be written?

A business plan, as we will see in this chapter, is a highly technical document, calling for the combined expertise of a marketing executive, an accountant and a production or operations manager.  If the business owner is confident in all these aspects, there are books on the market and pamphlets from the banks which will give guidance.  If the business owner needs assistance, an accountant or management consultant will be able to help, although, of course, at a price.  If you are undertaking a Young Enterprise or mini business scheme, you should consult your documentation.   It is recommended that the plan be produced on a word processor so that it can be printed out in a presentable format.  It should also be produced in at least two or three copies, so that a copy can be sent in advance of any interview to a prospective lender.

## why should a plan be written?

A business plan should be written if:
- the business owner approaches a bank for finance for a new or expanding business
- the business owner wishes to turn an existing sole trader or partnership business into a limited company, and needs to raise money from a specialist venture capital company which will invest in the new company's shares

A business plan is also a valuable exercise for the owner of the business.  It will enable him or her to assess the present situation and plan for the future.  It avoids the all too prevalent plan "on the back of an envelope" or "it's all in my head" mentality.

A further advantage of writing a business plan is that it enable a business to *monitor* its future performance against the projections contained in the plan.  Specifically it will be able to look at:
- *cash flow* – against the cash flow forecast
- *monthly profit and loss and balance sheet* (standard reports if the business has its accounts on a computer – against the projected figures in the plan (particularly at the year-end)
- *sales figures* – against sales targets in the marketing plan
- *production figures* – against the projections in the production plan

# Case Study: Sonic Deco Limited

In this Case Study we set out the five part business plan compiled by John Eliot and Edward Gardiner, the owners of Sonic Deco. They are forming a limited company to manufacture hi-fi loudspeakers. The product, the "Presence" loudspeaker, has already been successsfully launched on the market by John Eliot working as a a sole trader; he is now being joined by Edward Gardiner. A large increase in production is planned, and the two directors need to approach the bank for finance of £110,000.

You should now read the notes set out below and study the relevant sections of the business plan which follows. The notes refer to the specific sections of the business plan in the order of presentation in theplan.

## introductory page

A business plan, like any document, needs careful thought about the *order* in which material is arranged. The first page is critical. It should include:

- the name and address of the business
- a *summary* setting out the business idea positively and clearly, quoting appropriate detail
- a *list of contents* – so that the reader can find the information he or she wants without having to thumb through pages of material

## business objectives and mission statement

The nature of the business and its legal status (here a limited company) should be set out, together witht the objectives of the business. The short-term (12 months) objectives should state:

- the type of product – whether it be a manufactured item or a service
- the expected sales volume (number of items sold)
- the sales value (the amount of income to be received from sales)
- the projected market share
- the profit target, eg net profit figure and Return on Capital Employed

It has become fashionable to encapsulate these objectives in a pithy sentence known as a "Mission Statement".

It is also accepted practice to state the long-term (up to five years) objectives of the business.

## personnel

An important determining factor of the the success of a business is the people which it employs. It is customary to list in a separate section the management of the business, showing their qualifications and experience. If necessary their CVs can be attached as an Appendix. The extent of the other staff of the business should also be listed, although in less detail.

## marketing plan

As we have seen in the marketing section of this book, a successful business should invest time and money in marketing.  The business plan should convince the reader that the product or service will fulfil a specific need.  The plan should should set out details of:

- the product and its price (sales brochures could be included in the Appendix)
- the present market and the expected market share
- the competition, and why the proposed product is better
- promotion plans – showing timings
- distribution and sales
- the marketing budget (brief details)
- break-even calculations

It should be stressed that the marketing plan which appears in the business plan is an *abbreviated* version of a full marketing plan (see Chapter 48).

## production plan

The production will set out details of the physical resources needed for the production of the manufactured item.  It will contain:

- a summary of the production method
- the premises used, showing full details of cost, valuation, whether freehold or leasehold
- the machinery and vehicles required, together with details of cost, valuation and expected life
- raw materials needed, stating cost, supplier details and expected stock levels
- labour and training requirements

You should note that if the plan is presenting a *service*, the appropriate details will be listed, although there will obviously be no raw materials requirement.

## resource requirements

This section summarises in financial terms

- the resources that will be needed
- the amount of money being contributed by the owner(s)
- the amount of finance required
- the assets available for security

This section summarises for a potential lender the essential questions of

- *how much finance* is being requested in proportion to the *capital sum* being invested by the owner(s)?
- what assets are available for security?

## financial data

This section will contain for a *new* business:

- a twelve month cashflow forecast
- the balance sheet at the beginning of the twelve months
- projected trading and profit and loss account (or operating budget) for thefirst twelve months
- projected balance sheet at the *end* of twelve months

If the business is *already* trading, the financial data should also include past finanacial statements, normally over a three year period.

When looking at the figures in the financial statements in this Case Study, remember that the cashflow forecast will include VAT, and the profit statement will not.

You should also note that the financial projections contained in the plan will enable the business to *monitor* and *review* performance during the course of the year.

# BUSINESS PLAN ━━━━━━━━━━

**name**      Sonic Deco Limited

**address**      Unit 1b Severnside Industrial Estate
Link Road
Stourminster ST2 4RT

## summary ━━━━━━━━━━━━━━━━━━━━━

Sonic Deco Limited is a hi-fi loudspeaker manufacturing business founded by John Eliot and Edward Gardiner in 19-1.  John Eliot has fifteen years' experience of loudspeaker design and has pioneered as a sole trader a new Deco'Presence' speaker which is now in production in rented premises, and has already sold 500 units in six months to hi-fi dealers in London and the West Midlands. There is proven market demand for an estimated 5,000 units a year.

The new company proposes to takeover and expand the sole trader business. It will purchase an industrial unit, machinery and delivery vehicle. Total cost of assets will be £219k. The owners are contributing £125k of capital, and the company seeks a further £110k from the bank: £50k by way of commercial mortgage on the premises, £20k by way of business loan for the machinery, and £40k by way of overdraft for working capital purposes.

## contents ━━━━━━━━━━━━━━━━━━━━━

# business and objectives _____

**name**       Sonic Deco Limited

**address**      Unit 1b Severnside Industrial Estate
Link Road
Stourminster ST2 4RT

Tel 0605 577455  Fax 0605 577498

**legal status**   Limited company
Shareholders:
John Eliot 50%
Edward Gardiner 50%

**business**     Hi-fi loudspeaker manufacturer

**start date**    1 January 19-1

## mission statement

"Sonic Deco Limited will become a leading manufacturer of quality loudspeaker systems and a household name in the UK"

## short-term objectives

Sonic Deco will within the first twelve months of trading:
- produce and sell 4,800 units (pairs) of loudspeakers
- achieve sales turnover of £480,000
- achieve a pre-tax profit of over £45,000
- supply over 50 major hi-fi retailers throughout the UK
- take 10% of UK market in similar units

## long-term objectives

Sonic Deco will within the first three years of trading:
- increase the product lines to six loudspeaker models
- increase annual turnover to £1,000,000
- establish sales through agents in the EC, USA and Japan

# personnel _____

## key personnel

| name | age | qualifications | position | annual salary |
|------|-----|----------------|----------|---------------|
| John Eliot* | 35 | BSc. MSc | Managing Director -responsible for production, sales and R & D | £24,000 |
| Edward Gardiner* | 45 | BA.MBA.ACCA | Finance Director Company Secretary - responsible for finance and administration | £24,000 |

* CVs attached

## other personnel

| job description | number | expected weekly wage |
|-----------------|--------|----------------------|
| production line workers | 3 | £175 |
| despatch clerk/driver* | 1 | £150 |
| part-time packer* | 1 | £50 |
| clerical assistant | 1 | £150 |

*to be recruited

# marketing plan ─────────────

## product

Sonic Deco "Presence" loudspeakers (sold in pairs):

* matched pairs in high density chipboard laminate with moulded fascia
* attractive modern styling
* two colourways - black ash and light oak finish
* price £100 per pair (excluding VAT)

The product specifications and price have been arrived at following market research among existing customers:

* questionnaires sent with products and mailings
* customer comments made during telephone conversations

A copy of the brochure for the "Presence" loudspeaker is included in Appendix 1.

## the market

* domestic use, supplied by hi-fi retailers and mail order houses
* total UK sales in 19-0 of £45m for similar units
* expanding market (10% in 19-0) - especially B, C1, C2 social groupings
* further growth in market (forecast 7% p.a. to 19-5) stimulated by demand by consumers for CD-play and CD-record systems

Sonic Deco Limited realistically expect to take 10% of the UK market in 19-1.

## the competitors

Major names in the market are BEF, Rosedale, Session, M&W who take 80% of current total UK sales.  Their weaknesses are:

* staid image
* high unit price -an average of £115 for similar units
* slow delivery

We can gain market share by

* our bright "modern" image
* price-cutting to £100 per unit
* rapid delivery to suppliers
* responsive after-sales service

We also have the advantage of being a small company which is able to offer a more "personal" service to our customers.

# marketing plan (continued) _____

## promotion
Promotion is by way of
- monthly advertising in the hi-fi magazines
- mailshots to existing suppliers (quarterly from January 19-1)
- purchase of product-related mailing lists (January)
- John Eliot visiting retailers and mail order houses
- sending the speakers for review to the Hi-fi magazines

## distribution and sales
Distribution of the speaker units is in sealed cartons direct to hi-fi retailers and mail order houses. No wholesaler is involved.

Sonic Deco Limited is purchasing a van for local and urgent deliveries. It also has a contract with a carrier, SpeedDirect, which offers a 24 hour and three day delivery service within the UK.

## marketing budget
In the first twelve months the marketing budget has been estimated at £12,000. This will cover
- advertising costs in magazines
- mailings
- purchase of mailing lists
- postages related to mailings

In addition, £1,800 has been budgeted for postage and delivery costs.

## sales projections
Expected turnover for the first 12 months, based on the sale of 4,800 units: £480,000

*sales break-even figures:*

$$\frac{£145,275 \text{ (total overheads)}}{42\% \text{ (gross profit margin\%)}} \times 100 = £345,892$$

sale of units needed for break-even = 3,459

Sonic Deco Limited is confident of achieving this level of sales (72% of annual projected sales) in view of the existing good name of the speakers and the current demand shown in the order books.

# production plan _____

### production

Sonic Deco Limited will manufacture pairs of
"Presence" speaker units on a power saw and
welding production line set up in their
freehold premises. 3 production line workers
will produce 400 pairs of speakers per month.

The units will be packed on site in
double-walled cartons with high-density moulded
filling pads.

The units will be despatched from the premises
either in the company van or collected by
carrier.

The business will be administered from the
premises by the two directors and a clerical
assistant. An office will be set up on the
premises.

All Health and Safety at Work conditions will
be met.

### premises

*freehold factory*

Sonic Deco Limited will operate from:
    Unit 1b Severnside Industrial Estate
    Link Road
    Stourminster ST2 4RT

Freehold premises of 2,500 square feet
Purchase price £125,000
Professional valuation £127,500 (December 19-0)
Business rates £2,900 p.a.
No mortgage currently outstanding
Financed by capital and proposed £50K bank
commercial mortgage.

### machinery

*production line*

Sonic Deco Limited will purchase power saws and
other production machinery:

Cost: £45,000
Expected life 5 years (20% straight line
depreciation)
Financing: from capital and proposed £20k bank
business loan

*office machines*

Sonic Deco Limited will purchase a PC and other
office machines:

Cost: £12,500
Expected life 5 years (20% straight line
depreciation)
Financing: from capital

# production plan – continued

**vehicle**

Sonic Deco Limited will purchase a delivery van:

Cost: £12,500
Expected life 4 years (25% straight line depreciation)
Financing:  from capital

**raw materials**

*speaker units*
Sonic Deco Limited purchase high quality bextrene cone individual speaker units for building into the "Presence" cabinets.

Supplier is R & T of Cambridge.

Cost of the individual units is £20 (£40 per pair).

At present terms are cash, but from February 19-1 terms will be 30 days.

*speaker cabinets*
Sonic Deco Limited purchase high quality chipboard laminates, internal bracing and filling from two suppliers.

Total cost of materials per pair of speakers is £20.

At present terms are cash, but from February 19-1 terms will be 30 days.

*Total materials cost per pair of speakers: £60*

*Average stock to be held £10,000*

**labour costs**

The total annual labour budget is £43,750, calulated on the basis of employing the following for a 50 week year:

3 production line workers @ £175 per week

1 part-time packer @ £50 per week

1 despatch clerk/driver @ £150 per week

1 clerical assistant @ £150 per week

# resources requirements _____

## resources required

| item | cost (£) |
|------|----------|
| freehold premises | 125,000 |
| production machinery | 45,000 |
| office equipment | 12,500 |
| vehicle | 12,500 |
| materials and working capital | 40,000 |
| TOTAL | <u>235,000</u> |

## financial requirements

| item | finance(£) | |
|------|-----------|---|
| freehold premises | 50,000 | commercial mortgage* |
| production machinery | 20,000 | business loan** |
| stock/working capital | 40,000 | overdraft |
| TOTAL FINANCE REQUIRED | 110,000 | |
| | | |
| CONTRIBUTION FROM OWN RESOURCES | 125,000 | |
| TOTAL | 235,000 | |

\* commercial mortgage with annual repayments of capital and interest requested

\*\* business loan with first year interest only repayments requested

## assets available for security

| security | value (£) |
|----------|-----------|
| freehold premises | £127,000 (valuation Dec. 19-0) |
| other fixed assets | £70,000 (at cost) |

# financial data – cashflow forecast _____

| Name of Business: | Sonic Deco Limited | | | | | | | |
|---|---|---|---|---|---|---|---|---|
| Period: January - Dec 19-1 | | | | | | | | |
| | Jan | Feb | Mar | Apl | May | Jun | July | Aug |
| | £ | £ | £ | £ | £ | £ | £ | £ |
| RECEIPTS | | | | | | | | |
| Cash sales | | | | | | | | |
| Cash from debtors | | 47000 | 47000 | 47000 | 47000 | 47000 | 47000 | 47000 |
| Capital | 125000 | | | | | | | |
| Loans | 70000 | | | | | | | |
| Interest | | | | | | | | |
| TOTAL RECEIPTS | 195000 | 47000 | 47000 | 47000 | 47000 | 47000 | 47000 | 47000 |
| | | | | | | | | |
| | | | | | | | | |
| PAYMENTS | | | | | | | | |
| Cash purchases | 28200 | | | | | | | |
| Credit purchases | | | 28200 | 28200 | 28200 | 28200 | 28200 | 28200 |
| Capital items | 195000 | | | | | | | |
| Wages | 7645 | 7645 | 7645 | 7645 | 7645 | 7645 | 7645 | 7645 |
| Rent/rates | | | 290 | 290 | 290 | 290 | 290 | 290 |
| Insurance | 1500 | | | | | | | |
| Services | 200 | 200 | 200 | 200 | 200 | 200 | 200 | 200 |
| Telephone | | | | 300 | | | 300 | |
| VAT | | | | 7000 | | | 7000 | |
| Vehicle expenses | 200 | 200 | 200 | 200 | 200 | 200 | 200 | 200 |
| Stationery | 50 | 50 | 50 | 50 | 50 | 50 | 50 | 50 |
| Postages | 150 | 150 | 150 | 150 | 150 | 150 | 150 | 150 |
| Bank charges | | | 150 | | | 150 | | |
| Interest | | | 500 | | | | | |
| Loan repayments | | | | | | | | |
| Advertising | 1000 | 1000 | 1000 | 1000 | 1000 | 1000 | 1000 | 1000 |
| Packaging | 500 | 500 | 500 | 500 | 500 | 500 | 500 | 500 |
| | | | | | | | | |
| | | | | | | | | |
| TOTAL PAYMENTS | 234445 | 9745 | 38885 | 45535 | 38235 | 38385 | 45535 | 38235 |
| | | | | | | | | |
| NET CASHFLOW | -39445 | 37255 | 8115 | 1465 | 8765 | 8615 | 1465 | 8765 |
| OPENING BANK | 0 | -39445 | -2190 | 5925 | 7390 | 16155 | 24770 | 26235 |
| CLOSING BANK | -39445 | -2190 | 5925 | 7390 | 16155 | 24770 | 26235 | 35000 |

# financial data – cashflow forecast

| Sept £ | Oct £ | Nov £ | Dec £ | TOTAL £ | | |
|---|---|---|---|---|---|---|
| 47000 | 47000 | 47000 | 47000 | 517000 | | |
| | | | | 125000 | | |
| | | | | 70000 | | |
| | | | | 0 | | |
| 47000 | 47000 | 47000 | 47000 | 712000 | | |
| | | | | | | |
| | | | | | | |
| | | | | 28200 | | |
| 28200 | 28200 | 28200 | 28200 | 282000 | | |
| | | | | 195000 | | |
| 7645 | 7645 | 7645 | 7655 | 91750 | | |
| 290 | 290 | 290 | 290 | 2900 | | |
| | | | | 1500 | | |
| 200 | 200 | 200 | 200 | 2400 | | |
| | 300 | | | 900 | | |
| | 7000 | | | 21000 | | |
| 200 | 200 | 200 | 200 | 2400 | | |
| 50 | 50 | 50 | 50 | 600 | | |
| 150 | 150 | 150 | 150 | 1800 | | |
| 150 | | | 150 | 600 | | |
| | | | 7000 | 7500 | | |
| | | | 2000 | 2000 | | |
| 1000 | 1000 | 1000 | 1000 | 12000 | | |
| 500 | 500 | 500 | 500 | 6000 | | |
| | | | | 0 | | |
| | | | | 0 | | |
| 38385 | 45535 | 38235 | 47395 | 658550 | | |
| | | | | | | |
| 8615 | 1465 | 8765 | -395 | 53450 | | |
| 35000 | 43615 | 45080 | 53845 | 0 | | |
| 43615 | 45080 | 53845 | 53450 | 53450 | | |

# financial data – projected profit statement —

**PROJECTED TRADING AND PROFIT LOSS ACCOUNT OF SONIC DECO LIMITED FOR YEAR ENDING 31 DECEMBER 19-1**

|  | £ | £ |
|---|---|---|
| Sales |  | 480,000 |
| Purchases | 288,000 |  |
| Less closing stock | 10,000 |  |
| Cost of Goods Sold |  | 278,000 |
| Gross Profit |  | 202,000 |
|  |  |  |
| Wages | 43,750 |  |
| Directors salaries | 48,000 |  |
| Rates | 2,900 |  |
| Insurance | 1,500 |  |
| Services | 2,400 |  |
| Telephone | 1,200 |  |
| Vehicle expenses | 2,400 |  |
| Stationery | 600 |  |
| Postages | 1,800 |  |
| Advertising | 12,000 |  |
| Packing | 6,000 |  |
| Bank charges | 600 |  |
| Interest | 7,500 |  |
| Depreciation | 14,625 |  |
|  |  | 145,275 |
|  |  |  |
| Net profit |  | 56,725 |

Note:
The figures for purchases and sales on the cash flow forecast differ from those quoted above because the figures here *exclude* VAT.

# financial data – opening balance sheet

**PROJECTED BALANCE SHEET OF SONIC DECO LIMITED AS AT 1 JANUARY 19-1**

|  | Cost £ | Dep'n £ | Net £ |
|---|---|---|---|
| **Fixed Assets** | | | |
| Premises | 125,000 | 0 | 125,000 |
| Machinery | 45,000 | 0 | 45,000 |
| Vehicle | 12,500 | 0 | 12,500 |
| Office equipment | 12,500 | 0 | 12,500 |
| | 195,000 | 0 | 195,000 |

|  |  |  |
|---|---|---|
| **Current Assets** | | |
| Stock | | 24,000 |
| | | |
| **Less Current Liabilities** | | |
| Overdraft | | 24,000* |
| | | |
| **Working Capital** | | 0 |
| | | 195,000 |
| **Less Long-term Liabilities** | | |
| Bank Loans | | 70,000 |
| | | |
| **NET ASSETS** | | 125,000 |

**FINANCED BY**
**Authorised Share Capital**
125,000 ordinary shares of £1 each         125,000

**Issued Share Capital**
125,000 ordinary shares of £1 each, fully paid   125,000

*Note that the overdraft of £24,000 results from the initial stock purchase of £24,000. The full overdraft requirement of £40,000 shown in the Resources Requirement Section (p.8) will not be utilised until the end of the first month of trading.

# financial data – year-end balance sheet ___

**BALANCE SHEET OF SONIC DECO LIMITED AS AT 31 DECEMBER 19-1**

|  | Cost £ | Dep'n £ | Net £ |
|---|---|---|---|
| **Fixed Assets** | | | |
| Premises | 125,000 | 0 | 125,000 |
| Machinery | 45,000 | 9,000 | 36000 |
| Vehicle | 12,500 | 3,125 | 9,375 |
| Office equipment | 12,500 | 2,500 | 10,000 |
| | 195,000 | 14,625 | 180,375 |

| **Current Assets** | | |
|---|---|---|
| Stock | 10,000 | |
| Debtors | 40,000 | |
| Bank | 53,450 | |
| | 103,450 | |

| **Less Current Liabilities** | | |
|---|---|---|
| Creditors | 34,100 | |

| **Working Capital** | | 69,350 |
|---|---|---|
| | | 249,725 |
| **Less Long-term Liabilties** | | |
| Bank Loans | | 68,000 |
| **NET ASSETS** | | 181,725 |

*FINANCED BY*
**Authorised Share Capital**

| 125,000 ordinary shares of £1 each | 125,000 |
|---|---|

**Issued Share Capital**

| 125,000 ordinary shares of £1 each, fully paid | 125,000 |
|---|---|
| Profit and loss | 56,725 |
| | 181,725 |

## EVIDENCE COLLECTION EXERCISE

# 23

# *Writing and presenting a business plan*

| | |
|---|---|
| *Element 8.2* | *Produce and present a business plan* |

Suggested Sources:
- participation in a Young Enterprise or mini business scheme
- "How to Start a Business" booklets produced by the banks
- talks from bank officials, accountants and management consultants
- textbooks in libraries and resource centres

*Note: many of the activities in this exercise may already form part of a Young Enterprise or mini business scheme. If this is the case, they should be integrated with those schemes as part of the assessment process.*

## TASK 1

Form into groups (companies) of at least seven students. Allocate the roles of

- managing director/company secretary
- financial director and assistant
- marketing/sales director and assistant
- production director and assistant

## TASK 2

Decide on a product or service.

## TASK 3

Under the control of the managing director, carry out the necessary research and compile a five part business plan, each taking responsibility as follows:

- business objectives – group discussion and responsibility
- marketing plan – compiled by the marketing team
- production plan – compiled by the production team
- resource requirement – group discussion and responsibility
- financial data – financial team with assistance from the others

## TASK 4

The individual companies should give an oral presentation of the proposed plan to the whole class. Handouts, OHPs, flipcharts and videos should be used where appropriate and available.

It is suggested that a bank lending officer, a management consultant or a representative from a venture capital company should be invited to attend the presentations to comment and to help assess.

# 48 Producing a sales and marketing plan

## introduction

We have seen in Chapter 13 that part of the marketing process is careful planning. We have also seen in Chapter 47 that marketing forms an important part of the *business plan*, the marketing content of which is often a *summary* of a fully developed *sales and marketing plan*, the subject of this chapter.

Developing a sales and marketing plan for a business is not a process which involves difficult techniques. All you need is time and perseverance. The plan helps to co-ordinate diverse sales and marketing activities into effective total action. It involves seeking the best balance between the market's needs and the relative skills of the firm. For the plan to be useful, it needs to be based firmly on the principle of *responding to the needs of customers*. It also needs to be internally consistent, to 'add up', rather than allowing individual elements to conflict with each other.

In this chapter we examine how a typical marketing plan is constructed. We look at the following areas:
- the reasons for drawing up a plan
- the structure of a plan
- the marketing audit
- setting of objectives
- market strategy and action plan
- the marketing budget

## drawing up the sales and marketing plan

### reasons why a business should have a plan

There are many reasons why a business needs a sales and marketing plan, but the overall one is that it provides the owner(s) with an opportunity for better *control* of the business. In the course of running a business the plan will help management to:
- provide the opportunity to emphasise and concentrate upon the factors of competition *other than* price
- systematically analyse the business' capacity to expand

- prepare for problems that could arise, eg losing customers, a rise in interest rates
- quantify what is going to be done by setting goals
- outline what must be done in order to achieve the goals
- monitor progress by measuring performance against those goals
- provide a case when negotiating with banks and government agencies for finance and assistance

## what is involved in a sales and marketing plan?
The process of drawing up a sales and marketing plan involves a number of steps. These are:
- assessing the business' past and/or future potential performance
- assessing competitors
- looking at the world in which the business has to operate in order to find opportunities and avoid pitfalls
- deciding what objectives are required for the owners and their business
- deciding how the objectives will be achieved by the development of a strategy and action plan

## structure of the plan
In practice, sales and marketing plans vary in detail and sophistication. They tend to have a common structure which is sequenced as follows:

- *the information base*
This is an analysis of the position of the business, eg profits, revenues, product market shares, market sectors served, strengths, weaknesses and recent trends – economic, social, technical and competitive.

- *external assumptions*
On the basis of the best evidence available, the assessment is made of important economic factors likely to affect the forthcoming year(s) performance, eg
- government measures
- economic factors affecting, for example, labour and raw material costs
- social and technological changes influencing demand
- people's spending patterns
- known or probable competitive activity

- *basic overall objectives, policies and strategies*
In a business these include profit and investment goals and decisions regarding priorities and/or emphases on the products sold and the markets served, as well as strategies relating to the product (or quality of the service offered), pricing, distribution, advertising, promotion and sales.

- *specific goals and programmes of action*
These cover market segments in which products are sold, but are more detailed in terms of specific details regarding actions for product planning, selling, promotion, distribution after sales service etc. Responsibilities and time scales for the achievement of set tasks should be set out and agreed.

- *planned expenditure*
Details of the overall marketing budget which can be broken down into more detailed sub-group budgets (eg market research, advertising, sales) and set against measures of performance.

- *measures of performance*
The business should set clear long and short-term objectives, some of which can be included in the overall budgets of the business as well as in the plan itself. Important *quantitative* objectives – ie objectives which involve specific figures – include:
- sales figures
- market share(s) to be achieved
- profit expressed in monetary terms and as a percentage of sales

- actual costs of selling, advertising, promotion distribution, after sales service, against budget costs

Other objectives may not be so easily quantified, especially:
- providing the necessary manpower training and development
- providing effective plant and manpower utilisation
- avoidance of excessive variations in the level of business transacted
- maintenance and improvement of market position against the competition

### review of the plan
Most plans are written on a 'rolling plan' basis, revised maybe at quarterly intervals, but keeping the period covered to a minimum of one year. The precise timetable and scale should be designed around the business and the market conditions it faces. A broad guideline is to plan for at least one year to a maximum of three years. Looking further ahead would in most markets be highly speculative, with the possible exception of industries like capital goods, agriculture and mining.

Now examine the diagram set out below which illustrates the planning process explained in this chapter. Note the *stages* of the planning process as it moves from the top to the bottom of the diagram.

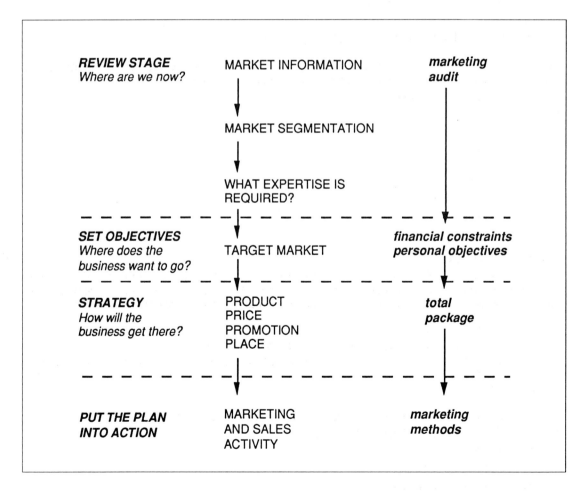

*Fig. 48.1  A framework for sales and marketing planning*

## the marketing audit – SWOT analysis

The starting point in the planning process is to undertake a Strengths, Weaknesses, Opportunities, Threats (SWOT) analysis divided into three parts:
- current situation
- competitor situation
- external/environmental situation

### current situation
This part of the SWOT analysis examines the business' present situation in relation to its trading patterns and performance.  The purpose of this is to ensure that the business capitalises on its *strengths*, for example:
- the skills of the owner(s) and other people working in the business
- the quality of product/service offered
- the location of the business
- the design facilities
- the business premises
- the equipment/machinery available in the business
- availability of the product/service on a local basis
- the ability to be able to provide quick delivery service

The *weaknesses* of the business must also be identified and made less vulnerable to the market, and where possible be rectified.  Weaknesses in a business could include:
- the business lacks the level of finance required
- lack of sales representation
- lack of modern equipment
- unsuitable premises
- lack of market knowledge
- lack of competitor knowledge
- poor distribution channels
- lack of promotional material

### competitor situation
The business should look at the market sectors served and analyse the competitors in these sectors. The business needs to understand competitors' capabilities and counter their strengths while attacking their weaknesses.  Possible opportunities open to the business should be identified.

### the external environment in which the business has to trade
The preparation of a sales and marketing plan cannot be done in a vacuum. It needs to  identify the range of outside factors that will have an impact on the business in the future, either by way of presenting opportunities or by posing threats.

There are a number of factors which every business needs to consider on a regular basis:
- trends in both the local and national economy
- changes in population
- developments in technology
- political or legislative changes
- changes in society

Within each of these broad categories there are many factors which will affect different businesses. Even a cursory examination of the changes likely to come in the next two to five years is likely to reveal both opportunities and threats to the firm's existence. A plan should help to prepare for these changes and also help avoid being caught completely unawares.

---

### student activity 48.1 – SWOT analysis

(a) Suppose that you are opening up a new shop in your local shopping street (choose a product area of your choice). Identify:

- the strengths of the business that could be used to marketing advantage
- the weaknesses that the new business would have to be aware of, and how they could be tackled
- the marketing opportunities that exist for your product – you will need here to outline the market sector and the competition
- the threats that you can see posed by the competitors – how can they be countered?

(b) List the external/environmental factors outside the control of your planned business which will affect your marketing planning process (eg technological, economic, social, demographic, political and legal factors)

---

# marketing objectives

## defining objectives

Information obtained in the marketing audit, together with market research, sales forecasts, financial considerations, personal considerations of the owner(s) will all play a part in defining the broad direction in which the firm is moving. This appraisal needs to be matched against the *objectives* of the business.

*Objectives are statements about what the business wants to achieve in the future.* They are often called goals and targets. In the case of small businesses it is often difficult to divorce the personal objectives of the owner(s) from the business objectives. So the first job is to sort out one from the other.

All objectives should meet the following criteria. They should be:

- *clear* – stated briefly and unambiguously
- *actionable* – probably the single most important feature – the business ought to be clear that with existing resources and skills, the objectives set must be realistic
- *consistent* – it is important that established objectives do not run counter to each other – unnecessary clashes or conflicts undermine the entire process
- *measurable* – wherever possible actual numbers should be included in the statement in order to provide a basis for measurement of the performance achieved

## matching marketing objectives with other considerations

The marketing objectives should be matched with the personal objectives of the owner(s), who should carefully consider what they want personally from the business, whether it is to run a bigger business, to start exporting or to take more free time. The owner(s) should have an overall view of how they want the business to develop.

Marketing objectives also have to be set in the context of the overall business objectives such as financial return expected on the overall investment. For example, the business objectives may require a 15% annual return on capital employed, or may aim to increase the workforce by a certain percentage. Business objectives will define many different boundaries.

## statement of marketing objectives

All the work carried out previously during the marketing audit will point out what needs to be achieved both

• in the *long term* (developing new market sectors)

• in the *short term* (preparing new sales literature, employing extra salespersons, training staff, etc).

Putting this in terms of *objectives* means making statements such as the following:

*"The business will achieve a growth rate in sales of 10% per annum above inflation  over the next three years."*

*"During the first year of the plan the business will break into the following new markets  . . ." (defined geographically, by customer group or by market need).*

*"The company will  increase its market share by 3% in year one of the plan."*

---

**student activity 48.2 – setting marketing objectives**
Refer to the shop which was the subject of the previous Student Activity.

(a)   write out your *personal* objectives in setting up the business

(b)   transfer those objectives into *sales and marketing objectives* which the business needs to achieve

It would be helpful in this exercise to investigate the current market conditions and restraints by visiting and interviewing shop owners, or arranging for a proprietor to come to talk to the class.

---

# strategy and action plan

## marketing strategies

Marketing strategies need to be developed which will outline broadly *how the business will achieve the overall marketing objectives and goals.*  A number of alternative strategies can be recommended for each objective and the ability to develop these strategies will depend on the knowledge of marketing ideas within the business.  The development of a strategy will lead into the specific marketing actions which will be required to put the plan  into action.

## action plan

*A marketing action plan identifies the specific policies and actions to be used by the business within the strategy to achieve the objectives.*  A useful way for developing what is required to be done in order for each strategy to be put into action is to use the "marketing mix" (described in Chapters  16 to 18).  The marketing mix involves the "4 Ps":

Product – what you are selling

Price – how you are going to price it

Promotion – how the product is to be packaged, promoted and sold

Place – how the product is to be distributed

Using the "4 Ps" approach will help to develop a  marketing action plan as outlined in fig. 48.2 on the next page.  In this case *three* different strategies are proposed to fulfil the overall objective of increasing sales by 10% in one year.  Note how elements from the "4 Ps" are defined in columns running down the diagram.

**ACTION PLAN – Objective: to increase sales by 10% in a year**

| strategy | product & price | distribution | selling | promotion |
|---|---|---|---|---|
| **STRATEGY 1** | | | | |
| "To expand sales to present customers this year by 10%." | • add a new line<br>• modify an existing line<br>• improve discount structure | • appoint a new agent to cover the area | • make four sales calls per year to each customer | • develop a new brochure |
| **STRATEGY 2** | | | | |
| "To open two new accounts per month." | • introduce extensions to present product range<br>• cut prices on certain lines | • appoint a distributor in Scotland, where your sales are negligible | • identify prospective customers and make three calls to each | • exhibit at the National Exhibition Centre in Birmingham |
| **STRATEGY 3** | | | | |
| "Identify a new product to complement exisitng ones and increase sales." | • find product ideas by visits to trade fairs<br>• examine competitors' products<br>• investigate the possibility of importing products | • investigate distribution requirements | • determine if staff can cope with new products | • develop a mailing campaign to sell to areas not covered by existing sales force |

*Fig. 48.2  A marketing action plan*

**student activity 48.3 – defining strategy**

Refer to the shop which was the subject of the previous Student Activities.

(a) choose one of the marketing objectives defined in the last Activity (or take as an example "increase sales by 10% next year")

(b) transfer that objective into *two* strategies

(c) devise an *action plan* for the strategies along the lines of the diagram set out above

# the sales and marketing budget

The control of sales and marketing expenditure or, to put it another way, the maximisation of benefits from any given level of expenditure, demands careful planning. The two major parts of the plan are a detailed statement of what is to be achieved during the period of the plan and a translation of that statement into its budgetary (financial) implications. The result is the sales and marketing budget related to a course of action to be taken by the business. Many businesses find this area very difficult and often do not undertake this part of the plan in any detail. A number of approaches may be used:

- *affordable or given-sum method*
  Here the business decides "what it can afford" relative to other company costs and profit levels required. This means a given sum of money is allocated to sales and marketing costs which often bears no relation to the actual requirements of the plan.

- *percentage of sales method*
  Here a fixed percentage is used, based upon sales in previous years, and the level of expenditure used to generate such sales. The problem is that conditions prevailing in the past may not apply in the future. Alternatively, a percentage can be based upon *forecast* sales. The problem here is that as sales increase or decrease the level of expenditure will do the same, whereas the *opposite* may be needed. "Sales" may relate to overall turnover or to revenue received for individual products or groups of products.

- *sales response method*
  The approach is to graph changes in levels of expenditure on the elements of the marketing mix being used, against the effect or response that these levels will produce in sales revenue. This approach tends to be theoretical, and again the relationships are in the future and are difficult to assess.

- *objective and task method*
  This is a logical approach which involves establishing the sales and marketing *objectives*, determining the marketing tactics to achieve these, specifying the *tasks* of the tactics, and costing out the tasks to provide the required level of expenditure. As this method provides a logical progression within the plan and starts with objectives, it is favoured by a number of larger companies.

For a worked example of a sales and marketing budget, see the Case Study which follows this chapter.

## reviewing the plan

When the written plan is put into action it needs to be reviewed at regular intervals – usually quarterly – and any necessary amendments made. A complete review and update of the plan usually takes place towards the end of year 1 in order to put more detail into year 2, which then becomes year 1. The existing year 3 is then updated and becomes year 2 and a new year 3 is written. This approach gives you a "rolling plan" basis.

## chapter summary

❑ Sales and marketing plans are working documents and should be as short and simple as possible. A typical sales and marketing plan will:
  - assess the current situation of the business
  - assess the competitor situation
  - review the overall environment in which the business has to trade
  - establish the sales and marketing objectives
  - develop an action plan to meet those objectives
  - prepare a budget which the business can afford and which will be appropriate to the promotional activity required to achieve the objectives
  - review the actual situation against the plan and provide for updating as required

❑ An extended Case Study presenting a sales and marketing plan for the Healthy Foods Catering partnership follows this chapter.

## Case Study: "Healthy Foods Catering " partnership – a sales and marketing plan

### introduction: writing a sales and marketing plan

In the previous chapter we examined the format of a *sales and marketing plan* in detail. In normal business practice no two plans are presented identically; the actual approach very often depends on the individual business and the main purpose for the development of the plan. The written plan is often an *internal* document within the business which identifies how the business is going to achieve the aims and objectives it has set.

The sales and marketing plan must be distinguished from the *business plan* which is an external document, and which will contain a *summary* of the sales and marketing plan.

Before the plan is written, an *outline* of the plan should be written so that the structure and contents remain clear in the writer's mind when the plan is being compiled. A typical outline might run as follows:

1  objectives, eg to increase market share by 3%

2  sales forecast

3  product policy

4  description of the markets to be entered

5  market segmentation

6  market research to be carried out

5  pricing policy

7  distribution policy

8  advertising and sales promotion policy

9  sales policy

10  budget statement – with an explanation of how it is to be used

11  outline timing for implementation of various selling and marketing activities

We now turn to the Case Study which is a sales and marketing plan developed for a new catering business "Healthy Foods Catering" run by Sarah and Louise Osborne, two sisters in partnership. The business is to commence trading in November 19-4 . The plan is of three years duration, with Year 1 presented in detail and Years 2 and 3 in outline.

# HEALTHY FOODS CATERING: MARKETING PLAN

## INTRODUCTION _____

The business will commence trading in November 19-4, manufacturing and selling a specialised range of healthy and vegetarian dishes (main and snack meals). Meals will be produced in the firm's own production kitchens, and will be sealed, vacuum-wrapped and chilled. Trial production of meals will commence early in October 19-4. Note that the term "meal" refers to an individual course.

Initially orders will be processed as they are received and then delivered to individual customers. The consumer (private customer) market will be developed during the first three months of trading, but it is part of this plan to introduce and develop a range of meals and dishes to meet the commercial market, ie food wholesalers and distributors.

Production of meals will be undertaken by one of the partners and a member of the partner's family. The other partner will undertake the day-to-day sales and distribution. Both partners will be involved in promotional events.

## OBJECTIVES _____

**Year 1**      To develop sales to the consumer and commercial markets to the value of £60,000 and provide a net profit return on sales of 10%.

To be selling on a regular basis (at least 2 orders per month) to five frozen food wholesale distributors.

To employ a salesperson/delivery person during the final quarter.

**Year 2**      To double sales during Year 2 and retain net profit margin at 10%.

To employ a salesperson/agent to develop the commercial market within a 50 mile radius of the production unit.

To employ a sales telephone/administration person.

**Year 3**      To increase sales by 50% and also increase the net profit margin to 11%.

To introduce the product range into two nationwide-based catering food suppliers.

## SALES FORECAST _____

**Year 1**      **Consumer Sales**
Total sales £60,000; consumer market sales target £45,000

The average unit price of a meal at sales price is £2.50 and therefore there is a need to sell at least 18,000 units during Year 1.

Research indicates that the average order value to be delivered will be £20 and a customer will purchase 15 times in a year. We will therefore require to build up a base of 150 regular customers to provide the turnover required.

Following all tasting/promotional events it is anticipated that initial response will be high but some fall-off will occur; however a base of 150 regular customers is possible. In addition, other customers will purchase spasmodically during the year.

**Commercial Sales**
Sales target £15,000.  Target customers 5

Average order value is expected to build up to £250 per order.  Commercial customers will only be available to the company for approximately eight months of the year.  Initial annual sales target will be as above.

**Year 2**        Total sales £130,000
Consumer sales £65,000
Commercial sales £65,000.  Target customers 10

**Year 3**        Total sales £190,650
Consumer sales £75,000
Commercial sales £115,650. Target customers 18

During Years 2 and 3 the commercial markets will become the important development area of the business.  Sales direct to the consumer will be restricted to the geographical area around the production unit, situated in Airedale.

## PRODUCT RANGE

**Year 1**        A range of 28 dishes (main and snack meals) of which 10 dishes will be available from the start of trading in November 19-4.  The other 18 dishes will be gradually introduced into the range as the year progresses on the basis of "the dish of the week or month".  In addition, certain recipes have a seasonal flavour and will be offered only during the appropriate season.  Popularity of individual dishes will be monitored carefully.  Consideration will need to be given to a basic group of at least 10 dishes each quarter.  Throughout the year a review of the dishes' popularity (over the full year and seasonally) will be undertaken in order to develop an appropriate menu to meet the market needs in Years 2 and 3. This will mean some slight variation of menus for the consumer and commercial markets.

**Years 2 and 3**  Development of new dishes will continue to meet market demands and tastes.  All existing dishes will be reviewed at least once a year with regard to costs of production, with the aim of providing a better contribution.

## MARKET GEOGRAPHICAL AREA
**Year 1**        **Consumer Sales**

Initial promotion will be within the boundaries of the area covered by Airedale Borough Council and the circulation area of the "Airedale Courier".

During the course of the year promotional activity will increase the area covered into areas adjacent to Waterdown, keeping the area covered within a radius of 15 miles of the production unit.

Areas to be developed will include: Cradwell, Wychwood, Laxdale, Thornhill, Knowle, Thornton, Wibsey and Morton.  Selling into this area will provide a potential market of 325,000 homes for delivery of individual meals.

**Years 2 and 3**  There will be a need to widen the geographical area to a maximum of 25 to 30 miles from the production unit.  More important will be the need to increase the total number of customers purchasing on a regular basis from the existing areas served.

**Year 1**   **Commercial Sales**
Following research during the early part of the year (January) to identify potential buying/decision-making people, the commercial market will be developed.

It is proposed to develop as customers a number of outlets which supply pubs, hotels, restaurants and other catering establishments, together with delicatessen and health food retailers. It is the firm's policy to develop a commercial base of customers in an area within a 30 mile radius of the production unit and by the end of Year 1 at least five suppliers will be purchasing at least twice a month.

**Years 2 and 3**   Development of wholesalers/catering purchasers will continue, and during Year 2 it is planned that the company will develop the market radius to within 50 miles of the production unit. During Year 3 it is planned to introduce into its customer list at least three nationwide-based catering suppliers.

# MARKET SEGMENTATION

**Consumer market**
Research has indicated that the potential market is as follows:

| | |
|---|---|
| Age | 20-45 years |
| Occupation | Professional people/middle class |
| Income | £12,000 and above |

Potential locations are to be identified in specific geographical areas. Airedale initially has been segmented as follows: Idle, Lightcliffe, Lidget Green, Bransford, Brant West, Hunts End, Walkwood, Southcrest, Westwood, Queensford, plus the villages of Holts End, Robin Green, Hebden and Crookhill.

Segmentation needs to take place on a geographical basis for further areas to be developed later in the year:

| *Area* | *Month* |
|---|---|
| Cradwell & Wychwood | March |
| Laxdale & Thornhill | May |
| Knowle & Thornton | July |
| Wibsey & Morton | October |

**Commercial market**
Sources of potential customer sectors identified:

- cash and carry wholesalers
- delicatessen wholesalers/retailers
- health food wholesalers /retailers
- frozen food wholesalers/retailers
- public house groups
- restaurants and cafes
- hotels and guest houses
- institutional caterers

## MARKETING RESEARCH

**Consumer market**
*Requirements* – to investigate the areas identified for future development in order to segment on a geographical basis. Also to investigate potential promotional approaches in the individual areas identified for expansion. Investigation of the areas to be conducted as follows:

| | |
|---|---|
| Crudwell/Wychbold | February/March |
| Laxdale/Thornhill | April/May |
| Knowle/Thornton | June/July |
| Wibsey/Morton | August/September |

**Commercial market**
*Requirements* – to identify potential customers in the following areas:

| | |
|---|---|
| Distributors | Cash and carry wholesalers, Delicatessen wholesalers, Health food wholesalers, Chilled/freezer distributors |
| Retailers | Hotels/Guest houses, Restaurants/cafes, Delicatessen retailers, Health food retailers |
| Catering Groups | Institutional caterers, Breweries, Restaurants and Hotels |

This work is to be undertaken during December 19-4 to January 19-5. The planned selling exercise will commence in March and will be repeated from time-to-time over the next two years as sales are developed in new geographical areas.

## PRICING

**Consumer Sales**
Production costs will be identified and a margin of 65% (minimum) will be added in order to cover overheads and profit. A comparison with competitor prices should take place. Consumer prices should be finalised by October 19-4. There will be a need for monthly reviews of costs of fresh ingredients and a quarterly review for other ingredients.

**Commercial Sales**
Once initial costings have been identified and appropriate margins (see above) added, a discount structure for bulk purchase will be required. This needs to be prepared by the end of January 19-5. A comparison with competitor prices should take place, and final decisions made by the end of December. Competitors' price lists must be obtained on a regular basis.

In Years 2 and 3 a policy of review of prices on a quarterly basis will continue, and towards the end of the first year's trading an overall review of price levels will be undertaken to see if prices can be increased in order to provide better profit margins.

## DISTRIBUTION

**Consumer Sales**
Orders will be delivered direct to customers' homes in the firm's own transport – delivery to take place 2 days after receipt of order – evening delivery will be available. As the business develops, a planned delivery schedule will be introduced and customers will be notified of its timings in their area. From the start of Year 2 all new areas developed will have a planned delivery system introduced.

**Commercial Sales**
Central bulk deliveries will be made to identified distribution outlets which can then sell on to individual small (retail) outlets. In the case of contracts with groups (eg breweries) distribution will have to be agreed with them at the time of negotiation. It is planned to deliver to central distribution warehouses as far as possible.

## PROMOTION

### Consumer Market

Three *tasting sessions* to be organised for the end of October and early November for approximately 35 to 40 people already identified as potential customers during initial research.

A *promotional leaflet* to be delivered to identified areas in Airedale – using the Airedale Courier distribution system during the first week of November.

*Press release* to be sent from mid-October onwards to five local newspapers.

### Commercial Market

*Mailing* – identified commercial/group buyers to be sent an individual addressed letter introducing Healthy Foods Catering, together with details of specimen menus/dishes. The letter to state that a follow-up telephone call will be made to arrange an appointment and a full presentation.

*Advertising/Promotion* – research to be undertaken with regard to a small advertising and press release campaign in appropriate local business journals.

*Brochure/Leaflet* – a simple cost-effective leaflet for Year 1 which can be used in both consumer and commercial markets. It will give brief details, including ingredients of dishes. The price list will be on a separate sheet for ease of reproduction, and to allow for price changes.

## SALES POLICY

### Consumer Sales

A telephone selling approach will be developed in order to contact customers on a regular basis and at the same time build up deliveries in planned areas. Initially this work will be undertaken by the partners; if it is successful, a part-time evening telesales person could be employed.

### Commercial Sales

Initial sales contact is to be undertaken by the partners. When sales have developed to a level which cannot be managed by them, an agent will be recruited to sell the range to appropriate outlets. During Year 2 there will be a need to appoint a telephone salesperson, who could take calls from both commercial and consumer customers and also ring specific customers to encourage them to place an order. This employee could also act as a clerk/typist.

## MARKETING BUDGET

| Year 1: | Sales Income | £60,000 |
|---|---|---|
| | Units produced | Consumer market 18,000 at an average price of £2.50 |
| | | Commercial market 10,000 at an average price of £1.50 |

Research suggests that the average expenditure in the industry is 5.5% of sales turnover for promotional costs. Therefore, on that basis the firm would have £3,300 available for sales and marketing budget in Year 1. This amount is considered not to be a large enough budget for a firm which wishes to grow in a very competitive market. Therefore, for Year 1 the company will have an initial budget of £5,500 (9.2% of turnover) which will be reviewed on a quarterly basis.

| Allocation of budget | £ |
|---|---|
| Press Advertising | 1,750 |
| Printing - Menus/price lists | 450 |
| Printing - Leaflets | 450 |
| Leaflet distribution | 350 |
| Food sampling at cost price | 1,250 |
| Sales folders | 20 |
| Direct Mailing campaign | 250 |
| Brochure | 650 |
| Miscellaneous/Reserve | 330 |
| TOTAL BUDGET | 5,500 |

## SALES AND MARKETING PLAN IMPLEMENTATION SCHEDULE

| TIMING | CONSUMER MARKET | COMMERCIAL MARKET |
|---|---|---|
| **19-4** | | |
| October | Invitations for tasting sessions | |
| October | Finalise pricing structure | |
| October | Press release to local press | |
| October/November | Tasting sessions | |
| Oct/Nov/Dec | Adverts/leaflets in local press | |
| November | Preparation of leaflet for house delivery | |
| November | Leaflets delivered to houses | |
| December | | Commercial market research |
| **19-5** | | |
| January | | Prepare pricing structure |
| January | | Prepare press release to trade press |
| February | Review menu and prices | |
| February | Review plan (first quarter) | |
| February/March | Research Cradwell and Wychwood areas | |
| February | | Develop mailing campaign |
| March | | Start sales campaign |
| April/May | Research Laxdale and Thornhill | |
| May | Review menu and prices | |
| May | Review plan (second quarter) | |
| June/July | Research Knowle and Thornton | |
| July | Organise the appointment of sales/delivery person | |
| August | Review plan (third quarter) | |
| August | Review menu and prices | |
| August/September | Research Wibsey/Morton | |
| August/September | | Prepare brochure for next year |
| October | Review pricing structure | Review pricing structure |
| October | Review and update the plan | Review and update the plan |

## EVIDENCE COLLECTION EXERCISE

# 24

# *Sonic Deco Limited – the sales and marketing plan*

| | |
|---|---|
| *Element 8.3* | *Produce a sales and marketing plan* |

Suggested Sources:
- Case Study "Sonic Deco Limited" in Chapter 47
- Case Study "Healthy Foods Catering" and Chapter 48
- talks by marketing managers
- investigation into other loudspeaker manufacturers
- textbooks in libraries and resource centres

## INTRODUCTION

Form into groups of at least four students. Read the following case studies in this book:

- Case Study "Sonic Deco Limited" in Chapter 47
- Case Study "Healthy Foods Catering" in Chapter 48

## TASK 1

Draw up a written sales and marketing plan for Sonic Deco Limited for Year 1 of trading and also (in outline) Year 2 and Year 3. You will use as your base document the marketing plan contained in Sonic Deco's business plan. You will also need to draw on other areas in the business plan, eg details of objectives and products. The sales and marketing plan should be drawn up under the headings set out below. Note the suggestions which follow each heading.

| | | |
|---|---|---|
| 1. | Objectives | These should be based on the objectives set out in the business plan. |
| 2. | Sales forecasts | Figures should be extracted from the business plan and projected for years 1, 2 and 3. Draw appropriate graphs. |
| 3. | Product range | Investigate different types of speaker (Sonic Deco plan to introduce six models). |
| 4. | Market segmentation | Investigate different types of consumer who buy speakers – what type of speakers do they need? |
| 5. | Distribution methods | Refer to the marketing section of the business plan |
| 6. | Pricing | What pricing strategies will you use? See Chapter 17. |
| 7. | Promotion | Refer to Chapter 18 for the different methods of promotion. |
| 8. | Sales Policy | Refer to Chapter 18 for the different selling methods. |
| 9. | Budget | See Chapter 47; make an allowance for an annual increase. |
| 10. | Implementation | Draw up an implementation schedule for Year 1. |

## TASK 2

Give an oral presentation of your group plan to the rest of the class, using visual aids wherever possible. You could, if resources permitted, design a brochure for the products. *Compare* your presentations.

# unit tests ———————————————

The eight tests set out on the following pages are designed to test assimilation of the range statements of each of the eight GNVQ Units. They are are intended both as a reinforcement of learning and also as a revision aid for students preparing for the external tests. They are set out in GNVQ Unit order.

The tests are *not* intended to be simulations of the external tests.

# UNIT TEST

# 1

## UNIT 1:  BUSINESS IN THE ECONOMY

1.  What does "specialisation" mean in economic terms?

2.  What do "needs" and "wants" mean in economic terms?

3.  What are the three main classifications of goods?

4.  What are the three main business sectors?

5.  List two possible motives for carrying on a business.

6.  What is effective demand?

7.  List three determinants of demand and three determinants of supply.

8.  Define "elasticity of demand".

9.  What is the "equilibrium price"?

10.  What is a free market economy?  List two advantages of a free market economy.

11.  What is the difference between income and wealth?

12.  How are income and wealth taxed in the UK?

13.  What is the difference between a monopoly and an oligopoly?  Give an example of each.

14.  How does the UK government intervene to resolve the problem of regional inequalities?

15.  What is a planned economy?

16.  Give two advantages and two disadvantages of a planned economy.

17.  What is a mixed economy?

18.  What is the difference between the private sector and the public sector?

19.  Give two advantages and two disadvantages of nationalisation.

20.  What are the four main aims of government economic policy?

21.  What is "fiscal policy"?

22.  What are the constituents of aggregate demand?

23.  State two causes of inflation.

24.  What is the balance of payments?

25.  What is the difference between wealth and welfare?

## UNIT 2: BUSINESS SYSTEMS

1. List six main administration functions within a business.

2. List four main provisions of the Health and Safety at Work etc Act 1974.

3. Does an employee have to have a written contract of employment? If not, what should he/she receive from the employer?

4. List three legal administrative obligations of a business set up as a limited company under the Companies Acts 1985 and 1989.

5. When should a business register for VAT? What are the administrative implications?

6. What is PAYE?

7. How does the Sale of Goods Act 1979 affect the producer?

8. What is "customer care", and how can its success be monitored?

9. What is BS5750?

10. What is Total Quality Management?

11. What are the stages in the communication process?

12. In what circumstances would you use a letter, and in what circumstances would you use a memorandum?

13. What are the main headings in a formal written report?

14. What is a file server?

15. What is the difference between a LAN and a WAN?

16. Give two advantages of ISDN2.

17. What are the three main methods of storing data in electronic systems?

18. What is the difference between a database and a spreadsheet?

19. Give two possible uses of a database.

20. What are the main advantages of Electronic Mail?

21. Give two possible uses of a spreadsheet.

22. List three overall benefits of information technology.

23. What are the security implications of information technology?

24. What are the main provisions of the Data Protection Act 1984?

25. What is the significance of EC Directive 87/391?

# UNIT TEST

## 3

### UNIT 3: MARKETING

1. Define "marketing".

2. List three instances where the ethics of marketing could be questionable.

3. What does SWOT stand for?

4. What are the 4 Ps in the marketing mix?

5. What is the difference between primary and secondary research?

6. List two sources of economic data published by HMSO.

7. What is a "population" in terms of marketing research?

8. List three methods of carrying out primary research.

9. List and briefly explain three types of sampling.

10. What is market segmentation? Give three examples.

11. Give examples of the consumer characteristics of lifestyle and conscience spending.

12. What are the four main types of trend used in forecasting?

13. What is a moving average?

14. What is linear regression?

15. Why are index numbers so useful when analysing trends?

16. What is the difference between a complementary and a competitve product?.

17. List the stages in the product life cycle.

18. What is a cash cow?

19. What is the difference between differentiated and undifferentiated marketing?

20. What are skimming and penetration pricing policies?

21. Define "break-even".

22. How is advertising controlled?

23. What is the difference between publicity and public relations?

24. What is the difference between branding and packaging?

25. What are the different distribution routes between manufacturer and consumer?

**UNIT TEST**

**4**

## UNIT 4: HUMAN RESOURCES

1. What is "human resource management"?

2. List three reasons why an employee may leave an organisation.

3. List five benefits of employee performance appraisal.

4. What are the four reasons for which an employer might dismiss an employee when the work is unsatisfactory?

5. What is the other reason for dismissal?

6. To what body could an employee take a case of apparent unfair dismissal?

7. What are the four main types of trade union?

8. What is the role of the Confederation of British Industry?

9. List and briefly explain three types of employee involvement and consultation.

10. What is multi-skilling?

11. Give three examples of how an employee with potential can be developed.

12. What are the main provisions of the Equal Pay Act 1970?

13. What is the difference between a partnership and a limited company?

14. What is the difference betwen a franchise and a co-operative?

15. What is the difference between a public corporation and a public limited company?

16. What is the difference between a public limited company and a private limited company?

17. List two advantages and two disadvantages of a "flat" organisation.

18. What is an hierarchical organisation?

19. What is the difference between the roles of director and manager?

20. What is the difference between a job description and a person specification?

21. What are the two main sources of candidates for a job vacancy.

22. What are the main headings to be found on a CV?

23. What is a testimionial?

24. List five points to remember when preparing for an interview.

25. List five points to remember when being interviewed.

## UNIT TEST
## 5

### UNIT 5: EMPLOYMENT IN THE MARKET ECONOMY

1. Define "division of labour".

2. Name two advantages of occupational specialisation.

3. What is meant by "capitalism"?

4. What is meant by "laissez faire"?

5. State three ways in which the Government intervenes in the labour market.

6. What are the characteristics of Optimum Population?

7. What is a "dependent population"?

8. Give an example of the way in which the current age structure of the UK population is affecting the labour market.

9. Define "de-industrialisation".

10. Give three examples of ways in which the UK government is encouraging employment.

11. Define "labour" and "capital".

12. What is the "equilibrium wage"?

13. What is the effect of the skills required by a job on the elasticity of supply of labour?

14. State three factors which will have an effect on the elasticity of demand for labour.

15. Explain briefly what is meant by the marginal productivity theory of labour.

16. What part of the population will be affected by the "natural" rate of unemployment?

17. What is the difference between frictional unemployment and structural unemployment?

18. What is the difference between seasonal unemployment and cyclical unemployment?

19. How can the management of demand in an economy affect unemployment?

20. Give three reasons why the labour market does not readily follow the simple laws of demand and supply.

21. What is the main reason for the increase of the number of women in work in the UK?

22. What is the main reason for the increase in part-time employment in the UK?

23. Explain the term "outworkers".

24. What is meant by an "Equal Opportunities Policy"?

25. Give two advantages to a business of flexible working practices.

# UNIT TEST

# 6

## UNIT 6: FINANCIAL TRANSACTIONS AND MONITORING

1. Give three reasons why financial transactions should be monitored.

2. What document is used to order goods?

3. What document accompanies goods when they arrive at the purchaser's warehouse?

4. What document formally states the amount that is due to the seller?

5. What document would be issued by the seller if the purchaser had been overcharged?

6. State five details you would expect to find on a payslip.

7. What two signatures would you expect to find on a petty cash voucher?

8. What is the significance of the words "Account payee" in a cheque crossing?

9. What would you do if you received a cheque through the post, and it had not been signed?

10. What is the main advantage to a shop when it receives payment by cheque accompanied by a cheque card or payment card?

11. If a shop receives payment by debit card, how does it receive payment from the bank?

12. What is the main advantage to the user of a credit card?

13. What is EFTPOS?

14. State five details which must be included on a bank giro credit.

15. Why should a limited company or partnership business prefer two signatures on a cheque which it is issuing?

16. What form would be used within a business when a large cheque has to be issued?

17. What is BACS?

18. What is the difference between a standing order and a direct debit?

19. Name three parties who would be interested in the financial statements of a business.

20. What does an aged debtors schedule show?

21. What is the current ratio, and how is it calculated?

22. What financial ratios would indicate the profitability of a business?

23. What is meant by "gearing"?

24. What does a cashflow statement show?

25. What financial statement would show the way in which a business is financed?

## UNIT 7: FINANCIAL RESOURCES

1. What type of bank finance would be suitable for a working capital requirement?

2. What type of bank finance would be suitable for premises?

3. How could a business finance machinery if it was not purchasing it?

4. State three other sources of business finance apart from bank finance.

5. How could a business raise finance from its book debts (debtors)?

6. What parties would be interested in a cash flow forecast?

7. What items, apart from sales income, would you expect to see in the receipts section of a cash flow forecast?

8. Sales income in a cash flow forecast can include VAT. True or false?

9. What does a bank balance in brackets on a cash flow forecast signify?

10. Goods ordered in January and paid for in February will be recorded in the January column of a cash flow forecast. True or false?

11. What are the three elements of the cost of a product or service?

12. What is the difference between direct and indirect costs?

13. What is the formula for the calculation of the unit cost of a product or service?

14. What is the main difference between a trading and profit and loss account and a balance sheet?

15. What is the difference between gross profit and net profit?

16. Explain the term "cost of sales".

17. Explain the term "depreciation".

18. What is the difference between fixed assets and current assets?

19. What is working capital, and how is it calculated?

20. In which financial statement are the overheads of a business shown?

21. In which financial statement are the drawings of a sole trader shown?

22. In which financial statement of a limited company are the salaries of directors shown?

23. What is the difference between authorised and issued share capital?

24. What does the profit and loss account on a balance sheet represent?

25. To whom would a business show its financial statements, and why?

**UNIT TEST**

**8**

## UNIT 8:  BUSINESS PLANNING

1.    What is a Mission Statement?

2.    State two advantages and two disadvantages of starting business as a sole trader.

3.    State three differences between a partnership and a limited company.

4.    State three legal considerations you would have in mind when taking up business premises.

5.    What age restrictions are there on employing staff?

6.    Does a business have to pay National Insurance for its employees?

7.    What is the difference between product liability insurance and public liability insurance?

8.    How can a business cover itself against a claim from an employee who has been injured at work?

9.    What are Non-Domestic Rates?

10.    What is the difference between freehold and leasehold premises?

11.    What are the advantages of leasing equipment?

12.    What is "Just in Time"?

13.    Give two examples of stock purchasing systems.

14.    What is cost benefit analysis?

15.    What is critical path analysis?  How can it be  illustrated?

16.    How would you set out the objectives of a business in a business plan?

17.    What details would you expect to see in the marketing section of a business plan?

18.    What details would you expect to see in the production section of a business plan?

19.    What financial statements would you include in a business plan?

20.    What are the main sections to be found in a sales and marketing plan?

21.    What three main areas would a SWOT analysis cover in a sales and marketing plan?

22.    What is the aim of an action plan contained in a sales and marketing plan?

23.    State three different ways of carrying out the marketing budget in a sales and marketing plan.

24.    Over what time scale would you draw up a sales and marketing plan?

25.    What is an implementation schedule in a sales and marketing plan?

# index

**notes** ────────────────────────────────

notes